A GUIDE TO HISTORICAL METHOD

A GUIDE TO HISTORICAL METHOD
GARRAGHAN

BY GILBERT J. GARRAGHAN, S.J.
Late Research Professor of History
Loyola University, Chicago

EDITED BY JEAN DELANGLEZ, S.J.
Research Professor of History
Loyola University, Chicago

FORDHAM UNIVERSITY PRESS
East Fordham Road, New York

A GUIDE TO HISTORICAL METHOD
Copyright, 1946, by Fordham University Press
Fourth Printing, 1957

Permissu Superiorum

BIBLIOGRAPHICAL CITATION IN THE SOCIAL SCIENCES
Copyright, 1940, by the University of Wisconsin

Printed and bound in the United States of America

FOREWORD

IT IS GENERALLY recognized that *Lehrbuch der historischen Methode*, by Ernst Bernheim, is the classic work in the field of historical method. Unfortunately, it has never been translated, nor have any of those who taught this subject in countries where German is not the mother tongue explicitly attempted to adapt Bernheim's book to the needs of their students. A suggestion to this effect was made by Langlois and Seignobos, who speak of using Bernheim with modifications, "leaving out metaphysical problems which we consider devoid of interest" and developing certain points which the author ignores, but "which appear to us to be of the greatest importance, both theoretically and practically."

A more recent writer, Allen Johnson, has noted that nearly all the books on historical method which have appeared since Bernheim, "flatter him by imitation," or lean heavily upon him in formulating in practical form "the approved modes of procedure in historical criticism."

Among this latter class is *Lehrbuch der geschichtlichen Methode*, by Alfred Feder, of which the same writer says that "it makes no advance beyond Bernheim," and "is, indeed, in many respects reactionary in its point of view, especially in matters concerning ecclesiastical history and tradition."

It may be conceded that in the essentials of historical methodology neither Feder nor any other writer has advanced beyond the work of Bernheim, but in specific details and in various interpretations Feder has made a notable contribution to this science. Further, the "reactionary" character of Father Feder's work consists in his having a metaphysical conception of the universe with which Mr. Johnson does not agree; a conception which leaves room for the supernatural, for God, for revelation, for miracles.

The initial intention of Father Garraghan was to translate and adapt Feder's book, but as the work progressed, his treatment of the subject became more independent. In its final form, as here presented to the reader, what he has done should be regarded as truly original, except for Part III, entitled "Criticism." Even in this third part, and throughout the whole book, wherever possible, his illustrative material is taken from American and English History.

In preparing the manuscript for the press, the editor has endeavored to make no change affecting the substance of the book, although there are points of detail, such as the requirement for establishing individual facts, which might be more strongly emphasized. It will be evident, also, that certain sections are purely academic, and that many problems are discussed which concern the philosophy of history rather than historical method. Their interest for the student of history amply justifies their inclusion, though they might well have been omitted if this were merely a textbook for classroom use. Such supplementary or divergent points of view as seemed necessary have been indicated in the footnotes.

Two main changes have been made in the original arrangement of the book. The sections in Chapter One, marked F, G, and H, were originally part of Chapter Four, and the remainder of this fourth Chapter now appears as section G, at the end of Chapter Sixteen. This change was suggested by Professor William J. Schlaerth, S.J., of Fordham University, whose help in editing the manuscript is here gratefully acknowledged.

The second major change consists in the complete revision, in Chapter Seventeen, of what now appears as subdivision C, paragraphs 395–403, inclusive. This section was entirely rewritten by Robert E. Holland, S.J. Director of Fordham University Press. He is also responsible for the reprinting of Miss Appel's booklet on bibliographical citation, which appears with her permission as an appendix to this book. Father Holland's long experience has been invaluable in every phase of the editing process; in fact, the features of presentation are all due to him.

Added to the original manuscript is a bibliography of books on historical method arranged chronologically.

Any inaccuracies which occur with regard to the text or the references are to be attributed solely to the editor.

JEAN DELANGLEZ, S.J.

Chicago, Easter Sunday
April 21, 1946.

FOREWORD TO THE SECOND PRINTING

READERS of this book will find no change in this second printing, except for some misprints which have been corrected. Some reviewers have expressed the wish that the book be thoroughly revised in a second "edition." Such a revision is entirely out of the question. In publishing Father Garraghan's manuscript, I was careful to present it to the public in its original form, because of my certain knowledge that the late Father Garraghan wanted his book to appear exactly as he wrote it.

My edition of his manuscript was *not* "compiled from notes without sufficient care" as may be seen by anyone who wishes to compare it with the original manuscript, which has been carefully preserved. The few changes which seemed to me absolutely essential were explicitly mentioned in the Foreword to the first printing.

To have changed his bibliographies by inserting books which he had not seen, including those published after his death, would have been dishonest. His omission of books in foreign languages was entirely deliberate. Deplorable though the fact may be, it is nevertheless a fact that "Catholic graduate students," to say nothing of others, have not mastered "French and German as well as . . . other modern languages."

I venture to hope that my conscientious endeavor to confine myself to the proper functions of an editor of a posthumous work will not prevent a competent teacher of historical criticism from supplementing these bibliographies by reference to later editions of the works listed and to more recent books on the various subjects treated herein.

JEAN DELANGLEZ, S.J.

Chicago,
August 31, 1948.

PUBLISHER'S NOTE

GRATEFUL ACKNOWLEDGMENT is made for permission kindly granted by copyright owners or by their representatives, to make extracts from the works here listed. Permission was asked for every extract, whether copyrighted or not, with some exceptions: where it was found impossible to trace author or publisher. This last is notably the fact in the cases of European publishing houses, damaged in the war. Fordham University Press asks indulgence if through any inadvertence the following list is not complete.

Readers of this book will be grateful to Miss Livia Appel and to the University of Wisconsin Press for granting permission to print *Bibliographical Citation in the Social Sciences* as an appendix. Fordham University Press makes special acknowledgment of this fine co-operation.

GEORGE ALLEN & UNWIN, LTD.
   H. Belloc, *The House of Commons and Monarchy*.
AMERICANA CORPORATION
   P. Shorey, art. "Homer" in *Encyclopedia Americana*.
D. APPLETON-CENTURY CO.
   H. E. Barnes, *The New History: Essays Illustrating the New Historical Outlook*.
   S. F. Bemis, *The Diplomacy of the American Revolution*.
BANCROFT-WHITNEY COMPANY
   B. W. Jones, *The Law of Evidence in Civil Cases* (3d ed.).
G. BELL & SONS, LTD.
   F. Gasquet, *Henry III and the Church*.
BENZIGER BROTHERS
   J. F. X. Pyne, *The Mind*.
   J. Rouseil, *St. Joan of Arc*.
THE BRUCE PUBLISHING COMPANY
   G. C. Ring, *The Gods of the Gentiles*.
CAMBRIDGE UNIVERSITY PRESS: THE MACMILLAN COMPANY
   R. E. Balfour, "History," in H. Wright ed., *Cambridge Historical Studies*.
   J. B. Bury, *An Inaugural Lecture Delivered in the Divinity School, Cambridge, on January 26, 1903*.
   Cambridge Modern History.
   G. Saintsbury in *Cambridge History of English Literature*.
   Selected Essays of J. B. Bury, H. W. V. Temperley, ed.
CHAPMAN & HALL, LTD.
   J. E. Holmstrom, *Records and Research in Engineering*.
   W. S. Lilly, *Christianity and Modern Civilization*.
THE CLARENDON PRESS (Oxford)
   H. Bradley, *The Collected Papers of Henry Bradley*.
   C. N. Cochrane, *Thucydides and the Science of History*.
   C. G. Crump and E. F. Jacob, *The Legacy of Greece*.

H. B. George, *Historical Evidence.*
G. Murray, *The Rise of the Greek Epic.*
Sir C. Oman, *Inaugural Lecture on the Study of History.*
W. Stubbs, *Select Charters; Seventeen Lectures on the Study of Medieval History and Kindred Subjects.*

COLUMBIA UNIVERSITY PRESS
E. R. E. Seligman, *The Economic Interpretation of History.*
J. T. Shotwell, *The History of History.*
J. T. Shotwell and L. R. Loomis, *The See of Peter.*

THE DIAL PRESS, INC.
M. L. W. Laistner, *Thought and Letters.*

DOUBLEDAY AND COMPANY, INC.
R. S. Baker, *Life and Letters of Woodrow Wilson.*

E. P. DUTTON & CO., INC.
Venerable Bede, *The Ecclesiastical History of the English Nation* (Everyman's Library).
A. J. Toynbee, *Greek Historical Thought from Homer to the Age of Heraclius.*

ENCYCLOPAEDIA BRITANNICA
E. Gosse, art. "Biography" in Encyclopaedia Britannica (11th ed.).
J. T. Shotwell, art. "History" in Encyclopaedia Britannica (11th ed.).

FISK UNIVERSITY PRESS
C. Wissler in Bernardino de Shagun, *A History of Ancient Mexico, 1547–1577.*

M. H. GILL & SON, LTD.
J. E. MacNeill, *Phases of Irish History.*

HARCOURT, BRACE & COMPANY, INC.
B. Croce, *History: Its Theory and Practice.*

HARPER AND BROTHERS
E. G. Bourne, *Spain in America* (The American Nations Series).

HARVARD UNIVERSITY PRESS
W. C. Abbot, *Adventures in Refutation* (1935).
M. M. Bober, *Karl Marx's Interpretation of History* (1927).

D. C. HEATH AND COMPANY
A. Nevins, *The Gateway to History.*

HENRY HOLT AND COMPANY
C. V. Langlois and C. Seignobos, *Introduction to the Study of History.*
F. J. Turner, *The Frontier in American History.*

HOUGHTON MIFFLIN COMPANY
H. Adams, *The Education of Henry Adams.*
J. C. Almack, *Research and Thesis Writing.*
A. J. Beveridge, *Abraham Lincoln.*
W. Wilson, *Mere Literature.*

HUTCHINSON & CO., LTD.
J. A. Spender and C. Asquith, *Life of Herbert Henry Asquith.*

ALFRED A. KNOPF, INC.
E. P. Cheney, *Law in History and Other Essays.*

LITTLE, BROWN & COMPANY
J. Fiske in Preface to Francis Parkman, *Works* (Champlain Edition).
J. H. Wigmore, *The Principles of Judicial Proof.*

Publisher's Note and Acknowledgments

LIVERIGHT PUBLISHING CORPORATION
  M. H. Mandelbaum, *The Problem of Historical Knowledge.*
LONGMANS, GREEN & CO., INC.
  B. Boedder, *Natural Theology.*
  R. W. Chambers, *England before the Norman Conquest.*
  M. Creighton, *Historical Lectures and Addresses.*
  H. Delehaye, *The Legends of the Saints.*
  C. Devas, *A Key to the World's Progress.*
  Sir J. W. Fortescue, *The Writing of History.*
  W. James, *The Will to Believe.*
  W. E. H. Lecky, *Historical and Political Essays.*
  Sir C. Oman, *The Unfortunate Colonel Despard.*
  J. Rickaby, *First Principles of Knowledge.*
  J. H. Wiley, *The Council of Constance.*
LOYOLA UNIVERSITY PRESS
  O. T. Kuhnmuensch, *Early Christian Latin Poets.*
MACMILLAN & CO., LTD. (London)
  Lord Cromer (E. Baring), *Political and Literary Essays.*
  E. A. Freeman, *The Methods of History: The Unity of History.*
THE MACMILLAN COMPANY (New York)
  Lord Acton, *Historical Essays and Studies. History of Freedom and Other Essays. Lectures on the French Revolution. A Lecture on the Study of History.*
  H. Belloc, *Essays of a Catholic.*
  A. E. R. Boak, *A History of Rome.*
  James Viscount Bryce, *Modern Democracies. The Study of American History.*
  Encyclopaedia of the Social Sciences.
  Sir C. Firth, *A Commentary on Macaulay.*
  F. Harrison, *The Meaning of History.*
  C. H. McIlwain, *The Growth of Political Thought in the West.*
  W. P. Montague, *The Ways of Knowing.*
  R. L. Patterson, *The Conception of God in Aquinas.*
  J. F. Rhodes, *Historical Essays.*
  A. Schlesinger in W. P. Gee, ed., *Research in the Social Sciences; New Viewpoints in American History.*
  H. W. V. Temperley, *Research and Modern History.*
METHUEN & CO., LTD.
  J. R. Bacon, *The Voyage of the Argonauts.*
  O. Barfield, *History in English Words.*
  H. Belloc, *First and Last.*
  Sir W. S. Holdsworth, *History of English Law.*
OXFORD UNIVERSITY PRESS (London)
  A. J. Carlyle, in F. S. Marvin, ed., *Progress and History.*
  Sir H. C. M. Lambert, *The Nature of History.*
  E. Scott, *History and Historical Problems.*
OXFORD UNIVERSITY PRESS (New York)
  L. M. Salmon, *Historical Material. The Newspaper and the Historian.*
PRINCETON UNIVERSITY PRESS
  J. F. Jameson, *The American Revolution Considered as a Social Movement.*

G. P. Putnam's Sons
 L. Sears, *Principles and Methods of Literary Criticism*.
Rivingtons
 W. Edwards, *A Medieval Scrap-heap*.
George Routledge & Sons, Ltd.
Kegan Paul, Trench, Trubner & Co., Ltd.
 E. A. S Dowes, *The Alexiad of the Princess Anna Commena: Being the History of the Reign of Her Father Alexius I, Emperor of the Romans, A.D. 1081-1118*.
 C. G. Crump, *History and Historical Research*.
Charles Scribner's Sons
 J. B. Bishop, *Theodore Roosevelt*.
 E. G. Bourne, *Essays in Historical Criticism*.
 G. F. Hoar, *Autobiography of Seventy Years*.
 A. Johnson, *The Historian and Historical Evidence*.
 J. Jusserand and Others, *The Writing of History*.
 J. E. Olson and E. G. Bourne, *The Northmen, Columbus and Cabot*.
 G. Santayana, *Winds of Doctrine*.
 H. M. Stephens, *A History of the French Revolution*.
 P. Van Dyke, *Ignatius of Loyola*.
Sheed and Ward, Inc.
 M. C. D'Arcy, *The Nature of Belief*.
 C. H. Dawson, *Enquiries into Religion and Culture. Religion and the Modern State*.
 L. Gougand, *Christianity in Celtic Lands*.
 O. Marucchi, *The Evidence of the Catacombs for the Doctrine and Organization of the Primitive Church*.
Society for the Propagation of Christian Knowledge
 C. G. Crump, *The Logic of History* (Helps, 6).
 J. P. Gilson, *A Student's Guide to the Manuscripts of the British Museum* (Helps, 9).
 G. F. Hill, *Coins and Medals* (Helps, 36).
University of California Press
 L. O'Brien, *The Writing of History*.
University of Chicago Press
 T. E. Strevey in W. T. Hutchinson, ed., *The Marcus W. Jernegan Essays*.
University of Colorado Press
 C. Sauer, "Historical Geography," in J. J. Willard and C. B. Goodykoontz, eds., *The Trans-Mississippi West*.
University of North Carolina Press
 F. H. Giddings, *The Scientific Study of Human Society*.
Yale University Press
 R. G. Adams in *Essays Offered to Herbert Putnam by William Warner Bishop and Andrew Keough*.
 F. M. Fling, *The Writing of History*.
 F. J. Teggert, *The Processes of History*.

Publisher's Note and Acknowledgments

AMERICAN HISTORICAL ASSOCIATION
 Report, 1904, 1932.
 American Historical Review, 1927, 1932, 1935.
THE BRITISH ACADEMY
 Proceedings of the British Academy, 1924.
ECONOMIC HISTORY SOCIETY (London)
 Economic History Review, 1929.
THE HISTORICAL SOCIETY (London)
 History, 1933.
ILLINOIS CATHOLIC HISTORICAL ASSOCIATION
 Illinois Catholic Historical Review (now Mid-America), 1918.
THE JOHN RYLANDS LIBRARY
 Bulletin of The John Rylands Library, 1918.
THE MISSISSIPPI STATE DEPARTMENT OF ARCHIVES AND HISTORY
 Publications of the Mississippi Historical Society, 1927.
THE MISSISSIPPI VALLEY HISTORICAL ASSOCIATION
 Mississippi Valley Historical Review, 1937.
PACIFIC COAST BRANCH OF THE AMERICAN HISTORICAL ASSOCIATION
 Pacific Historical Review, 1932.
YALE UNIVERSITY PRESS
 Yale Review, 1924.

ABBREVIATIONS

AHA, Report, American Historical Association, Annual Report, Washington, D. C., 1889——
AHR, The American Historical Review, New York, 1895——
CE, The Catholic Encyclopedia, 16 vols., New York, 1907–1914.
CHR, The Catholic Historical Review, Washington, D. C., 1915——
EHR, The English Historical Review, London, 1886——
Helps, Johnson, Charles, Whitney, J. P., Temperley, Harold W. V., eds., Helps for Students of History, 51 vols., London, 1918–1924.
HB, The Historical Bulletin (St. Louis University), St. Louis, 1922——
MA, Mid-America (Loyola University) Chicago, 1930——
MVHR, The Mississippi Valley Historical Review (The State University of Iowa), Iowa City, Iowa, 1914——

A GUIDE TO HISTORICAL METHOD

Table of Contents

PART ONE
PROLEGOMENA TO HISTORY

Chapter 1: THE MEANING OF HISTORY . . . . . page 3

A. History as Past Actuality. B. History as Record. C. Three Types of History as Record. D. History as a Method of Inquiry. E. Contemporary History. F. Continuity and Unity. G. Civilization and Culture. H. Progress. I. Erroneous Conceptions of History.

Chapter 2: METHOD IN HISTORY 33

A. Historical Method: Meaning. B. Historical Method: Uses. C. History as Science. D. The Competent Historian: Characteristics. E. Hallmarks of Critical History. F. Historical Method in the Making.

Chapter 3: CERTAINTY IN HISTORY 70

A. The Nature of Historical Belief. B. The Nature of Historical Certainty. C. The Possibility of Historical Certainty.

Chapter 4: THE AUXILIARY SCIENCES 81

A. Philosophy. B. Bibliography. C. Anthropology. D. Linguistics. E. Geography. F. Chronology. G. Diplomatic. H. Sigillography and Heraldry. I. Palaeography. J. Archaeology. K. Epigraphy. L. Numismatics. M. Genealogy.

PART TWO
FINDING THE SOURCES (Heuristic)

Chapter 5: THE NATURE AND CLASSIFICATION OF HISTORICAL SOURCES 103

A. What Historical Sources Mean. B. Classification by Origin. C. Classification by Content. D. Classification by Aim. E. The Narrative Type of Source. F. Official Records. G. Oral Sources (Tradition). H. Pictorial and Figured Sources. I. Written Sources.

Chapter 6: MECHANICAL AIDS TO RESEARCH 124

A. Note-taking: Systems. B. Note-taking: Technique. C. Questionnaires and Interviews. D. Libraries, Archives, Museums. E. Hints on Historical Research.

PART THREE

APPRAISING THE SOURCES (Criticism)

Chapter 7: LOGICAL PROCESSES IN HISTORY 143

A. Analogy. B. Generalization. C. Reasoning from Statistics. D. Hypothesis. E. Conjecture. F. The Argument from Silence. G. The Argument a priori.

Chapter 8: THE AUTHENTICITY OF SOURCES 168

A. The Genuine and the False Forgery. B. The Criteria of Authenticity. C. Errors in Questions of Authenticity. D. Dating Sources. E. Localizing Sources. F. The Determination of Authorship.

Chapter 9: THE ANALYSIS OF SOURCES 205

A. The Meaning of Source-analysis. B. Sources as Related. C. Sources as Derived. D. One Source Original, One or More Derived. E. One Source Derived, Several Original. F. Lost Sources.

Chapter 10: THE INTEGRITY OF SOURCES:
Textual Criticism 215

A. Textual Integrity: Meaning and Scope. B. The Criteria of Integrity. C. The Recension: Direct Tradition. D. The Recension: Indirect Tradition. E. The Recension: Relationship of Manuscripts. F. The Emendation and the Editing of Texts.

Chapter 11: THE CREDIBILITY OF SOURCES 232

A. The Problem of Error. B. The Credibility of Specific Written Sources.

Chapter 12: THE CREDIBILITY OF SOURCES (continued) 259

A. The Credibility of Popular Tradition. B. The Legend-making Process. C. Legend as a Historical Source. D. Sources Differentiated by Aim. E. Sources Differentiated by Type of Witness.

Chapter 13: THE CREDIBILITY OF SOURCES (concluded) 282

A. The Direct Witness: Knowledge. B. The Direct Witness: Veracity. C. The Indirect Witness. D. The Single Witness. E. Corroboration on Intrinsic Grounds. F. Miracles and the Historian. G. Moral Possibility and Impossibility. H. Concurrent Testimony. I. Concurrent Testimony in Remains. J. Concurrence in Formal Testimony. K. Concurrence of Formal Testimony with Remains. L. Conflicting Testimony. M. Problems in the Credibility of Sources.

Contents xvii

PART FOUR
PRESENTATION OF THE RESULTS OF RESEARCH
(Synthesis and Exposition)

Chapter 14: THE INTERPRETATION OF SOURCES . . . 321
   A. Verbal Interpretation. B. Technical Interpretation. C. Logical Interpretation. D. Psychological Interpretation. E. Factual Interpretation. F. Letting the Facts Speak for Themselves.

Chapter 15: EXTERNAL SYNTHESIS 338
   A. The Problem of Selection. B. Organizing Data.

Chapter 16: INTERNAL SYNTHESIS 346
   A. The Synthesizing Faculty at Work. B. Causation in History. C. Materialistic Determinism in History. D. Conditions and Means as Factors in History. E. Chance in History. F. Putting Oneself in the Past. G. The Philosophy of History.

Chapter 17: THE INDICATION OF SOURCES 381
   A. The Necessity of Giving References. B. Footnotes: Rationale. C. Footnotes: Technique. D. Bibliography. E. The Documentary Appendix. Source Books. Consecutive Documents.

Chapter 18: MAKING THE PRESENTATION EFFECTIVE 396
   A. Reconstructing the Past. B. The Literary Element in History. C. Vivid Writing. D. Synthetic Views. E. Quotation: Direct and Indirect.

Chapter 19: HISTORY—WRITTEN AND REWRITTEN . 408
   A. Studying Historians' Methods. B. Co-operative History. C. Why History is Rewritten. D. Historical Revisions. E. Examples. F. Historical Problems.

Bibliography of Historical Method 427

Index of Authors 433

Index of Matter 458

Appendix: *Bibliographical Citation in the Social Sciences*

Part One
PROLEGOMENA TO HISTORY

Chapter One

THE MEANING OF HISTORY

A. History as Past Actuality . . . . Page 4
B. History as Record 11
C. Three Types of History as Record 12
D. History as a Method of Inquiry 18
E. Contemporary History 19
F. Continuity and Unity 21
G. Civilization and Culture 24
H. Progress 26
I. Erroneous Conceptions of History 29

¶ 1   The term *history* stands for three related but sharply differentiated concepts: (a) past human events; past actuality; (b) the record of the same; (c) the process or technique of making the record.

The Greek ἱστορία, which gives us the Latin *historia*, the French *histoire*, and the English *history*, originally meant *inquiry, investigation, research*, and not a record of data accumulated thereby—the usual present-day meaning of the term. It was only at a later period that the Greeks attached to it the meaning of "a record or narration of the results of inquiry." In current usage the term *history* may accordingly signify or imply any one of three things: (1) inquiry; (2) the objects of inquiry; (3) the record of the results of inquiry, corresponding respectively to (c), (a), and (b) above.

For a similar triple division of the general concept of history, see Aloys Meister, *Grundzüge der historischen Methode* (2d ed., Leipzig, 1913), 1.

It has been pointed out that the German word for history, *Geschichte*, from *geschehen, to happen*, means radically not inquiry or the object of inquiry, but "things that have happened": history as past actuality.

History as *knowledge*, which is historical data as they exist in the mind and are material for record, may be recognized as a fourth use of the term. But history so conceived tends to become identical with history as record. The distinction between history as actuality and history as knowledge, is useful in analysis of the sophistical axiom that philoso-

3

phy and history are identical concepts. That philosophy is to be identified with history as actuality, must be denied; that it is identical with knowledge, may be granted, but only if philosophy be taken in an arbitrary sense, and not in its generally accepted sense of the science of ultimates [¶ 32].*

A. History as Past Actuality

¶ 2 History as past actuality includes in its range all things that have come to pass, whether they belong to the world of nature or the world of man; in a more restricted sense it includes only human events. We speak of the history of France or of the history of England, meaning to express thereby the complex of human events in the countries named. In a more general sense one may speak of a history of the earth, understanding by it the geological changes through which the earth has passed. The so-called "natural histories" of Pliny, Goldsmith, and others, in as far as they deal only with types and are treatises in descriptive zoology, are not history at all in any proper sense of the term. Again, since events connote change, so history as actuality regards only such things as pass from one state or condition to another. Anything that changes will have a history; God, who is unchanging and unchangeable, can have no history except (and this by analogy only) in what concerns the outward manifestations of His power. Any true conception of history necessarily posits the idea of change. Finally, to note still another use of the term, we speak of history-making in the sense of doing things more than ordinarily significant, such as deserve a place in history as record.

Human things that have happened are accordingly the material with which history as record deals. This is the objective side of history, the side that is permanently and irrevocably fixed. "But past who can recall, or done, undo!" No amount of learned discussion or research can make the actual circumstances of the death of Julius Caesar, for example, or of the battle of Waterloo, other than what they actually were. From this point of view history is absolute.

¶ 3 RELATIVITY IN HISTORY
While relativity cannot be predicated of history as actuality, it can, under certain aspects, be predicated of history as record.

(a) *The facts of history, apart from the few we may come to know directly* (by personal experience), *are known to us only indirectly,* that

---

* The style here used refers to numbered paragraphs or groups of paragraphs included under one number, throughout this book—not to pages.

is, from traces of them left behind in documents and other sources of information. In other words, what we apprehend directly are not the facts themselves, but somebody's knowledge or impression of them. Moreover, such impression is based, not on all the actual details of the reported fact, but on a limited number of them. These circumstances do not make it impossible to know the past *wie es eigentlich gewesen* (Ranke), to know historical facts "as they really occurred," and to know them with certainty. But because of the necessarily limited number of details which we know, history may be said to be *relative*. History as record, however, is not wholly and necessarily relative, for there are many facts which can be known absolutely.

(b) *Our apprehension of history as past actuality, our ability to understand and realize it, is conditioned by our knowledge of the world in which we live.* In many ways we view the past through the spectacles of the present, a process which need not, however, result in distortion or error. Our knowledge of Roman political institutions is made possible to a great extent by the knowledge we have of the political institutions under which we live, and therefore with which we are familiar. We can be said to know the past only to the extent that it is reflected in the present, as in a mirror; but there is nothing in the nature of things to prevent the resulting image from being true. Here again a certain relativity attaches to history. The reflection of the past in the present varies from age to age, and from one individual to another in the same age.

(c) *The past can be, and is in fact, viewed from varying angles of interest, as one generation succeeds another.* Aspects of history that appealed to students of one day may fail to intrigue those of another day. The same body of facts that make up, say, English medieval history may be looked at preferably on its political or social or economic side, according as human interest shifts with time from one aspect of life to another. The modern democratic movement has had the result of diverting the attention of historians from courts and camps and of fixing it in increasing measure on the people. The twentieth-century World Wars revealed the part to be played in wartime by the noncombatant elements of the populace. Doubtless there was a similar participation in previous wars, although not on so considerable a scale. Because this aspect of war has been almost uniformly overlooked in published accounts of the great military struggles of history, such accounts are inadequate. Any future large-scale history of the American Civil War, one may expect, will place in due relief the important part taken in it behind the lines by the civilians of both sides. Here again history has its relative side.

Briefly, the whole question of relativity in history reduces to this simple distinction: as actuality history is absolute; as record it is or can be relative, in certain regards. Events are a constant; what we know or think about them is a variable.

¶ 4 A spurious, irrational relativity would be this: to look upon "all things and all principles of things as no more than inconstant modes or fashions."—AHR, 37 (1932): 236.

Also spurious and irrational is the relativity of the Italian neo-Hegelian idealist, Giovanni Gentile: "There is nothing which we can really regard as existing absolutely either in the past or in the present."—See "The Transcending of Time in History," in Raymond Klibansky and Herbert J. Paton, eds., *Philosophy and History: Essays Presented to Ernest Cassirer* (Oxford, 1936), 91.

Against such a view of things common sense rebels [¶ 67]. If all things are relative, and the absolute does not exist, then the theory of relativity is itself relative, and therefore without intrinsic and permanent validity. Relativists in history are in general skeptics as regards the validity of historical knowledge. Their position is criticized in Maurice Mandelbaum, *The Problem of Historical Knowledge: An Answer to Relativism* (New York, 1938).

For a criticism of relativity wrongly understood, see AHR, 39 (1934): 225.

¶ 5 THE RANGE OF HISTORY

The range of history as the totality of past human experience, a range expressed by the *quidquid agunt homines* of the Latin poet, practically knows no limits. Anything that man has thought, said, or done, is material for history as record. The slightest detail under any one of these three categories may in certain circumstances acquire historical significance. The tendency to throw down all barriers to the universal reach of history in its specific field of past human experience, has become pronounced in recent years. Yet, that history can legitimately concern itself with all of man's doings in the past is not distinctly a modern notion. Thinkers centuries ago gave expression to it more or less clearly; but it is only in our own day that it has been fully grasped and urged with emphasis as a practical basis in history-writing.

¶ 6 COMMENT ON THE RANGE OF HISTORY

History has for its subject human nature. It is the record of what man has thought, said, and done.—James Viscount Bryce, *The Study of American History* (New York, 1922), 78.

The exclusive idea of political history, *Staatengeschichte*, to which Ranke held so firmly, has been gradually yielding to a more comprehensive definition which embraces as its material all records, whatever their nature may be, of the material and spiritual development, of the culture and the works of man in society from the stone age on.—John B. Bury, *An Inaugural Lecture Delivered in the Divinity School, Cambridge*, on January 26, 1903 (Cambridge, 1903), 35.

Gradually its scope has broadened, so that today history is becoming concerned, in the hands of some is already concerned, with the totality of man's experience in the past. No aspect of these experiences can be safely neglected, for there is nothing man has done or hoped for or feared that has not left its mark in some manner in the life of society. Thus history is as many-sided as life itself.—A. Schlesinger in Wilson P. Gee, ed., *Research in the Social Sciences: Its Fundamental Methods and Objectives* (New York, 1929), 222.

History has for its object everything that is intimate, everything that is passionate, everything also that is of trivial or daily occurence, all the color and all the infinite variety of the past.—George M. Trevelyan, "History and Literature," *Yale Review*, 14 (1924): 121.

¶ 7 HISTORY: A WORKING DEFINITION

While human activities of whatever kind are thus the raw material of history, practical historical research and writing are concerned only with human events of a certain type.

(a) The first thing to be noted about the facts with which history deals is that they are largely the product of the *free agency of man*. The freedom of the human will is an essential postulate of history. Without it history is unintelligible. But facts independent of human volition, such as physical environment, an earthquake, a plague, can also come within the purview of history, inasmuch as they affect or modify the social scene, and may thus be regarded as human events.

(b) Human activities, to be proper material for history, must be concrete, that is, *restricted in time and place*. If the activities of men, with the laws that regulate them, are dealt with in the abstract, then we are in the field not of history but of some other department of knowledge, such as psychology or sociology or anthropology. The vicissitudes of the John Smith family during its residence in Boston 1870–1880, is or might be a topic in history. The characteristics in general of the human family, considered in abstract as a social unit, is a topic of sociology. Group psychology discusses the typical reactions of a mass of men to certain stimuli; history narrates the pertinent concrete case of the French Revolution. So it has been said that sociology is "history without proper names," and that history is "illustrated sociology." This idea of definiteness in time and place, which forms the basis of the "individual," the "singular," the "unique," must be clearly grasped, since it furnishes the chief clue to the distinction between history and the other social sciences. Yet, while history deals in the first instance with the "individual," the "particular," it also deals, and inevitably so, with what are called "general facts." These are in reality generalizations [₡ 132]. That the Romans were a political-minded people is a general fact, and one, indeed, probably of more significance than most of the particular facts of Roman history.

(c) It must be pointed out that the singleness (unicity) or definiteness of the facts with which history deals is broad enough in its implications to include such complex facts as are spread over a protracted range of space and time: for example, movements (Renaissance, French Revolution); reigns, institutions (political, social, economic, religious, etc.); laws, manners, customs. Facts in such categories are not *generalizations* or *general facts*; they are concrete, definite, and therefore *single* facts, however complex, however diffused in space and time they be.

(d) Auguste Castelein has a suggestive treatment of general facts, which he reduces to three main classes: (1) *Character of an individual*. Appraisal of a person's character involves an induction or conclusion based on a number of individual acts. Nothing is more difficult than to determine the motive or passion which ordinarily inspires personal action. Is one avaricious or merely thrifty? prodigal or generous? needlessly severe or only just? The accuracy of Tacitus' portrayal of Tiberius is still a matter of debate among scholars. (2) *Character of a race, people, family, or any other group*. The same difficulties that occur in (1), present themselves here. Social facts are inductions the truth of which must be gauged by the laws which regulate inductive reason in general. (3) *Character of a period, age, reign, administration*. This is the most difficult of all classes of general facts to determine. Various phases of institutional life, such as the political, economic, religious, call for examination, and such an examination involves personal standards of value which differ from one historian to another. Was such an age enlightened or benighted, progressive or static, prosperous or the reverse?—*Cours de philosophie* (2 vols., Namur, 1887), 1:256.

(e) History, strictly understood, concerns itself with the doings of individuals, not merely as such, but as social beings, as members of this or that social unit—the family, the city, the state. The career of an individual has historical meaning only to the extent to which it influences an organized group of other individuals or is influenced by it. The details of the daily occupational or intimate family life of a person belong to history only to the extent to which they affect the development of some other social group, whether this be political, religious, or some other sort. The reason why history deals with the activities of men as social beings is that the tendency of historical development, as toward its proximate end, is the perfection of human society in general, and thereby of the individual. The result is that all the single elements in the highly complex tissue of historical development must look to this identical end. They do so only in as far as they bear a *social character*, that is, are linked together by a common objective, a common interest, common laws of development.

(f) But not all the doings of men as social beings are history. To be so, they must show importance or significance—which are obviously relative terms. The idea of historical significance postulates standards of measurement. What appears significant to one historian may not appear so to another. Philosophy of life, personal viewpoints and prepossessions, the scope of one's writing—for example, whether political or military or economic—can all be factors in determining for the historian whether he is to regard a given datum as significant or not. Summarily, it may be said that all facts are historically significant which have impressed themselves on the contemporary world in some marked or effective way. Their significance is therefore all the more obvious if they are seen to have helped to make the existing world what it is. Contemporary civilization is the inconceivably complex, many-sided outcome of an infinity of circumstances and conditions operating in a causal way in the past. The relation to it of these circumstances and conditions determines their importance and significance from the historical point of view. The consequence is that those individuals are of most concern to the historian whose influence over their environment has been particularly direct and far-reaching. At the same time, a human career of retirement and obscurity may become a source of inspiration to later generations, and so acquire historical significance. Moreover, the experiences of an altogether obscure individual may take on historical meaning to the extent that they are typical of life in the age or social environment to which he belonged; because through them we make acquaintance with the world in which he lived.

⁋ 8 For instance, it does not help to an understanding of the past to know merely as isolated facts what was the particular doctrine or system taught by some Cynic philosopher in the Rome of Marcus Aurelius; or what was the program of studies of some unknown schoolboy of the Carolingian era; or what was the reception ceremonial of a certain Byzantine patrician. But the cases differ when these facts can be regarded as representative of the *milieu* to which these individuals belonged. In such a hypothesis the first fact might add to our knowledge of philosophical thought in the second century A.D.; the second might throw light on educational practice in the Carolingian era; the third might aid to an understanding of the social position of the Byzantine nobility.—Alfred Feder, *Lehrbuch der geschichtlichen Methode* (3d ed., Regensburg, 1924), 4f.

To sum up, history, the most inclusive and many-sided of all the social sciences, may be defined as *the science which first investigates and then records, in their causal relations and development, such past human activities as are (a) definite in time and space, (b) social in nature, and (c) socially significant.*

¶ 9 ANTIQUARIANISM AND HISTORY

Thomas Arnold insisted nearly a century ago on the difference between antiquarianism and history. "[Mere antiquarians] have wanted, what is the essential accompaniment to all our knowledge of the past, a lively and extensive knowledge of the present; they wanted the habit of continually viewing the two in combination with each other."—*Introductory Lectures on Modern History* (New York, 1880), 109.

One may say that antiquarians are interested in the past for its own sake only, that is, in so far as it stimulates and gratifies curiosity or imagination or sentiment, while interest in the past as profoundly affecting the present is what stamps the genuine historian. For him the past has meaning only to the extent to which it can explain how the contemporary world came to be what it actually is. Naturally, the two fields, antiquarianism and history, tend to run into each other. Books of history often contain data which one must qualify as of only antiquarian interest or value. The important idea for the student to grasp here is that history as "living past" is essentially a practical thing, one which helps us to know and use to better purpose the world in which we live; by no means is it a matter of academic interest and speculation. Historians and antiquarians differ by their contrasting attitudes towards the past; they deal as a rule with different categories of topics. The antiquarian field is relatively narrow. It includes for the most part only such matters as local or regional manners and customs, place-names, archaeological survivals in the industrial and other arts. But politics, legislation, wars, broad social and economic conditions and movements are left to the historian.

¶ 10 While history thus derives its main value as a discipline from the light it throws on the present, and in a measure on the future also, it does not appear that such a consideration furnishes the average historian the real inspiration in his work. It may be questioned whether any conscious design to clarify the present in the light of the past is before him as he pursues his tasks; some other consideration or motive more personal to him exerts its influence. One can hardly conceive him as held to his labors, often discouraging enough, on a chance that the new data he turns up, for example, on early Assyrian social life is going to better present-day social life in any appreciable way. But the historian's attempt to recover a pattern of life obscured for centuries, can appeal to him on other grounds. It can stir his imagination, stimulate his curiosity, gratify his interest in the doings of our common humanity, however remote in time and place. Again, a sense of accomplishment can lure him on, the desire to achieve a firstclass piece of work. There is also the "collecting mania," the delight in searching out and assembling all available data, especially new ones, on a given topic; or the detective instinct, which urges one through a welter of conflicting evidence to the solution of some historical conundrum. Motives such as these operating in the historian's consciousness would appear to lie behind his pursuit, rather than any vague altruistic ambition to make the world in which we live better because of his researches.

B. History as Record

⟨11 The subjective counterpart to objective history, to history as past actuality, is man's attempt to recapture the latter, to fix it in words, to give it a meaning. This is history as record, which may take any one of an endless variety of shapes, from a hero-tale handed down by word of mouth to an inscribed coin, a letter, a charter, a narrative running into many volumes. And as the happenings themselves (*objective history*) are fixed beyond the possibility of change, so, on the contrary, the record of them (*subjective history*) will show an infinite variety of content and color from one recorder to another [⟨ 3c].

⟨ 12 DOCUMENTS

Any one of the multitudinous shapes which historical record takes, may in some general way be designated a *document*. The student of history has the term constantly on his lips; it is well that he learn to use it with precision. Three meanings in particular may be distinguished.

(a) *Anything whatever, written or unwritten, that lets in light on the human past, that informs or teaches us concerning it,* may be called a document (Latin *documentum* from *docere*, to teach). Thus used, the term may refer to any one of such various items as an oral tradition, a coin, a building, a parliamentary report, a diary, a history written at second hand. This meaning is a broad one, but it has its uses; it is the only meaning of the term which gives validity to the dictum, "there is no substitute for documents; no documents, no history." If *documents* in this context is meant for written records only, then the dictum is false; history in certain uses can be based, wholly or in part, sometimes on oral tradition, sometimes on archaeological remains.

(*b*) More strictly, a document is *any original written record, public or private, official or unofficial, printed or unprinted*. This is the usual meaning of the term, and as such will be verified in most contexts in this work. Thus, the nineteenth century has been labelled "the age of documents," in reference to the practice, then first introduced, or at least systematized, of basing history largely on archival or original material, especially official records. But what precisely are we to understand by an "original document"? Hardly anybody would hesitate to call Domesday Book such. In reality it is only a digest or compilation of reports turned in by the royal commissioners. So also in the case of Livy. His work is a recognized "primary" source or document for Roman history; substantially, it is a secondary work put together from earlier sources, of which few perhaps were primary in the accepted sense of the term. The ambiguity may be removed, in some cases at least, by qualifying as "original" any document beyond which one can not go for some particular data, because of the fact that the earlier sources on which it may have been based have disappeared. In this sense the works of Thucydides and Livy are "original" documents, while those of Gardiner and McMaster are not.

(*c*) In the strictest sense of the term a document is *any original written record of an official or public character*. It was especially in this sense that Ranke and his school contended that history should be based on documents.

The three definitions of *document* here set down are working definitions. The historian's terminology, because derived from common usage or borrowed from other branches of learning, never achieves or even approaches the precision of the terminology of the exact sciences. What really matters, is the realities behind the terms commonly used by the historian. So long as the realities are clearly grasped, so long as the terms that express them are used intelligibly, consistently, and with such measure of precision as is practicable, the historian will have done his duty to the vocabulary of his craft.

C. Three Types of History as Record

¶ 13   Three major types of historical record (history-writing, historiography) are recognized. What differentiates them is the particular angle from which they view the raw material of history common to all three. *Narrative history* looks at the facts of history as a series of interesting data following one another in a simple order of time, and worth reporting for their own sake; it is "a story that is told." *Didactic history* finds in these facts a repertoire of texts from which to draw lessons, political, moral, and otherwise, for individual or social guidance. Genetic history sees in the facts an elaborate complex of causes and effects, revealing "growth," "development," "evolution," as the basic phenomenon in history.

❡ 14 NARRATIVE HISTORY

This is the earliest of all the genres of history as record. It answers to one of the most elemental of human traits, readiness to tell a story or listen to one. Sagas, myths, ballads have been the first carriers of historical data, however distorted the data may become in the process. The inspiring motive of these vehicles is generally esthetic: to entertain, to please, by seizing the living recollections of a heroic past and fixing them in some engaging literary way. But narrative history can take shapes of a more businesslike kind, such as genealogical tables, lists of rulers and officials, and similar documents that have a practical use in political or social life. Also, narrative history can record the doings of kings, princes, or heroes, with a view to glorify them, as is the case in numerous annals and chronicles, Oriental, Greek, and Roman. Narrative history in these various forms continued to be written far into the Middle Ages, and during this period, as far as it bore a Christian character, it was penetrated with the idea of a Divine Providence guiding the destinies of men. Even today, history of the narrative or factual kind has its recognized place, and is perhaps the commonest of all types.

Herodotus is generally instanced as the typical exponent of narrative history. "To rescue from oblivion the memory of former incidents and to render a just tribute of renown to the many great and wonderful actions both of Greeks and Barbarians, Herodotus of Halicarnassus produces this historical essay."—Bk. 1, Belloe's translation.

❡ 15 DIDACTIC HISTORY

Didactic (G. διδακτικός), instructive history is sometimes designated pragmatic, a term borrowed from Polybius (ca. 210–128 B.C.), whose history professes to deal chiefly with affairs of state (πράγματα). The avowed purpose of didactic history is to treat past happenings as precedents for action, individual or social. The classic statement of it is by Lord Bolingbroke, who, however, said he merely quoted from Dionysius of Halicarnassus: "History is philosophy teaching by examples."— Letters on the Study and Use of History (London, 1779), 14.

"Battle history" ("drum-and-trumpet history") gives a disproportionate measure of space and emphasis to military facts. As a type of general history, it is now happily outmoded. Professedly military histories, needless to say, have, their legitimate place in historiography.

(a) *The Teaching-value of History*. It is a fashion in some quarters to call the teaching-value of history into question. "*L'histoire ne sert à rien*," said Fustel de Coulanges. Henry Adams is equally condemnatory: "In essence incoherent and immoral, history had to be taught as such—or falsified."—*The Education of Henry Adams: An Autobiography* (Boston, 1918), 300.

Yet both historians produced works which belie their pessimistic views. Fustel de Coulanges's prestige as an authority on French origins is outstanding, while Adams' treatment of the presidencies of Adams and Jefferson probably remains unsurpassed.

Recently, especially among the exponents of the so-called "new history," lively skepticism has been expressed as to the didactic uses of history. "The chief lesson of the newer history," says Harry Elmer Barnes, "would seem to be that the main purpose of studying the past is to lose our reverence for it, though not of course our interest in it." According to James Harvey Robinson, history, were we to have a completely comprehensive grasp of it, would function in the role of "teacher," not by furnishing us with "precedents of conduct," but by enabling us to base conduct upon "a perfect comprehension of existing conditions founded upon a perfect knowledge of the past."—*The New History: Essays Illustrating the New Historical Outlook* (New York, 1912), 21.

Even from this point of view, it will be noted, history is not a thing of speculative interest only.

(b) The starting point of the newer skepticism as to the practical uses of history is rejection of the familiar axiom that "history repeats itself." The fallacy of the axiom, it is alleged, is seen in its assumption that history returns on itself in closed circles, thus creating more or less parallel situations, with the result that knowledge of a past situation enables one to cope with a similar situation in the present. Rather, it is contended, history never returns on itself in closed circles; it has no lessons to offer to the individual or to society, each of which must work out its own salvation in the living present, namely, amid circumstances and conditions that are without parallelism of any kind in the past. In other words, the events of history are essentially "unique."

In all this there is a manifest lack of logic. No one may reasonably contend that the past ever repeats itself completely and in exact pattern. But a situation of today may resemble one of yesterday closely enough to make one's experience, direct or indirect, of the former, a guide to proper handling of the latter. In this sense, history, as past actuality, does unquestionably repeat itself. Sound thinking, ancient and modern, has never called the axiom into question; the normal human mind accepts it without demur. Thucydides meant to impart an "exact knowledge of facts which have not only actually occurred, but which are destined approximately to repeat themselves in all human probability."—Trans. in Arnold J. Toynbee, *Greek Historical Thought from Homer to Heraclius* (New York, 1924), 19.

Experience (individual history), kept present in the mind by memory, is an indispensable guide to correct personal conduct in the present; what memory does for the individual, by the same token, history, the "social memory," does for the community, and for the individual also.

(c) It should be sufficient to note that from the point of view of common sense the notion that historical events are wholly unique, is simply not tenable. In medical practice, for instance, no case, even of a relatively simple disease like pneumonia, is exactly like any other case; each patient presents to the physicians a problem in some way unique. But not wholly unique, else the medical profession could never have achieved the triumphs it undoubtedly has achieved. The physician expects to learn from experience—that is, from history. The fact is that most practical men—farmers, sailors, engineers—habitually act on what it is no mere quibble to call historical uniformities. They may make mistakes. If they act as if their experience gave them *absolute uniformities*, they are certain to make grave mistakes. But they would make even graver ones if they assumed that each problem they faced was wholly unique and unprecedented.—See Clarence C. Brinton, "Napoleon and Hitler," *Foreign Affairs*, 20 (1941): 213.

¶ 16 The idea that history is a storehouse of lessons for future use was common in classical antiquity. Thucydides has been mentioned; some of the later Greek historians elaborated the same idea with cleverness.

The following passages are from the prefaces written by Greek historians to their respective universal histories; the translations are from Toynbee, *Greek Historical Thought*.

> The knowledge of past events is the sovereign corrective of human nature. This duty, however, is far from having been exceptionally or perfunctorily performed. It is actually the note on which almost all historians have begun and ended their work when they have eulogized the lessons of history as the truest education and training for political life and the study of others' vicissitudes as the most effective or indeed the only school in which the right spirit for enduring the changes of fortune can be acquired.—Polybius (ca. 201–120 B.C.).

> [Thucydides] also introduces the idea of utility and of what is obviously the rational object of history, which is, as he explains, to enable mankind to cope successfully with current problems in the light of rec-

ords of the past, in the event of circumstances repeating themselves.—Lucian of Samosata (ca. A.D. 125–200).

[Historians] have discovered the secret of imparting the fruits, without the perils, of experience, and therefore have knowledge of inestimable value to offer to the readers of their works. Toil and danger are the price of the practical wisdom which is bought by the experience of daily life, . . . [but] history is able to instruct without inflicting pain by affording an insight into the failures and successes of others.—Diodorus of Agyrium (ca. 90–20 B.C.).

History will accordingly be found to be the universal teacher of mankind, who lays before us what we should attempt and what we should leave alone as being unlikely to succeed. . . . For the old she is a nurse and an unbroken reed; for the young she is an admirable and supremely intelligent tutor, who powders the head of youth with the hoariness of experience and thus anticipates the gradual knowledge that comes by time.—Theophylactus Simocatta the Egyptian (ca. A.D. 560–630).

₡ 17 TYPICAL MODERN STATEMENTS ON THE TEACHING-VALUE OF HISTORY.

We do not draw the moral lessons we might from history. On the contrary, without care it may be used to vitiate our minds and to destroy our happiness. In history a great volume is unrolled for our instruction, drawing the materials of future wisdom from the past errors and infirmities of mankind.—Edmund Burke, "Reflections on the Revolution in France," *The Works of the Right Honourable Edmund Burke* (12 vols., London, 1871), 3:418.

But there is no part of our annals more essential to be studied if the main object with which history is read be to gather examples and warnings for the future. There were no mistakes committed in that day which are not liable to occur again and again, because they are mistakes to which the Celtic race is prone; and to exhibit them is like setting up a storm-bell on a rock where shipwrecks have been common.—Sir Charles Gavan Duffy, *Four Years of Irish History, 1845–1849* (London, 1883), 25.

The knowledge of the past, the record of truths revealed by experience, is eminently practical as an instrument of action and a power that goes to the making of the future.—John E. E. Dalberg, Lord Acton, *A Lecture on the Study of History* (Cambridge, Eng., 1895), 3.

No political conclusions of any value for practice can be arrived at by direct experience. All true political science is, in one sense of the phrase, *a priori*, being deduced from the tendencies of things, tendencies known either through our general experience of human nature or as the result of an analysis of the course of history, considered as a progressive evolution.—John Stuart Mill, cited in Acton, *Lecture*, 75.

Fashionable skepticism has derided of late the worth of the "lessons of history," but no amount of deriding can make those lessons lose their worth. . . . The past teaches us, for example, that unbearable abuses breed revolutions; that a class which no longer justifies its privileges by its services is doomed.—Jean Jules Jusserand and Others, *The Writing of History* (New York, 1926), 29.

Considered in their application to practice, these conclusions of history have a real value not only to the student but also to the statesman. Many an error might have been avoided had a body of sound maxims been present to the minds of constitution makers and statesmen.—James Viscount Bryce, *Modern Democracies* (2 vols., London, 1929), 1:22.

Burke A. Hinsdale, "Educational Value of History," in *How to Study and Teach History, with Particular Reference to the History of the United States* (New York, 1914), chap. 1.

Bibliography on the teaching-value of history: AHA, *Report* (1889), 1:570 ff.

¶ 18   GENETIC HISTORY

Didactic history held the field from Greek and Roman times well into the nineteenth century. It was especially in honor in the heyday of the European national states of the eighteenth century, with their tendency to glorify heroic beginnings and pioneer patriotic leaders. But didacticism in history was destined to give place to a newer ideal, knowledge of the past as it really was. If history was to confine itself to being merely a storehouse of political and moral lessons, of precedents for future conduct, individual or social, it could never rise to the dignity of a science. This distinction was reserved for a third type of history, the *genetic* or *evolutionary*—the latter term not being taken here in a biological or Darwinian sense. The merit of having introduced the genetic concept and of making it the basis of a new school of historiography belongs to a group of German scholars, Herder and Niebuhr among them, who at the turn of the eighteenth century began to apply the idea of development to history. This idea of development in history as actuality was not unknown to earlier authors, but only at the period named was it grasped in its full implications and made the basis of a science of history. It must be observed here that while the genetic has supplanted the didactic type of history as more satisfying, it has not eliminated the latter altogether, nor is it desirable that it do so. Genetic history of the right kind may be, and generally is, virtually didactic. History which stresses cause and effect and the slow process of social evolution from past to present, has still its lessons of wisdom to impart, though it may not do so by deliberate aim or explicit statement. Moreover, situations and personalities that obviously convey some message of instruction to posterity must have place in genetic as well as in any other kind of historical record.

Genetic history regards the complex of historical events as an infinitely vast tissue of causes and effects, every event standing to certain other events in these two relations. This means, therefore, that historical events and conditions grow, develop, evolve out of those preceding. It is the function of the genetic historian to search out this growth, development, evolution, and to present it as the very core of history. In doing so he employs a rigorous method, which, more than anything else, is what makes history a science [₵ 40].

D. History as a Method of Inquiry

₵ 19 History presents itself under three distinct aspects, past actuality, record, technique or method of inquiry. The first two aspects have been considered; it remains to consider the third. We say of someone that he is a trained historian, which means that he is a skilled practitioner in the art of history. The art of history connotes something different from facts or the record of them. It connotes the method, technique, in fine, the whole process involved in making the record. Here, then, is a third use of the term history, which one must recognize and manage to keep distinct from the others. When we say of someone that he is a trained historian, we do not mean simply that he knows a great many facts about the past, though this may well be the case, but that he knows and can apply the right technique in searching out the facts. When the Greeks first used the term, it was in the sense of inquiry, investigation, research. This meaning is identical with that considered here. Briefly, then, history, in the third acceptation of the term, is equivalent to historical method or technique, the subject matter of this book.

Charles H. Haskins, "History," *Historical Outlook*, 16 (1925): 196.

Historical method may be regarded as an application, in one particular direction, of epistemology—a science that deals with the nature of human thought and the circumstances which condition its truth or validity. Just as epistemology establishes the mind's general capacity for knowing the truth and the conditions under which it must work in order to attain it, so historical method or technique demonstrates the correct procedure to be followed in attaining to a specific kind of truth, namely, truth in history.

E. Contemporary History

¶ 20 From a philosopher's point of view there can be no such thing as strictly "contemporary history." The two ideas "contemporary" and "history," when analyzed, are seen to be mutually exclusive. We act in the present; but the present is an infinitesimal point of time, which is relegated to the past in the very act of using it. When we speak of the present as a stage of history we have in mind what has been described happily as "the specious present": which though time really past, is separated from time present by relatively small intervals. "Contemporary" is more precisely "recent" history, though both terms are relative in their implications, since the exact range of time which they cover is determined by choice, convention, or other considerations. Lord Acton thought that contemporary or recent history was "the most pressing of all." A similar view was expressed by John B. Bury in regard to modern history, which he considered to be the only period in which "history could be set forth in its all-embracing range. You cannot portray an age in all its aspects unless you are in direct relation with it."—Harold W. V. Temperley, ed., *Selected Essays of J. B. Bury* (Cambridge, Eng., 1930), xxii. See also Robert W. Seton-Watson, "A Plea for the Study of Contemporary History," *History: The Quarterly Journal of the Historical Association* (London), 14 (1929): 1–18.

However, modern or at least contemporary history, being unfinished history, cannot be "set forth in its all-embracing range." See Toynbee's statement [¶ 21].

¶ 21 The importance of contemporary history is now widely recognized, especially in teaching. Textbooks and courses in this particular part of the historical field multiply; the proportion of space allotted to it in general histories steadily increases. Apart from the consideration that records for contemporary periods are more abundant than for the earlier, the emphasis laid on recent history appears to be based mainly on the general principle that present-day conditions have been shaped more decisively by recent events than by the remote. In many respects the principle is a sound one; but it admits of qualifications. As a matter of fact, certain remote events have been more far-reaching, more significant in their effects than any of the recent events. The most significant of all past happenings in its bearings on history as a whole, has been the advent of Christianity nearly twenty centuries ago. Again, increasing current interest in medieval history is due, among other causes, to a growing conviction among scholars that the Middle Ages hold the key to the solution of numerous social and economic problems. Lord

Morley thought that interest in medieval history is motivated by the fact that "the life of the nineteenth century strikes its roots in the thirteenth." As regards contemporary history, a drawback in it is the circumstance that we can never see it in full perspective and as a finished whole. It has yet to be seen in its final issue before we can grasp its true meaning and see its relations to history in general. Toynbee says of the history of ancient Greece: "We can sit as spectators through the whole play; we can say: This or that is the crisis; from this point onwards the end is inevitable; or, if this actor had acted otherwise in these circumstances, the issue would not have been the same."—Charles G. Crump and Ernest F. Jacob, eds., *The Legacy of Greece* (Oxford, 1923), 229.

⟨ 22 The formula of the Italian neo-Hegelian idealist, Benedetto Croce, calls for comment. Croce says "that every true history is contemporary history."—*History: Its Theory and Practice* (New York, 1921), 12.

(a) The formula is not to be interpreted simply and according to the obvious meaning of its terms; it is meant to express one of the many sinuosities of thought involved in the author's idealistic viewpoint. Taken at its face value, it is patently untrue. Tenth-century history is as much "true history" as yesterday's.

(b) The past lives on in its effects; the "living past" is with us today, and hence can be properly called contemporary. In this sense it is intelligible that "every true history is contemporary history."

(c) Since history as past actuality survives in a sense in the human consciousness, to which it is present as an object of thought, and since certainly the object of thought is contemporary with the thinker, all true history may in this qualified sense be called contemporary history. It is some such concept as this, it would appear, which Croce seeks to express by the formula in question. If, then, the only "true" history is that which is known here and now with accompanying insight and realization, and if, which is a fact, the object of thought (*conceptus objectivus*) is a thing coincident in time with the thinker, then it follows that every "true" history is necessarily "contemporary" history. This is an intelligible proposition, and as explained, a correct one; but it is also nothing more than a psychological or pedagogical truism. It is not anything new in philosophical reflection that the realities of history have value, significant for us of today, only to the extent that we can apprehend their meaning, the place they occupy in the historical process as a whole.

(d) It has been suggested that what Croce means to convey by his formula is that history in its true definition is "contemporary thought about the past."——*AHR*, 39 (1934): 219.

Such a concept is valid in the sense that the all-important thing in history is what we of today think about the past, how its realities impress us. But this is not by any means the concept to which Croce sought to give expression.——G. J. Garraghan, "The Crocean View of History," *The Modern Schoolman*, 16 (1939): 54–57.

F. Continuity and Unity

¶ 23   Edward A. Freeman, the English historian, was wont to stress two closely related ideas, the continuity and the unity of history. "The history of man is one in all ages," he said. "We must look at history as one unbroken whole, no part of which can be safely looked at without reference to the other parts."——*The Unity of History* (London, 1872).

History from this point of view is conceived as one uninterrupted process, which it is, from the earliest recorded incidents to the present day. There are no broken links in the complete chain of historical causes and effects. History, to borrow a concept from scholastic philosophy, is a *continuum*. The present always dovetails into the past; there is never any clear-cut line of cleavage between the two, not even in times of highly radical change, such as the French Revolution or the Russian Revolution. If, then, history is a *continuum*, by the same token it is a unit.

This reasoning led Freeman to two practical conclusions: that to know adequately any single period of history, one must know all the others; that the conventional blocking off of history into periods—ancient, medieval, and modern—is arbitrary and should be abandoned. The continuity and unity of history are valid concepts, but Freeman pushed them to unwarranted lengths. When he lectured at Cambridge on the history of modern Sicily, he approached his subject from the Greek period and with considerable detail; but the long-drawn-out treatment bored his hearers, and in the end he found himself addressing nearly empty benches.

¶ 24   The ideas of historical continuity and unity have had a profound influence on historiography, especially in modern times. The conventional device of furnishing "background" to historical accounts is an instance in point. Thucydides introduces his narrative of the Peloponnesian War with a brief survey of early Greek history. Lately there has been the tendency, in Lord Acton's happy phrase, "to descry dimly the Declaration of Independence in the forests of Germany," a tendency not conceded by all students as warranted by the facts. John Fiske, ardent disciple of Freeman, started his *Beginnings of New England* at A.D. 476, tracing ideas and institutions from the collapse of the Roman Empire to their appearance on the shores of the New World. Thomas Arnold pointed out "how impossible it is to study any age by itself, how necessarily our inquiries run back into previous centuries." Citing Comines, he showed that the marriage of Mary, Duchess of Burgundy, and sole heiress of Charles the Bold, with the Austrian Archduke Maximilian, had visible reactions in Belgian history as late as 1830.—*Introductory Lectures on Modern History*, 137.

The signing of the Vatican treaty, February 11, 1929, had a thousand years and more of history leading up to it.

Herbert E. Bolton makes United States history an integral chapter in the broader story of the "two Americas." Only in the light of New World development forward from the time of Columbus, can the essential character and significance of United States history be fully understood.—*The History of the Americas* (New York, 1935).

In all such uses of historical background the principle invoked is to see one's subject as an integral unit in a larger whole.

❡ 25 Freeman's objection to the conventional division of history into ancient, medieval, and modern, has failed to find support in modern historiography. One of the most elaborate of recent historical projects, the Cambridge series of histories, accepts the threefold division. The main reasons justifying periodization in history are two. First, some system of grouping historical data according to time-elements is indispensable. Without such system effective organization of the data is impossible, whether in teaching or writing history. Second, periods, eras and other time-divisions of the historical field are not necessarily mere mental figments; they often have reality independently of human record. William H. Mace distinguishes between *mechanical* historical wholes and *organic* historical wholes.—*Method in History* (Chicago, 1914).

(a) In the first group the only element fixing the whole, or unit, is one of time. A reign or a presidential term may be nowise different substantially as regards political, social, cultural, and other conditions from the reign or presidential term that preceded or followed it. In other words, it may be merely an external or mechanical block of history set off by accidental dates of beginning or end. On the other hand, a block of history as objective reality may have a distinctive character. Here it is not a question merely of a tract of time limited by dates. In political, social, economic character, in general conditions of whatever sort, this tract is more or less sharply differentiated from other tracts of time. Briefly, its distinctive character constitutes it an objective, organic unit or whole, prior to any attempt of the historian to reproduce it in record. Certain blocks or tracts of history do therefore stand out as organic wholes, as true periods, which the historian has to recognize if his record is to be true to fact.

(b) The Middle Ages had unquestionably certain characteristics about them which one fails to find in the Renaissance period, and vice versa. Each period had individuality, each was in many respects intimately and organically a cultural unit or whole. To call the medieval period "the age of faith," is to recognize the objective fact that for some ten centuries the greatest single force operating in the contemporary world was belief in dogmatic Christianity. Periodization is therefore not a thing left to the historian's option; it enters into the very essence of history as record.

The distinction between ancient and modern history is no mere accident nor yet a mere matter of chronological convenience. What is called modern history is in reality the formation of a new cycle of culture, . . .—Theodor Mommsen, *The History of Rome* (New York, 1871), 1:24.

There is no need to eliminate these old concepts which have become part of usage, antiquity, the Middle Ages, modern times, and which moreover, by dominating the labor of scholars, have acquired an incontestable practical value.—*Encyclopaedia of the Social Sciences* (15 vols., New York, 1930–1935), 8:367.

❡ 26 The objection that periods are time-divisions in appearance only and not in reality, since they gradually merge into one another, is without force. Though they do merge into one another by slow degrees, a moment comes when the process is complete, and one period stands out in contrast to the other. We cannot distinguish the precise moment when night becomes day, but the moment comes when we know for certain we have passed from one to the other.

(a) Since the passing of the Graeco-Roman era, periodization in history has been conventional. The early Middle Ages saw the "six ages" of St. Augustine come into vogue: Adam to Noah, Noah to Abraham, Abraham to David, David to the Babylonian Exile, the Babylonian Exile to Christ, Christ to the end of the world. Isidore of Seville and Venerable Bede were instrumental in popularizing this time-division throughout the Middle Ages. Dionysius Exiguus (sixth century), discarding the currently used Era of Diocletian, on the ground that he was loath to perpetuate the name of a persecutor of the Church, introduced the Christian Era, according to which dates are reckoned in two series, one back from, the other after the Incarnation. This central event he dated March 25, of the year 754 from the foundation of Rome. The concept of the four world-kingdoms, Babylonian, Mede and Persian, Macedonian, Roman, achieved wide currency in the European West, especially through the influence of St. Jerome. Christopher Keller

(1634–1707) popularized the classic division of history into ancient, medieval, modern. The limits of the medieval era (Middle Ages) have been variously set; some begin with the reign of Constantine the Great, others with the deposition of the last Roman emperor in the West, 476, and others with the crowning of Charlemagne, 800, ending the era with the fall of Constantinople, 1453, or with the Protestant Revolt (first half of the sixteenth century).

(b) Conventional periods are met with in most fields of history, such as, in the English, the eras of Tudor despotism, industrial revolution, political reform; in the French, the eras of monarchical growth, the Revolution, reaction; in the American, the eras of colonial development, "critical period" (1783–1789), "good feeling," slavery agitation, reconstruction, economic depression of the nineteen-thirties. William S. Lilly conveniently (if rather roughly) blocks off nineteen centuries of history into four periods, distinguished from one another by their relations to Christianity: Europe in process of Christianization, 1–800; Europe Christian, 800–1500; Europe un-Christian, 1500–1789; Europe anti-Christian, 1789.—*Christianity and Modern Civilization* (2 vols., London, 1903).

For comments on periodization in history, see Peter Guilday, *An Introduction to Church History* (St. Louis and London, 1925), 20ff.

G. Civilization and Culture

❡ 27 *Civilization is a condition of organized society in which political, social, economic, and intellectual life has reached a more or less advanced stage of development.*

(a) The German *Kulturgeschichte*, generally rendered into English by "history of civilization," excludes political history; in other words, *Kultur* includes non-political elements only, as the social, economic, intellectual, etc. But English texts on the history of civilization do not all exclude the political element. Thus Lynn Thorndike aims to present "those positive accomplishments in political and social institutions, in art and industry, in science and thought, which are denoted by the collective term, civilization."—*Short History of Civilization* (New York, 1927), 3.

Guizot's *General History of Civilization in Modern Europe*, also covers all aspects of development, the political included.

The English economist Charles S. Devas analyzes the concept "civilization" in all its implications. It is taken by him to mean the condition of a large group of men displaying the following seven characteristics: (1) the possession of a city worthy of the name; (2) some degree of political order and power; (3) some proficiency in the industrial arts, in agriculture, manufactures, mining, building, and transport; (4) some proficiency in the fine arts; (5) some knowledge of philosophy, history, and physical science; (6) a written literature; (7) the existence of a moneyed and leisured upper class.—*A Key to the World's Progress* (London, 1924), 3.

(b) Civilization may also be conceived as popular institutional life. But the two concepts are not altogether identical, because civilization implies a certain perfection or advanced degree of institutional life. The life of a people is many-sided; it presents various aspects or phases of activity. At least five such phases can be distinguished: political, social, religious, educational, and economic. Each of the phases tends to express itself in an institution: political ideas and activities in government; social, in the family; religious, in the church; educational, in the school; economic, in industry and occupation. The complex of these institutions with the activities centering about them is equivalently civilization, or popular institutional life. The life of a people is a closely knit and organic whole. A major movement or event makes itself felt in every member of the social organism. The French Revolution affected France on every side, just as the economic depression of 1929 and subsequent years, reacted visibly in the United States on government, family, church, school, industry, labor, and on other elements of national life. From this line of thought issues the corollary that history seeks to make known the life of a people as this is revealed to us in its institutions, just as biography seeks to portray a human personality as revealed in its words and acts.

For an exposition of the concept of history as institutional life, see W. H. Mace, *Method in History*.

(c) "Culture" stands generally for *intellectual* as distinct from *material* civilization. It includes therefore (4), (5), (6), in the series suggested by Devas. One must note the anthropological use of "culture," as expressing any development of society, however primitive. It is correct to speak of Siouan "culture" of a period when the Sioux were distinctly an uncivilized people. Anthropologists count over 650 "cultures" or primitive social developments.

(d) The term *civilization* can be understood as not necessarily including the notion of moral or religious development. "No doubt the word [civilization] can be stretched so as to include them, but becomes valueless by the inclusion and we should be involved in the fruitless paradox that the Romans in the height of their civilization were in some most important aspects less civilized than the illiterate barbarians of the North."——Devas, *Key to the World's Progress*, 3.

To some, however, this exclusion of morality and religion from the characteristics of civilization seems unwarranted.

(e) Civilization is a relative, not an absolute concept. There are civilizations; there is no civilization, unless one wishes to take in this sense such definitions of the term as are formulated above. Feudalism was probably a better, a more "civilized" system for the society contemporaneous with it than centralized government would have been. A people may be civilized (as for instance, were the Romans of the Empire) with a system of government other than democratic or parliamentary. Arnold J. Toynbee in *A Study of History* distinguishes twenty-one civilizations.

Ernest R. Hull, *Civilization and Culture* (St. Louis, 1915).

Moorhouse I. X. Millar, "Human Nature and Civilization," *Unpopular Essays in the Philosophy of History* (New York, 1922), 7.

Demetrius B. Zema, *The Thoughtlessness of Modern Thought Concerning the Ideas of Civilization, Culture, Science, and Progress* (New York, 1934).

H. Progress

¶ 28 Progress may be defined as "an increase in the quantity or quality of some good."——Devas, *Key to the World's Progress*, 4.

To say that a disease is "progressive," meaning that it tends to become worse, is good usage, but abstractly it does not verify the most logical application of the term. Progress in disease is in reality retrogression in health. As applied to society or civilization, the term *progress* has constantly to be distinguished. A people may be going forward materially and backward morally. Hence, to speak of progress in civilization as a whole, almost necessarily results in ambiguity and misunderstanding. Civilization is such a highly complex reality that one seldom if ever finds it advancing simultaneously on all fronts.

The idea of progress as the fundamental law of social evolution was first distinctly formulated by the Abbé de St.-Pierre in the first quarter of the eighteenth century. Later in this same century, Condorcet (1743–1794) wrote a notable tract on "the indefinite perfectability of man" (*Esquisse d'un tableau historique des progrès de l'esprit humain*)—and the nineteenth-century Darwinians, with their theories of the ascent of man from the lower forms of life, gave currency to the notion of progress, or evolution for the better, as underlying not only the physical order, but also the entire social structure, past, present, and to be. Eventually, the cult of "progress" rose almost to the proportions of a religion. According to James H. Robinson, it was only yesterday in world history that man "came to wish to progress, and still more recently that he came to see that he can voluntarily progress and that he has progressed. This appears to me to be the most impressive message that history has to give us and the most vital in the light that it casts on the conduct of life."—*The New History*, 251.

Perfect knowledge of the past, so Robinson explains, reveals above everything else the eternal law of progress, according to which the present system of things, including traditional ethics and dogmatic religion, is merely temporary and provisional, a preparation for something better to come, just as the past was the preparation for the better order of things that obtains today.

An elaborate exposition of the doctrine of progress is made by John B. Bury, in *The Idea of Progress; an Inquiry into its Origin and Growth* (New York, 1932). Bury admits that the doctrine itself of progress, in deference to the assumed everlasting relativity of all things, may eventually be displaced by an entirely different doctrine. "Will not the process of change for which Progress is the optimistic name, compel 'Progress' too, to fall from the commanding position in which it is now, with apparent security, enthroned?" The idea of historical progress as expounded by Robinson, Bury, and others of the rationalist school, obviously carries with it anti-Christian implications.

The studies by Dawson and Devas, here cited, are especially helpful. Also the following:

Ross Hoffman, *Tradition and Progress and Other Historical Essays in Culture, Religion, and Progress* (Milwaukee, 1938).

Jean de Plessis, *The Human Caravan: The Direction and Meaning of History*, trans. from the French (New York, 1939), 61 ff.

Christopher H. Dawson, *Enquiries into Religion and Culture* (London, 1933), 67 ff.

Douglas Jerrold, *The Necessity of Freedom: Notes on Christianity and Politics* (London, 1930), 1–17.

(a) In certain important respects there certainly has been progress or improvement. Mechanical inventions ministering to human needs and comfort are legion. Slavery has been abolished, the barbarous criminal codes of earlier periods have been replaced by humane; opportunities for education have been widened, diseases "conquered," or almost so; space and time "annihilated." And yet, the question is being raised with insistence whether mechanical aids and improvements cannot reach a stage in number and perfection where they are in many ways a liability rather than an asset to society in general.

(b) A concept of progress that postulates possible radical change in everything, including even fundamental ethics and revealed religion, is clearly inadmissible. No grounds whether of pure reason or historical proof have ever been produced to make valid the concept of progress in this sense.

(c) The facts of retrogression in history are probably as startling as those of progress. One of the amazing things in the human story is the apparently complete disappearance of whole systems of highly-developed cultures, such as the Assyrian, Egyptian, Minoan, East Indian, Mayan. One may correctly contend that the present modern age outdistances all others in merely material achievements; but in other regards, artistic and literary excellence, it is frankly conscious of inferiority to other ages. —See Devas, "The Manifold Facts of Retrogression," Key to the World's Progress, 8.

(d) In recent years the doctrine of progress has received a visible setback. "For two centuries it has dominated the European mind to such an extent that any attempt to question it was regarded as a paradox or a heresy, and it is only during the last twenty years that its supremacy has begun to be seriously challenged."—Dawson, Progress and Religion (New York, 1928), vii.

Various reasons have contributed to this result, among them, growing dissatisfaction with the present industrial system, increasing appreciation of medieval ideals and achievements, the World Wars, with their appalling destruction, and the disillusionment and economic distress following. The question whether men are really any better off on the whole than they were in past ages, is often asked and not always answered in the affirmative. Spengler's momentarily much talked-of *Decline of the West*, itself inconsequential as a philosophy of history, echoes the growing conviction that the nineteenth century did not achieve ultimate civilization. "It may even be questioned, as indeed it has been questioned by many, whether the modern advance of material civilization is progressive in the true sense of the word; whether we are happier or wiser or better than they were in simpler states of society, and whether Birmingham or Chicago is to be preferred to medieval Florence."—Dawson, Progress and Religion, 8.

Practically, the question whether or not the world is progressing, will be answered according to one's standard of values, one's philosophy of life. In any case *progress* is a term which the historian must contrive to use with caution and with a clear sense of its manifold and shifting implications.

(e) To conclude, it is not open to question that in many important ways men are better off today than were the men of yesterday. It is wisdom to recognize what is sound in present-day civilization, and to be thankful for it. Contrasting the present with the past at the expense of the former, is on occasion legitimate enough; but it is a procedure that can easily rest on mistaken views as to what past conditions really were. That "distance lends enchantment to the view" is a psychological fact which accounts for not a little distortion in interpretations of history. The past in retrospect tends to wrap itself in an illusory haze of poetry and romance. One must not overlook the truth that "golden ages," to recall Frederick Ozanam's dictum, have really no basis in historical fact. They may show certain traits which excite the admiration or envy of later ages; in all of them is the inevitable fly in the ointment.

A historian worthy of the name will use the common terms of historiography, such as progress, civilization, democracy, liberty, science, with precision and clear understanding of the realities to which they refer; he will carefully avoid an all too common perversion of truth by the misuse of such terms. Thus, "fascism," as bandied about in current discussions of world affairs, assumes a chameleon-like diversity of meaning; this renders its use by speakers and writers an almost inevitable source of misunderstanding, just as "democracy" has been made to cover realities which are the very negation of popular rule.

I. Erroneous Conceptions of History

⁋ 29   *That history is exclusively or primarily concerned with politics, with the state.* That "history is past politics and politics present history," was a favorite proposition with the English historian Edward Freeman.—*The Methods of Historical Study* (London, 1886), 148.

The viewpoint thus expressed owes the vogue it has had largely to the influence of the Hegelian philosophy, the author of which held the state to be "an absolute end in itself" (*sich absoluter Selbstzweck*), whereas its true, immediate, and necessary end, which is the public welfare, lies altogether outside the state. The state as an entity exists for the sake of the individual, the family, and not *vice versa*. The Hegelian conception of it is the philosophical basis of state-worship, political absolutism, totalitarian government. It carries with it denial of the "natural-rights theory," and the consequent assumption that all rights whether of the individual or the family originate with the state. The fact is that there are natural rights anterior to the state and independent of it, a truth which met with classic expression in the preamble to the Declaration of Independence.

As a matter of course, Freeman's own books (*History of the Norman Conquest, William Rufus*, etc.) are patterned after his theory. Literature, religion, social and economic life, are topics conspicuous by their absence.

So also non-political factors in English medieval life suffer neglect in Lingard's notable work. The shift from the political to the social point of view in English historiography was signalized by the appearance in 1874 of John R. Green's *Short History of the English People*. In the preface Green wrote: "I have preferred to pass lightly and briefly over the details of foreign wars and diplomacies, the personal adventures of Kings and nobles, the pomps of courts, or the intrigues of favorites, and to dwell at length on the incidents of that constitutional, intellectual, and social advance in which we read the history of the nation itself."

¶ 30 *That history is only another name for social phenomena produced by necessarily-operating laws of nature.* This is the positivist conception of history introduced by Auguste Comte and his school. The "sociology" or "social science" formulated by Comte has for its task the comparative study of social groups of all sorts as regards their functions, relations, transformations, and the like, with a view to eliciting therefrom certain laws of a mechanical type by which the activities of the various groups are determined. All history thus becomes the product of necessarily-operating laws of nature. Moreover, it is conceived as only a branch of sociology, and shares with sociology an identical aim and method. It is reduced by Comte to a "*histoire sans noms d'hommes ou même sans noms de peuples.*" The positivist view of history, though a century has passed since its formulation, has yet to find a recognized basis in experience or fact. Research in the field of sociology properly understood has produced no evidence of the existence of mechanical laws which positivism postulates as the explanation of social phenomena. Like Marx's materialistic interpretation of history, positivism has not got beyond the stage of gratuitous assumption of laws which common experience as well as scientific research thus far has failed to bring to light.

¶ 31 *That history is fine art rather than science.* The alleged grounds for this conception are chiefly two: history deals with the singular, the unique, the concrete, whereas science deals with the general, the universal; history, like fine art, has for its immediate purpose the stimulation of pleasure of an esthetic sort. In the Graeco-Roman World history was regarded as a branch of rhetoric; the typical historians of classical antiquity, such as Herodotus and Tacitus, owed their reputation as much to the good literary form as to the factual content of their productions. The right stand to take in this question is to hold that the immediate purpose of history is not to stimulate esthetic pleasure but to ascertain the truth regarding past human realities. To assume any other immediate purpose of history is as gratuitous as it is illogical. If the presentation of historical truth can be made at the same time satisfying, so much the better; but for the historian, literary quality and the satisfaction it begets, can never be more than by-products of his craft. As to history's dealing only with the unique, the singular, the concrete, this is an obvious misapprehension, since the general, the universal, can also in a true sense come within its range.

¶ 32 *That history and philosophy are one.* A paradox from Benedetto Croce. "There is neither philosophy nor history nor history of philosophy, but history which is philosophy and philosophy which is history and is intrinsic to history."—*History; Its Theory and Practice,* 83.

It is difficult to see in this statement anything but a futile playing with words, unless one arbitrarily invests the term *philosophy* with a meaning other than that generally accepted, as the science of ultimates; and this is precisely what Croce does. For him philosophy is "the thought of the eternal present"; it is history as *knowledge,* the activity of the mind playing in an intimate, in an understanding way upon the facts of the historical past, which, so it is assumed, never had existence external to the thinker. Thought and the object of thought are thus identified. But this cannot be, for outside the mind, lie innumerable objects of thought existing independently of the mind in the field of extra-mental reality.

> The idea that history took place in the past actuality outside the mind is accepted as the common sense view of the matter.—Charles A. Beard in *AHR,* 41 (1935): 82.
>
> Unlike Croce the true historian believes, prosaically if you will, but as the very first article of his faith in the objective reality of the facts of history.—Arthur S. Turberville, "History, Objective and Subjective," *History,* 17 (1933): 296.
>
> But the identity, if accomplished at all, makes of history something which is unrecognizable by those who have spent their lives in studying it, and endows it with features which they prefer that it should not have. Croce gives to the word *history* a meaning different from that which it ordinarily possesses, but one which it is convenient it should have in order to fit in with the requirements of his philosophy. One would not have expected such conduct from the author of a work on "Logic"; but philosophy is sometimes a very portentous form of frivolity.—Ernest Scott, *History and Historical Problems* (Melbourne, 1925), 35.

To Croce, philosophy is identical with history as knowledge; history as past actuality is ruled out of the scheme of things by his sweeping idealism. The net result of this fusion-into-one of two such primary concepts as philosophy and history, which, despite varying definitions of them, thinkers have traditionally managed to keep apart as fundamentally distinct, is a confusion of thought which, more than anything else, is the hallmark of Croce's philosophy. To Irving Babbitt he is a "neo-Hegelian confusionist." "He not only denies the validity of genres in literature and art, but finally identifies religion with philosophy and philosophy in turn with history."—*Yale Review*, 14 (1925): 379.

Certainly, in view of the verbal and logical contortions that must be resorted to in order to make it intelligible, to the extent that this result can be achieved at all, the formula, "philosophy and history are one," offers no illumination or guidance of any kind to the student or writer of history.

Chapter Two

METHOD IN HISTORY

A. Historical Method: Meaning . . . . Page 33
B. Historical Method: Uses 34
C. History as Science 37
D. The Competent Historian: Characteristics 43
E. Hallmarks of Critical History 54
F. Historical Method in the Making 59

A. Historical Method: Meaning

❰ 33 Every science, when it becomes an art by being reduced to practice, follows certain rules and directions which insure or help to insure accuracy of result. The complex of these rules and directions we call *method*, or *technique*. Surgical science has its method of performing a given operation; the musician has a method of handling his instrument; and success in the classroom is very much a matter of effective method. So also with the art of history, the direct aim of which is the attainment of historical truth. This is a complex process involving search for sources of information, critical evaluation of the same, synthesis and exposition of the results of research and criticism. This process must follow certain recognized rules, be regulated by method.

Historical method may therefore be defined as *a systematic body of principles and rules designed to aid effectively in gathering the source-materials of history, appraising them critically, and presenting a synthesis (generally in written form) of the results achieved.* More briefly it may be defined as "a system of right procedure for the attainment of [historical] truth."—Richard F. Clarke, *Logic* (London and New York, 1927), 462.

Conventional historical method, the theme of this book, is *per se* effective in leading to correct results. Failure of it to issue thus will be due to causes extrinsic to the method itself, generally to a faulty manner of applying it. Finally, it is to be noted that while "historical method" and "historical criticism" are sometimes used as convertible terms, the latter is in reality only one step, the second, in this threefold process of historical method. Hence, the adequate designation of this book is "A Guide to Historical Method."

John C. Almack defines scientific method in general as "the expert pursuit of knowledge," or "a mode of applying logical principles to the discovery, confirmation, and elucidation of truth."—*Research and Thesis-writing* (Boston, n.d.), 57.

¶ 34 There are three major operations, as such, in historical method. First, the search for material on which to work, for sources of information (*heuristic*). This is the initial step in all historical writing. Second, the appraisement of the material or sources from the viewpoint of evidential value (*criticism*). This is so important a step that the whole process of historical method often goes by the name of *historical criticism*. Third, formal statement of the findings of heuristic and criticism. This includes the assembling of a body of historical data and their presentation (generally in writing) in terms of objective truth and significance (*synthesis* and *exposition*).

In actual historical work these three operations are not necessarily taken up in strict succession. They scarcely stand apart (at least the first two); rather they overlap one another, and the historian has sometimes to use all three simultaneously. Heuristic cannot generally do its work without application of some of the principles of criticism. The trained historical craftsman reveals himself in the readiness and skill with which he performs the several operations. He handles a mass of material with dispatch, is quick in sensing its value, in seeing its bearings. This practical ease and dexterity in handling material and using it aright for the purposes of history-writing, implies, among other attainments, a critical sense. Fundamentally, this is a gift, rather than an attainment; but practice sharpens and perfects it. Of all a historian's mental equipment, none is more basic, more strictly indispensable. All the masters of historical science have had it.

Howard W. Odum and Katharine Jocher, eds., *An Introduction to Social Researches* (New York, 1929), chap. 14.

The various steps in historical method are outlined by Michael I. Rostovtsev, "History: Its Aims and Methods," *A History of the Ancient World* (2 vols., Oxford, 1925), 1:1–17.

B. Historical Method: Uses

¶ 35 Historical method is not a thing of utility only to the student or writer of history; anyone may profit by a knowledge of its principles.

For many things we all depend on information furnished by others; the extent to which we are thus influenced in our views, principles, and general attitude towards life is enormous. A person without proper criteria for evaluating the information that reaches him from the outside, runs the risk of a thousand deceptions and errors. This is especially the case when the information presents itself through the medium of print. Behind the expression, "the tyranny of the printed page," is a profound psychological fact. What has arrived at the dignity of print has a curious tendency to impress itself upon us as true. This tendency must be resisted if truth and error are not to have equal claims on the mind. Newspaper readers, especially, have to learn when and how far to suspend assent. They have constantly to put the principles of evidence to use.

¶ 36 METHODOLOGY A NEED IN HISTORY

Proper training of the historical craftsman, for the most part an apprenticeship in methodology, aims to give him skill in assembling material, assessing it critically, and setting out the results of his research and criticism with effect. Here, as in other matters, to be self-taught is not always the best preparation for the task; the self-taught worker in history easily falls into mistakes which formal apprenticeship enables him to avoid. Even the simplest document can offer so many problems as to content and interpretation, that the untrained student may be in no position to recognize them, much less to solve them.

At the same time it is easy to exaggerate the necessity of technical training for the historian. After all, critical method in history is in substance nothing else than sound judgment and common sense. Meister indorses the same view, pointing out that while the rules of criticism can be taught, their application to a particular problem is necessarily individual. But he is careful to add that this view "must not lead to a one-sided rejection of all the rules of historical criticism."—*Grundzüge der historischen Methode*, 8.

The English universities, unlike the German and the American, have not set (at least in the past), any great store by formal training in the case of history students.

> If a man cannot pick up the art of weighing and comparing facts and theories from studying his Aristotle and his Maine, his Hobbes, his Maitland, and his Stubbs, he will not pick it up from any lectures on method. If he cannot read all the prescribed books for his special subject without learning how to compare sources and evaluate their worth; if he cannot peruse Clarendon and Ludlow, Baillie and Cromwell's Speeches . . . without learning automatically the elements of historical criticism—then he is not a person about whom we need bother our heads at all. He will

never make a historian though you drive "method" into him with a hammer. In short, the true historian—and here lies the gist of my creed—is born, not made."—Sir Charles W. C. Oman, *Inaugural Lecture on the Study of History* (Oxford, 1906), 23.

But while sound judgment, or common sense, is unquestionably the historian's most indispensable aid, it is necessary to recognize its limitations in practical research. It takes one a long way but not the whole way. Sound judgment may enable a historian to sift a mass of conflicting evidence and to determine correctly which side of a disputed issue has the better claim to assent; but if he relies on sound judgment alone, many niceties in the skilful handling of historical data are likely to escape him. Moreover, apart from special scholarship in language, palaeography, and diplomatic, native judgment alone, however keen, will not qualify him to decipher, to date, to localize, or to interpret simple ancient, medieval, or even modern documents.

¶ 37 USES OF METHODOLOGY IN THE FIELDS OF PHILOSOPHY AND THEOLOGY

A wholly speculative method, one restricted to syllogistic reasoning, and one heedless of the facts of experience, often ends in nothing better than narrow, one-sided views. The logician, to cite an instance, may be tempted to set the requirements for trust in human testimony so high that these would scarcely ever be realized in practice. He needs the corrective supplied by the historian, who has learned to adjust himself to the rough-and-ready standards of everyday life, in the course of which, what is offered on evidence that none would pretend is a demonstration, is repeatedly accepted as certain, for all practical purposes.

In fundamental theology (the evidences of religion), the problem of the Gospels as historical documents must be dealt with in the spirit and according to the methods of critical historical research. In the exegesis or interpretation of Holy Scripture, one needs a sound hermeneutic or system of interpretative canons, which is a recognized step in historical methodology. Historical theology, or the history of dogma, takes the body of doctrine revealed by Christ to the Church, and traces its development, rightly understood, through the centuries; development implies change (in this case not in the doctrine itself but in men's apprehension of it), and where there is change, the first postulate for historical treatment is at hand. Here again the need of a correct historical methodology is evident.

Catholic Church legislation requires that the principles of scientific method be taught in ecclesiastical seminaries: "Let there be in each of the faculties, in addition to the lectures, exercises by means of which the auditors may learn the scientific method of investigation and the art of presenting even in writing what they have learned by study under the guidance of professors."—Apostolic Constitution of Pius XI, *Deus Scientiarum Dominus*, Tit. III, art. 30, §1, in *Acta Apostolicae Sedis*, 23 (1931): 254.

On the place of the "seminar" in Catholic seminaries of theology, see J. de Gellinck, *Les exercices pratiques du "Séminaire" en théologie* (Paris, 1935); also Leopold Fonck, *Wissenschaftliches Arbeiten* (Innsbruck, 1908), French adaptation, *Le travail scientifique* (Paris, 1911).

¶ 38 Any of the sciences, especially the social sciences can be approached from a historical point of view. Thus, in economics and political science one may either consider an institution or practice as it exists today, or as it existed at a definite period in the past; or he may trace out the processes of change through which the institution or practice came to be what it is today. In the latter case, the method of treatment is historical. Modern thought has been so permeated with the idea of development or progressive change that the historical treatment or approach has become familiar in all the sciences. In making this approach the principles and tools of methodology are indispensable.

For instances of the historical treatment of topics:

Charles M. Gayley and Fred N. Scott, "Historical Study of Poetry," in *An Introduction to the Method and Materials of Literary Criticism* (Boston, 1899), 350 ff.

George Saintsbury, *A History of Criticism and Literary Taste in Europe from the Earliest Texts to the Present Day* (3 vols., New York, 1902).

Sir Robert W. Carlyle and Alexander J. Carlyle, *History of Medieval Political Theory in the West* (6 vols., Edinburgh and London, 1903-1936).

John Eppstein, *The Catholic Tradition of the Law of Nations* (Washington, 1936).

Wilhelm Schmidt, *The Origin and Growth of Religion* (London, 1931); *The Culture Historical Method of Ethnology: The Scientific Approach to the Racial Question*, trans. by S. A. Sieber (New York, 1939).

C. History as Science

¶ 39 The question whether history is a science has been answered, sometimes affirmatively, sometimes negatively. Difference of opinion on the subject among historians is very probably more apparent than real. The discussion practically revolves around the meaning one chooses to attach to the term *science*. History is "simply a science, no less and no more," peremptorily said John B. Bury, the English historian, in a Cambridge inaugural lecture (1903). Later, Bury's Cambridge successor, Harold W. V. Temperley, countered with the statement: "In my own memory the idea that history is a science has perished."—*Research and Modern History* (London, 1930).

Years earlier (1889) Goldwin Smith in a presidential address before the American Historical Association, "The Treatment of History," had made a vigorous assault on the claims of history to be considered a science. The student will make his way through opposing views if he fortifies himself with a clear-cut and defensible definition of the major term in the dispute. Here, as happens repeatedly, controversy is largely a *lis de verbis*. If the parties to a dispute will use vital terms in the same sense, often enough the dispute is over.

Sir Henry Lambert contends that history is not a science; but the reasons he alleges for this contention prove only that it is not an *exact* science.—*The Nature of History* (London, 1933), chap. 3.

A familiar viewpoint appears in Bernard J. Muller-Thym, "Of History as a Calculus Whose Term is Science," *The Modern Schoolman*, 19 (1942): 41 ff.; 73 ff.

In practically all instances where the claim of history to be a science is denied, the denial is based on the assumption that the term *science* necessarily denotes an exact science. Thus, for Henry Adams all science was of the exact type.—"The Tendency of History," in *The Degradation of the Democratic Dogma* (New York, 1920), 125 ff. In the mind of Adams, history could become a science only by having its rigorously-operating and immutable laws. Plainly, with such a conception of science premised, history is certainly not a science.

¶ 40 WHAT SCIENCE IS

(a) In the first place, history, especially in educational practice, is now conventionally grouped with the so-called "social sciences," the disciplines concerned with man in his social relations, such as anthropology, sociology, economics, and the like. The nomenclature is established, and there is no reason to quarrel with it. We start, therefore, with the assumption that history in current educational nomenclature is a social science.

(b) As is clear, the precise meaning of science is the crux of the whole discussion. Unfortunately, there is no hard and fast definition of the term that has passed into general use. Probably, most careful thinkers on the subject would agree that every element essential to the general concept of science which we ordinarily seek to express by the corresponding term, is covered by the following definition: "A systematized body of general truths concerning a definite subject matter and established by an efficient [effective] method."—John F. X. Pyne, *The Mind* (New York, 1926), 20.

This definition gives us a *genre*, including within its range two *species*, the exact sciences and the non-exact (or social) sciences. It rec-

¶ 40   Chapter 2

ognizes four elements as being essential (or at least integral) to the concept of science, whether exact or otherwise:

(1) *A body of systematized* (ordered, organized, classified) *knowledge*, not a heap of isolated, disjointed facts or truths, but a complex of facts or truths closely knit together according to some principle of rational, logical order, such as of time, space, topic, causation.

(2) *An effective method.* It has been maintained that science spells method more than anything else. "Science is fundamentally a method of dealing with problems."—Frederick J. Teggart, *Processes of History* (New Haven, 1918), 1.

Obviously not every kind of method serves the purposes of history. What history desiderates is a correct, effective method. "A correct process is one that rightly followed necessarily leads to a correct result."—Henry M. Bowman, "Fundamental Processes in Historical Science," in *Proceedings and Transactions* (The Royal Society of Canada, 3d Series, vol. 6, 1912), Section 2, p. 140.

History cannot be written without some method, however primitive or defective. Herodotus and Thucydides had their methods, which were by no means unsatisfactory, especially that of the latter. But it is only in modern times that a systematic historical technique has been formulated, and has been accepted by scholars generally. History as record has therefore reached a stage where it employs a recognized correct and consequently effective technique or method, from which the writer of history, at least of professedly scholarly history, cannot afford to depart. The use of a recognized method is a prime factor qualifying history to rank as a science.

(3) *A definite subject matter.* There can be no difficulty on this head. The material on which a science works cannot be vague or limitless. A science must work within some more or less sharply defined department or field of human knowledge.

(4) *The formulation of general truths.* History deals primarily with particular happenings, with the unique. This seems to have been the only function assigned to history by Aristotle, and for this reason he did not recognize it as a science: "Science is of universals."—*Metaphysics*, X, 1. See also *Poetics*, IX, 1[¶ 54], for the statement that "history tends to express the particular." But a broader conception of history makes it pass at will beyond the unique to the general, to the universal.

The general truths which history can formulate are of two kinds: those not restricted as to time and place, and those thus restricted [¶ 134ff.]. Examples of the first kind are: Material prosperity tends to beget moral decay; extreme governmental repression provokes rebellion. An instance of the second kind of general truth is the statement that the Romans were skilful administrators. This clearly is not the statement of a particular or unique fact, but of a general fact or inductive truth, based on numerous particular instances of administrative skill recorded of Roman officials or groups of officials. It is, then, within the province of history to establish and state such generalizations. In fact, it is mainly from such broad, comprehensive truths that history derives whatever practical utility it has. For instance, the so-called "critical period of American history," which preceded the adoption of the Federal Constitution, may be said to have significance only to the extent to which, with parallel situations in history, it affords a basis for the practical inductive truth, "in union there is strength."—Charles A. and Frank M. McMurray, *Method of the Recitation* (New York, 1908), 34.

The objection, however, has been raised that the scope of history is necessarily descriptive, that "explanation," "interpretation," and especially "generalization," are so many trespassings on other fields of knowledge. The objection goes back to the view that history is concerned only with the singular, the unique. But there is no valid reason for thus contracting the historical horizon. History as a record of the human past has at all times been understood to include not only the reporting of particular facts, but also interpretation and generalization based upon the facts.

¶ 41 HISTORY A SCIENCE—NOT AN EXACT SCIENCE

Since history includes the four elements of *systematized knowledge, effective method, definite subject matter*, and (as part content) *general truths*, it may therefore be designated a science. At the same time it is sharply differentiated in a specific way from the exact (natural) sciences. Compared with these, history (and the same is true of sociology and other cognate disciplines) is a science only in the broad qualified sense explained above. Some of the differences between history and the exact sciences as a group, must be pointed out:

(a) The general truths or laws established by history are only morally uniform in their application, not rigidly uniform, as in the case of the truths or laws established by the exact sciences [¶ 138].

(b) History, apart from a few terms used in methodology, is without technical terminology. It employs, indeed, certain stock words, such as progress, civilization, democracy, liberty, etc.; but none of these or similar words are rigidly fixed in meaning by usage or convention. With different historians they stand for different concepts. The quantitative technical terms of the exact sciences, such as light-year, volt, ampere, gram, calory, etc., have fixed meanings; to scientists the world over they mean absolutely one and the same thing. Absence of technical terms is a weak side of history as science, the result being that a certain amount of vagueness and ambiguity inevitably enters into historical writing. The matters with which history deals are in the nature of things not subject to mathematical measurement.

(c) History works on its material, not directly, as the biologist or chemist works on his specimen in the laboratory, but indirectly, through the medium of traces left in past happenings. History is not a science of direct observation, and in this regard it is set off distinctly from the exact sciences, with their endless possibilities of immediate test and verification. The chemist may repeat the same experiment a hundred times on the same lump of mineral. The historian is in no such good fortune when he attacks a problem in his field, as when, for instance, he tries to ascertain what really took place at Waterloo. The historical battle has vanished irrevocably, and there is no possible way by which it can be recalled and set before one's eyes to be studied at close range. Nothing remains of it (apart from possible archaeological survivals) but the reports of it left by eyewitnesses and by hearsay. If we are to learn anything at all about it, we must give our attention first to the reports, and through them to the battle. Contrariwise, the natural sciences are based essentially on direct observation, and in this regard enjoy a distinct advantage over history. But the method of indirect observation, the only one open to the historian (except in the relatively few cases where he can draw on personal knowledge of the facts), is after all valid, and can become an instrument for genuinely scientific work.

(d) History, being the human story, has to deal with the self-determining agent, man. Free will is, therefore, a factor to be reckoned with in historical phenomena. It especially conditions historical generalizations and laws as bases of prediction. It introduces into history an "incalculable element," one to which the exact sciences are immune. On this topic Freeman has some excellent remarks: "It may be enough to say that if we have no free will, we live in a world of sheer delusion, not only as to historical knowledge, but as to all daily events, public or private.—*The Methods of Historical Study*, 148ff.

(e) Prediction in history is less reliable than in the exact sciences. One can foretell with certainty what will happen if certain chemical elements are brought into combination. Physical and chemical properties are constant, and the laws based upon them admit of no exception apart from divine intervention. But it is otherwise with the generalizations of history. From intimate understanding of an individual or a group, one may forecast with great probability, sometimes with moral certainty, how they will act in given circumstances. But, just because they are free to act this way or that, in last analysis it is impossible to make such forecast with the same rigorous certainty with which it is possible to predict the rising of tomorrow's sun or the precise amount of time it will take a falling body to pass through a given distance. Free will, the "incalculable element" in history, must be reckoned with.

Obviously, foretelling the future from one's knowledge of the past can be a hazardous business. As has been said, it is easier to lose a reputation at it than to make one. Palmerston is said to have declared the unification of Germany impossible, while Frederick the Great (and not he alone) gave the United States at its birth only a few years of life. Forecasts of the outcome of political campaigns are notoriously falsified by the event. A crop of discredited prophets was begotten of the first World War, and no doubt is being begotten of the second. Our military experts were quite unanimous in predicting Russia's overthrow within three months of the German invasion of June, 1941. Yet these considerations do not militate against the common-sense proposition that one may on occasion (though only with such assurance as the supporting evidence allows), reasonably predict the action of individuals or of groups in a given set of circumstances. "The crown of science," declared Goldwin Smith in the presidential address referred to above, "is prediction. Were history a science, it would enable us to predict events." The pertinent comment on these words is that history does enable us to predict events, though in the limited manner, as here explained, and that it is a science, though not an exact one.

¶ 42   HISTORY NOT LITERATURE

If history is science, it cannot, primarily at least, be literature, and as such, fine art. The first business of the historian is the methodical pursuit of truth in his own special field, which is the establishment and interpretation of the facts of history as past actuality. If he can in the bargain clothe his findings in attractive literary garb, all the better. But, insofar as he is a historian, the literary satisfaction he can afford his readers is supererogatory. He is not held to it by any requirement of his craft. It goes without saying that if he is a sensible person he will be at pains to write well, and to turn out something which is not literature and yet is excellent history. In other words, literary quality, however desirable in itself, belongs to the accidentals, not to the essentials of history. Much of history is of such a nature that it affords no occasion for literary treatment at all. Surviving data may be so meager, obscure, and mutually contradictory that the historian's task can be nothing more than a patient, rigorous, prosaic sifting of the evidence. It is especially when sources of information are abundant, as in contemporary history, that the opportunity comes to make the treatment literary.

¶ 43 AN ACADEMIC QUESTION

The question whether history is a science or not, is after all merely academic. Its resolution one way or the other will not help the historian to discharge his task more effectively. What is vital is that his work show the qualities which entitle it to be called scientific. The term itself is not at all important. An illusion often cherished among historians, but less so today than a generation or two ago, is that there is something of magic in the description *scientific*. But the term has stood and continues to stand for certain traits which may be lumped together under the virtually equivalent term *scholarly*, and which by common accord all history-writing that attains to the higher levels of the art should possess. In general, such traits are honesty, impartiality, thoroughness, accuracy, documentation. Let these traits obtain in a work of history and it is a matter of no consequence whether it be characterized as scientific or otherwise.

D. The Competent Historian: Characteristics

¶ 44 ZEAL FOR THE TRUTH

Zeal for the truth is as indispensable to the historian as a passion for beauty is to the artist. It postulates sincerity and frankness in stating the facts, however much the writer's feelings or those of others may be ruffled in the process. The principle to be followed here was stated in 1883, by Leo XIII, in a letter on the subject of historical studies. Appropriating a well-known saying of Cicero, the pontiff sets down the principles of genuine history in one sentence: "It is the first law of history that it dare say nothing which is false nor fear to utter anything that is true, in order that there may be no suspicion either of partiality or of hostility in the writer."

One drawback to honest, non-partisan history, if it is a drawback, is that it is seldom popular history. Lord Acton said that the impartial historian can have no friends. Exaggerated, misleading, or patently false accounts of personalities and events are cherished because they minister to national or local pride. The attempt to deal with them critically provokes resentment. Recent re-writing of the history of the American Revolution on the basis of due appreciation of all the interests involved, met with protest in many quarters. But always the historian's plain duty is to give the facts.—Joseph Donat, *The Freedom of Science* (New York, 1914), 93.

(a) *Suppressio veri est assertio falsi.* Honesty requires that all important facts and circumstances, good or bad, creditable or otherwise, regarding a person, an institution, an event, be recorded. To omit important facts, whether this be done deliberately or otherwise, can create an entirely wrong impression, and in truth be a virtual falsification of the matter in question. Prevarication in history is easily possible without any positive misstatement of fact. To detail the abuses of an institution and say nothing about its good side, may misrepresent it as effectively as though one deliberately lied about it. It used to be conventional with historians to enlarge upon the evils of medieval society and to pass over in silence its wholesome side, its contributions of value to the solution of social problems. Sins of omission are often to be charged against the biographers. They are prone to place their subject's virtues and achievements in relief and to obscure or altogether suppress the less creditable side of his career, if such there were. Einhard's life of Charlemagne (*Vita Caroli Magni*), by far the best biography of the Middle Ages, is at the same time an example of *suppressio veri*. The emperor's good points are duly mentioned; what might be to his discredit is omitted.—HB, 10 (1932): 36–38.

> It is not a question of errors of fact which can be set right in a footnote; by emphasizing certain facts and omitting others, Macaulay produces a false impression, which it would take pages of explaining to remove.—Sir Charles Firth, *A Commentary on Macaulay* (London, 1938), 92.

(b) But cases can occur in which failure to mention facts does not necessarily imply their non-existence. The reports of medieval visitations very often stressed abuses in monastic institutions, a legitimate procedure in view of the purpose of such visitations; that they fail to stress normal conditions in such institutions or keep silence about them altogether is no evidence that normal conditions did not exist. "The reports of visitors dealt with faults; they rarely commend the virtues that such visitations revealed."—William Edwards, *A Medieval Scrap-heap* (London, 1930), 270.

The normal is usually taken for granted, and comment on it is deemed superfluous. But the unwary historian, using material of the type referred to, easily falls into a trap. Here is a typical instance in which the "argument from silence" does not hold [¶ 149].

We are warned by Hilaire Belloc that "History should be written not from the Bar, but from the Bench."—"The Case of Mr. Coulton," *The Month*, 170 (1937): 500. The historian is not an advocate or a special pleader; advocacy or special pleading is fatal in historiography. Rather the historian is a judge. It is permissible to the advocate addressing the bench or the jury to stress the evidence in favor of his client and to suppress entirely the evidence against him. But the judge or the jury must attend to all the evidence, whether in favor of the defendant or against him. Similarly, the historian is forbidden a merely one-sided presentation of the evidence; he must present both sides of it. The following lively statement of this principle is from a seventeenth-century Jesuit historian, Francis Sacchini: "If things are true no historian can, without violating the laws of history and his own conscience, keep silent about them. . . . The reason is that since the essence of history is to narrate outstanding things good or evil . . . (which in the case of a biographer help to form a true judgment of the man), he who publishes a history relating only good things writes himself down as willing to deceive. . . . Truth is rightly called the soul of history. If she is absent because writers keep silent about what should be told, history dies. For it is against the truth not to say those things which ought to be said."— Cited in Paul Van Dyke, *Ignatius Loyola, the Founder of the Jesuits* (New York and London, 1926), 236.

(c) *A caution.* The principle of candor in stating the facts of history must not be strained. A physician, for instance, while in the discharge of his professional duties comes to know things compromising to his patient's good name. Later he becomes the patient's biographer. May he reveal in his book, to the patient's discredit, the compromising information he had picked up? Plainly not, any more than a lawyer is free to publish abroad the incriminating things he has learned professionally about his client. Again, apart from special circumstances, as in court procedure, correct ethics would frown upon the publication of family correspondence that compromises the reputation of persons still living, or seriously embarrasses them in any way. As a rule, free use by the historian of unpublished material of incriminating tenor would seem to be in place chiefly when the persons thereby affected are long deceased, especially if they already have a place in history which it is necessary in the interests of historical candor to investigate.

❡ 45 CRITICAL SENSE

Sound judgment, a critical sense, is the historian's primary asset [❡ 36]. It works quietly, controls investigation at every turn, distinguishes between essentials and non-essentials, and seizes on the truth with something like intuition.

(a) To sound critical judgment are opposed the two extremes, lack of criticism, and hypercriticism. Lack of criticism, or an injudicious attitude of mind can show itself in various ways: in credulity; in a mania for the extraordinary; in a narrow, exaggerated conservatism, which looks upon criticism as the natural enemy of all cherished traditions and as the starting point of a dangerous skepticism; in depreciation of the minute preoccupation with details, necessarily involved in research. As regards the last named item, the words of St. Jerome are pertinent: *Non sunt contemnenda quasi parva sine quibus magna constare non possunt.* For the unduly conservative, Pius X had words of admonition: "There are persons who, firmly entrenched in their own faith, rage against criticism as a thing of destruction. As a matter of fact, it is an innocent thing in itself, and, rightly used, aids investigation in the happiest manner."——Encyclical letter, *Jucunda sane,* in *Acta Sanctae Sedis,* 36 (1903–1904): 521.

The proved results of research are not for the critics only: the general public may be made acquainted with them. But the nature of the results will sometimes require that it be done cautiously and by degrees, and in the spirit of the fine saying of the Latin poet, *reverentia debetur pueris.*——J. Donat, *The Freedom of Science,* 93–95.

(b) On the other hand, *hypercriticism,* as being the abuse of a good thing, is also to be deprecated. It shows itself in an overrating of internal evidence, in an absorption in trifles, with corresponding neglect in the inner meaning and significance of things; above all, in an itch for novelties and an urge to upset (on no grounds of adequate evidence) established beliefs and traditions, especially those concerning the Church. This spurious criticism is the enemy of genuine science and serves only the cause of error.

(c) On the nature and true spirit of critical research, the Bollandist, Charles De Smedt writes: "It is enough to recall among numerous other enterprises of research those of the Bollandists and M. De Rossi, to show that criticism can do something more than upset and destroy."——*Principes de la critique historique* (Liége, 1883), 1 f.

One may easily get the impression that the net result of modern critical investigation of the sources of history, especially ancient and medieval, has been to throw suspicion on them collectively, and so justify a wholesale skepticism in their regard. This is far from being the case. The fact is that a considerable proportion of the old historians have stood successfully the rigid scrutiny to which they have been subjected. Thus, up-to-date critical scholarship is favorable on the whole to the trustworthiness of Herodotus, Xenophon, Plutarch, Gregory of Tours, Venerable Bede. This is an important consideration for the student of history, for whom an unfounded and therefore unhealthy skepticism would be the worst possible attitude to take up in face of his pursuit. Criticism at its best can be happily constructive in scope; it can be and often is preservative of traditional viewpoints.

⁋ 46 Objectivity

Zeal for the truth and objectivity are in reality only different aspects of the same ideal in history. By objectivity (or the virtually equivalent term, impartiality) is meant such a detached and neutral attitude in the historian as enables him to deal with his material in the light of the evidence alone. Ranke's enunciation of the principle is classic: the historian must record a thing "as it really occurred," (*wie es eigentlich gewesen ist*).——George P. Gooch in *Cambridge Modern History*, 12: 824ff.

The practicality of the principle has been warmly debated; but stripped of certain misconceptions arbitrarily read into it, the principle itself rests on solid ground. Some of the misconceptions are here set down.

(a) Objectivity does not require that the historian be actually free from prepossessions or prejudices—racial, political, religious, or of any other kind.

This would be to require a psychological impossibility. Education, environment, and other circumstances result in certain fixed views, likes and dislikes, which in most people, if not in all, become a second nature. No one can be said to be entirely free from them. What objectivity does require is that the historian allow none of his prepossessions and prejudices, whatever they be, to cloud his judgment, to draw him beyond the evidence, to distort his estimate of persons and things. This is by no means an impracticable ideal, though it means for the historian stern restraint, conscientious self-discipline. Yet unless he submit to the restraint, to the self-discipline, his work is vitiated from the start. The text *sanctus amor patriae dat animum*, which the editors of the *Monumenta Germaniae historica* adopted for their motto, suggests the truth that scholarship inspired by patriotism need not necessarily be spurious. In the words of Sir Henry Lambert, the historian "cannot stand outside his problem," as, for example, the physicist or chemist can. He carries into his problem his whole personality, with all the attitudes, mental, emotional, moral, that distinguish it.

That partisanship and good history do not mix, is such an obvious truth that men have grasped it in all ages. Cicero's dictum has already been noted. Josephus, who complained of the treatment received by the Jews from non-Jewish historians, said of his own work: "I shall maintain a strict objectivity." The twelfth-century Greek princess Anna Comnena presents thus the case for objective history: "But he who undertakes the role of a historian must sink his personal likes and dislikes and often award the highest praise to his enemies when their actions demand it; and often, too, blame his nearest relatives if their errors require it."——*The Alexiad of the Princess Anna Comnena: Being the History of the Reign of her Father Alexius I, Emperor of the Romans*, A.D. 1081–1118, trans. by Elizabeth A. S. Dawes (London, 1928), 20.

A severe neutrality was demanded of the historian by Fénelon:

> The good historian belongs to no time or country; though he loves his own, he never flatters it in any respect. The French historian must remain neutral between France and England; he must as willingly praise Talbot as Du Guesclin; he renders the same justice to the military talents of the Prince of Wales (the Black Prince) as to the wisdom of Charles V.—Cited in J. J. Jusserand and Others, *The Writing of History*, 22.

Precisely the same ideal was championed in the nineteenth century by Lord Acton, who as editor-in-chief of the *Cambridge Modern History*, urged upon his collaborators an absolutely flawless neutrality: "Our account of Waterloo must be one that satisfies French and English, German and Dutchman." But Sir Charles Oman, who wrote the account of Waterloo for Acton, held the task imposed upon him to have been impossible. He thought his account might please a Frenchman, but not to the same extent a Dutchman.

(b) Objectivity does not require that the historian approach his task free of all principles, theories, philosophy of life.

It is preposterous to suppose that the normal human mind can be made over into a blank, a *tabula rasa*, empty of all preconceived ideas or views that could possibly condition or shape its free approach to a subject of study. Working hypotheses, however, are not at all incompatible with the scientific temper. Behind every great work of history has been some dominating viewpoint to organize the material or give it meaning. A broad hypothesis, with room for newly discovered evidence, may be the historian's invaluable aid. Proved or disproved, it can open up unsuspected vistas of truth and in this among other ways serve the cause of history [₡ 145ff.]. Facts standing by themselves are generally without value. The value of facts, it has been said, is that they tell for or against some theory.—J. Donat, *The Freedom of Science*, 93; Alban Goodier, *History and Religion* (London, 1937), 1–12.

(c) Objectivity does not require that the historian be free from sympathy for his subject, be it a person, institution, or cause.

But the sympathy must be under control; otherwise it deteriorates into partisanship, which being the abuse of an intrinsically good thing, is evil. Wisely-regulated sympathy stimulates insight into persons and things, and so is an aid to the historian. "That I have written with sympathy goes without saying. Who could have the courage to undertake such a task in cold blood? And how, without sympathy, could there be understanding?"—Ray S. Baker, *Life and Letters of Woodrow Wilson* (8 vols., Garden City, N.Y., 1927–1939), 1:xxxiii.

Tacitus hardly meant to exclude a managed sympathy when he announced his intention of writing *sine ira et studio*. On the other hand, partisanship in history, once the reader becomes aware of it, is a boomerang; it can easily defeat, by its note of tactless and obtrusive challenge, any design the historian may have had for engaging the sympathies of the reader on behalf of the character or cause he supports.

(d) Objectivity does not require that the historian refrain from forming judgments or drawing conclusions.

Such things he must do unless history is to be nothing more than a mere mechanistic and statistical record of the past. Someone has written that "every sentence in a book of history holds a judgment in solution."

(e) Objectivity does not require that all the circumstances attending an event in history be known before the event can be recorded "as it really occurred."

To maintain, as has been done, the contrary proposition, is sophistry. It is sheer common sense that the fact of a murder, "as it really occurred," can be established beyond controversy, though a thousand unessential details concerning it may not have been reported, and therefore cannot be known. This is the attitude of the law in the matter, and the experience of all ages and countries does not call the attitude into question. It is the substance of the fact that matters, not the accidentals. The historical career of Christ was recorded and is now known "as it really occurred," though as St. John (21:25) says, the unrecorded side of it would fill so many books that the world itself could not contain them.

(1) The validity of the Rankean formula of objectivity has been repeatedly impugned, but on no convincing grounds. Criticism of it began in Ranke's own day, and at present, so some maintain, it is quite discredited.— AHR, 41 (1935): 74-85. Objection to the formula rests mainly on two alleged grounds: first, the historian, for psychological and other reasons, cannot really be objective (impartial); and secondly, an event of history cannot be recorded "as it really occurred," since it can never be known in all its circumstances and details. We have just dealt with this criticism. The correct notion of historical objectivity implies, then, two things: first, impartiality (rightly understood) on the part of the historian, which is a practical ideal; secondly, the recording, as far as the evidence permits, of events "as they really occurred," a result which in many cases can be satisfactorily achieved, even though numberless details about the events remain unknown. As is the case in the question whether history is a science, the question whether history can be objective is kept alive by loose and unwarranted use of the cardinal term in the dispute. For the rest, the dispute is mainly speculative,

with little practical bearing on the historian's actual tasks. Let him conform to the demands of impartiality as the term is ordinarily understood, and it will be of little import whether his product be called objective or subjective.

(2) A long list could be compiled of well-known works of history that have fallen short in varying degrees of objectivity, in the correct understanding of the term. Livy, in his patriotic ardor, does less than justice to the enemies of Rome. Matthew Paris, a leading medieval chronicler, is influenced by anti-papal prejudice. Macaulay is notoriously unfair to the anti-Whigs. From his ultra-democratic viewpoint, Grote could see no good in the Greek "tyrants." A recent reissue of his *History of Greece*, admittedly a work of value, omits the chapter on the "Tyrants" as a distortion of the facts. Froude's *History of England* is saturated with anti-Catholic feeling. Gardiner's *History of the Commonwealth* has not escaped the imputation of bias in favor of the Cromwellians. Bancroft's exaggerated nationalism often results in one-sided presentation of the facts. Parkman's stirring narratives of the French-English conflict in North America are out of focus as a result of his preoccupation with Anglo-Saxon "superiority." Mommsen's *History of Rome* has its patent prejudices, in regard to Cicero. Motley's *Rise of the Dutch Republic* is unfair to the Spanish actors in the drama. Rhodes' *History of the United States* betrays animus against certain political figures, against Douglas, for instance, while the accuracy of the picture he draws of slavery has been called into question. Osgood's *American Colonies* has been charged with prejudice against the Quakers. Von Holst, in his *Constitutional and Political History of the United States*, is against the South. Oberholzer's *History of the United States since the Civil War* has been arraigned for undue severity in its treatment of certain men and events.

Examples such as these point to the conclusion that among historians subjectivity has been the rule rather than the exception. Probably Lingard, in his *History of England*, has approached nearest of them all to the ideal of an air-tight objectivity.

An instructive study in the influence of bias on history-writing is Eugene C. Barker, "On the Historiography of American Territorial Expansion," in James F. Willard and Colin B. Goodykoontz, eds., *The Trans-Mississippi West* (University of Colorado, Boulder, Colo., 1930), 219–47.

> It is impossible to peruse Mr. Gooch's work [*History and Historians of the Nineteenth Century*] without being struck by the fact that amongst the greatest writers of history bias—often unconscious bias—has been the rule, and the total absence of preconceived opinion the exception. Generally speaking, the subjective spirit has prevailed amongst historians in all ages.—Evelyn Baring, Earl of Cromer, "The Writing of History" in *Political and Literary Essays* (London, 1913), 215.

> I do not think that freedom from bias is possible and I do not think that it is desirable. Whoever writes completely free from bias will produce a colorless and dull book. . . . Is there any event or transaction

worth investigating or writing about in which the writer can fail to have a definite bias if the subject really engages his interest? And it will be admitted that otherwise he cannot hope to produce anything that will engage the interest of the world. No history can be instructive if the personality of the writer is entirely suppressed; it will be dead and colorless and inhuman, however faultless it may be in detail, however carefully the rules of historical method may be applied.——H. W. V. Temperley, *Selected Essays of J. B. Bury*, 70.

Mommsen wrote his glittering *History of Rome* with one eye on events in contemporary Germany and did not deny that he was influenced by them. On the contrary he said, "Those who have lived through historical events as I have, begin to see that history is neither written nor made without love or hate."——Ernest Scott, *History and Historical Problems*, 195.

No great book ever has been or ever will be written by a historian who suppressed self as he wrote each word; what such a book may conceivably gain in accuracy it loses in spontaneity and conviction. The passionless scientist chronicling the antics of puppets with whom he feels no sympathy, for whom he has no moral like or dislike, does not tend to produce a readable literary output.——Sir C. Oman, *Inaugural Lecture on the Study of History*, 13.

Lord Acton has said that an impartial historian can have no friends; but even at this cost the historian must still aim at impartiality in his conclusions and in the statements of them.——Charles G. Crump, *The Logic of History* (Helps, 6:59).

For my part I do not see why an honest partisan should not write an honest book if he can persuade himself to look honestly at his subject and make allowances for his own prejudices.——William Stubbs, *Seventeen Lectures on the Study of Medieval History and Kindred Subjects* (Oxford, 1900), 125.

It was thought necessary only twenty years ago to demonstrate that impartiality was impossible in history. . . . Not only do we repudiate the ideal of Ranke that history should be colorless, new and impartial. We do not even suggest that it is desirable."——Harold W. V. Temperley, *Research and Modern History: An Inaugural Lecture* (London, 1926), 18.

There is [says De la Gorce in the preface to his *Histoire religieuse de la rèvolution française*] the impartiality born of indifference. That one I have neither the hope nor the desire to attain, and in narrating the Christian trials of our fathers I dare not affirm that I felt no heartbeat at their sufferings for the Church and for God. If, at the beginning of this book, I promise to be impassible, I should deceive both others and myself. . . . There is another impartiality, one that consists not in the abdication of personal thought, but in the strict observance of truth: that consists in never altering a fact, even a displeasing one; in never mutilating a text, even a troublesome one; in never knowingly misrepresenting the features of a human soul, were it that of an enemy. Such is the gift of a higher impartiality which I ask God to grant me.—Cited in Jusserand and Others, *The Art of Writing History*, 24–25.

The study of human societies . . . is of such a nature that no man, however balanced he may be, however determined to maintain himself on the line of strict impartiality, can ever escape from the thousand biases created in him by the many particular acquired or inherited traits of his personal nature. Nor can he avoid the influence of his own theoretical ideas concerning the relative value and the comparative role of the various factors, economic or religious, in the evolution of societies or the secret influence exercised upon him without his knowing it by his nationality, his religion, his social position, his avowed or unconscious affinities, with, for example, the bourgeoisie or the working class, etc.—*Encyclopaedia of the Social Sciences*, 7:367.

A mind devoid of prepossessions is likely to be devoid of all mental furniture. And the historian who thinks that he can clear his mind as he would a slate with a wet sponge, is ignorant of the simplest facts of mental life. "The objectivity on which some of them pride themselves," remarks a caustic critic [J. T. Merz, *A History of European Thought in the Nineteenth Century*, 1896], will (centuries hence) be looked upon not as freedom from, but as unconsciousness on their part, of the preconceived notions which have governed them.—Allen Johnson, *The Historian and Historical Evidence* (New York, 1926), 100.

(f) Ranke, pioneer of the modern school of scientific historians, had to defend himself against the charge that his method, however sound on the whole, had yet a good deal of the subjective about it. He had repeatedly to make an exercise of judgment. He selected typical events and characters to illustrate general laws; he attempted to extract from the particular the spirit or general truth of which it was the outward symbol.—See Edward G. Bourne, *Essays in Historical Criticism* (London and New York, 1901), 256.

A process like this presupposes personal standards of what is typical and of what is not, among a mass of details, of what is important and what unimportant. These standards may or may not be true, but the use of them by the historian makes it clear that he cannot dissociate himself entirely from the subjective. Even as regards the most scientific, confidence in their clearness and honesty of judgment, unless we are able to test for ourselves the value of their individual statements—is a manifestly prohibitive procedure. Scientific history is not always the highly detached and impersonal, the completely unobjective thing one must assume it to be, if claims often made for it by its devotees are to be taken at their face value.

(g) Writers here quoted, who say that history may or should be written with bias, are evidently to be understood as implying that the bias should be held in control, so as not to issue in distortion of the facts. Further, they seem to use the term *objectivity* with varying implications, not all of them legitimate. If, as has already been insisted on, to be sympathetic to one's subjects, or to have certain principles or prepossessions or philosophy of life, is not to be objective, then, needless to say, objective history is anything but desirable. But true objectivity, as we have explained it, remains what common sense and sound scholarship see it to be, a necessary ideal in the writing of history.

Two further personal traits marking the successful practitioner in history may be noted: industry, and ability to concentrate on his work.

¶ 47   INDUSTRY

Few pursuits levy a heavier tax on time, patience, and perseverance than the historian's. The nature of research makes it almost impossible to carry it on satisfactorily as a mere avocation in the spare hours saved from other employment. One must have abundant leisure in prospect, long stretches of time on which to draw freely. Nothing can be more time-consuming than grubbing in libraries and archives, tracking down minute points of research that elude pursuit, deciphering and collating texts, reducing a mass of data to unity and meaning, to say nothing of the long, tedious process of composition. Economy of time, the utilization to the best possible advantage of the working hours of the day, are principles of wisdom to the historian, as they are to the specialist in any field.

> It seems to me that the one counsel that can be given to the man who . . . wishes to set sail into the ocean of Research . . . is simply to work and work and work again. He will think many hours wasted—they are not really so; a negative result is often as valuable as (though less exciting than) a positive one.—Sir C. Oman, *Inaugural Lecture on the Study of History*, 23.

Leopold Fonck in his *Wissenschaftliches Arbeiten*, gives interesting data on the number of hours in the day, in some cases astonishingly many, which scholars in diverse fields have given to their tasks. Biographies of noted historians often afford instructive information on the same head.

> All this he [Justin Winsor] did by personal labor, for he always maintained that a historical student, to accomplish anything of value, must handle all the books and papers with his own hands.—Edward Channing, *AHR*, 3 (1898): 187.

¶ 48   CONCENTRATION

Allied to industry, probably only an aspect of it, is concentration, by which is here understood a mental alertness that makes one ready to recognize and put to account every piece of casual information that can help to mastery of one's subject. Charles G. Crump speaks of the importance of a "mind trained to seize any useful scrap of knowledge that may turn up by chance even when the attention is not specially directed to it."—*History and Historical Research* (London, 1928), 129.

Aspects that would escape persons not engaged in a student's particular field of research, automatically reveal themselves to him as useful to his purpose, at least if he is wide awake to his task. We are led by habit to view things from our particular angle of interest. A mass of masonry crashing from the cornice of a building to the sidewalk below will evoke different trains of thought in the passers-by. To an architect the incident may suggest a problem of faulty construction; to a lawyer, the question how far the proprietor is responsible for damages if anyone were hurt; to a reporter, the possibilities for an interesting story. So with the historian. By an instinct, partly innate, partly acquired, he is drawn to look at things, past and present, particularly in the light of their availability or aptness for historical record.

E. The Hallmarks of Critical History

❡ 49 Method in critical history

Method as a constituent of critical (scholarly, scientific) history, involves two things: first, the application of a correct technique to the finding and criticism of data; secondly, the arrangement and presentation of the data according to an effective plan. Correct technique in history-writing, which is the subject matter of this book, is comprehensive enough in its implications to include this second requirement; all questions pertaining to the orderly and effective presentation of data come within its range. As to method, it is well to recall here what has been stated [❡ 40-b-2], that more than anything else it makes science what it is. *Methodical* and *scientific* are therefore virtually convertible terms, as are also their negatives, *unmethodical* and *unscientific*. "Method, not genius or eloquence or erudition, makes the historian." —Lord Acton, *History of Freedom and Other Essays* (London, 1907), 235.

❡ 50 Candor

Critical history makes no attempt to pass for more than what it really is; it makes no pretense to any greater measure of scholarship or research than actually went into it. Further, it scrupulously observes the proprieties by making due acknowledgment of all appropriations made by the author from the pertinent sources, published or unpublished.

Finally, it is open and candid, which is to say, objective, not concealing or glossing over matters which cannot be so treated without sacrifice of the truth [⁋ 44]. If there is anything that marks the scientific temper, it is this spirit of honest candor, in which the true scholar takes up his task and carries it through.

For a helpful discussion of candor in history, see Heribert Holzapfel, *Handbuch der Geschichte des Franziskanerordens* (Freiburg, 1909), ix.

Dishonesty, in the sense of failure to give due credit for borrowed material finds its major exhibition in plagiarism. Literary plagiarism denotes either the act by which one appropriates another person's writing and gives it out as one's own, or the writing so appropriated. Needless to say, procedure of this sort is a breach of ethics. Yet there have been times when such procedure was not seriously frowned on, being, it would appear, more or less condoned as a sort of recognized literary licence. The extent to which even reputable historians could go, in openly pirating fellow craftsmen's work, is surprising.——See William A. Foran, "John Marshall as a Historian," *AHR*, 43 (1937): 51–64.

⁋ 51 ACCURACY

Accuracy is truth, and any history may do no less than aim at being true. Correctness of statement in all matters of fact, if not of interpretation, is therefore the irreducible minimum of requirement set for the historian. Nothing tends more to diminish interest in a history, at least for thoughtful readers, than the suspicion that they are not getting the facts. Accuracy often connotes not so much truth in its broader aspects as truth in matters of detail; more often, unimportant details. Here again a meticulous correctness of statement in all matters of fact, however minor and trivial, is the true historian's ideal. This means correct dates, correct proper names, correct figures and statistics, correct details.

(a) Needless to say, before a manuscript is allowed to go to press, it should be carefully checked for possible errors, especially in such details as dates, spelling of proper names, references, and the like. Justin Winsor's practice in this connection was not commendable. "Errors, too, in such matters as names and dates occurred, and were perpetuated in the printed page; for relying on his wonderful memory, he did not systematically verify every title and date in proof."——Edward Channing, "Justin Winsor," *AHR*, 3 (1898): 201.

The caution may be added that while checking of editorial accuracy may be done in proof, it should preferably be done in the manuscript. Corrections in proof are always expensive.

(b) But an ideal of perfect accuracy can scarcely be reduced to practice. Probably no great historical work ever written is altogether free from error. Scholarly standard works of reference generally have their quota of mistakes. The British *Dictionary of National Biography* is supplemented with a three-hundred page book of errata. A similar book of errata in the *Dictionary of American Biography* has been projected.

The fact is that historical accuracy is a relative term. A history is accurate when its mistakes are few and of the kind described as "slips"; these are for the most part mere accidents, as it were, and are by no means to be taken as indicating habitual carelessness or inexactness on the part of the author. On the other hand, a history is inaccurate when its mistakes are both many and of a nature to suggest that the author is really careless in matters of detail. Such temperamental or chronic inaccuracy results in work sometimes described as "sloppy." No history open to such criticism has a claim to be called scholarly.

(c) A corollary of the preceding paragraph is that no historian, young or old, should defer publication of a manuscript until he has achieved or thinks he has achieved an absolutely flawless text. No doubt a manuscript may often gain much by being held up even a long time in the interests of literary refinement or more thoroughgoing research. Some chapters in Beveridge's *Lincoln* were rewritten many times. But a manuscript ought not to be withheld from publication mainly through fear that when it is in print some lynx-eyed reviewer may convict it of this or that misstatement. This is a morbid attitude to take, for it is grounded in the illusion that perfecly accurate history is a practicable ideal. To point out inexactitudes is the book reviewer's privilege; but a book does not stand or fall by a few, or, it may be, even by a considerable number of inexactitudes.

> Every investigator knows of examples of the most competent scholars whose knowledge was lost at their death, because they were afraid to go into print with an incomplete story. If only some way could be found to induce a man who has done a piece of research to "dig in" in such a fashion as to indicate the limits of his findings, without at the same time allowing him to be worried by fears of not having been infallible, we might have a great many temporary advances made which could later be consolidated for the benefit of scholarship.—Randolph G. Adams in *Essays Offered to Herbert Putnam*, William Warner Bishop and Andrew Keogh, eds. (New Haven, 1929), 37.

> Do not be led away by megalomania; do not think that you can possibly write a book without mistakes; the man who imagines that he can do so will probably never write a book at all. . . . [The writer of history] must make up his mind that however hard he may strive for absolute accuracy, it is certain that there will be errors of detail somewhere—

perhaps even of more than detail. But he should not for that reason shrink back from production; I have known books hung up for years because the author had not the heart to confess himself fallible.—Sir C. Oman, *Inaugural Lecture on the Study of History*, 28.

(d) For instances of gross inaccuracy in recording figures, see Arthur Vermeersch, *Tolerance*, trans. by W. Humphrey Page (New York, 1912), 339.

A French school text gives 2,000,000 as the number of victims of the Spanish Inquisition in ten years. Alfred Rambaud, *Histoire de la civilisation française* (2 vols., Paris, 1885–1887), 2:327, has 300,000 for a period of three and a half centuries, while for the same period, Llorente (hostile to the Inquisition) has 30,000; and Pius B. Gams, *Die Kirchengeschichte von Spanien* (3 vols., Regensburg, 1862–1879), only 4,000.

Herbert Thurston discusses George C. Coulton's inaccuracies in *Some Inexactitudes of Mr. G. G. Coulton* (London, 1927); and those of Henry C. Lea, in *The Month*, 169 (1937): 51–61; 116–28.

Carlyle, in his account of the flight of Louis XVI from Paris to Varennes, is said to have gone wrong "in every single possible detail where a writer could go wrong," which is probably an exaggeration. For the truth of his description, "the sea-green Robespierre," his only evidence is said to have been the statement of an English lady that Robespierre wore "greenish" spectacles.—Lucy M. Salmon, *Why History Is Rewritten* (New York, 1929), 53 f.

James Anthony Froude was curiously inaccurate. "Froude's disease," or "Frouditis" are by-words coined to express incapacity for precise and accurate statement. In a new edition of Carlyle's *Reminiscences*, which Froude had edited, one hundred and thirty corrections were made in the first five pages. Brewer, the scholarly editor of the state papers of Henry VIII, affirmed that in Froude's account of Thomas Cromwell's early life, "scarcely a single statement was correct."—George P. Gooch, *History and Historians in the Nineteenth Century* (London and New York, 1913), 337. See also Andrew Lang, "The Mystery of Amy Robsart," in *The Valet's Tragedy and Other Studies* (London, 1903), for an instance of Froude's careless copying and translation.

❡ 52 THOROUGHNESS

Thoroughness in history implies two things in particular: first, use of all important sources bearing on the subject in hand; secondly, treatment of all significant phases of the subject. Thoroughgoing treatment does not stop at the surface; it goes beneath, often to the bottom, and in doing so tends to be exhaustive; in some instances it actually becomes so. Yet there is much relativity in the concept of thoroughness. Purpose, scope, and other factors have to be reckoned with in determining whether a given treatment is to be accounted thorough or superficial.

A student's thesis in view of the requirements he has to meet, may reasonably be called a thorough piece of work, though a professional historian's treatment of the same theme might go considerably beyond the thesis in scholarly depth and range. Practically, there are always working standards at hand to enable one to judge whether a work reaches or falls below the demands of thoroughness.

Probably no critic would hesitate to qualify as thorough Abel's *Slaveholding Indians*, or Osgood's *American Colonies*, or the Carlyles' *History of Medieval Political Theory in the West*.

When a work is not thorough, it has to be done over again, either by the author himself, who probably will not himself care to attempt the task, or by someone else. No judgment more damaging to a historian's product can be passed, than to say that it has to be done over again—as Gooch (*History and Historians*, 339) says of Froude's *History of England*.

(a) The ideal of thoroughness in historical research has been expressed by Fustel de Coulanges:

> The very origins of this régime [feudalism] are a great problem in themselves. A German school and a Roman school have tried to make the matter easy by having feudalism issue from a single source. But feudalism is neither German nor Roman. It shaped itself slowly. It was the outcome of a long series of facts, customs, rules, which became fixed by imperceptible degrees. Hence, the historian who attempts to understand it is committed to endless researches over a period of eight centuries. He has no right to neglect anything, for he does not know beforehand whether such an event, such an institution, such a rule of public or private law has not contributed to the birth of this régime. At every fact he encounters, at every law or usage he sees before him, he must ask himself whether the fact, the law, the usage stood in any relation to it. And yet all this is nothing. To arrive at a knowledge of feudal institutions he must also know about and be able to recognize the non-feudal institutions which mingle with and dovetail into the former. Thus, everything must needs come under observation, and this not on the surface only, for it is in the roots of things that their intimate relations or secret differences are ordinarily to be found.—*Recherches sur quelques problèmes d'histoire* (4th ed., Paris, 1923), ii.

¶ 53 VERIFIABILITY

By an accepted convention among scholarly historians, a work of history must be fortified with such indications of sources as will enable the reader, if he is so minded, to check the accuracy of individual statements and the reliability of the work as a whole. Guy Sidney Fisher took exception to the revised edition of Bancroft's *History of the United*

States, on the ground that its statements could not be verified, owing to the absence of references in footnotes [¶ 393]. Translations into English of important historical work in foreign languages, sometimes omit the footnotes of the original—an omission which renders them less adapted to the student's purpose.

(a) Checking an author's references as indicated in footnotes may yield curious results. The references, or some of them, may have been lifted from other authors, though this kind of irregularity is becoming rare; wrong page numbers or other inaccuracies may make it difficult to trace passages referred to; a reference may not always really perform its expected function of illustrating or supporting the text. The charge has been made against so careful a historian as Samuel Rawson Gardiner, that authorities cited by him to substantiate statements in his text, fail to do so. Such failure, however, may sometimes be explained on the ground that the source or authority quoted by an author is really open to more than one reasonable interpretation. The interpretation he adopts, so he may contend, really bears out the statement in the text.

F. Historical Method in the Making

¶ 54 With but few exceptions the ancients made no distinction between the writing of history and rhetorical exposition.

To Cicero history was a branch of oratory; he calls it an "opus . . . oratorium maxime."—*De Legibus*, I, 2.

Elsewhere Cicero describes history as a work "*in qua narratur ornate et regio saepe aut pugna describitur, interponuntur etiam conciones et hortationes.*"—*De Oratore*, 20, 26.

Quintilian declares it to be close to poetry, a sort of prose-poem: "*est enim [historia] proxima poetis et quodammodo carmen solutum.*—*Institutio Oratoria*, X, 1, 31.

Aristotle ranks poetry above history:

> The poet and the historian differ not by writing in verse or prose. The work of Herodotus might be put into verse and it still would be a species of history with meter no less than without it. The true difference is that one relates what has happened, the other what may happen. Poetry, therefore, is a more philosophic and higher thing than history; for poetry tends to express the universal, history the particular."

[¶ 40-b-4]—*Poetics*, IX, 1; trans. in Samuel H. Butcher, *Aristotle's Theory of Poetry and the Fine Arts* (London, 1902).

At the same time, Aristotle realized that scholarly treatment is possible only on the basis of source material, and so he studied the pertinent sources before composing his *Politics*, *Poetics*, and *Rhetoric*. Significant of the attitude of the ancients toward history is the circumstance that it never found a place in their definitely organized system of the sciences, such as politics, economics, and ethics, which were cultivated with zeal.

(a) The distinction of being the "father of history" is given by Cicero to Herodotus (ca. 484 to ca. 425 B.C.), the creator of "narrative recital."—*De Legibus*, I, 1. Often feeling it his duty to be doubtful in the face of uncertain or conflicting reports, he is still on occasion curiously naive and credulous. "It is incumbent upon me to record the different opinions of men, though I am not indiscriminately to credit them." Yet modern critics often commend Herodotus highly as an authority. James T. Shotwell calls him "the first scientific historian," and Arnold J. Toynbee protests against the conventional opinion of him as a "simple-minded Father of History."—*Greek Historical Thought*, xix. See also Lionel Pearson, *Early Ionian Historians* (London, 1939).

(b) Thucydides (460 to ca. 399 B.C.) is rated on good grounds the first genuinely scientific historian.—Charles N. Cochrane, *Thucydides and the Science of History* (London, 1929).

In the opening book of his *History of the Peloponnesian War* (I, 22) he reveals his methods of heuristic, which were rigorous enough:

> As regards the material facts of the war I have not been content to follow casual informants or my own imagination. When I have not been an eyewitness myself, I have investigated with the utmost accuracy attainable every detail that I have taken at second hand. The task has been laborious, for witnesses of the same particular events have given versions that have varied according to their sympathies or retentive powers.— Toynbee, *Greek Historical Thought*, 19.

The aim of Thucydides in writing his work was frankly instruction, not entertainment; he sought to produce (in oft-quoted words), "a permanent contribution to knowledge, κτῆμα ἐς ἀεί," and his work is accounted the first typical example of the didactic treatment of history. Speeches put into the mouths of leading participants in the war constitute a fourth or fifth part of his text. Modern criticism has on the whole upheld Thucydides in his adoption of this literary device, which he used under restrictions expressly declared.

(c) Though the ancients considered Xenophon (431–354 B.C.) inferior to Herodotus and Thucydides as a master of his craft, they classed him with them as one of the three leading Greek historians. His *Anabasis*, a well-told narrative of the famous march of the ten thousand mercenaries, which he personally conducted, has its recognized merits, among them accuracy in topographical detail. His *Hellenica*, planned as a continuation of Thucydides, is agreeably written, as are all of Xenophon's compositions, but is weak in criticism. More important than

Xenophon in the development of historiography, is Polybius (ca. 198–122 B.C.), an avowed pragmatist and searcher of causes, who penned in sympathetic vein an account of the rise of Roman imperial power in the Mediterranean basin, and the lessons to be learned therefrom. His reiterated views as to the function of the historian and the scope of his art, which he held to be instruction, are the most noteworthy on the subject to be found among the historians of the ancient world.

(d) In the van of the Roman historians are Sallust (86–35 B.C.), Livy (59 B.C.–A.D. 17), Tacitus (ca. 55–119). Sallust (*The Conspiracy of Catiline, Jugurthine War, History*) took Thucydides for his model. He is truth-seeking, relates in considerable degree from personal experience, and is skilful in depicting character; but he is under the spell of party tradition, fails to mention his sources, and is careless in chronology. Livy (*History*) is noteworthy for psychological delineation of character, and for a rare gift of presentation. But he has obvious defects. His work is deficient in documentary research, methodical testing of material, critical selection of data; moreover, his main interest is in the rhetorical. Tacitus (*Agricola, Germania, Histories, Annals*), is distinguished for lofty outlook and love of the truth; in his method of presentation he inclines to the pragmatic, and can be severely critical in its pursuit: His handling of the defeat of Drusus (*Annals*, IV, 11) and the death of Germanicus (*ibid.*, II, 82, III, 11 ff.) is masterly. He is an adept in character sketching and psychological analysis. On the other hand, he is influenced by party spirit (class-prejudices, Stoic standards of virtue, misconceptions of Christianity), and has a bent to pessimism of a distorting kind, and to rhetorical finery.

(e) Foremost among the later Jewish historians is Josephus (A.D. 37 to ca. 100), author of *Jewish Antiquities* and *The Jewish War*. The official documents incorporated in his works, and his accounts of events in which he personally participated are of distinct value. But his statements often need verification; he wrote according to the historical canons of his day, and was on the side of the emperor.

¶ 55 The leading historian of Christian antiquity was Eusebius of Caesarea (A.D. ca. 260 to ca. 340), author of a *Chronicle* (to A.D. 325), and a history of the Church. The *Chronicle*, as adapted and supplemented by St. Jerome, furnished the conventional chronological framework for historiography all through the Middle Ages, and beyond. The ecclesiastical history is a source of the first rank, both on account of the many important original documents, not elsewhere extant, which it embodies, and because of its method of treatment, which for his day was critical.

(a) During the "great thousand years" of the Middle Ages, historiography was by no means sterile. Annals, chronicles, regular histories and biographies were produced; measured, however, by the requirements of modern research, probably none of them rises to a high level. Discrimination in the use of historical sources was not typical of medieval scholarship. "The confusion between history and legend was never-ending. History in the Middle Ages meant everything that was told, everything that was written in books."——Hippolyte Delehaye, *The Legends of the Saints*, trans. by V. M. Crawford (London, 1907), 66.

At the same time, it is easy to exaggerate the incapacity or slowness of medieval chroniclers and historians to distinguish between fact and fiction. Not a few among them show more than a measure of caution and reserve in dealing with source material: examples are Gregory of Tours in his *History of the Franks*, Venerable Bede in his *Ecclesiastical History of the English Nation*, Otto of Freising in his *Two Cities*.

> Bede is strangely modern in his methods; he begins with a list of his authorities and appends to his history a bibliography of his own writings.——Raymond W. Chambers, *England Before the Norman Conquest* (London, 1926), xi [ℂ 404].

> In positing the objective and impartial aim of the historian, Ranke's *Wie es eigentlich gewesen ist*, is paralleled seven centuries earlier by Otto [of Freising] in language almost identical.——CHR, 17 (1931): 325.

> Yet we must not assume that there was no medieval criticism, and that it was left to moderns to apply the rules of common sense and evidence to bring the forger to book. So early as the ninth century a knavish bishop of Le Mans was convicted of forging charters to the detriment of the rights of the abbey of Saint Calais. A letter of Innocent III explained to the chapter of Milan with admirable lucidity why a false bull presented to them was suspicious in style and handwriting and the artful way in which a genuine seal had been adopted for the service of the spurious document. The pope's letter is a little treatise on the rules for detecting forged documents. Again, in the early fourteenth century, a French Dominican, Bernard Gui, employed in the criticism of suspicious documents principles which, as M. Delisle says, no modern scholar would disavow. And a little later, the letter in which Petrarch explained to the emperor Charles IV that there was no warranty for believing that Julius Caesar and Nero had conferred any privileges on the House of Austria, is a model essay in diplomatic criticism. It must, however, be admitted that in our period the critics were the exceptions to the general rule of unthinking credulity.——Thomas F. Tout, "Medieval Forgers and Forgeries," in *Bulletin* of the John Rylands Library, 5 (1918-1920): 217-218.

For a discussion of the topic, see also Francis X. Mannhardt, "Medieval Conditions and Historical Problems," *HB*, 10 (1932): 11.

(b) In his *De gubernatione Dei*, Salvian, the Marseilles priest, pictured vividly the moral and economic confusion that went with the barbarian invasions of the fifth century. His thesis, that the disintegration of the Empire was a triumph of barbarian virtue over Roman vice, is vigorously put, but it has met with criticism. Salvian stands on the dividing zone between the old Roman Christian world and the new world of the Middle Ages. To the latter belong Gregory of Tours, Bede, Einhard, Asser, Matthew Paris, Froissart, and Comines. Whatever shortcomings modern scholarship may allege against these productions, all have a place of interest and importance in the history of history.

Salvian, *On the Government of God*, tr. by E. M. Sanford (New York, 1930).

History of the Franks by Gregory of Tours, trans. by Ormonde M. Dalton (2 vols., Oxford, 1927).

Venerable Bede, *Ecclesiastical History of the English Nation*, Everyman's Library (London and New York, 1910); Latin text, ed. by Charles Plummer (2 vols., Oxford, 1896).

The Anglo-Saxon Chronicle, trans. by James Ingram, Everyman's Library (London and New York, 1913).

Einhard, *Life of Charlemagne*, trans. by S. E. Turner (New York, 1880).

Two Cities by Otto Bishop of Freising, trans. by C. C. Mierow (New York, 1929).

Asser, *Life of King Alfred*, ed. by W. H. Stevenson (London, 1904).

Ordericus Vitalis, *The Ecclesiastical History of England and Normandy*, trans. by Thomas Forester, based on the edition of Prévost and Delisle, Bohn's Antiquarian Library (4 vols., London, 1853–56).

Matthew Paris, *Chronicles*, Bohn's Standard Library (London, 1852).

Jean Froissart, *Chronicles*, Everyman's Library (London and New York, 1906).

Philip Comines, *Memoirs*, Bohn's Standard Library (2 vols., London, 1901).

¶ 56 The fifteenth-century Renaissance, largely an Italian movement, was the outcome of intellectual and cultural forces that had been active in Europe from the twelfth century onward. Two aspects of the Italian Renaissance are distinguishable, one Christian, the other pagan. Though the validity of the distinction has sometimes been called into question, the pagan Renaissance looked back to the Graeco-Roman world not only for patterns of excellence in literature and art, but also for standards of conduct in public and private life. Humanists of both groups worked diligently in the restoration of ancient classical texts, and after the invention of printing in the publication of critical editions of the same. The Italian scholar, Lorenzo Valla (1407-1457), attacked the authenticity of the so-called Donation of Constantine in a dissertation which is generally held to have been the earliest work of historical criticism to appear. Thus, in various ways the germs of the critical spirit were being planted by the Renaissance, while at the same time a beginning was also made of formal historical method.

(a) The critical attitude in history was given a pronounced impetus by the controversies incident on the Protestant Revolt. The Magdeburg Centuries, a church history written from an aggressively Protestant point of view, elicited from the Catholic scholar Baronius a notable rejoinder. the Annales ecclesiastici, a work marked by vast research and sound criticism.

Peter Guilday, ed., Church Historians (New York, 1926), 153–89.

For the attitude of the Counter-Reformation towards history, as exemplified in the work of an outstanding scholar on the Catholic side, see Edward A. Ryan, The Historical Scholarship of Saint Bellarmine (Louvain, 1936).

(b) Further steps in the direction of scientific history were taken with the launching by a group of Jesuits (Bollandists) of the monumental hagiographical series known as the Acta Sanctorum quotquot toto orbe coluntur, the first volume of which appeared in 1643. The Bollandists, so called after the chief original promoter of the enterprise, John Bollandus (Bolland) of the Society of Jesus, do not, as is sometimes erroneously thought, write new lives of the saints; they edit existing lives, especially contemporary ones, but do so with all the recognized apparatus of textual criticism and with learned discussions of authenticity, credibility, and similar problems. The standards of criticism adopted by the editors of the Acta are set high, and represent a landmark in the development of historical technique. "The Prolegomena with which the Bollandists preface the biographies of the individual saints," says Edward Fueter, "are the first examples of the methodical criticism of sources. Therein for the first time attempt was made on a large scale to group original authorities according to age and credibility." —Geschichte der neueren Historiographie (Munich and Berlin, 1911), 325.

Best account of the Bollandists is Hippolyte Delehaye, L'oeuvre des Bollandistes, 1615–1915, English translation under the title The Work of the Bollandists Through Three Centuries (Princeton, 1922). See also Guilday Church Historians, 190–211; CE, art. "Bollandists."

(c) Notewothy and permanent gains for the cause of critical history were made through the bella diplomatica, as they came to be called, academic controversies carried on chiefly between Jesuit and Benedictine scholars. Questions about the authenticity of certain medieval documents led to critical examination of their provenance. The attempt to determine their interdependence paved the way for the analysis of sources, while searching comparison of manuscript copies brought the causes of error usually at work in the process of handing down texts. The most important of the *bella diplomatica* in its results, was the one involving the Jesuit, Daniel Papebroch [Van Papenbroeck] (1628–1714), a Bollandist, and Jean Mabillon (1632–1707), member of the Benedictine Congregation of St. Maur, in Paris. Papebroch in a dissertation embodied in the second April volume of the *Acta Sanctorum* (1675), had challenged the genuineness of certain charters of the Merovingian period, belonging to the famous Benedictine Abbey of St. Denys. Mabillon, entering the lists in their defense, set himself the task of drawing up an elaborate body of principles and tests by which genuine medieval documents could be distinguished from the false. The results of his labors, the treatise *De re diplomatica* (1681), laid the foundation of the science of diplomatic, and to a certain extent, of paleography. Papebroch was the first to congratulate the Benedictine on his great achievement. The letter which he addressed to him on the occasion is a classic expression of the correct attitude in academic controversy.—See H. Delahaye, *The Work of the Bollandists*, 34 f.

(d) "Its canons [*De re diplomatica*] are the basis, indeed almost the whole of the science of diplomatic, the touchstone of truth for medieval research." Many of Mabillon's monastic associates followed him in making invaluable contributions to the auxiliary sciences, especially palaeography and chronology.

> The place of this school [St. Maur] in the history of history is absolutely without parallel. Few of those in the audiences of Molière returning home under the grey walls of St.-Germain-des-Prés, knew that within that monastery the men whose midnights they disturbed were laying the basis of all scientific history.—James T. Shotwell in *Encyclopaedia Britannica*, 11th ed., 13:530.

Reginald L. Poole, *Lectures on the History of Papal Chancery Down to the Time of Innocent III* (Cambridge, Eng., 1915), vii.

Joseph U. Bergkamp, *Dom Jean Mabillon and the Benedictine School of St. Maur* (Washington, 1928).

Henri Leclerq in *Dictionaire d'archéologie chrétienne et de liturgie*, art. "Mabillon."

James W. Thompson, "The Age of Mabillon and Montfaucon," AHR, 47 (1942): 225–44.

(e) While Jesuits and Benedictines were thus anticipating the spirit and methods of modern scientific historiography, history was gradually becoming self-conscious as a pursuit distinct from literature, with which

the ancients had largely identified it, and therefore as one requiring its own technique. Noteworthy among attempts to formulate a technique for the historian was the *Methodus ad facilem historiarum cognitionem*, of Jean Bodin (1566), the importance of which has been variously rated.
—John L. Brown, *The Methodus ad facilem historiarum cognitionem of Jean Bodin: A Critical Study*, (Washington, 1939); *John Bodin, Method for the Easy Comprehension of History*, trans. by Beatrice Reynolds (New York, 1945).

In the opinion of Allen Johnson, the *Ars historica* (1623) of G. J. Voss was the first effective statement "of the claims of history as an independent subject of study," and Mabillon's *De re diplomatica*, "the first methodology." The *Ars critica* (1696) of the Protestant theologian, J. Le Clerc discussed with penetration the causes of the errors usual in manuscript copying, and their emendation; it was rich in illustrative material drawn from Hebrew, Greek, and Latin sources. A widely used manual was N. Lenglet du Fresnoy's *Méthode pour étudier l'histoire* (1713). The *Réflexions sur les règles et sur l'usage de la critique* (1713), of the Carmelite Honoré de Sainte-Marie, marked a distinct step forward. Johann Martin Chladenius in his *Allgemeine Geschichtswissenschaft* (1752), broke new ground by discussing with insight the rules of historical evidence.

In 1769, appeared the Jesuit Henri Griffet's *Traité des différentes sortes de preuves qui servent à établir la vérité de l'histoire*.

> Ce petit livre est très remarquable pour l'époque à cause de l'esprit critique ferme et pénétrante, dont l'auteur est doué."— Frantz Funck-Brentano, "L'homme au Masque de velours," *Revue historique*, 56 (1894): 256.

Further, Griffet's treatise has been characterized as "the most significant book on method after Mabillon's *De re diplomatica*" and "the most clear-cut statement of the fundamentals of historical research that can be found in the French literature of the eighteenth century."— A. Johnson, *The Historian and Historical Evidence*, 114 f.

The gradual shaping of methodology thus going on, also owed much to the frankly atheistic and anti-Christian writings of Charles de Montesquieu. His *Considérations sur les causes de la grandeur des Romains et de leur décadence* (1734) sought to uncover factors of various kinds, as influencing the course of Roman history, while his *Esprit des lois* (1748) set forth the geographical and social conditions underlying the various forms which the state has assumed in different lands. The philosopher Leibnitz also had an influence on methodology, through his insistence on what he called the *lex continuitatis*, that is, the law of historical continuity, according to which every historical phenomenon is the effect of antecedent phenomena and the cause of phenomena that follow.

¶ 57 The closing decades of the eighteenth century and all of the nineteenth, were an era in which methodology made notable strides. Various causes operated to bring about this result, among them the following.

(a) *The idea of history as evolution or growth which began to dominate historical thinking*, owed its vogue chiefly to Johann G. von Herder (1744–1803), who exploited it in his *Ideen zur Philosophie der Geschichte der Menschen* (1785). While not all his views are admissible, he has the distinction of having opened the way to the genetic or evolutionary concept of history.

(b) *The rebirth and liberation of nations in the wake of the Napoleonic wars.* Nations became conscious of their past, of their individuality, of their unity. Historians began to grasp the various phases of civilization, which in the past had been treated more or less separately, as so many expressions of a single great national life. This new approach to history, resulting in the genre in historiography known as *Kulturgeschichte*, or "history of civilization," had been anticipated by Voltaire in *Le siècle de Louis XIV*, and in his *Essai sur les moeurs*.

(c) *The Romantic movement.* Directed largely against rationalism, this great intellectual current drew men's attention anew to the Christian viewpoint in history and the Middle Ages as the flowering of the Christian spirit. In the van of the romanticists was Chateaubriand: *Génie du Christianisme* (1802); *Les martyrs* (1809). "It was his [Chateaubriand's] chief achievement to unlock the Middle Ages."— G. P. Gooch, *History and Historians*, 161.

(d) *The cultivation of legal history.* Critical researches in the history of German and Roman law during the Middle Ages, especially at the hands of Eichhorn and Savigny, were a stimulus to methodology.

(e) *The new importance of philology.* This discipline took for its province the entire intellectual life of the classical age. The Homeric question, brought to the fore by Friedrich August Wolf (1750–1824) in his *Prolegomena* (1795), was dealt with by him and his followers in the spirit and with the tools of the destructive "higher criticism," later applied by the rationalists to the Bible. Wolf's theories in favor of a multiple authorship of the Homeric poems no longer find the favor once accorded them, but his method of procedure, especially his use of internal criticism, short of its excesses, has passed over into the conventional methodology of history.

(f) *The accession of Barthold G. Niebuhr to the chair of Berlin (1803).* This was in many ways a landmark in the evolution of scientific history. Niebuhr's *Romische Geschichte* (1811–1832) relegated the early periods of Roman history to the domain of fiction and unverified tradition. Probably his specific contribution to the growth of the critical spirit in history was the emphasis he laid on the historian's obligation carefully to appraise his sources from the viewpoint of evidential value.

(g) *Lingard's historical method.* John Lingard's avowed intention, implemented in practice, to go back to the original sources in writing his *History of England*, is noteworthy as a landmark in historiography. In his own words, this work was "in the first instance composed without any reference to modern historians. The author religiously confined his researches to the original, and wherever it was possible, to contemporary writers."

> Lingard represents, therefore, the transition in English historical writing from secondhand to firsthand sources. Although some of his authorities have been discarded in the light of later research, yet his return to the sources marks the beginning of a new epoch in the writing of English history.—Joseph B. Code, *Queen Elizabeth and the English Catholic Historians* (Louvain, 1935), 152.

(h) *The influence of Leopold von Ranke.* Called the "father of modern scientific history," Ranke is generally credited with the invention of the "historical seminar," or laboratory class for firsthand investigation of source materials under professorial direction. As Niebuhr stressed the critical appraisement of sources, Ranke called for the utilization of unpublished archival material, especially in the form of diplomatic and other official documents, as the proper basis of the new scientific history. The cult of the "document," especially the "official document," owes its development largely to Ranke. But the cult has been overdone. Altamira protested against what he calls the "idolatry of the document." It is now recognized that other sources of information besides strictly documentary, such as literature and archaeology, must sometimes be tapped by the historian if he is to exhaust the evidence available for his subject.

(i) *The publication, generally under government auspices, of elaborate collections of source materials.* One of the chief handicaps under which historical scholars had to work far into the nineteenth century, was the difficulty of access to the necessary sources. For all practical purposes, the sources were often inaccessible, because for the most part they were often buried in public or private archives, which were not open to students at all, or could be visited only at considerable expense of time and money. This state of affairs began to be remedied with the publication on a large scale, and in series, of chronicles, state papers, and other source material bearing on the history of various European countries. Thus appeared such voluminous collections as the *Monumenta Germaniae historica* (1826), in Germany; the *Documents inédits* (1836), in France; the *Rolls Series* (1858), in England. This series now includes ninety-nine separate works in two hundred and forty-three volumes. "The sources for the history of England are more varied and more continuously complete than those of any other European country."—G. M. Dutcher, Guide, 484.

(j) *Photographic reproduction of source materials.* The facility with which perfectly accurate copies of documentary material, even in quantity, can be brought by this technique within the reach of the historian, has made it a highly important factor in the promotion of research. "In August, 1839, [Louis]-Jacques-Mandé Daguerre published the details of his photographic process before the Académie des Sciences, and laid the foundation for the science and art of modern photography. It is significant that this first known application of photography to documentation may also be traced back almost a hundred years."—Vernon D. Tate, "Microphotography in Archives," *Staff Information Circulars*, No. 8, National Archives (Washington, 1940), 1 [₵ 99-d].

Chapter Three

CERTAINTY IN HISTORY

A. The Nature of Historical Belief . . . . Page 70
B. The Nature of Historical Certainty 74
C. The Possibility of Historical Certainty 77

A. The Nature of Historical Belief

❡ 58 Human knowledge is derived either from sense-perception or from a variety of mental processes, such as the analysis of ideas, reasoning, belief. The term *knowledge* is sometimes narrowly restricted to what we learn from experience or reasoning, thus excluding what we learn from belief. Knowledge logically includes within its range of meaning all facts and truths apprehended by the human mind, no matter from what source they are derived. It is correct to say that we *know* that Henry VIII existed, however true it be at the same time that our knowledge of the fact is rooted in belief. The knowledge which we call history as record, or historical knowledge, is based almost entirely on belief, which may be defined, *a mental assent to a truth or fact on the word or authority of another*. There are two parties, therefore, to the process. Someone (witness, informant) communicates knowledge, and someone (believer) receives it. *Testimony* is the actual communication of the knowledge, or testimony may signify the content of the knowledge communicated. *Authority* is the complex of reasons or motives which make a witness worthy of belief, which induce others to accept his testimony as true. Authority is integrated of two elements, the witness's *credibility* and the *established fact of his testimony*, namely, of his having rendered testimony on a given matter.

For a lucid discussion of the topic of belief, see William F. Poland, *The Truth of Thought, or Material Logic* (Chicago, 1916), chap. 14.

See also Patrick Coffey, *The Science of Logic: An Inquiry into the Principles of Accurate Thought and Scientific Method* (2 vols., London, 1918), 2:250 ff.

❡ 59 THE CREDIBILITY OF THE WITNESS

This is reducible to three elements: the actual possession by the witness of the knowledge which he undertakes to communicate; his intention and wish to communicate it just as he possesses it; his accuracy in communication of it [❡ 281].

(a) Before accepting the testimony of a witness, we must have some means of ascertaining whether he really has, or can be presumed to have knowledge of the thing to which he testifies. A member of a general staff writing on the major operations of a war in which he participated, elicits belief in his account on the strength of his official position; his relation to such operations creates a presumption that he knows whereof he writes. A private soldier's account of the same matter will be rightly discounted, unless he can produce convincing proof of acquaintance with what went on; under the circumstances, the presumption of adequate knowledge is against him. The account by an eyewitness of a battle, or a murder, for example, loses in credibility if it can be shown that his physical point of view was not favorable to accurate observation.

(b) A witness must be in good faith, must have the intention and desire to tell the truth, to report the facts as he knows them. Veracity is the most essential of all the qualifications demanded in a witness.

(c) But knowledge and veracity do not alone constitute the satisfactory witness; a third qualification is required in him, namely, ability for accurate communication of his knowledge to others. Persons with the very best of knowledge and intention may prove themselves unsatisfactory witnesses through such limitations as weakness of memory, imperfect power of expression, and unconscious habit of exaggeration. Knowledge, veracity, and accuracy of communication are therefore the three factors that guarantee the credibility of a witness.

❡ 60 THE FACT OF TESTIMONY

Together with the credibility of the witness, one must establish the fact of his testimony. A person may be perfectly competent to render testimony on a certain point, but it may be doubtful whether he has actually done so. One may accept in blanket-form the high authority of Thucydides on the Peloponnesian War, but find that question has been raised as to whether a certain passage in his history is not an interpolation; in other words, it may become doubtful whether Thucydides is really a witness or authority in regard to the content of the passage in question. As a preliminary to the acceptance of Christian revelation it is necessary to establish not only the principle that God must be believed when He speaks, but also the historical fact that He has spoken.

❡ 61 Belief a necessity of life

Belief is an inescapable condition of everyday social life. An enormous proportion of everyone's stock of knowledge has been acquired, not by personal experience or reasoning, but by credence given to others. The child believes his parents and teachers, the adult his associates in business or social intercourse. The most educated must take a thousand things on authority. "It is not scientifically certain assents, but beliefs based on authority that shape the conduct of men's lives. The multitudes of mankind are influenced and led by the authority of the few; and no less in the twentieth than in fifteenth, or tenth, or fifth century."
—Coffey, *The Science of Logic*, 2:252.

Science itself is in important ways the servant of authority. The scientist repeatedly accepts the findings of his fellow scientists without verifying them. If he could not so accept them, science would go round in a circle, and progress in it would be at an end. It is not the practice of the engineer, before using a standard table of logarithms, to satisfy himself of its accuracy by checking up its several items. The familiar injunction, "take nothing on authority but prove everything," is futile as a practicable axiom of conduct, whether for the scientist or the man in the street. Modern individualism may sometimes preach it, but in so doing only reveals its own naive lack of perspicacity, its misunderstanding of human nature. The words of St. Augustine are as true today as they were in the fifth century, and as they will be in the centuries to come: "It can be shown on many counts that human society would absolutely fall to pieces, were men to make up their minds to assent to nothing except what they learn by their own experience."—Cited in Feder, *Lehrbuch*, 23.

❡ 62 The motive of belief

The essential idea in belief is acceptance of something as true, solely on the word of another. The other person's word, not the evidence he produces or can produce in support of it, is the motive of belief. The motive comes to this: "I believe because the witness has said so," or, "The witness has said so, therefore I believe." Such an act of belief, perfectly reasonable as it can be in every regard, presupposes that the mind has formed, explicitly or implicitly, the judgment: "What this witness says is true."

On the other hand, belief may rest directly not only on the authority of the witness, but also on the evidence he can produce for the truth of what he says. It is often possible, with the aid of an author's references, as given in footnotes, to go back to the particular sources on which his statements rest; to do so is often necessary in order to quiet suspicion or doubt. But it would be scarcely practicable to adopt the stand that no statement in a history book may be admitted unless it can be traced back to ultimate sources. Even the most exacting critic, if he accepts Channing, for example, as a reliable source of information, will have in practice to accept the bulk of his statements on the ordinary basis of all historical belief; he must accept them on Channing's own authority. The critical attitude in historical belief demands above everything else that the claim of a historian to rank as a trustworthy witness or authority, be submitted to thoroughgoing examination. The historian's personality, means of knowledge, veracity, affiliations, whether social, political, religious, have to be investigated if his general trustworthiness is to be set on a satisfactory basis. Once his general trustworthiness has been ascertained, we may confidently accept him as a guide, while being ready at the same time to suspend assent if doubt arises as to the accuracy of individual statements.

(a) Belief is *doctrinal* when assent is given to a truth or doctrine; *historical* when assent is given to a fact. It is *human* or *divine* according as the witness is man or God. Human belief is the inevitable foundation stone of history. Divine or supernatural belief (faith), which is assent to a truth or fact on the basis of revelation, is on an immeasurably higher level than human faith; but considered as mental operations, which they both are, the two are psychologically alike. The difference between them is that human belief is elicited by the natural forces of the soul, while divine belief, or faith, is accompanied by a special aid called grace, which elevates the soul from a natural to a supernatural plane of operation, thus enabling it to elicit an act which is beyond its merely natural powers.

> We all start life with beliefs which we have learned from others. . . . We stand on the shoulders of the past and learn to the end of our lives from the accumulated experience of mankind.—Martin C. D'Arcy, *The Nature of Belief* (London, 1931), 207.
>
> It is necessary for an individual to trust other individuals in matters which he cannot investigate for himself; and unless there is reason to suppose that the witnesses are biased or incompetent, their testimony should be put on a par with his own. . . . The ultimate premises of the historian must nevertheless rest upon the testimony of other minds than his own and it is both justifiable and inevitable that he should at least give provisional credence to all disinterested authorities.—William P. Montague, *The Ways of Knowing; or The Methods of Philosophy* (London, 1928), 225.
>
> Upon human testimony all our inferences and conclusions from

narrative and statistical data ultimately rest. When we have discovered that historical and statistical documents are genuine as records, we still have to inquire whether the story they tell is credible.—Franklin H. Giddings, *The Scientific Study of Human Society* (Chapel Hill, N. Carolina, 1924), 101.

There is no such thing as historical knowledge in the strictest sense of the word, beyond the very few things of which our own senses have been cognizant. It is, strictly speaking, belief based on the testimony of others, and that belief may be of any degree, from such complete confidence that it is virtually equivalent to certainty, downwards.—Hereford B. George, *Historical Evidence* (Oxford, 1909), 218.

A speaker at a convention of historians once claimed as a merit of the source system in the teaching of history, that it impresses on the student's mind the fact that evidence, not authority, is the only rock-bottom basis of history. The speaker's plea was that historians cease to be "the bondmen of authority": the words of St. Anselm, *credo ut intelligam*, "I believe in order that I may understand," were cited as expressing a principle the very opposite to that which should guide them. As a matter of fact, the most superficial analysis demonstrates that every historian is the veriest "bondman of authority," and that his adoption of St. Anselm's principle is the indispensable condition of his being a historian at all. The medieval churchman was stressing the need of faith as the basis of supernatural or revealed knowledge; but the principle which he laid down has its application in the field of historical knowledge as well. "Evidence" and "authority," far from being opposite concepts, are in reality identical in the case of history, because the only evidence we have for what happened in the past is, in the main, the testimony, the authority of trustworthy witnesses.

B. The Nature of Historical Certainty

❡ 63 The capital function of methodology is to indicate the ways and means of arriving at historical certainty, which may be defined as a *firm assent of the mind to a historical datum without reasonable fear of its being false.* According to the nature of the motive on which it is based, the certainty may be moral, physical, or metaphysical.

(a) The motive grounding or justifying *moral certainty* is the known uniformity or regularity of some moral law. Examples of the moral laws which people usually recognize and reckon with in their judgments are these: parents love their children and will safeguard their lives; a son will defend the good name of his father; a person of recognized integrity of life will not commit a shocking crime. Two quite fundamental laws in the same order are the following: people are eager to know the truth when such knowledge is of advantage to them and is within easy reach;

people do not lie when there is no advantage in lying. Moral laws admit of exception, but in general they operate with a steadiness and regularity that afford a solid basis of certainty. As history is largely a matter of belief on the testimony of others, and as testimony is a matter conditioned in its very nature by moral laws, it follows that for the most part historical certainty is of the moral order. Moreover, the certainty attainable in history is often the result of a converging series of probabilities issuing in that very high degree of probability which is scarcely distinguishable from certainty, and which accordingly logicians often label "moral certainty." *Moral* in this usage of the term has the connotation of *virtual*, not of *ethical*. Proof by "converging probabilities" was the method used by the archaeologist De Rossi to establish his brilliant interpretations on the subject of the Roman catacombs. The method seldom finds application in philosophy. Here, as a rule, a cumulus of probabilities does not yield more than probability.

"Moral certainty" as applied to history, may also be defined as "a certainty excluding all reasonable doubt," the assurance, namely, of which juries are instructed by the law to be in possession before pronouncing the defendant guilty. On the general notion of "moral certainty," see John Rother, *Certitude* (St. Louis, 1911), 12 ff.

(b) Historical certainty is of the *physical* order when its basis or motive is the known uniform operation of a physical law, such as those of astronomy, mechanics, chemistry, biology, physiology, and even psychology. We have no documentary evidence that the four seasons followed one another in due order in America in the year A.D. 500; but it is a physical certainty that they did, since there is no reason to assume any suspension of the usual course of nature in that year and region.

Physical laws and conditions play an 'important part in the critical assessment of evidence. We know, for instance, that the time consumed in a journey is necessarily conditioned by the distance to be covered and the means of transportation available; that certain illnesses bring on death; that unconscious color-blindness leads to erroneous perception of colors; that lack of attention prevents one from seeing clearly what is going on; that careless wandering of a copyist's eyes may result in omission of words, and even of entire sentences.

(c) *Metaphysical certainty* finds its basis in principles which are absolute in their application, and admit of no exception. Such are the principle of *contradiction* ("a thing cannot exist and not exist at the same time") and of *sufficient reason* ("nothing exists without a sufficient reason," a variant of the principle of causation.)—R. F. Clarke, *Logic*, 72.

The metaphysical certainty possible in history is reductive in character—the meaning of which appears from this example: "The alleged historical fact A is reported by several independent witnesses. But their agreement cannot possibly be explained except by the objective truth of the fact reported (principle of sufficient reason). Consequently the alleged fact A is metaphysically certain." Taking their stand on this reasoning, logicians sometimes contend that many outstanding facts in history such as the Roman Empire, Charlemagne, the Crusades, the French Revolution, Napoleon, Washington, are absolutely or metaphysically certain. But the question whether anything in history can be metaphysically certain is only of speculative interest. It suffices as a practical issue that we are able to establish the possibility of at least moral certainty in regard to historical data. Such certainty, which excludes all reasonable doubt, is certainty of the kind we look for, and when found, on which we act "in the gravest concerns of life" (Freeman's phrase).

☾ 64 Probability in History

What are the chances or probabilities that an alleged historical datum is true? Can the chances or probabilities be expressed in mathematical form? "Mathematically speaking, probability is the ratio between the factors favorable to an event and the total number of factors involved, favorable or unfavorable."——J. C. Almack, *Research and Thesis Writing*, 183.

Thus, of twenty factors involved, if five are favorable and fifteen unfavorable, the chances are 3-to-1 that the event did not happen. Again, of thirty factors involved, if twenty are favorable and ten unfavorable, the chances are 2-to-1 that the event happened. The results in such calculations can also be expressed in terms of percentage. Thus, in the first instance probability that the event happened is twenty-five per cent. But it must be pointed out that in these and similar calculations it is assumed that the factors conditioning the problem are all of an equal degree of probability, an assumption not generally borne out in the type of evidence (moral, not mathematical), with which history deals. Practically, the considerations affecting the probability or improbability of alleged events are to be weighed rather than counted: *non sunt numeranda sed ponderanda*. One may produce ten reasons why a supposed event could not have occurred, and only five why it must have occurred. The ten outnumber the five; it does not follow that they outweigh them. Hence, mathematical calculations such as those exemplified, are seldom decisive in rating the probability of alleged historical facts. But they may have their use, provided due regard be had for weight as well as number in assessing the probabilities, and the resulting figures be interpreted broadly.

George H. Joyce, *Principles of Logic* (London, 1926), 373–79.
Patrick Coffey, *The Science of Logic*, 2:268.

C. The Possibility of Historical Certainty

❡ 65 Can we really be morally *certain* about any of the supposed facts of history? This is an important question, which on reflection is seen to include three: First, is the human mind capable of knowing historical truth? Second, is such truth *in se* knowable? Third, is such truth ever presented to us on grounds adequate to guarantee its certainty? We distinguish, therefore, between the subjective and the objective possibility of historical truth. The two are correlative; one goes along with the other.

❡ 66 THE MIND'S CAPACITY FOR TRUTH
That the mind has a capacity for knowing the truth is a proposition set out in any sound treatise on epistemology. Instinct bids us acquiesce in the proposition, for it is really a necessary postulate, and to deny it is to commit intellectual suicide. Attempts have been made to erect skepticism into a philosophical system, but to no purpose. Fundamental common sense rebels; all such efforts to upset the foundations of knowledge are labor lost. Nor is there any ascertainable ground for the type of skepticism which would allow the human mind to be an instrument for the attainment of truth in all fields of knowledge except that of history. For if the mind is no fit instrument for the pursuit of historical truth, neither is it a fit instrument for the pursuit of any other kind of truth.

John F. X. Pyne, *The Mind* (New York, 1926).
William F. Poland, *The Truth of Thought, or Material Logic* (Chicago, 1916).

❡ 67 IDEALISTS AND SKEPTICS
Critics of the objective possibility of historical certainty may be grouped into two classes: *philosophical idealists*, especially those of the schools of Kant, Hegel, Croce, Gentile, and others, who undermine in some way or other the foundations of extra-mental reality; and *skeptics* of various colors, who exaggerate the difficulties in the way of reaching truth in history.—Désiré Mercier, *The Origins of Contemporary Psychology* (London, 1918), 249–62.

(a) An idealistic viewpoint in the philosophical sense crops up at times in writings on historical science. Thus Allen Johnson: "To say that a historian should tell the truth is a counsel of perfection. It assumes that there is absolute truth to which he may attain. Such a quest, however, is as hopeless as the metaphysician's search after 'things-in-themselves'—that hypothetical outside world of things which are supposed to stimulate our sense-organs to activity. The most that philosophers can know is the world as given in consciousness; and the most that historians can know is that historical past which has been perceived and reported by human intelligence."—*The Historian and Historical Evidence*, 146.

This passage has a Kantian ring; the author takes the "outside world of things" to be "hypothetical" only, and goes no farther than to "suppose" that it "stimulates our sense-organs to activity."

(*b*) Benedetto Croce propounds a system of philosophical idealism as applied to history. His *History, Its Theory and Practice*, a tissue of fanciful and obfuscating speculation, offers nothing of value to the student of history [₵ 32]. The radical and decisive objection to idealistic systems in philosophy, and in history as well, is "their divorcement from the principles of common sense."—Gilbert J. Garraghan, "The Crocean View of History," *The Modern Schoolman*, 16 (1939): 54–57.

That history as record is "relative," may be admitted, in the sense that deriving as it does from the perception and testimony of men, it often borrows shape and color from the subjective medium through which it passes. Furthermore, the objective facts are perhaps never reproduced in their full range of authentic detail. But it is folly to leap thence to the conclusion that nothing can be *absolutely* known about the historical past. That Napoleon Bonaparte existed, that he fought Europe, was worsted at Waterloo, and died at St. Helena, are facts which we can be said to know absolutely. On the other hand, that his personality was such or such, that he was dominated by this passion or that, may very well be matters about which we have not, and probably cannot have knowledge that is final and irreversible. What knowledge we have about them is almost of necessity provisional and relative. History as record is therefore part absolute and part relative. It is important that "historical relativity" be understood in its legitimate sense, for under cover of the term there often masquerades the illusion that all historical knowledge is necessarily and in every respect in a state of flux, that nothing of the content of history as reality can be known with the calm assurance of one possessing undeniable truth [₵ 1 ff.].

₵ 68 The skepticism bred of the falsity of so much that passes or has passed muster for actual history finds classic expression in the saying generally attributed to Fontenelle (1657–1757): "*L'histoire n'est qu'une fable convenue.*" An American captain of industry once said the same thing less elegantly: "History is bunk." Modern critical investigation with its frank exposure of the uncertainties, gaps, contradictions, and downright falsehoods in recognized historical sources, has brought with it a tendency in many quarters to question the reliability of history as a whole. Even the French methodologists, Charles V. Langlois and Charles Seignobos, strike a somewhat skeptical note.

> The facts which it is possible to establish [in history] are chiefly those which cover a large extent of space or time (sometimes called *general facts*), customs, doctrines, institutions, great events; they were easier to observe than the others and are now easier to prove. . . . In the case of antiquity and the middle ages, historical knowledge is limited to general facts by the scarcity of documents. In dealing with contemporary history it is possible to include more and more particular facts.—*Introduction to the Study of History*, trans. by G. G. Berry (New York, 1925), 203.

Allen Johnson thinks that the historian is fortunate "if he can reach a high degree of probability, a probability beyond reasonable doubt.—*The Historian and Historical Evidence*, 141.

But "probability beyond reasonable doubt," if we overlook the contradiction involved in this statement, is equivalent to certainty. What we hold "beyond reasonable doubt," we hold with certainty. Finally, it may be noted, a morbidly skeptical mind can call into question the most unequivocally attested facts. Such a mind can prove to its own satisfaction that Napoleon never lived—a theme elaborated by Archbishop Whateley in his famous satirical pamphlet, *Historic Doubts Relative to the Existence of Napoleon Buonaparte* (1819).

¶ 69 THE GROUNDS OF HISTORICAL CERTAINTY

These are either one's own personal experience, or the testimony of others. Personal experience, where it exists, can be relied upon as a source of certain knowledge. To deny this, is to deny the reliability of one's own senses as sources of information. Testimony, to be reliable, must meet certain requirements, the nature of which is discussed in Chapter 13 [¶ 279ff.]. But where these requirements are met, the content of the testimony may and should be accepted without reasonable doubt: which is to say, with certainty. The common-sense attitude on the question may be expressed in the formula: "Human testimony, oral or written, direct or indirect, under given conditions is a dependable source of certain knowledge." The truth of the formula issues with logical rigor from analysis of its separate terms and the implications they bear.

> Although the historian can never attain the same certainty which is attained by the mathematician, the physicist, or the chemist, nevertheless, especially in the case of converging lines of evidence, he is able to reach such moral certainty as is the basis of nearly all our actions. The "evidence on which we act every day, the evidence on which we stake

our fortunes, our honour, and our lives, is the kind of evidence which we get in our historical studies."——E. A. Freeman, *The Methods of History*, 152.

It is not because the historian's work is subjective in character, or because his findings are almost inevitably colored by religious or political prejudices, that one is justified in casting "doubt over the truthfulness of any history. Carlyle referred to it as the great Mississippi of falsehood; another speaks of it as a fable upon which there is agreement. Such harsh comments are undeserved. The historian who selects all the sources, who subjects them to criticism after the approved tenets, who checks the testimony of one witness against the testimony of the others, who records all the facts of his subject faithfully, who reports his facts accurately, and who makes reasonable generalizations on the basis of his facts, runs no more risks of emotional upset than his fellows in experimental and normative science."——J. C. Almack, *Research and Thesis Writing*, 182 f.

Chapter Four

THE AUXILIARY SCIENCES

A. Philosophy . . . . Page 82
B. Bibliography 83
C. Anthropology 84
D. Linguistics 85
E. Geography 87
F. Chronology 89
G. Diplomatic 91
H. Sigillography and Heraldry 93
I. Palaeography 94
J. Archaeology 95
K. Epigraphy 97
L. Numismatics 98
M. Genealogy 99

¶ 70 "A man writing good history," says Hilaire Belloc, "is driving more horses abreast in his theme than a man writing any other kind of literary matter"; for what he aims to achieve is a synthesis, more or less complete, of the results of research of whatever kind which bear on his specific theme. Almost any topic of investigation will send the historian in various directions for data, but, as a rule, the narrower the limits within which he works, the less will be his need for the broader and more inclusive types of information.

In general, all the social sciences (and some of the non-social) furnish grist to the historical mill. *Anthropology* enables the historian to trace the course of social and cultural evolution through the dim, nebulous centuries of the prehistoric and proto-historical, or as some prefer to call it, the pre-literary era. In a measure psychology initiates him into the mysteries of group-behavior, not a negligible factor in the correct analysis of such important social phenomena as revolutions, popular movements, mass-reactions to oratory, or it may furnish him with important clues to the behavior of historical characters. In *historical geography* he may learn much of the influence of physical environment on man and his affairs. *Economics* has its lessons in the manner in which the immemorial quest for a livelihood and material goods influence social development and therefore history. *Political science* supplies principles for a correct appreciation of the highly important group of human relations which center around the institutions of civil government. The historian must be a man of the broadest possible knowledge and interests, refusing no light from whatever quarter it may come. But it is plain in view of these considerations that his task becomes possible only on the principle of the division of labor. He must utilize the researches of others, beginning in many cases where they leave off. This becomes clearer when account is taken of the sometimes highly technical nature of what are conventionally called the "auxiliary sciences of history." These bear rather on the method than on the content of historical research, and in any case are of the utmost importance as aids to the historian.

A. Philosophy

¶ 71 A grounding in the principles of sound philosophy in its various branches is an important step in the training of the historian. *Logic* or *dialectics* acquaints him with the laws of clear, orderly, accurate thinking. The normal mind is obedient to these laws more or less automatically; but formal study of them has its advantages. Any critical use of historical material involves the application of one or more of the ordinary forms of logical proof, such as deduction and induction. *Epistemology*, in its analysis of the nature and objective value of human knowledge, bears on the all-important question of the possibility and conditions of certainty in history. *Metaphysics* may not seem to touch the historian's business at all; in reality it does. For instance, it safeguards the principle of causality against the attacks of theorists, and sets it in proper relief as a universal factor in the historical process. *Ethics* furnishes correct principles and standards of private and public morality, an equipment necessary for the historian if his interpretations of past events are to have validity. *Theodicy* supplies the principles and proofs which validate the theistic outlook on life. It furnishes the only basis on which it is possible to build up a satisfactory philosophy of social evolution in its broadest ascertainable range; for history cannot be written without reference to ultimates. Its narrower themes can be so written, but not its broader ones. Any attempt to handle the latter will prove ineffective without a comprehensive view of the scope and meaning of the historical process as a whole. This is an attitude which finds increasing favor with the historians, even such as are not committed to a Christian or even to a theistic point of view.

B. Bibliography

❡ 72 From an etymological point of view bibliography may be defined broadly as "a description of books," or as "the science of books." The description or the science may regard either the format of a book, or its content. Bibliography as a practical tool of the historian is concerned mainly with the latter element, its function being to bring to his notice what is available in the way of source material, chiefly printed, on the subject of his investigation. "Knowledge is of two kinds," said Samuel Johnson. "We know a subject ourselves or we know where we can find information upon it." A Latin adage expresses the same idea: *qui scit ubi sit scientia, proximus est scienti*. Knowledge is largely a matter of building upon other people's knowledge. To neglect doing so is to condemn oneself to useless expenditure of time and labor.

Since historical erudition is progressive, the more recent a book, the more likely it is to embody the results of the latest research on its theme. Works in the fields of Oriental, Greek, and Roman history produced half a century ago necessarily have their shortcomings, as they lack the data supplied by recent archaeological and other research. Sometimes up-to-dateness is of a spurious kind, being merely a mask for rash and sensational speculation and hypothesis; but if a work be of the really scholarly kind, its up-to-dateness will be a large factor commending it to the student. Where more than one edition of a work has appeared, use should be made of the latest, unless the so-called new editions are merely reprints of the original without change of content. In bringing out new editions of their works authors often subject them to important and even drastic changes correcting errors in earlier editions, adopting new viewpoints and interpretations, and revising the text in the light of new additions made to knowledge of the subject concerned. In such cases use of an edition other than the most recent might be unsafe. The original edition (1895) of Rashdall's *Universities of Europe in the Middle Ages* has been displaced by the thoroughly revised edition prepared by F. M. Powicke and A. B. Emden (1936).

❡ 73 REFERENCE WORKS OF BIBLIOGRAPHY
Ronald B. McKerrow, *An Introduction to Bibliography for Literary Students* (Oxford, 1928).
Henry B. Van Hoesen and Frank K. Walter, *Bibliography: Practical, Enumerative, Historical: An Introductory Manual* (New York, 1928).
Edith M. Coulter and Melanie Gerstenfeld, *Historical Bibliographies: A Systematic and Annotated Guide* (Berkeley, California, 1935).

Theodore Bestman, A World Bibliography of Bibliographies (2 vols., London, 1939).

International Bibliography of Historical Sciences [Annual] (New York, 1930——).

Bibliographies in the Various History Fields

GENERAL: George M. Dutcher and Others, A Guide to Historical Literature (New York, 1931).

MEDIEVAL: Louis J. Paetow, Guide to the Study of Medieval History for Students, Teachers, and Libraries (rev. ed. New York, 1931).—— August Potthast, Wegweiser durch die Geschichtswerke des europäischen Mittelalters bis 1500 (2d rev. ed., 2 vols., Berlin, 1896).——Ulysse Chevalier, Répertoire des sources historiques du moyen âge (4 vols., Paris, 1894-1907).——George Sarton, Introduction to the History of Science (2 vols., Washington, D. C., 1927——).

GERMAN: Friedrich C. Dahlmann and George Waitz, Quellenkunde der deutschen Geschichte (8th ed., Leipzig, 1912).

FRENCH: Auguste Molinier et. al., Les sources de l'histoire de France (18 vols., Paris, 1901-1926).

ENGLISH: Charles Gross, The Sources and Literature of English History to 1485 (2nd ed., New York, 1915).——Godfrey Davies, Bibliography of British History: Stuart Period, 1603-1714 (Oxford, 1928).——Conyers Reid, Bibliography of British History: Tudor Period, 1485-1603 (Oxford, 1933).——Clyde L. Grose, A Select Bibliography of British History, 1660-1765 (Chicago, 1939).

IRISH: James F. Kenney, Sources for the Early History of Ireland (to 1172) (New York, 1929), vol. 2.

AMERICAN: Henry P. Beers, Bibliographies in American History: Guide to Materials for Research (New York, 1928).——Edward Channing, Albert B. Hart, Frederick J. Turner, Guide to the Study and Reading of American History (rev. ed., Boston and London, 1912).——Samuel F. Bemis and Grace G. Griffin, Guide to the Diplomatic History of the United States, 1795-1925 (Washington, 1935).

CHURCH HISTORY: For bibliography of Church History, see P. Guilday, An Introduction to Church History, chap. 8; Shirley J. Case and Others, eds., A Bibliographical Guide to the History of Christianity (Chicago, 1931).

C. Anthropology

❡ 74 Anthropology, in its broadest range of meaning, the science of man, has also been defined as the science of primitive or undeveloped man. It derives its data chiefly from *palaeontology*, which deals with fossil and skeletal remains; from *archaeology*, which works with physical survivals or remains of extinct cultures or civilizations; and from *ethnology*, which treats of racial and tribal characteristics as expressed in customs, manners, arts, religious beliefs. Ethnology, so defined, is equivalently *cultural anthropology* as distinguished from *physical anthropology*, which is concerned mainly with the problem of the origin and growth of man on his physical or biological side.

Culture in the anthropologic sense is "a common way of life—a particular adjustment of man to his natural surroundings and his economic needs."—Christopher H. Dawson, *The Age of the Gods; A Study in the Origin of Culture in Pre-historic Europe and the Ancient East* (London, 1933), xiii.

Culture or civilization, taken in its widest ethnographic sense, is that complex whole which includes knowledge, belief, arts, moral, law, custom, and any other capabilities and habits acquired by man as a member of society.—Edward B. Tylor, *Primitive Culture* (2 vols., London, 1871), 1:1.

As all history may be conceived to be "the manifestation of the growth and mutual interaction of living cultural wholes" [Dawson], the dependence of the historian on the cultural anthropologist is manifest, more particularly for data on the prehistoric (pre-literary) era, or the very earliest periods of documented history.

A principle of wide acceptance among present-day anthropologists, especially American, is that cultural growth is effected, not by mere development from within, but largely by development from without, by borrowing from existing civilizations and cultures. In other words no people lifts itself by its own bootstraps from savagery to civilization. This is the so-called "diffusion theory," as opposed to the evolutionary theory of uniform, unilinear development according to rigidly operating laws.

Christopher H. Dawson, *Progress and Religion* (London, 1929), 49 ff.
Albert Muntsch, *Cultural Anthropology* (Milwaukee, 1934), 13.
For illustrations of the use of anthropologic data in history, see Dawson, *The Age of the Gods*, passim.
William H. Rivers, *History and Ethnology* (Helps, vol. 48).
Albert Muntsch, *Evolution and Culture* (St. Louis, 1923).
William Schmidt, "Primitive Man" in Edward Eyre, ed., *European Civilization, its Origin and Development*, (7 vols., Oxford, 1937–1939), 1:1–82.
Eva Ross, *Social Origins* (London, 1936).
Sylvester A. Sieber and Franz H. Mueller, *The Social Life of Primitive Man* (St. Louis, 1941).
Joseph J. Williams, "Boas and American Ethnologists," *Thought*, 9 (1936): 194–209.

D. Linguistics

₡ 75 LINGUISTIC DATA AS AIDS TO HISTORY

Scientific study of the development of language and the principles which regulate it supplies valuable data to the historian. Thus, one important use he can make of such study is based on the principle that "if a word occurs today in a fair sprinkling of the Aryan languages, then that word existed in some form or other in the Aryan civilization."—Owen Barfield, *History in English Words* (New York, 1926), 11.

This is an illustration of the nature of the evidence which linguistics can furnish the historian. Similarly, by a comparative study of the earliest languages of Italy, Mommsen brought to light numerous facts regarding the country's primitive racial stocks.——*History of Rome*. trans. by W. B. Dickson, (3 vols., New York, 1854–1856), vol. 1, chap. 2.

Such words as inch, kitchen, mile, mill, street, wall, and table, brought over by the Anglo-Saxons to England, suggest close contacts between them and the Romans of the Continent.——Owen Barfield, *History in English Words*, 31.

The negligible number of Celtic words (about a hundred) surviving in English has been pointed to, rightly or wrongly, as evidence of the sweeping nature of the Anglo-Saxon conquest. Finally, a good deal of social history is reflected in the process by which the English language evolved slowly out of Anglo-Saxon and Norman-French elements. Often a word helps to fix, at least in rough working fashion, the earliest possible date of a document. Knowing the time when the following words were coined or when they first came into use, we know consequently that the dates (indicated in parentheses), are the earliest which can be assigned to documents containing the respective words: beef-eater (1671); flabbergast (1772); Mrs. Grundy (1798); communism (1840); microbe (1878).——See Ernest Weekley, *An Etymological Dictionary of Modern English* (New York, 1921). See also Lucy M. Salmon, "The Record of Language," *Historical Material* (New York, 1933), 77–90.

⁊ 76   FOREIGN LANGUAGES

The first requirement for intelligent work with source material is ability to read it, and to do this the student must necessarily know the language in which it is written. If he works in the medieval field, he is lost without medieval Latin, just as he is lost in the Hispanic-American field without Spanish. What the indispensable language or languages are, depends on the material dealt with. Classical Latin alone will not put one at ease among medieval texts. Medieval Latin has its own specific vocabularies with which the student of medieval texts must become familiar. He must know, for example, that in the Middle Ages *quia* might mean "that," and *seu*, "and," meanings that are foreign to classical usage of the same words. Even in St. Augustine's time, classical words were taking on new technical meanings. His treatise, *De rudibus catechezandis*, is concerned with religious instruction, not of illiterates (*rudes*, in classical Latin), but of "catechumens," persons, whether illiterate or not, who were being prepared for baptism. On the other hand, in St. Augustine's day *sacramentum* had not yet taken on its later theological sense, and hence theological arguments based on his use of the term are generally not to the point. To what grotesque results inadequate acquaintance with a language will lead, is illustrated by the translation in an American book of the Latin *quatuor tempora* as "four times" instead of "ember days." A certain cleric is represented as having been ordained "four times a year," whereas he was ordained once, and that during one of the ecclesiastical seasonal periods known as "ember days," which occur four times a year.

¶ 77   How much the solution of a historical problem may depend on the precise meaning to be attached to certain terms is illustrated in an archaeologist's answer to the question, "What was the population of ancient Rome?" By using the Latin words, *domus*, *insula*, and *coenacula*, in what he contends are the only correct meanings to be attached to them, Jerome Carcopino reaches the conclusion that the population of Rome at the time of the Antonines was approximately 1,200,000.—See *Daily Life in Ancient Rome: The People and the City at the Height of the Empire*, translated from the French by E. O. Lorimer, edited with Bibliography and Notes by Henry T. Rowell (New Haven, 1940), 16–20.

¶ 78   Apart from the necessity of knowing the pertinent languages for the reading and criticism of documents, a knowledge of French and German is virtually indispensable if the history student is to keep abreast of the most recent scholarship in his field. He needs also an immense amount of specialized study and research, the results of which are set out in contemporary books, monographs, and learned reviews in the principal Western European languages. Contact with such secondary literature must be steadily maintained, if one's published product is not to fail in a recognized hallmark of scholarly work: up-to-dateness.

E. Geography

¶ 79   Chronology and geography have been happily called "the two eyes of history." The description derives from the very notion of history as record, which deals with human events not as suspended in midair, but as tied down to time and space. The category of place (called "ubication," by Scholastic philosophers), as being one of the two inevitable physical settings of the events of history, falls within the purview of geography, which may be taken to be the science of the earth viewed as the stage on which the human story unfolds.

Geography is divided into three branches: First, *physical*, which deals with climate, configuration, land-and-water distribution, soil, natural resources, fauna and flora, and other features of the earth's surface as it appears today; second, *political*, which indicates (often with accompanying descriptive data), the location, boundaries, organizations, of present-day political units of whatever sort (countries, cities, towns, etc.); and third, *historical*, which combines the physical and political points of view in its study of the earth's surface. Historical geography aims accordingly to present both political geography as it evolved in successive periods of world-history, and the results of the past mutual interaction of man and his physical environment.

The physical and political types of geography are, therefore, concerned with the earth's surface only as it exists today; the third type, the historical, is concerned with it as it existed in successive periods of the past. The first two are mainly descriptive in treatment; the third is both descriptive, and to a considerable extent, interpretative. It is a fact of historical geography that the Mississippi Valley, as a result of progressive settlement, is less thickly wooded than it was when white men first made its acquaintance.

> The three major questions in historical geography are: (1) What was the physical character of the country, especially as to vegetation, prior to the intrusion of man? (2) Where and how were the nuclei of settlement established, and what was the character of the frontier economy? (3) What successions of settlement and land utilization have taken place?——Carl Sauer, "Historical Geography," in J. F. Willard and C. B. Goodykoontz, eds., *The Trans-Mississippi West*, 277.

(a) Geography of whatever type usually presents its data through the graphic devices of maps (cartography). How these serve the needs of students of history is obvious and needs no elaboration.

Encyclopaedia Britannica, article "Map" (brief and comprehensive).
Edward A. Reeves, *Maps and Map-Making* (London, 1910).
Henry N. Dickson, *Maps: How They are Made and How to Read Them* (London, 1912).
Sir Herbert George Fordham, *Maps, Their History, Characteristics and Uses: A Handbook for Teachers* (Cambridge, Eng., 1927).
Erwin Raisz, *General Cartography* (New York, 1938).
John P. Goode, "The Map as a Record of Progress in Geography," *Annals* of the Association of American Geographers, 17 (1927): 1–14.

(b) Physical geography in as far as it supplies the data for the study of the influence of the material world on man and on his social evolution, is of prime interest and importance to the historian; but its significance in the interpretation of history has been overstressed by Buckle and by other economic determinists, for whom material forces are primary in history [☾ 352 ff]

(c) The influence of physical environment in history has been offered in exaggerated form by Friedrich Ratzel, *Anthropogeographie* (1st ed., Stuttgart, 1882–1891), and his American popularizer, Ellen C. Semple, *Influ-*

ences of Geographic Environment, on the Basis of Ratzel's System of Anthropo-geography (New York and London, 1925). See also American History and its Geographic Conditions (Boston, 1903).

Ratzel's anthropo-geography has also been called human geography. A typical study of the relations of physical environment to historical development, with due account taken of non-physical factors, is Albert P. Brigham, Geographic Influences in American History (Boston, 1903). A brief treatment is by Herbert J. Fleure, Geographical Factors (Helps, vol. 44). See also Arthur M. Schlesinger, New Viewpoints in American History (New York, 1922), chap. 2; Archer B. Hulbert, Soil, its Influence on the History of the United States (New Haven, 1930).

F. Chronology

¶ 80 Means of dating events and documents must be at hand to the historian. Events that cannot be made to fit into some chronological scheme are scarcely ever material for the historian to handle.

In so-called pre-history or the pre-literate period of social development, dating of the series of successive cultures revealed by paleontological remains is possible as regards order of succession; their absolute age cannot be determined except within a broad margin of accuracy. So also a dateless and undatable document is in many cases useless for the historian's purpose.

Chronology or the science of time-measurement furnishes the principles by which it becomes possible to assign events a definite position in the stream of time. Needless to say, the evidence which enables one to fix the date of an event or document falls outside the province of chronology proper; but such evidence cannot be formulated without aid of the computations and time-schemes which chronology provides. It furnishes the framework into which occurrences must be made to fit if their relations to one another in point of time are to become intelligible. Historical or practical chronology, which is based on mathematical or theoretical chronology, deals with such matters as time-units great and small, eras, beginning of the year, comprehensive systems of time-reckoning such as the Julian (Old Style) and Gregorian (New Style) calendars, civil and ecclesiastical, indictions, regnal years, and the like.

(a) *Beginning of the Year*. The year, civil or ecclesiastical, has begun variously in different ages and countries. In the Middle Ages, and even later, it began, now on December 25, now on January 1, now on March 25. Even today the years according to which papal bulls are dated commence on December 25.

(b) *Old Style, New Style*. By the sixteenth century the civil year was ten days in arrears of the solar year, and this because of an original miscalculation in the Julian calendar then in use. To remedy this defect Pope Gregory XIII reformed the calendar, 1582, by dropping from it ten days, October 5–14, and making other provisions calculated to keep the civil year in accurate step with the solar year. Thus, October 4 of 1582, was followed immediately by October 15, of the same year. The reformed calendar came to be called New Style (N.S.) and the one it supplanted Old Style (O.S.). Many countries delayed for a long period to introduce the New Style, with the result that discrepancies arose in the dating of events. Thus England introduced the Gregorian Calendar in 1752, Holland in 1700, and Russia after the Bolshevik Revolution.

At present, dates in history books are given according to N.S., at least as regards the year; but in printed works and especially documents of generations ago, O.S. is often followed. Sometimes it becomes convenient or necessary to indicate a date according to both systems. To illustrate, the death of Queen Elizabeth took place on March 24, 1602, O.S. At this period the year in England began on March 25; hence the Queen died on what was the last day of 1602. Adjusted to N.S., the date in question becomes April 3, 1603; and the two dates are indicated:

$$\frac{\text{March } 24}{\text{April } 3}, \frac{1602}{3}.$$

It is important when dealing with events in countries where the Gregorian reform was not in vogue at the time, to attend to the date here obtaining (according to O.S.) for the beginning of the civil year. This was generally March 25.—See Peter Archer, *The Christian Calendar and the Gregorian Reform* (New York, 1941).

(c) *Regnal Years*. One method of dating events and especially laws, grants, and other official acts, is to refer them to a particular year of a sovereign's reign. The famous decree of Parliament (1536) dissolving the lesser English monasteries was passed in the "twenty-sixth year of Henry VIII." Obviously such a method of dating documents is incomplete unless we know when precisely the sovereign began to reign. Practice in computing the beginning of a reign varied from one European country to another, and in the same country underwent change in the course of time. In England of the earlier centuries it was reckoned from the sovereign's coronation; later (the present practice), it was reckoned from his predecessor's death, deposition, or abdication. In the case of the popes and other elective rulers, reigns have begun, sometimes with election, sometimes with coronation. Lists of regnal years for all classes of rulers have been compiled and made accessible in print, thus making special research in these matters unnecessary to the student. With the aid of such lists one can readily ascertain the calendar year or such parts of it as correspond to the regnal year.—John E. Wallis, *English Regnal Years and Titles* (*Helps*, vol. 40).

(d) *Saints' Days and Feast Days*. In medieval and even later records, events are sometimes fixed merely by mention of the saint's day or the ecclesiastical feast on which they occur. (The "Massacre of St. Bartholomew's," August 24). Marquette, the missionary-explorer, writes somewhere that the Indians will be absent on the hunt until "St. Luke's" (October 15). *Hilary* and *Michaelmas* terms designate seasonal sessions, or terms in the English law-courts and universities.—Wallis, *English Regnal Years*, 84.

Easter, Pentecost and other festivals of the ecclesiastical year furnish convenient reference points for dating events. Lists of saints' days, and ecclesiastical calendars showing the dates of the major church festivals year by year according to the shifting Easter date, are accessible to the student.

(e) *Day of the Week*. Dates given in history books do not ordinarily include the day of the week. Various simple methods of ascertaining this item, when desirable, have been devised. See *CE*, article "Chronology," 3:740; Peter Archer, *The Christian Calendar*; Walter J. Miller, "The Calculation of the Day of the Week in any Year," *Jesuit Science Bulletin*, 10 (1933): 120-24.

Hermann Grotefend, *Zeitrechnung des deutschen Mittelalters und der Neuzeit* (2 vols., Hannover, 1891-1898); idem, *Taschenbuch der Zeitrechnung des Deutschen Mittelalters und der Neuzeit* (5th ed., Hannover, 1928).

John J. Bond, *Handy Book of Rules and Tables for Unifying Dates with the Christian Era* (4th ed., London, 1889).

James C. McDonald, *Chronologies and Calendars* (London, 1897).

Alexander Philip, *The Calendar: its History, Structure and Improvement* (Cambridge, Eng., 1921).

Reginald L. Poole, *Medieval Reckonings of Time* (*Helps*, vol. 3).

Frederick M. Powicke, ed., *Handbook of British Chronology* (London, 1939).

Adriano Cappelli, *Cronologia, Cronografia e Calendario Perpetue* (2d ed., Milan, 1930).

G. Diplomatic

¶ 81 Diplomatic (L. *diploma*) investigates the date, place or origin, and authenticity of written documents—especially ancient and medieval. One may call it simply "the science of documents." Its principal objective is to assemble evidence on which to rate documents as genuine or false. For the most part, this general objective resolves itself into four subsidiary purposes. To be able to declare a document as genuine or false, one must, though all steps need not be taken in every case, decipher it, date it, localize it, determine its authorship. The principles and rules in use for deciphering documents of the classical and medieval periods have been erected into a special science, palaeography, which in reality is but a branch of diplomatic.

Diplomatic finds its major application in the mass of manuscript material which has come down to us from ancient and medieval times. But with regard to questions of date, authorship, and genuineness, the principles it employs are applicable to modern documents also. If doubt is raised as to the authenticity of a hand-written document purporting to be an original official copy of a bill of Congress, one would set about solving the problem by applying virtually the same criteria, internal and external, as apply in the case of a thirteenth-century charter.

Diplomatic in a stricter sense has to do with official documents only; but its uses are broad enough to extend also to non-official or private documents. Thus, an inquiry into the authenticity of a poem, a personal letter, a literary or a scientific treatise, in cases where the matter must be settled by manuscript evidence alone, falls within the scope of diplomatic.

In the Middle Ages the office practice of the various European chanceries varied from one country to another, from one period, one reign, or in the case of papal documents, from one pontificate to another. The various characteristics of medieval official documents as regards formalities, signatures, seals, writing material, script, were carefully catalogued by Mabillon, the founder of diplomatic, and others after him for the more important chanceries [¶ 56-d]. The result was that it became practicable to assign a document, within a slight margin of error, to the particular chancery—imperial, royal, or papal—from which it issued, and to ascertain its approximate date, if this were missing. Raised thus to the dignity of a systematized body of principles, rules, and criteria, diplomatic took on the character of a science, and as such has won for itself a recognized place in the scholarly investigation and study of documents. For students of medieval history it is an essential instrument of research, but practically all fields of history, if worked to any depth, must on occasion call its services into requisition.

Mabillon's classic work on diplomatic, *De re diplomatica*, first published in 1681, was reprinted at Naples in 1789. For a brief analysis of the typical medieval diploma or charter, see Wallis, *English Regnal Years*, (*Helps*, vol. 40), 87 ff. For a bibliography of diplomatic, see Dutcher, *Guide*, 33–35.

H. Sigillography and Heraldry

❡ 82 The usefulness of seals

The science of sigillography or sphragistics (L. *sigillum*, G. σφραγίς, *seal*) is of interest to the historian chiefly for the aid it lends to diplomatic, a science which finds that its specific task of investigating the authenticity and provenance of documents is advanced in many cases towards a solution through evidence furnished by seals. The term *seal* denotes either the instrument with which an impression is made on some plastic substance, such as clay, wax, lead; or it means the impression itself. The latter sense is usual in methodology.

The function of a seal is in general to identify or guarantee a document as coming from a certain individual or group of individuals or institution. Its purpose, therefore, is identical with that of a signature, for which it may be a substitute, though often both seal and signature are attached to the one document. The characteristics of seals in regard to material, shape, legend, method of attaching, have been carefully noted and catalogued by scholars on a scientific basis, and this for seals of whatever provenance, such as those of kings, princes, popes, bishops, officials (lay and ecclesiastical), institutions, corporations. There is thus available, at least for the medieval period, a body of accurate and carefully organized information on the subject which can aid the investigator in ascertaining the authenticity and dates of documents. This help is afforded for the most part through the legend of the seal and the personal data which it embodies.

The seal was at first attached to the face of the document (*en placard*); later it was suspended from it by leathern thongs or silken or hempen cords. The later practice appears to have become general in Europe about the middle of the eleventh century. Knowledge of this fact may enable one to fix roughly a *terminus post quem* for the date of a medieval document, otherwise undated, but provided with a pendent seal.

❡ 83 Heraldry

As the "science of armorial bearings" heraldry has its uses on occasion for the searcher in history. The practice of marking armor with a personal device or a symbolic design (coat of arms, armorial bearings) to identify the bearer, was common in the Middle Ages. The device was also attached to tombs, buildings, and other objects, with a view to identifying them as the property of an individual or of a family or a corporation, civil or ecclesiastical. Armorial bearings as a token of identification can thus perform the same function in regard to armor, buildings, books, as seals do in regard to written documents.

Hugh S. Kingford, Seals (*Helps*, vol. 31).
Reginald L. Poole, "Seals and Documents," *Studies in Chronology and History*, Collected and Edited by Austin Lane Poole (Oxford, 1934), 90–111.
Walter de Gray Birch, *Seals* (London, 1907).
Francis J. Grant, *The Manual of Heraldry* (Edinburgh, 1924).
C. Wilfrid Scott, "The Shorthand of History," *The Romance of Heraldry* (London and Toronto, 1929), chap. 1.

I. Palaeography

¶ 84 Palaeography, "the science of ancient writing," is an offshoot of diplomatic, of which it is properly an integral part. But the apparatus peculiar to it is special, and its immediate purpose, which is to decipher manuscripts, differs from the purpose of diplomatic, which in the main is to investigate their authenticity. Hence, for these and other reasons it has become an independent science. Palaeography does more than merely provide helps for the deciphering of manuscripts; it can also furnish evidence bearing on the date, place of origin, and authorship of manuscripts.

Handwriting or script has not been static. It has evolved through various styles and idiosyncrasies from age to age, from country to country. The different stages in the evolution of script, together with their characteristics, have been minutely studied, catalogued, and marked off by tolerably definite chronological limits, with the result that manuscripts can be assigned a fairly accurate date, and even place of origin, upon the evidence of script alone. Evidence furnished by ink and writing material, whether this be papyrus, parchment or paper, linen or pulp, is also helpful in fixing the dates of written documents.

Palaeography (G. παλαιός, old), as the name indicates, is concerned with old writings, those especially of ancient and medieval times; but there is such a thing as modern palaeography. "Old" is a relative term. The script of an English or French manuscript of the sixteenth century may be sufficiently unfamiliar or forbidding to require the services of an expert to decipher it. Moreover, problems regarding the provenance or authorship of modern manuscripts must be settled by the same principles that hold in the case of the earlier.

(a) The art of ascertaining the authorship of documents by handwriting now commonly goes by the name of "bibliotics." The present-day bibliotist, or "handwriting expert," has developed a degree of accuracy in his findings which gives his testimony standing in the courts. His method is essentially one of comparison. The questioned writing is confronted with some other piece of writing unquestionably in the hand of the person supposed to have written the document under examination. The standard of comparison applied is commonly the supposed author's "writing habits." [₡ 165-d-2].

John E. Sandys, A Companion to Latin Studies (3d ed., Cambridge, Eng., 1935), 765–790.

Sir Edward Maunde Thompson, Introduction to Greek and Latin Palaeography (Oxford, 1912).

E. A. Lowe, "Handwriting," in C. G. Crump and E. F. Jacob, The Legacy of the Middle Ages.

Hilary Jenkinson, Palaeography and the Practical Study of Courthand (Cambridge, Eng., 1915).

Maurice Prou, Manuel de paléographie latine et française du sixième au dix-septième siècle (3d ed., Paris, 1910).

Francis Ehrle and Paul Liebaert, eds., Specimina codicum Latinorum Vaticanorum (Berlin and Leipzig, 1932).

(b) The discovery in modern times, in Egypt, of numerous documents written on papyrus, has given rise to a special section in the field of palaeography—papyrology. Papyri finds have thrown light both on Egyptian secular history and on Christian origins. What appears to be the oldest extant Christian manuscript, a collection of deeds and words of Christ, perhaps derived from St. John's Gospel, is a papyrus document brought to light in 1934.—H. I. Bell and T. C. Skeat, eds., Fragments of an Unknown Gospel and other Early Christian Papyri (London, 1935).

For good accounts of the Egyptian papyri finds, see Sir E. M. Thompson, An Introduction to Greek and Latin Palaeography, 93-101. For illustrations of historical evidence furnished by papyri, see John G. Winter, Life and Letters in the Papyri (Ann Arbor, Mich., 1933); A. S. Hunt and C. C. Edgar, Select Papyri, Loeb Classical Library (London and New York, 1932), vol 1.

J. Archaeology

₡ 85 Archaeology is in substance the science of "antiquities," or "ancient remains," these being physical or material objects of various sorts surviving from a vanished culture or civilization. Light has been thrown on the historical past in a thousand ways by such physical survivals. Products of the fine and industrial arts, such as buildings, statues, paintings, inscriptions, bridges, clothing, implements, weapons, coins— all have something to tell us as to the cultural and economic levels reached in different lands and periods.

> As to the codices [manuscripts] doubt may arise, however unfounded, as to whether they were corrupted when they were copied in later times and whether they really hand down to us the text of ancient Christian writers. But confronted by our monuments, it is impossible

to doubt the authenticity of inscriptions and scriptures which we see in the catacombs and museums, for they have reached us as they left the hands of the men of their day.—Orazio Marucchi, *The Evidence of the Catacombs for the Doctrines and Organization of the Primitive Church* (New York, 1929), vi.

On the whole, archaeological survivals are so much more reliable in their testimony to the past than written records, that archaeologists are sometimes prone to stress their importance unduly, as though the only real source material in history is what is dug out of the ground or found above it in weather-beaten remains of bronze or stone. The fact remains that the bulk of historical sources is in writing. The evidence furnished by archaeology, while it can be, and is repeatedly of the highest importance, especially in regard to dates and proper names, is often merely supplementary or corroborative. Moreover, archaeological survivals are seldom self-explanatory but need interpretation in the light of criticism and written texts.

On the necessity of supplementing archaeological by documentary evidence, see Ettore Pais, *Ancient Legends of Roman History* (London, 1906), 241.

The nineteenth century saw new and highly important additions made to our knowledge of the ancient world through archaeological research, especially in the Near East and the Orient. Layard brought to life the buried ruins of Babylonian and Assyrian palaces; Petrie and his contemporaries worked among tombs and other monuments to lay an adequate basis for the science of Egyptology; Schliemann uncovered a site of ancient Troy, and thereby did much to vindicate the historicity of the Homeric poems; De Rossi in a series of brilliant investigations solved the problem of the Roman catacombs; Pompeii, rescued from its sepulchre of ashes, came again into view as a Roman town, through a ruined one, of the classical period. Sir Arthur Evans unearthed in Crete the remains of an impressive but long-forgotten civilization.

No period, however, has witnessed more large-scale and varied archaeological enterprises than the years following the first World War. Much money was spent by governments, more often by private agencies as represented by universities, by foundations or museums, in financing expeditions to various fields of archaeological research. Excavations in Iraq have disclosed abundant new data on the Sumerians and on other primitive inhabitants of the region. The exploration of Egyptian tombs has led to sensational finds, such as those connected with King Tutankhamen. In Palestine biblical archaeology has attracted numerous European and American scholars, whose field-work has issued in significant discoveries. In Persia monumental ruins have been unearthed comparable in importance to those laid bare on the sites of Babylon and Ninive. The remarkable Central American remains of the mysterious Maya culture have been, and still are being investigated. Classical archaeological research has been pursued with spectacular results. The Athenian Acropolis is being cleared of the debris of the centuries, while in Rome a whole group of imperial forums, long buried underground or hidden behind modern structures, has been uncovered. Under the ancient church of San Sebastiano, in the environs of the same city, one may now look upon numerous invocations to Saints Peter and Paul (*graffiti*) scratched on the walls of what was once a restroom for pilgrims in the first centuries of the Church. These recent finds are of acknowledged significance for the history of Christian origins.—Marucchi, *The Evidence of the Catacombs*, chap. 8.

"The Relation of Archaeology to History," *Cambridge Ancient History*, 1:112–15.

William M. F. Petrie, *Methods and Aims in Archaeology* (London and New York, 1904).

Grant Showerman, *Monuments and Men of Ancient Rome* (New York, 1935).

Orazio Marucchi, *Manual of Christian Archaeology*, translated and adapted by Hubert Vecchierello (Paterson, N. J., 1925).

Louis Laurand, *Manuel des études grecques et latines* (Paris, 1928), 839–42.

K. Epigraphy

❡ 86   Under certain aspects inscriptions rank first in value among the various types of source material utilized by the historian [❡ 254]. Hence the importance to his purpose of epigraphy, or "the science of inscriptions," which discusses their physical characteristics, technique of production; edits their texts and assembles them in collections on the basis of language, country or period. Doubtful readings can often be cleared up, and missing dates supplied by the epigraphist. Just what collections of inscriptions will prove useful to the student, depends on his field of research. If he is engaged in Oriental or Greek or Roman history, he cannot ignore this species of primary material, which may be abundant. On the other hand, inscriptions serve the medievalist only slightly; in modern history they may be said to be negligible.

Edward L. Hicks, *Manual of Greek Historical Inscriptions* (2d. ed., revised by G. F. Hill, Oxford, 1901).

James C. Egbert, *Introduction to the Study of Latin Inscriptions* (2d. ed. rev., New York, 1906).

Leonard Wibley, ed., *A Companion to Greek Studies* (2d. ed., Cambridge, Eng., 1906), 581–96.

John E. Sandys, *Latin Epigraphy* (Cambridge, Eng., 1919).

Orazio Marucchi, *Christian Epigraphy: An Elementary Treatise with a Collection of Christian Inscriptions, Mainly of Roman Origin*, trans. by J. Armine Willis (New York, 1928).

H. P. V. Nunn, *Christian Inscriptions* (Texts for Students, No. 11, London, 1920).

Adhémar d'Alès, ed., *Dictionnaire Apologétique de la Foi Catholique* (4 vols., Paris, 1925–1928), 1:1404–57.

¶ 87 IMPORTANCE OF INSCRIPTIONS

Rich as have been their bequests to us in other lines, the Hindus have not transmitted to us any historical works which can be accepted as reliable for any early times. And it is almost entirely from a patient examination of the inscriptions, the start in which was made more than a century ago, that our knowledge of the ancient political history of India has been derived. But we are also ultimately dependent on the inscriptions in any other line of India research. Hardly any definite dates and identifications can be established except from them, and they regulate everything that we can learn from tradition, literature, coins, art, architecture, or any other science.—J. S. Cotton and Others, eds., *Imperial Gazetteer of India* (2 vols., Oxford, 1928), 2:3.

L. Numismatics

¶ 88 Numismatics or the classification and description of coins according to countries and periods, has reached a degree of development which entitles it to rank as a science auxiliary to history. The legends usually found on coins often embody historical data of value, especially for fixing the duration of reigns and administrations, and the succession of rulers individually or by houses or dynasties. Gaps in history may frequently be filled from the information supplied by coins, which can also furnish evidence for the distribution of ancient religious cults. Under the Roman emperors coins sometimes performed the function of the modern newspaper by communicating to the public at intervals information on current happenings of note. For knowledge of the Greek kingdoms set up by Alexander the Great in northwestern India, we are dependent almost entirely on contemporary numismatic data.

> There are coins and groups of coins which afford the sole evidence for the existence of cities and federal organizations or reveal the names and dates of rulers otherwise unknown. Silerae, a Sicilian town in the time of Timoleon is not mentioned by any ancient author.—Hill, *Coins and Medals*, 7.

Bibliography for Numismatics

Harold Mattingly, *Roman Coins from the Earliest Time to the Fall of the Western Empire* (London, 1928).

Charles Seltman, *Greek Coins* (London, 1933).

George F. Hill, *Historical Greek Coins* (London, 1906); *Coins and Medals* (*Helps*, vol. 36).

George McDonald, *The Evolution of Greek Coinage* (Cambridge, Eng., 1916).

On numismatic evidence in history

Stanley L. Poole, *Coins and Medals: Their Place in History and Art* (3d. ed., London, 1894).

Cambridge History of India (6 vols., Cambridge, Eng., and New York, 1922–1932), 1:582–92.

Lucy M. Salmon, Historical Material, 71–75.

Joseph S. Milne, Greek and Roman Coins and the Study of History (London, 1939).

Robert H. McDowell, "The Indo-Parthian Frontier," AHR, 44 (1939); 781–801.

M. Genealogy

❡ 89   Genealogy is "the science of pedigree"; but as a science auxiliary to history, it has a broader range. It includes in its field of research not only pedigrees or "family trees," but also such types of data as lists of officials, civil or ecclesiastical. The compilation of such lists entails minute and accurate investigation. This is labor well spent, for dynastic tables of ruling houses and lists of administrative heads of whatever kind, with accompanying dates, are reference tools indispensable to the historian. For students of church history, works of the type of Gams' *Series episcoporum* are a necessity, supplying as they do information not easily accessible elsewhere. Genealogical research properly so called can yield results of importance to the historian and to the biographer. Records of family descent are sometimes the only sources that can be drawn upon for the solution of a historical problem.

William P. Phillimore, *How to Write the History of a Family: A Guide for the Genealogist* (2d. ed., London and Boston, 1888).

Walter Rye, *Records and Record Searching: A Guide to the Genealogist and Topographer* (London, 1888).

Part Two

FINDING THE SOURCES: *Heuristic*

Chapter Five

THE NATURE AND CLASSIFICATION OF HISTORICAL SOURCES

A. What Historical Sources Mean . . . . Page 103
B. Classification by Origin 104
C. Classification by Content 109
D. Classification by Aim 109
E. The Narrative Type of Source 111
F. Official Records 113
G. Oral Sources (Tradition) 118
H. Pictorial and Figured Sources 122
I. Written Sources 123

A. What Historical Sources Mean

¶ 90 The term *sources* in reference to history covers a body of material vast in range and diversified in character. Written records, oral traditions, remains of prehistoric villages, ancient inscriptions on the sides of rocks; in short, any bit of testimony, any object that can throw light on the human story, finds place in the category, "historical sources." One may define the term as "human remains and such products of man's activity as either were meant by their authors to communicate knowledge of historical facts or conditions, or by their nature are calculated to do so."—Feder, Lehrbuch, 84).

The words *human remains*, are meant to include all persisting elements of the human body, for instance, skeletal survivals of prehistoric man, and ecclesiastical relics. The division of *products of human activity* into such as were designed to communicate historical knowledge, and such as by their character automatically serve the same purpose (archaeological survivals), is based on the very nature of sources and is of much importance in their systematic treatment.

(a) A suggestive way to look at historical sources is to regard them as "traces" left behind by past events. The events of history are no longer realities, though they once were. All that survives of them is the impression they made on observers, which impression the observers themselves, or other persons relying directly or indirectly on the reports of observers, fixed in writing or in some other medium of record. The recorded impressions are, therefore, the only traces which past events have left in their wake. The historian must work directly on the recorded impressions and through them on the events. No other approach to the past is open to him. Yet the real objective of historical research is not the sources themselves but their contents, namely, what the sources can furnish us in the way of information about the past, or what we can by reasoning deduce from them. Sources are only a means to an end. Heuristic is therefore in the nature of a mining process, having for its object to bring the raw material of history to light. From this point of view Niebuhr was led to describe it as a "working underground."

B. Classification by Origin

₡91 The author of a historical source may be God, as well as man. Hence the distinction between *divine* and *human* sources. Divine sources are identical with what is known as divine revelation; their scientific treatment belongs to Christian apologetics and to theology. Historical method is concerned with human sources, and with divine sources only in as far as these come to us from the mouth or hand of man, and confront us in the guise of historical testimony.*

Human sources may be classified on a threefold basis: of origin [₡ 91], of content [₡ 92], of aim [₡ 93].

Discussion of the origin of a source turns on such factors as (a) the time of production; (b) the place of production; (c) the manner in which the author came by his information; (d) the author's personal status or position.

(a) *Origin of Sources: the Time of Production*
According to the time when they were produced, sources are *contemporary* and *remote*. The first group emanate from persons who were alive at the period of the events they profess to narrate; the second group, from persons not living at such period, or, if they were so living, were not of an age to make them competent witnesses. *Quasi-contemporary* sources are the product of persons living shortly after the events reported. In general, contemporary sources are to be preferred to remote ones; yet, a contemporary source is not *ipso facto* a reliable one, for other factors besides contemporaneousness enter into the question

* The discussion of sources in the present chapter is descriptive only. Other treatment, under the aspects of authenticity, integrity, credibility, will be found in Chapters 8–13.

¶ 91

of a witness's reliability. Thus Matthew Paris, the thirteenth-century chronicler, was contemporary with much of the history which he records; but he wrote with a distinct anti-papal bias, and for this reason his statements often need correction from other sources.

Moreover (and this is a very important consideration in the evaluation of sources), a good critical remote source can be fuller, more accurate, and, on the whole, more reliable, than any contemporary account of the same matter. The remote or secondary account may have utilized all the primary and contemporary sources, collated their data for possible errors and contradictions, thrown light on the topic in question from archaeological and other sources, and, in general, given the reader the benefit of a critical summing up of the evidence coming from numerous scattered and not easily accessible quarters. Nevertheless, in the abstract, the superiority of contemporary to remote sources remains unquestioned. They stand closer to the events they deal with, and being in many instances the reports of eyewitnesses of the events and even participants in them, have a freshness and realism about them which later accounts rarely take on.

How much may depend on using contemporary sources in preference to later evidence can be illustrated by the history of the First Crusade. Historians formerly employed as their principal source for this topic William of Tyre, who, following Albert of Aix, had depicted Peter the Hermit as the chief promoter of the movement. But about 1840 Ranke suggested and Sybel proved that Albert of Aix was unreliable. Sources more strictly contemporary were needed. Sybel accordingly based his treatment of the First Crusade on three contemporary accounts, all by eyewitnesses, the anonymous Gesta Francorum, Raymund of Agiles, and Fulk of Chartres. Sybel's estimate of Albert of Aix was generally accepted by historians and proved a turning point in the historiography of the First Crusade. As a result Peter the Hermit, whose intimate connection with it was vouched for mainly by Albert of Aix, thenceforward assumed only a secondary place in the history of the movement.—Ernest Barker, The Crusades (London, 1923).

For a study based entirely on contemporary or quasi-contemporary sources, chiefly as found in the Monumenta Germaniae historica, see Joseph E. Hansbery, "The Children's Crusade," CHR, 24 (1938): 30–38.

(b) Origin of Sources: the Place of Production

According to place or country where sources originate, they are domestic or foreign. This is a convenient division, in cases where it is desirable, in assessing the credibility of a group of sources, to distinguish between those produced by residents of a country and those produced by travelers or other persons having residence outside it.

(c) Origin of Sources: the Author's Manner of Obtaining
According to the manner in which authors came to a knowledge of the data they record, sources are *immediate* or *mediate*. The author of a source may be either an eye-and-ear witness of the events he narrates or even a participant in them, or he may have gathered his information from persons who were witnesses, direct or indirect, of the events in question. In the first case the source is immediate, in the second, mediate.

Immediate sources may also be designated as *original* (in a restricted sense) or *primary*; mediate sources, as *derived* or *secondary*. This classification of sources into immediate (primary) and mediate (secondary) is a highly practical one in historical research. "A vital principle in historical method requires the investigator of any datum of history to follow it back as far as possible to its actual origin, to link it up with its first immediate source" (Feder).

When Sir Cornwall Lewis assailed the credibility of early Roman history, he laid down the same principle, insisting that nothing in history is certain unless we can connect it directly or indirectly with the testimony of eyewitnesses. It was only in the nineteenth century that the distinction between primary and secondary sources was fully grasped in all its far-reaching implications, and was consistently applied in historiography. But the distinction was by no means unknown in earlier periods, even the classical.

Primary Sources distinguished from secondary
(1) The eighteenth-century Jesuit, Henri Griffet [₵ 56-c] anticipated the typical methods of the modern scientific school in history. In his *Traité des différentes sortes de preuves qui servant à établir la vérité de l'histoire*, he insists on the use of primary, or, as he chooses to call them, "authentic" documents (*pièces authentiques*) in preference to secondary documents. He cites three instances of the importance of primary or firsthand material in history.

First: The assassination of Henry III by Jacques Clément is misrepresented by the French historians Jacques-Auguste de Thou and Pierre Bayle. For the true account one must refer to the letter of M. Laguesle, an eyewitness, and to the deposition made an hour after the assassination by another witness. "All the testimony furnished by contemporary authors is valueless; it must of necessity collapse and come to nothing in all points where it is negatived by documents of this description."

Second: Richelieu is shown to have instigated a Portuguese rising against Spain with a view to setting the house of Braganza on the throne of Portugal. The evidence is to be found in a document, certainly Richelieu's, which contains secret instructions to his agent in Spain to foment the rising.

Third: Hume's account of Mary Tudor is refuted with the aid of the dispatches of the French ambassador at the court of St. James's. Griffet's own history of Louis XIII, in three volumes, carries marginal references to primary sources.

(2) To the category of *primary sources* must be assigned accounts from eyewitnesses of a murder, a battle, a railroad accident, a debate in Congress; many "acts of the martyrs" (*acta martyrum*); minutes of parliamentary, congressional, judicial proceedings; laws, treaties, papal briefs and bulls, and, in general, all official papers of church and state; personal memoirs, autobiographies, etc. As *secondary sources* are to be rated, for the most part, the classical and better known histories of all periods, these being generally based on earlier and more original accounts. Thus, Herodotus, Livy, Tacitus, Bede, Prescott, Gardiner, Pastor.

Often a single source is by turns primary and secondary according as the author drew upon firsthand or secondhand information. Thucydides in the brief outline of early Greek history which prefaces his account of the Peloponnesian War is a secondary source only; for this section of his work he was dependent on sources of information supplied by others. As regards events of the Peloponnesian War itself, with which he was contemporary and in which he was himself a participant, he is a primary source. Yet a distinction is needed here. Thucydides did not himself witness all the incidents, the plague at Athens, for instance, which he records. A rigorous use of the term "primary" would entitle only those parts of his history to be described as such which he wrote from personal observation or experience. For much, perhaps for most of what he tells, he had to rely on accounts furnished him by others, in which case, however, he took every pains to ascertain the truth. "Where I have not been an eyewitness myself, I have investigated with the utmost accuracy attainable every detail that I took at second hand."

Even the commanding officer in a battle, present though he be on the scene and directing the movements, will not see everything that goes on. When he comes to make a detailed report of the action, he finds himself dependent more or less on the observations of his staff. Yet it seems captious not to characterize his report as a primary source.

So also one scarcely hesitates to call Thucydides a primary source for the Peloponnesian War. The difficulty may be met by using the term *primary* now in a rigorous, now in a less rigorous sense. Strictly, Thucydides is a primary source only for what he records from firsthand knowledge; less strictly (the term being here used as equivalent to contemporary), he is a primary source for everything he records about the war in question. This double use of the term *primary* can aid towards solving certain problems met with in the classification of sources.

> Louis O'Brien, *The Writing of History*, adapted from Paul Harsin's *Comment on écrit l'histoire* (Berkeley, Calif., 1935), 43, cites a French author who maintains that common soldiers can furnish valuable testimony on what they witness, and who rejects the theory that only "commanders-in-chief are competent to describe battles."

(3) An apt illustration of a primary source is Fray Bernardino de Sahagun, *A History of Ancient Mexico, 1547–1577* (Nashville, Tenn., 1932). Clark Wissler writes in the preface:

> He [Sahagun] is usually spoken of as the first great historian in the New World, but we can now recognize him as the first true ethnologist. His method should please even the ultra-modern field-worker, because he gathered about him selected native informants, first writing down in the original language what these informants narrated. Yet, not content with this procedure, other informants were sought out to listen to these texts and comment upon their accuracy. Further, natives were encouraged to sketch and write in their own symbols, and finally, with all these original materials in hand, the good Father sat himself down to write.

> The Greek historian Procopius, who accompanied Belisarius in his campaigns, and kept a diary from which he composed the eight books of his history, concentrates all his attention on events of which he was an eyewitness, and is meager on contemporary events which he did not witness.— John B. Bury, *A History of the Later Roman Empire from Arcadius to Irene*, A.D. 395 to A.D. 800. (2 vols., London, 1889), 2:482.

(d) *Origin of Sources: the personal status of the author*

According to the status or position of the person producing them, sources are *private* or *official*. One may write in a merely private capacity, representing no one except oneself, or one may write as the incumbent of an office or as the representative of a community, a corporation, a group. From this point of view sources are either private or official. One holding office may also write as a private individual. A purely personal letter of a president of the United States to a friend is a private, not an official document. But it is often a teasing problem whether a given historical source is to be classified as private or official. In view of the general legal character of early medieval records, all such documents emanating from popes and bishops, as well as from independent or semi-independent lords, such as emperors, kings, princes, are to be regarded, at least broadly, as official. On the contrary, all other early medieval records, no matter who their authors may be, may be labeled as private.

C. Classification by Content

¶ 92 In general, the classification of sources on the basis of content runs parallel with the division of the history field according to subject matter, and more particularly according to periods and countries. As to the distinction between religious (sacred) and profane (secular) sources, the former have a content bearing directly on religion, while the latter have no such content. Sources of uniform, general bearing, but showing a wide diversity of specific content, may be grouped for purposes of evaluation, into political, social, religious, economic.

D. Classification by Aim

¶ 93 If we fix our attention on the aims which motivate their production, we shall find the sources to be either *formal* (speaking) or *informal* (mute, factual, virtual). From the same point of view, sources may be classed as strictly informative and not-strictly-informative [¶ 275 ff.].

(a) *Formal* sources comprise all the thousand-and-one ways which human testimony can take when it becomes a channel of historical information of whatever kind. The distinctive note of any source belonging to this group is *a conscious intent on the part of its author* (direct or indirect witness) *to communicate information of a historical nature*. Whether the communication be by word of mouth or in writing or in any other way, the deliberate design to render testimony as to something that happened is never absent in a formal source. In the light of this explanation, the term *formal* (speaking,), as applied to this group of sources, explains itself.

(b) *Informal* sources comprise all such material objects or non-material phenomena as were connected with historical events or conditions, and by their nature are calculated to give information about them. There was a purpose motivating their production, but it was not the purpose of giving information about the past. They are either natural growths, such as the human body or language, or artificial products designed to serve some purpose of the arts, such as shelter, clothing, defense, entertainment, or satisfaction of an esthetic kind. Of themselves they are silent, mute; but we can give them voices, as it were, inasmuch as they offer a basis for inference as to what took place in the past. For the reason that they thus testify indirectly in some way or other to the historical past, they may be described as "virtual witnesses." Following

Bernheim, most authors on methodology describe them as remains. Bernheim defines them as "everything immediately surviving from past occurrences and present at hand." John M. Vincent calls them "historical relics."—*Historical Research: An Outline of Theory and Practice* (New York, 1911), 18.

Formal Sources distinguished from informal
(1) It is to be noted that one and the same source may be formal or informal, according to one's point of view. A copy of the New York *Journal*, for October 12, 1775, is a formal source insofar as it supplies information on current events; it is informal insofar as it is a physically surviving specimen of the newspaper-making of that period. The immediate object of the paper was to furnish the public with news, not to aid the future historian of American journalism; but now, as we hold the hundred-and-fifty-year-old copy in our hands, we learn many interesting facts about the makeup of an American journal of that date, as regards paper, ink, headlines, choice and arrangement of news, advertising. So also old coins, with their dates, legends, and portraits, are formal sources; in their mechanical features they are informal, witnessing as they do to the development of the metallurgical and numismatic arts at the periods to which they belong. A Roman inscription in marble may record important historical data; it will also, though its producer was not inspired by this motive, reveal the contemporary degree of perfection reached by the epigraphist's art. The great Gothic cathedrals of Europe illustrate the principles of medieval architectural technique.

(2) Informal sources or remains are exemplified in documents, objects or phenomena of the greatest variety and range, such as bones, skulls, "relics"; traces of climatic or geographical influence on human life; products of the technical or fine arts, such as weapons, tools, articles of clothing, buildings, bridges, coins, statues, paintings; public records; business documents and papers; footprints, fingerprints, an article of wear mutilated by a weapon; a bullet hole in a door, and similar clues utilized in criminal investigation; finally, all non-material phenomena which may be described collectively as "survivals." These may be linguistic "holdovers," customs, institutions, and religious, moral, or intellectual viewpoints. It is obvious from this enumeration that the category *remains* is highly elastic. The test in every case to determine whether a thing belongs to this category or not, is its physical connection in some way or other with facts or conditions of the historical past.

¶ 94 CONTEMPORARY LITERATURE
Presenting a certain analogy to archaeological remains is contemporary literature, whether poetry, drama, fiction, or some other type. Products

of this kind were not meant to furnish source material to the historian; yet they do so most effectively. In any national literature we put our fingers on the beating pulse of a vanished society, or of a culture, and come to know it as a living reality in a manner scarcely possible in any other way. Literature at bottom is a record, however undesigned, of the thought, the feeling, and of life in general of contemporary man.

(a) Theodore Roosevelt declared in his confident way that the fifteenth idyl of Theocritus throws more light on Greek life in the second century B.C. than all the ancient inscriptions ever recovered. Probably not all scholars would indorse the sweeping statement; yet the hyperbole is not without its point. It remains true that the idyl mentioned is a delightfully human document. The chatter of the women, as Andrew Lang commented, has changed no more in two thousand years than the songs of the birds. Shakespeare is of vast aid to the student of history in helping to understand the Elizabethan attitude towards life. The letters of Madame de Sévigné introduce one to the tinselled life of the French upper classes in the reign of Louis XIV. Horace Walpole's letters bring us face to face with interesting phases of English social life of the eighteenth century. *Vanity Fair* mirrors the manner of life led by English folk of rank and means in Napoleonic days. In like fashion, the novels of Dickens picture to us the middle and lower strata of English society in the Victorian age. The emotions and ideals that lay behind the efforts put forth by the North in the Civil War are vocal in Lincoln's Gettysburg Address, in his Second Inaugural Address, in Julia Ward Howe's "Battle Hymn of the Republic." In like manner, the feelings of the South at the end of the struggle are eloquent in Father Ryan's "Conquered Banner."

(b) See George M. Trevelyan, "History and Literature," *Yale Review*, 14 (1924): 112 ff.

> If there is a desire to know the spirit of an age so often concealed under a body of facts, events, and commonplace life, nothing will so reveal it as its writings nor anything explain them in turn like contemporary activities.—Lorenzo Sears, *Principles and Methods of Literary Criticism* (New York, 1898), 199.

E. The Narrative Type of Source

❡ 95 Compositions of a simply narrative tenor, which have for primary end the transmission of historical fact, are either addressed exclusively, or mainly, to contemporaries, or are produced with a view to transmit the memory of historical happenings to posterity. To the first class belong newspapers and letters communicating current news; to the second class belong the bulk of merely narrative sources as exemplified in the following types:

(a) *Inscriptions*. Next to coins, inscriptions are the oldest of all forms of written historical record. The Monumentum Ancyranum, the Behistun Inscription, the Rosetta Stone, are well-known examples. The great collections of inscriptions, such as those made by Mommsen and De Rossi, are storehouses of historical data.

(b) *Genealogical material.* This category includes pedigrees, family trees, dynastic tables, lists of officials, civil and ecclesiastical: emperors, kings, princes, presidents, popes, bishops, abbots. Though the materials here listed, and under (c), are not strictly narrative, they approximate the narrative type, and for purposes of classification may be regarded as belonging to it.

(c) *Calendars,* that is, tables of the days, divisions of the civil and ecclesiastical years, martyrologies, and similar lists.

(d) *Annals and Chronicles.* These are brief notices of historical events arranged consecutively by the year or its divisions. Originally loose and jejune compilations, annals later evolved into the type of connected narrative found in the chronicle. As a form of historical record, annals were known to the Assyrians, Greeks, and Romans. With the passing of classical literature annals degenerated into mere marginal notes and similar records, or into collections of tabulated data in which biblical and secular incidents were mingled in chronological order. Shaping the whole course of medieval historiography of the annalistic type, and not without influence even in the modern age, was the Greek *Chronicon* or *Chronicle* (to A.D. 325) of Eusebius of Caesarea, in the Latin version prepared by St. Jerome, and containing supplementary data from his own hand up to A.D. 378. The annals of earlier periods find a present-day analogy in the so-called annual or yearbook.

The first volume of the *Monumenta Germaniae historica* contains a number of medieval chronicles in which the development from simpler to more complex types can be traced. See also G. A. Giles, ed., *Old English Chronicles* (London, 1912); Thomas F. Tout, "The Study of Medieval Chronicles," *Bulletin* of the John Rylands Library, 6 (1921–1922): 414–38. A general treatment of the topic will be found in Reginald L. Poole, *Chronicles and Annals: An Outline of their Origin and Growth* (Oxford, 1926).

(e) *Histories of any kind conceived as records of the past.* In works produced in periods of more developed historical instinct, a merely chronological succession of events is generally subordinated to a topical or similar arrangement. This category includes in its range the classical and standard histories of all periods.

(f) *Biographies.* "That form of history which is applied, not to races or masses of men, but to an individual."—Edmund Gosse, "Biography," in *Encyclopaedia Britannica.*

On the ground that biography deals with the details, even the most intimate and personal, of a person's career, it has been objected that it cannot be classed as history. These details, it is alleged, are without social significance, and therefore fall outside the purview of history as record. Moreover, no account of a person's life can present an adequately consecutive and rounded treatment of any historical situation or series of events. But the objection is without force, because biography is concerned in most cases with personalities who either have had a real influence on international, national, or local affairs, or if they have had no such influence, can at least be regarded as types of certain social groups or classes. In the Middle Ages the saints were the favorite subjects of biography, so that an entirely distinct branch of historical research and writing dealing with them, hagiography, was eventually developed [¶ 56-b]. Examples of medieval biography are Asser's *Alfred*, Einhard's *Charlemagne*, Joinville's *St. Louis*, and St. Bernard's *St. Malachy*.

(g) *Autobiographies, memoirs, diaries, journals, letters*. All these closely related types may be listed broadly under the general head of biography. Evaluation for the historian's purpose of these and of the other types of source material here mentioned is treated in ¶ 237.

F. Official Records

¶ 96   Official records (acts, *diplomata*) comprise all such documents as are produced in the routine administration of church or state, or of any corporation or group, secular or ecclesiastical. These can be classed under the following heads.

(a) *Government records*

The term is used here broadly and not in the restricted sense which would limit it to the more important papers of a diplomatic nature. Furthermore, what is here envisaged is civil government of whatever period or form: imperial, royal, republican, municipal. Civil government in the ordinary discharge of its threefold function, legislative, judicial, and administrative, produces quantities of written material of every description. The content of such material includes legislative measures of all kinds, such as laws, statutes, ordinances, enactments, decrees; judicial decisions and other court declarations; writs, grants, charters, proclamations, manifestoes; diplomatic, military and other correspondence; minutes of parliamentary and congressional proceedings; reports of officials and commissions; treasury and other financial records, account books, tax and census lists, statistics; military orders, war-bulletins; and the like. Any document, however trivial, originating in any department of an organized civil government may be described as a "government record." In the United States the term "government documents," or "government publications" is commonly used to describe printed material of this kind. The term "state papers," in general use in England, is not unknown in the United States, where we have the *American State Papers, Documents, Legislative and Executive of the Congress of the United States* (38 vols., Washington, 1832–1861).

The importance and the use of official records

Léopold Delisle stressed the importance of the official acts of Philip Augustus for an understanding of his personality and policies. "They make it possible for us to understand the play of institutions, to learn about the king's plans, the means he made use of, the ministers who served him, the obstacles he met with, the results he achieved."

With the aid of the 2,236 documents listed by Delisle in chronological order, and bearing in each case the name of the place where they were signed and issued, it becomes possible to follow the king's movements as in an itinerary, since there is every reason to assume that he and his court were actually present in the places where the documents were signed and issued. An exact chronology of Philip's reign is thus worked out, in this regard supplying the deficiencies of French contemporary chronicles, which are notorious for omitting dates or giving wrong dates. An anonymous chronicle records the surrender of Rouen to Philip by Pierre de Préaux, who was commanding it for the king of England. The "acts" at this juncture show us Philip making handsome gifts to nephews of Pierre de Préaux, and gaining other persons and provinces to his side by similar means. Further, the "acts" record the measures taken by Philip Augustus to build up the royal authority and depress that of the feudal lords. Thus, an important period of French history is set in new and revealing light.—*Catalogue des actes de Philippe Auguste* (Paris, 1856), introduction.

What Delisle did for Philip Augustus of France was done for Frederick II of Germany, by Jean L. A. Huillard-Bréholles, in his *Historia diplomatica Friderici Secundi* (7 vols., Paris, 1852–1861).

Official records and their use
Vivian H. Galbraith, *An Introduction to the Use of the Public Records* (London, 1935).
Lawrence F. Schmeckebier, *Government Publications and their Use* (Washington, 1936).
L. F. Rushbrook Williams, *Four Lectures on the Handling of Historical Material* (London, 1917).
Eric J. Dingwall, *How to Use a Large Library* (Cambridge, Mass., 1933), 56–60.
Margaret Hutchins, Alice S. Johnson, and Margaret S. Williams, *Guide to the Use of Libraries* (4th ed., New York, 1929).

(b) *Church Records: Catholic*
From a research point of view the written records of the Catholic Church are of the first importance. They are more extensive in quantity and range of time, more historically significant than those of any other religious body. They fall for the most part into five distinct groups.

(1) *Papal records.* These include papers of every kind emanating from or originating in the papacy on its administrative side. Such are the codified canon law, papal bulls, briefs, encyclicals and other letters; conciliar statutes, disciplinary and liturgical decrees or decisions; dispensations, rescripts, and other pronouncements of the various papal commissions known as the Roman Congregations; concordats and treaties; papers of a fiscal or economic nature bearing on papal administration in all its branches; official liturgical books, such as the missal, the ceremonial, the breviary. To the same category must be referred all papers having to do with the civil administration of the former papal states.

On the chancery practice of the Holy See during the Middle Ages, see Reginald L. Poole, *Lectures on the History of the Papal Chancery down to the Time of Innocent III.*

Since the opening of the Vatican archives by Leo XIII, in 1883, scholars have been engaged in the critical editing and publication of various papal registers or collections of letters, and of other papers of the popes, especially those of the medieval period. The registers of the popes of the thirteenth and fourteenth centuries have been published under the auspices of the French School of Rome. The correspondence of Gregory VII and of John XXII, now printed, throws new light on important phases of papal history. The published letters of Innocent IV alone run into the thousands.

For an instance of papal records put to capital account by present-day scholarship, see William E. Lunt, *Papal Revenues in the Middle Ages* (*Records of Civilization, Sources and Studies*, vol. 19 [in 2 parts], Columbia University, New York, 1934).

(2) *Episcopal records.* These include all documents issued in the routine administration of a diocese, such as pastoral letters, synodal statutes, episcopal enactments and decrees, dispensations, registers of ordination, reports of visitations, account-books, and other fiscal documents. English medieval history, to cite one instance, draws heavily for source material on episcopal registers and similar documents.——Robert C. Fowler, *Episcopal Registers of England and Wales* (*Helps*, vol. 1).

Ecclesiastical and social conditions in the pre-Reformation period have been elucidated from data preserved in episcopal registers of visitation. Letters written by pioneer clergymen to their bishops detailing experiences in the organization of missions and parishes, are valuable sources for social and economic history. Such letters, being often in the nature of official or quasi-official reports, may be properly listed under episcopal records. The Catholic archdiocesan archives of Baltimore and St. Louis, and the collection of papers from episcopal archives now housed at Notre Dame University, contain much material of this type.

(3) *Parish records.* These are commonly restricted to baptismal, marriage, confirmation, and burial registers. Such registers frequently contain a great amount of genealogical and other data of the first importance to the researcher. In numerous instances they are the earliest extant records for a given locality, as in the cases of St. Ignace (Mich.), Vincennes (Ind.), Kansas City (Mo.), St. Louis. Circumstances sometimes invest parish history with more than a parochial range of interest and significance.—See Gilbert J. Garraghan, *St. Ferdinand de Florissant: the Story of an Ancient Parish* (Chicago, 1923).

Alexander H. Thompson, *Parish History and Records* (Helps, vol. 15).

Indexing of parish records in the United States was undertaken as a WPA project. See the published reports (1937–1938) for Seattle (Wash.), and for the State of New Hampshire.

(4) *Monastic and similar records.* Within the Catholic Church are found numerous religious orders, congregations, and confraternities, which in the course of time have accumulated in their archives quantities of papers bearing on their respective affairs. A large proportion of this material is in the form of correspondence. It is often of importance, not only for the history of such corporative bodies, but also for history in a broader sense. Heribert Holzapfel, *Handbuch der Geschichte des Franziskaner Ordens*, and Thomas A. Hughes, *The Society of Jesus in North America, Colonial and Federal*, are examples of large-scale works based mainly on the domestic records of the religious orders with which they deal.

(5) *Records of mission-aid societies and similar associations of charitable scope.* Catholic mission-aid societies preserve in their archives important material for religious and social history, material which has begun to be utilized only in recent years.—Edward J. Hickey, *The Society for the Propagation of the Faith 1822–1922* (Washington, 1922); Theodore Roemer, *The Leopoldine Foundation and the Church in the United States, 1829–1839* (New York, 1933); idem, *The Ludwig-Mis-*

sionsverein and the Church in the United States, 1838–1928 (Washington, 1934).

(c) *Church records: non-Catholic*
Records of the Oriental churches not in communion with Rome exist in quantity in Russia, Turkey, Greece and other Near-East countries. So also, organized Protestantism, both in the Old World and the New, has its achival depositories, episcopal and parochial, often of marked importance in quantity and quality of content. The archives of Fulham and Lambeth palaces, London, contain much material on the history of the English Established Church, part of it throwing light on Anglican activities in the pre-Revolutionary American period.——Claude Jenkins, *Ecclesiastical Records* (*Helps*, vol. 18).

Baptismal, marriage and other records of the Dutch Lutheran Church in colonial New York are included in the collection, Hugh Hastings, ed., *Ecclesiastical Records of the State of New York* (7 vols., Albany, 1901–1916).

The extensive correspondence preserved in the archives of early Protestant missionary societies in the United States has begun to be utilized as fresh source material for the history of the American West. In this regard the archives of the American Board of Foreign Missions, Boston, are noteworthy. Putting such material to account, Archer B. Hulbert was able to throw a new light on the much-discussed topic of the Whitman ride. The American Society of Church History is active in seeking out and indexing the manuscript sources for the history of the various Protestant denominations in the United States.——William W. Sweet "Church Archives in the United States," *Church History*, 8 (1939): 43–53. See also Kenneth S. Latourette, *A History of the Expansion of Christianity* (7 vols., New York and London, 1937–1945).

(d) *Private organization records*
By private organizations of a civil nature are understood all such associations of men or women or of both, as are not integral elements of civil government proper. Such associations include guilds, benevolent and fraternal societies, labor and other unions, organized groups of professional men, corporations of whatsoever kind, commercial, educational. The feature common to all is that they are private and voluntary, not public or governmental bodies. They may be organized loosely and informally, or on a stable basis of legal recognition and even incorporation. In any case, such associations transact business of a certain type which is officially recorded in papers of varying extent and value. Medieval guild records offer data for a study of prices. Denifle and Chatelain's *Chartularium Universitatis Parisiensis* (4 vols., Paris, 1889–1897)

and their *Auctarium Chartularii Universitatis Parisiensis* (2 vols., Paris, 1894–1897) are rich in official documents illustrating administration and studies in the University of Paris in the Middle Ages. Business papers of the Hudson's Bay Company, the Missouri Fur Company, the American Fur Company, the McCormick Harvester Company, are important material for a study of certain early phases of American economic life.

In many cases the purpose of a document is to lend credit to a transaction by giving it legal standing. This is exemplified in a marriage contract, a charter, a deed of purchase or sale, a promissory note, a will. Such documents may be described as "written records designed through the observance of recognized forms to accredit certain proceedings or acts for the future as legal." Papers answering this description are obviously official. But a contract, a donation, a purchase, a sale, a will, can all be made in written form but on a purely private basis, and with neglect of legal formalities. The resulting papers are not official, and constitute a group of sources lying outside the two main groups already indicated, namely, purely narrative accounts, and official records.

With regard to the preceding or any other precise classification of historical sources, it must be noted that their practical bearing on research in general, is not considerable. Independently of the question as to what specific category a given source is to be referred, it is often possible for the historian to ascertain its merits as evidence, and to determine thereby the use he can legitimately make of it. At the same time, the consideration whether a document is to be regarded as official or non-official can sometimes be important as regards its use as historical source.

G. Oral Sources (Tradition)

¶ 97   There are three media by which historical data can be transmitted: by word-of-mouth; by picture or figure; by writing. Hence arises a threefold classification of formal sources: oral, pictorial or figured, and written [¶ 90 ff.]. For a long time it was the practice—not obsolete even today—to attend to written sources alone in historical research and writing, with the neglect of archaeological remains and other non-written means of information about the past. Such procedure is obviously unscientific, and issues in unsatisfactory work in cases where archaeological survivals and tokens of the past are available to the historian.

¶ 98   The category of sources by *oral transmission* is inclusive of all such material as involves communication through the spoken word. In the critical evaluation of sources the fact that many of them have their origin in word-of-mouth transmission must not be overlooked. Prior to the composition of the Gospels, their content existed in great measure as oral tradition. The Icelandic sagas of the fourteenth century were borne along in the living memory of successive generations before they were fixed in writing in the sixteenth. Events carried by oral transmission may be recent or remote. If recent, the author of the tradition may be known or unknown. If known, a number of mediate reporters of the tradition may intervene between the author and the last person to report it. If the author of the tradition is unknown, we have the phenomenon known as "rumor."

(a) *Rumor, anecdote, historical proverb.* By rumor we understand an anonymous report of a current happening, especially a sensational one, bandied about from mouth to ear. In times of public excitement, a few days, sometimes a few hours, may be enough to distort an incident completely and to fix the distortion so firmly in the popular mind that subsequent efforts to substitute the true version of what happened for the false, are fruitless. The anecdote and historical proverb are also to be regarded as species of anonymous oral tradition.

The *anecdote* is generally a report of some "personal or biographical incident." In many cases it is impossible to trace its source. Anecdotes are often transferred from one person, or from one set of circumstances, to another.

The *historical proverb* gives brief and striking expression to some incident or generalization of historical import. "When Greek meets Greek, then comes the tug of war." Another example is St. Paul's "The Cretans are always liars" (Tit. 1:12), a saying borrowed from Parmenides.

(b) *Popular tradition.* Oral transmission of incidents or events from the remote past generally goes under the name of "popular tradition." To serve as a trustworthy historical medium it must meet certain requirements, the discussion of which is made in Chapter 12 [₡ 257]. As a rule, popular tradition is found only in periods when written records are meager. Moreover, it generally comes to the surface, that is, is first heard of long after the date or period of the occurrence which it transmits [₡ 260].

(c) *Historical ballad.* This, like the saga, has generally a concomitant non-historical motif, mostly entertainment. It is the oldest of all the forms of historical transmission. With it history as record makes its earliest appearance. Possessing all the freedom of song, it perpetuates the memory of famous exploits from one generation to another. It owes its final fixed form to the rhapsodists and poets, who not infrequently have the artist's gift in a high degree. Most historical ballads in their earliest stages of growth receive fanciful accretions, which generally disappear with the progress of civilization and education. We meet ballads with a history-content chiefly in times of violent struggle for national or political independence, as in the periods of the Greek tribal displacements or the early medieval "migrations of the nations." Frequently such songs find their way as accredited history; it is from sources of this kind that data were taken over by the earliest historians of the Germanic peoples, such as the Goth, Jordanes, the Frank, Gregory of Tours, and the Lombard, Paul the Deacon. It was a theory of the German historian Niebuhr that the classic stories of early Roman history found in Livy were survivals from historical ballads, which he attempted to reconstruct, but without success.

(d) *Saga*. In its original meaning, the saga is a *spoken* historical tale, in contrast to the historical ballad, which was sung or meant to be sung. In present-day usage saga signifies more particularly a Scandinavian (and especially Icelandic) hero tale. In a wider sense, the term may be understood of any orally transmitted recital of past events, of heroic tenor, untrustworthy on the whole, but retaining withal a kernel of historical truth. Though sagas attach themselves to historical persons, incidents, localities, inventive popular fancy embellishes the historical facts until they are no longer recognizable. Sagas usually become the common and highly-prized possession of some large social group: of a race, of a nation. In the dim past where sagas take their rise, they are fairly beyond the reach of criticism. The more feeble the historical sense of the people who cherish them, the more luxuriantly they thrive. Thus understood, the saga does not differ in character from the legend, which is the English term more in use to express the concept. It is probably better usage, however, to speak of the Arthurian legend, or of the legend of the Holy Grail, than of the Arthurian saga, or the saga of the Holy Grail [₡ 263].

A widely-spread genre of the local saga is that usually called *etiological* (cause-explaining).

This centers around some local circumstance to which the play of popular imagination attaches a fanciful meaning by way of accounting for its origin. Opportunity for doing so may present itself, for example, in a curiously-shaped hill or rock that seems to suggest a human face, in names of persons or places no longer explicable by neighborhood folk, in venerable institutions and customs. Naive attempts to explain such phenomena often give rise to the etiological saga or myth. Thus, we have the supposed invention by the early Romans of the popular hero Romulus as a means of accounting for their national origin.

In the "wandering saga" the content of the story is transferred from one person, period, or place to another person, period, or place. This is exemplified in the sagas centering around Alexander the Great, and in certain East Indian sagas which found their way to the West at the time of the Crusades. The Holy Grail is a typical example of the wandering saga.—CE, 6:719.

A hero-tale is a saga celebrating the exploits of a popular or national figure who lived and struggled, perhaps died that a people might survive or achieve liberty or greatness.

(e) *Myth*. In general a myth is any recital which lifts merely mundane happenings to a supra-mundane or divine sphere. It takes two forms, one of which transforms physical elements and forces, or even moral forces, into deities or quasi-deities who demean themselves as human beings. Thus, the savage sees in the north wind, the sun, the moon, in winter, spring, drought, disease, intelligent superhuman beings, benevolent or malevolent, as the case may be. These are more often called nature myths.

Another form of myth celebrates in naive fashion certain happenings of significance in racial or national history; or it may glorify a historical figure to whom a nation traces back its origin, or to whom it believes it owes its political or military greatness. Through the agency of the myth such ancestral heroes pass beyond the limits of simple human nature and life into a supramundane world where they appear as gods or as messengers of the gods, with magical powers. These two technical meanings of myth cover the whole range of the stories known collectively as mythology. In present-day general usage the term is taken universally to signify a baseless fictitious story.

(f) *Legend*. Etymologically legend signifies "things to be read" (L. *legenda*). The reference is to certain texts which the Catholic liturgy requires to be read in the divine office. These texts include numerous "acts of the martyrs" and "lives of the saints." From the thirteenth century, the term *legend* meant specifically these two types of narrative. As such narratives were often marked by historical errors and distortions, legend came eventually to mean an untrustworthy account, such as is likely to grow up around the memory of great personalities or events. The use of the term in this sense is widespread, for example, the legends of the Holy Grail, of the Wandering Jew, of Faust.

It is to be noted that legend, myth, and saga are often interchangeable terms. We may speak with equal verbal propriety of the Washington legend, the Washington myth, the Washington saga, when there is question of the numerous unverified stories which attach to the first president's name. The common feature of all three types of recital is that they are to some degree unreliable as channels of information, whatever be the elements of historical fact they may contain [₵ 262]. Note, however, the frequent present-day use of "saga" to designate a hero-tale wholly or in part historical in content.

H. Pictorial and Figured Sources

₵ 99   Transmission of historical data by picture or figure is made in various ways.

(a) *Monumental transmission.* Here monuments is used in the restricted sense of self-standing, non-graphic memorials produced by art and handicraft. Such are: pyramids, temples, churches, commemorative tombs; historical memorials, sculptured or painted, such as the triumphal arches of Constantine and Titus in Rome, the columns of Trajan and Marcus Aurelius in the same city, paintings or frescoes of historical persons or scenes; historical memorials of the lesser arts, such as those of the garment-maker, the gem-cutter, the goldsmith; seals, armorial bearings, insofar as these bear some pictured or figured presentation of historical facts.

(b) *Ornamental transmission,* or such as is made through decorative detail. This comprises painted or sculptured work of historical content on buildings; historical pictures on parchment, in books; historical details on coats-of-arms.

(c) *Graphic transmission,* or such as is effected by drawings, as in maps, topographical sketches, plans of towns and cities; by statistical tables, anthropometric measurements in criminal records, such as fingerprints, and the like.

(d) *Photographic transmission.* This includes all the various processes of photography: the photostat, the microfilm, the microprint, the moving picture, and the "talkie"; the last is also an instance of sound transmission. Photographic reproduction of documents has proved an invaluable aid to historical research in securing absolutely reliable copies of source material.

The Use of Photography in the Reproduction of Documents
Robert C. Binkley, *Manual on Methods of Reproducing Research Material* (Survey Made for the Joint Committee on Materials for Research of the Social Science Council and the American Council of Learned Societies, Ann Arbor, Mich., 1936); idem, "New Tools for Men of Letters," *Yale Review,* 24 (1935): 519–37.

M. Llewellyn, ed., *Microphotography for Libraries* (Chicago, 1936).

Vernon D. Tate, "Microphotography as an Aid to Research," *American Library*

Association, *Public Documents* (1935): 210-17; *idem*, "The Use of Microphotography in Manuscript and Archival Work," American Library Association, *Archives and Libraries* (1939): 103-108; *idem*, "Documentary Photography" in Morgan and Lester, *Graphic Graflex Photography* (New York, 1940), 227-45; *idem*, "Microphotography in Archives" (*Staff Information Circulars*, No. 8, National Archives, Washington, 1940).

The Journal of *Documentary Reproduction* (American Library Association, Chicago) is a quarterly review of the application of photography and allied techniques to library, museum, and archival sciences.

(e) *Phonographic transmission*. The preservation of the human voice and other forms of sound through the medium of the phonograph has interest for the historian.

I. Written Sources

¶ 100 According to the material employed and the manner of writing as conditioned thereby, written transmission may be of two kinds.

(a) Transmission by chiselling, casting, stamping, scratching or other like processes. This comprises two main groups of sources: first, *inscriptions*, which have been preserved in extraordinarily large numbers, especially from ancient times. Only a few inscriptions have remained *in situ*; the bulk of them have been removed to public or private museums and collections. As regards content they range over every activity of public and private life from treatises and laws, executive orders and other official pronouncements, to data on lamps, drinking vessels, and boundary stones, to trade marks on bricks and earthen pitchers. A large proportion of extant inscriptions are from tombs. Second, coins, medals, seals, coats-of-arms with writing of any kind.

(b) Transmission through the medium of solid material, as stone, plaster (*graffiti*); or writing material properly so-called, such as clay or wax tablets, papyrus, parchment, paper. Here also finds place printed transmission in all its various forms.

Attempts to fit historical source material into moulds of rigid, logical classification are not always successful, nor need they be. Overlapping and duplication can easily occur without affecting in any way the proper use of the material itself. The general lines of division into primary and secondary, contemporary and remote, formal and informal, are of course important, and should be grasped; but whether a given source is to be classed under one head or some other, is not always a question that must be resolved before the historian can proceed to put it to account. The classifications here set out have their value in directing the student's attention to the vast range and variety of the material with which history must deal.

Chapter Six

MECHANICAL AIDS TO RESEARCH

A. Note-taking: Systems . . . . Page 124
B. Note-taking: Technique 126
C. Questionnaires and Interviews 130
D. Libraries, Archives, Museums 131
E. Hints on Historical Research 136

A. Note-taking: Systems

⟨ 101 Nothing is more inevitable in scientific research of any kind than note-taking. Any venture into the field means the assembling of a quantity of items which one must manage somehow to hold in suspense until the time comes to fix them in writing. No researcher, though endowed with the memory of a Mezzofanti, ever reaches a point where he feels he can place on it the entire burden of carrying around, subject to instant and accurate recall, the data he has accumulated. Literary workers in all ages have recognized the limitations of memory and the need of supplementing it by artificial aids. Pliny the Younger received from his uncle, the elder Pliny, one hundred and sixty notebooks packed with items. St. Augustine, calling memory *infida custos excogitatorum* (the *faithless custodian of one's thoughts*), made written notes of important conversations he wished to remember. The sixteenth-century educator, John Sturm, deplored his failure in earlier years to make memoranda of his reading: "I did not do it, to my bitter regret. Would that my teachers had admonished me to do so! I should be of greater help to you than I am now."

How to take notes in the right way is accordingly one of the first lessons the history student must learn. Wrong ways have been learned at regrettable loss of time and labor. Here, as in so many other matters, proper direction at the outset, supplemented by one's own common sense, will bring ample returns later on. Personal experience also counts for much; only after repeated mistakes may one hit upon the system of note-taking best suited to one's tastes and needs. "Anyone who has had experience in original records work, certainly in the social sciences, knows that the taking of notes and the arrangement of these notes is more than half the battle" (Broadus Mitchell).

¶ 102 *Systems: blankbooks, cards, slips, loose leaves.* Systems of note-taking are in the main two. One makes use of blankbooks or copybooks, the other of cards, slips, or loose leaves. The first held the field from classical times to the latter part of the nineteenth century and is not quite obsolete even now. George Bancroft, at work in the forties on his voluminous history, had on hand a number of quarto-size blankbooks, in which one or more pages were given to the successive days of the years. Data gathered by him in reading and research were duly entered in these books on the page or pages corresponding to the particular day and year to which they belonged.——See John S. Bassett, *Middle Group of American Historians* (New York, 1917), 208.

Even as late as the nineties another American historian, James Ford Rhodes, made use only of blankbooks for his notes, the card system being at the time something of a novelty. Towards the close of the last century, public and other libraries began to discontinue the practice of getting out printed catalogues of their books, chiefly for the reason that the catalogues were out of date and in need of supplementing as soon as printed. As a substitute for the printed catalogue, the card system was introduced. Its use eventually became widespread, not only in libraries but among students and research workers in all fields, and even in business and commercial offices, where now the card index is generally an indispensable feature of equipment.

¶ 103 The old blankbook system labors under the disadvantage that it does not easily admit of insertions. Moreover, it is difficult to adjust it to any satisfactory order, logical or topical, in the succession of the notes. To remedy this defect, an index to the contents of the blankbook system is not wholly unsatisfactory. The advantages of cards are that they are self-indexing, can be rearranged to suit convenience or necessity, and can receive additions of new cards indefinitely, and in the proper place, as the note-taking proceeds.

A disadvantage of cards is that it requires time and often patience to finger them when they have run into large numbers. There is no doubt that a series of titles of books can be read off with more ease and rapidity from a few consecutive pages of a blankbook than from some fifty or a hundred cards. But in most cases the data will not appear in the blankbook in the consecutive and satisfactory order in which they can be entered on cards. Thus, to this extent at least, the drawbacks of either system are balanced.

On the whole, there can be no doubt of the essential superiority of the card system to the blankbook; all workers in history should early become accustomed to its use. The student working in a library or in the archives should have a supply of cards with him for note-taking. But a notebook of some kind is still a desideratum on such occasions, for there will often be references and other data to record which will not conveniently find place on cards.

❦ 104   Cards of various sizes for note-taking are easily obtainable. The size mostly in use for the purpose is the same as that of the standard library catalogue card, 3 x 5 inches. Cards of larger dimensions are expensive; but they have the advantage of offering more space for writing, a convenience when a note is long and would run over into several cards of smaller size. In contrast to stiff cards, slips of paper cut in a size to suit the user's convenience have much to recommend them. Half a sheet (8½ x 5½ inches) of typewriting paper of standard size (8½ x 11 inches), furnishes a slip or loose leaf that can be used with satisfactory results. When only a few words are to be noted down as in the case of a bibliographical entry, a smaller sized slip will be preferable. When slips are grouped according to topical or other headings, the groups can be filed vertically in individual folders.

Filing cases or cabinets in various materials, steel, wood, or pasteboard, for either cards or slips, are obtainable from stationers and dealers in library or office supplies. The 5½ x 8½ slip can be filed in the case made for the full-sized typewriting sheet. This is often desirable, since together with the slips, one may wish to file away in the same case, but in separate folders, other pertinent material, such as manuscripts, pamphlets, of larger size than the slips. The loose-leaf blankbook has most of the advantages of a card-system or slip-system. The leaves or large-sized slips, preserved between the covers of the binder and not in a filing case, can be handled with the same ease with which one handles an ordinary book.

B. Note-taking: Technique

❦ 105   DIRECTIONS FOR NOTE-TAKING

Procedures in note-taking should be intelligently systematic.

(a) The cards will fall into two main groups, according as they contain bibliographical entries only, or extracts, summaries, or comments. The two groups being distinct in purpose must be filed separately.

(b) Only one side of the card should be written on. Occasionally the reverse side may be used for cross references, but such additions should be noted on the face side of the card. It is better to use an additional card.

(c) Only one item should be entered on a single card. Manuals that offer directions for note-taking allow of no exceptions to this particular rule. But it is often a problem to determine whether the extract to be copied contains only one item or several, in the sense of the rule. Thus, a passage of some length from a contemporary letter commenting on Washington's attitude on the Federal Constitution, internal improvements, and the Jay Treaty may be handled in either one of two ways. First, the passage may be divided in three parts, each being entered as a unit on one or more cards, which are then filed under one of the three topics, with cross-references on separate cards to the other two topics. The second way is as follows: If the three parts of the passage are of interest to the student only as so many illustrations, let us say, of Washington's conservatism, then really only one item is involved; hence a single card, appropriately headed, suffices, and cross-references will be unnecessary. The rule, separate cards for separate items, may seem at times to be burdensome and to swell the volume of cards unnecessarily; but it should be rigorously adhered to, since it justifies itself in the long run.

⁋ 106   An obvious excellence of the card-system is that it is self-indexing. But to be so, headings or captions must be given the cards or slips. This is not always as simple a matter as may appear. To file away notes merely in the order in which they were taken would be manifestly illogical. Some organization of notes into groups according to an intelligible plan is necessary. This plan will be for all intents and purposes identical with the outline or scheme of treatment of the topic in hand, formulated by the student at the outset of his research. Such an outline, orderly and comprehensive, and set out at least tentatively under heads and subheads, may and should be a guide to him at every stage of his task [⁋ 121]. The heads and subheads of the outline will furnish the topical captions for the notes. When he reaches the stage of composition, he will find himself in the happy position of having all his data, as far as they are furnished by the notes, arranged more or less in the same order in which they are to be embodied in the article, monograph, or book. This is an advantage which amply repays time and labor spent in careful and systematic taking of notes.

⁋ 107   As explained above, a collection of notes on any topic of research will fall into groups, each of which carries a common caption or sub-topic heading. In what order will the notes constituting any single group be arranged? Generally, in a chronological order. Thus, if the general topic treated is the diplomacy of the American Revolution and a sub-topic is the French-American alliance, notes bearing on the latter point can follow one another in the order of date, which may be entered at the upper righthand corner of the card or slip, the opposite corner (sometimes the center) being reserved for the sub-topic heading. The advantage of such arrangement is that successive steps in the origin, development, and operation of the alliance will be presented by the notes in the actual order in which they occurred. At the same time, a modification or adaptation of this general pattern may be called for at times in view of the content of the notes or of the plan of treatment followed in the composition. Here, as in other problems of note-taking, the student's understanding of his own needs in the particular research he pursues, and in the way he pursues it, coupled with his own ingenuity, will be the decisive factors.

¶ 108 FORM OF THE NOTE

Except for bibliographical data, notes may take any one of five typical forms: (a) *word-for-word extract*; (b) *summary*; (c) *reference*; (d) *comment*; (e) *factual memoranda*.

(a, b) *Word-for-word extract, summary.* Whether a passage from a source is to be copied verbatim or summarized in the note-taker's own words, is a question he will have to settle for himself in each particular case. Sometimes the passage may be of such importance to illustrate or prove a point that he will wish to have the exact wording at hand for close study later on; perhaps he may even wish to incorporate it textually in the finished work. In these cases nothing remains but to transcribe the passage word for word.

(1) The copying of passages requires painstaking care; after the copy is made it should be checked carefully with the original for possible errors. Sometimes a passage is seen to be useful for the particular line of research the investigator is pursuing, but there is no likelihood that it will be needed subsequently for closer study or formal quotation; moreover, it may be too long to quote textually. In such cases it will be enough to summarize or condense it, a process which requires the utmost care. The sense of the original must be reproduced substantially and accurately without distortion of any kind. This is a matter of the first importance. When the time comes to use the note, the original may be entirely out of reach; one cannot be checked with the other. Hence, implicit confidence must be put in the summary and its accuracy. If anywhere, caution and conscientious attention to the matter in hand are imperative in note-taking.

(2) Whenever a passage is copied textually or is condensed, an inexorable rule requires that the source from which it was drawn be entered in the note. If one fails to do so, results are likely to be embarrassing. Perhaps no researcher, however practised, has escaped altogether the experience that when he came to cite a passage from his notes he could not do so, because reference to the source was missing. Even if the title of the source can be

recalled, reference to it without page-number may be unsatisfactory, while searching out the passage may be prohibitive, because of the size of the work or the absence of an index. Anonymous quotations in history are generally useless for purposes of proof or confirmation; the name (when known) of the source from which the quotation is cited should be indicated. In the familiar phrase, one must "give chapter and verse." Hence, no card or slip containing a quotation or summary should be allowed to leave one's hands until an exact reference to its source has been entered thereon. To insure accuracy, the reference should be entered directly from the source, and the exact reference should always be the first item entered on the card.

(c) *Reference.* Often a mere reference to a passage will be all that need be entered on the card. This will happen when one wishes merely to cite an authority in illustration or proof, in the expectation that the critical reader, if interested, will look up the passage for himself. Again, one may be pressed for time, while the source will be within easy and convenient reach later. It is folly to spend valuable time in a library making extracts from works that are on one's bookshelf, or that are easily procurable later. The citation of the source should be clear and accurate. Only as much of the title need be reproduced on the card as serves to identify the source, the complete title of which should be entered on a bibliography card.

(d) *Comment.* In a mood "mulling," the investigator may form a judgment connected with his topic of research and wish to record it. The story of Alexander Pope having once had a candle brought to his bedside at night that he might jot down a happy phrasing or idea which occurred to him in a waking moment, may have its whimsical side, but it suggests withal a principle of wisdom. A person's best and most fruitful ideas sometimes break into the field of consciousness in moments of relaxation or distraction.——Henry V. Gill, *Fact and Fiction in Modern Science* (New York, 1944), chap. 1.

Not to fix ideas immediately in writing may be to run the risk of having them fade from the memory beyond possibility of recall. Needless to say, when one is absorbed in the actual process of research or in serious study of one's sources, ideas and judgments will occur which it may be wise to note down at once, and not to trust memory alone.

(e) *Factual memoranda.* Dates, statistics, facts of any kind, which the student finds useful for his theme, and which he foresees may have to enter directly or indirectly into his written work, should be noted down, especially when the sources which supply them will not be accessible later. Sometimes a mere reference to the source may suffice. But as an immediate preliminary to the actual process of composition, factual data will often have to be carried in the memory, at least for a while. Only when all the material is clearly outlined and well organized in his mind, will the author start the process of setting it down in written words. Books are made in the mind before they are made on paper. It is an illusion to suppose that one can write history directly from cards and notebooks. A reliable memory, to say nothing of good judgment and constructive imagination, is a *sine qua non* in the art of history-writing. Historians differ in their methods of composition. No two will go about the task in precisely the same way; but the general procedure for all is much the same. The data they seek to present must first be assimilated, organized in due sequence, made alive in their own minds, before they take the final step of committing them to paper.

¶ 109 *Manuals on note-taking*
Samuel S. Seward, Jr., *Note-taking* (Boston, 1910).

John M. Manley and Edith Rickert, *The Writer's Index of Good Form and Good English* (New York, 1923).

Earle W. Dow, *Principles of a Note-system for Historical Studies* (New York, 1924).

Henry Van Hoesen and Frank Walter, *Bibliography, Practical, Enumerative, Historical* (New York, 1928).

Charles G. Crump, *History and Historical Research*, 119–49.

Homer C. Hockett, *Introduction to Research in American History* (New York, 1931).

Arthur H. Cole and Karl W. Bigelow, *A Manual of Thesis Writing for Graduates and Undergraduates* (New York, 1934).

Sherman Kent, *Writing History* (New York, 1941).

"Memorandum of a Method of Noting and Arranging Material in Research," *Historical Outlook*, 10 (1919): 192 f.

C. Questionnaires and Interviews

¶ 110 THE USE OF THE QUESTIONNAIRE

In seeking information from persons presumably qualified to give it, it may be advisable to do so through the medium of a series of formal written questions, the "questionnary" or "questionnaire." Two points are to be attended to in this device: it should be properly drawn up; its recipient should be properly approached. The questions ought to be specific and bear on distinct, clear-cut points of inquiry. Vague, perplexing queries should be avoided, as also broad questions, at least when too broad to be satisfactorily answered without considerable expenditure of time and labor. How far one may go in soliciting information through a questionnaire depends in general on one's personal relations to the addressee. If there be no acquaintanceship at all between the two, the sender of the questionnaire will often find it prudent to obtain first an introduction to the person addressed. Happily this is not always necessary. The amenities of academic intercourse often suffice to induce busy scholars or officials to attend with courtesy and diligence to the questionnaires addressed to them by students and investigators personally unknown to them. But always there is the duty on the student's part of considerateness and tact when he sends out his queries for information. Good judgment, always the ultimate resource in the practical things of life, necessarily conditions any success in research by questionnaire.

¶ 111 INTERVIEW

There is no substantial difference between the questionnaire and the interview as media of historical research. In both cases an individual is approached for information, in one case in writing, in the other by personal visit. Hints and directions for making a questionnaire effective are applicable also to the interview. Pioneers and old settlers are often interviewed by investigators, and their reminiscences set down as source material for history. In this manner Lyman C. Draper and Hubert H. Bancroft garnered masses of data of varying value, not accessible elsewhere, for the history of the midwestern and Pacific Coast States, respectively. Pioneers and old settlers will generally have abundant time at their disposal, and will not begrudge it to the visiting inquirer. The same will not ordinarily be the case with the professor, librarian, or other professional person, who is considerate enough to grant an interview. Here the recipient of the favor should be particularly careful to weigh beforehand the precise nature of the information he is seeking, so as to be able to put his questions pointedly and briefly. Without such preparation time will be lost in needless queries and answers.

William C. Schluter, *How to do Research Work* (New York, 1927), 81–88.
Ward G. Reeder, *How to Write a Thesis* (Bloomington, Ill., 1930), 34–38.
Manual on Research and Reports (Amos Tuck School of Administration and Finance, Dartmouth College, 1937), 29–36.

D. Libraries, Archives, Museums

¶ 112 THE USE OF LIBRARIES IN RESEARCH

Libraries and archives are the historian's chief reliance in his tasks of research. The day is past when manuscript materials must be secured as personal property by the historian himself, as was done at great expense by such scholars of means as Bancroft and Prescott. George Bancroft is said to have made an outlay of over seventy thousand dollars in obtaining the books and transcripts of documents which he needed for his history. Of course, it is an advantage at all times for the worker in history to have personal copies of the books and documents he utilizes in research, especially if resort to them must be frequent. Every craftsman in the field has ambitions for a library of his own, however modest in content. But merely private or personal libraries, however extensive, seldom meet all the needs of investigation; one has almost invariably to seek needed material in the great public and institutional collections of printed and manuscript sources, organized and maintained chiefly in the interests of students and scholars. That such collections are as a rule now easily accessible is an advantage which the searcher of two or three generations ago did not enjoy.

Libraries, considered here as depositories of historical source material, are often individualized by exceptional resources in some specific line of research. For medieval and Renaissance history, for papal history of all periods, the Vatican Library is unsurpassed. The Bibliothèque Nationale is one of the world's great storehouses of medieval material; it is notably rich in other fields. All the broader divisions of the historical field are fully represented in the British Museum; its collections of medieval manuscripts are outstanding. In the United States, the Library of Congress ranks first in range and quality of unpublished material bearing on American history, while its increasing accumulation of photostats and microfilms of documents from Paris, Seville, and from other archival centers will eventually make it virtually unnecessary for searchers to travel abroad. The John Carter Brown Library, Providence, Rhode Island, and the Huntington Library, San Marino, California, contain treasures in Americana of the colonial period. The Gage, Germain, Clinton, and allied papers assembled in the William L. Clements Library, Ann Arbor, Michigan, make it a research center of the first importance for students of the American Revolution. The Edward E. Ayer Collection of the Newberry Library, Chicago, is noteworthy for material on Indian ethnology, frontier Americana, and Hispano-Americana. The collection of papers on the western fur trade in the Missouri Historical Society Library, St. Louis, is the largest available on this subject. At Notre Dame University is an extensive collection of original letters and other documents illustrating the early history of the Catholic Church in the United States.

(a) What library or libraries to use depends on whether or not they contain material pertinent to one's topic of research. On this point it may not always be easy to obtain satisfactory information. If the library be within convenient reach, it will be possible to visit it, and so to ascertain by inquiry or examination of its catalogue, what help it has to offer. Further, there will be the possibility of consultation with directors, professors, workers in the same field as one's own. When a library is at a distance, various devices can be employed to learn its resources in the material one needs. A request for information can be addressed to the librarian, or one may consult persons acquainted with its contents, or one may find at hand printed catalogues or lists of books on special subjects issued by the library. Sometimes such preliminary inquiries reveal the existence of material in various and widely-scattered localities, so that travel may become necessary, if there is no other practicable way of reaching the material.

(b) How to use a library is an art every student in history must learn if he is to economize time and labor. The art regards chiefly the use of the catalogue. This may sometimes have its intricacies, but the broad features of the system employed, whether Dewey decimal, Library of Congress, or any other, can and should be understood, to give one the best results in using the catalogue with intelligence and dispatch. Unless this be done, not only will valuable time be frittered away in fruitless turning over of catalogue cards, but helpful material may be overlooked through failure to appreciate the uses of author, title, subject, cross-reference, and other types of cards.

(c) The device of the inter-library loan has become common in the United States. By this means the student can obtain books not available in local libraries. Sometimes, as in the Library of Congress, the privilege extends also to photostats, microfilms, and written transcripts.

(d) Patrons of libraries are sometimes allowed access to the stacks or open shelves. The advantages of such a privilege in the way of preparing a bibliography, surveying the resources of the library on a certain topic, or familiarizing oneself with the individual books, are manifest. Sometimes as much may be accomplished in a few hours at the open shelves as could be accomplished in as many days, if the books had to be called for individually and consulted in the reading room.

M. Hutchins, A. S. Johnson, and M. S. Williams, *Guide to the Use of Libraries.*
E. J. Dingwall, *How to Use a Large Library.*
William T. O'Rourke, *Library Handbook for Catholic Students* (New York, 1935).
William T. Kane, *Catholic Library Problems* (Chicago, 1939).

❡ 113 ARCHIVES

In the opinion of Worthington C. Ford, "an archive cannot be defined in sufficiently precise terms to make it worth while." Primarily, according to modern ideas, archives have been defined as "the proper place of deposit for documents preserved for administrative purposes relating to any department of national or other public affairs."—Julian P. Gilson, *A Student's Guide to the Manuscripts of the British Museum* (Helps, vol. 31), 8.

This definition, good as far as it goes, omits an item which any adequate definition of an archive apparently should include, namely, the qualification that the documents preserved, owing to their back dates or for other reasons, are not needed in the actual administration of the office to which they belong. Accordingly, we may define an archive as *a depository for papers that have accumulated in the routine administration of an office, public, or private, and are no longer needed for current business.*

❡ 114 It is noteworthy that this definition limits the term defined to a place of deposit of papers of a specific kind, namely, such as originate in an administrative office, public or private. A depository for manuscript material is not necessarily an archive. The distinction is seen in the use of the term as applied to the great archival depositories of the world, such as Vatican Archives (Archivo Vaticano); the National Archives (Archives Nationales), Paris; the Dominion Archives, Ottawa; the National Archives, Washington. The function of the Public Record Office, London, is sufficiently indicated by its name. All the great collections here named are more or less limited to administrative or official papers emanating from their respective governments.

Furthermore, the great national libraries generally have two departments, one of printed material, the other of manuscripts not having place in the category of state papers. This is the case at the Vatican Library (Biblioteca Vaticana); National Library (Biblioteca Nazionale), Rome; the National Library (Bibliothèque Nationale), Paris; the British Museum; the Library of Congress. One goes to the Vatican Library for medieval manuscripts of the classics or treatises in theology, to the Vatican Archives for the correspondence of papal nuncios. Similarly, in London, the state papers of Henry VIII will be found in the Public Record Office, while the collections of miscellaneous private papers known as the Harleian and the Cottonian, are in the manuscript division of the British Museum. So also, in Washington one finds the old business papers of the Indian Office in the National Archives; the personal papers of deceased presidents of the United States in the Library of Congress, Manuscript Division.

❡ 115 It is not practicable to offer here directions on the use of archives. Existing government archives differ from one another in arrangement, cataloguing, methods of administration, rules for patrons. Actual experience in the use of a particular archival depository is the only real solution of the difficulties a student may expect to meet with who resorts to it for research. A few visits will be enough to make him familiar with its physical layout and the regulations governing the use of material. Government archives in Europe and America are open from five to eight hours daily. Students traveling a great distance to do research are sometimes annoyed to find themselves thus restricted in the use of an archive to this limited time. But, except in the Dominion Archives, custom has fixed the relatively short working-hours in public archives.

On archive administration
Charles Johnson, *The Care of Documents and the Management of Archives* (Helps, vol. 5).

M. R. James, *The Wanderings and Homes of Manuscripts* (Helps, vol. 19).

John C. Fitzpatrick, *Notes on the Care, Cataloguing, Calendaring and Arranging of Manuscripts* (3d ed., Washington, 1928).

Hilary Jenkinson, *Manual of Archive Administration, Including the Problem of War Archives and Archive Making* (Oxford, 1922).

Grace L. Nute, *The Care and Cataloguing of Manuscripts as Practiced by the Minnesota Historical Society* (St. Paul, 1936).

Samuel Muller, J. A. Feith and R. Fruin, *Manual for the Arrangement and Description of Archives*, trans. from the 2d ed. by Arthur H. Leavitt, (New York, 1940).

Charles M. Andrews "Archives" in AHA, *Report* (1913).

Guide to the Material in the National Archives (Washington, 1940).

Philip C. Brooks, "What Records Shall we Preserve?" (*Staff Information Circular*, No. 9, National Archives, Washington).

❡ 116 MUSEUMS

Museums, as far as they concern the historian, are mainly storehouses of that important class of material for his purpose which is generally classified under the rubric "historical remains" or "historical relics." Written sources are the historian's main reliance in his searchings, but he cannot neglect the important evidence to be found in objects physically surviving from the cultures and civilizations of other days. Only with these objects before the historian does firsthand, accurate knowledge of numerous aspects of the economic and cultural life of early periods become possible. Here one does not have to recur to the "historical imagination" to realize the past. The household furniture and agricultural implements in the Egyptian Museum, Turin; the thousands of well-preserved articles from Pompeii in the National Museum, Naples; the splendid collections of Greek vases in the Louvre and in the British Museum; the medieval antiquities in the Cluny Museum, Paris; the specimens of the industrial and fine arts in the Victoria-Albert Museum, London, and in the Metropolitan Museum of Art, New York —things such as these help the student to visualize history and portray it true to life.

Many state and local historical societies of the United States maintain museums of the strictly historical type, which have their utility for special lines of research. The rare documents of historical interest sometimes on display in museums, besides yielding information, can be especially intriguing. The genuine student of history will be moved when standing at close quarters in the British Museum with Magna Carta, or with the famous bull of Innocent III, accepting England as a papal fief, or in Washington, with the parchment copy of the Declaration of Independence, signed by the members of Congress.

E. Hints on Historical Research

¶ 117 *The initial step in historical research is the choice of a topic.* Sometimes there may be no question of choice at all. For students, the topic may be assigned by a professor, or circumstances may make a particular selection expedient or necessary. When the investigator is really free to choose his topic of research, various factors will have to be reckoned with in making a suitable selection. Among these are the amount of space, as also the nature and amount of source material available for treatment; it would be folly to attempt to treat certain subjects thoroughly within the limits of a thousand-word paper. Broad, comprehensive subjects are, as a rule, to be avoided, at least by the average student, chiefly because it is impracticable for him to treat them satisfactorily within the limits of space and time at his disposal, not to speak of his presumed lack of equipment and general fitness for such major tasks. "Learn to be definite at all costs," Sir Charles Oman warns the beginner; "be limited, if it is necessary, stick to a single century or to a single reign, but write something—knowledge not committed to paper is lost." Very much futile wit has been expended on the practice of setting graduate students to work on what look like ridiculously trivial and inconsequential minutiae of research. No doubt the practice of assigning topics of narrow scope for investigation can be, and sometimes is carried too far; but behind it is the sound principle that the narrower the field of research, the more intensive it is; and therefore, its cultivation is more likely to be successful. Moreover, training in method can come as well, sometimes better, through handling a narrow rather than a broad topic.

¶ 118 *A topic having been chosen, look up its bibliography, if such there be.* Research, if it is to be fresh and thereby justify itself, ought to start, at least in a general way, where previous research left off. Thus, it is necessary to find out the present status of scholarly investigation on the subject in hand. This can be ascertained from reliable, up-to-date bibliographical surveys, such as are sometimes found in the more scholarly type of history books now appearing, and from standard bibliographies, general or special, supplemented by notices of new publications in the current historical reviews. Graduate students have their professors and directors to consult in the matter, while investigators not working under direction will find it helpful, sometimes perhaps necessary, to seek information from experts in the field. It is paramount to have in one's possession the findings of previous investigation on the subject dealt with; otherwise one may lose valuable time and labor threshing out old straw, already winnowed by others, who may have practically exhausted its possibilities. Such an unhappy result will scarcely occur in the case of a graduate student of history working on a subject previously approved by his director.

(a) Lists of doctoral dissertations in history, in course of preparation at American and Canadian universities, contain historical projects in general, and are issued periodically by the American Historical Association (*American Historical Review*, Washington). Similar lists for Canadian history appear at intervals in the *Canadian Historical Review*, Toronto. The Medieval Academy of America, through its organ, *Speculum*, has kept students informed of published articles and books relating to its special field. Dissertations and other projects in research are listed in *Progress of Medieval and Renaissance Studies in the United States and Canada. An Annual Bulletin*, edited by S. Harrison Thomson of the University of Colorado. The London Institute of Historical Research, University of London, publishes regularly in its *Bulletin* helpful summaries of graduate theses issuing from the British Universities. Useless duplication of research tasks may be avoided by consultation of such lists.

(b) The graduate thesis is meant to be a "contribution to the sum of knowledge." But it must be noted that there is a tendency in American graduate schools to allow students to write their dissertations on previously treated subjects, and even without the support of fresh material, provided that the old material be submitted to some new and significant organization or interpretation, so that approach to the subject may be new. The new organization, the re-interpretation of the old material, on the assumption that it is really significant, is understood to be in its way "a contribution to the sum of knowledge."

¶ 119 *Before definite choice of a subject is made, ascertain whether enough material is available to make satisfactory treatment possible.* One may begin research on a subject only to find out that the material needed to develop it properly is non-existent, or inaccessible. If little time or labor has been spent in the research, no great loss may have to be deplored; but getting into such a blind alley sometimes proves a costly mistake. Bibliographies, guides to manuscript material in libraries and archives, consultations with experts in the field, must here be put to account.

❡ 120 Definite choice of a subject being made, master enough of its historical background to make research intelligent. This means becoming familiar from reliable secondary accounts with the larger historical whole of which the topic to be worked out may be only a very small part. It would be folly to start gathering material for a study of a thirteenth-century Yorkshire manor if one had no adequate idea of the manorial system as a whole, or was ignorant of general political and social conditions in the English contemporary scene. Documents and other material with important bearing on a topic of research may be passed over lightly or neglected altogether, simply because the searcher does not know enough of the setting of his topic to see the implications contained, and to interpret them aright.

❡ 121 Sketch out under heads and subheads the treatment one expects to give the topic, the plan of development to be followed. Two things are to be noted about such a plan. First, it is indispensable as a guide to reading, note-taking, and research in general on the topic treated. Secondly, in its first draught it is always almost necessarily tentative, and subject to revision as investigation proceeds, for it will open new vistas and perhaps reveal new and unsuspected source material, or indicate the absence of certain source material one expected to find. Some such elastic, readily convertible plan must therefore be in mind as the student goes forward in his work of research. Lacking it, he may flounder about amid books and documents, wasting valuable time and energy by making notes or in reading matter which later he finds to be useless for his purpose. The plan should be written out to insure definiteness, as far as this is possible in the beginning. Further, its main points should be perfectly familiar to the student, so that he can recall them easily without having to refer to a memorandum. Very possibly a plan such as is here in question cannot be framed in the earlier stages of research. One has generally to make some progress in a subject by reading and study, in order to become familiar with it, before any outline of treatment, however tentative, will suggest itself. But the formulating of a plan must not be delayed too long. To repeat, a plan in some shape or other is an indispensable aid to insure definiteness of aim, economy of time and labor, satisfactory research, and in the end, a worthwhile piece of history writing.

❡ 122 The question of plan implies that of scale. Sometimes this is a matter with which the writer need not be concerned at all. It is determined for him. A limit of so many thousand words may be set, and he must conform to this limit, imposed by professor or editor or publisher. But even within these imposed limits for the production as a whole, there is the question how much space should be given to the individual parts or divisions that fill out the plan. This is a problem which the writer himself must solve. Considerations of relative importance, artistic effect, available data, will be among those that determine the solution. At all events, this question of proportion in developing the integral members of the plan should be disposed of satisfactorily before the actual work of composition is begun. In cases where the space limits of the article, dissertation, or book are not imposed but are left to the writer's choice, the question of scale should be faced early in the research, not left to subsequent accident or caprice. But it is intelligible (as is true of the plan of treatment), that determination of scale is not a thing that can always be effected satisfactorily at the outset. As research or composition proceeds, an adopted scale may have to be modified, either in absolute magnitude or in the proportionate treatment of individual topics.

¶ 123 *Work first on primary material, then on secondary.* In actual research primary and secondary sources will not generally be found sorted out neatly in distinct groups, but mingled together; in note-taking, for example, the student must utilize the sources in the order in which they occur. The important direction here given does not concern heuristic, but the later step of critical study of a subject based upon the material assembled. Careful, thoroughgoing study of the subject requires that one go back to the original sources, and be not satisfied to take things merely at second hand or third hand. Recourse to firsthand material is the fundamental rule of all scientific work. Much, perhaps most of the perverted history of the past owes its origin to the unscholarly passing on of statements or interpretations from one secondary authority to another [¶ 437].

Even where secondary treatments of a topic are of the scholarly type, it is best to defer reading of them until one has carefully sifted the primary material and has reached conclusions of one's own, based on its evidence. At the same time, scholarly, up-to-date articles, monographs, books, may bear with more or less directness on the investigator's topic of research; it is a matter of importance to him to acquaint himself with their findings. Gaps in his own work may be filled in, statements corrected, interpretations modified. It will be reassuring to find himself in agreement with other scholars, just as it may be, but not necessarily so, disconcerting to find himself at odds with them—a situation which may entail a revision of the manuscript.

(a) Fonck calls attention repeatedly to a danger to which beginners in research are exposed. They may easily allow their interpretation of primary sources to be influenced by what they have read in secondary sources. This is not the way to attain to the habit of independent thinking so vital to the historian. The danger mentioned may be real, not only for beginners, but even for professional researchers. Fonck insists strongly that reading of the scholarly special and monographic literature of one's subject should follow, not precede, reading of the primary material.—*Wissenschaftliches Arbeiten*, 132.

Lingard said appositely in the preface to his *History of England* (2d ed.):

> To render these volumes more deserving of public approbation I did not hesitate, at the commencement of my labors, to impose on myself a severe obligation from which I am not conscious of having on any occasion materially swerved; to take nothing upon trust; to confine my researches, in the first instance, to original documents and the more ancient writers; and only to consult the modern historians when I had satisfied my own judgment and composed my own narrative. My object was to preserve myself from copying the mistakes of others, to keep my mind unbiased by their opinions and prejudices, and to present to the reader from authentic sources a full and correct relation of events.

❡ 124 *Adequate exploitation of sources often requires incursions into special fields of knowledge.* Not only must the historian summon to his aid on occasion the auxiliary sciences, such as diplomatic, palaeography, archaeology, if the topics treated require their use, but almost any field of knowledge may at times serve his purpose by helping to the elucidation of a text. Certain documents cannot be fully understood without some, or considerable acquaintance in many cases, with the principles of economics or psychology or theology. Any complete study of the miracles of Christ presupposes some knowledge of medical science. The phenomenon of nationalism is in many ways a problem in group psychology; so also are revolutions, riots, popular movements of any kind. The layman, John Baptist Rossi, "Father of Christian Archaeology," sat for years on the benches learning theology, because he felt that this science was indispensable for the proper interpretation of the inscriptions and other monuments of Christian antiquity. In a sense, the true historical searcher is prepared to annex the whole domain of human knowledge to his own province. If the Roman moralist broke down all barriers to his range of interest by his *nihil humanum a me alienum puto*, the historian is by the same token committed to a like catholicity of outlook. All and sundry data furnished him by various fields of knowledge, even the most disparate, if they help him to understand his documents, to interpret them aright, are grist for his mill.

Part Three

APPRAISING THE SOURCES: *Criticism*

Chapter Seven

LOGICAL PROCESSES IN HISTORY

A. Analogy . . . . Page 143
B. Generalization 146
C. Reasoning from Statistics 151
D. Hypothesis 153
E. Conjecture 160
F. The Argument from Silence 162
G. The Argument a priori 166

¶ 125 Historical method is largely a matter of reasoning about sources and the data they contain. Not all knowledge of the past now in our possession was originally accessible in explicitly recorded statements; much of it was contained only implicitly in the sources and had to be extracted therefrom by various operations of the mind. Any attempt to order a mass of historical data into a coherent and intelligible narrative, with accompanying interpretation, calls for constant exercise of the reasoning powers, especially in certain forms of logical proof. These forms include: analogy, generalization or induction, hypothesis, conjecture, the argument from silence, and the argument a priori.

A. Analogy

¶ 126 THE MEANING OF ANALOGY
"Analogy may be defined as inference based on resemblance."—Joseph A. McLaughlin, *An Outline and Manual of Logic* (Milwaukee, 1932), 138. See also George H. Joyce, *Principles of Logic*, 259. Anthony C. Cotter, *Logic and Epistemology* (Baltimore, 1930), 71.

Analogy argues from the resemblance of two things in one or more respects to their necessary or supposedly necessary resemblance also in other respects. The basis of an argument of this kind is the double principle that every being shows certain attributes or traits corresponding to its nature, that every efficient cause has a corresponding effect; consequently, similar beings show similar attributes or traits, while similar causes have similar effects, and vice versa. Historical analogy applies the principle of analogy to historical data as a method of logical proof. For its validity it rests largely on the broad fact (or on concrete application of the double principle mentioned) that men of different times and places act more or less alike when placed in like circumstances, and this in virtue of their common nature.

¶ 127 Analogy can aid historical investigation: first, by revealing new aspects and relations of facts, by bringing out points of disagreement even more so than of agreement; secondly, by opening up new problems, suggesting new hypotheses and affording new data for proof by induction; finally, by bringing to light a relation of dependence between two things, on the principle that "similar things are related in origin." This principle finds frequent application in historical reasoning as well as in everyday life. We use it by a certain necessity of nature, as we do the principle of causality; but it is easily misapplied. One or more of the possibilities that condition a problem can be and often are overlooked, with faulty analogy as a result. Erroneous applications of the principle in question are repeatedly met with, especially in the fields of history, ethnology, and comparative religion.

¶ 128 EXAMPLES OF HISTORICAL ANALOGY

From the fact that the Romans had a priesthood with high priest and sacrifices, to conclude that other peoples having a priesthood also had a high priest and sacrifices.

From the resemblance in certain respects between the French Revolution and the Russian Revolution, to argue that they will also resemble one another in having a military dictatorship as their common issue.

Louis XVI might have saved himself by making concessions; therefore the last Russian czar might have saved himself by doing likewise.

To see in the dependence of modern labor on capital, of the workingman of today on the capitalist, a "new feudalism" analagous to medieval feudalism with its dependence of peasant and serf on the lord of the manor.

An analogy once much discussed is that alleged by Sir Henry Maine between the English village community and the village community of India.— George L. Gomme, *The Village Community with Special Reference to the Origin and Form of the Survival in Britain* (London, 1896).

¶ 129 FAULTY ANALOGY IN GENERAL

To argue from the mere co-existence or succession of two similar facts to the immediate dependence of one on the other (*post hoc, ergo propter hoc*).

To infer intrinsic dependence from merely extrinsic and accidental points of resemblance.

To conclude with certainty from the agreement of two things in one trait or one relation, to their agreement also in other traits or other relations.

To bring together in some relation or other things which lie far apart in time and content, for instance, to transfer ideas, views, institutions, from one period to an entirely different period, from one sphere to a wholly disparate sphere.

To go on the assumption that the development of peoples and states has in all cases followed similar lines.

To assume that social phenomena are governed by laws similar in their rigidity to the laws that govern physical phenomena (Buckle, Comte, Taine).

To transfer the characteristics and traits of the animal organism to social and political institutions, especially the state, unless for purposes of broad comparison and illustration.

❡ 130 FAULTY ANALOGY IN PARTICULAR
From the resemblance in anatomical structure between man and the anthropoid apes, to conclude that one is descended from the other.

To set up on the ground of certain external points of resemblance a relation of dependence between the heathen office of financial overseer (ἐπίσκοπος) and the Christian office of bishop. (Edwin Hatch, *Organization of the Early Christian Churches* [London and New York, 1909]), or between the religious notions of the Greek mystery-religions and Christian baptism.

To seek to establish from certain external features common to both, a connection between the Christian legends of the saints and heathen legends.

To interpret ancient texts according to the ideas and customs of one's own time.

To argue that, because some persons subject to strange psychic experiences were hypnotics, the saints also were hypnotics (See Joyce, *Logic*, 286).

> Coke read into Magna Carta things that were not there, but which did pertain to the quarrels between James I and his Parliaments. Alluring parallels spring up in which resemblances are emphasized and important differences overlooked; and no fallacies are so misleading as supposed historical parallels [analogies]. They have been the occasion of an appalling amount of bad political argument.——E. Scott, *History and Historical Problems*, 191.

Green's *Short History of the English People* has been described as "a democratic manifesto," an attempt to read history backwards by seeing democratic phenomena long before they had actually put in their appearance.

Faulty analogy is stressed here because the process is used oftener with invalid than with valid results. But sound analogies or parallels in history do occur. For a likely example see the comparison made between the Graeco-Roman world of the time of Christ and the world today in William F. Albright, *From the Stone Age to Christianity: Monotheism and the Historical Process* (Baltimore, 1940), 311.

⁋ 131   SUGGESTIONS FOR USE OF HISTORICAL ANALOGY

The texts or facts which one seeks to bring into relation must first be subjected to accurate and thoroughgoing study.

A conclusion based on analogy is false if found to be at variance with known facts, even a single one.

The value of an inference by analogy is not "in direct proportion to the number of points of resemblance which can be discovered. We must weigh points of resemblance rather than count them; they must represent some deep-lying characteristic of the things concerned."—McLaughlin, *Logic*, 139. See also Joyce, *Logic*, 262, where it is shown against John Stuart Mill that "the mere number of resemblances is in fact a point of little moment."

Inference by analogy can never issue in more than a probable conclusion, as the major premise in such inference, because it is only probable that "a thing similar to another in one respect is similar to it also in other respects."

Interdependence in the case of texts or facts may be affirmed only when some certain nexus or relationship has been established. Hence in determining whether A depends on B, or B on A, or A and B on C, the various possibilities must be carefully weighed. Thus, to maintain that customs, institutions, viewpoints, have been taken over by one people or period from another, is logical only when a direct relation of dependence between the two peoples or periods has been established.

B. Generalization

⁋ 132   THE NATURE OF GENERALIZATION

History is concerned immediately with single, individual facts; mediately with such generalized truths as can be derived from the individual facts Generalizations in history may be applicable only to the past, or they may be of universal application, and as such, independent of time and place. Examples of the two types are respectively the statements, "the Athenians were an art-loving people"; "a strongly centralized government is the best in war time." It is only in the case of the latter type that we can speak with consistency of "historical laws." The logical process employed in arriving at either kind of generalization is known as *induction* or, more specifically, *incomplete induction*, which may be defined as "the legitimate derivation of general laws or truths from a limited number of individual cases." From certain recorded instances of individual bravery among the early Romans, one may with more or less accuracy derive the general statement, "the early Romans were a brave people."

(a) The conditions under which inductive reasoning is valid are carefully indicated in manuals of logic; disregard of them results in fallacy.—McLaughlin, Logic, 144 ff.

It is especially to be noted that the validity of incomplete induction as a method of proof does not rest merely on the number of individual cases on which the generalization is built. What is essential is that a causal relationship be established between the individual cases and the resulting general truth. This causal relationship, generally expressed in the form, "like causes produce like effects," or "like natures have like properties," must be verified in each case. Thus, from ten individual instances of classical manuscripts having been preserved from loss by a medieval monastery, we may conclude to the general truth that the medieval monasteries preserved the classics. Here, the force of the proof lies in the circumstance that the tenfold repetition of the same phenomenon cannot be explained except on the assumption that it was a characteristic or effect more or less uniformly found in the institution in question.

(b) As we accept "historical laws" on the ground of experience, so also must we accept *historical induction* as a valid process of logical thought, for it is the only means by which we can arrive at a knowledge of the laws in question. Its validity rests, as was said, on the principle of causality, according to which a definite cause operating under definite conditions always produces a definite effect. Furthermore, induction together with the general truths it puts us in possession of, is a necessity of everyday life. Ordered social life is possible only to the extent that we can enjoy a measure of assurance in regard to future transactions and events. But such certainty would be unthinkable were human conduct not to show a certain regularity according to law. We recognize this exigency of social life when we say of history that it is a *magistra vitae*, meaning thereby that its laws are guideposts for the future, and enable us to forecast events with varying degrees of assurance.

℃ 133   THE VALUE OF HISTORICAL GENERALIZATION

Only in the light of general truths does history become intelligible. General truths simplify history by reducing whole masses of facts to brief, easily-apprehended formulas. The facts, individualized, may stagger us by sheer weight of numbers; generalized, they are readily grasped as a manageable unit. A striking, far-reaching generalization can illuminate a vast area of the historical field. To say that medieval culture was the net product of three great streams of influence—Graeco-Roman, Christian, Teutonic—is to help to clarify a thousand years of world history; it is to give meaning to millions of isolated facts, which, left to themselves, are incapable of telling their own story.

Ability to generalize on his data is indispensable to the historian. Where it is lacking history as record is reduced to a mere barren annalistic recital of facts, without the vitality and significance which it is possible to inject into them by means of broad, general views. And yet, generalization can be overdone. A historian may be too "viewy," too speculative, too eager to dispatch his business in broad, sweeping judgments, which it is difficult, perhaps impossible, for the reader to test with anything like satisfaction.

¶ 134 The laws of economics, sociology, and the social sciences in general are for the most part inductions or generalizations based on human experience, and on history. That parents love their offspring; that men are gregarious by instinct; that the prices of commodities are affected by supply and demand; that extreme political repression begets revolution: these are general truths derived by inductive reasoning from bodies of individual facts. These truths, or laws, as we may not improperly call them, belong somehow to the category of history as past actuality.

But here a difficulty may be raised. Has history, in last analysis, any laws of its own? It would seem merely to furnish the material for generalizations such as those stated, which, once established, are the property, not of history but of one of the other social sciences. That extreme repression by authority begets revolution is a proposition which cannot be verified a posteriori without the aid of history; but of itself it is apparently a proposition or law, not of history, but of political science.

The question is academic; it does not involve any important issue in its resolution, one way or the other. As was already noted, the generalizations supplied by history are either restricted in time and place (the Greeks were a mentally gifted people) or they are not (material prosperity tends to moral decay). To call those of the first kind "laws" would be a misnomer. Those of the other kind are by a recognized convention often referred to as "laws of history." No serious reason can be alleged for impugning this convention, even though on analysis such laws may appear to belong to other social sciences rather than to history. It is beyond question that certain uniformities and regularities may be observed in historical phenomena; there is no difficulty in designating these as "laws" in the broad sense which this usage requires.

In *Law in History and Other Essays* (New York, 1927), 1–29, Edward P. Cheyney attempts to state some of the fundamental laws behind the historical process; but his discussion has a deterministic slant [¶ 138-d]. For an exposition of certain uniformities or "laws" which reveal themselves in political and social upheavals, see Clarence C. Brinton, *The Anatomy of Revolution* (New York, 1939).

¶ 135 Laws may also be classified as those of the *individual* and those of the *group*. Group-laws express certain uniformities in the behavior of groups or masses. Uniformities of this kind have their roots in the identity of human nature as it is shared by all the members of the group, as well as in the reciprocity of influences of the same tenor obtaining among them. Sometimes also, suggestion or instinctive impulse has its place, as in the dancing-mania frequently epidemic in the Middle Ages and in the tulip-mania of seventeenth-century Holland.

¶ 136 HUMAN VOLITION IN HISTORY

The most significant finite factor in history is human free will. But freedom is limited both within and without; it is influenced not only by subjective conditions in the human agent, but also by his physical environment. The result is that an event in history ordinarily presents itself as the net product of various factors which operate according to their own proper laws and under the influence of which the will shows a certain regularity in its activities. On the other hand, precisely because of the freedom of the will, such regularity can only be relative. An individual can make himself an exception to the general law; he can reverse the ordinary and normal course of development and set things going in an entirely new and unexpected direction. Free will has been described as "the incalculable element" in history.

¶ 137 FACTORS INFLUENCING HUMAN VOLITION

These fall into three groups: first *physical factors*, or those of external nature, such as space (geographical features of land and water), time (the seasons), weather and climate, the non-intelligent animal world; second, *human factors*, or those of the human agent, such as bodily growth and decay, instincts, ideas, emotions, knowledge; and third, *social and economic factors*, such as those of family and community life. Because it is subjected to these various groups of influences, the will normally operates in certain uniform ways, which may be roughly described as "laws."

Examples of such uniformities or laws corresponding to each of the three groups of factors indicated are:

The seasons regulate choice of food and clothing; the nature of a building-site conditions the type of building; northerners possess more energy and capacity for work than inhabitants of the tropics.

Hunger and thirst lower the resistance of an army; personal mental and moral characteristics help to determine choice of a career; an urge to knowledge is typically human, especially when knowledge promises to be remunerative; hard things are not attempted without a prospect of corresponding gain.

A surplus in production lowers prices; better communications speed up the circulation of goods; earnest cultivation of the moral and religious factors in life promotes good relations between individuals and nations.

¶ 138   THE USE OF HISTORICAL INDUCTION

(a) The logical procedure in historical induction is on the whole the same as in induction in general. But the resulting generalization or law, when applied to individual cases, yields moral certainty only, and sometimes not more than probability.

(b) As in general induction, so in induction of the historical type, John Stuart Mill's four methods of verification (agreement, difference, residue, concomitant variations) may be usefully applied.

(c) Inductive generalizations in history may form the basis of a prudent forecasting of events; but they find their chief application in the interpretation of past events and conditions.

(d) One must not look for too much uniformity and law in history. It is an illusion to expect that men will some day discover laws in the sense of ultimate generalizations, in the light of which all the events and processes of history can be explained with mathematical exactness. Generalizations of this kind postulate an entirely mechanistic world without place in it for free will or divine intervention. Buckle, and Marx, viewing history from an entirely materialistic angle, sought to reduce historical processes to the rigid uniformity characteristic of physical law. The attempt was futile, as must be any attempt that runs counter to nature; but the mirage of some ironclad law or laws, as yet undiscovered, that will unravel the skein of history and make its processes as clear as the solution of a geometrical problem, has still power to intrigue the unwary.

Henry Adams played audaciously along this line.—See William R. Thayer, "The Vagaries of Historians," AHA, Report (1919).

> The laws of history will most certainly eventually be established.—*Encyclopaedia of the Social Sciences*, 7:362.

> If we knew the laws of history, we might reason and act with the same intelligence and precision and anticipation of success with which the engineer acts in conformity with the known laws of physics, or the astronomer with the laws of astronomy, or the cattle breeder with the Mendelian law of inheritance [heredity?]—Edward P. Cheyney, *Law in History*, 28.

Historical laws conceived according to the foregoing mechanistic points of view are non-existent and therefore unknowable [¶ 39, 355].

It is folly to speak of the laws of history as of something inevitable, which science has only to discover and whose consequences any one can then foretell but do nothing to alter or avert.——William James, "Great Men and their Environment," *The Will to Believe and Other Essays in Popular Philosophy* (New York, 1909), 244.

(e) The individual facts on which a generalization is based should be carefully tested for objective truth.

(f) An inductive conclusion gains in probability the more the items on which it is based agree in essential points and differ in non-essential. It is peculiar to historical data that circumstances of time and place frequently belong to the essential.

(g) "Sweeping generalizations" are based on inadequate data either in quantity or quality. They follow for the most part the fallacious principle *ab uno disce omnes*. In all sound generalizations the individual cases examined are numerous and typical enough to warrant conclusion from the particular to the general by an application of the principle of causality. With the historian, as with anybody else, generalization is a logical process; to be valid it must conform rigorously to certain rules.

For examples of hypothesis interpretation, refer to ₵ 146, 329.

For suggestive generalizations in the American history field, see Turner's volumes on the frontier and the sections; Dixon R. Fox, *Ideas in Motion* (New York, 1935); and Walter P. Webb's discussion of the technique of western settlement [₵ 146-d].

C. Reasoning from Statistics

₵ 139 STATISTICS IN HISTORY

As a method of investigation in history, the use of statistics may be taken to mean the collection, tabulation, and analysis of numerical facts of a given category, with a view to deducing therefrom averages, proportions, and other uniformities or laws, useful to the historian. Broadly, the term expresses the idea of mere figures or numerical data bearing on a certain topic; for example, findings of the United States Census for a given year. More precisely, it expresses the idea not only of numerical data, but also of certain computations based upon them, such as the rate of increase of the population of the United States, by decades.

Government statistics are as old as history. The Romans took the census of the empire by methods that made for precision and accuracy of result. Elaborate records of custom receipts for London and other English ports under Edward III are extant. Historians of earlier days were scarcely alive to the value of statistical data for their purpose. More recently an amount of excellent history based on statistics, public or private, especially of the economic order, has been produced. A pertinent example is James E. Thorold Rogers, *History of Agriculture and Prices in England, 1259–1793* (7 vols., Oxford, 1866–1902). The range and general accuracy of the data of this work, derived mostly from manuscript sources, have been commended; but the computations based upon the data and the conclusions drawn therefrom have sometimes been called into question.

¶ 140 UTILIZATION OF STATISTICS IN HISTORY

(a) Statistical data, and the conclusions based thereon, often enable us to arrive at the meaning and interrelationships of whole groups of facts. Consider, for instance, the case in which several such groups of the same category present, under varying circumstances of time and place, certain identical features or characteristics. We rightly conclude that these characteristics are not accidental but belong to the very nature of the facts.

(b) Application of the so-called *method of differentials* enables us to ascertain relationships of cause and effect. We compare, for instance, the death-rate for a certain time and place with corresponding weather conditions, or with the prevalence of a certain disease. A parallel rise or fall in the two groups of phenomena may evidence a relationship of cause and effect between them.

(c) Any uniformity or ratio based on statistics is valid for the mass or group only, not for the individual units composing it; any single unit can form an exception to the character or behavior of the group as a whole. Statistics may prove that education in a given country at a given period was, in general, on a high level; it is not proved thereby that the education of an individual belonging to the country and period in question, was on a high level, though a more or less probable inference that he was well educated, may be justified.

(d) Uniformities based on statistics are fixed, but in a restricted sense; they afford only moral certainty or a high degree of probability.

The general use of statistics in the social sciences
P. Coffey, *The Science of Logic*, 285 ff.
Valère Fallon, *The Principles of Social Economy*, trans. by John L. McNulty (New York, 1933), 21–25.
A. M. Schlesinger, in W. Gee, ed., *Research in the Social Sciences*, 233–35.

Instances of statistical data as bearing on history
James W. Thompson, "The Statistical Sources of Frankish History," AHR, 40 (1935): 625 ff.
Clarence C. Brinton, *The Jacobins: an Essay in New History* (New York, 1930).
Donald Greer, *The Incidence of the Terror during the French Revolution: A Statistical Interpretation* (Cambridge, Mass., 1935).

Robert R. Palmer, "The French Jesuits in the Age of Enlightenment," *AHR*, 45 (1938): 44–58.

D. Hypothesis

❡ 141 A hypothesis is a "provisional or tentative explanation," or "a supposition made with evidence recognized as insufficient, in order to account for some fact or law known to be real."—Joyce, *Logic*, 354.

An intelligent use of hypothesis conditions all progress in scientific research. As a rule it is only by thinking out various likely explanations of a phenomenon, by testing them one after the other, and rejecting such as are unsatisfactory, that the true explanation is finally brought to light. This is the course pursued by the physicist and other specialists in the natural sciences; it is a necessary procedure in the social sciences as well. Historical hypothesis may be applied not merely to the data supplied from sources, but to the sources themselves in the whole range of problems which they present, such as authorship, textual integrity, interpretation, trustworthiness. A favorite field for its exercise is found in the highly complex causes of the major events and movements of history.

> But technical equipment alone does not make a historian. If this is his sole qualification, he is destined to remain a mere hodman, performing only the most menial offices. Theoretical training alone makes the true historian. No theory—no history. Theory is the prerequisite to any scientific writing of history.—Werner Sombart, "Economic Theory and Economic History," *Economic History Review*, 2 (1929): 3.

Two kinds of hypothesis can be distinguished: the *explanatory*, the purpose of which is to account for a phenomenon, to ascertain its cause or causes; and the *descriptive*, which aims to supply a framework for the orderly grouping and presentation of data.

❡ 142 THE EXPLANATORY HYPOTHESIS
(a) *Seeking the reasons of things.* Man has never been satisfied in the face of his environment with a merely passive attitude of admiration or wonder; he wants to know the why and the wherefore, he seeks to bring the facts of everyday life together in relationships of cause and effect. This human impulse is rooted in the mind's capacity for knowledge, and in the resulting urge to seek out the reason of things. The plain citizen, noting some untoward happening about the house—a broken lock, the track of an animal, a bit of scorched woodwork—vexes himself in an effort to solve the mystery. The physicist, the historian, feel it incumbent on them to seek behind the veil for the hidden agencies that account for physical or social phenomena. The mental procedure usual in ferreting out the explanation of things is essentially the same, whether

the investigator be the plain citizen, exercised over some trivial occurrence of the day, or the physicist, or the historian. Various possible explanations or hypotheses are thought out, the facts applied, and then cast aside if they fail to square with them; the process is continued until either the true explanation is found or the search for it given up. Kepler framed twelve distinct hypotheses about the satellites of Mars before he hit on the correct one. The mental trait most in service in the handling of hypotheses is intuitive insight. Under its influence one readily makes guesses, sometimes brilliant ones, that turn out to be true. But, apart from any special gift of divination, a plodding industry, a dogged perseverance can accomplish much. There is comfort and no little truth in the view that genius is a capacity for taking infinite pains.

(b) *Dangers of hypothesis.* While there is no progress in scientific research without hypotheses, they contain certain dangers. Chief among these is the tendency often seen in investigators to put the cart before the horse, to reverse the legitimate order of procedure by trying to make the facts fit into the hypothesis instead of to make the hypothesis fit into the facts. The author of an explanatory hypothesis is likely to be partial to his own creation, to see in it more than it really contains, to stretch conclusions beyond the limits set by the evidence. The only corrective of this false attitude is rigorous self-discipline and intellectual honesty. Such moral safeguards will save the investigator from undue attachment to his hypothesis, make him disinterested and objective in applying it to the facts, and ready to abandon it promptly if the facts tell definitely against it.

Discredited hypotheses litter the pathways of all the sciences, history included. Dogging the footsteps of every historian who has a theory, is the temptation to distort the facts in the effort to make them dovetail neatly into the theory. "What historians distrust is really not hypotheses that invite investigation—fluid hypotheses, if one may use the term—but fixed theories that control investigation. The literature of history is strewn with examples of such ruling theories."—A. Johnson, *The Historian and Historical Evidence*, 160.

(c) *Disproved hypotheses.* From the circumstance that a hypothesis is eventually disproved, it does not necessarily follow that it was futile or useless. The net result of even a false theory may be gain, not loss. The Ptolemaic theory, though unproved and recognized as such by the ancients, was a helpful device for systematizing the astronomical knowledge of the day and thereby making it useable. The theory advanced by the foremost student of the Roman catacombs, John Baptist de Rossi, that the Christian communities of the era of persecution were legally recognized *collegia tenuiorum*, finally proved untenable; but it led to discoveries which threw important light on the problem of the catacombs. It is conceivable that in time scholars may reject Turner's hypothesis as inadequate, but in that contingency it would still have rendered distinct service to American historiography by opening up new vistas and points of view, and by stimulating research in fresh and inviting fields.

❡ 143 THE DESCRIPTIVE HYPOTHESIS

The descriptive hypothesis is an assumption, not made to explain a phenomenon, but to serve as a framework or center of reference for scattered data, thereby giving them a coherence and a meaning which otherwise they would not possess. The Ptolemaic theory of the heavens, which served descriptive as well as explanatory purposes, may be cited as an example. Sound descriptive hypotheses, therefore, have a legitimate place, in fact, are often necessary, in the writing of history.

> The general thesis which underlies this whole series of lectures is the thesis that all the varied activities of men in the same country and period have intimate relations with each other, and that one cannot obtain a satisfactory view of any one of them by considering it apart from the others.—J. Franklin Jameson, *The American Revolution Considered as a Social Movement* (Princeton, 1926), 158.
>
> Facts are like beads; they require a string to hold them together, to connect them. But if there is no string, if there is no unifying idea, then even the most distinguished authorities cannot help producing unsatisfactory work.—Werner Sombart, "Economic Theory and Economic History," *Economic History Review*, 2 (1929): 5.

A *working hypothesis* in history, as in other fields of study, may be either explanatory or descriptive. In either case what is specific about it is its practical character. Avowedly tentative and provisional, a working hypothesis is conceived directly with a view to facilitate and promote research.

❡ 144 FAULTY HYPOTHESIS

Faulty hypothesis frequently has its origin in a mere desire for novelty. An explanation put forward may have no solid ground of probability from the outset. Interpretations of texts often fail to satisfy because the scholar was bent merely on advancing an explanation unheard of before, without taking due account of the historical background that might be supposed to condition it. Further, not a few hypotheses put out by historians have their source in a mistaken identification of historical method with the method of the natural sciences. The aims and technique of the natural sciences are carried over into historical research, while the fact is overlooked that the immediate aim of the latter is not the discovery of general laws, but the knowledge of individual facts or groups of facts. Besides, no account is taken of the circumstance that whereas growth and decay in physical bodies proceeds more or less along uniform lines, in historical phenomena uniformity asserts itself only to a limited degree. The result is that every single phenomenon in history, and every phase of it, must be submitted to separate examination.

In popular and even scientific usage the terms *theory* and *hypothesis* are used indifferently to express the same idea. One may speak with equal propriety of the "frontier theory" and the "frontier hypothesis." But it has been pointed out that hypothesis connotes rather the idea of an unproved proposition, while theory can be used of a demonstrated truth, for example, the Copernican theory. The "theory of evolution" and "the evolutionary hypothesis" may suggest opposite attitudes towards the same scientific concept.

¶ 145 The use of historical hypothesis

(a) Never frame a hypothesis, at least with a view to serious support of it in print, without previous thoroughgoing study and analysis of the data on which it is based.

(b) Never frame a hypothesis without at least some supporting grounds of probability; these must be exactly weighed while opposing grounds are to be given due consideration. At the same time, only a slender degree of probability may sometimes justify one in giving tentative support to a theory. Time and the progress of research will determine whether the probability tends to grow in volume and to develop into a certainty.

(c) A hypothesis that runs counter even to a single established fact must be abandoned. But this rule "must not be so strictly interpreted as to signify that the consequences inferred from the proposed hypothesis must so agree with all the facts as to leave no perplexities."—Joyce, *Logic*, 360.

(d) Applying several distinct hypotheses to the same problem at the same time is to be avoided. To do so dissipates one's working powers and leads to confusion.

(e) What is only a hypothesis must not be allowed to appear in a narrative, or in a line of argument, as though it were an established fact. Historians sometimes start out with a hypothesis, present it in the earlier stages of discussion as merely probable, and end by speaking of it as a demonstrated fact. Herbert Thurston speaks of a certain author's "propensity to present as demonstrated facts, speculations which at best can only be regarded as more or less plausible hypotheses."—*The Month,* 162 (1933): 562.

(f) The more complex and many-sided the body of facts dealt with, the more need there is of caution in handling the hypothesis. Circumspection is especially required in the case of hypotheses meant to ascertain unknown effects proceeding from human agency, since a given free cause can produce entirely different effects.

(g) It should be possible to express a hypothesis in terms of a single central and unifying concept to which all the items in the group of facts under examination can be referred.

₡ 146 EXAMPLES OF HYPOTHESIS

(a) The various theories invented by rationalist criticism in its attacks on the authenticity of the Gospels.—William A. Dowd, *Gospel Guide,* 81-83.

The "economic interpretation of history," or "historical determinism," the theory that economic factors alone determine the course of history. In its extreme form it eliminates all spiritual realities, including free will. It is the official philosophy of Soviet Russia. [₡ 353].

Thomas Carlyle's "Great Man Theory" (*Heroes and Hero Worship*), the assumption that universal "history is at bottom the history of the great men who have worked there." Inadequate as a key to history. Great men are the creatures as well as the creators of their times.

William M. McDougall in *The Group Mind* (2d ed., New York, 1928), 306 ff., reviews various theories devised to account for "English independence," "French sociability," and other racial traits.

It used to be a favorite view of the anthropologists that the cultural development of primitive peoples proceeded in all cases by precisely the same stages, being mostly, so it was maintained, a uniform process of growth from within, in obedience to rigorously-operating laws of evolution. Today, a widely accepted view is that such development is largely a process of borrowings from without.—See Christopher H. Dawson, *Progress and Religion,* 49-52 [₡ 74].

Henry Adam's theory that the physical law of the dissipation of energy (second law of thermodynamics) is also the controlling law of history. A piece of nebulous and baseless theorizing, like most of Adams' speculations on the philosophy of history [₡ 138-d].—See *The Degradation of the Democratic Dogma,* 140 ff.

Max Müller, the Anglo-German orientalist, attempted to explain the origin of Greek religious myths by the principles of comparative philology. Thus, Athene signifies "dawn," as indicated by the alleged connection of this proper name with the Sanscrit for "dawn." Hence, everything predicated of the Greek goddess was originally predicated of the "dawn." An interesting theory, but groundless.—See Albert Muntsch, *Cultural Anthropology*, 201-202.

(b) The first recorded imperial edict directed against the Christians was that of Decius, A.D. 250. Various theories to account for the legal basis of proceedings against the Christians prior to this date have been advanced. Such basis has been held to be: common statute law including the laws of lèse-majesté, sacrilege, etc.; the ordinary police power of the state, *jus coercitionis* (Mommsen); customary law; some unrecorded formal edict of the tenor "*Christiani non sint.*"—Paul Allard, *Ten Lectures on the Martyrs*, trans. by Luigi Cappadelta (New York, 1907), 82.

Hypotheses in explanation of the fall of the Roman Empire run the whole gamut of conjecture, from that of Gibbon on the refusal of the Roman soldiers to wear armor, to moral corruption, over-taxation, overpopulation, disintegration of the Roman army through its being staffed with barbarian officers (John B. Bury), soil exhaustion, "climatic pulsations" (Ellsworth Huntington). At the 1932 meeting of the British Association for the Advancement of Science, a speaker hazarded the conclusion that "nobody knows anything about it," which is probably not far from the truth. At all events, not a single cause, but many working concurrently must have brought about the great collapse. Theories in explanation of it are reviewed in Michael I. Rostovtsev, *Social and Economic History of the Roman Empire* (Oxford, 1926). See also idem, "The Decay of the Ancient World and its Economic Explanation," *Economic History Review*, 2 (1930): 197-214. The speculations thus multiplying around the breakdown of one of the world's famous empires, furnish copious material for a study of the subject of historical hypothesis in all its aspects.

(c) Theories concerning the origin of the French commune and the English borough are discussed by Carl Stephenson in *AHR*, 37 (1932): 451 ff.

As regards the Pragmatic Sanction of Bourges, De Smedt, *Principes*, 259 ff., concludes that it was never issued under authority of Saint Louis, but bears nevertheless all the marks of a document contemporary with him, and is therefore not a fabrication of a later period. To account for its origin De Smedt offers the explanation that it was actually presented to St. Louis for approval, was rejected by him as prejudicial to the Holy See, and then remained buried in some archive, whence it was brought to light several generations later, in order to support the Gallican pretensions of the French episcopate and court.

The controversy between the French and the German-English schools of historians over institutional origins in Western Europe, the one stressing Roman, the other Germanic influences. Various hypotheses are reviewed by Paul G. Vinogradoff, *Villainage in England: Essays in English Medieval History* (Oxford, 1927), introduction. See also Herbert Thurston, "Celt, Roman and Teuton," *The Month*, 146 (1925): 20-35.

Seven theories on the origin of the medieval town are listed in James W. Thompson, *Economic and Social History of the Middle Ages* (New York, 1928), 765 ff. See also Henri Pirenne, *Medieval Cities: Their Origin and the Revival of Trade* (Princeton, 1925).

Theories as to the significance of Charlemagne's coronation by Pope Leo III, A.D. 800, are mainly two: a translation of the empire from East to West (St. Robert Bellarmine and other authors); a restoration of the western Roman Empire, the emperor to be the "advocate" or official protector of the papacy and the Church [(329-b].

(d) Frederick J. Turner's frontier hypothesis is formulated as follows: "The existence of free land in the West explains American history." This is challenged on various grounds; but, according to Frederick L. Paxson, "no major historian has ever called it into question." Turner's paper in which he announced the hypothesis at the Chicago (1893) meeting of the American Historical Association is republished in his volume, *The Frontier in American History* (New York, 1920).

Estimates of the theory and its influence

F. L. Paxson, "A Generation of the Frontier Hypothesis, 1893–1932." *Pacific Historical Review*, 2 (1933): 34 ff.

John C. Almack, "The Shibboleth of the Frontier," *Historical Outlook*, 16 (1925): 197 ff.

Dixon R. Fox, ed., *Sources of Culture in the Middle West, Backgrounds Versus Culture* (New York, 1934).

Murray Kane, "Some Considerations on the Frontier Concept of Frederick Jackson Turner," *MVHR*, 27 (1940): 379–400.

Gilbert J. Garraghan, "Non-economic Factors in the Frontier Movement," *MA*, 23 (1941): 263–71.

"His [Turner's] thesis made a greater impression upon the teaching and writing of American history than any other single idea and it put the West permanently on the map" (Frank H. Hodder).

For bibliography of the frontier influence in American history, see Ina Faye Woestemeyer and J. Montgomery Gambrill, eds., *The Westward Movement: A Book of Readings on Our Changing Frontiers* (New York, 1939), 478 ff.; Everett E. Edwards, *References on the Significance of the Frontier in American History* (United States Department of Agriculture, Bibliographical Contribution, No. 25, 2d ed., Washington, 1939).

For an application of the frontier hypothesis to German eastward expansion during the Middle Ages, see *AHR*, 18 (1913): 494 ff.

Cognate to Turner's frontier theory is the safety valve doctrine, according to which free land in the West relieved the East in times of depression and panic by affording an outlet for unemployed labor. See Murray Kane, "Some Considerations on the Safety Valve Doctrine," *MVHR*, 23 (1936): 169 ff.

(e) Frederick J. Turner, *The Significance of the Sections in American History* (New York, 1932). New, suggestive viewpoints.

Walter P. Webb, in *The Great Plains* (New York, 1931), maintains that the opening up and economic exploitation of the Plains Region of the United States was conditioned by a new "technique of settlement," based on certain mechanical inventions, such as barbed wire, the six-shooter, the water mill. An original and noteworthy hypothesis.

The radical Reconstruction policy was abandoned by the North as being less profitable for northern business interests in the South than a policy of conciliation—an economic theory of Reconstruction. See William B. Hesseltine in *MVHR*, 22 (1935): 191–210.

E. Conjecture

₡ 147 Conjecture does not greatly differ from hypothesis. Both terms are often used as synonyms in every day speech, technically, however, they differ in meaning. Conjecture generally regards individual facts or phenomena, while hypothesis, being of wider range and significance, deals typically with bodies of facts, general situations. Historical conjecture may assume three forms.

(a) *Conjectural emendation*, or the restoration of lost or corrupted words, or shorter passages, in texts. This is a process often productive of valuable results in textual criticism, whether of literary or historical material. Critical editions of the classical and medieval historians furnish numerous instances of readings based on conjecture. Yet the device is not without its dangers and in the hands of the uncritical has been responsible for a large output of fanciful and arbitrary emendations [₡ 219].

(b) *Conjectural restoration of longer passages or entire documents* [₡ 203].

(c) *Conjectural detail*. Even scientific historians, but more especially biographers, often amplify the meagerness of their sources with conjectural detail. It is especially to fill out a picture or supply defective background that the device is employed. Thus, according to Constant Fouard, *The Christ, the Son of God* (2 vols., New York, 1902), 2:59, the words of Christ, "I am the Light of the world, he that followeth me walketh not in darkness," were occasioned by the lighting at the moment, and subsequent extinction of two great candles in the Temple. But the connection between the two data is conjectural only.—Louis C. Fillion, *The Life of Christ: A Historical, Critical and Apologetical Exposition* (3 vols., St. Louis, 1928), 3:57.

Portrayals of persons and events in Mommsen's *History of Rome* are often highly circumstantial. One feels that not all the details were found in the sources; many are merely inferential or conjectural.

¶ 148 USE OF HISTORICAL CONJECTURE

(a) Conjecture of details, situations, and the like, should not be made except on some sound supporting basis of probability. What is merely fanciful or gratuitous should be avoided.

(b) If the conjectured detail is at least likely, it may find place in the narrative. But the reader must be made aware that the detail is a conjecture and nothing more. To leave him under the impression that it is established fact, is not sound literary ethics. Qualifying terms, such as "perhaps," "probably," "one may suppose," "no doubt," are to be employed. The following will illustrate: "As was his wont, Mr. Jefferson withdrew to his study after breakfast and doubtless ran over the pages of a manuscript which he had been preparing with some care for this Fourth of March. It may be guessed too that here as at Monticello he made his usual observations, noted in his diary the temperature, etc." —Allen Johnson, "Jefferson and his Colleagues," in *Chronicles of America*, (50 vols., New Haven, 1918–1921), 15:20.

Just how Thomas Jefferson filled out the morning of his first inauguration day cannot be ascertained from documents, and so the historian felt that what statements he made on the subject would have to be made with reserve.

Jules Jusserand puts the matter happily when he suggests a parallel between the historian's method of presenting conjectural data and the archaeologist's skeleton map of an ancient wall. Actually-standing sections of the wall are indicated by heavy lines, gaps in the wall, by dotted lines. Similarly, when historical data stand above ground, that is, when they are of certain record, the narrative should make this plain. When they are below ground, that is, where there is doubt or uncertainty regarding them, such gaps in the evidence must be brought in some manner to the reader's notice. If statements of fact and statements of mere probability are jumbled together on one level of apparently unqualified assertion, then the first law of history, which is that it should tell the truth, no more, no less, is obviously flouted, and the barriers between history and historical fiction are broken down.

Homer C. Hockett, "The Literary Motive in Writing History," *MVHR*, 12 (1926): 478–482, protests against "mere conjecture" in history.

For an example of studied caution and reserve in historical statement, see George Saintsbury's sketch of Shakespeare. "No biography of Shakespeare, therefore, which deserves any confidence has ever been constructed without a large infusion of the tell-tale words, 'apparently,' 'probably,' 'there can be little doubt,' and no small infusion of the still more tell-tale 'perhaps,' 'it would be natural,' 'according to what was usual at the time,' and so forth."—*Cambridge History of English Literature*, 5:187 f.

F. The Argument from Silence

¶ 149 The argument from silence aims to prove the non-reality of an alleged fact from the circumstance that contemporary or later sources of information fail to say anything about it. It is sometimes misleadingly called the negative argument; but this can easily be taken to mean something false, namely, that the argument rests on an explicit denial of some fact. A writer's silence regarding a fact may be because of ignorance, or by deliberate omission, or from lapse of memory.

(a) To be valid, the argument from silence must fulfil two conditions: the writer whose silence is invoked in proof of the non-reality of an alleged fact, would certainly have known about it had it been a fact; knowing it, he would under the circumstances certainly have made mention of it. When these two conditions are fulfilled, the argument from silence proves its point with moral certainty. Both conditions have their explanation in the human instincts which urge us to ascertain the truth, as also to give expression to it when self-interest so requires.

(b) In applying the argument from silence, the first step is to determine by rigorous analysis of the evidence whether or not the conditions laid down really exist. The first condition presupposes that the alleged fact was of some importance, was easily knowable, and would certainly have come directly or indirectly to the notice of the informant whose silence regarding it is under examination. The second condition presupposes that suppression of the fact would have been prejudicial to the informant by compromising his reputation for honor, justice, patriotism, learning; by injuring his family, political party, religious denomination; or by giving comfort and aid to his enemies.

¶ 150 Uses of the argument from silence

The argument from silence may serve two ends: it may establish the non-reality of a supposed fact when all contemporary or quasi-contemporary sources fail to record it; or it may prove the untrustworthiness of a witness who testifies to a supposed fact when other contemporary or quasi-contemporary witnesses are silent about it. In such cases the silence of even one important witness may be tantamount to proof.

(a) *Non-reality of an alleged fact.* The Latin word *adorare* is found in common use among writers from Vergil and Livy forward; it is not found in earlier writers: Plautus, Varro, Cicero, who use other words in its place (*venerari, colere*). One may argue validly: the earlier writers would have used *adorare* had it found a place in the current vocabulary; hence, it had no place in that vocabulary.

Lyons (*Lugdunum*) is not mentioned by Caesar, hence one may infer that at the time he was in Gaul, it had not yet been founded, at least as a settlement bearing a name.

The list of the bishops of Lyons begins with Pothinus (second century); hence, one may conclude that Lyons was not organized as a diocese before his time.

(b) *Untrustworthiness of a witness* (or source). In the so-called Chronicle of Turpin (*Historia de vita Caroli Magni et Rolandi*) exploits are ascribed to Charlemagne of which the first men of the empire, his courtiers in particular, were said to be witnesses. Einhard, Charlemagne's contemporary biographer, is silent concerning these exploits. In view of Einhard's exceptional authority, Turpin's account may be rejected as untrustworthy.

¶ 151 CAUTIONS IN THE USE OF THE ARGUMENT FROM SILENCE
In using the argument from silence two cautions are recommended.

(a) In our modern age with its immense facilities for the communication of news, an event of importance no sooner happens than it becomes known far and wide, among all classes of people. But such was not the case in earlier times. Because of poor means of communication, events of major interest and importance could remain unknown for long periods of time, even to persons in high position, even though they could command all existing sources of information on current happenings. Instances in point, so astonishing that one would scarcely credit them if they were not attested by unimpeachable evidence, are on record.

(b) Present-day standards in the selection of data for historical record often differ from those which obtained among the ancient and medieval authors. They had their own ideas as to what was important and unimportant, and hence could easily pass over in silence incidents or facts which might appear to us in every way deserving of record.

> Many incidents may be adduced of the most extraordinary silence of historians relative to facts with which they must have been acquainted and which seemed to lie directly in the course of their narrative. Important facts are mentioned by no ancient writer though they are unquestionably established by the evidence of existing inscriptions, coins, statues or buildings.—Isaac Taylor, *The Transmission of Ancient Books to Modern Times together with the Process of Historical Proof* (Liverpool, 1875), 120.

¶ 152 St. Augustine knew (ca. 405) nothing of the great orthodox Synod of Sardica, ca. 343–344, though he was aware of the parallel Arian Council held at that same time, and later in the neighboring Philipopolis.

He was also uninformed as to the great controversial writings of St. Athanasius and St. Hilary, which make frequent mention of the same Synod of Sardica. Again, when St. Augustine was consecrated bishop, neither he nor the aged Bishop of Carthage, Valerian, was aware of the eighth canon of the Council of Nice, which forbade that two bishops have their sees simultaneously in the same city.—Feder, Lehrbuch, 284 f.

Josephus makes no mention of the massacre of the infants in Bethlehem. Either he never heard of the incident, or if he did, he probably thought the massacre of a few infants too minor an incident in the criminal career of Herod to deserve record.—Constant Fouard, *The Christ, the Son of God,* 1:72.

Numerous long-standing problems bearing on legends, traditions, and the authorship or authenticity of writings have been satisfactorily solved by critical use of the argument from silence. On the other hand, attempts to apply it in certain cases have been unsuccessful.

❡ 153   VALID USE OF THE ARGUMENT FROM SILENCE

The alleged existence of the Popess Joan is disproved mainly from the silence of contemporary sources about her.—See *CE,* 8:407.

The Donation of Constantine, and other documents constituting the so-called False Decretals, are shown to be spurious from the absence of any reference to them for centuries following their supposed dates of production.—John Morris, ed., *Historical Papers* (5 vols., London, 1897–1904), 1:25–44.

The writings attributed to Denis the Areopagite, St. Paul's disciple, could not have been written by him, because, among other reasons, they were unknown to the Fathers of the Church and other early Christian writers.—See "Dionysius the Pseudo-Areopagite," *CE,* 5:13–18 [❡ 173-a].

The "Pragmatic Sanction of St. Louis," cited by the Council of Bourges (1438) cannot be authentic in view of the circumstances that had it really existed in the time of Philip the Fair and of later French kings, they would have appealed to it in their attacks on the Holy See.—De Smedt, *Principes,* 259 ff.

This case and that of the medieval *Chronicle of Turpin* [❡ 150-b] are especially instanced by De Smedt as legitimate uses of the argument from silence.

Villani, a contemporary writer, asserts that the English used cannon at Crécy (1346), while Froissart and Baker of Swinbrook, also contemporaries, make no mention of cannon in their accounts of the battle. Hereford B. George argues that Villani must have been misinformed and that the argument from silence should prevail. He appeals to the principle that the force of such argument is not necessarily destroyed by a documentary statement in the opposite sense.—See *Historical Evidence,* 175.

Hartmann Grisar, *Martin Luther: His Life and Work* (St. Louis, 1930),

578, rejects the story that Luther when dying chalked on a wall the celebrated verse, "Pestis eram vivens, moriens ero mors tua, papa." Ratzeberger is the only author to mention the incident. Says Grisar: "The silence of the other sources, particularly that of the panegyrics . . . render Ratzeberger's account rather incredible."

Edward G. Bourne, "The Legend of Marcus Whitman," *Essays in Historical Criticism,* 3–109; and William I. Marshall, *The Acquisition of Oregon and the Long Suppressed Evidence about Marcus Whitman* (2 vols., Seattle, 1911), make effective use of the proof from silence in their destructive analysis of the "Whitman-saved-Oregon" story.

¶ 154 INVALID USE OF THE ARGUMENT FROM SILENCE

Biblical references to the Hittites used to be impugned on the ground that no mention of this people is to be found in the Greek and Roman authors. But modern archaeological research has placed their historicity beyond doubt.—See Archibald H. Sayce, *The Hittites: the Story of a Forgotten Empire* (London, 1925); John Kavanagh, "The Hittite Empire," *The Month,* 160 (1932): 121–29.

Pliny the Elder, though he records with detail many striking physical phenomena of his day, such as the earthquake and shower of stones which occurred at Stabiae, makes no mention of the destruction of Herculaneum and Pompeii, with which events he was contemporary. Tacitus, also a contemporary, says merely that "certain cities were consumed or buried." Suetonius makes no allusion to the two ruined cities. The first historian to refer to them was Dion Cassius, who wrote about a hundred and fifty years after Pliny.

All naturalists who have searched into the memorials of the past for records of physical events must have been surprised at the indifference with which the most memorable occurrences are often passed by in the works of writers of enlightened periods. . . . We have no hesitation in saying that had the buried cities never been discovered, the accounts transmitted to us of their tragical end would have been discredited by the majority, so vague and general are the narrations, so long subsequent to the event.—Charles Lyett, *Principles of Geology* (2 vols., Philadelphia, 1837) 1:30.

That St. Gregory the Great wrote no hymns used to be maintained on the ground that none are ascribed to him by any author down to the sixteenth century; but "after long debate, the question whether or not he was the author of any hymns seems now to have been definitely settled in his favor."—Otto J. Kuhnmuench, *Early Christian Latin Poets from the Fourth to the Sixth Century* (Chicago, 1929), 133.

Spinoza's friend, Oldenburg, who was in London during the great plague of 1665, when ten thousand victims perished in a week, has only a casual reference to the calamity.—See John Rickaby, *First Principles of Knowledge* (4th ed., New York, 1901), 386.

Reuben Parsons, *Some Errors and Lies of History* (South Bend, Ind., 1893), argues plausibly from the absence of any mention of the incident in contemporary accounts that the friar, Giordano Bruno, was never actually burned at the stake, as has been generally believed; but in an appendix in the same volume he states that evidence coming to light after the account in the text was written, places the historicity of his death at the stake beyond question.

Thorold Rogers, on the basis of the absence of salt from the records of price-quotations, denied that this commodity was mined in medieval Cheshire. Research later proved that this district actually had its salt products.— *American Economic Review*, 20 (1930): 5, note 1.

The silence of Wyclif and his contemporaries regarding his putative translation of the Bible has been urged as an argument against its existence. —See Francis A. Gasquet, "The Pre-Reformation English Bible," in *The Old English Bible*, (London, 1908), 97.

The silence of contemporaries bearing on the question of the authenticity of Mirabeau's reply to Dreux-Brézé, on June 23, 1789, is discussed in Fred M. Fling, *The Writing of History, An Introduction to Historical Method* (New Haven, 1920), 123.

To sum up, the argument from silence is an invaluable logical tool for the historian; but to be such it must be used with due caution and reserve. There is certainly no reason for calling this species of reasoning "heretical."—*MVHR*, 25 (1939): 611.

G. The Argument a priori

¶ 155 The argument a priori is based on antecedent probability or improbability. Direct evidence may be lacking that a man is guilty of a crime imputed to him; but his known character, antecedents, habits, make it likely or unlikely that he is guilty. Here the reasoning concerns facts or circumstances prior in time to the occurrence of the event in question. A priori reasoning of this kind can be legitimately applied to historical sources and data. Thus, one may argue on a priori grounds that it is unlikely that Mary Stuart wrote the Casket Letters, or Thomas a Kempis the *Imitation of Christ*, or George Washington his alleged letter of 1781, in which he repudiates the revolutionary cause. In like manner, from what we know of the loyalty of Louis IX to the Holy See, it is improbable that he sponsored the anti-papal document known as the Pragmatic Sanction of Bourges, which has been attributed to him.

On the other hand, in view of Aaron Burr's character and antecedents, one might wish to argue that when in 1806 he went down the Ohio with his sixty men, he really had it in mind to attempt to detach the West from the Union. This is an interpretation, however, which most present-day historians are not disposed to accept. Finally, to cite an instance from literary criticism, anyone who has read the doggerel verse known to have been written by Francis Bacon will conclude to the antecedent improbability that he could have written the plays attributed to Shakespeare.

A priori reasoning, as other processes of logic, can be abused in history, and so can issue in error, not in truth. Everything depends on the actual degree of antecedent probability or improbability that obtains. If this be slender, then an inference a priori can never have more than a slender degree of probability. If it be considerable, the inference rises to a proportionate level of assurance. Wherever the historian has to reason on his sources, only clear thinking and sound judgment will enable him to keep the proper balance between the evidence at hand and the deductions he makes from it.

Chapter Eight

THE AUTHENTICITY OF SOURCES

A. The Genuine and the False: Forgery . . . . . Page 169
B. The Criteria of Authenticity 174
C. Errors in Questions of Authenticity 190
D. Dating Sources 194
E. Localizing Sources 201
F. The Determination of Authorship 203

¶ 156 Heuristic, or the finding of sources, the initial step in the mechanical processes of the historian, is followed by criticism (κρίσις, judgment), which is appraisement of the nature and evidential value of the source material found. This is a complex process involving, at least in theory, six distinct inquiries or problems, for each and every source put to account.

(a) When was the source, written or unwritten, produced (date)?
(b) Where was it produced (localization)?
(c) By whom was it produced (authorship)?
(d) From what pre-existing material was it produced (analysis)?
(e) In what original form was it produced (integrity)?
(f) What is the evidential value of its contents (credibility)?

In practice this last query will resolve itself into an attempt to fix the degree of certainty or probability (falsity or doubt) to be attached to the several statements which the source contains.

These six distinct inquiries exhaust the whole process of historical criticism, which may be defined as *the use or application of a body of rules and principles for testing the genuineness of historical sources, restoring them as far as possible to their original form, and determining their evidential value.*

¶ 157 By a convention first introduced by Bernheim, the steps a to e are known collectively as *external criticism*, while step f designates *internal criticism*. Moreover, a to d are generally grouped together as constituting *higher criticism*, the term *lower* or *textual criticism* being applied to e. Unfortunately, higher criticism, though a legitimate instrument of historical research, has taken on a sinister connotation, owing to the use made of it in nineteenth-century rationalistic attacks on the Bible, most of which were concerned with questions of date, authorship, and derivation of content.—Hugh Pope, *The Catholic Student's Aids to the Study of the Bible* (5 vols., 2d ed. rev., London, 1922–1937), 3:282–94.

Having for its purpose the inquiry into the origin or provenance of sources, higher criticism investigates first, their genuineness or authenticity, namely, their date, place of composition, and authorship; secondly, their derivation and dependence in regard to content.

The three outstanding and most significant points of inquiry in the entire process of the critical examination of sources are *genuineness, integrity* and *credibility*. All three are vital for the historian's purpose. A document may be genuine but not textually intact; it may be genuine and textually intact, and still not be credible as a source of information. Again, to be credible, it must be of proved integrity, at least substantially. If the document fulfils all three conditions, if it is genuine, textually intact, and credible, then its contents (at least in the large) must be accepted as true.

⟨ 158   *Criticism*, external and internal, is to be differentiated from *evidence*, external and internal. *Internal evidence*—that based on such elements as handwriting, style, content—may be used in solving a problem of *external criticism*, such as the authorship of a manuscript. But the two sets of terms are often interchanged with resulting ambiguity. What many, if not most writers have in mind when they speak of internal criticism, is not discussion of a problem of credibility (Bernheim), but the application of internal criteria of evidence to any problem whatsoever of criticism, whether external or internal.

A. The Genuine and the False: Forgery

⟨ 159   When we say that a source is *authentic* or *genuine*, we mean that it has the origin which it pretends to have, that it has for its author the person under whose name it appears and to whom it is commonly ascribed. If it be anonymous, it is at least the work of some unknown author of the period to which it is generally assigned. Hence, criticism of the authenticity of a source has for its object to determine whether or not the reputed origin of the document is the real origin. If the reputed origin is the real origin, the source is *genuine*, or *authentic*; otherwise, the source is *spurious*, or *false* (apocryphal, counterfeit, suppositious). Sources, the authenticity of which is vouched for on probable grounds only, may be described as *doubtful*.

(a) The term *authenticity* is too often used to express two ideas: genuineness and credibility. The usage is deplorable, for it is misleading. Here *authenticity* will be employed to express solely the idea of genuineness, no account at all being taken of the question whether the source is trustworthy or not; such question has place only in the specific problem of credibility. While it may be conceded that a spurious source is also, as a rule, untrustworthy, the fact remains that the truth or falsity of the content of a source is no decisive criterion for determining its authenticity; a demonstrably spurious source can still be reliable throughout. A, writing from firsthand information on current events, may turn out an accurate and trustworthy account of them, though the account may go before the public under the name of B, with a view to securing greater authority for it. B is generally but mistakenly credited with having written the book, which thereby must be described as not authentic but spurious, inasmuch as the reputed author is not the real author.

(b) The assignment of a source to the wrong author may be due to conscious fraud or unconscious error. In either case the falsification may be complete or partial, according as it extends to the entire source or only to a part of it. Partial falsification takes such forms as outright fabrication of one or more passages, serious garbling of a genuine passage, omission of parts of the original text. Omissions are not always to be referred to an intention to deceive. Conscientious copyists of manuscripts have often been puzzled by illegible words, especially proper names and foreign terms, with resulting omission. Had these copyists been conversant with the modern practice, they would have noted the omission in their transcripts by some conventional device or symbol.

¶ 160 INTERPOLATION

Of the various ways of partially garbling a written text the most serious is interpolation. This is the deliberate insertion, generally by a copyist, of extraneous matter into a genuine document for whatever reason, as a rule in order to fill out gaps in the text, or to supplement or correct or interpret the author's words. Interpolation may be done in good faith or in bad faith; the copyist may be led merely by a well-meaning desire to perfect the text, or he may consciously intend to distort or falsify it. Genuine texts have been thus tampered with through party or sectarian interests.——See Frederick W. Hall, *A Companion to Classical Texts* (Oxford, 1913), 100 ff.

From interpolation must be distinguished a few analogous practices affecting textual authenticity.

(a) *Continuations* or *additions by various hands and without fraudulent intent*, as in the case of medieval chronicles. The most important of medieval chronicles, the *Chronica majora* of Matthew Paris, a continuation of Roger of Wendover's chronicle, was itself continued in another chronicle, the *Flores historiarum*, erroneously ascribed to Matthew of Westminster.

(b) *Explanatory, supplementary or emendatory additions or changes made by the author himself.* Criticism of alterations of this nature in a text is beset with special difficulties. Obviously such alterations cannot usually be recognized except with the aid of the author's original manuscript. With only copies to depend on, the problem would seem to be insoluble.

(c) *Glosses* are *interlinear* or *marginal insertions* made by copyists with a view to explain, supplement, or improve the text; they are often subsequently drawn into the text itself so as to become a part of it in later copies. The author of the gloss had no intention of incorporating it into the text. Such incorporation was due in most cases to inadvertence, some later copyist mistakenly taking the gloss to be an integral part of the text. Whether the *Comma Johanninum* is an interpolated gloss or an integral part of the original text is a moot point in biblical criticism.— H. Pope, *The Catholic Student's Aids*, 5:331–36.

⁋ 161 FORGERY

Forgery or counterfeiting may occur in products of any of the arts, but it is notably frequent in the case of historical records. Here, besides the usual incentive to forgery, namely, pecuniary gain, other motives may come into play, such as notoriety-seeking, scholar's vanity, jealousy, party interest, and inordinate religious zeal. The motive of gain is generally the one at work in the fabrication of works of art, inscriptions, and the like. The desire of art fanciers to fill out gaps in their collections is played upon by designing persons, who supply them with spurious objects for genuine. On the other hand, the pursuit of publicity and fame often leads to the faking of literary works, as was notably the case in the Renaissance period. Every period, ancient and modern, has seen falsifications of this nature.

Numerous instances of counterfeiting may be found among the sources classified as oral traditions [⁋ 255]. Such also is the case with many sagas, insofar as their contents purport to go back to ancient times, whereas in reality they belong to a later period or have been appropriated from other sagas and transferred to persons or places to which they do not properly belong. Behind fabrications of this sort are usually such motives as family pride, nationalism, local pretensions, false piety. In the Middle Ages, some countries, and especially some churches and monasteries, sought by such "pious frauds" to throw an air of dignity and importance over their beginnings.

(a) Counterfeit local traditions are not limited to older periods of history.

Earthen fortifications attributed to the [De Soto] expedition begin at the mouth of the Muskingum River at Marietta, Ohio, and as they extend to the southward they increase in number until nearly all the Gulf States are well represented. Indeed, there are so many of them that De Soto with 1,000 able-bodied men could not have constructed them in a century.

Tradition and local pride locate his forges in southern New York, Pennsylvania, Ohio, and many of the States further south; innumerable battlefields and camping places are to be found throughout the region mentioned; relics, numerous and of great variety, are scattered over a wide territory never visited by De Soto or his men.—Theodore H. Lewis, "The Chroniclers of De Soto's Expedition," in Dunbar Rowland, ed., *A Symposium on the Place of Discovery of the Mississippi River by Hernando de Soto* (Jackson, Miss., 1927), 1.

(b) Among forgeries may also be reckoned the so-called "wandering sagas" [ℭ 98-d]. In their peregrinations these have undergone so many changes in content as to be radically transformed. An example is the William Tell story, which is found in various countries: Norway, Denmark, Iceland, England, and the Rhineland. Numerous falsifications are also to be met with in the categories of legend, anecdote, and famous sayings. Fabrication in such cases consists in giving to reports of recent origin, either expressly or by implication, the semblance of a respectable antiquity, or in transferring data from a genuine source to persons, localities, times, not at all identified with the source in question [ℭ 261 f.]

(c) In hagiography the paramount motive of fabrication has been a mania for the marvelous. Sober, well-grounded tradition has not sufficed to satisfy popular belief, which would envelop the lives of the saints in a blaze of the extraordinary. It has looked upon them, particularly the martyrs, as invulnerable; as a result, God had to protect them at all times and from every danger, from fire, wild beasts, the tyrant and the executioner. The persecutors had to pay the penalty of their crimes even on earth; they met with notorious and dire punishment, or else returned to God by a striking conversion. This mania for the marvelous has led popular belief not only to supplement or falsify the content of existing genuine legends, but even to invent entirely new, or fix extraneous legends on favorite saints, or on countries held particularly in honor. Often also, naive national or local vanity, or predilection for a particular patron saint has led to myth-making. Many a person in high repute for holiness has been claimed for a particular land or city, but on no serious grounds of evidence. Thus, Cyprus folk claimed Catherine of Alexandria; the inhabitants of Marseilles, the sisters of Bethania; the people of Paris, Denis the Areopagite.

It is pertinent to note that what is said above does not militate against the reality of the many extraordinary happenings recorded of the saints on unimpeachable evidence, such as the miracles attributed to St. Bernard, which, according to Bernheim [₡ 296], cannot be questioned as objective historical facts. To be noted also is the rigorous criticism employed by the Catholic Church in testing the historicity of the miracles accepted in processes of beatification and canonization. The proper attitude in hagiography, at once reverential and critical, is exemplified in the revision (London, 1925–1938) of Alban Butler's *Lives of the Saints*, by Herbert Thurston and his collaborators. Other instances of studies which achieve a proper adjustment between scholarship and piety are: Brodrick, *Robert Bellarmine* (1928); Battifol, *St. Gregory the Great* (1929); Concannon, *St. Patrick* (1931); McCann, *St. Benedict* (1937).

(d) *Counterfeit oral tradition*

Sagas: numerous tales of the Romans from the Trojans; the founding of the "city of the seven hills" (Rome); the Roman kings; Arnold von Winkelried; the burning of Magdeburg.

Wandering sagas: William Tell; tales about the medieval German emperors.

Etiological sagas: the mouse tower of Bingen; Mount Pilatus at Lucerne; St. Crispinus; the seven cities of Cíbola; Ponce de León's fountain of perpetual youth.

Hagiographical legends: the martyrs Procopius of Caesarea, and George, as officers or knights; pretended founding of certain churches immediately by the Apostles or disciples of the Apostles—thus Marseilles by Lazarus, Paris by Denis the Areopagite, Cologne by Maternus; legends about the historically accredited martyr, St. Christopher.

Anecdotes: Many about Pythagoras, Caesar, Napoleon; Columbus' egg; Charles V and Anthony Fugger at Augsburg; the end of Don Carlos.

Famous sayings: *Noli turbare circulos meos* (Archimedes); *Alea jacta est* (Caesar); *Credo quia absurdum* (Tertullian); *In necessariis unitas, in dubiis libertas, in omnibus autem caritas* (St. Augustine); *Virtutes paganorum splendida vitia* (St. Augustine); *E pur si muove* (Galileo); *Moriamur pro rege nostro* (Diet of Pressburg); *La garde meurt et ne se rend pas* (Cambronne); *L'état c'est moi* (Louis XIV).

On the historicity of some famous sayings, see [ℭ 261-a]. For examples of counterfeit or spurious documents, [ℭ 173-a].

B. The Criteria of Authenticity

Criteria for determining the authenticity of documents fall into two main groups, external and internal.

External Criteria

ℭ 162 *A manuscript or printed work should be attributed to the author whose name it bears unless there are reasons to the contrary.* As applied to works produced before the use of printing, the criterion may take this form: As a rule, a work should be attributed to the author whose name appears in the title, subscription, or other similar part of genuine early manuscript copies of the work in question. We say, as a rule, for the principle needs qualification. Writings have come out under false names, or if originally anonymous, have had false names attached to them later. Moreover, it is to be borne in mind that authors' names appearing in very early manuscripts were not put there by the authors themselves. This was done at a later period by copyists or revisers. More specific directions follow.

(a) If a work appears under the name of a living author, it may safely be taken to be his. If the attribution were false, he would, unless in very exceptional circumstances, repudiate it, or, on the supposition that he had fraudulently put out someone else's composition as his own, protest would be made by the true author or by someone else.

(b) In the case of an author not long deceased, the question of the authenticity of a work attributed to him may frequently be disposed of with ease.

(1) If the work was published in the lifetime of the reputed author, the criterion indicated in (a) may be applied.

(2) For the case where a work has not been published, though the original manuscript of it together with other admittedly genuine manuscripts of the same author, are available for comparison, see ℭ 165.

(3) It may happen that it is impossible to compare the original manuscript with other extant manuscripts of the same author, or that the work has not come down to us in the original manuscript, but only in one or more copies. In these circumstances, a work may ordinarily be accepted as genuine if the deceased author in a letter, memorandum, or any other authentic writing from his pen, claims the work as his own, or if some reliable contemporary or quasi-contemporary authority assigns the work to the author in question (*extrinsic testimony*).

(c) The aforementioned principles are also to be applied to written works of remote date which bear a definite name. Here we must be sure, through unmistakable references made by the author himself or other trustworthy contemporary authorities, that we have the genuine original work and not a forgery substituted in its place. Genuine writings have often been lost, and spurious works carrying the same titles were made later, to replace them. This is the case with certain pretended works of Justin the Martyr. The originals disappeared, but fabrications under the same titles have come down to us.—Eusebius, *Ecclesiastical History*, IV, 18, 3–4. Yet, on the other hand, a reference in a letter of Pliny the Younger (IX, 10, 2) to the dialogue *De oratoribus* (IX, 26) as a work of Tacitus, is sometimes accepted as evidence that the latter wrote it.—Alfred Gudeman, ed., *Tacitus De Oratoribus* (Boston, 1898), vi). Another reference in Pliny the Younger (*Letters*, III, 5) to the writings of his uncle, the elder Pliny, is taken to settle the question of their authenticity. So too, St. Augustine in his *Rectractationes* lists the bulk of his earlier works (ninety-three in all) according to date, occasion, purpose, idea and method of composition.

(d) Evidence of genuineness based on the original manuscript is almost paralleled in weight by evidence based on agreement in a series of mutually independent manuscript copies. Such agreement is explicable only on the ground that the copies are all derived from the original, or from some nearly contemporary copy, and that the alleged authorship was denied neither by the reputed author nor by any of his contemporaries.

Manuscript copies of the Bible, or parts of it, in various languages, are extant in great numbers. The earliest of these, such as the Greek codices *Sinaiticus* and *Vaticanus*, and the Latin *Codex Vercellensis*, date from the fourth century. Of manuscript copies of the Greek New Testament, some ten belong to the fifth century, and more than two hundred to the period from the sixth to the tenth centuries, while the total number of manuscripts of the Greek New Testament in its entirety or in part is nearly four thousand. It may be affirmed without exaggeration that the New Testament writings enjoy a degree of extrinsic certification without parallel in the case of the non-Christian writings of classical antiquity. Vergil's record as regards manuscript transmission is next to the Bible's; various copies of his works from the fourth and numerous copies from the following centuries are extant. How comparatively recent is manuscript evidence for many of the classical texts is seen in the cases of Herodotus (ca. 425 B.C.) and Thucydides (ca. 396 B.C.). The oldest manuscripts of Herodotus date from the eleventh century, the oldest of Thucydides from the tenth.

(e) The criterion of extrinsic testimony to authorship from contemporary or nearly contemporary witnesses is the more convincing the more numerous and independent are the witnesses that can be cited for the alleged author. It grows in probative value the more the witnesses are differentiated by nationality and habitat, the shorter the interval between the date of the work and the date of the testimony, the greater the interest which the witnesses, in view of the nature or importance of the matters reported, may have had in exposing immediately any fraud that was possibly perpetrated. Again, the testimony gains in weight if it comes from witnesses who are of another school, or of another party than the author's, who do not stand at too great an interval from the period of the work in question, and who in case of attempted fraud would not have failed to challenge the pretended authorship.

(1) These principles may be illustrated in the case of the four Gospels. Witnesses from various Christian communities may be cited to prove that by the middle of the second century their authenticity was recognized on all hands. The witnesses include not only second century Catholic writers, like Papias, for Hieropolis in Asia Minor; Justin the Martyr for Palestine and Rome; his disciple Tatian (ca. 172) a schismatic, for Syria; Irenaeus for Lyons; Pantanaeus and Clement for Alexandria; Tertullian (schismatic after 200) for Carthage; but also heretical writers who did not venture to call the apostolic origin of the Gospels into question, though they interpreted them in their own favor. Such, for example, were Basilides, Valentinus, and their disciples Heraclion and Marcion, all of the second century. Also to be regarded as witnesses are pagan adversaries, such as Celsus (second century) and Porphyry (third century), who sharply attacked the content of the Gospels, but in no wise impugned their authenticity.—See William A. Dowd, *The Gospel Guide: A Practical Introduction to the Gospels* (Milwaukee, 1932), 71–77.

(2) How great must have been the interest of the first Christians in preserving the sacred books intact, may be inferred from the fact that they contain the very foundations of Christianity. Their genuineness must have meant as much to the Christians as the truth of Christianity itself. Further, it was the easier for them to detect any adulteration that may have occurred, since many of them were contemporaries of the evangelists, and the books, in view of their widespread diffusion by the middle of the second century, were found in numerous hands. Moreover, that the first Christians guarded the genuine books of Christian revelation with exceeding circumspection and care, appears from their rejection and prevention of circulation of apocryphal writings, and even from the occasional challenge to many writings which later met with general acceptance.

Among writers of the classical age a simple case of extrinsic testimony to authorship is furnished by the *Anabasis*. Both Plutarch and Diogenes Laertius state explicitly that it was written by Xenophon.

¶ 163 A work is not to be attributed to a given author if it has been attributed to someone else by undoubtedly trustworthy authorities.

¶ 164 When extrinsic testimonies contradict one another, the degree of reliability to be attached to each must be accurately gauged, and the various degrees weighed one against the other.

If more recent manuscripts bear an author's name different from the name appearing in older manuscripts, the testimony of the more recent, provided they are seen to be merely derivatives of the older, is to be ignored. But if the later manuscripts show an independent transmission, the relative value of the two transmissions must be assessed and the conflicting claims to authorship rated accordingly.

Often great caution is required in the application of external criteria. Thus, there are documents which are spurious in a juridical, but not in a technical sense. An instance is that of medieval papers which bear a definite date, while external mechanical features point with certainty to a later date of production. These papers were fabricated with a view to establish anew the title to possession already legally held. Owing to theft or to the ravages of fire or war, it was a common occurrence in the Middle Ages that the archives of monasteries, churches, or towns, with their papal bulls, royal diplomas, charters, and other documents, perished utterly. After order was restored, the survivors were at pains to provide new legal papers to safeguard their property rights or privileges. Either from memory, or perhaps from some surviving copy, the text of the old record was drawn up anew by some public notary or other official, was furnished with the seal of a prince, a bishop, or other powerful lord of the neighborhood, and then deposited in the archives as a perfectly valid instrument.

Internal Criteria

¶ 165 *A work is probably to be attributed to a given author if it resembles other admittedly genuine works of his in internal form.* In this rule the word *internal* refers to the content, so that internal form covers such features as formalities, diction, style, versification, handwriting, and art-form in products of the industrial and fine arts.

(a) *Formalities.* In every age and country certain more or less uniform characteristics have marked the mechanics of literary composition in its various ways of writing a letter, of organizing books (as by sections, chapters, and paragraphs), of drawing up writs, charters, wills, and other legal papers. In the Middle Ages the various European chanceries, ecclesiastical and civil, had their respective individual styles, which they regularly adhered to in drafting official papers. By noting formalities observed in the matter of date, invocation, name and title of writer or granter, salutation, introduction, conclusion, subscription, and sealing, many problems of authenticity of medieval documents may be solved.

(b) *Language.* This is subject to development in which such elements as vocabulary, syntax, sentence-form, undergo change from one age to another. Livy's first-century Latin is not the same as Einhard's ninth-century Latin, any more than Chaucer's fourteenth-century English is the same as Tennyson's nineteenth-century English. Various recognized features of a given language in its various stages of growth are so many clues to the historian, enabling him to fix at least in some rough way the age of documents before him. Chatterton knew that he could not win acceptance of his poems as fifteenth-century products unless he dressed them out in fifteenth-century diction.

Application of the test of language requires special caution. The *Medieval Latin Word-list from British and Irish Sources*, appearing under the auspices of the British Academy, gives 735 for the earliest occurrence of *forinsecus*. But St. Augustine had used the word three centuries before. Hence, one may not argue that a manuscript containing *forinsecus* cannot be of earlier date than 735. Dictionaries that trace the usage of words historically can be consulted when there is question of the language test. Thus, *The Shorter Oxford English Dictionary* (1933) gives the following dates for the first recorded appearance of the words: elective (1530); loyal (1531); braggadocio (1590); hobnob (1601); heterodox (1619); imbroglio (1750) [₵ 75].

For examples in French, see Leon E. Kastner and Joseph Marks, *A Glossary of Colloquial and Popular French* (London, 1929). Thus grognard (literally *grumbler,* or *growler*) was a name given to Napoleon's soldiers of the Old Guard, and by extension to an old soldier or veteran in general. *Poilu* for a French soldier, with connotation of bravery and strength, dates only from the first World War.

Americanisms are treated from the historical angle in Sir William A. Craigie and James R. Hulbert, *A Dictionary of American English on Historical Principles* (4 vols., Chicago, 1938–1944). See also, Henry L. Mencken, *The American Language* (4th ed., 8th corrected printing, New York, 1936); *Supplement I, The American Language* (New York, 1945).

(c) *Diction and style.* That style is something intimately personal, and as such serves to identify an author is a commonplace of literary criticism. *Le style est l'homme même.* Characteristics of style or even of diction alone often enable one to assign an anonymous literary or historical composition to a definite author. But that this criterion has limitations, see ₵ 170 f.

¶ 165   *Chapter 8*   179

(*1*) Tacitus' mannerisms of style and diction individualize his writing and make its identification relatively easy. He indulges in ellipses and other peculiarities of construction. He affects certain sonorous words, such as *primores* and *qua tempestate*, in place of *primi* and *quo tempore*; frequentatives, such as *ostentare, clamitare, imperitare*; intensive verbs formed with the prefix *per*, such as *perdomare, pervigere, permunire, perstimulare*.

Apart from tradition and other indications, characteristics of style prove the Acts and the third Gospel to be from the same hand. Certain expressions common to both authors are not found in other authors. Thirty-three words occur in the Acts and third Gospel, and not elsewhere.

The word ὁμοούσιος occurring in an official document justifies the conclusion that it is later than the Council of Nice (325).

Unus Dominus dates a writing after the Third Ecumenical Council (Ephesus, 431); enumeration of the seven sacraments places it after the ninth century.—A. Castelein, *Cours de philosophie*, 1:256.

(*2*) As an illustration of the aid which linguistic evidence can lend to questions of authenticity and chronology, the brilliant results achieved by the European scholars, Lewis Campbell, Wincenty Lutoslawski, and others, in connection with Plato's dialogues, deserve mention. Previous to their discoveries the problem of the chronology of the dialogues was thought to be practically insoluble. Attempts made to determine their dates on the basis of doctrinal content were particularly unsatisfactory. Nowhere was there unanimity or quasi-unanimity. The *Phaedo* may be cited as an illustration. Efforts made by nine different scholars to determine its relative position in order of composition among twenty-five dialogues of Plato recognized as authentic, yielded the following results: nine, seventeen, seven, twenty-four, eleven, twenty-one, twenty-two, sixteen, twenty-one.—A. Diès, *Autour de Platon: Essai de critique et d'histoire* (2 vols., Paris, 1927), 2:249.

The method applied by Campbell and his successors (called "stylometry" by Lutoslawski) rests on the general principle that an author uses any given word or expression at the same rate of frequency during the same period of his literary development. Stylometry helps to fix the order of composition of an author's works rather than their precise dates. With its aid it became possible to determine what dialogues of Plato are authentic, and also to follow the development of his thought, a problem previously thought to be scarcely soluble.—Wincenty Lutoslawski, *The Origin and Growth of Plato's Logic with an Account of Plato's Style and the Chronology of his Writings* (London, 1897). Lutoslawski, however, by going beyond Campbell, made claims for stylometry that appear to be excessive.—John Burnet, *Platonism* (Berkeley, Calif., 1928), 9–12.

(*d*) *Handwriting*. Like literary style, handwriting is a distinctly personal trait. Though the prevailing style of penmanship may be more or less uniform in a particular country or age, individuals will use it with certain personal variations of their own, usually referred to as their "writing habits." Bibliotics, or the art of referring handwriting back to its producer, has apparently reached a stage where its findings are readily accepted in courts of law. Even the layman, unversed in the mysteries of bibliotics, will often find it a comparatively easy task to determine the authorship of a document when he has the original manuscript in his hands together with other material in the known handwriting of the same author, with which to compare it. If such material be not available, it may be possible, at least with the aid of palaeographical principles, to assign the document to a definite period, country, or school. Often, too, the writing material, watermarks, abbreviations and other such features furnish clues to period or place of origin. Methods similar to those employed in investigating the genuineness of handwritten documents are applicable in the case of typewritten papers.— See the interesting chapter in Osborn, *Questioned Documents*, 581–608.

A typewritten will purporting to be signed by John Brown in 1910, may be proved a forgery from the circumstance that the type-forms appearing in the document had not been introduced at that date.

(1) Firsthand study of medieval documents obviously requires acquaintance with their difficult script. Charters of the Merovingian period exist for the most part only in copies preserved in chartularies. Medieval copyists in making transcripts for the chartularies naturally made mistakes. The script of the originals was perplexing to a degree, and the Latinity was barbarous. In many cases the mistakes made by the copyists later found their way into printed editions of the texts, even into the *Monumenta Germaniae historica*.

Julien Havet, the French medievalist, studying the original of an act of Clovis III, August 12, 692, was able to show that the Latin form of the name of a French village occurring in the document and usually printed as Childulfovilla (a name which could not be identified) should be Duldulfovilla. This was the Latin for Doudeauville, a village which could be identified. The other form was a wrong reading persistently repeated from one edition to another. Havet gives some specimens of Merovingian script in "Questions Mérovingiennes," *Bibliothèque de l'École des Chartes*, 51 (1890): 213–37.

> (2) A person's "writing habits" include such matters as the slant of the lines, the slant of individual letters, the slant of single words, the absolute and the relative size of the letters, the length and width of loops, the use of the right or the left nib of the pen, the variety of alphabet employed, the location and character of the shading, the habit of dotting or not dotting *i*'s (and of crossing or not crossing *t*'s), the relationship of the writting to the left margin of the paper, the degree of

pressure employed, the speed of the writing, the presence or absence of linking strokes between certain letters, the location and character of ornamental flourishes, the arrangement of the writing on the page or envelope, the presence or absence of loops, the omission of initial or terminal upstrokes, the position and shape of the *i*-dots and *t*-crossings, the forms and positions of punctuation marks, etc.—Samuel A. Tannenbaum, *The Critical Crown* (New York, n.d.), 9.

For an application of the principles of bibliotics to the question whether a scene in the play, *Sir Thomas More* (Harleian MS 7368, British Museum) is in Shakespeare's hand, see Sir Edmund Maunde Thompson, *Shakespeare's Handwriting: A Study* (Oxford, 1926); Samuel A. Tannenbaum, *Problems in Shakespeare's Penmanship, Including a Study of the Poet's Will* (New York, 1927), chap. 10. Thompson concludes that the script is Shakespeare's, Tannenbaum, that it is not.

(3) Douglas Blackburn and Waithman Caddell, *The Detection of Forgery: A Practical Handbook for the Use of Bankers, Solicitors, Magistrates, Clerks and All Handling Suspected Documents* (London, 1909).

Jerome B. Lavay, *Disputed Handwriting: with Illustrations and Expositions for the Detection and Study of Forgery by Handwriting of all Kinds* (Chicago, 1909).

Charles Johnson, *English Courthand* A.D. *1066 to 1500, Illustrated Chiefly from the Public Records* (Oxford, 1915).

Simon Gratz, *A Book about Autographs* (Philadelphia, 1920), 40–68.

Charles A. Mitchell, *Documents and Their Scientific Examination* (Philadelphia, 1922); idem, *Scientific Detective and Expert Witness* (New York, 1931).

Albert S. Osborn, *Questioned Documents with Citations of Discussions of the Facts and the Law of Questioned Documents from Many Sources* (2d ed., Albany, 1929).

R. B. McKerrow, "On Fakes and Facsimiles," in *Introduction to Bibliography*, 231–38.

Samuel A. Tannenbaum, *The Handwriting of the Renaissance* (New York, 1930).

Edward K. Rand, *A Survey of the Manuscripts of Tours* (Cambridge, Mass., 1929).

Charles G. Crump and Ernest F. Jacob, eds., "Handwriting" in *The Legacy of the Middle Ages* (Oxford, 1926), 197–226.

(e) *Art-form.* Periods, countries, individual artists have their own conceptions of art, their own ways of expressing their conceptions. By applying the comparative method one may sometimes settle questions of authenticity in the case of art products.

℄ 166 *A work is probably genuine if its content, as regards details of time, place, conditions, etc., fits in with the environment in which it is supposed to have been produced, as far as such environment is known to us from reliable sources.*

(a) The accounts of the martyrs of Lyons, in Eusebius, are recognized as genuine from their minuteness and accuracy of detail in topography, chronology, and contemporary life. One feels that they came from a hand that could draw on immediate and firsthand knowledge of the incidents narrated.

The evidence for the authenticity of the Gospels from their content is discussed in Dowd, *Gospel Guide*. See also Pope, *The Catholic Student's Aid*; Fillion, *The Life of Christ*; Léonce de Grandmaison, *Jesus Christ; His Person, His Message, His Credentials* (3 vols., London, 1932).

On the internal evidence from language that St. Luke was a physician, see Fillion, *The Life of Christ*, 1:58.

On the freshness and immediacy of information revealed in the narrative of the third evangelist, see John A. Scott, *Luke, Greek Physician and Historian* (Evanston, Ill., 1930).

(b) The rule given in ¶ 166 may be expressed negatively: *A work is probably false if its contents are in any respect at variance with the environment in which it is supposed to have been produced.* A certain caution, however, is necessary in applying the rule in its negative form. Inconsistencies can creep into genuine sources because of negligence or inadvertence on the part of the writer. Caution is particularly needed in the case of posthumous works, for since these lack the advantage of the author's revision in the process of publication, they are sometimes marred by defects. Often, too, one must take into account the possibility of an author's putting out two or more editions of his work, as was the case with Tertullian's *Apologetic* and Eusebius' *Ecclesiastical History*.

(c) Inconsistencies in the category of time, which often make it possible to pronounce a work spurious, include the following: passing over in silence otherwise well-known and highly-significant events; introducing events, conditions, viewpoints which belong to a later or perhaps to an earlier period (anachronisms); assigning the composition of a source to a time when the alleged author was not alive, or at least was not in a position to produce the source in question. The *Athenian State* (ca. 425 B.C.) has been credited to Xenophon, a manifestly false attribution in view of the date of his birth, 434 B.C.

¶ 167 *Discovery or transmission of a source under strange and hardly credible circumstances points to spuriousness, as also does the much belated appearance of a tradition.*

(a) Many hagiographical sources of antiquity and of the Middle Ages betray their apocryphal character by the incredible explanations presented to account for their origin. Thus, their authors pose naively as eyewitnesses under cover of the principle in St. John (I John, 1:1), *quod vidimus oculis nostris, quod perspeximus;* for example, the *Passion* of St. Andrew, 1, and the Acts of St. Barnabas, 1. The acts or lives are alleged to have been found on writing tablets or in rare old manuscripts. The Passion of St. Alban was discovered in the ancient Roman town of Verulam in an old British codex, which on being deciphered immediately fell into dust. St. Placidus related his own life story after his death, and even allowed his portrait to be taken. Certain hagiographers made pretentions to be disciples or servants of the saints whose lives they wrote. Thus, Euripus appears as a disciple of St. John the Baptist, Pasicrates as a servant of St. George, Augarus as a scribe of St. Theodore, Athanasius as a stenographer of St. Catherine, Florentius as a servant of St. Cassiodorus.—Feder, Lehrbuch, 142.

For a brief treatment of the principles of scientific hagiography, see Hippolyte Delehaye, Cinq leçons sur la méthode hagiographique (Brussels, 1934).

(b) In attempts to palm off spurious documents as genuine, one of two circumstances generally helps to detection of the fraud: either its perpetrator will go no farther than to produce only a copy of the document, declining on one or other pretext to produce the original, or, if he does produce what purports to be the original, he will fail to explain satisfactorily how it came into his possession.

For late appearance of a tradition as making it suspect, see ⁋ 260.

⁋ 168 *Incomplete authenticity; interpolation; change.* Often the question is not whether a document as a whole is authentic, but whether certain passages or parts of it are so; in other words, whether there has been interpolation or change at the hands of someone other than the author himself. Here various criteria or tests are applicable.

(a) *Palaeographical tests.* Interpolations or changes made in an original text can be easily recognized from erasures or from differences in the characters, or composition of the ink. Pages inserted at a later date may often be recognized by a difference in the quality of the paper or other writing material. If only copies of the garbled original are at hand, it may be that one or more copies of earlier date, if such can be found, will fail to show interpolations or changes. In the case of pictorial or plastic work, additions are often recognizable by contrasts in material or color or by perceptible seams.

(b) *Tests by language and style.* Interpolation or change is often revealed by breaks in the uniform flow of diction and style. In official papers the use of formalities different from those employed in the body of the document may point to garbling.

(c) *Tests by content.* Inconsistencies; lack of logical sequence in ideas; certain details out of place chronologically and clearly referring to some other period (anachronisms). Here again one must proceed circumspectly. Even competent authors will sometimes err in making additions to their own work. The evenness of the text is spoiled, sequence of thought and theme is upset, even contradictions may be found. Hurry, negligence, change of mood, interruption of work, and other reasons may account for the untoward result.

Whether or not the passage in Josephus (*Jewish Antiquities*, XVIII, iii, 3) referring to Christ is an interpolation, is a moot question among scholars.—See De Grandmaison, *Jesus Christ*, 1:8 f., 193; *The Month*, 144 (1924): 57 ff.

⟪ 169 FALSIFICATION BY OMISSION

Sometimes the original copy, if extant, shows deletions or erasures; or copies of the original may show space left open for an omission, while probably other manuscripts show the omitted passage intact. It may be that the verbal context shows gaps, or that logical or factual coherence is not preserved. Often the nature of the gap can be determined so accurately that it becomes possible to restore the omitted passage in broad outline. "In the study of forgery the bibliotist devotes himself to searching out evidences of tampering, mending, patching, erasures, unlikely breaks in the writing, unnatural pauses, artificial joinings, unnecessary alterations, suspicious identities, etc." (Samuel A. Tannenbaum).

(a) Application of the various internal tests of script, formalities, language, or the like, to a question of authenticity, is illustrated by Léopold Delisle, the French medievalist, who proved a letter of Charles VI of France, dated March 15, 1403, to be spurious on the following grounds.

The style differs from that obtaining in letters of Charles VI known to be genuine.

The script differs obviously from the script in use in that king's chancery; it points to a period later than the beginning of the fifteenth century.

The signature does not bear the least resemblance to genuine signatures of the king. Delisle's article presents in facsimile two typical signatures of Charles VI, and below them the signature of the letter under investigation. The mere juxtaposition suffices to show they could not have come from the same hand.

The date, *Donné a Paris CE XVe jour de mars*, should, according to the usage of Charles VI's chancery, read *Donné a Paris LE XVe jour de mars*.

The latter part of the date reads: *mil IIII^c trois*. But Charles VI's notaries were accustomed to write *mil CCCC* and not *mil IIII^c*; moreover they inserted the conjunction *et* between the hundreds and the units—*mil CCCC et trois*, not *mil CCCC trois*.

The notary's signature is misplaced, being below the king's at the bottom of the letter. "In private letters the notary was accustomed to put his name at the extreme right of the sheet almost on a level with the king's signature or the line which contained the date."—L. Delisle, "Une fausse lettre de Charles VI," *Bibliothèque de l'École des Chartes*, 51 (1890): 87–92.

As is plain, the erudition thus put to account by Delisle in testing the authenticity of the document in question is of a very specialized nature. Only one quite at home in royal chancery usage under Charles VI is competent for the task.

⟨ 170   THE PITFALLS OF INTERNAL EVIDENCE

The criticism of documents by internal tests is a legitimate process *in se*, and has to its credit many valuable results; but as a process it is peculiarly liable to abuse. The field of scholarship is strewn with the debris of theories built on alleged internal evidence. Two great productions in particular have been made the target of misdirected criticism of this sort, the Bible and the Homeric poems.

⟨ 171   Modern critical study of the Homeric question began with the appearance (1795) of Wolf's *Prolegomena*, which attacked the unity of authorship of both the Iliad and the Odyssey, mainly by an application of the higher criticism, and set up the hypothesis that they were late compilations of ballads and other poetic pieces from various hands. It was assumed that the compilations were made at Athens in the time of Pisistratus. The best classical and historical scholarship in recent decades has discarded the Wolfian theories; "a gigantic bluff," the humanist, Paul Shorey, described them. According to this authority, "neither the facts nor the arguments of any one of the twenty or thirty most prominent books of this literature will endure scrutiny. This so-called science always breaks down when challenged by a competent scholar who knows the texts."—"Homer," *Encyclopedia Americana*. See also John A. Scott, *The Unity of Homer*, (Berkeley, Calif., 1921); *Cambridge Ancient History*, 2:498–517.

The exaggerations of internal criticism are dealt with satirically in Ronald Knox, *Essays in Satire* (London, 1930), 201–19; 223–35.

⟨ 172   Application of theories of multiple authorship, on supposed grounds of internal evidence, to the books of the Old Testament has resulted in the publication of the so-called "polychrome" or "rainbow" bibles, in which the sections assigned to the various alleged co-authors are set out in various colors. The theories themselves have proved abortive. In the case of the New Testament the important problem of the date of composition of the Gospels has been a favorite with the destructive critics. The general trend of their speculations has been to assign dates far later than those of tradition, thereby impugning the credit which the books had previously enjoyed as contemporary documents. But the best scholarly opinion has come to accept the traditional dates as correct after all, because the weight of evidence bearing on the problem is decisively in their favor. "The chronological framework in which tradition co-ordinated the sources is exact in all principal points from Paul's epistles to the writings of Irenaeus. The historian is obliged to take no account of all the hypotheses which deny the framework."—A. Harnack quoted in Fillion, *Life of Christ*, 1:296

The so-called "we"-sections in the Acts of the Apostles long held to "be pages from the diary of a journey kept by a companion of St. Paul," are now seen to have come from the same hand as the rest of the Acts. —De Grandmaison, *Jesus Christ*, 1:78–82.

(a) Other traditional viewpoints besides those concerning Homer and the Bible have found corroboration in modern critical research. Cicero's *Pro Marcello*, and his third Catilinarian oration were formerly accounted spurious by the critics, on the alleged ground that they were too unlike his demonstrably authentic orations to be assigned to him. Today classical scholars generally have no hesitation in accepting these two orations as Cicero's. Present-day critics are more ready than their predecessors of some decades ago to recognize that a writer's style is not necessarily quite the same throughout all his works or even within the limits of the same work. It may vary according to subject matter, whether it was composed at an earlier or later period of the writer's life. Tacitus in his *History* writes otherwise than in his *Dialogue*. Goethe's older and younger *Fausts* are not in the same literary manner. Tennyson's early poems bear no stylistic resemblances to the best of his later work.

For an informing discussion of the abuses of the higher criticism in historical research see Louis Laurand, "Progrès et recul de la critique," *Études*, 130 (1912): 601 ff.

(b) The net result of all the exposure of false conclusions arrived at by destructive critics in the name of internal criticism, has been to throw on it a large measure of suspicion. The suspicion is a healthy one for the student to nourish, if it does not blind him to the advantages undoubtedly inherent in a right use of the process. Internal criticism is a legitimate tool for solving problems of authenticity and has led to important results.

¶ 173 A selection of examples of the application of the principles of criticism to problems of authenticity, especially in connection with forgeries, real or alleged, are given here.

(a) *Early Christianity*

The apocryphal gospels.—See Otto Bardenhewer, *Patrology*, trans. by Thomas J. Shahan (St. Louis, 1908), 90 ff.

The famous works (*Areopagitica*) formerly attributed to Denis (Dionysius) the Areopagite, the disciple of St. Paul (Acts, 17:34). Two European scholars, Hugh Koch and Joseph Stiglmayer, after working independently on the problem of the authorship of the Areopagitica, published the results of their research in the same year, 1895. The conclusion which they reached was identical: the Areopagitica were in reality the product of some unknown author living at the earliest in the second half of the fifth century. Though the anonymous author of these remarkable works represents himself as the Dionysius mentioned in the Acts, proof that he lived several centuries later is conclusive. HB, 10 (1932): 41; CE, 5:13–18.

Experts generally appear to accept the authenticity (in the sense that it is not a modern fabrication) of the so-called "Antioch chalice"; but they assign it a much later date (third to sixth century) than that (first century) originally claimed for it.—See Henri Leclercq, Dictionnaire d'archéologie chrétienne et de liturgie, 8:853; G. de Jerphanion, Le calice d'Antioche, les théories du Dr. Eisen et la date probable du calice (Rome, 1926); Herbert Thurston, The Month, 148 (1926): 450–53.

(b) The Middle Ages

Herbert Thurston, "The False Decretals," The Month, 139 (1922): 158–68; idem, No Popery: Chapters in Anti-papal Prejudice (London, 1930), chap. 8.

Erwin J. Ruch, "The So-called Donation of Constantine," HB, 8 (1930): 23–25.

Robert Grosseteste's letter in Matthew Paris, in which he tells of his excommunication by the dying Innocent IV, is held to be spurious by Arthur L. Smith, Church and State in the Middle Ages (Oxford, 1913), 103 ff.

The "Prophecies of St. Malachy" concerning the popes. "Before 1148 they reproduce the erroneous data of a sixteenth-century papal historian Onofrio Panvinio and perpetuate his mistakes."—Herbert Thurston, "The Mistakes of Pseudo-Malachy," The Month, 124 (1914), 527 ff.; see also idem, The War and the Prophets (New York, 1915), 161.

For another pretended prophecy of St. Malachy, which deals with Ireland, see Paul Grosjean, Analecta Bollandiana, 51 (1933): 318 ff.

The History of the Monastery of Croyland, long attributed to Ingulf, an eleventh-century writer, the date of composition being supposedly 1089, embodies numerous charters said to have been granted in favor of that monastery. The work has been proved by its numerous anachronisms to be of much later date than that alleged. See Richard L. Marshall, Historical Criticism of Documents (Helps, 28:19–21); Thomas F. Tout, Medieval Forgers and Forgeries (2d ed., Manchester, 1890).

A circumstantial description of Roman Britain, published in 1757, under the title De situ Britanniae, purported to be a genuine work of Richard of Cirencester, a fourteenth-century monastic writer. In reality it was fabricated in the mid-eighteenth century by one Charles Julius Bertram, who was successful in palming it off on scholars as authentic. Internal and external evidence, and especially comparison with the genuine works of Richard of Cirencester, eventually showed it to be a forgery. The decisive step in the exposure was taken when Karl Wex pointed out, in 1845, that its quotations from Tacitus were borrowed from modern editions of that historian, and included emendations which a fourteenth-century scholar could not have known.—See Marshall, *Historical Criticism of Documents*, 17–19; J. A. Farrar, *Literary Forgeries* (London, 1917), chap. 2; Thomas F. Tout, *Medieval Forgers*; "Bertram," in the *Dictionary of National Biography*.

J. A. Twemlow, "John de Nigravalle, A Fictitious Librarian of the Vatican," *Miscellanea Francesco Erhle* (5 vols., Rome, 1924), 3:219–26.

(c) *English History*

The *Casket Letters*, alleged to have been written by Mary, Queen of Scots, implicate her in the murder of her husband, Henry, Lord Darnley. This is a classic problem in the criticism of documents.

Thomas F. Henderson, *The Casket Letters* (2d ed., Edingurch, 1890).

Andrew Lang, *The Mystery of Mary Stuart* (London, 1912).

Reginald A. Mahon, *Indictment of Mary, Queen of Scots* (Cambridge, Eng., 1923).

Sir Edward P. Parry, *The Persecution of Mary Stuart* (London, 1931).

Jean Héritier, *Marie Stuart et le meurtre de Darnley* (Paris, 1934), "perhaps the best thing in print" on the Casket Letters; unfavorable to authenticity.—*AHR*, 40 (1935): 777.

"If on the one hand, their authenticity still lacks final proof, no argument yet brought forward to invalidate them has stood the test of modern criticism."—John H. Pollen, *CE*, 9:765.

Bibliography of the Casket Letters in *Cambridge Modern History*, 3:814 f.

The "Squire Papers," forged by William Squire, an antiquarian, were accepted by Thomas Carlyle as genuine letters of Cromwell, and published by Carlyle as an appendix to the first volume of his *Letters and Speeches of Oliver Cromwell*. See the Lomas edition (London, 1904), and Marshall, *Historical Criticism of Documents*.

On the numerous Shakespeare forgeries, see Sir Sidney Lee, *Life of Shakespeare* (New York, 1917), 646 ff.

Thomas Chatterton (1752–1770) passed off poems of his own as the work of Thomas Rowley, a fifteenth-century monk. To give them the proper air of antiquity he borrowed words from the *Dictionarium Anglo-Britannicum*, and in doing so copied the dictionary's mistakes, writing "cherisaunei" for "cherisaunce" (comfort). Skeat in his edition (1871) of Chatterton definitely exposed the fraud.—See *Cambridge History of English Literature*, 10:265–69.

James Macpherson (1736–1796) published verses of his own under the name of Ossian, third-century Gaelic hero and bard.—See *Cambridge History of English Literature*, 10:256 ff.

(d) *French History*

For certain remarkable forgeries of letters of Marie Antoinette, and of other celebrities, see Lord Acton, *Lectures on the French Revolution* (London, 1910).

Raoul Hesdin, *Journal of a Spy in Paris During the Reign of Terror, January–July, 1794* (London, 1895). Proved a forgery; its anachronisms especially helped to the exposure. *EHR* 9 (1896): 594–99.

The third volume of Bailly's *Mémoires* is a mere compilation from contemporary newspapers.—F. M. Fling, *The Writing of History*, 52–56.

(e) *Irish History*

An incriminating letter alleged to have been written by James Stewart Parnell the day after the Phoenix Park murders, was published in facsimile in the London *Times*, April 18, 1887. The misspelling *hesitency* for *hesitancy* was a major item in the evidence that led to exposure of forgery.— See Francis L. Wellman, *The Art of Cross-examination* (New York, 1924), 263–76.

(f) *American History*

Letters purporting to be Washington's were forged during his lifetime with a view to impugning his loyalty to the revolutionary cause and his private morals.—John C. Fitzpatrick, "The George Washington Scandals," *Scribner's Magazine*, 81 (1927): 389–95.

An issue of the Cape Fear *Mercury* for June 3, 1775, cited in support of the alleged authenticity of the Mecklenburg Declaration of Independence has been pronounced a fabrication.—Worthington C. Ford in *AHR*, 11 (1906): 548 ff.

With a view apparently to upsetting the stock market, a bogus proclamation of Lincoln calling for 400,000 additional troops, was published in the New York *World* and in the *Journal of Commerce*, May 18, 1864.—See Otto Eisenschiml, *Why Was Lincoln Murdered?* (Boston, 1937), 453–56; Lucy M. Salmon, *The Newspaper and the Historian* (Oxford, 1920), 418 f.

The forged "Morey-Motley letter" (1880) is discussed in J. B. Lavay, *Disputed Handwriting*.

Margaret C. Schindler, "Fictitious Biography," *AHR*, 42 (1937): 680–90. Sketches in a standard work of reference of persons that never lived.

Wilfrid Partington, *Forging Ahead: the True Story of the Upward Progress of Thomas James Wise, Prince of Book Collectors, Bibliographer Extraordinary and Otherwise* (New York, 1941).

That the day of the literary forger is not over was seen by the appearance in the *Atlantic Monthly*, 1928–1929, of a series of alleged Lincoln documents, which were pronounced spurious by experts immediately on their appearance. The usual tell-tale indications of forgery, especially anachronisms, are many. In a letter of May 9, 1834, Lincoln is made to speak of *section 40* in a land-survey, whereas there are only 36 sections in a township. In the same letter, he speaks of a friend of his as going to "Kansas."

At the period in question that region was not open to white settlement, and the word *Kansas* was used only in reference to the river of the same name. Anne Rutledge is made to say that she copied out of a Spencerian copy-book "every time I can spair"; but Spencer's first book on penmanship did not appear until thirteen years after her death.—See Paul M. Angle, "The Minor Collection," *Atlantic Monthly*, 143 (1929): 516–25.

On the "Kensington Stone," an allegedly fourteenth-century (1362) relic of Norse origin, found in Minnesota, see Hjalmar R. Holand, *The Kensington Stone* (Ephraim, Wis., 1932); Laurence M. Larson, "The Kensington Rune Stone," *Minnesota History*, 17 (1936): 20–37; Milo M. Quaife, "The Myth of the Kensington Stone: The Norse Discovery of Minnesota, 1362," *New England Quarterly*, 8 (1934): 613–45; Hjalmar R. Holand, "The Myth of the Kensington Rune Stone," *New England Quarterly*, 8 (1935): 45 ff.; Francis S. Betten, "A Belated Viking Adventure," *From Many Centuries: A Collection of Historical Papers* (New York, 1938), 56–62.

A legend on a contemporary map, indicating that La Salle descended the Ohio River, is an interpolation.—Jean Delanglez, *Some La Salle Journeys* (Chicago, 1938), 29 ff.

The authenticity of the inscribed brass plate found near San Francisco in 1936, and claimed to be the one actually set up by Sir Francis Drake in that locality in 1579, is controverted.—See "Drake's Plate of Brass," California Historical Society, *Publications* (San Francisco, 1937) Nos. 13, 14; C. G. Fink and E. P. Polushkin, *Drake's Plate of Brass Authenticated: The Report on the Plate of Brass* (San Francisco, 1938), reviewed in *AHR*, 44 (1939): 879 f.

C. Errors in Questions of Authenticity

¶ 174 THE MEANING OF ERROR

In regard to the authenticity of a source, error or mistake consists in taking a genuine source for spurious, or the converse—a spurious source for genuine. When the author himself has tampered with the source, with intention of leading astray, this practice is deception.

¶ 175 The causes of error in questions of authenticity are many, among them credulity, hypercriticism, wilful dogmatism. *Credulity* is a mental infirmity, being an unthinking proneness to believe or judge on slight or only apparent grounds, such as was common in periods before the rise of the critical spirit. The opposite of credulity is *hypercriticism*. Assuming a guise of thoroughgoing research, this is in reality a one-sided attitude towards a subject of study, an attitude motivated by preconceived theory or by other prepossession; or it may be a preoccupation with minute detail, which leaves the larger aspects of the subject unrecognized. *Wilful dogmatism* is especially manifest in cases where the evidence is really not decisive, but leaves the door open to honest doubt. Often error as to the authenticity of sources is attributable to mere ignorance or carelessness. Thus, similarity of name or content may be the occasion of mistake. The well-known apologetic dialogue *Octavius*, of Minucius Felix (second century) both in the only extant manuscript (*Codex Parisiensis*, 1661, ninth century) and in the first printed edition (1543), was joined as a ninth book to the eight books of Arnobius *Adversus gentes* (beginning of the fourth century). As a consequence, the *Octavius* came to be attributed to Arnobius. In other cases, works of various authors were bound together and later published under one name. Not infrequently, a mere exercise in rhetoric or style was accepted as a serious work.

❡ 176   ERROR IN THE VARIOUS TYPES OF SOURCES

(a) *Remains.* Mistakes in dating remains in the fields of palaeontology and anthropology have been endless. Remote origins have been assigned them which later research proved to be groundless. In archaeology claims have been made which subsequent investigation failed to verify.

The case of the German scholar, Schliemann, is interesting. Though the net result of his excavations represented an epochal advance in Greek archaeological research, he was on more than one occasion in substantial error in his calculations. At Hissarlik he thought he had discovered Homer's town among the remains of what was actually a pre-Homeric settlement; the actual Homeric Troy, if such existed, he had passed by in an upper stratum practically unnoticed. Misinterpreting a passage in Pausanias, he undertook to find the graves of the Atrides in Mycenae, where actually he brought to light other tombs of the utmost significance. At Tiryns he uncovered a Homeric stronghold, but thought it was a construction of the Roman or medieval period.

(b) *Literary productions.* The speeches introduced by the Greek and Roman historians into their narratives, formerly were taken at their face value as orations actually delivered, but now are recognized to be merely literary devices once in fashion. Similarly, dramas, romances, and other products of literary invention have been taken for genuine historical sources. A whole series of ancient writings, now generally distinguished by the prefix "pseudo," once passed muster as genuine works of their reputed authors. On the other hand, a number of writings from classical antiquity—certain works of Aristotle, Cicero's *Pro Marcello*, several odes of Horace—once held to be spurious, are now accepted as genuine.

(c) *Oral tradition.* Sagas, myths, legends, popular tales, whether in prose or verse, were long rated as genuine historical sources. Their *true* character was first brought to light in the nineteenth century. The contribution of Niebuhr to this result was noteworthy. His call to a professorship of history in the University of Berlin (1810), marked the beginning of critical treatment of the legendary material that forms the warp and woof of early Roman history. Both Niebuhr and Mommsen in their histories of Rome wrote from the new viewpoint of the general unreliability of Livy, and of other similar sources for the earlier periods of their subject. The new critical spirit was seen in Jacob Grimm for German history, Ranke for European, and Lingard for English.

Mere rumor and similar types of oral tradition were invested in ancient, medieval, and not rarely even in modern times, with the dignity of trustworthy historical sources. It has been asserted that in the preface of his *Ecclesiastical History*, Bede gave expression to this attitude in a principle which other historians both of the ancient and medieval world put into practice: *Quod vera lex historiae est, simpliciter ea quae fama vulgante collegimus, ad instructionem posteritatis litteris mandare studuimus.* [⁋ 55-b]. But Bede's meaning cannot be that he relied only on hearsay for his information; he knew the value of written sources and indicated the more important sources which he used. "In all that he relates he is careful to give his authority. 'I would not that my children should read a lie,' was one of his last utterances. He quotes documents if they are available and whether for ordinary or extraordinary events he gives when he can, firsthand evidence, and, if that is not forthcoming or if he has nothing to rely upon save common report, he frankly says so."—Loeb translation, xv.

(1) *Examples.* Errors as to the historical character of many sagas and myths in numerous historians of antiquity, such as Herodotus, Livy, Cornelius Nepos.

St. Jerome (*Vita S. Pauli*, 7, 8, Migne, *Patrologia Latina*, XXIII, 22) on the existence of centaurs and satyrs.

Witiking, *Res gestae Saxonicae*, on the descent of the Saxons from the Greeks. The interpolated chronicle of Martinus Polonus (after 1278); the chronicle *Flores Temporum* (to 1290); many medieval theologians on the popess Joan.—See John J. I. Döllinger, *Fables Respecting the Popes of the Middle Ages* (London, 1871), 3–67.

(2) The so-called letter of Aristeas, which contains a romantic account of the origin of the Septuagint, was supposed to be the composition of Aris-

teas, an official of high rank in the court of King Ptolemy Philadelphus (285–246 B.C.). In reality it is the invention of a Hellenistic Jew, probably of the period 96–63 B.C. But it was held to be genuine by the Church Fathers and scholars generally, down to the sixteenth century.—CE, 13:722.

Baronius and others regarded the acts of the Sixth Ecumenical Council relating to the Honorius controversy as spurious.

For fifteen hundred years the letter of the Synod of Sardica (ca. 343–344) to the emperors Constantius and Constans was thought to be a petition addressed by St. Hilary of Poitiers to the Emperor Constantius.—See André Wilmart, *Revue Bénédictine*, 24 (1907): 149–79, 291–317; Alfred Feder, *Studien zu Hilarius von Poitiers*, (1912), 133–51.

The continuations by other hands of the *Epitoma Chronicon* of Prosper were held to be the original work of Prosper himself.—*Monumenta Germaniae historica*, "Chronica minora," 1:486 ff.

(d) *Inscriptions*. Here mistakes have come about in various ways. Thus, the script or the writing-material or certain external formalities, especially in the case of Christian inscriptions, were thought to be inconsistent with the period to which the objects in question were supposed to belong; or the manner of transmission seemed to give the lie to genuineness; or certain abbreviations were misunderstood, with the result that the inscription was assigned to the wrong locality or date; or the content or the language, seemingly at odds with the supposed provenance, gave rise to misunderstanding.

The abbreviation B.M. (*Bonae Memoriae*) following the name of a deceased person was in a certain case mistakenly read as *Beatus Martyr*, and accounts of the supposed martyr were accordingly drawn up.

A church in Spain interpreted the fragmentary inscription, S VIAR, all that remained of the original text [PRAEFECTU]S VIAR[UM], to be the name of a saint, St. Viar, and thereupon made petition to Pope Urban VIII for a grant of indulgences, which was not allowed.—De Smedt.

A Roman inscription RRRFFF was made out to be a Sibylline prophecy: *Roma Ruet Romuli Ferro Flammaque Fameque*.—Döllinger, *Fables*.

The abbreviation M.XI.V. (*martyres undecim virgines*), in an inscription, came to be read *millia undecim virginum*, and this reading was alleged as evidence for the eleven thousand virgins of Cologne.

(e) *Art products*. Attempted identification of architectural remains and works of art has often proved incorrect. Buildings, paintings, sculptures, have been assigned to architects, artists, schools, periods, to which they did not actually belong. In particular, a one-sided and undiscerning use of "stylistic analysis" has led to repeated errors in attempts to identify works of art.

"The bust-portraits on Carolingian seals, which were made from ancient gems, were erroneously taken to be the portraits of Frankish rulers."—Feder, *Lehrbuch*, 2d ed. 140; Charles H. Hart, "Frauds in Historical Portraiture or Spurious Portraits of Historical Personages," AHA, *Report* (1913), 87–94.

Rules for the detection of errors are the same as those for the detection of forgeries; in the former there has been no conscious falsification of the source or object by its author, but some error in regard to it on the part of the investigator.

D. Dating Sources

¶ 177   The problem of the origin of a source is complex, for it involves inquiry as to *when, where, by whom* and *from what material* it was produced. These four lines of investigation exhaust the question of origin in the case of historical sources. If any one of them turns out unsatisfactorily, the historian may well find his use of a document limited, if not cut short altogether. An undated or undatable document is in most cases of no use to him. A document which has not been, and cannot be localized, may in consequence present special difficulties of interpretation. To know when or where a letter was written can be a decisive factor in grasping its real import. Whether the False Decretals were compiled at Constantinople or Rome, or in northern France, is a question with practical bearing on the motives that lay behind those famous fabrications.

(a) Questions of origin or provenance are concerned as a rule only with sources more or less remote in date. Yet even in the Middle Ages official papers of corporate bodies customarily each bore the name of such a body, as well as the date and place of issuance. In letters, the year was sometimes omitted (not an infrequent occurrence even today), as being presumably known to the addressee. A manuscript often embodies data, explicit or implicit, which point to its origin, or such data may be inserted by a hand other than the author's. Printed books usually indicate on the title-page the name of author and publisher, or printer, together with date and place of publication. Date of publication may be traced, if not on the title-page, in the copyright notice.

(b) The number of historical writings that lack designation of any or all of the three items, author, date and place of composition, is greater than one might suppose. Even printed books are sometimes deficient in these respects. The abbreviation "n.d." (no date), used by cataloguers of current publications, is evidence that even today publishers and printers depart on occasion from the conventions. Before the days of printing, purely literary productions were circulated in manuscript copies, with no indication as to when or where they had their origin. Even state papers, including official letters and decrees of parliaments, have in many cases no date at all, or a defective one. Moreover, numerous writings and records have come down to us only in copies, wherein designation, at least of date and place of issuance, was omitted as superfluous. This is especially the case in the larger collections of letters (Cicero's, Pliny's) and of laws, either civil (Justinian Code) or ecclesiastical (papal decrees).

¶ 178 THE IMPORTANCE OF DATE

Except in critical studies of the growth of an author's literary art, the date of composition of a work of mere literature is generally not a matter of any consequence. Whether *Macbeth* was written this year or that is not a question that affects our enjoyment of it or the place it holds among the literary classics of the world.

With historical sources, whether these be written documents or archaeological remains, it is frequently of the first importance to the historian to know when precisely they originated, to know, for instance, when a chronicle was written, a law passed, an institution founded, a coin minted, or a custom introduced. Parliamentary or congressional proceedings would scarcely have any significance for the historian if the minutes came to him undated and undatable. The character and motives of statesmen and other persons in public life cannot as a rule be properly gauged from their speeches or other declarations, unless these fit into a definite chronological scheme. Again, the reliability of reports made by witnesses, immediate or mediate, cannot be duly evaluated unless we know how much time intervened between the reports and the events reported; likewise, the same reports can be properly interpreted only in the light of the precise time at which they were made. An error of one day made in the dating of an originally undated letter may lead to the imputation to its writer of a grave delinquency of which he is entirely innocent.

It must be emphasized that an undated document is in most cases useless. And yet, even a wrong date assigned to a document, if it does not differ widely from the correct date, will frequently add to its value as a historical source instead of vitiating it. Whether a charter of King John of England is to be dated March 1, 1213, or March 10 of the same year, may not be a question that necessarily affects its value to the historian.

Sometimes the question of dependence, as between two literary works known to be related, can be settled only by ascertaining their dates. Is Shakespeare's *Hamlet* dependent on Marston's *Malcontent*, or vice-versa?—

See Harold R. Walley, "The Dates of Hamlet and Marston's The Malcontent," *Review of English Studies*, 9 (1933): 397–409.

¶ 179 CRITERIA OF DATING

Criteria used in the dating of historical sources are partly external, partly internal. The terms external and internal are used here with reference to the source investigated.

¶ 180 EXTERNAL CRITERIA

(a) A document of known date can help fix the earliest or latest possible time of composition of a document that is dateless. The diary of Simon Foreman, a London physician, has an entry, April 20, 1610, which records his presence at a performance of Macbeth. The play was therefore written before this date.

(b) Sometimes an author in one of his works of known date, will refer to another work of his as already written. Of course, this information merely establishes the priority of one work to the other; it does not fix the actual date of composition.

(c) Similarly, a work of known date may refer by citation or by allusion, to another issued without date, or may even make explicit statement of the date of the latter. But here one must proceed wih caution. Definitely-dated minor sources have sometimes by fraud or error been incorporated into larger source units. It would be rash to fix the date of the latter by that of the minor source. Archaeology furnishes an illustration. An inscription on the façade of the Pantheon, at Rome, assigns the famous structure to the time of Agrippa (reign of Augustus). In reality the body of the structure dates only from the time of Hadrian, during whose reign the inscription was put in place.

(d) The circumstances attending the finding of a source often help to fix its date. A number of objects belonging to the Cretan-Mycenean civilization can be accurately dated because together with them were found Egyptian objects of ascertained date, for example, scarabae and cartouches from the time of Amenophis III (first half of the fourteenth century B.C.)

The Porta Nigra of Treves, probably Germany's most famous Roman architectural survival, together with an adjoining section of a city wall, is built on ground which was in use as a burying ground up to at least the middle of the second century A.D. The Porta Nigra, therefore, belongs to a period later than this date.

Traces of violent destruction by natural or human agency often furnish evidence for dates. The Acropolis of Athens shows signs of ravages by the Persians. Its construction therefore antedates that event (ca. 480–479 B.C.).

(e) Sometimes technical conditions of which we have certain knowledge and which affected the production of an undated source, may be a starting point from which to argue to its date. The time it took to forward a letter, or to print a book, may be a factor aiding us to fix the time of composition of one or the other, provided we know when the letter arrived or the printing was finished; and how long such processes usually lasted. But interruptions in the forwarding of a letter or the printing of a book may render this method of calculation unreliable.

(f) The fragmentary character of a source is sometimes a clue that leads eventually to its date. Investigation may reveal that the fragment is part of a source, the date of which has already been satisfactorily established.

(g) The quality of paper and of ink used in a manuscript or book has often furnished a clue to its date.——See Julius Grant, *Books and Documents: Dating, Permanence and Preservation* (London, 1937).

₡ 181 INTERNAL CRITERIA

(a) *Comparison of a source with other sources evidently belonging to the same period often results in fixing its date, at least approximately.* Sources of the same period show common characteristics, more frequently these are external, such as format, writing-material, script, style of printing. Together with evidence furnished by content, comparison is the palaeographer's usual method of determining the date of manuscripts.

(b) *Similarly, literary traits, such as diction and style, often help to date a source, if not with precision at least within certain limits.* Frequently, too, they supply negative evidence by showing that a source does not belong to the period or age to which it has been generally assigned. Language undergoes change from one period to another, old words drop out of the vocabulary, new ones are taken in. Each period has its laws regulating literary style both in poetry and in prose. The result is that a body of criteria may be evolved by the aid of which the investigator, fixing his attention merely on the verbal and stylistic features of the document, can in many cases determine the period to which it belongs. Mere style, however, understanding by this an author's distinctive manner of expression apart from vocabulary and grammatical usage, is in many cases too elusive an element to be made a safe standard for objective measurement. The application of merely stylistic tests has led to well-known vagaries in Biblical and Homeric criticism. [₡ 165-c-2].

(c) *Content is the major test for determining the date of documents.*

(1) There may be a dedication to a known person, or the author may make statements from which one may reasonably infer that the document was written within the limits of a certain period. The words "James Madison being President of the United States," occurring in an otherwise undated state paper, at once fix the date of origin at some time during the period 1809–1816.

(2) The sequence of events, for example, of a war, may end abruptly, while subsequent events of the war are left unnoticed. It is a fair inference that the narrative was composed prior to the later period of the war, unless other evidence points to the contrary.

(3) An astronomical phenomenon (an eclipse of the sun or moon, the appearance of a comet, a conjunction of planets) may be mentioned in the document as having occurred shortly before it was written. Such a mention enables one to date the document.

(4) From an author's silence about certain events he would have known about at the time he wrote, and would certainly have mentioned, it may be concluded that he wrote before the events, not after them [❰149 ff.].

(5) Viewpoints, ideas, theories, customs, which find mention in a document, are often a clue to date of composition. The same holds for surviving objects in the field of the plastic arts. A Roman statue of a bearded man in early Christian times (excepting statues of philosophers, for whom wearing of the beard was conventional), must be assigned to the post-Hadrian period, since only under Hadrian had the wearing of beards again came into vogue. Every Roman empress introduced a new fashion in the wearing of women's hair. Hence, it is frequently an easy matter to fix the date of statues of the empresses, in cases where head and frisure are hewn from the same stone.

❰ 182   TERMINI IN DATES

Frequently the available evidence is not of such a nature as to enable us to fix the precise date of composition of a document, though it does make it possible to establish limits within which the precise date occurs. These limits are designated as the *terminus post quem* (earliest possible date), and the *terminus ante quem* (latest possible date). Thus a *terminus ante quem* for such of Shakespeare's plays as are mentioned in Francis Meres's *Tamia Palladis*, is 1598, since that is the year in which the *Tamia* appeared. In *Henry V* (V [Prologue], 30–32) there is an allusion to the Earl of Essex as being still in power. Essex left for Ireland April 27, 1599, and news of his disastrous campaign did not reach England until the end of June. This last circumstance accordingly determines the *terminus ante quem* of *Henry V*; the play could not have been written later than the end of June, 1599, on the reasonable assumption that its author was aware of Essex's disgrace. The *terminus ante quem* of Caesar's *Commentaries on the Gallic War* is 46 B.C., for this work is mentioned in Cicero's *Brutus* (LXXV, 262), which appeared in that year.

Having established as accurately as possible the two *termini* within the limits of which the document must have been produced, generally the investigator will next proceed, with the aid of whatever evidence is at hand, to fix the date of composition more precisely.

(a) The method of fixing the *terminus post quem* and *terminus ante quem* of an undated document, through evidence furnished by content, is illustrated in the following, from Bernheim's *Lehrbuch* (1908), 397 f. It has to do with the Annals of Lorsch (*Annales Laurissenses*) in the *Monumenta Germaniae historica* (vol. 1). Nothing is known from direct statement as to the authorship or time of composition of these annals, which cover the years 741-829. Analysis shows the work to consist of several parts written by different authors. For our purpose we take only the first part (741-791), which is the product throughout of a single hand. The annals were not compiled year by year; the author betrays at times a knowledge of later events. Assuming that these references to later events are not interpolations, we determine the *terminus post quem* by this line of proof:

772—*et inde perrexit* [*domnus Carolus*] *partibus Saxoniae prima vice* ("and [Lord Charles] proceeded thence for the first time to the parts of Saxony"). The author evidently knows of Charles' second expedition to Saxony, 775; hence, the words cited must have been written subsequently to 775.

777—*tunc domnus Carolus rex sinodum publicum habuit ad Paderbrunnen prima vice* ("then Lord Charles held a public synod [reichstag] at Paderborn for the first time"). It is a safe inference that these words were written after Charles' second synod or reichstag at Paderborn, 785.

781—*sed non diu promissiones quas fecerat conservavit* ("but he did not keep his promises for long"). The writer must have known of the fresh revolt, 788, of Tassilo of Bavaria. Hence, the passage was written after 788. From the three passages just cited it is possible to fix the *terminus post quem*, that is, 788. There is only one indication pointing to the *terminus ante quem*.

785—*et tunc tota Saxonia subjugata est* ("and then the whole of Saxony was brought under"). This could hardly have been written by one who knew of the total defection of Saxony in 793; hence, it was written before that date. The Annals of Lorsch (first part) were therefore compiled some time during the period 788-793. Whether this conclusion is certain or only probable, depends on the value to be attached to the reasoning at each step of the process.

(b) Dates of composition of the Gospels are discussed in Fillion, *Life of Christ*, 1:66 ff.; 495 ff.; also in De Grandmaison, *Jesus Christ*, 1:118, 228-33.

When did Caesar write the *Commentaries on the Gallic War*, and when were they published?—See T. Rice Holmes, *Caesar's Conquest of Gaul* (2d ed., Oxford, 1911), 201-202.

English royal charters from the Norman Conquest to the accession of Richard I, are normally undated. Léopold Delisle noted that the change in the style of Henry II's charters from *Rex Anglorum* to *Dei Gratia Rex Anglorum*, took place during the biennium 1172–1173. Accordingly, it became possible to group that sovereign's charters in two series, one dated before, the other after the biennium indicated.—See also Reginald L. Poole, "The Date of Henry II's Charters," *Studies in Chronology and History*, 302 ff.

Dugdale's *Monasticon* is dated in Maurice W. Keatinge, *Studies in the Teaching of History* (London, 1913).

Date of the treatise of Frederick II on falconry, *De arte venandi cum avibus*, is discussed in Charles H. Haskins, *Studies in the History of Medieval Science* (Cambridge, Mass., 1927), 299–326.

The dating of Shakespeare's plays exemplifies, for the most part along rather simple lines, the general technique employed in the dating of documents.

Harris Fletcher, "Grierson's Suggested Date for Milton's *Ad Patrem*," in *The Fred Newton Scott Anniversary Papers* (Chicago, 1929), 199–205.

(c) The dating of archaeological remains, especially of the very remote past, is easily liable to error. The dates assigned by Charles L. Wooley, *The Sumerians* (Oxford, 1928), to the remarkable finds in Iraq, have been questioned as being too remote. The point is important, for only on the assumption of the more remote dates can Wooley's claim that the Sumerian is older than the Egyptian civilization, be established. At the same time archaeology is often a reliable aid to chronology. Flinders Petrie, the Egyptologist, used pottery as a clue to dates. "Thanks to Professor Petrie it is possible to date a Palestinian mound as unambiguously as if it had been full of inscriptions."—*Cambridge Ancient History*, 1:114.

A recent method of calculating dates has been evolved from evidence furnished by tree-rings. See Florence M. Hawley, *Tree-Ring Analysis and Dating in the Mississippi Drainage* (Chicago, 1941), bibliography.

¶ 183 THE DATING OF PRINTED BOOKS

The date of composition of printed books presents a special problem. Generally, the publisher's date is the chief guide, since it supplys an approximate *terminus ante quem*; but such indication fails when a considerable interval occurs between the actual time of composition and the time the manuscript is submitted to the publisher, or actually published. A better index is the author's dated preface. This again will supply a *terminus ante quem*; but a considerable interval may separate the actual date of composition from the date of the preface. It will then be necessary to have recourse to internal evidence in order to fix the latest date covered by the contents of a book or any part of it. This is sometimes an important point to determine. Thus, undated economic facts stated in a book are not necessarily to be taken as of the year of publication. And yet, the reader will often like to know, and probably should know in the interests of accuracy of information, just to what precise year or period the facts are to be referred.

E. Localizing Sources

¶ 184 To know where a piece of literature was composed is generally not of greater consequence than to know when it was composed. But historical sources must often be localized if we are to evaluate them properly. A survey of American newspaper opinion which aims to ascertain sectional attitudes on an important past national issue, such as slavery or reconstruction or the tariff, will necessarily check the localities to which the newspapers belong.

¶ 185 CRITERIA OF LOCALIZATION
(a) The place where a manuscript or work of art was found is often a circumstance helping to determine where either was produced. Yet with only such evidence for a guide, one must proceed with caution. Works of art have been removed from their original sites to other sites, even to distant lands, while manuscripts have been transferred from one library or archive to another. In the case of a printed book it obviously does not follow, especially today, that the place of publication or printing is also the place where it was written. Roman coins in considerable quantities have been found in England; but no one concludes offhand that they were minted there. In 1913 a leaden marker left behind by the La Vérendrye exploring party of 1742, was found at Pierre, South Dakota. Discussion ensued as to whether it had remained in its original site or had been removed therefrom by Indians. The point had significance, for only on the first supposition could the finding of the marker at Pierre be adduced as evidence of the route of the expedition. Similarly, in 1937, a stone inscription referring to the Coronado expedition of 1540, was found in Kansas, near the Missouri River. Without raising the question of its authenticity, was that its original *locus*, or was it moved there from elsewhere?

(b) Place of origin can be indicated in manuscripts by peculiarities of script (calligraphical schools of Tours, St. Gall, Bobbio); in printed books, by style of typography (numerous sixteenth-century presses, such as the Aldine, Moretus); in sculpture and painting, by technique (schools of Phidias, Raphael).

(c) Characteristics of language, especially in dialect forms, and of literary style, often supply evidence that a document was produced in a distinct locality or region. Thus, certain expressions occurring in the Latin version of the *Imitation of Christ* suggest that the great spiritual classic was composed somewhere in the Rhine country, more particularly in the Dutch Netherlands. But this criterion, like so many others resorted to in the criticism of documents, has its limitations. As a language develops, it tends to absorb local idioms; even dialects of the same language often borrow from one another. Moreover, authors sometimes write in a language other than their own vernacular. The Provençal of the French medieval troubadours was in frequent use by poets of various countries. In past times Italian authors often wrote in French, and Spanish writers in Portuguese. In other words, a source, literary or historical, did not necessarily originate in the country of the language in which it is written. Finally, details of content often furnish a clue. The writer may betray a particular interest in a certain locality, monastery, or other institution, or show himself especially well informed as to persons or things of a definite area. Reasoning of this kind, it may be added, is more convincing, the more difficult was access to the place in question; hence, the more unlikely was the transfer of the documents from one place to another.

(d) Bernheim examines an instance of localization of a source—Lehrbuch, 399 f.—In the twenties of the last century a German scholar, Wedekind, found in the register of the monastery of St. Michael's, Lüneburg, Saxony, a Latin manuscript containing annals covering the period 1057–1130. Author, date, and place of composition were unknown. The handwriting showed traits of the twelfth century, but no regional characteristics, while the Latinity was the usual variety of the period. The place where the manuscript was found pointed to Saxony as its original home, but not conclusively. It was necessary to fall back on internal evidence. Forward from 1100, this was of uniform tenor. Saxon events are told with particular detail, in contrast with the manner in which events from other parts of Germany are either passed over lightly or ignored altogether. Such appointments to episcopal sees and such deaths as are recorded, chiefly regard Saxony. Deaths occurring in the Saxon family of the Counts of Stade are regularly mentioned, and the author takes for granted that his readers are acquainted with this relatively unimportant family. The interest he takes in it was so great that in the midst of the struggle of Henry IV with his sons, he pauses to relate that Count Liuderus, of the family of Stade, was brought sick to the convent of Rosenfeld, and died there. A clue is now at hand in the association of this convent with the Counts of Stade. The convent was in the territory of these counts; they had founded it. Who would be interested in the details referred to, except one writing in the convent of Rosenfeld for a local circle of readers? In fine, an entry for 1130 throws decisive light upon the problem: *Cono abbas obiit*, "Abbot Cono died." Only a person in the abbey where Cono died could refer to him in so casual a manner and without further identification. As a matter of fact, Cono is known *aliunde* to have been Abbot of Rosenfeld up to 1130. The conclusion is accordingly reached that the annals in question, as far as they were original, were written in the Convent of Rosenfeld, and hence they were published in the *Monumenta Germaniae historica* under the title *Annales Rosenveldenses*.

F. The Determination of Authorship

⁌ 186 Numerous published monographs or articles bear on questions of authorship in the field of historical sources. Acquaintance with this literature will repay the student. A few of the problems here listed regard works of literature rather than history; but the criteria of evidence applicable in either category are the same.

⁌ 187 The authorship of the fourth gospel is discussed by John Donovan, "Did St. John Write His Gospel?" *Thought*, 6 (1932): 569–87; also by De Grandmaison and Fillion.

Otto Bardenhewer, *Patrology*, contains numerous discussions of authorship in the field of the patristic writings.

Tertullian is probably the editor of the original text of the *Passio* of Saints Perpetua and Felicity.—See H. Shewring, *The Passio of SS. Perpetua and Felicity: A New Edition and Translation of the Latin Text* (London, 1931).

The authorship of the life of St. Martin of Tours, traditionally attributed to Sulpicius Severus, is discussed in William E. Brown, *Pioneers of Christendom: Bishops* (London, 1929).

Who wrote the *Stabat Mater Dolorosa?*—See Hugh T. Henry, "The Two Stabats," *American Catholic Quarterly Review*, 28 (1903): 291–309; Frederick J. B. Raby, *A History of Christian-Latin Poetry from the Beginnings to the Close of the Middle Ages* (Oxford, 1927); John Julian, *Dictionary of Hymnology* (New York, 1892), 1081.

Who wrote the *Adeste Fideles?*—See Hugh T. Henry, *American Catholic Quarterly Review*, 39 (1914): 617–22.

⁌188 The authorship of *The Imitation of Christ* is still a stock subject of controversy. Recent criticism unfavorable to the case for Thomas a Kempis, is offered by Leonard A. Wheatley, *The Story of the Imitatio Christi* (Oxford, 1891); James E. G. De Montmorency, *Thomas a Kempis: His Age and Book* (London, 1906); Albert A. Hyma, *The Christian Renaissance: A History of the 'Devotio Moderna'* (Grand Rapids, Mich., 1924), chap 5; *The Following of Christ: The Spiritual Diary of Gerard de Groote, 1340–1384, Founder of the Brethren and Sisters of the Common Life*, trans. by Joseph Malaise (New York, 1937).

The spiritual treatise, *Hundred Meditations on the Love of God*, by the Spanish (or Portuguese) Franciscan, Diego de Estella, was formerly attributed to Blessed Robert Southwell, S.J.—See *The Month*, 146 (1925): 443–45.

On the Bacon-Shakespeare controversy, see Sir Sidney Lee, *The Life of William Shakespeare* (New York, 1917), 651–55; William A. A. Neilson and Ashley H. Thorndike, *The Facts about Shakespeare* (New York, 1924), 156–66; bibliography in the *Cambridge History of English Literature*, 10:501.

The Bible attributed to Wyclif probably is not his, but identical with the Catholic version of the Scriptures in use in England before the Reformation.—See Francis A. Gasquet, "The Pre-Reformation English Bible," *The Old English Bible and Other Essays*.

Raymond W. Chambers, "The Authorship of the 'History of Richard III,'" in *The English Works of Sir Thomas More* (London, 1931), 1:24–53, assigns this work to More, against the *Cambridge History of English Literature*, and the *Dictionary of National Biography*.

A manuscript published for the first time in 1923, has been attributed to George Buchanan as being the original version of his well-known *Detectio*.—See Reginald A. Mahon, *The Indictment of Mary, Queen of Scots* (Cambridge, 1923).

The letters of Junius have been assigned to as many as sixty-four different authors.—*Cambridge History of English Literature*, 10:454 ff.; C. W. Everett, *The Letters of Junius* (London, 1927); Frank Monaghan, "A New Document on the Identity of Junius," *Journal of Modern History*, 4 (1932): 68–71.

The provenance of the Memoirs attributed to Charlotte Robespierre, is discussed by Hilaire Belloc, in *Robespierre* (new ed., London and New York, 1927), 399 ff.

❡ 189   The authorship of *The Federalist* is examined by Edward G. Bourne, *Essays in Historical Criticism*, 113–45, and by Paul Leicester Ford, *The Federalist, a Commentary on the Constitution of the United States by Alexander Hamilton, James Madison and John Jay* (New York, 1898).

"A New Madison Manuscript Relating to the Federal Convention of 1787," *AHR*, 36 (1930): 17 ff.

John T. Lee, "The Authorship of Gregg's Commerce of the Prairies," *MVHR*, 16 (1930): 451–66.

Francis H. Herrick, "Thomas Ashe and the Authenticity of his *Travels in America*," *MVHR*, 13 (1926): 50–57.

"Lincoln's First Inaugural Address," *AHR*, 36 (1931): 550–52.

William A. Dunning, "George Bancroft Author of President Johnson's First Message to Congress, December 4, 1865," in *Massachusetts Historical Society, Proceedings*, 1905.

"The Diary of a Public Man: Unpublished Passages of the Secret History of the American Civil War" was published anonymously in the *North American Review*, 129 (1879). Neither the authenticity nor the authorship of the document "has been proved beyond the possibility of reasonable doubt. The problem is very baffling when one gets into details." *AHR*, 41 (1936): 277 f.

Chapter Nine

THE ANALYSIS OF SOURCES

A. The Meaning of Source-analysis . . . . Page 205
B. Sources as Related 206
C. Sources as Derived 208
D. One Source Original, One or More Derived 209
E. One Source Derived, Several Original 211
F. Lost Sources 212

A. The Meaning of Source-analysis

¶ 190 The dissection of historical writings with a view to ascertain the sources of information from which they were compiled, is a conventional method of inquiry in scientific history. The process must be conducted with meticulous care. For credibility of a narrative, as conditioned by the sources on which it draws, is not necessarily a constant; it may fluctuate according to the credibility of the individual sources.

(a) Thucydides distinguishes three categories of facts recorded in his history: those he knew by personal experience; those he knew at second hand, if one may say so; and at third hand, from the written tradition of his day. To the last category belongs the survey of Greek history with which he introduces his narrative; the reliability of this survey must be assessed according to the usual criteria for testing tradition. On the other hand, the vivid account of the retreat from Syracuse has all the weight of personal firsthand testimony [¶ 91-c-2]. The sources for Livy and Tacitus are minutely discussed in critical editions of these authors, or in the special monographic literature bearing on them. The discussion naturally runs into questions of credibility [¶ 311].

(b) An elaborate critical analysis of sources is involved in discussion of the Synoptic Problem, which is concerned with the relations of dependence between the three gospels of Matthew, Mark, and Luke. Study of the problem resolves itself into an attempt to ascertain, as far as may be, the sources of information on which the evangelists severally drew.—See Fillion, *Life of Christ*, 1:28 ff.; De Grandmaison, *Jesus Christ*, 1:56 ff.; Henry Schumacher, *Handbook of Scripture Study* (3 vols., St. Louis, 1922–1923), 3:42 ff.; CE, 14:389–94.

(c) Source-analysis applied to the life of Columbus, written by his son Ferdinand, reveals that this work is unreliable up to 1492, reliable after that date since it is based for the later period on the discoverer's journals and letters.—Edward G. Bourne, *Spain in America* (New York, 1904), 323.

Las Casas made an abridgment of the journal of Columbus' first voyage, and drew upon it for his *Historia de las Indias*. Sometimes the journal is quoted in Columbus' own words, sometimes in those of Las Casas, sometimes the reader must decide for himself whether it is Columbus' own thought or that of Las Casas which is expressed.—John Boyd Thacher, *Christopher Columbus* (3 vols., Cleveland, 1903-1904), 1:512 ff.; 604 ff.

¶ 191 THE PRINCIPLES OF SOURCE-ANALYSIS

The analysis of sources as a method of investigating whether and to what extent they are derived from other sources, is based in the main on three facts of psychology and on the "principle of community of origin."

(a) When two or more persons observe the same facts or series of facts, their reports will not tally in all minor details.

(b) When two or more persons give expression to the same ideas or report the same facts, they will not do so in the same order and in identical words, spoken or written.

(c) When a person appropriates another person's literary work, he usually betrays his dependence thereon by the substantial identity of his own version of the appropriated matter with the original.

(d) The application of "the principle of community of origin" to source-analysis is made as follows: When two or more sources (witnesses) report the same fact or series of facts in the same way, the sources are mutually related. If the sources are two in number, one is derived from the other, or both are derived in common from a third. If the sources are more than two, various relationships of dependence may exist between them.

B. Sources as Related

¶ 192 The general problem of relationship in the case of two or more sources can be worked out according to the following rules.

(a) *If there is agreement in content and form, the sources are certainly related.* Agreement in content can be recognized by various criteria: the narrative parts tell the same facts; digressions and abrupt breaks in the text are identical; the sources present the same general conception of things, the same viewpoints, political, religious, the same motives for identical acts. Agreement in form appears in the diction, style, distribution of data, and in other elements. Thus, Einhard in his life of Charlemagne, betrays dependence on Suetonius (especially on the latter's Augustus) by imitation of the Roman author's treatment and style.

As regards agreement in form, it must be noted that in narrative as a type of record, mere chronological succession of data has generally no probative force as a criterion of dependence, since such succession is postulated by the very nature of narrative itself. But the case is different when the facts narrated present a great complexity of detail, or cover a wide range of time and are reported by authors whose affiliations, political or religious, and general intellectual outlook are not the same. Under such circumstances one and the same time-order of events may point to some relation of dependence between the sources involved; but in other cases an identical time-order of facts found in different sources may well have its origin in the exigencies of narrative as a literary type, or in current fashions of thought and speech. Thus, two or three informants, independently of one another, may easily follow one and the same natural order in reporting facts, as they also may make common use of certain locutions current in the particular environment they share together. Attempts to identify Francis Bacon as the author of the plays attributed to William Shakespeare on the ground that numerous expressions occurring in Shakespeare occur also in Bacon's writings, are discounted because such expressions were more or less in common use among Elizabethan writers.

(b) *If, in the case of two or more sources, there is agreement of content but not of form, the sources will certainly be related.* Here the supposition is that the sources agree closely in matters of detail. Differences of form can be explained on various grounds.

(1) The author's individuality, literary mannerisms. One given to "fine writing" may show these traits in his version of material appropriated from another.

(2) Variation in literary practice according to time, place, race. Convention once tolerated, even authorized, a more literal reproduction of borrowed material than would be thought proper today. Even failure to make acknowledgment to the original source was not frowned upon. Present-day usuage is rigorous in requiring that in all literary borrowings due mention be made of the immediate source drawn upon.

(3) The literary genre of the original source. If this differs from the genre of the derived source, differences of literary form almost necessarily ensue. Thus, a poetic version of events will vary in form from a matter-of-fact narration, and a strictly annalistic version from one artistically conceived.

(4) The author's methods of work. In borrowing from the same

source historians will not do so in precisely the same way. Direct quotation, paraphrase, summary, citation from memory, are only some of the ways in which an identical fund of borrowed material can be put to use by various hands.

(c) When there is difference in form with doubtful agreement of content, the following rule may be applied: *If the same momenta in a large group of facts, or the same facts in a broad range of time are found in different sources, or if authors with different intellectual viewpoints make the same selection of facts, we may safely assume that the sources are related.* Experience proves that two or more authors handling a given body of facts do not make precisely the same selection of momenta; nor do they do so when the facts are spread out over a broad range of time. Moreover, when they do happen in some case to select identical momenta, their treatment of these is not identical, nor are their syntheses of facts identical in conception.

In a group of related sources, one independent, the rest dependent, only the independent group is to be credited with the evidential value of a primary source for the fact or facts in question. The others enjoy only the degree of evidential value which attaches to the independent source.

C. Sources as Derived

¶ 193 Indications that a source is dependent or derived, wholly or in part, include the following.

(a) *Identity or close agreement with another source of prior date in content* (or data and their arrangement) *and literary form.* This is the most decisive criterion by which to judge whether a source is dependent on one or more other sources, wholly or in part.

(b) *Differences in diction and style between an author's alleged composition and his known work.* This test has serious limitations; it must be applied with caution. If only parts or passages have been borrowed, the "purple patches" will sometimes furnish proof of the borrowing.

(c) *Digressions from theme or subject matter, or obvious additions which disrupt unity or coherence.* A source appears more clearly as derived, the more awkwardly the borrowing has been done, or in the case of additions, the more evidently these disrupt the order of the data as presented in the original text.

(d) *Different or entirely opposite motivation assigned for the same act.* When an author attributes to a person a definite motive, but elsewhere in his account attributes to him an entirely different motive for the same act, there may be room for the suspicion that one of the explanations offered is not original with the author, but has been borrowed.

(e) *Discrepancies between an author's portrayal of allegedly contemporaneous events and his actual environment, with its current viewpoints.* A forged manuscript purporting to be the journal of a spy, written during the French Revolution, embodied factual details and points of view that belonged to earlier or later periods [¶173-a–f.].

(f) *Mention of details and viewpoints alien not only to the author's own period, but also to the period of the events narrated.* Such details and viewpoints, it may be inferred, derive from a source which was composed before the events narrated, or else between them and the period of the author.

(g) *Of an author's writings, one may show him borrowing on a considerable scale, while another may bear the surface-marks of scholarly, independent treatment.* That he was certainly a borrower on the one occasion may justify a presumption that he was a borrower also on the other occasion.

For illustrations under these rules, all from ancient or medieval historiography, see Feder, Lehrbuch, 159.

D. One Source Original, One or More Derived

¶ 194 Relations of dependence between sources can be various according to the number of sources involved. The problem may have baffling complexities. In general, three cases demand consideration, differentiated by the number of sources.

¶ 195 TWO SOURCES

If two sources, A and B, agree in content or in form or in both, we must assume them to be related. Then, on the supposition that one is original in regard to the other, only two possibilities occur: either A derives from B, or B from A. To determine the actual relation, various tests may be applied.

¶ 196 TESTS

(a) One of the two sources may reveal itself as the original by its perceptibly greater age, as indicated by writing-material, script, and the like.

(b) Both sources contain passages which either in content or style harmonize only with one of the two, and therefore, as found in the other source, are clearly seen to be borrowed. One source may contain numerous anachronisms, or abrupt transitions from direct to indirect discourse, while the other source is written throughout in direct discourse only, which may be an indication that the latter source is the original.

(c) Dependence is not infrequently brought to light through additions or omissions. As a rule, the more detailed source is the original, especially when there are other indications to mark one of the sources as derived. A derived source may betray itself through omissions, when these result in ambiguity or lack of logical sequence.

(d) Alterations of content which have apparently been made with tendentious design sometimes indicate that a source is derived.

(e) In many cases greater finish and purity of style distinguishes the derived source. The clever borrower usually aims to improve on the style of the pattern, and this often enough with the design of covering up his tracks. But one must not overlook the possibility that the borrower may have had before him a copy of the original that was really finished in point of style, while only poorly-worded drafts of the original have come down to us.

❡ 197 THREE SOURCES

Here there are nine possibilities of relationship. In the first place, of three sources, A, B, C, each can be the original source of the other two. Moreover, in each of these three cases there are three possible combinations of the three units, or nine in all. For example, take the case where A is the original and only source of B and C. Here B and C are derived from A, either directly or indirectly; that is, either B is derived from A through C, or C is derived from A through B. These relationships are shown in the following *Figures*.

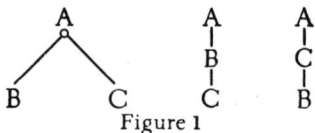

Figure 1

Note (Fig. 1) that in each group the letters, A, B, C, can be arranged in three different ways; for, the three sources, according as we take any one of the three to represent the *original* source, can stand to one another in nine different relations.

If we suppose that of the three related sources, the dependent source has put two independent sources to account, then six possible relations can occur, for B could have drawn on A as well as on C and, C on A as well as on B. The relations are indicated in Fig. 2.

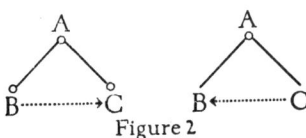
Figure 2

¶ 198 TESTS

To ascertain precise mutual relations in the case of three sources, the same tests or directions may be applied as were indicated for two sources. One or more special directions may be added.

(a) If, of three related sources, two show numerous points of agreement with the third, while at the same time they differ from one another in many respects, it is a reasonable inference that they have been derived from the third.

(b) Again, one must assume a direct dependence of two derived sources (B, C,) when B and C show clear reciprocal points of agreement as against A (the assumed original source), while, on the other hand B (C) shows clear points of agreement with A as against C (B). Hence, a special relation must be recognized between the Greek version of St. Matthew's Gospel and the Gospel of St. Mark, both of which made use of the Aramaic version of St. Matthew, for the Greek St. Matthew shows itself to be directly dependent on St. Mark.

¶ 199 MORE THAN THREE SOURCES

The more numerous the sources, the greater the number and variety of the relations that may exist among them. The process employed in fixing the relationships is always one of analysis. Various lines of investigation will have to be pursued, with the eye fixed on two or three sources at a time. This process is quite adequate for clearing up even the most complex relations, such as are met with in the pedigree of manuscripts. But caution is required at every step, since the bulk of the evidence uncovered will have been supplied by internal tests. As past experience in the field of critical scholarship abundantly witnesses, nothing is easier than to apply such tests with an arbitrariness that leaves a rich crop of errors and misconceptions. Internal criteria or tests work both ways. They are as capable of leading the investigator astray as they are of putting him on the right way in his search for truth.

E. One Source Derived, Several Original

¶ 200 THREE SOURCES

Here three combinations are possible according as any one of the three related sources A, B, C, is derived directly from the other two (Fig. 3).

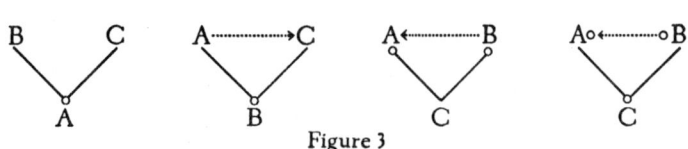

Figure 3

The two originals can be independent of each other, or can be mutually related, one being derived from the other or each having drawn upon the other. Further, the case may occur in which the two originals go back to a common source.

❡ 201 TESTS

(a) If of three sources (A, B, C), A contains data also found in B and C, while B and C contain entirely different data, or the same data in an altogether different form, then A is to be regarded as a derived source, which has drawn at once upon B and C.

(b) If, on the contrary, A contains data from B and C (one of which borrowed the data in question from the other), then we must first determine whether A drew on both the other sources, or only on one. This problem can be solved by the application of rules given ❡ 197.

(c) The most reliable internal test for the dependence of a source, A, on two others, B and C, as originals, is the circumstance that it exhibits so-called "doubles," that is, it presents the same content one time in the form of source B; another time in the form of source C (Fig. 4).

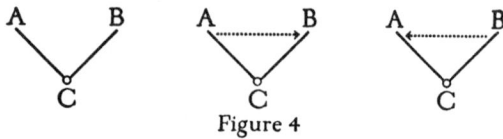

Figure 4

❡ 202 MORE THAN THREE SOURCES

The same tests, mutatis mutandis, apply as those indicated in ❡ 199. Numerous indications of relationship between several original accounts and a derived narrative, are met with in critical investigation of the early Church historians, Socrates, Sozomen, and Theodoret of Cyrrhus.

F. Lost Sources

❡ 203 One of the happy results of source-analysis in its task of dissecting historical material is the recovery, or rather the restoration of lost sources. These may be either the originals in their entirety, or in part. Thus, from certain aspects of actually existing conditions, customs, institutions, one may argue back to their original form. A fund of similar data, of similar passages in a group of sources may furnish a basis on which to build up the common source no longer extant, but on which they all drew. So also, various citations from a lost source, which occur in authors, may be pieced together, and thus the original text reconstructed with more or less completeness and accuracy. Sometimes pictorial representations may help us to restore in outline the content of a lost text.

¶ 204   The following three examples of restoration of lost sources are from Feder, *Lehrbuch*, 165.

Extracts made by Paul the Deacon, the historian of the Lombards, from the *Tractatus mysteriorum* of St. Hilary of Poitiers, have made it possible to recover lost sections of that treatise.

From the fact that Sulpicius Severus in his *Historia Sacra* drew almost verbatim for certain data on the Roman imperial period, from the *Annals* of Tacitus, a German scholar, J. Bernays, conjectured that the account in Severus of the burning of the Jewish temple in Jerusalem, which deviates in substance from the account in Josephus, was also drawn from the *Annals* of Tacitus. Moreover, he made a very clever attempt to reconstruct the lost passage of Tacitus, and to show the reconstruction to be correct.

From the data furnished by the Roman annalists of various periods, Theodor Mommsen sought to restore the consular lists (*Consularia Italica*), from which more data were taken.

¶ 205   The German historian, W. von Giesebrecht, observed that a group of medieval historians had all drawn on a common eleventh-century chronicle, which was missing. From excerpts embodied in the derivatives he was able to piece together the missing chronicle which on its discovery in 1867 was found to be in agreement with Giesebrecht's reconstruction.— Bernheim, *Lehrbuch*, 406.

For a reconstruction of the substance of Urban II's lost sermon delivered at the Council of Clermont, see Dana C. Munro, *AHR*, 11 (1905): 231 ff.

J. Franklin Jameson restored from available data the lost Pinckney plan, which was discussed in the Federal Convention of 1787. The original of the plan was later discovered and found to be substantially identical with Jameson's version. AHA, *Report* (1902) 1:111–32.

¶ 206   The historiography of all periods furnishes problems in the analysis of sources.

On Livy's sources, see *Cambridge Ancient History*, 7:312 ff.; J. Wight Duff, *A Literary History of Rome* (New York, 1928), 637 ff.

On Tacitus' sources, see Walter C. Summers, *The Silver Age of Latin Literature* (London, 1920), 162 ff.; Frank B. Marsh, "The Sources of

Tacitus," *The Reign of Tiberius* (London, 1930), 233 ff; Gaston Boissier, *Tacitus and Other Roman Studies* (New York, 1906), 43–68.

Felix Liebermann, "Nennius the Author of the Historia Brittonum," *Essays in Medieval History Presented to Thomas Frederick Tout* (Manchester, 1925).

Francis Tschan, "Helmold: Chronicler of the North Saxon Missions," *CHR*, 16 (1931) 380 ff.; idem, ed., *The Chronicle of the Slavs by Helmold, Priest of Bosau* (New York 1935).

W. G. Boswell-Stone, *Shakespeare's Holinshed: The Chronicle of the Historical Plays Compared* (London, 1896).

R. H. Carr, *Plutarch's Lives of Coriolanus, Caesar, Brutus and Antonius in North's Translation* (Oxford, 1906).

William of Tyre depends for the first crusade on contemporary chronicles; for the second crusade, on his own knowledge and on the information of contemporaries. See E. Barker, *The Crusades*, 108 ff.

Chapter Ten

THE INTEGRITY OF SOURCES
TEXTUAL CRITICISM

A. Textual Integrity: Meaning and Scope . . . . . Page 215
B. The Criteria of Integrity 218
C. The Recension: Direct Tradition 219
D. The Recension: Indirect Tradition 221
E. The Recension: Relationship of Manuscripts 223
F. The Emendation and the Editing of Texts 225

A. Textual Integrity: Meaning and Scope

¶ 207   The utility of a source for the historian's purpose, is conditioned in many ways by the correct answer to the question: "By whom, when, where was the source produced?" Another question must also be asked and answered: "Is the source in the same form textually as that in which it left the author's hands?" This is the question of integrity, or wholeness. Historians are sometimes led astray through basing conclusions on corrupt or otherwise defective versions. Had the original source been in their hands textually intact, they would have seen matters in a different light.

¶ 208   The task of textual criticism is twofold: first, to ascertain what errors, if any, have crept into the original text in the process of transmission; and second, to correct the errors and to build up a text identical, as far as possible, with that produced by the author. The process must be carried on by the application of a sound method, which makes it necessary to work out a body of safe and effective criteria. The reconstruction or restoration of texts in all their original purity is therefore the prime business of textual, or, as it is sometimes called, philological criticism. This particular field of critical research has striking results to its credit. The outstanding instance is the restoration of the text of the New Testament.

¶ 209   It has been estimated that the number of doubtful passages of the New Testament does not exceed a thousandth part of the entire text. Only some fifteen texts of any importance are in this doubtful part; no dogmatic truth has perished nor has any been added by these variants.—

See Dowd's *Gospel Guide*, on this topic; see also, on the general principles of textual criticism, Leo Vaganay, *An Introduction to the Textual Criticism of the New Testament*, trans. by V. B. Miller (London, 1932).

An enterprise in textual criticism now under way is the restoration of the text of the Vulgate, St. Jerome's Latin translation of the Scriptures. This enterprise engages the services of a group of Benedictine scholars in Rome, organized as a papal commission. Serious use of this new edition will perhaps be made only by students of Scripture or theology, but even a cursory examination of the volumes that have already appeared (*Genesis*, in 1926; *Exodus* and *Leviticus*, in 1929), will repay the student of history by bringing home to him the enormous research and intricate mechanical processes involved in the critical editing of ancient texts.

¶ 210 Critical scholarship has reached today a stage in which the historian finds ready to hand accurately prepared editions of many texts of the standard sources, for ancient, and to a certain extent, for medieval history. The writing of history, as pointed out more than once, posits a division of scholarly labor. The historian begins where the critical editor of texts leaves off. Had the historian to prepare on his own account reliable editions of Thucydides, Livy, Gregory of Tours, Venerable Bede, or other important sources, according to his needs, he would never come within hailing distance of his specific task. Moreover, much of the history that is being written today draws on new and previously unused material. Thus, numerous recent studies in the field of American history have the merit of being based wholly or in part on fresh and hitherto unknown sources. Hence, if a historian wishes to use new material, and especially if he incorporates in his book the original text of unpublished documents, he will have to face many of the problems of critical textual editing. Moreover, graduate students of history sometimes embody in their master's or doctor's theses the text, entire or partial, of unpublished material they have been fortunate enough to acquire. Here again, a knowledge of at least the essentials of textual criticism is necessary. Hence, for all workers in the field of history, the principles and directions that follow have one or another practical application.

(a) The French have a name for the person who gives himself exclusively to the tasks of heuristic and editing; they call him *un érudit*, a term probably best rendered in English by "critical scholar." He does the pioneering work in history, but does not go the whole length; he helps to lay the foundations but does not build the superstructure. This he leaves to the historian, who capitalizes on the labors of bibliographers, editors, and other specialists, and is enabled thereby to turn out at a minimum cost of time and labor the finished written product which alone can be dignified by the name of history.

(b) It is a mistake to assume that problems of textual criticism concern only documents of ancient or medieval date. There are doubts about the correct text of Lincoln's Gettysburg Address, though five copies in his own hand are extant.—See William E. Barton, *Lincoln at Gettysburg*, (Indianapolis, 1930); "Gettysburg Address in Autograph," *Michigan History Magazine*, 17 (1933) 127 ff.

For a textual study of the Declaration of Independence, see Carl L. Becker, *The Declaration of Independence; a Study in the History of Political Ideas* (New York, 1922), 5, note 1; 135–93.

(c) The importance of correct texts in historical research is exemplified in the letter of the missionary, St. Cosme, of January 2, 1699, in which a passage offers the only contemporary evidence available for the exact location of the Mission of the Guardian Angel, which stood somewhere on or near the site of Chicago in the last decade of the seventeenth century. Prior to the appearance of Louise P. Kellogg's translation of the letter (*Early Narratives of the Northwest 1634–1679* [New York, 1917]), the passage in question, previously available only in the text edited by John G. Shea (New York, 1861), stated that on one side of the mission was "a little lake." In the course of expert testimony taken in 1912, in an important law suit involving the location of the old Chicago Portage Route, the site of this Indian mission came up for discussion. On the strength of the reference, in St. Cosme's letter, to "a little lake," it was conjectured by one of the professional historians testifying, that the mission stood either on the banks of Mud Lake, or near the "Skokie," both being small inland bodies of water. As a matter of fact, the correct text of the letter as published (in translation) by Kellogg, omits the qualification, "little," and says merely that the mission had "the lake on one side," the reference being apparently to Lake Michigan (p. 346).

(d) Similarly, whether Vergil was born at Pietole, his traditional birthplace, which is three miles from Mantua, or at some place thirty miles from that city, is a question hinging on the correct reading for a single word in the text of Probus' *Vita Virgilii*. Is the *trigenta* of the manuscript copies a transcriber's mistake for *tria*? Edward K. Rand who contends that it is, discusses the point in his *In Quest of Virgil's Birthplace* (Cambridge, Mass., 1930), and in "Virgil's Birthplace Revisited," *Classical Quarterly*, 17 (1932): 1–13. The alleged erroneous transcription appears to have been made about 1460.—See Robert S. Conway, "Vergil, Probus, and Pietole Again," *Classical Quarterly*, 26 (1932): 209–14.

¶ 211   The integrity of a source may be understood in two senses, one narrow, the other broad. In the narrow sense the term implies that the holograph, or author's original copy, has come down to us. This is seldom verified in the case of writings of ancient date. No part of the Scriptures and none of the Greek or Latin classics survive in holograph.

All that is left of Shakespeare's handwriting are six signatures, if we except the fragment, held by some to be in his hand, of the play, *Sir Thomas More*. On the contrary, the original manuscripts (or typescripts) of probably most histories of recent date are extant. In the broad sense, integrity postulates that while we may not have the original, we have at least a more or less exact reproduction or copy of it. Whether the term be used strictly or broadly, integrity is perfect or imperfect according as it extends to the whole or only to a part of a document.

What is said here of textual integrity has reference chiefly to written sources. The "wholeness" of other types of historical sources, buildings, works of art, may sometimes become a subject of inquiry. To give an instance, it may conceivably be important for an investigator to know whether and to what extent the Castel S. Angelo (Mausoleum of Hadrian) in Rome exists in its original shape, or whether it exists only with alterations and additions of later date. The fact remains, however, that the bulk of source material with which historians have to do, is of the written kind, a type of record peculiarly liable to corruption and decay in the course of time. All this source material once existed (much of it still does exist) in autograph copies, or in copies dictated by the authors. All sorts of vicissitudes have befallen these original copies. Though they may not have perished altogether, today they may be illegible, torn, mutilated, damaged in a score of ways. Physical, sometimes human agencies, are responsible for the damage; dampness, rust, fire, water, insects, mice, thieves. Not only originals, copies also of documents may suffer such mishaps.

B. The Criteria of Integrity

¶ 212 In research bearing on the integrity of documents (sources) the following criteria find application.

(a) Proof that a document is either the original or a reliable copy can be supplied by the handwriting, provided this be otherwise known; by physical features, (formalities, seals, quality of writing material); by reliable extrinsic testimony, such as the declaration of a notary public or other witness that a document is an exact copy of the original.

(b) If there are numerous copies substantially identical in form and belonging to various times, places, and schools of thought, we may conclude that the copies all go back to an early copy, or even (at least in part) to the original.

(c) If the source is extant in a number of translations which meet the conditions indicated in (b), or if its contents are vouched for by numerous extracts, paraphrases, and citations, it is safe to conclude to the substantial integrity of the text.

(d) Use of mutually-agreeing copies of a source by men of opposite schools of thought is often proof of integrity. If the copies were defective on the score of integrity, one of the schools would have called attention to the fact.

(e) Important evidence in favor of integrity may result from the circumstance that great care was taken to preserve the source in its original purity, especially by mutual comparison of manuscript copies, as was particularly the case in certain times of critical development, for instance, during the Alexandrian period, the Carolingian Revival.

The last four criteria (b, c, d, e) have been applied with marked success to various books of the Bible, especially the four Gospels.

With a good critical text edition of a source in his hands, the historian is saved the time and labor he would otherwise have to expend in settling textual questions for himself; but should no critical edition of the sources be available, or should the existing editions be unsatisfactory, he may have to work out a correct text for himself. This process involves two major steps; first, recension or study of the manuscript tradition in order to trace the source back to the earliest extant copies, and in order to ascertain the best accredited text; secondly, emendation, which aims to reconstruct or restore the text, where it is defective, on the basis of the results yielded by the recension.

Feder (*Lehrbuch*, 187) uses the term *recension* for study of the manuscript tradition. The use is technical and may give rise to ambiguity. In English, recension ordinarily means revision, or a revised version or edition of a book or document. Feder's use of the word, however, is retained as being a recognized term in the terminology of textual criticism.—See F. W. Hall, *A Companion to Classical Texts*, 108 ff.

C. The Recension: Direct Tradition

₡ 213 (a) Critical assessment of the tradition. The tradition or handing down of a written text can be effected in two ways: directly, through manuscript copies of the text; indirectly, through sources outside of the text. An editor of a text must first see that its direct manuscript tradition is familiar to him in all its stages. Nowadays this is an easier task than it used to be. Library and archive catalogues and guides in many cases furnish exact information as to the whereabouts of the pertinent manuscripts, and often even supply reliable data as to their characteristics. Further, printed editions of the text, when such exist, can also be consulted with profit. In some cases previous textual studies of importance on the source under study will be found in books or learned reviews. International intercourse between scholars is now organized through many practical media: universities, institutes of research, and learned societies and journals, with the result that the labor involved in the critical editing of texts has been notably lightened. The copying of manuscripts as a stage in the collation and restoration of texts has been greatly facilitated through the photographic processes of photostating and microfilming [⊄ 99-d].

(b) Tracing the manuscript tradition involves also the task of determining the value in each case of the extant manuscripts, with a view to selecting one or more as the basis of the textual restoration. Here a knowledge of the pedigree (genealogy, filiation) of the text, that is, the family relations existing between manuscript copies of the text, will be necessary. This is ordinarily obtained by means of the process known as *collation*, which is the minute examination and comparison of the available copies. Collation is not an easy procedure when the number of manuscripts is considerable, reaching perhaps into the hundreds. In such cases one may employ a selective process, consisting in a comparison of the manuscripts in important or doubtful passages. This process will result in fixing certain relationships, and in many cases will bring the best manuscripts to light. In making a selection from the manuscripts two dangers are to be avoided. One is to rate the value of a manuscript by age alone. In not a few cases the more recent of two manuscripts is the better, having been based on more correct exemplars, which are now lost. The other danger is that of giving the preference to the manuscript which is within easiest reach.

(c) Collation of a manuscript should extend to the various readings, to all errors in the text insofar as these may furnish a key to correct conjectures upon the proper reading. Where a reading or an abbreviation is doubtful, because of difficult or illegible script, a drawing in exact imitation of the original should be made, for any single letter or mark may be of importance. Moreover, all lacunae are to be noted; corrections also, especially those made by later hands, since these are to be sharply distinguished from corrections made by the first hand; similarly, erasures, which often betray deliberate changes made at a later date.

(d) It is often desirable in a critical edition of a text to give an exact description of the more important manuscript copies. The description will include data on such matters as the present home of the manuscripts, with library or archival call-number; date and place of origin; writing material (papyrus, parchment, paper) with trade- or watermarks; shape, size, and number of leaves; lacunae in the text and their location; style or school of writing; ink and colors; comments on flyleaves, and in the body of the text; subscriptions; condition of preservation; history of the manuscript.

(e) Sometimes a printed edition of a source aids in fixing the manuscript tradition. If only a single manuscript copy has survived, the printed edition has all the value of a transcript. If the printed edition was based on different manuscripts, the book will have the character of a quasi-manuscript, and its value is to be judged by the manuscripts used and the editorial care exhibited. Printed editions based on reliable manuscripts of early date which are now lost, have a particular importance. Old editions of a text may be of service to the editor of a new one through hints given in the dedication, or introduction, as to the manuscript's tradition; or by supplying variant readings, erudition of value, and important critical comments.

The manuscript copies of the Shakespearean plays, from which the first printed editions (quartos and folios) were made, have all disappeared. Hence, for knowledge of the text we are dependent on the first printed edition. For the probable errors made by Elizabethan compositors in setting up Shakespeare's copy for publication, and for the problems peculiar to the printed transmission of texts, see R. B. McKerrow, *An Introduction to Bibliography*, 252 ff; Thomas R. Lounsbury, *The Text of Shakespeare* (New York, 1908).

D. The Recension: Indirect Tradition

℆ 214 THE CHANNELS OF INDIRECT TRADITION

The indirect tradition of a text is often a factor to be reckoned with in attempts to solve the problems of transmission and textual restoration. It can, moreover, throw light on the circulation or popularity of a text as shown by translations, commentaries, and excerpts. Indirect tradition or transmission means in general the handing down of a text through channels outside the text itself. The more important of these are here noted.

(a) *Author's sources.* Sources utilized by the author, either through verbatim extracts or quotations or by appropriation of content, can be a help in supplying missing passages or correcting garbled passages.

(b) *Excerpts.* The practice of compiling "books of selections," containing choice passages from standard authors was widespread in the classical period. The passages, reproduced with more or less textual fidelity, varied in length from entire sections to paragraphs or sentences. Important texts from the classical authors, from the Fathers of the

Church (in the *catenae* or *chains* of selected passages), and from medieval chroniclers, have thus been preserved. Numerous excerpts from older sources are especially to be found in certain works of an encyclopedic or scientific character, such as the lexicons of Pollux (second century, the comedies and tragedies); Harpocration (third century, the Attic orators); Photius (ninth century, numerous ancient authors); Suidas (tenth century, Aristophanes, Thucydides, Hesychius of Miletus, and others). Selected texts are also to be found in many of the ancient grammars and in the *florilegia*.

(c) *Quotations*. Contemporary or later writers may borrow from a source, the quotations being perhaps passages which in the extant manuscripts are either missing or corrupt. But before taking over such quoted passages into a critically edited text, one must determine whether they were meant to be reproductions or only free renderings or paraphrases of the original, and these perhaps based on memory.

(d) *Translations*. As a rule, translations made in the ancient era are fairly true to the originals. The most important translations are those which furnish the only evidence we have for lost texts. Thus, except for some fragments, the very important *Chronicle* of Eusebius, which was composed in Greek, has survived only in the Latin translation by St. Jerome, and in an Armenian version. Another case in which the value of a translation is enhanced, occurs where the source survives, indeed, in its own language, but only in late and defective copies, while the translation was made from earlier and better copies now no longer extant. This is exemplified in various translations of the original Hebrew text of the Old Testament. While the Hebrew manuscripts are scarcely older than the tenth century, A.D., the Greek version goes back to the second century B.C., and the Syriac, Latin, and Coptic versions to the second and third centuries, A.D. At the same time, even with all such advantages on the side of a translation, one must not overlook the fact that even the most accurate of translators must be guided by the genius of his own language. Hence, under pressure of necessity he will not infrequently depart from the original text in such matters as grammatical construction, sentence connection, and use of particles. It would be quite unwarranted to give the preference to an isolated translation in the face of a well-accredited version in the mother-tongue. On caution in the use of translations, see ₵ 322.

(e) *Paraphrase*. This is a reproduction of a text or of passage in different and generally in fuller diction, made with a view to bring out the sense of the original. Meant primarily to serve the purposes of verbal interpretation, it may on occasion help to clear up a doubtful reading.

The *Paraphrases* of Themistius on Aristotle (fourth century A.D.) made the Stagyrite's difficult Greek more intelligible to contemporaries.

(f) *Glosses.* Glosses are elucidations of single words, a sort of partial paraphrase. They were eventually assembled into *glossaries*, which have become important aids in the scientific investigation of language, especially in its dialect forms. Of works of this nature probably the most famous is Du Cange's *Glossarium ad scriptores mediae et infimae Latinitatis* (Paris, 1678). Its interesting citations from authors and documents, illustrating the meaning of medieval Latin terms, make it one of the most readable of lexicons.

(g) *Commentaries and scholia.* A commentary is a body of running explanatory or illustrative notes on a text, especially on its more difficult passages. A *scholion* is a critical marginal note; for the most part *scholia* are excerpts from commentaries and lexicons. Subjects chosen for commentary were: in the ancient world, chiefly the philosophers (such as Plato and Aristotle), and the poets (such as Hesiod and Homer), but rarely the historians; in the early Christian period, particularly the Holy Scriptures; in the Middle Ages, the philosophers, old and recent. Both commentaries and scholia, with their abundant textual citations from authors, can sometimes be drawn upon to determine the correct reading of a doubtful text.

E. The Recension: Relationship of Manuscripts

₡ 215   The most important step in evaluating the manuscripts of a given source is to establish the relations that exist not only between the individual manuscripts themselves, but especially between them and a common first exemplar (prototype or archetype). The process applied here is essentially analytic and comparative, usual in historical method when there is question of establishing relationship between documents [₡ 190 ff.]. The inquiry is the more complex the more numerous the manuscripts, especially those of the class known as "conflated" or "mixed" (*codices mixtae*), which follow various exemplars, and which in turn influence "mixed" manuscripts of older dates. "Mixed" manuscripts of the Renaissance period are especially numerous.

₡ 216   VARIETIES OF RELATIONSHIPS
The net result of the assessment of the tradition, direct and indirect, will usually be (where sources from antiquity are in question) to establish one of the five following cases, which, however, are also to be met with in medieval and even in later sources, but with such differences as the circumstances entail.

(a) The text is at present attested by a printed edition made on the basis of one or more manuscripts now lost. This is the case with the Roman history of Velleius Parterculus (first century, A.D.), which was published by the humanist Beatus Rhenanus, in 1520, from the lost *Codex Murbacensis* (Murbach in Alsace). The text of Book X of Pliny's *Letters* depends on a lost manuscript, from which printed copies were made while it was still extant.——See Elmer T. Merrill, "The Tradition of Pliny's Letters," *Classical Philology*, 10 (1915): 9 ff; Dora Johnson, "The Manuscripts of Pliny's Letters," *Classical Philology*, 7 (1912): 66 ff.

A somewhat parallel modern instance, in which only printed sources are involved, is that of the *Ulster County Gazette*, Kingston, New York, January 4, 1800. Of this issue, which reported George Washington's funeral, only a single original copy is known to exist (Library of Congress), though sixty-seven reprints of the issue have been accounted for.——*Michigan History*, 15 (1931): 688 ff.; Edmond S. Meany, "The Ulster County Gazette," *Washington Historical Quarterly*, 22 (1931): 26-31.

(b) Only a single standard manuscript is now extant. This is either first, some ancient or medieval examplar, for example, a papyrus manuscript for Hyperides, Herondas, Bacchylides, or the *Codex Mediceus* for the *Histories* of Tacitus, the *Codex Wirceburgensis* (Wurzburg in Germany) for Priscillian, the Arles Manuscript for the *Tractatus mysteriorum* of St. Hilary of Poitiers; or second, a manuscript which is demonstrably the archetype of all other existing manuscripts, such as the *Codex Laurentianus* for Varro's work *De lingua latina*, or the *Codex Parisiensis* for Justin the Martyr.

The *Codex Mediceus* (*Laurentianus*) of the *Histories* of Tacitus is in Beneventan script, made at the monastery of Monte Cassino in Italy in the tenth or eleventh century. "All other manuscripts are copies of the *Mediceus* and comparatively useless except to supply the text in two passages now missing in the parent manuscript."——*Tacitus: the Histories* (Loeb ed.), xiv.

The text of Beowulf is based upon a single manuscript (ca. 1000) now in the British Museum.——*Collected Papers of Henry Bradley* (Oxford, 1928), 198 ff.; *Cambridge History of English Literature*, 1:24.

(c) A number of medieval manuscripts, and some of later periods, survive, all deriving from a single medieval archetype now lost. This is the case with Caesar's *Commentaries*, the *Germania* and *Agricola* of Tacitus, and the letters of Cicero to Atticus.

For the textual tradition of Caesar's *Commentaries*, see T. R. Holmes, *Caesar's Conquest of Gaul*, 166. There are two groups of manuscripts, both derived from a common original or archetype now lost.

(d) Medieval manuscripts, more or less numerous, are extant. Their texts disagree with one another in numerous readings, as in the works of Plato, Sallust, and many of the early Christian authors. The manuscripts can usually be distributed into various groups and families.

(e) Two sharply differentiated transmissions of a text can be traced, one ancient, the other medieval. The texts of Homer, Demosthenes, Plato, Vergil, Cicero, are examples.

The pedigree (genealogy, filiation) of manuscripts can be shown graphically by a stemma or "family-tree," after the manner of the Figures in ❡ 197, 200, 201.

Scholarly editing of a text requires thorough research into the manuscript tradition and careful evaluation of the extant copies. Alfred Feder was engaged at the time of his death (1926) on a critical edition of St. Jerome's *De viris illustribus*, a sort of bibliographical survey of the ecclesiastical writers of the first four centuries. He listed one hundred and sixty-two manuscripts, fourteen of which he considered to be of particular importance. He used the oldest manuscript of all, one of Bamberg, sixth century, which was unknown to previous editors of the text, as were also three of the fourteen he selected.—*EHR*, 43 (1928): 640.

Falconer Maden, *Books in Manuscripts: A Short Introduction to Their Study and Use* (2d ed., rev., London, 1921).

F. W. Hall, "Recension," *A Companion to Classical Texts*, chap. 6.

Albert C. Clark, *The Descent of Manuscripts* (Oxford, 1918).

Montague R. James, *The Wanderings and Homes of Manuscripts* (*Helps*, vol. 17).

Basil Williams, "Migrations of Historical Manuscripts," *Nineteenth Century and After*, 106 (1929): 35–48.

F. The Emendation and the Editing of Texts

❡ 217 Emendation, the second major step in textual criticism, aims to restore the original verbal form of a document. Using as a basis the results arrived at in the tracing of the manuscript tradition, it builds up, as far as can be, the author's actual text. In doing so, it employs two processes in particular, selection and conjectural emendation.

❡ 218 SELECTION

When research on the manuscript tradition has been completed, the editor finds himself, as regards many passages of the text, in possession of a number of variant readings, some of them, it may be, mutually contradictory, and none of them beyond cavil of doubt the original. (Variants in manuscripts of the Gospels number two hundred thousand.) It then becomes necessary to choose from among the various readings of a particular passage, the one more likely to be the original and true.

In determining the choice, the editor will be guided by various criteria, some external, others internal.

Among *external* criteria will be the older date, the greater authority, the general reliability in its undisputed passages of a particular manuscript. The same criteria may obtain in the case of a group of manuscripts. Harmony of a reading with the source or sources used by the author is also a point in its favor. *Internal* criteria to be made use of will include accord of a reading with the grammar, the logic, the author's mentality and character; verbal and stylistic traits of the author or of the period of the documents; the causes and circumstances of errors in copying and, in particular, the possibilities of progressive deterioration in regard to erroneous forms.—Feder, *Lehrbuch*, 190.

Errors of copyists have been classified on the basis of certain laws, physiological and psychological, which explain their origin or causes.—Feder, *Lehrbuch*, 170–77; F. W. Hall, *A Companion to Classical Texts*, chap. 7; F. Maden, *Books in Manuscript*, 68–87.

Copyists are especially liable to error, the most common of which is *omissio*, committed where *homoioteleuton* occurs: "The eye of the writer wanders from a particular word or portion of a word to a similar word or portion of a word elsewhere in the context, with the result that the intervening words are omitted."—A. C. Clark, *The Descent of Manuscripts*, 1.

Compositor's errors in printed texts are discussed in R. B. McKerrow, *An Introduction to Bibliography*, 252 ff.

¶ 219 CONJECTURAL EMENDATION

Sometimes it is impossible to recover with certainty the original reading of a word or other part of a text which obviously became corrupt in manuscript transmission. An effort is then made to conjecture from the context or from other evidence what the original reading must have been. Such emendations, commonly called *conjectural*, are sometimes happy, sometimes doubtfully successful.

(a) Madvig's six conjectural readings in Cicero's *Pro Coelio* appear to have been confirmed by the discovery of an important manuscript of the speech.—John E. Sandys, *A History of Classical Scholarship* (3 vols., Cambridge, Eng., 1901), 3:323.

A famous emendation by conjecture is Theobald's substitution (1734) of the words " 'a babbled of green fields" for "a table of greene fields," in Henry V, II, iii, 16 f. The latter reading failed to make sense and had long been a puzzle to editors of Shakespeare.—Thomas M. Parrot, *Shakespeare* (New York, 1938), 448, note.

Conjectural emendations are frequent in critical editions of the ancient classics; most of such conjectures furnish pertinent illustrations. It is a frequent practice for an editor, in selecting from a number of variants a particular reading for adoption in the text, to indicate the variant readings in footnotes.

(b) An instance of conjectural emendation, sometimes cited in textbooks, regards a passage in Seneca (Letter LXXXIX) which usually took this form in critical editions: *Philosophia unde dicta sit apparet; ipso enim nomine fatetur. Quidam et sapientiam ita quidam finierunt, ut dicerent divinorum et humaniorum sapientiam.* . . . These words yielded no meaning; the passage, it was assumed, had become corrupt. Then Madvig, realizing the possibility that a copyist had incorrectly divided certain words which in the original copy ran together without separation of any kind between the letters, as was usual in ancient manuscripts, made a new division of the words with this result: . . . *nomine fatetur quid amet. Sapientiam* . . . With this emendation the text became intelligible.—See, however, Louis Laurand's criticism of this emendation, "Les auteurs classiques et la critique des textes au XXe siècle," in *Études*, 136 (1913): 44.

Other examples of conjectural emendation.
F. W. Hall, *Companion to Classical Texts*, chap. 8.
Walter C. Summers, "Notes and Emendations to Seneca's Letters," *Classical Quarterly*, 2 (1908): 22–30; 3 (1909): 40–45, 180–88.
Henry M. McCracken, *Introduction to Shakespeare* (New York, 1916), 126.
W. A. Neilson and A. H. Thorndike, *The Facts about Shakespeare* (New York, 1924): 130 ff.
Collected Papers of Henry Bradley, 237 ff.

¶ 220   Conjectural readings may be certain or highly probable, in which cases they may be incorporated in the text; but their conjectural nature should be plainly indicated by a footnote. Certain pitfalls are to be avoided in the correction of texts, such as an attempt to introduce absolute verbal uniformity. It must not be assumed that an author everywhere and at all times used the same verbal forms, where choice was possible. One may on the same page write, now "do not," now "don't." A French author may write *si on*, and elsewhere *si l'on*. Cicero in his *De Oratore* used various admissible forms, *nosse* and *novisse*, *judicasse* and *judicavisse*, *scripserunt* and *scripsere*. This comment, however, is not to be taken as contradicting the fact that authors do tend to be somewhat uniform in their choice of equivalent word-forms, at least when the demands of variety in diction do not require an opposite procedure. —On the subject of conjecture in textual editing, see L. Laurand, *Manuel des études grecques et latines*, 800–802.

Conjectural emendation as a critical process has met with censure in recent years on two alleged grounds: first in general, papyrus discoveries fail to confirm the conjectural readings of modern editors. When they do so, the variation is, on the whole, very slight. In no case has any considerable change been justified by the papyri. Second, as a body, former conjectural readings do not conform to certain recently discovered laws of rhythm in classical prose.—L. Laurand, *Manuel*, 799 f.

❡ 221 THE TRANSCRIPTION

The transcription of a text from a manuscript is a process sometimes necessary as preliminary to its editing or translating. This is not always an easy process. It postulates in the copyist acquaintance with the language in which the document is written, especially in the form in which the language existed at the date of the document; acquaintance, too, when this is possible, with the stylistic characteristics of the author, with the palaeography, and the general background of the period to which the document belongs.

Grace L. Nute, *Copying Manuscripts: Rules Worked out by the Minnesota Historical Society* (St. Paul, Minn., 1936).

"Transcription of Manuscripts," in Henry G. T. Christopher, *Palaeography and Archives* (London, 1938).

R. B. Haselden, *Scientific Aids for the Study of Manuscripts* (London, 1938).

"Transcription," in J. Villasana Haggard, *Handbook for Translators of Spanish Historical Documents* (Archives Collection, University of Texas, Austin, Texas, 1941).

❡ 222 THE EDITING OF TEXTS

The text should be reproduced exactly as it is in the original; no attempt should be made to correct or modernize spelling, to amend faulty grammar or to substitute other words for the author's. This is an accepted present-day convention in the critical editing of texts; departure from it is frowned on as unscholarly procedure. Formerly, editors felt at liberty to tamper with texts in various ways. In editing Washington's writings for publication, Jared Sparks corrected the spelling. He apparently took the view that it would be an impropriety to allow the distinguished author's orthographical lapses to go before the public. On the other hand, Reuben G. Thwaites' edition of the Lewis and Clark journals (1904–1905), and Howard Beale's edition of Edward Bates' diary (1933), leave all spelling mistakes uncorrected. An exception to this rule of reproducing a text exactly as it is in the original, is allowed in cases where the purpose is not to furnish a critical edition, but one intended for the general reader, or for school use. Here it is permissible, provided the sense of the original is not impaired in the process, to amend or modernize the text by ridding it of verbal oddities and solecisms, which would only distract or perplex the ordinary reader, or perhaps even deter him altogether from its perusal. An example of this kind of popular editing is Milo M. Quaife's edition of George Roger

Clark's Memoir (Indianapolis, 1927). An analogous practice obtains in the case of popular and school editions of Shakespeare, and of other early English classics, in which it is customary to modernize the spelling and capitalization.

⟪223 CRITICAL APPARATUS

By critical apparatus (*apparatus criticus*) is meant the complex of signs, symbols, and other conventional devices used to insure clearness and accuracy in the reproduction of texts. By extension the term may be taken also to designate the complex of aids (introduction, footnotes, appendixes, tables) employed for adequate editing of the text.

(a) *The use of brackets* [. . .].

(*1*) Brackets are used in pairs to indicate editorial interpolation, explanation, correction, supplementation. The intention is to show that matter so enclosed in brackets is not found in the original, but has been inserted by the editor. Thus:

An outstanding contribution to philosophical thought was made by the Stagyrite [Aristotle].
America was discovered in 1493 [1492].

Parentheses (. . .) around a portion of the text are presumed to proceed from the author, not from the editor.

(*2*) Brackets are used to indicate an uncertain reading. Here the question is not raised as to the sense or truth of the reading, but only as to its verbal form found in manuscript. A word or expression may be illegible: if the meaning intended falls into doubt on this account, the editor adopts what he considers the more plausible reading, and indicates its doubtful character by the abbreviation [MSS?].

An interrogation point only, enclosed in brackets [?], indicates editorial doubt as to the meaning or truth of a statement. Thus:

Columbus derived most of his geographical knowledge from the *Ymago Mundi* of Pierre d'Ailly [?].

(*3*) Strange or erroneous reading is indicated by [sic], or less commonly by [!]. Thus:

Charlemagne became emperor in 798 [sic].
Charlemagne became emperor in 798 [!].

It is often preferable to indicate the correction in the text. Thus:

Charlemagne became emperor in 798 [800].

(b) *The indication of lacunae or gaps in the text*. Whether in textual editing or in printed reproduction of extracted matter a lacuna or gap (ellipsis) is indicated in various ways.

(1) Especially in law texts, by three 3-to-em spaced asterisks: * * *
(2) In other than law texts: by three periods, 3-to-em spaced: . . .

The use of three periods will be observed as common practice in a vast number of well-edited books. But see University of Chicago Press, *A Manual of Style* (10th ed., rev., Chicago, 1937, 9th impr., 1945), 102, where the use of *four* periods is ruled, and in such wise that after a complete sentence the preceding period is not to be considered as part of the elipsis marks (four periods).

Where there is elipsis of a whole paragraph, the gap is indicated by a full line of periods, em or 2-em spaced, on the exact measure of the text.

Where the original manuscript is torn, faded, or has some other physical defect, lacunae are indicated by the use of one period for each illegible letter.

Since practice in the use of some of the signs and symbols for the critical editing of manuscripts or texts is not uniform, a note is sometimes needed to inform the reader upon the precise significance in which the editor employs them.

(c) The specialized critical apparatus necessary for the more elaborate types of textual editing will best be understood by inspection. Such details are beyond the scope of this book.

¶ 224 INFORMATION ON CRITICAL APPARATUS
The handling of manuscripts:

Grace L. Nute, *The Care and Cataloguing of Manuscripts as Practiced by the Minnesota Historical Society.*

F. Maden, "Treatment and Cataloguing of Manuscripts," *Books in Manuscript,* 135–66.

Textual Criticism:

Louis Laurand, "Établissement des Textes," *Manuel des études grecques et latines,* 795–805.

F. W. Hall, *A Companion to Classical Texts,* 98–108.

F. Maden, *Books in Manuscript,* 68–87.

J. E. Sandys, *A Companion to Latin Studies,* 791–805.

Leonard Whibley, *A Companion to Greek Studies* (4th ed., Cambridge, Eng., 1931).

"Textual Criticism," *Encyclopaedia Britannica* (11th ed.).

Editing texts:

Brief directions for the editing of texts were published in "Editing of Medieval Latin Texts in America," by S. Harrison Thomson, *Progress of Medieval Studies in the United States and Canada. Bulletin No. 16* (April, 1931).

"The careful editing of a text affords excellent exercise. It stimulates initiative and sharpens the critical faculties."—Paul Studer, *The Study of Anglo-Norman* (Oxford, 1920).

⟨ 225   SCHOLARLY EDITIONS OF SOURCES

Examination of the editorial features of scholarly editions of historical sources can be instructive.

Ormond M. Dalton, translator and editor, *The History of the Franks by Gregory of Tours* (2 vols., Oxford, 1927).

Acton Griscum, translator and editor, *The Historia Regum Britanniae of Geoffrey of Monmouth with Contributions to a Study of Its Place in Early British History* (London, 1929).

Edmond Buron, ed., *Ymago Mundi de Pierre d'Ailly* (3 vols., Paris, 1930).

Ernest Nys, ed., *Franciscus de Vittoria, De Indis et de Jure Belli Selectiones* (Washington, 1917).

Leo F. Stock, ed., *Proceedings and Debates of the British Parliaments Respecting North America* (3 vols., Washington, 1924–1930).

Reuben G. Thwaites, ed., *Jesuit Relations and Allied Documents* (73 vols., Cleveland, 1896–1901).

Thomas A. Hughes, *History of the Society of Jesus in North America, Colonial and Federal* (2 vols., London, 1908–1910).

Elizabeth Donnand, ed., *Documents Illustrative of the History of the Slave Trade in America* (2 vols., Washington, 1930–1932).

Max Farrand, ed., *Records of the Federal Convention* (3 vols., New Haven, Conn., 1911, reprinted 1923).

Philip A. Rollings, ed., *The Discovery of the Oregon Trail: Robert Stuart's Narrations* (New York, 1935).

Herbert E. Bolton, ed., *Anza's California Expeditions* (5 vols., Berkeley, Calif., 1930).

Walter L. Fleming, ed., *Documentary History of Reconstruction, Political, Military, Social, Religious, Educational, and Industrial, 1865 to the Present Time* (2 vols., Cleveland, 1906).

Chapter Eleven

THE CREDIBILITY OF SOURCES

A. The Problem of Error . . . . Page 232
B. The Credibility of Specific Written Sources 240

A. The Problem of Error

¶ 226   ERROR IN INFORMAL SOURCES
Informal sources (remains) are always trustworthy *in se*. Error in regard to them is possible only in attempts to explain, to interpret, or to draw conclusions from them. Thus, frequently a mistake is made in the attempt to account for a phenomenon that results from some routine process of nature, or that occurs independently of observation. A skeleton may show traces of violent death, but whether by murder or accident or the play of some physical force, is a question it may not be possible to answer beyond doubt. So also a variety of causes may be invoked to account for the ruinous condition of a building—mere deterioration, neglect, deliberate wrecking, fire, earthquake. Any attempt to isolate the true cause can easily result in error.

¶ 227   ERROR IN FORMAL SOURCES
Formal sources are the favorite breeding places of factual error in history. To trust them implicitly is to court all sorts of deception. On the other hand, to distrust them altogether, on the ground that criticism so often shows them to be unreliable, would be equally unreasonable. It is possible to know the causes of historical error in general; such knowledge is indispensable to the historian.

(a) Two illusions in regard to formal testimony are frequently encountered. One, more common in past times than in our own, is that testimony given by a perfectly conscientious person must be presumed to be true; the other is that testimony given seriously and apparently in good faith, but later found to be false, must be regarded as deliberate falsehood, or at least as proof of criminal carelessness. Experience belies both illusions. Conscientious witnesses, without being aware of it, can deviate from the objective truth; the possibility of unintentional deception is considerable and must always be taken carefully into account.

(b) Testimony in history can be trustworthy without this qualification extending to minor and unessential details. To require that a source be trustworthy in every detail would be impracticable. At the same time, the source gains in value the more it can be shown to be reliable in both substance and details.

(c) Witnesses, direct or indirect, whose testimony the historian finds incorporated in written sources, as a general rule may be taken to be normal-minded persons. Chronic mental cases, proved to be such, are ruled out of the category of acceptable witnesses. In doubtful cases, such as lie on the borderline between the normal and the pathological, account is to be taken of the possibility of the witnesses not being normal; distinct abnormality is easily recognizable and quite exceptional.

℃ 228 Some writers on the subject see in the numerous and complex processes involved in giving testimony or making a report, a reason for throwing doubt on the credibility of witnesses in general. No doubt it may be conceded, the processes being what they are, that frequency of possible error is high. A glance at the various steps taken in the act of testimonial evidence is enough to show this. A witness first perceives something by one of his sense-organs, then fuses the perception with the general content of his experience, and further elaborates it. Next, perhaps after a long lapse of years and under entirely different conditions, he seeks for the perception in his consciousness, puts it into words, and gives it outward expression. The individual acts of perception, synthesis, reproduction, and expression are factors under the influence of which the content of the original perception is constantly exposed to the danger of taking on new and alien shapes. Yet even in face of this fact, it is to be insisted upon that the possibilities of change thus to be reckoned with, in general, concern only the non-essentials of a historical source. This truth emerges from the nature of the processes by which information is obtained and communicated to others, and is amply borne out by experience. Finally, criticism equips us adequately with means of checking these processes, as they occur, and of detecting any errors that may enter into them.

℃ 229 ERROR IN SENSE-PERCEPTION

(a) Any incident finding a place in history as record is in reality a series of single perceptible incidents knit together by time, space, or causal relations. Knowledge of historical occurrence is, therefore, built up (according as the occurrence is simple or complex), on a greater or lesser series of sense-perceptions; on the basis of these, reason exercises its faculty of judgment. If the sense-perceptions were erroneous, they become the occasion of erroneous judgments and conclusions.

(b) Psychology analyzes systematically the conditions under which sense-perception must be exercised if it is to issue in an accurate report. The organs must be organically sound and in normal working condition. They must be applied properly to their specific object, that is, in a manner suited to the perceptive capacity of the particular sense, and to the perceptibility of the object. The medium connecting sense-organ and object must be such as to leave to the organ the free and normal exercise of its activity. Finally, the will must bear upon the mind to bring to the entire perceptive process the necessary degree of attention.

(c) The imagination, "the faculty of forming mental images or representations of material objects apart from the presence of the latter," also has a role to play here. It renews the image or phantasm of the external fact as originally observed. The renewed image is often substantially like the original; but often, it differs from it in important respects, certain elements of the first image having fallen out, or extraneous elements having been added. The imagination, the "phantasy" of the older philosophers, is therefore a faculty party reproductive, partly productive. It inevitably comes into play when the witness undertakes to report what he has seen or heard. That on these occasions it may operate in such a manner as not to vitiate his testimony, whether oral or written, it must be in a normal, healthy state, and must limit itself to the data presented in the original act of perception.

(d) When any of the necessary conditions for correct sense-perception are missing, error will result in the perception, as also in the judgments based upon it. Color-blindness, myopia, deafness, functional disorder of the organs, fatigue, are conditions which result in mistaken observation. Similar conditions are: too great a distance of the object from the eye, too little light in vision, too low a pitch of voice in hearing. Inattention on the part of a witness is a prolific source of error. The careless, distracted, wool-gathering observer may not be trusted.

Contrariwise, a witness aware beforehand of the importance of what he is about to observe and of the necessity for his own good of making an accurate report, will be on the alert to observe correctly. But over-anxiety, and especially an uncontrolled desire that the observation may bear out some special theory, are not conditions favorable to correct observation. Without being aware of it, the too expectant witness projects images of the past into the foreground of consciousness and confounds them with the image of what is before him as he observes.

Mental quiet and poise, removed as far from lassitude or inattention as from emotional stir, is the mood in which observation will yield its best results. To what extent fear, fright, and similar states of emotional disturbance incapacitate a witness for observing properly, is a matter of common experience. Interesting experiments in experimental psychology furnish evidence to the same effect. A shot is fired in a classroom, and a brawl suddenly breaks out between certain groups of the students in attendance. After some moments of confusion the professor informs the class that it is all make-believe, and requests the students to prepare severally a written report of what was witnessed. Amazingly discrepant reports are handed in.—See A. Johnson, The Historian and Historical Evidence, 35.

(e) Erroneous judgments in history often result from the fact that the evidence on which they are based is vitiated by false play of the imagination. Where the necessary organic or physical conditions for normal use of this faculty are wanting, images corresponding only partly or not at all to the objective reality will ensue. The nervous system may be upset by mental or bodily strain; conditions such as sleeplessness, long continued hunger, or loss of blood, may have induced physical and psychical exhaustion. So also, the imagination operates abnormally under the influence of certain drugs, such as alcohol or opium; under mental depression, violent emotion, such as great fear or terror. In these circumstances phantasms may be generated of such vividness and intensity that reason or memory takes them for actual perceptions.

¶230 ILLUSIONS, HALLUCINATIONS

Two types of erroneous mental images have particular bearing on the question of objective truth in history. These are *illusions* and *hallucinations*. The two types mutually shade off into each other; it is not always easy (or necessary) to draw a clear line between them. A *positive* hallucination has nothing actual to correspond to it, as when the inebriate sees snakes, or the fever patient beholds his empty room full of people, or the lunatic fancies himself Napoleon. In *negative* hallucinations what can be seen under normal circumstances is not seen at all, as when a person awake and with eyes open, fails to see someone standing before him.

In *illusion* a physical object is actually perceived, but elements find their way into the image produced which do not properly belong to it. The result is that the perception is one-sided or false. In illusion there are data of actual sense-perception evoked by external stimuli, while in hallucination such data are altogether wanting. The victim of hallucination sees persons and objects or hears voices and noises which really do not exist, whereas the victim of illusion is led by his phantasm to give a false turn to what he does see or hear. He takes a tree for a human form, moonbeams playing in open spaces in the woods for living beings, the soughing of the wind for human voices, the murmur of the waterfall for music.

¶ 231 Numerous well-known cases of hallucination are on record. Descartes saw himself followed for a long time by a mentor, who admonished him not to falter in the pursuit of truth; Pascal, after a fall he once experienced, always beheld a black abyss yawning beside him; Byron was visited by ghosts; Schumann believed that Beethoven and others dictated melodies to him which he wrote down. Luther's illusions of eye and ear are recorded in H. Grisar, *Martin Luther, his Life and Work*, 202 ff.

(a) On the other hand, what seemed to be hallucinations were found in certain cases to be actual experiences. The two cases of St. Joan of Arc and St. Bernadette Soubirous are instructive in this connection. Even so judicious a historian as Lingard pronounced Joan's "voices" to be "the workings of her own imagination."—*History of England* (8 vols., London, 1849) 4:28.

> We must place Joan of Arc among the ecstatic saints, who enjoyed real interventions of supernatural spirits.—F. W. H. Meyers, quoted in Justin Roussel, *St. Joan of Arc: Study of the Supernatural in her Life and Mission* (New York, 1925), 28.

The Catholic Church also holds the apparitions of the Blessed Virgin to Bernadette Soubirous, at Lourdes, to have been real, not illusory.—See Georges Bertin, *Lourdes, A History of the Apparitions and Cures* (London, 1928); Johannes Jorgensen, *Lourdes* (London, 1914); bibliography in Cyril C. Martindale, *Bernadette of Lourdes* (London, 1925).

On *illusion and hallucination*:
Camille de la Vaissière, *Elements of Experimental Psychology*, (St. Louis, 1926), 149–64.
Michael Maher, *Psychology, Empirical and Rational* (9th ed., London, 1933), 171–78.
Herbert Thurston, *Beauraing and Other Apparitions: An Account of Some Borderland Cases in the Psychology of Mysticism* (London, 1934).

¶ 232 ERROR IN THE SYNTHESIS OF FACTS PERCEIVED
An eyewitness of a murder, a battle, a railroad accident, a shipwreck, is witness, not of a single happening, but of a whole series of successive and separate happenings, each of which must be apprehended by a distinct perception. Going back over these distinct perceptions, the witness must contrive in some way to connect and combine them, to make a synthesis of them, if he wishes to picture the happening as a whole. But such a mental synthesis of a whole series of distinct perceptions is an exceedingly delicate operation. The very nature of it makes a wide margin of possible error, at least as regards details. Factors of every kind can conspire to put the resulting synthesis out of step with the reality. Among them are defects of the sense-organs, memory, judgment; also, prejudice, passion, and in general, such emotional and moral states as inhibit one from making a synthesis that is perfectly objective, and in keeping with the facts.

Two persons of opposite political sympathies, witnessing a brawl between adherents of their respective parties, observe the same objective happening. *Ceteris paribus*, the resulting trains of perception in the two cases ought to be the same. But it is very unlikely that the resulting synthesis of perceptions will be identical. Political prejudice, not to mention other factors, can easily intervene, causing the witnesses to suppress or overemphasize details, disarrange their natural order, and adjust the synthesized picture to a political way of thinking. It is obvious that all this can have an effect on the shaping of history.

¶ 233 ERROR IN REPRODUCTION

Before a witness can communicate his perception of a happening to others, he must first reproduce it in his own mind. This may be done repeatedly, just as often, in fact, as individual desire or the association of ideas dictates. Here again is another perilous step to take. The factors which make it fraught with danger to accuracy of reproduction, are emotion, prejudice, defective attention, and especially the inadequacies of memory.

A certain degree of erroneousness, if only in non-essentials, is to be assumed in the normal act of recollection; a perfectly flawless recollection is the exception, not the rule. Memory ordinarily loses its effectiveness in direct proportion to the remoteness of its object in point of time. Occurrences lying far back in one's experience tend to become blurred in the memory; details vanish or merge into one another, so that a distinct, clear-cut recollection of the object in its proper outline becomes quite difficult, often impossible. Moreover, memory has its caprices, placing details where they do not belong, confusing persons and events, mistaking dates by wide margins, and in other ways resulting, however unconsciously, in erroneous recollection.

The psychological problem of accuracy in personal reminiscence has direct bearing, as is plain, on autobiography and memoirs as sources of history. The problem has been investigated on a scientific basis by German scholars. The outcome of the research was to place in strong relief the influence which the inherent limitations of human memory has on these two types of sources. It would, however, be an unwarranted inference from such conclusions that memory over a long period of time cannot be trusted in any case, not even for the substance of facts.

Inexact or mistaken recollection often proceeds from the fact that the original sense-perception made too feeble an impression. Again, under the influence of uncontrolled impulse or emotion, images of past happenings blend together. Thus, images are often distorted by a tendency to exaggeration, especially in matters involving quantity: size, distance, duration. Hence, numerous false data as to population of cities and losses of men by plague, famine, or war, are met with in the Greek, Roman, and medieval historians. Anguish, terror, sensationalism, heighten the dark side of past experiences; levity and unconcern may make them less gruelling in recollection than they really were.

¶ 234   ERROR IN COMMUNICATION

Immediate communication. On witnessing an event, a person makes a mental synthesis of the details, and recalls it in order to communicate it to others. This may be done by word of mouth, in writing, or through pictorial or plastic media. Anyone who has tried to describe an event to others knows how difficult it is and how easily he may be misunderstood.

(a) The prime factor inducing error or inaccuracy in oral or written communication is the limitations of language. In essentials language is a marvellous instrument for its purpose, but its effectiveness in transmitting human thought and feeling is never complete. A certain quota of the thought and feeling to be expressed is lost in the process. No writer, however great his mastery of words, can ever hope to give his account the same precision of detail, the same vividness that it has in his own mind. The handicaps of language make themselves particularly felt in the case of children, who cannot find the words needed to express their thought.

(b) But other causes besides the deficiencies of language can operate to make the communication of historical data inexact and misleading. These are the same as those already noted for the other steps in the complex process of knowledge, such as prejudice, passion, self-interest, or party-interest [¶ 232]. Again, an informant's attitude toward the person he informs may influence in various ways the character or quality of the information he gives. He may not tell the whole truth for fear of giving offense, or of compromising others or himself; or the sheer satisfaction he finds in communicating his information to hearers or readers of a certain type, may lead him to modify his data in a way prejudicial to the truth.

(c) One of the most important factors influencing the communication of thought is suggestion. This is the stimulation by one person in another of a mental attitude or viewpoint which the latter unconsciously adopts as his own. A common example is the type of question frequently put by lawyers in cross-examination, with the intention of eliciting a predetermined answer from witnesses. Suggestion can work through such agencies as a magnetic or forceful personality, public opinion, the press, mass-movements. Any one of these agencies can have its influence in lending this or that color to a person's testimony when he undertakes to report his observations to others.

¶ 235 *Mediate communication.* Everyday experience demonstrates that the reliability of a report decreases with the length of time that separates it from the facts reported. An eyewitness of an incident is handicapped, as was seen, in so many ways in the processes of observing exactly the details of the incident, making a proper synthesis of them, recalling the synthesis faithfully to memory and passing it on faithfully to others. The synthesis may then be passed on from one person to another, down a long stretch of years. In transmissions of this kind some distortion of the original synthesis is likely to occur. All the difficulties that beset the immediate observer also beset the mediate. The situation becomes still more unsatisfactory from the standpoint of credibility when the report is taken up and spread about by groups or masses. As individuals, so masses are subject to illusion, hallucination, suggestion, especially in times of social crises and physical disturbance: war, pestilence, earthquake, flood. Mass or collective hallucination furnishes the explanation of many putative historical happenings.——On illusions of memory, see Johannes Lindworsky, *Experimental Psychology*, (New York, 1931), 278–82.

¶ 236 THE LIE IN HISTORICAL RECORDS

The discussion of lying in its mental and moral aspects belongs respectively to psychology and ethics. Here it suffices to recall that a lie, taken broadly, means a conscious verbal departure from the truth as known to the speaker or writer. From the ethical viewpoint, a lie is *formally* wrong, when it is accompanied by consciousness of moral guilt; or *materially* wrong, when it is not so accompanied. From the psychological view point a lie is *pathological* when it is occasioned by some morbid or abnormal psychical condition in the subject. Moreover, on the basis of the various motives that can determine the deception, lies can be classified as those of jest, necessity, utility, defamation. Instances of all these kinds of prevarication occur in historical sources.

(a) Clearly, the historian's chief concern in the matter is to be able to recognize lies when they occur. Often this may be done without particular difficulty; but often also it may require considerable acumen on his part to detect a lie lurking in a document. When there are reasons to suspect its presence, investigation may have to be pursued in various directions. The author's antecedents, character, environment, will call for scrutiny, while the statement in question will have to be checked with data supplied by other documentary sources. Written history is prolific of deliberate misstatements of fact motivated by passion, by national, political, or religious prejudice.

Political speeches, especially those of the "campaign" variety, the aim of which is the discomfiture of opponents, are notorious for reckless liberties with the truth.

(b) In the criticism of documents, lies of necessity and utility come under especial consideration. In several passages of his *Republic* Plato is seen to have permitted lying as a means of escape from a greater evil. Moreover, men of the type of Philo and Quintilian, the Stoics, and even ecclesiastical writers, such as Clement of Alexandria, Origen, Cassian, and others, taught the lawfulness of the lie of utility or necessity, under certain circumstances. In view of these facts, one need not be surprised to find material lies in the old writers.

(c) A common cause of untruthfulness among the historians of antiquity and the Middle Ages was the wrong view of the purpose of history which then prevailed, inasmuch as it was regarded as serving primarily the ends of rhetoric, art, edification. The disregard for truth in certain biographies of saints and other medieval sources, as shown in invented details, covert borrowings from other sources, deliberate transference of data from one set of persons and places to another, exaggerated portrayals of virtue, and suppression of human weaknesses, indicates a moral point of view different from our own.

(d) Modern biography has likewise its lapses from the truth. What is looked for in a biography is the whole truth about its subject; one wants to know him as he really was and lived. But often the biographer presents an arbitrarily idealized portrait instead of the real man or woman. Discreditable personal traits, compromising incidents are explained away in uncritical fashion or altogether passed over in silence; doubtful data are accepted as certain; and free rein is given to a flair for the sensational and the extraordinary. In this wise, untruthfulness, negative or positive, easily finds its way into the text [₵ 239].

B. The Credibility of Specific Written Sources

₵ 237 The errors to which testimony as a basis of history is often liable, make it necessary to consider the question of the respective credibility of the various types of formal sources. This, however, is not to indorse in any way a spirit of skepticism or to deny the possibility of certainty in history. On the contrary, such inquiry will make it possible to bring to light the subjective influences which affect the perception and reproduction of historical facts, and with this knowledge in hand, to extract the kernel of the facts from the shell. The sound criteria provided by methodology for arriving at truth in history only confirm the plain fact of experience that happenings observed by competent witnesses can be reported by them exactly and according to the substantial truth.

(a) As our science [methodology] progresses, considerations of a skeptical trend have been steadily overcome by subjecting them to rigorous canons of criticism. We thereby fix the limits within which statements become more or less controllable and therefore usable for a knowledge of the facts. . . . Any lapse into a skeptical frame of mind will be avoided if one keeps in mind the high percentage of cases of successful observation and reproduction yielded under normally favorable conditions, objective and subjective, by experimental inquiry into accuracy of observation.—Bernheim, cited in Feder, Lehrbuch, 233.

Pertinent here is Paley's well-known dictum that the usual character of human testimony is "substantial truth under circumstantial variety."

(b) Informal sources or remains are *ipso facto* objective, and therefore reliable. Comparison of Semitic and Indo-European linguistic families demonstrates with certainty the original connection of the two groups of families. In numerous cases we can argue safely from the names of places, mountains, countries, to the identity of the persons who gave the names, to the time when the names were given and to other data. Business and official papers throw light on the administrative practices which occasioned them. Sagas enlighten us on the political and religious ideas of the people or particular environment from which they sprang.

¶ 238 ANNALS AND CHRONICLES

Annals and chronicles are distinctly medieval types of historiography. Formal history-writing in the Middle Ages assumed as a rule one or other of them. Medieval annals and chronicles constitute together a specific group of sources with the same general characteristics and much the same problems to engage the attention of the critical historian. Criticism was generally an undeveloped art in the Middle Ages, so that the written records which they produced leave much to be desired when measured by the standards of modern scientific history. To speak in general, every medieval chronicle or book of annals is a problem by itself as regards reliability. Scholarly editions of these sources, such as are found in the Monumenta Germaniae historica, and the Rolls Series, generally contain a critical discussion of their trustworthiness.

¶ 239 BIOGRAPHY

Practically the same problems in the use of source material confront historian and biographer alike. Each is bound by the same rules of rigorous criticism in testing first the authenticity, and then the trustworthiness of the sources on which he draws. Each, no matter how bent on turning out a readable and even entertaining book, is held by the same inexorable canons not to do violence to the facts, not to go beyond the evidence. Probably the temptation to do so may be the greater in the case of the biographer, whose understandable sympathy with his subject may easily lead him to overstep the bounds of truthful and verifiable statement. Again, the biographer has very often to base his work on private correspondence, diaries, memoirs, and similar personal material, the use of which for purposes of accurate information can easily have its risks. All the greater need for him, therefore, to be discriminating in the use of his sources. It is evident that the method according to which a biography has been written, conditions its use as a historical source.

¶ 240 The "New Biography"

Following in the wake of the first World War, the "New Biography" made a widespread bid for the favor of the reading public. This was a genre of "life" marked by certain manifest departures from the methods usually employed by the older biographers. It developed more or less along three distinct lines, giving rise to as many types, each of which presents special problems of credibility to the historian when he undertakes to use it as source material.

(a) *The "debunking" type.* Here the characteristic method is to throw into relief the limitations, foibles, defects, or worse than defects of the subject, in order to create the impression that his reputed greatness is exaggeration or sham. Honesty requires that the whole truth, shadow as well as light, be worked into the literary portraits of men and women. A half-truth may sometimes have the effect of a downright lie. Every individual statement made about a person may be correct and amply vouched for by documentary evidence; but the net result will be a falsehood if only one side of the picture, be it the good or bad one, is set before the reader. The correct attitude of the biographer in face of his subject finds classic expression in the words of Othello:

> Paint me as I am.
> Nothing extenuate nor aught set down in malice.

In the opinion of James Truslow Adams, our highly mechanized civilization, with its worship of science, has so weaned us away from appreciation of moral and spiritual values that we feel uncomfortable in the presence of their great traditional exponents, of the men and women of history who were successful in giving them expression. The result is that people, indulging a perverse instinct of nature, are gratified to see such persons brought down to their own lower level at the hands of skeptical and irreverent biographers.—See "New Modes in Biography," *Current History,* 31 (1929): 257.

Whatever be the motive inspiring it, biography of the "debunking" sort is too patently non-objective to qualify for safe use by the historian, if one assumes that the motive behind it is really sinister. If the author's design is merely to state the facts, good or bad, of his subject's career, even though in the process the subject should lose a reputation which he did not deserve, no objection may be raised to the procedure. Such a case is only a sincere and legitimate attempt to apply the principles of objective history.

(b) *The psychological type.* This is illustrated in the work of Lytton Strachey and by his feeble imitators. The distinctive note of its method is repeated conjecture as to what were the thoughts and emotions that engaged the subject on specific occasions. The sources may say nothing about the thoughts or emotions; the omission is supplied by the biographer with a free use of inference, or more correctly, of imagination employing "psychology" as its tool. Lytton Strachey makes Philip II regret on his deathbed that he had not been more drastic in his treatment of heretics. The biographer's sources make no mention of such a circumstance, which is the merest invention.—*Elizabeth and Essex* (New York, 1928), 175.

The net result of psychological biography is that without being aware of it the reader gets a medley of fact and fiction. The fiction is set before him under the guise of genuine history, or at least in such manner as inevitably to lead him to accept it as genuine. The method has its uses in professed historical romance; it is plainly out of place in serious biography, except under the restrictions which regulate the use of conjecture in history [₡ 147 f.].

(c) *The psychoanalytic type.* Here an attempt is made to apply the technique of Freudian psycho-analysis to the interpretation of historical characters. Thus, Jefferson is assumed to have had an anti-authority complex, which is traced back to certain unpleasant relations existing in his younger days between himself and his father. Psychoanalytic biography cannot be any sounder than the basis on which it rests, and this, which is Freudian psychoanalysis, has yet to find a recognized place in sound psychology. "History is no place for the naive and now discredited fantasies of the psychoanalyist."—J. C. Almack, *Research and Thesis Writing,* 194.

(d) A usual feature of modern scholarly biography is more or less detailed indication of sources.

"The Sources of Biographical Knowledge," in Sir Sidney Lee, *Life of William Shakespeare,* appendix 1.

Peter Guilday, *Life and Times of John Carroll, Archbishop of Baltimore* (2 vols., New York, 1922); idem, *John England, His Life and Times* (2 vols., New York, 1927).

Johannes Jorgensen, *St. Francis of Assisi, A Biography,* trans. by T. O'Connor Sloane (New York, 1922).

Louis C. Fillion, *The Life of Christ: A Historical, Critical and Apologetical Exposition* (3 vols., St. Louis, 1928).

James Brodrick, *Life and Works of Blessed Robert Francis Cardinal Bellarmine* (2 vols., London, 1928).
Douglas S. Freeman, *R. E. Lee, A Biography* (4 vols., New York, 1934–1935).
Arthur Bryant, *King Charles II* (London, 1931).
Louis Ponelli and Louis Bordet, *St. Philip Neri and the Roman Society of His Time, 1515–1598* (London, 1932).
Léonce de Grandmaison, *Jesus Christ; His Person, His Message, His Credentials* (3 vols., London, 1932).
Pierre Coste, *The Life and Labours of St. Vincent de Paul* (3 vols., London, 1934).
Raymond W. Chambers, *Thomas More* (London, 1935).
Pierre Janelle, *Robert Southwell, A Study in Religious Inspiration* (London, 1936).

An instructive example of a brief but comprehensive survey of the source material available for a biographical subject is Tenney Frank's "What Do We Know About Vergil?" The material reviewed is grouped under four heads: the poet's own statements; the few casual references to him by friends; the *Vitae Vergilianae* written in the fourth century and later; late scholia.—*Classical Journal*, 26 (1930): 3 ff.

Sir Sidney Lee, *Principles of Biography* (Cambridge, Eng., 1911).
Dana Kineman Merrill, *The Development of Biography*, (Portland, Maine, 1932).
Edward H. O'Neill, *A History of American Biography, 1800–1931* (Philadelphia, 1935).
Allan Nevins, "Biography and History," *The Gateway to History* (Boston, 1938).
Joseph R. Strayer, ed., *The Interpretation of History* (Princeton, 1943), chap. 4. "Biography and History," by Dumas Malone.
Wallace Notestein, "History and the Biographer," *Yale Review*, 22 (1933): 548–58.

₵ 241 MEMOIRS

Personal recollections or memoirs can contain valuable material for the historian, but he must be circumspect in their use. Two things in particular make them peculiarly liable to error.

(a) Based as they are to a great extent on memory, memoirs share the inherent fallibility of that faculty, and this the more so, the more remote the experiences recalled. This deficiency may be supplied, as is often done in the better type of memoirs and autobiography, when the author calls to his aid journals, diaries, letters, memoranda, and similar personal material of contemporary date. On the other hand, reminiscences of pioneers and old settlers, generally recorded in advanced age, with the help of memory alone, rarely inspire confidence as historical sources.

The first part of the memoirs of General de Caulaincourt rely on contemporary memoranda, especially of conversations with Napoleon.—*With*

Napoleon in Russia: The Memoirs of General de Caulaincourt . . . from the original memoirs as edited by Jean Hanoteau. Abridged, edited, and with an introduction by George Libaire (New York, 1935).

Francis A. McNutt, *A Papal Chamberlain: The Personal Chronicle of Francis Augustine McNutt* (New York, 1937); William Lyon Phelps, *Autobiography with Letters* (Oxford, 1939). Both make use of diaries. On the other hand, George F. Hoar admits: "I never kept a diary except for a few and very brief periods: so for what I have to say I must trust to my memory." —*Autobiography of Seventy Years*, (2 vols., New York, 1903), 1:17.

(b) Since memoirs, more than other classes of sources, labor under a complex personal equation, this must be solved before they can be used by the historian with safety. Very frequently their authors have an axe to grind, especially if they are statesmen, diplomats, military commanders, public officials. Their chief concern, sometimes openly avowed, is to set themselves right with contemporaries or with posterity, and this they undertake to do by placing their careers in the best possible light. Clearly, this is not an attitude making for honest and objective statements of the facts. Even without such conscious design, a person's account of his own exploits tends to run into apology, self-exculpation, exaggeration.

This, however, is not to say that all memoirs are vitiated by such defects. Numerous examples of this type of source which have passed muster with the critics as reliable in varying degrees, could be cited [⟪ 243 f.]. Moreover, even memoirs that are otherwise untrustworthy may often be securely drawn upon for data which the author had no reason to misrepresent. It is also to be noted that while writers of memoirs often exaggerate their part in history, the fact that they are writing about themselves may also have a precisely opposite effect: to lead them through modesty not to give themselves credit which is really their due. Cicero was not anxious to write the story of his consulate; he wished it written by someone else.

⟪ 242 Leonard Rice-Oxley deals with the value of memoirs as an informal record of contemporary manners and customs.—*Memoirs as a Source of English History, Stanhope Essay, 1914* (Oxford, 1914), 49–51.

See also John Campbell Major, *The Role of Personal Memoirs in English Biography and Novel* (Philadelphia, 1935).

(a) Memoirs can sometimes be shown to be in error, intentional or otherwise, by checking them with the author's correspondence. The Marquis de Bouillé wrote his recollections in 1797, to clear himself of responsibility for the flight of Louis XVI to Varennes; but the Marquis' own letters, contemporary with the incident, contradict the account given in his recollections.—Acton, *Lectures on the French Revolution*, 367.

The undercurrent of motive is to explain or explain away the earlier fact of his [Talleyrand's] career; to expose his incomparable services to the crown, the country and the dominant party; to show that nothing in the various past disqualifies him for the just place in the councils of the monarchy he had restored.—Acton, "Talleyrand's Memoirs," *Historical Essays and Studies* (London, 1907), 393.

The recollections of the actors in important political transactions are doubtless of great historic value. But I ought to say frankly that my experience has taught me that the memory of men, even of good and true men, as to matters in which they have been personal actors is frequently most dangerous and misleading. I could recount many curious stories which have been told me by friends who have been writers of history and biography, of the contradictory statements they have received from the best men in regard to scenes at which they have been present.—G. F. Hoar, *Autobiography of Seventy Years*, 1:2.

(b) France has led all other countries in memoirs, as England has in biographies. Griffet has a critical survey of the more notable of them in print in his day (eighteenth century), including those of Turenne, Sully, La Rochefoucauld, and Cardinal de Retz.—*Traité des differentes sortes de preuves*, chap. 6 f.

The French Revolution was productive of scores of memoirs, but as Acton shows, there was no means of controlling or testing this material until publication of contemporary documents was begun at about the middle of the nineteenth century. Up to that time official documents and private letters dating from the Revolution were rare. Mirabeau's secret correspondence, which first appeared in 1851, showed this popular leader as in the king's pay.—Acton, *Lectures on the French Revolution*, 361.

A large part, perhaps the bulk of the memoir literature touching Marie Antoinette must be discounted, as its authors were inspired in most cases by a desire to curry favor with the restored Bourbon regime.—Stefan Zweig, *Marie Antoinette, the Portrait of an Average Woman* (New York, n.d.), 466 ff.

Gustav Wolf has a detailed critical appreciation of the literature of French memoirs.—*Einführung in das Studium der neueren Geschichte* (Berlin, 1910).

The memoirs of Las Cases, Montholon, Gourgaud, and other intimates of Napoleon who lived with him at St. Helena, can be used only with caution, having been written more or less for purposes of propaganda. The *Mémorial de Sainte Hélène*, of Las Cases (1823), was compiled from the ex-emperor's conversations, with a view to creating a Napoleonic legend. On the other hand, the memoirs (first part) of General de Caulaincourt, covering Napoleon's Russian campaign and his flight back to Paris, and published for the first time in 1933, appear to be trustworthy.

The Franco-Prussian war of 1870, or aspects of it, are portrayed in numerous memoirs both on the French and German side, such as Busch's Memoirs of Bismarck; the Memoirs of Doctor Thomas W. Evans (Napoleon III's American dentist, who saved the French empress from the fury of the Parisian mob by spiriting her away to England); the Memoirs of Sir Edward Blount, English consul at Paris during the days of the siege; the Recollections of the Empress Eugénie, by her secretary, Auguste Filon, a book replete with dramatic detail.

The great body of printed diplomatic correspondence and other official papers bearing on the first World War serves as a check on the vast memoir literature from statesmen and military leaders who participated in it. In dealing with this literature, as also with the pertinent diplomatic correspondence, severe standards of criticism are indispensable [⟨ 251].

⟨ 243 AUTOBIOGRAPHY

There is only an accidental difference between autobiography and memoirs; essentially they are one and the same genre of historical record. Autobiography, as a rule, embraces the subject's entire career as far as he can reconstruct it from memory, aided in many cases by contemporary personal memoranda and other literary helps. Memoirs may or may not cover his career in its full range; they may chronicle only a part of it, for example, his participation in an event, or in a series of events. Grant's memoirs deal only with his Civil War experiences, Pershing's with his World War career. In some cases memoirs stress not so much the biographical element as the author's personal views and impressions of contemporary events.

The credibility of autobiography in general is subject to the same limitations as that of memoirs and must be evaluated by the same tests.

On the various motives that can inspire the autobiographer, see D. K. Merrill, The Development of American Biography, 12.

At all events, the life-stories, told by themselves, of men and women who influenced their contemporaries in some notable way, have a place among the legitimate sources of history. St. Augustine's Confessions and Newman's Apologia pro Vita Sua are classic instances of frank revelations of inner moral and religious experiences, and as such are of value to the social historian.

> He [Asquith] suffered as an autobiographer (Memories and Reflections) from one of the most fatal of disabilities—an insufficient interest in himself. He was too seldom the object of his own attention to ask, let alone discover, how he impressed other people.——John A. Spender and Cyril Asquith, Life of Herbert Henry Asquith, Lord Oxford and Asquith (2 vols., London, 1932), 2:324.

The autobiography of Thomas Jefferson, written in 1821, when he was seventy-seven, is typical in its errors of the defects often found in this species of record. Thus, against the fact, he says that the Declaration of Independence was signed on July 4.—Paul L. Ford, ed., *Autobiography of Thomas Jefferson, 1743–1790* (New York and London, 1914), 33, note 2.

Martin Van Buren's account of his political career is rated as a dependable and valuable document, by John C. Fitzpatrick, ed., *The Autobiography of Martin Van Buren*, in AHA, *Report* (1918), vol. 2.

Among other American autobiographies of note are those of Rutherford B. Hayes, George F. Hoar, Theodore Roosevelt, Calvin Coolidge.

For a survey of autobiographic and reminiscent material in a specific field, see Carl R. Fish, *The Rise of the Common Man, 1830–1850* (New York, 1927), 343 ff.

The field of hagiography furnishes numerous examples of autobiography of the highest degree of credibility. See the article, "Autobiographies spirituelles," in Marcel Viller and Others, eds., *Dictionnaire de spiritualité*, 1:563–77.

Fueter ranks St. Ignatius Loyola's autobiography as the best of the Renaissance period.—*Geschichte der neueren Historiographie* (3d ed., Munich, 1936), 282.

¶ 244 DIARIES AND JOURNALS

The diary or journal derives its chief merit as a historical source from the circumstance that at least in theory it is a record of personal experiences and external happenings made on the same day on which they occurred. The contemporaneousness of the diarist's record goes a long way to guarantee its accuracy. Sometimes gaps which are allowed to occur in diaries are later filled in from recollections or other sources, a procedure which is a species of deception if the reader is left under the impression that these entries were made on the dates to which they are assigned.

The various criteria to be employed in appraising the credibility of any form of human record are also applicable to the diary. It has been said, that "no one lies more boldly than to himself." As in the case of autobiography and memoirs, the distinctly personal character of the diary or journal renders it peculiarly liable to a subjectivism that is at cross purposes with the simple truth. But this is only to abuse a legitimate medium of expression. Given a competent and conscientious diarist, there is no reason why his product should not measure up to the requirements of accurate, objective record.

¶ 245 Two types of diary are distinguishable, the *intimate* or *introspective* (*journal intime*), and the *factual* or *objective*. The intimate diary is a self-revelation of inner mental and moral states, of the thoughts, fancies, emotions of the writer. It can interest the general reader; it can also be an aid to the historian, the biographer, and the psychologist. The factual diary can likewise be self-revealing, but in most cases only indirectly; it eschews in the main any expression of personal thought and feeling, and records for the most part only external happenings. The Washington diaries are a pertinent example. They afford little insight into the workings of the author's mind, for they consist largely of data about the weather, crops, visitors to Mount Vernon, and other more or less relatively unimportant matters. Yet indirectly they are a witness to Washington's methodical habits, business instincts, preoccupation with material things, steadiness and strength of will. Few things test volitional power more than the keeping of a daily journal.

> To the social historian, the elements of value in a diary usually fall into one or the other of two categories: objective contributions, such as firsthand descriptions and illustrations of conditions and customs of the time; subjective contributions, revealing the philosophy, the ideals, the soul of the writer. The latter element is particularly valuable when the writer may be regarded as either typical of a large group, or a leader of influence.—L. G. Van der Velde, "The Diary of George Daffield," *MVHR*, 24 (1937): 25.

¶ 246 Students of history soon come to know how useful diary entries often are in fixing unknown or doubtful dates. Further, such entries furnish in many cases conclusive, firsthand evidence for happenings of questionable historicity, or for data left obscure in some of their circumstances.

A contemporary journal discovered in 1925, in the Archives Nationales, Paris, seemingly the work of a French government agent, contains a reference to Patrick Henry's famous "treason speech" in the Virginia Assembly, introducing the Virginia Resolves on the Stamp Act, May 30, 1765. Under that date the writer, who was present when Henry spoke, records: "Shortly after I came in, one of the members stood up and said he had read that in former times Tarquin and Julius had their Brutus, Charles had his Cromwell and he Did not Doubt but some good american would stand up in favor of his country, etc." The entry is interesting corroborative evidence for an incident none too clearly vouched for in other contemporary sources.—*AHR*, 26 (1921): 745.

¶ 247 Diaries, like memoirs, often supply abundant vivid detail which enables the historian to visualize historical situations and to lend color to his accounts of them. Probably few documents of the period bring home to one with more telling emphasis the abrupt changes introduced by the Protestant Revolt in the religious life of Germany than the graphic diary kept by the Nürnberg nun, Charitas Pirkheimer.—

See *An Heroic Abess of Reformation Days*, edited with an introduction by Francis X. Mannhardt (St. Louis, 1930); Johannes Janssen, *History of the German People at the Close of the Middle Ages* (16 vols., London, 1896–1910), 4:68 ff.

London's plague and great fire of 1665 became realistic in the pages of Pepys' diary.

Student life and academic conditions at Harvard College towards the end of the eighteenth century are mirrored in the diary of John Quincy Adams.

The tragedy of the Missouri River smallpox epidemic of 1837, comes home to the reader in Francis A. Chardon's *Fort Clark Journal*.

¶ 248 *Examples of diaries*
English diaries of the higher type.

Samuel Pepys, *Diary*, ed. by Henry B. Wheatley (9 vols., London and New York, 1893–1899).

John Evelyn, *Diary*, ed. by Austin Dobson (3 vols., London and New York, 1906).

The Journal of Sir Walter Scott, 1825–1832 (Edinburgh, 1891).

P. W. Greville, ed., *The Greville Diary* (2 vols., London, 1927).

Philip Morrell, ed., *Leaves From the Greville Diary* (London, 1929).

American diaries of varying quality are plentiful. These afford material for a study of the technique of this type of record in the different shapes it can assume.

George Washington, ed. by John C. Fitzpatrick (4 vols., Boston, 1925).

Diary of James Monroe in *State Papers and Correspondence Bearing Upon the Purchase of the Territory of Louisiana* (Washington, 1903), 165 ff.

John Quincy Adams, ed. by Charles Francis Adams (12 vols., Philadelphia, 1874–1877); abridged edition, ed. by Allan Nevins (London, 1929).

Edward Bates, ed. by Howard K. Beale, AHA, *Report* (1930).

Orville Hickman Browing, ed. by James G. Randall, in the *Collections* of the Illinois State Historical Library (2 vols., Springfield, Ill., 1931–1933).

Meriwether Lewis and William Clark, several editions.

Herbert E. Bolton, ed., *Anza's California Expeditions* (5 vols., Berkeley, Calif., 1930).

Annie H. Abel, ed., *Chardon's Journal at Fort Clark, 1832–1839* (Pierre, S. Dakota, 1932).

Charles M. Gates, ed., *Five Fur Traders of the Northwest; Being the Narrative of Peter Pond and the Diaries of John MacDonnell, Archibald N. McLeod, Hugh Faries and Thomas Connor* (Minneapolis, Minn., 1933).

(a) On the use of diaries and journals by the biographer, see Wallace Notestein, "History and Biography," *Yale Review*, 22 (1933), 551; Arthur Ponsonby, *English Diaries: A Review of English Diaries from the Seventeenth to the Twentieth Century with an Introduction on Diary Writing* (London and New York, 1923).

(b) The general accuracy of a diary can sometimes be established by verifying a limited number of its statements about current events and conditions; the verification may be made by a check with other contemporary records. By inductive reasoning it may then become possible to conclude that a diary which is found to be accurate in the statements tested is accurate as a whole.* On the other hand, it may be possible to convict a work of inaccuracy or of worse, by confronting it with a diary kept by its author. In his published *Travels*, Jonathan Carver narrates journeys up the Mississippi and Minnesota rivers. That he never made such journeys, appears from his manuscript journals preserved in the British Museum.—Louise P. Kellogg, *The British Régime in Wisconsin*, (Madison, Wis., 1935), 71.

For exposure of a spurious diary, see Albert F. Pollard, "An Essay in Historical Method: the Barbellion Diaries," *History*, 6 (1921): 22–31; 183–94.

⟪ 249 LETTERS

As a literary type, letters stand by themselves with certain principles regulating their technique. When they contain description or narration, they take on more or less the character of record, and thereby become source material for the historian. Their value as recitals of contemporary events or as pictures of existing customs, manners, viewpoints, institutions, is often of the highest. When utilized as sources, their trustworthiness must be tested by the criteria applicable to testimonial evidence in general. The writer's opportunities for correct information, his veracity, his ability to state things accurately must all be taken into account. Sainte-Beuve said that the letter writer tends to take the point of view of the addressee. To the extent to which this is done, the result may be failure to state things precisely as the writer knows them to be. The correspondence of Madame Roland furnishes an illustration.— *AHR*, 33 (1928): 802 f.

⟪ 250 *Correspondence, public and private.* Letters, whether official or non-official, allow of a broad classification into public and private. Letters of a private, confidential character, such as were not meant for publication, are assumed to be more reliable in their contents than letters written with a view to publication. The assumption is correct on the whole, and is often borne out by the eventual publication of letters originally confidential. A person's private letters running simultaneously with his public correspondence, and dealing with the same matters, will sometimes show the latter to be unreliable. An instance in point is Horace Greeley's correspondence, public and private, on Civil War events [⟪ 252-d]. So also the letters or reports of a correspondent of a business firm may tell different stories according as they are meant for

---

* It merely follows that the presumption is in favor of the diarist, not that his uncorroborated statements are necessarily accurate.—Ed.

private consumption by the officials of the firm or are to be given to the press for advertising purposes.

¶ 251 *Diplomatic correspondence.* This is notoriously the happy hunting grounds of reserve, dissimulation, half-truths, often sheer prevarication. Edward A. Freeman said of it, though perhaps too sweepingly: "Here we are in the very chosen region of lies; everybody is by the nature of the case trying to over-reach everybody else."—*The Methods of Historical Study,* 258.

To what extent such correspondence will show lapses from the truth depends much on the status of the person or persons to whom it is addressed. Official letters exchanged between governments are obviously the most liable to misrepresentation. Letters sent by a diplomat to his own government are more likely to report conditions as they are. Yet even here, misinformation, bias, personal interest, can easily lead the writer to color or garble his accounts. The reports sent to Washington by Walter Hines Page, American ambassador to Great Britain during the first World War evince his intense sympathies for the Allied cause.

Moreover, it is not uncommon for a government's foreign agent to transmit two sets of report, one, to be given to the public, the other strictly confidential, and addressed to the responsible heads of government. The published reports can of course easily fail on the side of accuracy and candor. Even though they contain no positive misrepresentations of fact, they can mislead in a negative way by the suppression of embarrassing truths. It is also possible for such communications to remain entirely within the bounds of the truth, and yet say nothing worth while. On the other hand, private or confidential communications, which often eventually get into print, will presumably tell the whole truth, supposing of course that the writer is properly informed and does not misrepresent or color things for personal ends. Examples of diplomatic correspondence of every type and of all grades of credibility abound in the enormous printed mass of official communications exchanged between the governments that engaged in the first World War.

On the use of diplomatic correspondence by the historian, see William E. Linglebach, "Sources of Diplomatic History and the Control of Foreign Affairs," in Louis J. Paetow, ed., *The Crusades and Other Historical Essays Presented to Dana C. Munro by His Former Students* (New York, 1928), 289 ff.; see also George P. Gooch, *Recent Revelations of European Diplomacy* (London, 1929).

(a) Samuel F. Bemis says of a well-known work, Henri Doniol, *Histoire* de la participation de la France à l'établissement de États-Unis d'Amérique: "What appears at first as a monemental work [5 vols., Paris, 1886–1892] of great objectiveness is uniformly really dominated by strong national bias. . . . The author uniformly regards Vergennes's despatches as statements of fact, whereas they were constantly and studiously couched for the purpose of putting desired ideas into the minds of the foreign governments near which his envoys were stationed."—*The Diplomacy of the American Revolution* (New York, 1935), 265.

Diplomatic negotiations (1797–1798) between the American and French governments occasioned by the Jay Treaty are illustrated in "The X. Y. Z. Letters," *Translations and Reprints from the Original Sources of European History* (University of Pennsylvania, VI, n.d., No. 2).

(b) An instance of official government correspondence of varying types with varying degrees of credibility, is seen in the letters exchanged between the governors and intendants of New France (Canada) and the ministry at Versailles. Both governors and intendant sent at intervals individual reports to the minister on the affairs of the colony, these being accompanied by a joint report from the two on the same subject. It often happened that the Canadian officials said in their individual reports the opposite of what they said in the joint report, and vice versa. On the other hand, the ministry replied in individual letters to the official, addressing, however, at the same time, a joint reply to the two. Here again, instructions sent the officials individually were sometimes at odds with those sent to them in common.

(c) Letter-writers, unconsciously as a rule, lay up stacks of useful data for the future historian. Thus, Cicero's correspondence—trans. by Evelyn S. Schuckburgh (4 vols., London, 1908–1912)—is valuable both for the light it throws on Cicero's personality and for the fidelity with which it mirrors the stirring political and social events through which he lived. For the true character of the days that saw the fall of the Roman Republic, it is the most revealing document extant.

The correspondence of Pliny the Younger—trans. by Melmoth (Loeb. ed., 2 vols., London, 1923–1925)—lacks the spontaneity of Cicero's, having been composed with a view to publication; but it is a contemporary source of the first value, reflecting varied aspects of Roman life in the first century of the Empire. Pliny's letter to the Emperor Trajan (X, 96) asking for instructions on the policy to be adopted towards the Christians, and Trajan's answer, "*Conquirendi non sunt*" (X, 97), are classic documents for the history of the Christian persecutions.

The letters of Apollinaris Sidonius are rich in sidelights on conditions in Roman Gaul at a time when the empire was slowly toppling to ruin.—See Samuel Dill, *Roman Society in the Last Century of the Western Empire* 2d rev. ed., London and New York, 1899).

Charles H. Haskins, "The Life of Medieval Students as Illustrated in their Letters," *Studies in Medieval Culture* (Oxford, 1929), 1–35.

"Letters of the Crusaders," ed. by Dana C. Munro, in *Translations and Reprints from the Original Sources of European History* (University of Pennsylvania, I, 1910).

The Paston Letters are rich in data on English fifteenth-century social and economic life (Everyman's Library, 1924); also ed. by James Gairdner, (3 vols., London, 1910).

The Fugger News Letters: Being a Collection of Unpublished Letters from the Correspondents of the House of Fugger during the years 1568–1605, ed. by Victor van Klarwill (London, 1925); second series (Queen Elizabeth), 1926.

Upper social circles in France under Louis XIV are mirrored in the charming letters of Madame de Sévigné (ed. by R. Aldington, 2 vols., New York, 1927), unrivaled in literature for delicacy of touch and distinguished style.

Cross sections of English mid-eighteenth century society life are found in the correspondence of Horace Walpole, Earl of Orford, standard edition by Mrs. Paget Toynbee (16 vols., Oxford, 1903–1905).

❰ 252 NEWSPAPERS

Whether and to what extent newspapers may be relied upon as sources is a practical problem for the historian. As a matter of fact, they have come to be used widely by students and writers of history, and often to excellent purpose. Some directions for their critical use are therefore in order. The contents of the typical newspaper may be classified under three heads: news accounts, editorials, advertisements.

(a) *News accounts*. The newspaper, being designed primarily as a chronicle of current events, belongs to the category of history as record, and as such is liable to misstatements of fact. But its average of error is higher by a wide margin than that obtaining in other typical forms of historical record. This is caused by the haste with which a newspaper must be got out; to its ephemeral character, which does not tend to impress on its makers the need of accuracy; and to its general attitude towards the news, which is determined in large measure by party, business, family, and other interests. The pages of the average daily are seldom without errors of fact. Persons are made to say in interviews what they never really said; they are reported as having attended a political rally, a social function, when actually they were not present. Someone dies in an insane asylum, and the papers report that he died at the family residence. Misstatements of fact such as these are numerous and continual, so much so that the discerning reader may ask himself whether he can believe anything at all that "stands in the paper." In practice he must contrive to find a *via media* between naive credulity and thoroughgoing skepticism.

Present-day reputable journalism makes a serious and on the whole a successful effort, through trained news gatherers and elaborately organized press agencies, to obtain the substantial facts in happenings of news value, at home and abroad. No one has a right to be skeptical about the historicity of an earthquake, a conflagration, a shocking crime, when such news items are reported by several journals or even by only one, however much one may feel inclined to be skeptical about details. It is chiefly in matters of detail that newspapers lapse from the truth, though at times, through misinformation or even bias or malice, they may publish stories that are substantially untrue.

Practically, an investigator drawing data from the news columns of a paper should apply the proper tests, internal or external, to determine its reliability both in general and as concerns the specific data which he extracts. These tests are identical with those employed in estimating the trustworthiness of formal sources in general. The inquiry should extend to the paper's general policy, the personal views and standards of its editors, its political and other affiliations, its record as a conscientious dispenser of the news, and to those circumstances that might lead it to color or misrepresent the facts in any way.

For the attitude of the law toward newspapers as dependable sources of information, see T. W. Hughes, *An Illustrated Treatise on the Law of Evidence* (Chicago, 1907), 88.

(b) *Editorials*. On the assumption that the press reflects local or regional sentiment in politics and other matters, recourse may be had to it for data under this head. The assumption is probably correct in general, but exceptions to it are not infrequent. An editor's opinions are not necessarily those of the community in which he lives or of the reading public which he addresses. At the same time, public opinion on current events may often be satisfactorily gauged by the attitude of representative journals.

The cleavage of popular sentiment in Missouri on slavery, the Union, and other Civil War issues was reflected in the two contemporary influential St. Louis dailies, *The Missouri Republican* and *The Missouri Democrat*.

> In *The Voice of the Negro*, R. P. Kirben, through a compilation from the negro press in America for the four consecutive months immediately succeeding the Washington riots of 1919, has shown how the negro feels in regard to national affairs, what his own grievances are as well as what are his hopes and aspiration.—L. M. Salmon, *The Newspaper and the Historian*, 487.

Material for a study of public opinion as reflected in newspaper editorials may be found in Allan Nevins, ed., *American Press Opinion, Washington to Coolidge: A Documentary Record of Editorial Leadership and Criticism, 1785–1927* (Boston, 1928); Dwight L. Dumond, ed., *Southern Editorials on Secession* (New York, 1931); Cuthbert E. Allen, ed., *The Slavery Question in Catholic Newspapers, 1850–1865* (New York, 1936).

(c) *Advertisements.* These often furnish reliable data to the economic or social historian. They record, for example, current prices of commodities or furnish numberless descriptive details about articles of every kind meant to supply the human needs and luxuries of the day. Social conditions are often revealed with realistic touch. The conventional picture of the runaway slave, with his personal effects hanging from a stick over his shoulder, which may be seen in the advertisement columns of pre-civil-war newspapers, is an instance in point. An obvious caution in the use of newspaper advertising as a historical source, is to be slow to take at their face value alluring descriptions of articles announced for sale.

(d) Newspaper items often help to fix dates and can be reliably informative in other ways; on the other hand, press dispatches are frequently misleading. As an illustration James F. Rhodes cites the letters sent by Horace Greeley to the New York *Tribune*, in 1856, when Greeley was Washington correspondent for that journal. While the public letters contain no misstatements of fact, they fail to bring out clearly situations as he really knew them to be, and as he revealed them in private letters sent at the same time to the *Tribune* editor, Dana.

> A comparison of the newspaper accounts of Civil War battles with the history of them which may be drawn from the correspondence and reports in the Official Records of the War of the Rebellion, will show how inaccurate and misleading was the war correspondence of the daily journals.—James F. Rhodes, "Concerning the Writing of History," *Historical Essays* (New York, 1909), 32.

So also under the pressure of the Soviet government, newspaper correspondents in Moscow passed over in their dispatches the great Russian famine of 1932–1933, though they were aware of its magnitude.—See Eugene Lyons, "The Press Corps Conceals a Famine," *Assignment in Utopia* (New York, 1937), 572–80.

Despite certain manifest drawbacks under which newspapers labor as sources of reliable information, they remain an important aid to the historian; if he uses them, it should always be with the necessary reserve.

(e) On the use of newspapers as sources.

William T. Hutchinson, ed., *The Marcus W. Jernegan Essays in American Historiography by his Former Students at the University of Chicago* (Chicago, 1937), index, "Newspapers."

Charles H. Metzger, *The Quebec Act: A Primary Cause of the American Revolution* (New York, 1936), draws largely from the contemporary press for data on the reaction of the American colonies to the Quebec Act.

William Nelson, "The American Newspapers of the Eighteenth Century as Sources of History," AHA, *Report* (1908), 201–222.

Fred J. Hinkhouse, *Preliminaries of the American Revolution as Seen in the Eng-*

lish Press, 1763–1775 (Columbia University Studies in History, Economics and Public Law, No. 276, New York, 1926).

Herman E. von Holst, The Constitutional and Political History of the United States (7 vols., Washington, 1876–1892).

John B. McMaster, History of the People of the United States from the Revolution to the Civil War (8 vols., New York, 1883–1913).

James F. Rhodes, "The Newspapers as Historical Sources," Historical Essays, 83–97.

Ole S. Rice, Lessons on the Use of Books and Libraries (Chicago, 1920).

Lucy M. Salmon, The Newspaper and the Historian (Oxford and New York, 1920).

Dix Harwood, Getting and Writing News (New York, 1929) chap. 19.

Carl L. Weicht, "The Local Historian and the Newspaper," Minnesota History, 13 (1932): 45 ff.

Edgard Dale, How to Read a Newspaper (New York, 1941).

¶ 253 PROPAGANDA

The term *propaganda* was originally used in connection with the Roman "congregation," or commission of Cardinals charged with superintendence of Catholic foreign missions (*Congregatio de Propaganda Fide*). Later it became the name of a seminary in Rome for the education of priests (College of the Propaganda). Stripped of the odious connotation it has come to have in present-day usage, the term means strictly any attempt, especially organized, to influence public opinion through the press or other means, for any purpose, good or bad.

> In this sense every advertiser, or political party, every school of thought or church, has recourse to propaganda; in this sense Christ and his Apostles were propagandists. It follows that as the end, the means, and the motives are good or bad, propaganda is good or bad.—Charles H. Metzger, "Propaganda in the American Revolution," MA, 22 (1940): 243.

In quite recent times the term *propaganda* has taken on a sinister connotation, implying that the cause it seeks to promote is not worthy, or, if worthy, that the means it employs are not. Whether the attempt made in any particular case to win public opinion through the press, radio, or other media, is to be labeled propaganda in the sinister sense, is to be determined by the circumstances. Certainly praiseworthy causes can and do appeal for public support through such media. What we call propaganda, is not a recent introduction, there was propaganda in the Thirty Years War, in the American Revolution, in the Civil War, as well as in the World Wars. The *Jesuit Relations* or reports of missionary experience and achievement, having for their aim to engage popular sympathy and economic support on behalf of the Jesuit missions of New France, were propaganda.

For the historian, the tendentious character of all propaganda makes it necessary that he determine with caution the extent to which he may lend it credence. In the nature of things, material containing it presents with particular insistence the teasing problems which confront him when he undertakes to appraise the trustworthiness of witnesses.

Horace C. Peterson, *Propaganda for War: The Campaign against American Neutrality* (Norman, Okla., 1939).

Harold Lavine and James Wachsler, *War Propaganda and the United States* (New Haven, 1940).

Elmer A. Beller, *Propaganda in Germany During the Thirty Years War* (Princeton, 1940).

John C. Miller, *Sam Adams, Pioneer in Propaganda* (Boston, 1936).

¶ 254 INSCRIPTIONS

It was said of Theodor Mommsen that he did a greater service to historical science by his planning of the *Corpus inscriptionum latinarum*, with its two hundred thousand items, than by his monumental history of Rome. The former is a permanent and indispensable aid in the field of history it bears on; the latter has no guarantee of permanence as an authority, and in its early parts has already been superseded, because of advances in archaeological research and historical criticism.

A vast amount of political, legal, economic, social, and religious data, illustrating especially the history of the ancient Orient, Greece, and Rome, has been fixed in the form of inscriptions on stone, bronze, or other solid material. Two famous monuments, the Rosetta Stone and the Behistun Inscription, furnished the key to the Egyptian and cuneiform languages, respectively. By their very nature inscriptions are among the most dependable of sources; but they are none the less exposed to the falsifications common to all forms of historical record. Wrong dates, and explicit statements of events that never happened, may be found recorded in marble or bronze as well as on parchment or paper. The motive, whatever it be, patriotism, family pride, self-glorification, which dictated the inscription, must be reckoned with in assessing its evidential value.

A pertinent illustration is the famous Monumentum Ancyranum, the so-called "Deeds of Augustus." What precisely was the emperor's design in leaving to posterity this remarkable survey of his reign, has been a bone of contention among scholars.——Text in *Translations and Reprints from the Original Sources of European History* (University of Pennsylvania, No. 1, 1898). See William L. Westermann, "The Monument of Ancyra: an Interpretation," *AHR*, 17 (1911): 1–11; *Cambridge Ancient History*, 10: 593 ff.

Chapter Twelve

THE CREDIBILITY OF SOURCES
(Continued)

A. The Credibility of Popular Tradition . . . . . . Page 259
B. The Legend-making Process 265
C. Legend as a Historical Source 269
D. Sources Differentiated by Aim 277
E. Sources Differentiated by Type of Witness 279

A. The Credibility of Popular Tradition

¶ 255 ORAL TRADITION

Oral transmission of recent events. Knowledge of these may reach us in one of three ways: first, directly, from one or more immediate witnesses; second, indirectly, from mediate witnesses, through whom, however, it is possible to trace the report back to immediate witnesses.

In the first and second way it becomes possible to accept the information, since the first witness is known to us, and accordingly can be appraised by the usual tests.

The *third* way is from mediate witnesses, but with impossibility of reaching back to the immediate witness. Here, since the identity of the immediate witness is entirely unknown to us, we must be slow to accept information as true.

Rumors and a large proportion of anecdotes fall under this third way. These deserve little or no credence *in se*, while their content is generally something that has happened in private circles, where verification is generally very difficult, if not impossible. In the main, anecdotes have no other ground to support them except rumor or gossip about persons, what they did or said. Often, too, they merely retail a perverse popular feeling of envy, are sensation-mongering, or take delight in belittling persons of prominence.

Raymond W. Chambers, "Doubtful Development of Anecdote,"

Thomas More, 42–45, where the story of More and the cut-purse is discussed.

On the psychology of rumor, see Wilhelm Bauer, *Einführung in das Studium der neueren Geschichte* (2d ed., Tübingen, 1928), 238.

₵ 256 Oral transmission of remote events. This is tradition strictly understood, which may also be called oral tradition, or simply tradition. Its essential note is transmission by word of mouth of some happening in the past. The immediate witness or observer of the occurrence is unknown to us, as well as the mediate witnesses, except the last, who communicated the information to us; consequently, the testimony in question is anonymous.

In this age of literacy, when every occurrence of any note is at once committed to writing in various ways, oral tradition of this kind scarcely has place; but it was otherwise when writing was rare, when the chief means for the transmission of historical data was oral tradition. This process is therefore of the utmost interest to the historian, for numerous written records of earlier times are based demonstrably on tradition of the popular kind, and have no other evidential value than the tradition itself on which they rest. The question, then, is whether such tradition possesses any credibility at all, and if so, to what degree.

Oral tradition in the strict sense, which has for its content some remote but significant occurrence, usually runs through three stages. First, it takes the form of a recital or story handed down from father to son, from teacher to pupil, from one generation to the next, and so is borne along down a considerable period of time. In the second stage these historical recitals give occasion to the introduction of customs, usages, civil or religious institutions and festivals, and sometimes to the invention of new names. Finally, in the third stage the recitals in question are saved for posterity by being fixed in written or pictorial form.

₵ 257 EVALUATION OF TRADITION: SCHEME OF TREATMENT
For the reliability of the popular tradition of a historical fact, certain conditions must be fulfilled.

(a) *Broad conditions*: (1) Unbroken series of witnesses; (2) several parallel and independent series of witnesses.

(b) *Particular conditions*: (1) Content a public event of importance; (2) general belief for a definite period; (3) absence of protest during that period; (4) relatively limited duration; (5) influence of the critical spirit, and application of critical investigation; (6) absence of denial by the critically minded.

₵ 258 DISCUSSION OF THE CONDITIONS FOR RELIABLE TRADITION
The analysis here presented follows De Smedt and Feder.

(a) *Broad conditions stated.*

(1) The tradition should be supported by an unbroken series of witnesses, reaching from the immediate and first reporter of the fact to the living mediate witness from whom we take it up, or to the one who was the first to commit it to writing.

(2) There should be several parallel and independent series of witnesses testifying to the fact in question.

Comment: The realization of such conditions eliminates all possibility of error, for the concurrence of independent lines of testimony can be explained only on the ground that the fact in question is objectively true. A tradition which would realize these two conditions may be accepted without reserve; but it may well be doubted whether traditions of this kind really exist, such, namely, as alone and without corroborative evidence from other sources, afford a basis for certain belief. As has been explained [₡ 255 f.], in popular traditions not only are the intermediate witnesses unknown to us, but the earlier witnesses, as well —those to whom the tradition must be carried back. But where a tradition has really been carried along by parallel independent series of witnesses, the earliest of whom were eyewitnesses of the fact, that tradition may be regarded as reasonably certain; not, however, because of the tradition *per se*, but because of the mutual agreement of the independent series of witnesses among themselves.

The same conclusion holds also in the case in which a tradition is reinforced by archaeological remains. Here, however, it must first be shown that the remains are not vitiated by error of any kind. Place-names, which may have their origin in a false as well as in a true tradition, are an example in point.

(b) *Particular conditions formulated.*

(1) The tradition must report a public event of importance, such as would necessarily be known directly to a great number of persons.

(2) The tradition must have been generally believed, at least for a definite period of time.

(3) During that definite period it must have gone without protest, even from persons interested in denying it.

Comment: While these three conditions are necessary for the realization of a popular tradition, *alone* they do not suffice to guarantee it. Three others must be added.

(4) The tradition must be one of relatively limited duration.

(5) The critical spirit must have been sufficiently developed while the tradition lasted, and the necessary means of critical investigation must have been at hand.

Comment: This fifth condition was frequently wanting in the Middle Ages.

(6) Critical-minded persons who would surely have challenged the tradition, had they considered it false, must have made no such challenge.

Comment in general: A tradition which meets the six required conditions, must be considered as "in possession," and therefore as meriting belief.

The argument from prescription, or "possession" alone (conditions 2 and 3), lacks validity. Each case of a popular tradition must be examined on its own merits. In the end, some traditions will be found altogether groundless, others certainly, or at least probably true.

The bulk of traditions that can claim any truth at all, will not rise above the level of probability. At the same time, research has established a considerable number of cases of traditions which satisfy the six conditions. These should, accordingly, be accepted as objectively true. Examples in point are certain jealously preserved traditions of civil or ecclesiastical privileges, granted to cities, churches, or families.

⁋ 259 SUGGESTIONS ON THE CRITICISM OF TRADITION

(a) A popular tradition may have importance both as a formal and as an informal source; in the first instance because of the residuum of historical truth which it contains, in the second, because of the light it throws on existing conditions. Thus, apart from its possible content of truth, the legend of a medieval saint generally witnesses to the lively religious faith of the times, also to the existence of certain popular practices, such as pilgrimages, veneration of relics. Popular tradition also has its uses in corroborating or supplementing sources of other kinds.

(b) A tradition fixed in writing by a conscientious and critically minded narrator is probably reliable.

(c) A tradition failing to satisfy conditions [⁋ 258-b-5, 6], but current in the same form in widely separated localities or regions, between which there is no reciprocity of intercourse, must be regarded as highly probable, and this because of its repetition in the manner explained.

(d) To prove a tradition untrustworthy, it is not by any means required that its origin be satisfactorily accounted for. Many traditions are known to be false, and yet their origin baffles investigation.

(e) The oral tradition of illiterate groups enjoys a double advantage over that of literate peoples; it is carried along by means of an exceptionally developed power of memory, and in a set form of words.— Marcel Jousse, Le Style Oral et mnémotechnique chez les Verbo-Moteurs (Paris, 1925).

(1) The Icelandic sagas are often cited as striking examples of popular versions of history carefully and substantially handed down by word of mouth.

The general trustworthiness of this saga-telling period has been attested in numerous ways from foreign records. Thus, Snorri Sturlason's "The Sagas of the Kings of Norway," one of the great history books of the world, written in Iceland in the thirteenth century, was based primarily on early tradition brought over the sea to Iceland. Yet the exactness of its descriptions and the reliability of its statements have been verified in countless cases by modern Norwegian historians.—Julius E. Olson and Edward G. Bourne, eds., *The Northmen, Columbus and Cabot* (New York, 1906), 7.

Laurence M. Larson, "Old Norse Sources of English History," AHA, *Report* (1908), 103–108.

Geoffrey M. Gathorne-Hardy, *The Norse Discoverers of America, The Wineland Sagas*, (Oxford and New York, 1921).

Unfavorable estimates of the credibility of the Norse sagas: Fridtjof Nansen, *In Northern Mists, Arctic Exploration in Early Times*, trans. by G. Chater (2 vols., New York, 1911); Lord Raglan, *The Hero, a Study in Tradition, Myth and Legend* (London, 1936) chap. 5.

(2) Sometimes oral tradition can be more reliable than written records, as is exemplified in the Icelandic sagas. Official story-tellers repeat the same literary version without mistake; but the mistakes made by copyists are notorious. The point is discussed in Edward F. Gray, *Leif Erikson. Discoverer of America, A.D. 1003* (Oxford, 1934), 17.

(3) Ordinarily, however, written transmission has a permanency about it that does not in most cases belong to transmission by word of mouth. "Tradition fades, but the written record remains ever fresh," reads the inscription of the façade of the William L. Clements Library, Ann Arbor, Mich.

> Tradition, if indeed it is tradition, is worthy of all reverence. It is not infallible. Tradition is a people's memory, and a people's memory, like yours or mine, has its limitation. There are fields of historical inquiry in which tradition is the most faithful witness.—J. Eoin MacNeill, *Phases of Irish History* (Dublin, 1920), 105 f.

The question of how long the memory of historical events can be preserved accurately through oral tradition is interesting, but not easy to answer. Raglan (*The Hero*, 13) estimates the maximum period at about one hundred and fifty years. On the other hand, Merrill writes:

> Little attention seems to have been paid to the length of time that elapsed between the discovery of Vinland in 1003, or thereabouts, and the earliest possible date at which the narratives could have been reduced to writing, about 1250. The Icelanders were noted for the accuracy of their oral traditions; but to determine just how far details of events have

been preserved in their first integrity through two hundred and fifty years, is no easy task.——William S. Merrill, "The Norse Voyages to America," *MA*, 14 (1932): 226.

(4) The well-known tradition affirming the martyrdom of St. Peter in Rome finds abundant support in documentary and archaeological evidence. Rudolph Lanciani, an Italian archaeologist of note, declared that for men of his profession the tradition is verifiable beyond dispute. The first to deny it was Marsilius of Padua, in his *Defensor Pacis*. It was denied by Calvin in the sixteenth century, and in the nineteenth by Baur, and by the rationalist school generally. A reaction in favor of the tradition has set in, with the result that it now meets with support even in rationalist quarters.

The martyrdom of Peter in Rome was challenged first by Protestant, and then by critical prejudice. That this is a mistake is as open as day to any investigator who is not blinded by prejudice. The whole critical apparatus with which Baur contested the old tradition is today accounted worthless, and justly so.——Adolf Harnack, *Geschichte der altchristlichen Litteratur bis Eusebius* (2 parts, in 3 vols., Leipzig, 1893–1904), 2d part, 1:244.

The tradition current in classical times that kings once ruled in Rome is accepted as genuine by modern scholarship. "The kingship itself is beyond dispute, owing to the strength of the Roman tradition on this point and the survival of the title *rex* or king in the priestly office of the *rex sacrarum*."—— Arthur E. R. Boak, *A History of Rome to 565 A.D.* (New York, 1929), 36.

An instance of a local tradition ultimately verified by documentary evidence occurs in the early history of St. Louis. The name of the Rivière des Pères, or Fathers' River, at the southern boundary of the city, was traditionally accounted for as referring to certain missionaries who were supposed to have resided at one time in the locality. No documentary proof for the tradition was available until 1920, when the existence of an eighteenth-century mission-post at the river named, and concomitantly, the truth of the tradition were established beyond doubt by contemporary evidence.——See Laurence J. Kenny, *St. Louis Catholic Historical Review*, 1 (1919): 151–56; Gilbert J. Garraghan, *Chapters in Frontier History* (Milwaukee, 1934), 74–84; 86–88.

(5) An instance of gratuitous popular tradition is the anti-Catholic legend as it developed in England. It was subjected to acute analysis by John Henry Newman in his *Lectures on the Present Position of Catholics in England* (London, 1851).

For the American phase of the anti-Catholic legend, see Sister Mary Augustana Ray, *American Opinion of Roman Catholicism in the Eighteenth Century* (New York, 1936); Ray A. Billington, *The Protestant Crusade: A Study of the Origins of American Nativism* (New York, 1938).

The popular belief that the log-cabin was the usual type of dwelling built by the English colonists in America from their first arrival, is discussed by Harold R. Shurtleff, *The Log Cabin Myth: a Study of the Early Dwellings of the English Colonists in North America* (Cambridge, Mass., 1939).

₡ 260 LATE APPEARANCE OF TRADITION
It is typical of popular tradition that it is first heard of long after the time when the events it reports are supposed to have occurred. Almost invariably there is a gap, more or less broad, between the events and their first appearance in recorded history. Such a gap occurring in the case of any report is enough to make it suspect from the start. Instances of such reports, found on examination to be unverified, are without number. Thus, unaccountably tardy first-mention of them in written record of any kind is a major argument used by critics in discrediting such one-time general beliefs as the False Decretals, the Popess Joan, the authenticity of the reputed works of Denis the Areopagite. Again, no contemporary biographer of St. Thomas of Canterbury records that his mother was a Saracen princess whom his father had married in the Holy Land.—John Morris, "Legends about St. Thomas," *The Life and Martyrdom of St. Thomas Archbishop of Canterbury* (2d ed., London, 1885), 523–25.

That Luther committed suicide is a story first heard of some twenty years after his death, when it began to be circulated by persons hostile to his memory.—H. Grisar, *Martin Luther, his Life and Work*, 575–78.

The "Whitman-saved-Oregon" story first became public many years after Whitman's death.—See Edward G. Bourne's *Essays in Historical Criticism*.

The Ann Rutledge-Lincoln episode appears to be mainly legendary. No mention of it occurs until thirty-one years after her death.—*AHR*, 41 (1936): 283.

A crucial point to be noted about such beliefs as those indicated is that when mention of them in written record emerges for the first time, no reason is forthcoming to explain why mention of them had not been made earlier.*

B. The Legend-making Process

₡ 261 ALTERATION OF CONTENT
Change in the content of a historical fact as it passes over into legend may take one of five different directions.

(a) *Exaggeration*. This lifts historical persons to some higher, im-

* This fundamental principle is abundantly illustrated in Ulysse Chevalier, *Notre-Dame de Lorette. Étude historique sur l'Authenticité de la Santa Casa* (Paris, 1906).—Ed.

aginary, and at times to a quite supramundane sphere, as is found in the classical myths of the Graeco-Roman world. Incidents in a hero's career or traits in his character may be embellished out of all semblance to reality, as in the case of many of the lawgivers and philosophers of antiquity: Solon, Lycurgus, Pythagoras, Socrates. A hero is metamorphosed into an ideal type, sometimes even escapes the common destiny of death, as St. John the Evangelist at Ephesus, Charlemagne at Untersburg, Frederick Barbarossa at Kyffhäuser. In the Beatrice Cenci legend a historical character has been transformed by exaggeration from bad to good. "Thanks to criticism European literature has lost a tragic story. Beatrice Cenci was a common criminal, not a tragic heroine."—Cheldowski, cited in Ludwig von Pastor, *The History of the Popes from the Close of the Middle Ages* (34 vols., St. Louis, 1898–1941), 24:420, note 2.

By a process of exaggeration legend gives a more striking, a better-sounding form to famous sayings than they originally had. Thus, *Tout est perdu, fors l'honneur!* ("All is lost save honor!")—words of Francis I, but greatly diluted in the original letter which contains them. *L'état c'est moi* ("I am the state")—attributed on doubtful grounds to Louis XIV, though it expresses accurately enough his viewpoint in politics. *Roma locuta est, causa finita est* ("Rome has spoken, the case is settled")—words of St. Augustine, but the original version is less striking.

For a critical examination of the credibility of several such "historical apothegms," see L. O'Brien, *The Writing of History*, 85–95.

Legend likewise exaggerates by converting possibilities or probabilities into certainties. According to Tacitus (*Annals*, XV, 39) it was uncertain (*pervaserat rumor*) whether the burning of Rome was accidental or the deliberate work of Nero, who sang during the conflagration in mockery of the Romans. In the version of the incident that later gained currency, the guilt of Nero was taken for granted as a matter of historical fact.

Constantine was baptized a few days before his death; in legendary tradition he was baptized years earlier when he was in vigorous health.

Legend often extends to an entire territory, city, building, what is true of only a part of it. Attila never actually got below the Po in his invasion of Italy; in legend he overruns and devastates also the cities and provinces south of that river.

In history, Charlemagne wrested from the Moors only the country around Barcelona or the territory between the Ebro and the Pyrenees; in legend he frees the whole peninsula from the Moorish yoke.

(b) *Concentration*. This gathers together the deeds and achievements of different persons, whether contemporary or not, or of different nations, periods, or lands, and crystallizes them in a single person, nation, period, or land. In a line of princes, to cite a typical instance, one stands out as the heir of all the virtues of his forebears; he sums up in his person the whole past history, all the ancestral traits of his people. In general, concentration has its source in popular incapacity to follow clearly the great stream of history and its phenomena, or else in onesided admiration of certain great men, periods, lands. Also, it may be motivated by national pride or by similar tendencies, which result in an effort to bring together into artificial connection separated periods of time or developments, or to trace back a later development to an earlier. Illustrations of this process are the putative founding of Rome by Aeneas of Troy, the introduction of letters by the Phoenician Cadmus, the descent of medieval German princes from Roman heroes.

By concentration the actual course of events gains in intensity what it has lost in extent, as regards time and place. Instances of this are to be found in the national epics, such as the *Iliad* and the *Niebelungenlied*, and in sagas, such as those celebrating the Assyrian royal pair, Ninus and Semiramis, Dietrich of Bern, (the Theodoric the Great in German legend), and Charlemagne.

A modern example of concentration is the Code Napoléon, the historic French collection of laws, which popular belief is wont to attribute to the great emperor as his exclusive achievement, whereas in reality it was the outcome of a hundred years of effort on the part of kings, parliaments, and corporations. One particular kind of concentration is the acceptance of certain personalities as finished types of a virtue or a vice: Socrates, Marcus Aurelius, Nero, Richard III.

(c) *Confusion*. This assigns the performances of one person to another of the same name, as in the case of Charles the Great (Charlemagne) and Charles Martel. Other examples of confusion occur in medieval lives of the saints, Cyprian of Antioch and Cyprian of Carthage, Dionysius of Athens and Dionysius (Denis) of Paris, St. Louis of France and St. Louis of Toulouse.

The story told of Belisarius, Justinian's famous general, though familiar in literature and art (Longfellow's "Belisarius"), that, disgraced and with his eyes put out as a punishment, he was reduced to the necessity of begging his bread, is legendary. It arose possibly from confusion of Belisarius with John of Cappadocia, of whom a similar experience is recorded. The legend is discussed in George Finlay, *A History of Greece from the Conquest by the Romans to the Present Time* (7 vols., Oxford, 1877), 1:429-32.

(d) *Accretion*. This amplifies or embellishes a historical fact with fictitious details. It finds particular application in the case of national heroes who have caught the popular fancy; the hero is made to be an actor in all important events, and nothing noteworthy or inspiring happens without him. The actual fact of the meeting of Pope Leo I with Attila, King of the Huns, is, by a process of accretion, enlarged upon with the legendary detail that on this occasion the Apostles Peter and Paul appeared high in the heavens supporting with threats the words of warning uttered by the saint.

(e) *False interpretation.* This is often a factor in the legend-process. Types of false interpretation are wrong etymological derivations, wrong explanations of names and expressions. Popular accounts of the origin of place-names are often curiously fanciful and far-fetched. Complex and not easily intelligible historical situations are given a simplicity that is foreign to them, causes and effects are interchanged, occurrences of importance, especially the downfall of such great personages as Richard the Lion-hearted, Frederick Barbarossa, Wolsey, Napoleon, are set off against a background of imaginary causes or circumstances.

The growth of the Attila legend is interesting as an "illustration of the myth-creating faculty of half-civilized nations." Three versions of the legend were developed among the Latin, German, and Scandinavian peoples, respectively.——Thomas Hodgkin, *Italy and her Invaders* (8 vols. in 9, Oxford, 1880–1899), 2:175–81; Sidney G. Fisher, "Myth-making Processes in Histories of the American Revolution," American Philosophical Society, *Proceedings*, 51 (1912): 69.

❡ 262 Origin of religious myths

To explain the origin of myths (in particular the religious myths of the Greeks and Romans) various theories have been advanced. Most of the explanations, however, are unsatisfactory.

(a) *Euhemerism*, from the name of the Greek philosopher Euhemerus (third century, B.C.), regards myths as tales of the deeds and achievements of earthly heroes and heroines raised to the dignity of deities [❡ 98-e].

(b) The *symbolical* explanation, sponsored by Crates among the ancients, sees in myths symbolical embodiments of the processes of nature, of ideas about the physical world [❡ 98-e; 263].

(c) The *etymological* explanation (Max Müller) finds the origin of myths in the names borne by mythical persons [❡ 146-a]. Today it is recognized among scholars that in view of the great variety of relations which can exist between myths and historical realities, no one of the theories named can claim general validity. Each myth must be explained separately in the light of its own historical setting and characteristics. This manner of accounting for myths might be called the *historical* explanation.

Albert Muntsch, *Cultural Anthropology*, 198 ff.

Charles M. Gayley, *The Classical Myths in English Literature* (Boston, 1893), chap. 1.

Padraic Colum, "The Origin and Elements of Myth," in *Orpheus, The Myth of the World* (New York, 1930).

George C. Ring, *The Gods of the Gentiles: Non-Jewish Cultural Religions of Antiquity* (Milwaukee, 1938) 112 f.; 194-96.

C. Legend as a Historical Source

❧ 263   In English and in other languages there is a whole group of terms signifying a recital in some way at variance with the truth. Thus, we have fable, tale, story, myth, legend, saga. In ordinary usage no hard and fast line is drawn between these terms; they are often used indifferently to express one and the same idea of a fictitious or untrustworthy account. But critical study of the fictitious element in historical sources makes it necessary to determine with some precision the exact meaning to be attached to each of the terms in question [❧ 98].

The definitions here given follow largely those of Francisco Lanzoni, *Genesi, svolgimento e tramito delle legende storiche* (Rome, 1925), the standard work on the subject.* With Lanzoni, *legend* is a sweeping term covering historical falsification of any kind.

(a) *Fable.* A recital in which the actors are beasts, birds, or other non-intelligent beings, or even abstract notions personified, which take on human characteristics and talk and act like human beings. Classic examples are the fables of Aesop, Phaedrus, La Fontaine.

(b) *Tale* (story). A recital dealing with indeterminate times, places, persons, the conventional beginning for it being: "Once upon a time there was a king, a little boy, etc." Fairy tales, collections of which have been made in most languages ever since the Grimm brothers brought out their famous work in 1827, are examples. But fairy stories are only one type of tale, as the term is generally understood. The term is broad enough to include also the parables of the Gospels, which lack determination of time, place, and person.

(c) *Myth.* A recital or account of any kind which purports to be historical, but is really fictitious, wholly or in part. This definition is general and transcends the specific meanings which the term may bear [❧ 98 e]. The usual explanation of "nature myths," as they are called, is to regard them as attempts on the part of primitive peoples to account for physical forces or phenomena by personifying them. Homer's Greeks, seeing a pestilence raging and unable to account for it, conceived of an

---

* The genesis, development, and transmission of legends in general are briefly treated in H. Delehaye, *The Legends of the Saints*, chaps. 1-3.—Ed.

angry sun-god discharging his arrows at the defenceless victims. The nature myth, therefore, deals not with human beings as legend does, but with superhuman beings. Myth is the term to apply to the classic stories (mythology) of the Greek and Roman deities, legend to the unverifiable experiences often recorded of the medieval saints.

(d) *Legend.* In ordinary usage a legend is a recital or account at variance with the truth. For the etymology of the term see ⁋ 98-f. The historical or real element in a legend—time, place, persons—is only a peg on which the fictitious element is hung. Legends, whatever their origin, are first carried along for more or less considerable periods of time by oral or popular tradition. Eventually they are fixed in writing; but the principles regulating their use by the historian are the same as those which apply to popular tradition.

(e) *Saga.* In its original meaning a *saga* is a Scandinavian, especially an Icelandic hero-tale. But the term may be applied to any narrative of heroic tenor, as in Carl Wittke, *We Who Built America: The Saga of the Immigrant.* Again, the term may be used broadly to designate any narrative which departs from the literal truth, especially by way of exaggeration and coloring. Thus, we have the Lincoln saga to express the growth of exaggerations and unverified reports which surround the Emancipator's name. Often also, saga is used to describe any story of heroic contents without raising doubt as to its historicity [⁋ 98-d].

⁋ 264 The nature of oral or popular tradition and the caution to be employed by the historian in its use are discussed by De Smedt, *Principes.* His main contention is that popular tradition when critically examined, turns out to be true in some cases and false in others. It is scarcely practicable to lay down general rules for determining its reliability. Every popular tradition is a problem by itself and must be examined on its own merits. Often there is no foundation whatever for the report, which is merely a product of popular imagination. De Smedt illustrates this by the popular German legend of Count Gleicher of Thuringia, a thirteenth-century crusader, who having married in the Orient in the belief that his first wife was dead, found her on his return home to be alive. Thereupon, so it is alleged, he was granted a dispensation by Pope Gregory IX to live with both, a statement which has no foundation whatever. The tradition appears abruptly for the first time in 1584. There was a later Count Gleicher, who died in 1494. On his tomb was shown a knight standing between two female figures. This probably gave rise to the story. After citing this and other illustrations, De Smedt comments:

> This is enough to show how illusory is the rule which assumes that a core of truth is always present in popular tradition, so as to allow one to entertain doubt only as to details. It is not rash to affirm that the cases

in which this rule has been discredited are much more numerous than those in which it has been verified. The residue of truth yielded up by certain traditions when critically examined, attaches more often to the details than to the substance of the fact.

De Smedt thus disposes of the not uncommon misapprehension that "every legend contains a kernel of truth." Some contain no direct truth whatsoever, as in the instance he cites. The following direction is important:

> Criticism in its earlier stages thought that all details of a legend which did not conflict with history or which seemed possible a priori, could be retained. This false method is not yet outmoded. But it is to be rejected. Details of the simpler and more natural kind, such as seem more likely, more credible, occurring in an account, do not necessarily derive from genuine tradition, nor are they sure tokens of historicity; they can be the product of clever imagination, generalization, plagiarism.
> —Lanzoni, *Genesi*, 264.

It was conventional to use the sources for early Roman history according to this false method.

ℂ 265 An illuminating analogy between oral tradition about past events and public rumor about present-day occurrences is pointed out by De Smedt. Both are alike in two respects: first, numerous witnesses can be cited in their support, all agreeing as to the substance of the report but differing in details; secondly, no immediate witnesses can be cited for them. In the case of rumor, especially when it regards happenings in far-away countries, a prudent person will not accept it freely, but will try, as far as circumstances allow, to run it to ground. He will seek information from persons familiar through residence or travel with the distant country whence the rumor comes, or perhaps consult books or other printed sources of information; but in any case, he will not permit himself to believe the rumor until after diligent investigation he finds some positive basis of evidence on which to justify belief.

Instances in which legends and rumors have been discredited by research are many. See Thomas E. Bridgett, "The Rood of Boxley or How a Lie Grows," *Blunders and Forgeries* (London, 1890); John Morris, ed., *Historical Papers*, 2:61–118.

The mass of legends that grew up around the Bastille was exposed by the discovery, in 1840, of the archives of that famous prison.—Denis A. Bingham, *The Bastille*, (London, 1888); Frantz Funk-Brentano, *Legends of the Bastille* (London, 1899).

ℂ 266 Problems regarding the origin of legends and the isolation of the historical elements in their content can be as elusive as they are complex. Thus, various possible origins for the *chanson de gestes* (French *épopée*, epic) have been suggested. Were they compiled from accounts contemporary with the persons and events portrayed? Such accounts were handed down by oral tradition, to the end of the eleventh century, the period of composition of the chansons. Or were they based on popular songs? Or were they the product of pure invention practised in monasteries, with a view to entertain or edify merchants and pilgrims? Or were they derived simultaneously from oral tradition and invention? A considerable part of the stories in the *Little Flowers of St. Francis* are demonstrably either pretty invention or rhetorical embellishment, or else a recasting of facts related by biographers of St. Francis. But in regard to many incidents of the book it is impossible, in default of adequate evidence, to conclude whether they are fact, fiction, or dramatization.——Lanzoni, *Genesi*, 261.

That our own age can be as naively credulous as any other, is borne out by Sir Charles Oman's critical discussion of the many rumors that gained credence in England during the first World War, for example, those about "the angels of Mons," and the mythical "hundred thousand Russian troops from Archangel." The moral is "that we are the children of our fathers, that we should not jest too much at 'medieval credulity,' and that we should recognize in the rumor-phenomena of our own day the legitimate descendants of those which used to puzzle and amaze our ancestors, whom we are too often prone to regard with the complacent superiority of the omniscient nineteenth century."——*The Unfortunate Colonel Despard and Other Studies* (London, 1922), 69–70.

⁋ 267 DIRECT HISTORICAL VALUE OF LEGEND
A significant development in recent critical historiography is its increasing regard for tradition as a historical source.

The historical value of myths and legends . . . is distinctly on the rise again.——Reginald W. Macan, ed., *Herodotus, the Fourth, Fifth, and Sixth books* (2 vols., London, 1895) 1: lxxxi.

Undoubtedly the tendency to reject tradition went too far in the nineteenth century. It is now generally agreed that tradition, while losing or distorting the details, very commonly embodied some historical elements.——James T. Shotwell and Louise R. Loomis, eds., *The See of Peter* (New York, 1927), xxiii.

The changed attitude of scholars in this respect is due chiefly to the striking confirmation which numerous old and often questioned traditions has received, in the last generation or two, from archaeological research. It is now generally recognized that a long-standing tradition or a legend can and frequently does carry with it an actual content of historical fact.

Thus, the discoveries of Schliemann and others at Hissarlik and around the site of ancient Troy, together with other archaeological finds, have revealed the nucleus of historical fact around which the Homeric poems are woven.——*Cambridge Ancient History*, 1: 510–517.

Again, reference to Athens in Homer (*Odyssey*, VII, 80; *Iliad*, II, 546–55) had been arbitrarily assumed to be late interpolations made by the Athenians, in order to enhance their historical past. But excavations made on the site of Athens have uncovered Mycenean remains, thus linking up the city with the Homeric age.—John A. Scott, "Athenian Interpolations in Homer," *Classical Philology*, 6 (1911): 418-28; 9 (1914): 395-407.

The stories told by Herodotus, traditional target of attack ever since his day, have in nearly all instances where he alleges personal experience in proof of them, received striking confirmation through archaeological discoveries. Probably the most interesting of the services thus rendered by archaeology in substantiation of old traditions is in the case of the great sea-empire of King Minos of Crete, as described by Thucydides (I, 4). As the account seemed to be nothing more than tradition or legend, historians used to reject it as without any basis in fact. But the remarkable excavations conducted in Crete by Sir Arthur Evans, toward the close of the last century, showed Thucydides to be substantially correct. Remains of various culture-periods were uncovered together with traces of a vast sea-empire belonging roughly to the period 2250-1200 B.C.—*Cambridge Ancient History*, 1:138 ff.

¶ 268 INDIRECT HISTORICAL VALUE OF LEGEND

Lanzoni, following De Smedt, distinguishes two types of legend, *mere* legends, and *historical* legends. The former have no direct or explicit historical content whatever, the latter have content of this kind in varying degree. Both types can be of use to the historian by preserving data of value, whether implicitly or explicitly. The legend itself may be pure fiction, and at the same time incidentally (or, as the philosophers say, *praeter intentionem*) may picture vividly and even accurately various phases of a vanished culture or civilization.

The *Iliad* and *Odyssey* set before us Greek military and social life of the heroic age. The *Ramayana* portrays ancient Indian civilization; the *Niebelungenlied*, the men and manners of the eleventh and twelfth centuries. Equally much is done for the Persians by the *Shanameh*, for the Finns by the *Kalevala*, for the Scandinavian's by the *Edda*. The stories of Brutus, the Fabii, Coriolanus, however exaggerated in late historiography, reflect the ideas and spirit of the better classes of Romans in the fifth century before Christ. Feudal France survives in the *chansons de geste*. Spain of the eleventh and twelfth centuries, as regards its social life and psychology is mirrored to the life in the *Song of the Cid*.—Lanzoni, *Genesi*, 261-64. See also Grace Frank, "Historical Elements in the Chansons de Geste," *Speculum*, 14 (1939): 209-14.

¶ 269 Recognition of the indirect or implicit historical value of legend is now general among scholars. Lanzoni is especially emphatic on this score. He insists that one who has read of the Middle Ages, and in particular of the medieval church, in the historians only, has gone only half-way towards grasping the medieval spirit. One must become familiar also with the contemporary Christian legends if there is to be understanding of the real mentality of medieval folk and of their sentiments and ideals, their family and social life, all of which was intimately bound up with the legends.

> For an understanding of the history of Rome and the medieval West, the *Donation of Constantine* is worth more than a hundred chronicles of the period. . . . The celebrated false Isidorian [Decretals] explain better than all the documents of the ninth century the revolution which was going on at that time in the organic life of the Church in France. . . . Moreover, legends that reflect, not the mere imaginings of an individual but the prevailing mentality of an entire milieu, give expression to sentiments which the historian cannot afford to neglect. The growth of a legend around an event or a name shows the importance attached at the moment to the event or the name. The legend of Theodosius at the feet of Ambrose, on the floor of a basilica in Milan, reveals to us in its glowing colors the importance which Christians rightly attached to this significant episode in the history of the relations between the political and the religious authorities, of a bishop imposing a penance and a guilty emperor accepting and performing it. The legends of Theodoric the Great, related by St. Gregory the Great and by other Italian writers of the sixth and seventh centuries belong to the biography of that Ostrogoth king no less than the historical documents themselves, for they reveal the sinister impression which his last deeds made upon the Catholics of Italy.—Lanzoni, *Genesi*, 264–65.

ℂ 270 Delehaye is at one with De Smedt and Lanzoni in contending for the indirect value of legend.

> Their [the saints'] life . . . is in truth the concrete realization of the spirit of the Gospel, and from the very fact that it brings home to us this sublime ideal, legend, like poetry, can claim a higher degree of truth than history itself.—Hippolyte Delehaye, *The Legends of the Saints*, 230.

Roy T. Basler, in *The Lincoln Legend: A Study in Changing Conceptions* (Boston, 1935), adopts a similar viewpoint, stressing the educative and ethical uses of legend as illustrated in the case of Lincoln. Lloyd Lewis, *Myths After Lincoln* (New York, 1929), discusses the enormous growth of exaggeration and fiction which gathered around the memory of the Emancipator, and is eloquent testimony to the growth of his influence on the popular imagination.

ℂ 271 Chesterton comments caustically that people, being denied by the historians any truth that takes the form of legend, are led "to believe in the much more fabulous fable, the legend of the learned."—Gilbert K. Chesterton, "On the Truth of Legend," *All is Grist: A Book of Essays* (London, 1931), 150–53.

> It is in the essence of Legend that its historical value is not in question. It has not to be believed as witness to an event but as examples; or

even no more than a picture which does us good by its beauty alone. We are not in using legend approving a belief in a particular occurrence, but listening with profit to a story; and if the moral of the story is sound, if its effect is towards truth, goodness, beauty, that is all we ask of it. Humanity has lived on such stories and when a false philosophy banishes them or lets them die out, humanity is starved. . . . Most legends have history behind them, and take it by and large, there is more history in legend by far than fantasy.—Hilaire Belloc, "On Legend," *Essays of a Catholic* (London, 1931), 161 f.

After all, why should we reproach the hagiographers for their shortcomings as witnesses? Their aim in writing was by no means to fulfil the office of the historian. The methods on which the modern historian prides himself were altogether foreign to their purpose, as well as to the demands of the public for whom they wrote. Their sole object was to provide edification by means of narratives abounding in marvelous incidents or striking traits of virtue calculated to impress the mind of the reader and stir up his feelings to reverence and emulation. It would be doing them great injustice to judge their naive productions by the severe canons of modern criticism.—Louis Gougaud, *Christianity in Celtic Lands. History of the Churches of the Celts, their Origin, their Development, Influence and Mutual Relations* (London, 1932), 53.

Much of the hagiographical literature, like some mirror, reflects not merely the beliefs, but the hopes and fears, the daily labors, pleasures and sorrows of the people. Yet many inquirers into the life and spirit of the Middle Ages, deterred by a certain uniformity in these records, and still more swayed by the rationalism of a supposedly more enlightened age, have totally neglected this unique body of evidence. They have done so at their peril, for in setting aside what they deemed unworthy of serious notice, the self-declared enemies of "superstition" have closed for themselves one of the main avenues to enlightenment.—Max. L. W. Laistner, *Thought and Letters in Western Europe A. D. 500 to 900* (New York, 1931), 232.

¶ 272 A standing problem in the criticism of legends as sources for the historian is furnished by Livy's charming stories about early Rome. The general attitude of modern criticism is to regard them as unhistorical but enclosing in many cases a kernel of truth, "like flies in amber."

E. Pais, *Ancient Legends of Roman History* (London, 1906).

Cambridge Ancient History, 7: 363 ff., 498–500.

J. W. Duff, *A Literary History of Rome*, 637 ff.

E. T. Salmon, "Historical Elements in the Story of Coriolanus," *Classical Quarterly*, 24 (1930): 96–101.

The story of St. Christopher from the "Golden Legend" in Alban Butler, *The Lives of the Saints*, ed. by Herbert Thurston and Donald Attwater (12 vols., London, 1926–1938), 7: 358–63.

George O'Neill, ed., *The Golden Legend: Lives of the Saints, Translated by William Caxton from the Latin of Jacobus de Voragine* (Cambridge, Eng., 1914).

Jacobus de Varagine, *The Golden Legend of Jacobus de Varagine*, translated and adapted by Granger Ryan and Helmut Ripperger (2 vols., New York, 1941).

W. Lewis Jones, "The Arthurian Legend," *Cambridge History of English Literature* (New York, 1933), 1: 270–308.

Joseph Dunn, "The Brendan Problem," *CHR*, 6 (1921): 395–470.

Herbert Thurston, "The English Legend of St. Joseph of Arimathea," *The Month* 158 (1931): 43–54.

Mary Hayden and George A. Moonan, "Mythology and Legend," *A Short History of the Irish People from the Earliest Times to 1920* (Dublin, 1921), 3–8.

Andrew Lang, "Homer and the Saga," *The World of Homer* (London, 1910), chap. 16.

The whirligig of time brings its revenges and the historian of today goes to the tales discarded by his predecessors for a far from contemptible part of his material; folklore has become a historical science and mythology is acknowledged to be instructive if not literally true.—Janet R. Bacon, *The Voyage of the Argonauts* (London, 1925), 3.

If the *Iliad* and *Odyssey* were all fiction, we should still learn from them a great deal about early Greek customs, about practices of war and of government, about marriage, land-tenure, worship, farming, commerce, and above all, the methods of seafaring.—Gilbert Murray, *The Rise of the Greek Epic* (London, 1907), 179.

Magna Carta is an interesting example of legend in the form of misinterpretation, having a good issue. A later age read into it meanings which were not intended by its framers. "The greatness of Magna Carta lies not so much in what it was to its framers in 1215 as to what it afterwards became to the political leaders, to the judges and lawyers, and to the entire mass of the men of England in later ages."—William S. McKechnie, *Magna Carta; A Commentary on the Great Charter of King John* (rev. ed., Glasgow, 1914), 158.

On the new attitude of scholarship towards legend as a historical source, see L. M. Salmon, *Historical Material*, chap. 5.

⦅ 273 This discussion of legend as a historical source may be summarized as follows: first, some legends have a content of greater or less fact, and therefore possess direct historical value; secondly, others, have no content of fact at all, and therefore possess no direct historical value; and finally, legends of either class possess or may possess indirect historical value in the sense explained.

⦅ 274 Besides oral transmission (tradition), three other types of transmission may be recognized: *pictorial, figured, written* [⦅ 99].

Transmission by picture or figure is similar to that by writing, insofar as from the start it takes a shape, fixed and controllable, which even in copies is not so much liable to suffer the changes frequent in oral transmission. Figured sources of solid material are superior in permanence to written sources. On the other hand, the special character of pictorial representation often tends to obstruct clear understanding of the historical facts which it transmits. Hence, more so than the oral or written types, transmission by picture or figure needs interpretation, chiefly because in the nature of things it can present only a single moment or phase of an event, not its entire course. A painting of Waterloo, naturally can show any one juncture in the battle. A unique position in pictorial transmission is held by the movies, with their power of reproducing to the eye a complex happening in all its living actuality.

Artistic representations of historical scenes by picture or figure are often idealized, with the result that they cannot be taken to represent the literal truth. A contemporary engraving of the capture of the Bastille, July 14, 1789, reproduced in the *Encyclopaedia Britannica* (14th edition), article "Bastille," shows uniformed soldiers in ranks attacking the fortress. The attacking forces, as a matter of fact, were neither orderly nor for the most part uniformed.

As regards transmission by writing, the illusion is not uncommon that written documents may be trusted simply because they are written, as though an account gained in trustworthiness by being put in writing. Such procedure, indeed, tends to make the writer more attentive and more exact, while the consciousness that his reputation before the public may be at stake, can be an effective incentive to tell the truth. Written sources have a further advantage over oral sources in having their content rigidly shaped and defined from the beginning, so that they are subsequently less exposed to distortion or arbitrary change.

D. Sources Differentiated by Aim

⁋ 275 By its nature any historical source has for its primary aim the communication of historical data in their objective truth. But it may have at the same time a secondary aim, for example, to entertain, to inculcate a doctrine or moral lesson, to influence by propaganda. Historical sources can therefore be classified as *strictly informative* and *not strictly informative*. Knowledge of the aim or aims which inspire the composition of a historical source is therefore of the first importance in estimating its value as evidence.

⁋ 276 SOURCES STRICTLY INFORMATIVE
In the case of sources strictly informative, some means must be devised for testing their accuracy. As regards secondary sources, especially, serious doubt may arise regarding the correctness of the informant's data; such doubt will be greater, the greater his distance in point of time from the facts reported, and the less critical the age in which he lived.

Reports of a strictly informative nature, committed to writing by a competent hand shortly after the occurrence of the events, as a class, are to be regarded as worthy of credence. One may, accordingly, rate as reliable most of the annals, chronicles, and similar strictly historical narratives written by contemporary authors, as also the bulk of historical inscriptions and coins. In general, inscriptions and coins can be depended upon as regards both the information they furnish on public events and their chronological data. On the other hand, certain other types of the strictly informative source, books of travel, for instance, must be used with reserve. Sometimes we are reliably informed of the traveler's competence as an observer and reporter; in such a case we can trust his account more or less implicitly.* But cases will not be rare in which guarantee of this kind is wanting, so that we must attempt to determine just how far we may safely go in accepting the account. The literature of travel is a vexing body of source material which requires all the resources of the historian's critical faculty to evaluate it aright. Marco Polo and Sir John Mandeville, in China; Lahontan and Hennepin, in New France; Arthur Young, in France; and Dickens, in America, have left on record their impressions of the lands which they visited. No critical-minded student of history feels that he may accept these impressions at their face value; inevitably he subjects their authors to previous cross-examination to determine just how far their testimony may be depended on.†

⁋ 277 SOURCES NOT STRICTLY INFORMATIVE

(a) To this class belong *historical plays* and *novels*, which are designed primarily for enjoyment or esthetic satisfaction. The conventional license allowed playwrights and novelists necessarily discounts their productions as sources of accurate information, at least for factual data. Yet the influence of the drama in shaping popular impressions of the figures of history is far-reaching, as we see illustrated in the case of Shakespeare's historical plays.—Beverly E. Warner, *English History in Shakespeare's Plays* (New York, 1916); William J. Tucker, *College Shakespeare* (New York, 1932), chap 2.

As to historical novels, Walter Scott's are outstanding in the effect they have had in impressing certain definite pictures and estimates of the past on their countless readers. Presenting a more engaging view of the Middle Ages than the English public was accustomed to, in the

---

* What was said with regard to diaries [⁋ 248-b] is applicable to books of travel.—Ed.

† This is clearly insufficient. All important statements must be checked on independent evidence.—Ed.

opinion of Cardinal Newman they became one of the factors that prepared the way for the Catholic revival in England. This estimate of the influence of Scott's novels finds warrant in their general atmosphere and spirit, not in their factual content, which is full of inaccuracies.

(b) Also to be classed with sources not strictly informative are *sermons*, which often contain statements of a historical nature. To what extent the historian may accept these statements is a question which will sometimes require all his critical acumen to answer. Sermons denouncing prevalent moral abuses may easily run into exaggeration. To take such denunciation at its face value may easily leave one with an impression of a state of affairs at variance with the facts. The fifth-century priest Salvian's *De gubernatione Dei* is not precisely a sermon, but it is in the nature of such. The picture which he draws of current moral corruption is appalling; but its fidelity to fact has been called into question.—Sir Samuel Dill, *Roman Society in the Last Century of the Western Empire*, 141; Thomas Hodgkin, *Italy and her Invaders*, vol. 1, part 2, p. 921.

(c) State papers and office records of any kind may be classed among those sources the object of which is not wholly or even primarily to impart historical information. Primarily, they serve the purpose of administration; secondarily, they may serve the purpose of the historian. His use of them is limited by considerations of the object for which they were compiled, and by the circumstances of their compilation.

Charles G. Crump comments on what he takes to be a present-day tendency to use original documents or records uncritically. He points out that most so-called original or official records are not original at all in the strict sense of the term, but are compilations from reports, returns, and other such material, for example, the Domesday Book, pipe rolls; that records are drawn up in such manner as to conceal the true character or true opinions of the writer, and even of the person who caused them to be made. Hence, in view of these two facts, records are not likely to tell the whole truth. The utilization of original or official records calls, therefore, for a large measure of critical insight and reserve.—"A Note on the Criticism of Records," *Bulletin* of the John Rylands Library, 8 (1924): 140–49.

E. Sources Differentiated by Type of Witness

₡ 278 Witnesses may be grouped in different types or classes, differentiated on the basis of certain factors, of which the chief are race, age, sex, temperament, education, and occupation. This is an important classification, for such factors affect in various significant ways the trustworthiness of human testimony.

(a) *Race*. Veracity, as a social virtue, would appear to enjoy more credit in industrial than in non-industrial nations, for mutual confidence based on regard for the truth is a necessary support of commercial and industrial life. Besides, different attitudes toward truth-telling and toward the opposite vice, differentiate civilized from uncivilized peoples. Practically, to make racial or national origin one of the factors determining the veracity of a witness, is invidious; yet there are times when the test has its uses. Sweeping statements made by Lamothe-Cadillac, the founder of Detroit, have been discounted on the ground that he was a Gascon, with all the proverbial proclivity of his countrymen to exaggerate.

(b) *Age*. Children as witnesses enjoy certain advantages over adults; but on the whole they are at a distinct disadvantage. On the one hand, passion and selfishness do not influence them greatly, while their regard for truth, and their sense of justice, are still unimpaired. On the other hand, children lack a mature sense of responsibility, their imaginations are not duly checked, their notions of time and space are less accurate than those of adults, and they are easily liable to suggestion.

(c) *Sex*. It has been held that while apparently superior to men in accuracy of recollection and keenness of observation, women are inferior to men as witnesses, because of their higher emotional level, their greater credulity, and their liability to suggestion. (Feder, *Lehrbuch*, 210.) However, the opinion that the testimony of women does not differ materially in evidential value from that of men is not uncommon.—Charles E. Moore, *A Treatise on Facts; or The Weight and Value of Evidence* (Northport, N. Y., 1908), 1:914–20.

(d) *Temperament*. The choleric may observe keenly, but their strongly individualistic bent often renders them untrustworthy, and liable to distort the truth violently in order to serve their own ends. The sanguine are characteristically vivid in their perceptions, but at the same time are restless and unsteady, and consequently lose somewhat in dependability. Moreover, their statements tend to exaggeration and embellishment. The melancholic as a rule bring poise and attention to their observations, but their statements easily take color from their subjective attitude toward life. Tacitus' gloomy and pessimistic outlook left its impress on his estimates of persons and things. The phlegmatic are uniform in observing quietly and discreetly, in stating things soberly and dispassionately.

(e) *Education*. The testimony of the illiterate is different from that of the literate in much the same way as the testimony of children is different from that of adults. Observation by illiterates, and their manner of presentation are untrained; their critical faculty is not adequately developed; they have a higher suggestibility. On the other hand, evidence given by the illiterate is often conspicuous for soberness, and for simple, unaffected candor.

Besides education or the lack of it, environment also has its influence on the testimony of a witness. Informants of whatever period or nation tend unconsciously to give to characters and to events the shape and color they possess in the eyes of contemporaries. Testimony given on the witness-stand, as well as in written records, tends to align itself with current public opinion.

(f) *Occupation*, position in life. A person who has lived all his life in the country, who knows no more about a big city than what he has picked up from a single flying visit to New York or Chicago, may record some interesting impressions; but as a reliable informant on actual conditions in the city visited, his credit will not be rated high. His case has its counterpart in that of the life-long urban resident who finds himself a casual visitor on a farm, and lacking the most rudimentary notions about crops or anything else agricultural; any report he might make on country life would naturally have little weight.

It is often possible to infer from a person's occupation or position in life what his strong point is in the matter of observation. The farmer or hunter has naturally a keener eye for all aspects of life in the open than the confirmed city-dweller, who never leaves the municipal limits. The detective has a quicker and surer eye than most other people. His daily tasks tend to develop more and more in him the keen observer. It may be safe to believe persons in official position, liable on that account to public criticism, when they confine themselves to a bare statement of facts; it may not be so safe to believe them when they assign reasons or motives for the facts, for in such cases, private interest can warp their reports. Statements made by persons in private life, who have nothing to fear from speaking out, as a type, are more credible than statements coming from those whose position makes it necessary to consult the feelings and interests of others. Hence, confidential letters to relatives and friends are more likely to represent things correctly than letters or reports meant for publication.

Chapter Thirteen

THE CREDIBILITY OF SOURCES
(Concluded)

A. The Direct Witness: Knowledge . . . . Page 282
B. The Direct Witness: Veracity 287
C. The Indirect Witness 292
D. The Single Witness 294
E. Corroboration on Intrinsic Grounds 295
F. Miracles and the Historian 298
G. Moral Possibility or Impossibility 303
H. Concurrent Testimony 304
I. Concurrent Testimony in Remains 306
J. Concurrence in Formal Testimony 307
K. Concurrence of Formal Testimony with Remains 309
L. Conflicting Testimony 311
M. Problems in the Credibility of Sources 314

A. The Direct Witness: Knowledge

❰ 279 THE GENERAL POSTULATES OF CREDIBILITY
We may know some historical facts directly, by personal experience; we must know the mass of them, if we know them at all, through the medium of others. In this relaying process, a fact, as it originally stood, may lose much that is intrinsic to it, just as it may also take on much that is extraneous. What finally emerges is not precisely the fact as such, but a witness' impression of it. A witness' impression, however, very often means not merely reflection, but also refraction of what he has seen. If he were perfectly efficient as a medium of transmission, if the objective truth came through unmodified in any manner by the personal equation, we should be confident of being in complete possession of the fact as it really was. But circumstances of many kinds, such as poor observation, ignorance, prejudice, insincerity, malice, singly or in combination, can render a historical fact as reported wholly or in part unlike its original self. On the other hand, successful transmission of at least the substance of a historical fact can be proved to satisfaction.

(a) One must, therefore, in every individual case of historical testimony, inquire into the witness' efficiency as a medium of transmission; to establish, if possible, his knowledge, veracity, accuracy as an informant, for these are the elements necessary to render his testimony worthy of belief. Once we are assured that he is alert and painstaking as an observer, is truth-telling, and is accurate in passing on his information to others, we are not warranted in refusing assent to what he tells us. Even events of the first significance may be reasonably believed if only we can be certain of the authority of the witness who reports them. Hence, from a purely historical point of view, the account we find in the Fourth Gospel of the life and discourses of Christ, based as it is on the personal observations of His disciple, John, merits every belief. John's own words portray the ideal witness: "That which was in the beginning, which we have heard, which we have seen with our eyes, which we have looked upon and our hands have handled of the word of life ... we declare unto you." (I John, 1:3).

(b) In many cases it may not be possible for us to establish the general credibility of a witness. It then becomes necessary to inquire on critical grounds whether his credibility can be ascertained from the nature of the facts reported by him, or from his relation to the circumstances that accompany them. Here it is to be noted that a habitually veracious person is not necessarily a satisfactory witness on every count. A public official whose veracity is beyond all cavil, may be an excellent witness for what went on in his department while he held office, but not for what went on under his predecessor. An absolutely truthful person may be handicapped as a witness by a feeble memory or lack of knowledge.

¶ 280 THE CRITERIA OF KNOWLEDGE

As regards the criteria that follow, it is by no means necessary that they be applied in each and every case of testimony under examination. All that is necessary is that the competence of the witness on the score of knowledge be established as the first element guaranteeing his testimony.

Three steps can be recognized in the apprehension of a fact of history and its communication to others.

(a) The witness' *perception* of it by sight, hearing, or other sense. Subjective phenomena, such as bodily pain or mental or emotional experience, may also come within the range of history as reality, but the great bulk of historical phenomena are external.

(b) The witness' *retention* of the perception in memory, recall, or reproduction of it at need, and when recalled, recognition of it as identical with the original perception. This step comprises the specific acts of the memory, which has been defined as the "faculty of retaining, reproducing, and recognizing representations of past experiences."

(c) *Externalization* of the recalled perception by means of words, writing, or other medium.

(a) Perception.

(1) We can frequently be assured, either from personal knowledge or from the testimony of experts, that an informant's senses are sound and function normally, and that as a matter of habit he is a careful observer. It would be unfair to entertain doubts as to the capacity of such an informant for correct sense perception.

In numerous cases we can be certain by investigation that all conditions required for the elimination of error have been met. There is no room for doubt that the informant's sense organs are in normal condition. Abnormality in this respect is easily recognized, and in fact generally reveals itself to the most casual observer. Personal organic defects, such as blindness, deafness, short-sightedness, as a rule, are obvious. Similarly, we can often ascertain that the informant was not in any condition of bodily or mental fatigue or emotional excitement. If a person be subject to hallucination or illusion, this abnormal condition will usually be known to the circle of his friends, perhaps beyond, and hence will easily be open to investigation. Further, it will frequently be possible to interrogate the informant himself as to the reliability of his sense-organs, and on their condition at the time the observation was made. Finally, where several informants are available, it would be unreasonable to presuppose abnormality in the sense-organs of all.

We often know from a person's occupation or calling that his faculties of sense are especially adapted to observations of a certain kind. A seasoned hunter is an apt observer of the things of field and forest; a skilled physician, of the course of a disease; a veteran mariner, of happenings at sea.

(2) Certain adjustments of the sense's perceptive power to the object to be perceived, are necessary if the observation is to be correct. It is often possible to have certain knowledge that such adjustments were made. The witness was at close quarters with the object or incident observed. A staff officer on a nearby height, with fieldglass in hand, followed undisturbed the course of the battle. The event observed was simple, for instance, the throwing of a hand-grenade into a crowd of people; a single act of perception sufficed to grasp it.

(3) Again, one can frequently be assured that the medium between the sense-organ and its object was favorable for observation. The event took place in broad daylight, and the surroundings were quiet.

(4) Finally, we can know that the nature of the incident was such as to attract the attention of the observer and to stimulate him, as well as others present at the scene, to keen observation. The incident was noteworthy, and was probably of very great personal concern to the observer, so that it could not have failed to leave with him a lively impression, whether of wonder, of delight, or of pain. Under circumstances such as these, even a solitary witness could not easily become the victim of deception. Pertinent instances are: the discourses and the miracles of the Messiah as told in the Gospels; the solemn entry of a victorious army; murder in the open; the sudden healing of a sick person in public view. Where the bare fact is reported, without accompanying details, as in statements alleging the existence of a certain person, city, or custom. account should be taken of the slender degree of attention necessary in observations of this kind.

(b) Synthesis and inner reproduction.

(1) We can often be assured of an informant's sound judgment, ability to analyze his perceptions and arrange them in due logical and causal sequence, trustworthy memory and freedom from prejudice and uncontrolled emotion. Hence, we can be reasonably certain that the informant's attitude toward the facts perceived was objective.

(2) In doubtful cases critical investigation of the informant's mentality, prejudices, emotions, and relations to the facts reported, will often assure us that possible errors in synthesis and reproduction have been eliminated. The event was so momentous that it must necessarily have left a deep and indelible impression on his memory; it happened at a stage in his career when memory was at its best, so that a lapse of this faculty is not easily to be assumed; he wrote down the observation at once; his personal prejudices were not concerned; such of his sympathies as might have distorted his account were not engaged; the fact reported was in the nature of a permanent condition, so that it could easily be held under observation: thus, a custom, an economic or social situation, a person's character. The informant had every reason to be accurate in his reproduction, for otherwise he would be held to account for negligence, as in the case of a public official or of a traveler in a foreign land under commission from his government.

But in spite of the foregoing grounds of assurance, one must not overlook the fact that internal synthesis of a complex series of the facts is a difficult process, and as experience shows, often turns out badly. Hence, if doubt be raised as to its accuracy, it will be necessary to establish the informant's competence in detail.* One has only to recall the

* A witness' competence must be established for every particular fact.—Ed.

picture of German customs given by Caesar and Tacitus, the incorrect data about foreign countries to be found in travel books or in official reports of government envoys, to understand how easily this process of synthesis and inner reproduction can go awry.

(c) External reproduction.

Here also we may frequently be assured that the informant is a person accustomed to set down his observations soberly and exactly. He is not embarrassed by inordinate personal attachments or by external influence of any kind; perhaps he even makes it a practice to jot down more important happenings at once. In doubtful cases, investigation of the content of the report may also lead to the conclusion that the informant has expressed his thought faithfully, especially if the following circumstances be verified: the report is so clear and intelligible as a composition that we cannot but conclude to the informant's ability to express himself accurately in words; the data embodied in the report are so remote from the informant's emotional life that we have no right to assume that feeling or sentiment has colored it, at least in important ways; likewise we have no grounds for supposing that the informant allowed himself to be led by undue regard for others or was under alien influence or suggestion. Finally, there is nothing in the report to indicate the presence of any secondary motive prejudicial to historical truth, such as a design to use history for purposes of propaganda.

Caesar's testimony in numerous passages of his *Commentaries* can be accepted only with considerable reserve. This holds even when there is no deliberate intent on his part to misrepresent. He arranges the facts in many ways, with an eye to his own advantage, places his own person and services in relief, represents his motives and doings as just, but shows no insight into the motives of his enemies, who after all were only defending their rights. Further, we meet in him a callous warlord, one quite without sympathy for the peoples he invaded. At the same time, we may safely accept as trustworthy the details of matters in which Caesar himself played no part, or regarding which he was not influenced by selfish motives, such as geographical or ethnological data, or simple military operations. In this respect Caesar gains credence, for his *Commentaries* were based on the plain, realistic service-reports which as a man of clear and sober judgment he had to send annually to the senate, and which accordingly were subject to official scrutiny.

A notable instance of accurate reporting is found in the notes taken by James Madison, of the proceedings of the Federal Convention of 1787. See H. C. Hockett, *Introduction to Research in American History*, 84 f.; Max Farrand, *Records of the Federal Convention of 1787*, 3: 550.

B. The Direct Witness: Veracity

⁋ 281 Experience reveals that we usually accept testimony as true if there is nothing in the character of the witness or his testimony to raise a suspicion of falsehood. But the critical historian cannot be satisfied with this merely negative judgment, for it does no more than say of a witness, who must be presumed to be disposed, like every moral person, to tell the truth, that falsehood has not been and cannot be proved against him. A positive estimate is necessary. It must be established either that the witness' character is such as to exclude every suspicion of deliberate misrepresentation on his part, or that such misrepresentation is ruled out by the circumstances of this particular case.

(a) As a result of protracted familiar dealings with a person, or of assurances in his favor coming to us from reliable sources, his moral character may become so well established that any doubt about his veracity would be unreasonable.

(b) In doubtful cases investigation of the informant's antecedents and of the nature of the information he sponsors, may result in ruling out (on the principle *nemo gratis mendax*) the probability of his having prevaricated.

In most cases, either our own past dealings with a witness or the experience of others will reveal whether or not he is mendacious in a morbid way or whether there is anything else pathological about him. For the rest, pathological lies generally betray themselves in various ways; they are uttered recklessly; are promptly detected, when spoken in the presence of persons who know the facts; and elicit obviously awkward answers from the witness when he attempts to justify them.

⁋ 282 CRITERIA OF VERACITY

(a) Testimony may be accepted as truthful when its contents is of such a nature that lying would be of no advantage whatever to the informant, whereas telling the truth could not harm him in any known way. Regard for the truth is inherent in human nature; no one goes counter to it unless moved by the prospect of some advantage to be gained.

(b) Testimony may be also accepted as true when telling the truth would be only to the advantage of the informant, while lying would do him obvious and serious harm.

A normal witness will not testify falsely in court if he foresees that his false testimony will be easily detected and that he will incur some grave penalty as a result. In like manner, a defendant who has reason to believe that a frank, unvarnished statement of his case can result only in his acquittal, will hold to the truth. It should be taken for granted that an informant's testimony is true if by falsifying it he would suffer loss in reputation or goods.

This same principle finds application in the case of products of the pictorial and plastic arts that have a historical content. Such products should be accepted as reliable for the data they contain, if the artist had nothing but harm to expect from misrepresenting the facts. Accordingly, when we find myths or mythical figures, otherwise unknown, shown pictorially in an antique work of art, as a rule we may assume the existence of such stories for the period in question, on the elementary principle that a purchaser, trusting in the current myths of his childhood, would not easily allow himself to be offered a representation of a religious nature that had anything absurd about it. Thus, a Ruveser vase gives the sequel to the myth of the brazen giant Talos, the watchman of Crete, a saga which embodies an episode of the Argonautic expedition. One may learn about a pre-Hesiodic form of the old nature-myth of the goddess Pandora, and Epimetheus, from a Pandora vase in Oxford.—Feder, *Lehrbuch*, 255.

(c) Witnesses are sometimes so honest, candid, disinterested, so inspired by religious motives that we lend their testimony implicit credence from the start. Many accounts of the early Christian martyrs, immediate products of the harrowing experiences of the age of persecution, are of this type. A pertinent example is the well-known letter addressed by the Christians of Lyons and Vienne to the Christians of Asia, in the persecution of A.D. 177–178. For this and similar documents, see Beresford J. Kidd, *Documents Illustrative of the History of the Church* (2 vols., London, 1920–1923), vol. 1.

(d) Situations occur in which the witness is constrained by the public character of his testimony to keep within the limits of the truth. He may give the testimony in the presence of others, as in a court room, or in writing which can come to the knowledge of others. Should it be false, persons in possession of the facts will be found to challenge it, especially if it be injurious to them personally, or to a party or group with which they are identified. Under such circumstances fear of exposure and disgrace will act as a powerful deterrent from prevarication. No sane person (unless possibly the prospect of some enormous gain induces him to run the risk) will take chances of being branded publicly as a conscienceless liar. Assurance as to a witness' trustworthiness grows in proportion to the publicity and importance of the facts to which he testifies, and proportionately to the number of persons capable of bringing him to book.

To the type of testimony here discussed belong accounts which report contemporary events of importance with such detail of time, place, and local color, that in the case of falsification, exposure would surely and promptly follow.

(e) A witness' truthfulness is particularly in evidence when in consequence of the blame he imputes to persons or groups, he has good reason to fear contradiction and enmity, and to suffer loss of fortune, even life itself.

Successful application of these criteria of veracity can be made in the case of the writers of the four Gospels. They were plain, honest, unsophisticated characters, uninfluenced by personal interest or human respect. They tell in all candor of their own weaknesses and mistakes; they give us a pattern of objective, dispassionate reporting, which betrays no astonishment even at the most astounding events, no indignation over the most revolting. As a consequence of their reports they had later to endure aggression and persecution. When witnesses so thoroughly sincere protest that their only desire is to tell the historical truth (I John, 1:1–3; John 19:35), and this after careful and conscientious inquiry (Luke, 1:1–4), it is clearly unreasonable to refuse them credence. Moreover, any attempted misrepresentation of facts on the part of the Evangelists would have promptly been discovered and exposed by contemporaries.

(f) In some cases circumstances may require us to recognize an informant as reliable in certain of his statements, though otherwise demonstrably he may violate the truth through party interest or other motive and make no secret of doing so. On the principle already stated, *nemo gratis mendax*, the testimony of informants of this type may be admitted as trustworthy in matters in which their own private interests or those of their party or group are not involved. It is readily understood that they can be quite veracious when they relate things which it is not pleasant for them to relate, or which are to their own discredit or that of their party, or contrariwise, to the credit of their personal or party enemies.*

In the case where a witness of whom nothing is known or who is even known to be unreliable, confesses to a crime, and there are reasons to suspect that the confession is false, the motives that inspired it should be ascertained. Oftentimes self-incrimination of this kind is nothing more than a device whereby to gratify some passion, such as notoriety-seeking, hatred, revenge, envy. A person may inculpate himself in order thereby to inculpate someone else whom he seeks to ruin at the price of his own dishonor.

(g) If the content of a testimony does not affect the interests of the

---

* The principle is not as general as the author seems to think: Catholics have falsely discredited the Church; Protestants, members of their own denominations; and Democrats, and Republicans, their respective parties.—Ed.

informant or of his party, one way or the other, and no attempt to falsify can be proved against him, we may assume his veracity. This case is exemplified in reports dealing with events, persons, customs, or institutions, not touching in any manner the personal interests of the reporter.

Testimony given by a member of a party which contains several groups calls for special scrutiny. In this case the informant's interest can be less in the party as a whole than in the group standing nearest to him, less in the nation than in a section of it, less in religion than in a particular sect.

> Don't let us utter too much evil of party writers, for we owe them much. If they are not honest, they are helpful, as the advocate aids the judge, and they would not have done so well from the mere inspiration of disinterested veracity.—Acton, Lectures on the French Revolution, 373.

At the same time, it must be recognized that documents of political propaganda are very often, perhaps generally, unreliable as historical sources; not a little of Macaulay's history is vitiated by uncritical reliance on party pamphlets.

¶ 283 Doubtful criteria of veracity

The expressions "an air of sincerity," or "an impression of truth," are often on people's lips as standards by which they measure the reliability of testimony. A certain ingenuousness in the witness' manner, or in what he says, creates a feeling from the start that he is telling the truth. Testimony, written or oral, may undoubtedly be rendered under circumstances which inspire the utmost confidence in its reliability [¶ 282]. At the same time, in not a few instances the so-called "air of sincerity" may be nothing more than a semblance of plausibility which a witness manages to give to statements he knows to be false, or mistakenly believes to be true. It may be only clever deceit masked under an appearance of candor. As to the "impression of truth" conveyed by a witness' testimony, this again may easily be, not a reasoned conviction of the witness' honesty, but only a quasi-judgment born of sentiment and feeling.*

Instances where "an air of sincerity" holds good as a test of truth could be multiplied. Thus, opinion that the four Gospels meet this test is general. The same may be said of the authentic "Acts of the Martyrs." Hippolyte Delehaye rejects the theory that the testimony of the martyrs in court was a

---

* Taken by themselves, the "air of sincerity," the "impression of truth," are not only doubtful criteria of the witnesses' veracity, but in many cases they are not criteria at all.—Ed.

kind of stage performance previously rehearsed, and declares that nothing could be more contrary to fact, "as everyone knows from the impression left by the reading of the historical Acts, where everything is simple and spontaneous, especially the martyr's language, conformably to the precept of the Lord, 'Nolite cogitare quomodo aut quid loquamini.'"——*Analecta Bollandiana*, 50 (1932), 155.

The narrative of the Coronado expedition by Pedro de Castañeda, a participant, written twenty years after the event ". . . bears every evidence of honesty and a sincere desire to tell all he knew of the most remarkable expedition that ever traversed American soil."——Frederick W. Hodge and Theodore H. Lewis, eds., *Spanish Explorers in the Southern United States 1528–1543* (New York, 1907), 276.

℟ 284 Fullness and particularity of detail is sometimes taken as an indication of truth in reports which do not treat of contemporary events or cannot be easily checked. People say of a highly circumstantial account, "this surely cannot be made up." As a matter of fact, the details in accounts of this kind need not be fabricated; in many an instance they were borrowed by the author from other narratives or from places or times not his own. Consequently, the test in question is not valid in all cases. But it must be allowed as a broad principle that copious detail in the reporting of an incident or event creates a certain presumption (not necessarily a proof) of the truth of the report.* Cases occur in which the critical historian feels warranted in accepting particularity of detail in a report as a guarantee of its accuracy, or at least of the fact that the reporter was an eyewitness, or else derived his information from someone who was.

(a) Sir William Ramsay and other scholars have expressed the opinion that the intimate particulars in the account of the childhood of Christ in the first two chapters of St. Luke's Gospel, point to Mary, the Mother of Jesus, as the source of the Evangelist's information. Again, the account in Thucydides (II, 28) of the eclipse of August 3, 431 B.C., is quite circumstantial. "He [Thucydides] describes the phenomenon so accurately and with so many details that we can hardly doubt that he observed it himself."—— J. A. R. Munro, *Classical Quarterly*, 13 (1919): 127 f.

(b) Examples of direct human testimony of a high degree of credibility are to be found in the processes of beatification and canonization in the Catholic Church. Thus, in the case of St. Jean-Marie-Baptiste Vianney (the Curé d'Ars) numerous testimonials of his virtue were given by relatives and friends immediately after his death, a circumstance which precluded the

---

* One should not overlook the not uncommon cases in which an abundance of details is simply a proof of the witness' vivid imagination when he is sincere, and of his impudence when he is not.—Ed.

growth of legend.—See Francis Trochu, *The Curé D'Ars: St. Jean-Marie Baptiste Vianney (1781-1859)*, trans. by Ernest Graf, (London, 1927), viii.

(c) Certain causes for beatification and canonization introduced long after the decease of all direct witnesses to "the life, the virtues, the martyrdom, or the immemorial *cultus*" of the candidate, are called "historical causes." A *Motu Proprio* of Pius XI, dated June 6, 1930, was promulgated in order that the manner of examining such causes "should be somewhat modified so as to be more in accord with the peculiar nature of these causes and their special requirements . . . especially in view of the progress that has been made in historical sciences and the improved methods which they now employ."—*Acta Sanctae Sedis*, 22:87; English translation in T. Lincoln Bouscaren, *Canon Law Digest* (Milwaukee, 1934), 166 f.

The Pontiff defined historical causes as "those . . . in which there is neither contemporary testimony to the facts in question nor any certain proof of depositions properly taken at the right time."

The *Motu Proprio* sets up within the Sacred Congregation of Rites a *Historical Section*, "composed of a sufficient number of consultors who are specialists in historical methods and research." The *Relator General* (chairman) of the Historical Section "will be in charge of the historical work," for which rules and procedures are given.

A striking instance of the many applications of the functions of the Historical Section is found in the cause of Venerable Kateri Tekakwitha.—See *The Positio of the Historical Section of the Sacred Congregation of Rites on the Introduction of the Cause for Beatification and Canonization and on the Virtues of the Servant of God Katharine Tekakwitha* (New York, 1940).

C. The Indirect Witness

❡ 285 Most of our information about past happenings comes to us not from direct, but from indirect witnesses; that is, from persons who did not themselves see or experience what they report to us, but learned of them from others. Often the information is passed along from one to another through a whole series of individuals before it finally reaches us. To evaluate such information, we must inquire into the credibility of the entire series of informants, beginning with the one from whom we directly received the information, and going back to the one who immediately witnessed the occurrence and was the first to report it. But such a long queue of informants may become so unwieldly that one can scarcely grasp it in its individual units. In these circumstances it is not advisable to pursue the investigation, especially if other sources of information can be drawn upon to establish the truth of the facts in question.

❡ 286 TRUSTWORTHINESS OF THE INDIRECT WITNESS: CRITERIA In formulating criteria for the trustworthiness of indirect witnesses or informants, we must distinguish whether there is only one such witness or informant, or whether there are more than one.

(a) Knowledge of a single intermediary's antecedents and character will often make it possible to be certain that he did not accept the report of the direct witness blindly, but where doubt was justified, put the credibility of the report to the test. If the character of the indirect witness is unknown to us, critical inquiry into the relations existing between him and the events he reports may frequently result in certain proof of his trustworthiness. The process is the same as that employed in the case of the direct witness [₡ 279 f.]. In the case of written accounts, special tests to be applied will be the informant's industry in looking up and using primary sources critically, his zeal in evaluating the oral testimony of persons whose memory reaches back to the events reported. When the trustworthiness of the direct witness has already been ascertained, it is enough to make sure that the indirect witness understood the account delivered to him by the direct, and reproduced it accurately.

(b) If several successive indirect informants have transmitted the account, the same process that was applied to the case of the single intermediary must be repeated for every indirect informant in the series. If the desired conditions are met by every single intermediary, the account must be rated as trustworthy. But see ₡ 285.

(1) It has been objected that the trustworthiness of an account decreases with every new mediate version of it, since every new informant can claim only a portion of the trustworthiness of his predecessor; hence, in the long line of intermediaries the final degree of trustworthiness will be so insignificant as to be negligible. The objection may be met as follows: It is incorrect to say that an account necessarily loses in trustworthiness by passing through an intermediary. All that need be conceded is that the possibility of garbling and falsification is always present in indirect transmission, and increases with the number of intermediaries. Hence, the expediency, when the thing is possible, of drawing for corroboration on other sources of information. At the same time, the fact remains that at least the substance of numerous historical data has been correctly handed down through a long succession of mediate informants. A pertinent illustration is the body of early Norse history which was carried along for centuries with substantial accuracy by oral tradition or through a series of indirect informants [₡ 259-e-1].

(2) Objection has also been raised that the application of these criteria for the trustworthiness of several indirect witnesses is a begging of the question (*petitio principii*). Certain witnesses are used to prove the trustworthiness of other witnesses, while this same qualification in the case of the former must be proved by other witnesses, and so on indefinitely. The objection is

without force. It is often possible in the case of a single witness, sometimes even of several, to ascertain their trustworthiness directly from their antecedents or from their character as known to us immediately. In this manner the way is prepared for further investigation along safe lines. An example of careful weighing of testimonial evidence of different types is found in Henry E. Bourne, "The Personality of Robespierre," *Historical Outlook,* 9 (1920): 177 ff.

D. The Single Witness

¶ 287 It is a corollary of the principle set out in ¶ 285-a, that the testimony of a single witness whose competence in every respect is above suspicion, may be accepted as true. This is the position taken by De Smedt (*Principes,* 131), and by Bernheim (*Lehrbuch,* 536). Gaston Sortais in his *Traité de Philosophie* (3 vols., Paris, 1912–1921), 1:738, is in agreement with them, though he admits that the case of a single witness who is a source of certain information is seldom found, on the ground that it is very difficult to assure oneself of such a witness' perfect competence. It follows, accordingly, that the legal maxim, *testis unus, testis nullus,* does not apply to witnesses in history.

(a) De Smedt insists that the assurance we have of the competence of the single witness must not be merely negative, for this would mean only the absence of any explicit evidence discrediting it. There must be also, so he maintains, unimpeachable positive evidence that the witness has all the qualifications necessary to guarantee his testimony. De Smedt uses the illustration of a person picking up a report from a stranger in the street. There may be no positive reason for suspecting the stranger's information and good faith, but neither is there any positive reason for believing these qualifications to be present. It would be rash under the circumstances to give unqualified credence to the report.

> Busy with these considerations about the value of a multiplicity of vouchers, sometimes people are led into the assertion that never can a single witness be a sufficient authority for a certain assent. Without entering into detail, we may protest that this declaration, in its universality, is a calumny against human nature.—J. Rickaby, *First Principles of Knowledge,* 381.

> What is the historian's attitude in the presence of a single source? It must be assumed, of course, that he has tested it by all the rules hitherto presented and that it has survived their critical application. In such a situation there is nothing further left for him to do but to accept the testimony it contains.—L. O'Brien, *The Writing of History,* 56.

(b) Langlois and Seignobos, Fling, Johnson, and others require more than one witness for historical certainty.

It is a principle common to all sciences of observation not to base a scientific conclusion on a single observation; the fact must have been corroborated by several independent observations before it can be affirmed. History, with its imperfect modes of acquiring information, has less right than any other science to claim exception to this principle.— Langlois and Seignobos, *Introduction to the Study of History*, 195 f.

As a rule, then, the condition of certainty is the existence of at least two independent witnesses to the same detailed fact.—F. M. Fling, *The Writing of History*, 103.

It may be noted as a commentary on these opinions, that numerous alleged facts have been and continue to be accepted as true by historians generally, on the authority of a single primary source, such as Thucydides, or Caesar.*

(c) That Plato fled to Megara after the death of Socrates is a statement which rests on the authority of a single source—a source moreover, which is dubious. Yet scholars generally have accepted it as true, and even speak of the "Megaric" influence on the philosopher's work.—See Wincenty Lutoslawski, *The Origin and Growth of Plato's Logic*, 43.

That Henry VIII contemplated a divorce from Catherine of Aragon long before he met Anne Boleyn has been affirmed on the basis of a document discovered in recent years in the Vatican archives. No corroborative evidence for the alleged fact is forthcoming. Nevertheless it is admitted as credible by Alfred F. Pollard against Hilaire Belloc, who rejects it.—See Andrew Beck, "Pollard, Belloc and the Abbé Constant," *Clergy Review*, 9 (1935), 190 ff.

It is to be noted that in the cases here mentioned the facts in dispute are questioned or altogether denied, not on any general principle of the insufficiency of a single witness in historical testimony, but on the ground that the single witness as cited does not qualify individually as competent.

E. Corroboration on Intrinsic Grounds

⟨ 288 POSSIBILITY; IMPOSSIBILITY

(a) *Metaphysical (intrinsic) possibility; impossibility.* According to the principle of contradiction, a thing cannot be and not be, at the same time, under the same circumstances. Yet, historical records teem with statements which run counter to this principle. Here it is declared that such a thing happened, elsewhere, that it did not happen; here an individual is referred to as Jones's brother, there, as his son; or, some heroic deed wins a man a title of distinction, but another record attests that the title of distinction antedates the deed of which it is supposed to be a reward. In all historical inconsistencies the first thing to determine is

---

* In such cases as in the examples given in the following paragraph, it is safer to write: "Thucydides says . . .," or "Caesar says . . ." The general acceptance by historians adds nothing to the intrinsic value of the testimony itself. See ⟨ 303.—Ed.

whether they belong to the substance of the reported fact or only to its accidentals. If the latter be the case, the reported fact may be admitted, provided the document reporting it is itself thoroughly credible. Moreover, closer analysis of the report may bring to light the reason for inconsistency. Here, in a somewhat modified sense, avails the principle: *Distingue tempora et concordabunt jura.*——On conflicting testimonies, see ₡ 308.

(b) *Physical possibility; impossibility.* Facts may be reported which seem to stand in contradiction to the *laws of physical nature.* In such cases investigation must be made as to whether the contradiction is real or only apparent. Even learned men and learned societies, on grounds of supposed physical impossibility, have rejected phenomena which from the standpoint of natural science were not impossible at all.

The Town Council of Juillac, France, reported to the Academy of Sciences of Paris an extraordinary hailstorm, alleged to have occurred at Juillac, on July 29, 1790. Over three hundred trustworthy witnesses testified to the occurrence. Though there was no serious reason to disbelieve it, the Academy expressed official disbelief on the ground that the phenomenon was physically impossible. In our own day, phenomena which have actually occurred have been discredited by scientists of reputation before complete verification was at hand.

It may happen that the trustworthiness of witnesses reporting facts contrary to the laws of nature cannot be satisfactorily established. In general, witnesses of this type ought not to be believed, especially if they lived in uncritical times. For example, miraculous occurrences—which are the exception, not the rule—should not be admitted without certain proof, especially since their efficient cause is to be sought outside the visible world. On the other hand, if the trustworthiness of a witness to a miraculous occurrence is beyond all doubt, the investigator must accept the occurrence without reserve, for a witness' perfect trustworthiness carries along with it the complete truth of the content of his testimony [₡ 294 ff.]. Just as genuine criticism condemns unconsidered zeal, or hasty acceptance of the miraculous, it also condemns a dread of it or a readiness to reject a priori all miraculous occurrences as impossible [₡ 290].

(c) *Moral possibility; impossibility.* Distinguished from the moral law as treated in the science of ethics (obligation), "moral law" in a more special sense is referred to the *mores,* to those deep-rooted customs of men by which they react in a uniform way under given circumstances. This is so much the case that actions alleged as facts, but contrary to "moral law," are said to be morally impossible [₡ 298].

❡ 289   CORROBORATION OF A SOURCE BY A PRIORI REASONING

The full credibility of a source depends on acceptance of what it alleges as fact, without reasonable doubt of the contradictory. Where a source seems weak if taken solely on the merits of its own assertion, doubt of its credibility arises. Such sources must be put to the test of a priori reasoning. There are three steps in the process.

(a) Inspect the alleged fact in relation to its intrinsic possibility. Alleged facts that involve a contradiction in terms must necessarily be rejected as metaphysically impossible; the source on which they depend are without credibility with regard to these facts. But even if investigation reveals the intrinsic possibility of the alleged fact, this of itself is no guarantee of its reality: intrinsic possibility is necessary, but not sufficient. *A posse ad esse non valet illatio.*

(b) Thus, a second step is necessary, involving both physical and moral possibility. (1) Given an agent capable of actuating the possibility of the alleged fact, is there evidence that such an agent really operated? Without such evidence the source is still dubious. (2) But given the capable agent really operating, is there anything in the alleged fact contrary to acknowledged physical law or to "moral law"? If there is nothing of the kind contrary, the source may gain in credibility, but it may still remain dubious in some instances, if it can be shown that some power capable of suspending the action of physical law has operated; or that forces likely to cause exception to "moral law" have been brought to bear.

Suppose the case of an alleged fact which has successfully withstood the test of intrinsic possibility and of physical possibility, but leaves some doubt about moral possibility: for example, that although ordinarily men do not hate their parents, this man is alleged to have done so. Is there yet means of establishing credibility in such a case, at least with probability, if not with certainty?

(c) This introduces the third step in corroboration by a priori reasoning. It involves the matter of *probability*. Probability is likelihood-to-be or happen, based on good reasons. Probability is intrinsic if it arises from the nature of the matter involved; extrinsic, if based on the external authority of an expert (who himself must have been satisfied upon the intrinsic probability).

To the case supposed above: Say that investigation of the alleged fact—this man hated his parents—reveals in association with other facts, that the man's parents did him a series of grossly unjust acts. This might well have made him disregard the morally universal way men behave, of not hating their parents, and so have come to hate his own. In fact, he has now fallen, in a sense, under another moral law, by which men do not always successfully withstand continued injustice. In this way, the source which says that this man hated his parents, may have intrinsic probability.

(d) Inference from the intrinsic probability of a fact to its reality, is only a probable inference, since its harmony with other facts may find some other possible explanation. Investigation of the intrinsic probability of a fact is especially necessary when only a single witness is available, and that witness unreliable; or when we have to deal with several mutually contradicting witnesses of approximately the same degree of dependability.

(e) The process of corroboration a priori may well have application in the matter of conjecture or of hypothesis. It may be applied also to the case of any startling report, especially to the account of a miracle. Insofar as miracles require verification, they enjoy no status of advantage or privilege. In fact, by their very nature they have an air of improbability, so that their reality as historical fact demands particular scrutiny.

F. Miracles and the Historian

❡ 290 WHAT MIRACLES ARE

Belief in miracles is a perfectly rational attitude of mind. Happenings of this kind do, it is true, run counter to the ordinary course of nature; but they are possible *in se*, and what is no less important, are knowable as such by the human mind.

(a) By a *miracle in a broad sense* is understood a preternatural effect, whether perceptible to the senses or not, which is beyond (*praeter*) an agent's natural or ordinary powers. In this sense even the internal workings of grace in a soul may be designated a miracle.

(b) A miracle *in a strict sense* is a preternatural effect perceptible to the senses, and calculated by its unusual and extraordinary character to excite wonder. Its immediate agent is either God Himself, or some supramundane spiritual power (angel), which produces such effects in unison with the will of God. Accordingly, a miracle may be defined as *a sensible phenomenon contrary to the ordinary course of nature, and effected by divine power*.

From miracles in the proper sense are to be distinguished so-called *mira* or "wonders," which are prodigies wrought by evil spirits, with permission of the Deity.

❡ 291 MIRACLES: POSSIBILITY

Miracles, properly understood, do not contravene the immutability of God, who from all eternity has willed not only the laws of nature, but also certain exceptions to them. Nor do they contravene the wisdom of God, who must not be conceived as calling miracles to His aid to improve upon a presumably defective established order, and to help it along, as it were, by extraordinary means. What God aims to do is to reveal in a visible way His unlimited dominion and His special providence over men. Moreover, the laws of nature are no obstacle in the way of miracles. These laws possess a conditional necessity only, so that God in working a miracle does not change their character but merely suspends their operation.

The possibility of diabolic "wonders," which transcend *in se* the powers of matter, but not those of created spiritual natures, must also be admitted where they do not run counter to the wisdom of God. They do not so run when God on occasion permits evil spirits to exercise their power of working such seeming miracles for the trial of the good or the punishment of the wicked.

¶ 292 MIRACLES: KNOWABILITY

The knowability of miracles is a truth as well established as their possibility. Knowability here denotes that the human mind can know or recognize a miraculous occurrence under the threefold aspect of its *historical truth*, or objective reality; its *philosophical truth*, or extraordinary and preternatural character; its *theological truth*, or divine origin.

Since a miracle is a fact perceptible to the senses, we can recognize its historical truth by precisely the same means by which we recognize any other historical fact, and often more easily so, because the exceptionally striking character of a miracle at once arrests attention in the highest degree. Again, it is often possible from the very nature of the miraculous occurrence to recognize its philosophical truth, namely, to know that it transcends the inherent powers of physical nature. Any normal-minded person will agree that the raising of a dead person to life is an effect that cannot be produced by the mere powers of physical nature. Finally, it is possible to ascertain also the theological truth of a miracle, that is, to recognize that the occurrence is to be referred to God as its author. A miracle, which is certainly beyond the power of any created nature, must be referred to the Creator.

(a) As concerns miraculous happenings of doubtful provenance (that is, whether of divine or diabolic origin), the circumstances will determine their true character.

(1) *Negative criteria* to establish divine agency include these: the miracle is not wrought in confirmation of a doctrine otherwise known to be false, nor is it wrought from motives of vainglory, ostentation, or gain; it is free from any suggestion of magic, occultism, superstition.

(2) *Positive criteria* include the content, the purpose, the manner of performance of the miracle. As a physical phenomenon, a miracle in the strict sense must in every case be something ethically good or at least ethically indifferent; its purpose must be the glorification of God and the good of creatures; the manner of performance must be such that only what is morally licit enters into the phenomenon. That we are able to recognize these three momenta in any single case, results from the reality of a Divine Providence, which sees to it that sincere and truth-loving men are not led by evil spirits into invincible error.

(b) Instance of the perfectly reliable testimony often available in evidence of miracles as actual happenings, whatever may be their explanation, may be seen in Migne, *Patrologia Latina*, 185: 367–415.

See also *Monumenta Germaniae historica*, 26: 121–37. This document contains various reports of the miracles performed by St. Bernard of Clairvaux in the course of a journey which he made through Germany, in 1176, for the purpose of preaching the Second Crusade. It includes among other pieces of firsthand evidence, the individual testimony of ten of the saint's companions, to miracles wrought by him in the Upper Rhine provinces. The testimonies record numerous miraculous cures wrought in favor of persons of every age and condition in life, among them, blind, dumb, lame and crippled people of every degree. The witnesses are persons of mature age, sober judgment, more than average mentality, who report only what they have personally observed, and who in so reporting insist repeatedly that their sole intention is to tell the truth, no more, no less. Further, the testimonies report things done in public view, with crowds of people looking on. In fine, the witnesses are men whose moral authority is so fully accredited by their confidential relations with the great wonderworker, by their high position in Church or State, and by the esteem they enjoyed with the public, that to question their testimony would be to question historical testimony in general.—See Feder, *Lehrbuch*, 266; Bernheim, *Lehrbuch*, 328 f.; Ailbe J. Luddy, *Life and Teachings of St. Bernard* (Dublin, 1927), 523 ff.

The rigorous, scientific method employed by the Catholic Church in verifying alleged miraculous facts is revealed in the *Acta* or minutes of the official processes of beatifications and canonizations. CE, 2:364; *The Month*, 125 (1915): 250–63.

⁋ 293 Miracles: Their critics

(a) Modern critics of miracles fall for the most part into two groups. The first group deny the intrinsic possibility of miracles, and therefore regard all reports of them as untrustworthy; they maintain that there has never been an adequately certified miracle. Among such critics are in general all adherents of anti-Christian and rationalistic schools of thought. Their arguments are mainly two. Miracles interrupt the course of nature's laws; but as these work with absolute uniformity, miracles in themselves are simply impossible. Again, we always have physical certanity that there is no exception to the laws of nature. On the other hand, we have only moral certainty that an informant is reliable. Hence, as the weaker certainty must yield to the stronger, a report of a miracle can never be recognized as credible, no matter how insistently the witness appeals to his knowledge and veracity.

(b) The second group of critics also take issue with the intrinsic possibility of miracles in a theological sense, but do not reject reports of them, when these are found to be admissible according to the rules of evidence; they only deny the miraculous character of the events in question, and attempt to refer them back to merely natural forces as yet unknown to us. Accordingly, they have recourse to the analogies of magnetism, hypnotism, spiritism. This is Bernheim's attitude towards miracles (*Lehrbuch*, 328 f.).

¶ 294 The procedure of critics who reject the possibility of miracles is manifestly unscientific. That the laws of nature are absolutely uniform is gratuitously assumed to be true, and on the basis of this assumption all accounts of miracles are ruled out as inadmissible, a priori.

The only evidence we can have for the general uniformity of natural laws is human experience; but human experience witnesses not only to the general uniformity of natural laws, but also to their occasional suspension. To regard evidence of the same nature as validating the one fact, and not the other, is unreasonable. Hence, Hume's contention that it is more probable that testimony to miracles is false than that the miracles are true, breaks down. Hume held that history does not record any miracles attested by competent witnesses numerous enough to make it certain that they were not the victims of illusion. The fallacy latent in this contention is evident from the fact that a miracle, for its accurate observation and reporting, does not require a greater number of witnesses, or witnesses of a higher caliber, than are required for the accurate observation and reporting of any other external fact. The truth is that miracles, by reason of their extraordinary character, are often more easily perceptible than ordinary phenomena and engage the observer's attention to more than an ordinary degree.

An immense number of happenings justly described as miraculous have been attested by persons whose testimony in other matters, even of the gravest importance, would be accepted without question. The attack on miracles is really, therefore, an attack on human testimony as such. Behind it as its inspiring motive, from Hume's day down to our own, has been theological bias, especially towards Christianity, the evidence for which is partly based on miracles. Yet the Christian position in the matter is secure, and has so remained against all the objections of rationalistic criticism. Belief in a personal Supreme Being necessarily carries with it the possibility of miracles and their evidential value for the accrediting of a revealed religion.

₡ 295 The only argument a priori which rejects miracles on the ground of antecedent improbability, has therefore been largely discarded. An uncommonly keen thinker, John Stuart Mill, concluded that Hume's argument against miracles is valid only on the supposition that God does not exist. This supposition excluded, as it must be, Hume's "uniform sequence of natural phenomena" is no objection against the reality of miracles. As Huxley admitted, the whole question is one of evidence.

> That argument [Hume's, against miracles] lasted into the nineteenth century and troubled even such a scientist as Professor Huxley, who regarded it as wholly indefensible. As he properly observed, a law of nature was only based on observation and experience and they might well be incomplete.—Wilbur C. Abbott, *Adventures in Reputation* (Cambridge, Mass., 1935), 144.

See also H. B. George, *Historical Evidence*, 166, where it is pointed out that antecedent improbability is no argument against an alleged fact, if the fact be reported on credible grounds.

₡ 296 Ernest E. Bernheim (*Lehrbuch*, 328 f.), and others, admit miracles as historical facts; they deny, however, their miraculous character, on the ground that in them are involved merely natural phenomena, the explanation of which is at present beyond us. "Of the reality of the occurrences in themselves in the case of St. Bernard and a hundred other cases there is no reason at all to doubt. . . . We declare the facts to be the natural processes of certain nervous phenomena effected with the aid of psychology and medicine."

In answer to this position it may be said that in order to know whether or not a given effect is beyond the power of a natural agent, it is not necessary to know positively every effect which such an agent is able to produce. It is enough to know that there are at least certain effects which the agent is not able to produce. One may not know everything an extraordinarily strong man is able to do, but one does know for certain that he cannot push over a skyscraper. So also, it is wholly gratuitous to assume that at some future day we shall discover in merely human words the secret of imposing quiet on an angry sea, or of passing through closed doors, or of raising a demonstrably dead person to life. As regards magnetism, hypnotism, spiritism, suggestion, and similar psychic agencies, whatever cures have been effected thereby, have been cures of diseases of a nervous nature only. The sudden cure of the blind, the deaf, the maimed, or others organically afflicted, is unknown to such agencies. Moreover, they presuppose the application of definite curative media, while the Christian wonderworker produces his effects merely by a word, a blessing, a laying on of hands. Finally, the supposititious "hidden forces" of nature work after the manner of a law of nature, and then they contradict other forces of nature; or they work at the mere will of a magician, and then we have magical or diabolic prodigies, the possibility of which is also rejected by the critics in question.—John Rickaby, "The Explanation of Miracles by Unknown Natural Forces," *The Month*, 29 (1877): 68–85.

H. C. Hockett, *Introduction to Research in American History*, 104, qualifies accounts of miracles as "types of discredited statements." His criticism is the conventional one, and is met in what has been said. Unlike Bernheim, he holds that accounts of miracles are "no more usable [for the historian] than if they were proved to be untrue."

A similar rationalistic position towards miracles is taken by Langlois and Seignobos, *Introduction to the Study of History*, 206–208; F. M. Fling, *The Writing of History*, 106; and by Walter E. Spahn and Rinehart J. Swenson, *Methods and Status of Scientific Research with Particular Application to the Social Sciences* (New York, 1930), 133–35.

¶ 297 Sidney Smith, "Contemporary Miracles," *The Month*, 124 (1914): 561–76; 125 (1915): 113–26; idem, "Ecclesiastical Miracles," *ibid.*, 250–63; 371–84.

"Miracles," in *CE*, 10: 338–48; *Dictionnaire Apologétique de la Foi Catholique* 3: 513–78.

F. de Grandmaison de Bruno, *Twenty Cures at Lourdes Medically Discussed* (St. Louis, 1912).

E. Le Bec, *The Medical Proof of the Miraculous*, (London, 1922); idem, *A Study of the Four Miracles Accepted in the Cause of St. Theresa of the Child Jesus*, trans. by Grace Haren (St. Louis, 1929).

Bertam C. A. Windle, "Some Plain Facts about Miracles of Healing," *On Miracles and Other Matters* (New York, 1924), 25–47.

John Oxenham, *The Wonder of Lourdes: What It Is and What It Means* (London, 1924).

R. Marchand, *The Facts of Lourdes and the Medical Bureau*, trans. by F. Izard (New York, 1925).

Richard P. Phillips, *Modern Thomastic Philosophy* (2 vols., London, 1935), vol. 1, chap. 7.

James A. McWilliams, *Cosmology*, (rev. ed., New York, 1937), chap. 15.

G. Moral Possibility; Impossibility

¶ 298 Things are said to be *morally possible*, in reference to man, if they can be performed without reasonable difficulty or inconvenience;

otherwise *morally impossible*, even though they may be both metaphysically and physically possible.

Certain things seldom or never happen in the ordinary course of human life. That a normal-minded man should throw away his life with no other motive than notoriety-seeking is rightly accounted a thing morally impossible. That the Cynic philosopher Proteus did so, only proves that he was not a normal person. Hence, if an alleged fact is on the face of it morally impossible, its circumstances as well as the character of the person involved are to be carefully investigated. The result may be either that the person is shown to be abnormal, or that the fact itself was not correctly reported. Again, if a perfectly trustworthy report embodies a fact against the reality of which only some moral impossibility in a broad sense seems to militate, in view of the certain attestation of the fact, it should be admitted. Thus, in the case where a judge has to pass sentence on a defendant charged with a peculiarly revolting and scarcely credible crime, all doubt on the judge's part as to the possibility of the crime should vanish as soon as the fact of it is established beyond reasonable doubt. The adequate answer to the objection that may be raised to this conclusion is the fact of the free will of man.

H. Concurrent Testimony

⁋ 299 Sources which concur in attesting a historical fact can be all of the same evidential grade, that is, they can be all certain, or all probable. If all are certain, they are individually so many separate proofs of the historicity of the fact they attest, while collectively they usually yield a higher degree of certainty than any single one of them does individually. If the sources are probable only, they yield, taken together, only a degree of probability—though this degree may be high. But in many cases they result in genuine certainty, because their mutual agreement can be explained only on the assumption that the facts attested are objectively true.

⁋ 300 CIRCUMSTANTIAL EVIDENCE

Proof by circumstances (indirect, presumptive, circumstantial evidence), as differentiated from proof by testimony (testimonial evidence), is used to establish the reality of an alleged fact, or to render a doubtful fact certain. Very often circumstances or indications of varying number and significance for each particular case point to one and the same conclusion. Taken individually, they yield as a rule only probability; taken collectively, they issue in certainty when their concurrence is such that it cannot be explained except by the reality of the alleged fact or facts to which they point.

(a) Circumstantial evidence or proof by circumstances has its best-known field of application in court procedure. There has been a tendency in some quarters to magnify circumstantial evidence at the expense of that which is called direct or testimonial. An authority on criminal psychology has written: "As the science of criminal investigation proceeds, oral testimony falls behind and the importance of realistic (circumstantial) proof advances; 'circumstances cannot lie,' witnesses can and do."—Hans Gross, *Criminal Investigation* (Toronto, 1921).

The dictum "circumstances cannot lie" is Paley's. It is a sophism. Circumstances can lie, just as witnesses can. Left to themselves, they may be dumb, inarticulate; what meaning they have is more frequently that which we attach to them, and entirely different meanings can be attached (by opposing counsels in court) to the same circumstances. Both types of evidence, testimonial and circumstantial, have their advantages and disadvantages; both, properly employed, can be of service to the historian as well as to the lawyer.

(b) [The critics] present the two species of evidence [testimonial and circumstantial] in adverse relation to one another as though they were naturally in conflict and as though one species could be employed or relied on only at the other's expense. But this is obviously an incorrect view of the subject, the two species being parts of one system or means, natural as well as judicial; intended, when they are faithfully used in the cause of truth, to aid and not to thwart each other; and when legitimately employed, having such effect.—John H. Wigmore, *The Principles of Judicial Proof or the Problem of Proof as Given by Logic, Psychology, and General Experience, and Illustrated in Judicial Trials* 2d ed., Boston, 1931), 641.

It is misleading to declare that either kind [of evidence] is in a legal sense inferior to the other.—Owen W. Jones, *The Law of Evidence in Civil Cases* (3d ed., San Francisco, 1924), 1426.

¶ 301 Cumulative or converging evidence is virtually circumstantial. It is "a heaping up" (L. *cumulus*) of bits of evidence, individually never more than probable, and often only slightly so, until they form a mass of evidence, the net result of which is certainty. But, as already noted, the resulting certainty does not issue directly from the mass or cumulus of probabilities, since no number of mere probabilities added together can logically produce certainty. To produce such effect, one must invoke the "principle of sufficient reason," by arguing that the only possible explanation why so many bits of evidence point to the same alleged fact, is that the fact is objectively true.

Examples of careful sifting of circumstantial evidence may be seen in

Herbert Thurston, *The Gunpowder Plot*, (London, 1930); O. Eisenschiml, *Why Was Lincoln Murdered?*

A thorough treatment of circumstantial evidence is found in John H. Wigmore, *The Principles of Judicial Proof*, chap. 28.

I. Concurrent Testimony in Remains

¶ 302 Concurrent testimony supplied by various archaeological remains, their authenticity being assumed, can issue in certain proof of a fact or of a conclusion logically derived therefrom.

(a) Individually, the remains may not prove anything definitely; collectively, they may do so, and this because they all agree in pointing to one and the same fact or conclusion. But archaeological remains which thus concur in attesting the same fact or facts offer a basis of certain proof only if the several remains are mutually independent, that is, are originals, not merely copies of one another. Moreover, the conclusions drawn must be genuinely certain. Conclusions in this matter, grounded as they often are on mere analogy or hypothesis, may easily lack any well-founded probability.

(b) A conclusion based on the concurrent testimony of remains is naturally the more probable (or the more certain, as the case may be), the greater the number of remains or indications which point to the fact in question.

Frequently the conclusion is of an inductive character, which will be the case when the remains discovered are fairly numerous, are similar or equivalent in character, and can be explained only as survivals of a precise and definite fact. If one finds a Roman coin in a field, it is no proof that there was once a Roman settlement on the spot; the coin could have been brought from elsewhere. But if one finds in the same field a large number of such coins, as well as other objects of Roman origin, such as household utensils, fragments of decorative art, broken pillars, foundation stones, then it is a safe conclusion that a Roman house once stood there. Here again, as so often in historical criticism, the probative value of the argument rests on the "principle of sufficient reason." It is inconceivable that a considerable quota of remains, individually without necessary relation to a supposed fact, but collectively capable of explanation by it alone, should exist without the supposed fact being real.

(c) To argue from a merely possible or intended fact to its reality is in most cases to argue falsely. *A posse ad esse non valet illatio.* Such spurious logic is sometimes employed in the interpretation of documents which intend or envisage effects or events never realized. It would be rash to conclude, at least in all cases, from the existence of the document to the existence of the effect or event which the document has in view. Thus, a contract can be drawn up and signed but not executed; invitations to a function, public or private, can be issued, and yet those invited fail to appear. Laws are often promulgated but not enforced; a threat can be made but not carried out. It is often argued from legal prohibitions and penalties that the evils prohibited really existed. Logic of this nature is no doubt frequently valid, but not always so. The prohibitions and penalties of the law do not necessarily envisage existing evils only; they may be framed with an intention of preventing evils in the future.

J. Concurrence in Formal Testimony

⟨ 303   NO CORROBORATION WITHOUT INDEPENDENT TESTIMONY
If witnesses are to corroborate one another, their testimony must be independent. Merely to repeat another person's testimony adds nothing to its weight. The same principle holds for archaeological and other remains. Mere copies or imitations of an artefact cannot, at least ordinarily, heighten the evidence afforded by the original. There is only one case in which repeated testimony can be regarded as independent; namely, when the witness has really independent knowledge of the facts in question, and presumably would not reproduce them from another source unless they were set forth therein as he knew them to be.

Dependence takes various shapes. Data may be deliberately appropriated from writings not one's own. Statements may be influenced by suggestion, as happens in court testimony; or by party views or by the mental and moral atmosphere of the times as illustrated in the way in which heathen writers regarded the first Christians; or in the attitude of medieval and even post-medieval judges towards witches.

(a) The usual procedure followed in determining dependence (or independence) is that of analysis, which makes it possible to recognize and therefore isolate all borrowed or secondary elements, so that these can be eliminated in the summation of evidence according to the basic principle: *testimonia non sunt numeranda sed ponderanda.* Even in the case of a single informant, it can happen that he merely repeats testimony given to him on a previous occasion. Hence, from a critical point of view, the later testimony normally loses all independent value, though some importance may attach to it from the circumstance that it shows the witness still persisting in his previous testimony.

Again, the case can occur in which various press reports of a parliamentary or congressional session or of a lawsuit, are all based upon the same official minutes or report of the proceedings; presumably not having been present at the proceedings, the reporters were in no position to verify them by personal knowledge. Press reports made under such conditions evidently lack any value as independent sources.

The story of the so-called Thundering Legion is vouched for by Tertullian, Appollinaris of Hierapolis, Eusebius, St. Gregory Nazianzen, Orosius, and by numerous other authors. As a matter of fact, the letter of Marcus Aurelius, in Tertullian, is generally reputed a forgery. In this letter the Emperor mentions the miraculous rainfall, gives the name *Fulminans*, or "Thundering," to the Christian legion whose prayers are supposed to have brought it about, and forbids further persecution of the Christians. Tertullian's version of the incident, identical with that of Appollinaris, was copied by Eusebius. All later versions can be traced back to Tertullian or to Appolinaris, who are the only independent authorities for the incident.—CE, 14:711.

⁋ 304 A conclusion drawn from concurrence in formal testimony rests on two grounds: first, a datum of experimental psychology; second, "the principle of sufficient reason."

Psychology furnishes the datum that two or more persons will not, independently of one another, invent the same alleged fact, or in their reports of it, differ in precisely the same way from the objective truth. "The principle of sufficient reason" validates the inference that a number of independent witnesses or groups of witnesses, whose views, aims, and interests differ or even mutually conflict as a result of education, environment, and other circumstances, will not agree by mere accident in reporting something alleged as a fact (something fixed and stable by its very nature), if what they report is *not* a fact. In the given circumstances collusion against the truth is impossible, for the supposition is that the witnesses are mutually independent of one another.

Two independent accounts preserving the same body of tradition are found in the "Saga of Eric the Red" and in "The Vinland History of the Flat Island Book," J. E. Olson and E. G. Bourne, eds., *The Northmen, Columbus and Cabot*, 3–66.

⁋ 305 THE USE OF CONCURRENT FORMAL TESTIMONY

(a) On the grounds set forth above, sources, even when not fully accredited, can be rated as trustworthy if they agree with one another. This holds for oral tradition also. But it must be shown that the sources are not dependent on one another, since the probative value of the argument hinges on this particular point.

(b) If a fact is reported by a single direct witness whose reliability is fully attested by several indirect witnesses of credit, their unanimous stand can in certain circumstances raise the testimony of the direct witness to a certainty.

(c) The more numerous the independent witnesses, the greater the certainty of the matter they report in common, since agreement between them increasingly excludes the possibility of error.

(d) Divergence in unessential points cannot affect the substance of the testimony in which several witnesses concur. Such divergence follows as a matter of course from accidental differences in observation, perception, and communication of the facts.

K. Concurrence of Formal Testimony with Remains

¶ 306 CONVERSE RELATIONSHIP OF FORMAL TESTIMONY AND REMAINS

(a) First is the case in which formal testimony is confirmed by remains. Here the confirmation may be so decisive that no reasonable doubt as to the truth of the facts narrated can be entertained. Thus, the Gospel accounts, with their wealth of detail on the topography, customs, and manners of the Holy Land, are borne out by archaeological, linguistic, cultural, and other vestiges, to an extent which places their trustworthiness beyond dispute.

Even accounts of dubious value may be so corroborated by archaeological survivals as to take on a degree of reliability which they did not possess before. Remains are particularly significant when they supplement the testimony of a single witness. This is frequently the case in mere oral tradition of long standing, of itself a rather uncertain medium of transmission. When oral tradition of this kind is supported by such physical remains as inscriptions, coins, documents, it is to be accepted as reliable, at least insofar as it finds corroboration in the remains. In this way many sagas salvage a kernel of historical fact, the reality of which is attested with certainty by such archaeological remains as art products and monuments, by legal traditions, language, and custom.

Statements made in Thucydides and other historians of the classical period have received striking confirmation through archaeological research [¶ 267]. So also the testimony of Strabo and other ancient authors of books of geography and travel, has in numerous cases been vindicated by recent finds.

For confirmation of Old Testament accounts through recent excavations, see, H. Pope, *The Catholic Student's Aids*, vol. 3, chap. 1.

Sometimes archaeological findings upset the interpretations of historians. Thus, a belief, common at one time, that the Gallic fire of 390 B.C., in Rome, destroyed the old temples and their records, has been disproved by excavations. Much indeed of the tradition rejected by Mommsen and his successors has been verified by archaeological evidence.—See Tenney Frank, "Roman Historiography before Caesar," *AHR*, 32 (1927): 237.

(b) The second relationship of formal testimony and remains, is the converse of the first: remains or rather the conclusions drawn therefrom by competent investigators, can be corroborated by formal testimony. A familiar instance is the surviving objects of Egypt's ancient civilization, such as her temples, pyramids, tombs and tombstones, household utensils, wine jars, toilet articles, and other concrete survivals. The picture it was possible to draw on the basis of these remains of Egyptian cultural life has found striking corroboration in the inscriptions, official papers, letters, and literary texts brought to light, especially in modern times. Impressive also are the physical survivals from the Babylonian and Assyrian empires uncovered in the nineteenth century by Layard and his successors. The witness of these remains as historical sources has been corroborated or supplemented on a large scale by later finds (such as in Assurbanipal's library at Ninive) of great quantities of cuneiform tablets with their literary and other texts.

⁋ 307 PLACE-NAMES

These, viewed as archaeological survivals, often have value for the historian. To what extent they can be trusted as evidence of past happenings is a problem which cannot be resolved by general rules; every place-name, like every popular tradition, is a problem by itself. *Mont César* is the name of several hilltops in France and Belgium; but this is not to assure that Julius Caesar was ever in their neighborhood. *Cinq Hommes*, the name of a river in eastern Missouri, popularly explained by a tradition that five men were drowned in its waters, is in reality a corruption for *St. Cosme*, the name of a pioneer French missionary associated with that river.—See J. M. Breckenridge, ed., *William Clark Breckenridge, Historical Research Writer and Bibliographer of Missouri: His Life, Lineage and Writings* (St. Louis, 1932).

On the other hand, the *Rivière des Pères*, or Fathers' River, also in eastern Missouri, was usually explained by a current tradition that a group of missionaries once resided on its banks. The name of the river was the only evidence that could be alleged for support of the tradition until, in recent years, documents brought to light proved it to be true [⁋ 259-e-4].

These are two instances of place-names which to all appearances could be invoked to substantiate a tradition; research proved the reasoning invalid in one case, valid in the other.

(a) Place-names sometimes offer a clue as to the early inhabitants of a locality and their character. The name of the river Avon in England is of Celtic origin; hence, it may be inferred, its valley must have been occupied at one time by the Celts. But there are limitations to this method of reasoning. Numerous towns in western America bear French or Indian names; but this circumstance is no proof that their founders or first inhabitants were Frenchmen or Indians.

The Latin word, castra (camp), surviving in the suffix chester in the names of many English towns, indicates that they were originally the sites of Roman camps. "As false local etymology has in the past been the source of a great deal of historical error, so sound local etymology may sometimes be a valuable help in the discovery of historical truth."—Collected Papers of Henry Bradley, 82.

(b) Bernard W. Henderson, "The Use of Place-names in History," Classical Review, 12 (1898): 11–16.

P. W. Joyce, The Origin and History of Irish Names of Places (2 vols., London, 1898–1913).

Edmund McClure, British Place-names in Their Historical Setting, (London, 1910).

Henry Bradley, "English Place-names," Essays and Studies by Members of the English Association (Oxford, 1910), 1: 7–41.

Hereford B. George, The Relations of Geography and History (5th ed., Oxford, 1924), 49 ff.

Allen Mawer, English Place-name Study; Its Present Condition and Future Possibilities (Oxford, 1921); idem, Problems of Place-name Study (Cambridge, Eng., 1929).

Frederick M. Powicke, "Names of Trade in English Place-names," Historic Essays in Honour of James Tait (Manchester, 1933).

"Celtic Saints and Rome," The Month, 163 (1934): 454–55.

George R. Stewart, Names on the Land (New York, 1945).

L. Conflicting Testimony

¶ 308 THE RECONCILIATION OF CONFLICTING TESTIMONY

The historian frequently finds in his sources statements that disagree with one another, or are even flatly contradictory. The difficulty of reconciling them must be met. Some directions for correct procedure in the matter follow.

(a) Where statements are really contradictory, the first step is to evaluate the individual witnesses (or sources) in regard to the degree of probability or certainty that attaches to their respective testimonies. This done, it will be possible to check them one against the other. If the test results in showing that each of the witnesses (or sources) making up the group can claim approximately the same degree of probability, and that the contradiction cannot possibly be explained, we must conclude that the witnesses are really at odds with one another, and suspend judgment as to the historicity of the alleged fact. Writers often violate this rule in their eagerness to reconcile contradictions at all cost, and are thus led into strained interpretations or compromises foreign to the true spirit of critical research.

(b) Testimony devoid of any sort of probability must be disregarded.

(c) If a certainly reliable witness contradicts one who is only probably so, the testimony of the former must prevail.

(d) If testimony of the highest probability is contradicted by testimony from less reliable sources, the precise degree of probability attaching to the highest must be tested anew, while the less reliable sources must be examined for possible relations of interdependence. In many instances examination will show the less reliable to be mutually dependent, and so reducible to a single source, which, in the case supposed, cannot stand up against the first testimony with its very high degree of probability. Scholars, especially before the rise of criticism, often violated this rule by preferring a later (but less reliable source) to an older. Perhaps even a contemporary source held this preference, merely on some dubious ground of internal evidence.

(e) If the contradiction can be traced to party interest, the truth will often lie in the middle. With both sides to a contest claiming ascendency, it is safe to assume that neither side scored a complete victory.

(f) When a witness gives contradictory versions of the same incident, the circumstances under which the various versions are given will sometimes render it possible to recognize which is correct. Las Cases said of Napoleon that he had three different ways of commenting on the execution of the Duc d'Enghien. Speaking in private with a confidant he regretted it; in a circle of friends he mildly apologized for it; before strangers, he boldly defended it.

(g) If reliable accounts contradict one another only in incidental data but agree in essentials, the contradiction can be disregarded as far as the substance of the content is concerned. On the other hand, where unreliable witnesses are in agreement as to essentials, the test of possible contradiction in details can lead to sure detection of unreliability in the testimony as a whole. Such was the case of Susanna and the false witnesses in Daniel, 13:2–63.

(h) In certain cases the contradiction may be only apparent, not real. The witnesses may not be referring to precisely the same thing; they may tell of different situations, or report the same occurrence from different points of view, different angles of observation. Criticism along these lines sometimes succeeds in reducing apparently conflicting statements to agreement, at least substantial. Where reconciliation is impossible, the only course is to suspend judgment, and await possible new evidence toward a secure conclusion.

For elaborate treatment of the topic, see H. M. Bowman, "The Origin and Treatment of Discrepancy in Trustworthy Records," The Royal Society of Canada, Proceedings and Transactions, 3d Series, vol. 5 (1911), Section 2; John H. Wigmore, "How to Analyze a Mixed Body of Evidence," The Principles of Judicial Proof, 46–71.

⟨ 309 De Smedt (*Principes*, 131) sums up neatly the problem of conflicting testimony under three heads. First, conflict or disagreement in testimony may regard details only, not substance. This situation may be taken to imply that the thing reported is true; witnesses do not report the same thing in the same way. Second, conflict may be apparent only, not real. Examination of circumstances, language, etc., may reveal substantial agreement, accidental disagreement. Third, conflict may regard substance. In this case each of the individual witnesses or reports is to be examined to see what relative degree of credence can be given to them severally. One may then give provisional assent to the more probable report, or suspend assent altogether until new evidence is available to make a solution possible.

⟨ 310 Caesar (*Gallic War*, IV, 1; VI, 22) denies the existence of private property among the ancient Germans. Tacitus, on the other hand, affirms its existence, or at least leaves the point doubtful (*Germania*, XXVI). Fustel de Coulanges was of the opinion that the two authors are really not in contradiction, but are speaking of different things.

> When we meet with texts or facts in history which seem to contradict one another, this is due in most cases to the circumstance that historical truth is highly complex. Things very much at variance with one another can be found to be equally true, for a society is composed of very different organs. No doubt these organs have some relation between them, some bond, but rarely is there a perfect unity.—N. D. Fustel de Coulanges, *Recherches sur quelques problèmes d'histoire*, 292.

William of Malmsbury (*Gesta Pontificum Anglorum*) and Hugh the Chanter of York (*Historia quattuor archiepiscoporum ecclesiae Eboracencis*), give accounts, contradictory in many details, of the controversy (1070–1138) between Canterbury and York over primacy of jurisdiction.—See Charles E. Schrader, "The Canterbury-York Controversy," HB, 12 (1933): 11 f.

⟨ 311 The intricacies of the Cabot problem yield to a careful classification of our sources of information: first, into English state documents; secondly, contemporary reports by Italian and Spanish envoys in England, derived in part from John Cabot himself; thirdly, narratives in the Spanish and Italian archives derived fifteen or twenty years later from Sebastian Cabot. The first two classes agree with each other and are at variance with the third, which in accordance with principles of sound historical criticism must therefore be rejected.—Edward G. Bourne, *Spain in America*, 59.

Contemporary accounts of the assassination of the explorer La Salle (March 19, 1687), contradict one another in important details.—Jean Delanglez, ed., *The Journal of Jean Cavelier* (Chicago, 1938) 149 ff.

Accounts by Adams and Jefferson of the origin of the Declaration of Independence do not agree.—Carl L. Becker, *The Declaration of Independence*, chap. 5.

Contemporary accounts of the visit of Louis XVI to Paris, July 17, 1789, after the fall of the Bastille, conflict.—F. M. Fling, *The Writing of History*, 114–17.

[Aulard] denies Danton's complicity in the crimes of September. As Danton himself admitted his guilt to no less a witness than the future King of the French, this is a defiance of a main rule of criticism, that a man shall be condemned out of his own mouth.—Lord Acton, *Lectures on the French Revolution*, 372.

Count Rostopchin claimed to have set fire to Moscow (1812), and later denied it. Which of his accounts are we to credit?—H. B. George, *Historical Evidence*, 90.

There are two discrepant versions of Abraham Lincoln's use of an almanac in a court room to save a client under trial for murder.—See F. L. Wellman, *The Art of Cross Examination*, 55 ff.

Almost any critical history that discusses the evidence for important statements will furnish examples of discrepant or contradictory accounts and the attempts which are made to reconcile them.

M. Problems in the Credibility of Sources

¶ 312   As was emphasized in ¶ 157, the three major aspects of any historical source (authenticity, textual integrity, credibility) are to be carefully distinguished. A source may be authentic without being credible; on the other hand, it may be credible without being authentic, for it may be the work of a reliable author who concealed his authorship by publishing under the name of another. Historians differ in their attitude towards the problems raised in a study of sources. The great Mabillon concentrated on questions of authenticity. Once he proved a document genuine, he seemed almost to assume its credibility, which of course is an unwarranted procedure.—See *AHR*, 47 (1942): 36.

On the other hand, Fustel de Coulanges was drawn particularly to interpretation, to questions of credibility; whether a document was genuine or not, did not concern him greatly, so it is said, and he was led at times into taking spurious documents for genuine.—G. P. Gooch, *History and Historians*, 212.

¶ 313 European and American scholarship has to its credit an immense amount of learned inquiry into the credibility of concrete sources. This has been put to account in the various fields of historiography. Careful reading in the literature under this head will repay the apprentice in history.

(a) On the credibility of Herodotus, see R. W. Macan, *Herodotus; the Fouth, Fifth and Sixth Books*, introduction; Walter W. How and J. Wells, *A Commentary on Herodotus* (2 vols., Oxford, 1928).

Scholarly criticism has long been engaged with the trustworthiness of Livy, especially with the earliest parts of his history [¶ 272].

"The credibility of Caesar's Narrative" is discussed by T. R. Holmes, *Caesar's Conquest of Gaul*, 211–55; see also, idem, "Signor Ferrero's Reconstruction of Caesar's First Commentary," *Classical Quarterly*, 3 (1909): 203–215.

John Burnet, ed., *Plato's Eutyphro, Apology of Socrates and Crito* (Oxford, 1924) urges the serious historical character of the Apology.

Recent criticism tends to impugn the credibility of Tacitus. "If a writer does not correctly summarize in the form of general statements the facts narrated by himself, we are justified in entertaining the greatest suspicion regarding his general character as a historian."—Thomas S. Jerome, "The Tacitean Tiberius; a Study in Historiographic Method," *Classical Philology*, 7 (1912): 265. See also J. S. Reid, "Tacitus as a Historian," *Journal of Roman Studies*, 11 (1921): 191 ff. For a favorable estimate, see Louis E. Lord, "Tacitus the Historian," *Classical Journal*, 21 (1925), 177 ff.; Frank B. Marsh, "The Sources of Tacitus," *The Reign of Tiberius*, 233 ff.

(b) The merits of the four Gospels and the Acts of the Apostles as historical documents have been subjected to minute and exhaustive investigation by Hugh Pope, "The Historical Trustworthiness of Matthew's Gospel," *Aids*, 2: 180 ff. See also John M. Simon, "The Sources of St. Luke's Gospel," *A Scripture Manual Directed to the Interpretation of Biblical Revelation* (2 vols., New York, 1938), 2: 210; John Arendzen, *The Gospels, Fact or Legend?* (London, 1924); J. A. Scott, *Luke, Greek Physician and Historian*.

(c) John Morris, *The Life and Martyrdom of Saint Thomas Becket, Archbishop of Canterbury*, xiii-ff.; 104–117.

W. E. Brown, *Pioneers of Christendom; Bishops*, upholds the reliability of the contemporary *Vita B. Martini* (St. Martin of Tours) by Sulpicius Severus.

Johannes Jorgensen, *St. Francis of Assisi*, 351 ff., discusses the credibility of the sources.

Einhard, *Vie de Charlemagne*, Louis Halphen, ed. (Paris, 1923): The editor has been taken to task for the severity of his judgment on Einhard.

John H. Round, "Wace's Authority," *Feudal England: Historical Studies to Eleventh and Twelfth Centuries* (London, 1909), 403 ff.

The reliability of Boccaccio's *Vita di Dante* is discussed by Charles A. Dinsmore, *Aids to the Study of Dante* (Boston, 1903).

(d) The sources for the history of the De Soto Expedition are evaluated in

F. W. Hodge and H. Lewis, eds., *Spanish Explorers in the Southern United States*, 129–32; in Woodbury Lowery, *The Spanish Settlements Within the Present Limits of the United States, 1513–1561* (New York, 1901), 458 ff.; and in the *Final Report of the United States De Soto Expedition Commission* (76th Congress, 1st session, House Document, No. 71, Washington, 1929).

"The truthfulness of Fray Marcos," is examined by W. Lowery in *The Spanish Settlements*, 467 ff., and by Carl Sauer in *The Road to Cíbola* (Berkeley, California, 1926), 21 ff.

The trustworthiness of Lahontan is discussed by Reuben G. Thwaites, ed., *Lahontan's New Voyages to North America* (2 vols., Chicago, 1905), and by J.-Edmond Roy, "Le Baron de Lahontan," The Royal Society of Canada, *Proceedings and Transactions*, series I, vol. 12 (1895), section I, 63–192.

Carl L. Becker, checked the memoirs of Madame Roland with her correspondence, with a view to ascertaining their trustworthiness. *AHR*, 33 (1928): 782–803.

R. C. H. Catterall, "The Credibility of Marat," *AHR*, 16 (1910): 24–33.

Stanley Pargellis critically examined eight eyewitness accounts of "Braddock's Defeat," *AHR*, 41 (1936): 253–69.

Howard K. Beale, "Is the Published Diary of Gideon Welles Reliable?" *AHR*, 30 (1925): 547–52.

The data in Mrs. John H. Kinzie's *Wau-Bun The Early Day in the Northwest*, are discussed in Louise P. Kellogg's edition (Menasha, Wis., 1930); also in Milo M. Quaife's edition (Chicago, 1932).

Milo M. Quaife, "Critical Evaluation of the Sources for Western History," *MVHR*, 1 (1914): 167 ff.

The reliability of the Memoir of George Rogers Clark is discussed in James A. James, *Life of George Rogers Clark* (Chicago, 1928), Appendix 1. The memoir was not written thirty or forty years after the events, as Theodore Roosevelt asserted, but it was written for the most part between 1790–1791, some twelve years after the capture of Vincennes.

A critical sifting of a story affecting the integrity of a high government official of Reconstruction days may be seen in W. Norwood Brigance, "Jeremiah Black and Andrew Johnson," *MVHR*, 19 (1932), 205–13.

In general, minute scrutiny of any historical source will run into questions of dependence and credibility. Especially apt material for a study of the technique of investigation in this field is offered by the documents bearing on the great sixteenth-century North American explorations, mostly Spanish. The more significant of these documents with accompanying critical apparatus are available in the series, J. Franklin Jameson, ed., *Original Narratives of Early American History*, reproduced under the auspices of the American Historical Association (19 vols., New York, 1906–1917). Many of the critical essays on sources in Justin Winsor, *Narrative and Critical History of America* (8 vols., Boston, 1884–1889), are still unsurpassed.

₡ 314 To conclude, by far the most pressing of all the problems before the historian regards the credibility of his sources. The following exposition of right procedure in resolving this problem is pertinent.

As Gregory of Tours is by far the most important of our historical sources for a knowledge of Frankish origins, it is essential that we form a just estimate of his authority and the value we may properly attach to the information which he gives. Is he correctly informed? When does he speak with a perfect knowledge of the facts? When is he merely an echo of the popular voice, a registrar of legend? To these first questions must be added another not less important; in the recital of events with which he is acquainted, in his appreciation of the men he brings upon the stage, are his sincerity and impartiality perfect or are they influenced at times by passion or prejudice? . . . The scope of my work will be threefold. In the first part, I will study the man, his character, his mentality, his intellectual and moral attitudes, his education. The second part will show how he conceives his task of historian and in what manner he prepared for it. Finally, in the third part one will see, in the light of the data ascertained through this double investigation, the precise value of his work.—Godefroid Kurth, "De l'autorité de Grégoire de Tours," Études franques (2 vols., Paris, 1919), 2: 212 f.

Part Four

PRESENTATION OF THE RESULTS OF RESEARCH
(Synthesis and Exposition)

Chapter Fourteen

THE INTERPRETATION OF SOURCES

A. Verbal Interpretation . . . . Page 321
B. Technical Interpretation 326
C. Logical Interpretation 327
D. Psychological Interpretation 327
E. Factual Interpretation 330
F. Letting the Facts Speak for Themselves 336

A. Verbal Interpretation

⟨ 315 Interpretation as an essential step in historical method seems to lie on the borderline between criticism and exposition. On the one hand, it cannot be carried on without constant exercise of the critical faculty; to know what a document means is as much a challenge to critical judgment as to know when or by whom it was written, or whether one may trust it. On the other hand, the literary exposition of historical data is greatly conditioned by the interpretation one places upon them. For the rest, the question whether interpretation belongs logically to criticism or to exposition, is one of speculative interest only. It does not bear in any practical way on the problems of the historian.

⟨ 316 At least four different methods may be applied in the effort to arrive at the meaning of a document or any part of it. Attention may be focussed, first, on the words, taken individually or in groups (*verbal* interpretation); next, on the author's purpose in writing, and on the specific literary form he adopts (*technical* interpretation); then, on the author's mind and character, especially as influenced by environment, physical, social, and intellectual (*psychological* interpretation). Finally, having ascertained as far as possible the meaning of the document, or any part of it, on its textual side, by application of one or more of these three methods, one may proceed to determine the meaning or significance of the data which the document contains (*factual* interpretation).

Everyone who has made the endeavor will recognize how difficult it is accurately to determine the sense of even one document and what stern self-discipline is requisite as the first condition of every critical enquiry or historical investigation.—Francis A. Gasquet, *Henry III and* the English Church, A Study of his Ecclesiastical Policy and of the Relations between England and Rome (London, 1905), ix.

₵ 317 LANGUAGE

The major approach to the meaning of a document lies in its words taken singly or in groups. To explain the meaning of words and sentences, to extract from them the ideas they were meant to convey, is the task of verbal interpretation. Clearly, the task cannot be attempted without knowledge of the language in which the document is written. Not only must the interpreter be familiar with its language, he must be familiar with it in precisely that stage of development which it had reached at the period to which the document belongs. One who is expert in classical Latin only is not thereby equipped for the correct verbal interpretation of sources in medieval Latin, any more than one knowing only present-day English is thereby qualified to grasp with ease Chaucer's English, or even in full measure, Shakespeare's. A handicap often felt by students of medieval history is their inability to read postclassical Latin, or for that matter, Latin of any kind. Scholarly firsthand work in any field of historical research is impossible without at least through an exact knowledge of the language or languages in which the pertinent source material is found.

₵ 318 VOCABULARY

Grasp of vocabulary implies accurate knowledge, not only of word-units as such, but also of synonyms, idioms, and other distinct elements of speech. Usage very often fixes on a word, a connotation of which the dictionary does not take account. The connotation must be felt, and as a rule it is felt only by one perfectly conversant with the language as a practical instrument of expression. Furthermore, an author can have his idiosyncrasies in the use of words, so that anyone undertaking to interpret him must reckon with his departures from normal verbal usage. Concordances and special dictionaries are now available for a study of the vocabulary of some of the older historians, such as Caesar, Tacitus, Bede.

In the evolution of languages the same word has meant different things at different times. The Latin *reserare* meant in the classical period "to open," in the medieval period, "to close." *Orare* meant first, "to speak," later, "to beg," still later, "to pray." *Vel*, meaning "or," or "even" (in the classical age), was widely used in the Middle Ages in the sense of "and." *Sacramentum*, "a sacred thing," came eventually to express the Christian concept of a "sacrament."

Merovingian Latin is a language one must know exactly and such knowledge is acquired only by protracted use of texts. The sense of words has often changed: for example, *intentio* means a "law-suit"; *suffragium*, "protection" or "recommendation"; *solatium*, "support" or "aid"; *scandulum*, "complaint"; *hostis*, "army"; *electio*, "choice," and not "election," unless it is the people who makes the choice; *testamentum*, "a written act," as well as "a will"; *auctoritas*, "a royal diploma." —N. D. Fustel de Coulanges, cited in *Revue des questions historiques*, 113 (1930): 5–11.

The French *viande* was used up to the seventeenth century for any kind of meat, later only for flesh meat. In English *villain* originally signified "peasant," while "knave" for "boy," and "daft" for "modest" were once in common use.

₡ 319 GRAMMAR AND CONTEXT

To arrive at the meaning of a sentence, it is not enough to know the sense of the constituent words; one must also know their grammatical context, namely, their relation to one another as fixed by the rules of grammar; for instance, the relations between subject and predicate, object and predicate, adjective and noun, preposition and noun, and the like.

Furthermore, to arrive at the meaning of even a single sentence, one must know what may be called its syntactical context, that is, its relations of co-ordination or subordination to other sentences as indicated by conjunctions, sequence of moods and tenses, position of the sentence. Often the only factor settling decisively the meaning of a sentence is its context. On the other hand, to detach a sentence from its context is often to give it a false meaning. The importance of looking to the context in verbal interpretation has been realized from the earliest times. In the fifth century, St. Jerome urged the matter on the prudent reader, admonishing him to consider "*priora, media et sequentia*." A modern master in the interpretation of texts, Fustel de Coulanges, was ever insistent on the "law of the context."

Comparison of parallel texts whether of the same author or of authors closely related, is an important aid to interpretation. The parallelism may be in diction only, or in content, or in both. In such comparison of texts two rules frequently call for application:

First, ambiguous or obscure passages must be explained by others, clear and unequivocal. Sometimes two passages, alike obscure, may yield up their meaning when confronted with each other.

Second, by a similar process of mutual juxtaposition of texts, brief allusions and laconic expressions may sometimes be clarified, with the aid of the more detailed presentations of the same content that may occur.

¶ 320 A passage on the Roman primacy in St. Irenaeus, *Adversus haereses* ("ad hanc enim Ecclesiam propter potentiorem principalitatem necesse est omnem convenire ecclesiam"), is said to be capable of one hundred and eight interpretations, if one takes into account the various meanings of single words and phrases, and the possible logical combinations between them.—*CHR*, 16 (1931): 415.

See also the meticulous interpretation of a famous passage, "The Duo Sunt" of Gelasius.—Robert Hull, *Theories of the Medieval Papacy* (London, 1934), 13–28.

¶ 321 "Agri pro numero cultorum ab universis in vices occupantur, quos mox inter se secundum dignationem partiuntur. . . . Arva per annos mutant et superest ager" (Tacitus, *Germania*, XXVI). The interpretation of this passage, which is complicated by the different readings *vices*, *invicem*, *in vices*, has given rise to prolonged discussion. The capital point at issue is whether the passage proves or disproves the existence of private ownership of land among the early Germans. Fustel de Coulanges reviewed the various interpretations placed upon this text, and then advanced his own, in "Les Germains connaissaient-ils la propriété des terres?" *Recherches sur quelques problèmes d'histoire*, 263–89. See also on the same passage in Tacitus, Frederic Seebohm, *English Village Community* (London and New York, 1905), 343.

A discussion of the meaning of a passage in an Anglo-Saxon chronicle will be found in Edward Jenks, *Law and Politics in the Middle Ages* (New York, 1907), 191.

> A historian's only cleverness consists in drawing out of the documents everything they contain and in not adding thereto anything which they do not contain. The best historian has no other ambition than to see the facts clearly and grasp them accurately. It is not in his imagination or his logic that he seeks them; he seeks them, he arrives at them by minute observation of the texts just as the chemist finds his facts in minutely conducted experiments. . . . he keeps as closely as possible to the texts, interprets them with all possible exactness, and does not write or even think except in harmony with them.—N. D. Fustel de Coulanges, cited in *Revue des questions historiques*, 113 (1930): 9.

Henri Grégoire contends that misinterpretations of classical texts are of common occurrence even among scholars. With regard to the long-standing controversy as to the scene of the battle of Salamis, whether in the strait or outside it (The *Sund* and *Nicht-Sund* schools), he maintains that the passage in Herodotus (VIII, 83–96) describing the battle is "decisive," but only on condition "that it be taken literally and interpreted without prejudice." —"La légende de Salamine ou comment les philologues écrivent l'histoire," *Les études classiques*, 4 (1935), 519–31.

On a misinterpreted passage in Seneca, see Edward G. Bourne, "Seneca and the Discovery of America," *Essays in Historical Criticism*, 221 ff.

¶ 322 TRANSLATION

As a species of verbal interpretation, translation may be taken to be a literary process by which a passage in one language is so expressed in another as to stir in the reader the same thoughts and emotions as are stirred in one reading the passage in the original. This standard, so high as to be almost impracticable, can and ought to be approximated. The process postulates the threefold knowledge of a language as in ¶ 317.

Translations, even from presumably competent hands, are often inaccurate, in the sense of distorting the meaning of the original. "Distrust translations," is a wise caution though not always practicable. Sometimes the original text is not accessible, or the student may be unacquainted with its language. But if he has the original text of a document at hand and can read it, it is safer for him to rely on his own understanding of it than to have recourse to a translation.

Translation of historical material especially attends to accuracy and readability, the latter quality connoting smoothness, together with such clearness and propriety of language as offers no difficulty to the reader.

¶ 323 Common mistranslations of Scripture texts are listed in Jean V. Bainvel, *Les contresens bibliques des prédicateurs* (2d ed., Paris, 1906).

In translating Greek, βάρβαρος should not be rendered by "barbarian," the usual equivalent, but by "non-Hellenic," or "Oriental." In English, the word *barbarian* has connotations which are absent from the Greek βάρβαρος.—A. J. Toynbee, *Greek Historical Thought from Homer to the Age of Heracleius*, xxv.

In German, as an example, one might mention the word *sogenannte* as one which an unfastidious translator might render as *so called*, without appreciating the slight suggestion which attaches to this English but not to the German word, that the thing in question ought not properly to be so called.—J. Edward Holmstrom, *Records and Research in Engineering: A Guide to the Production, Extraction, Integrating, Storekeeping, Circulation and Translation of Technical Knowledge* (London, 1940), 263.

Malcolm V. Hay, "Some Mistranslations of the Word 'Missa,' " *A Chain of Error in Scottish History* (London, 1927), 236–38.

Sir Clement R. Markham's translation of a chronicle of Peru, published by the Hakluyt Society, in 1864, was everywhere accepted as reliable until Bailey W. Diffie in the *Hispanic American Historical Review*, 16 (1936): 96 ff., pointed out its gross defects. The numerous omissions and mistranslations put the Spaniards in a worse light than is warranted by the original text; hence, the writer entitled his article: "A Markham Contribution to the Leyenda Negra."

On translating in general, see Herbert C. Tolman, *The Art of Translating*

(Boston, 1901); J. Percival Postgate, *Translation and Translations: Theory and Practice* (London, 1922); E. Stuart Bates, *Modern Translation* (London, 1936).

On the translation of historical documents, see J. Villasana Haggard, *Handbook for Translators of Spanish Historical Documents*, 1–6.

B. Technical Interpretation

⟪ 324 The technical interpretation of a document is based upon two considerations: first, the author's *intent* in composing it; secondly, its *precise literary form*. Here recurs the important distinction already pointed out [⟪ 276 f.], between sources of strictly informational intent and those of mixed intent, such, namely, as are designed not only to impart information, but to attain some purpose also, whether primary or secondary. Thus, the controlling aim in poetry and the drama is to stimulate intellectual and emotional enjoyment, esthetic pleasure; what information may be conveyed incidentally in a ballad, an epic, a historical play, is secondary in intent. It is true that literary productions are at times conceived primarily with a view to propaganda, to the inculcation of a theory or doctrine; but in such cases the productions, if they are to answer to the notion of literature at all, must compass immediately the reader or hearer's enjoyment, his esthetic satisfaction, and only mediately the purpose of propaganda. Hence, to penetrate the meaning of a document, it is often important to look to its outer form, both as revealing the author's design in producing it, and as carrying with it a technique that places certain limitations on the presentation of the literal truth. The authors of poems, plays, novels which introduce historical facts and persons, do not deal with them in the same way they are dealt with by the historian. Poets, dramatists, novelists are granted the immemorial license of taking liberties with the facts. They may disarrange the time-order, introduce purely fictitious details, incidents, situations, and exaggerate the qualities, good or bad, of the characters portrayed. Spenser's *Faerie Queen*, Shakespeare's historical plays, Scott's romances, are examples.

The idealizing process peculiar to poetry and the drama, is scarcely possible without sacrifice of the objective truth. Moreover, the very nature of poetic diction, with its metaphors and other figures, with its colorful epithets, militates strongly against strict historicity in the presentation of facts. Other types of discourse in which the literal truth is not to be expected, owing to the purpose inspiring them, but which, nevertheless, the historian must sometimes draw upon, are lawyers' pleas in court, eulogies, funeral orations, public declarations of diplomats, treaty covenants. State papers and public documents of any kind are to be used with special caution, since other designs besides that of conveying accurate information can easily preside over their compilation. The formalities customary in official papers often furnish problems of interpretation. These formalities differ from one age, country, chancery, to another. The student must know the precise meaning they bore at the time and in the place where the document was produced. Salutations, expressions of good will, formal phrasings, are not to be taken at their face value. No one supposes that "Dear Sir" or "Dear Madam," at the head of a present-day letter are necessarily expressions of genuine affection, any more than "Your obedient servant," at its end, necessarily implies readiness on the part of the writer to be at the service of the addressee. The strongly Christian language occurring in Shakespeare's will is not necessarily to be taken as an expression of his personal religious conviction; it was the conventional phraseology used by lawyers in drawing up instruments of this kind.

C. Logical Interpretation

⁋ 325 Grammatical context is based upon and presupposes logical context, which is a certain connection and cohesion between the various parts of a composition, according to the laws of correct thinking. Logical context postulates, therefore, that a given passage be connected in thought with what precedes and follows, whether immediately or mediately. The main connecting thread is generally some leading idea in the entire composition, or in the case of historical sources, the unity arising from treatment of one and the same event or series of events. As a consequence, logical interpretation, through its effort to bring out the logical context, can be a valuable aid in establishing the correct sense of a passage, or of a composition as a whole. Thus, if doubt should arise as to the sense of a particular passage in a document, the doubt can be solved in numerous cases by taking into account the sense of the document as a whole.

D. Psychological Interpretation

⁋ 326 Psychological interpretation of a document is an attempt to read it through its author's eyes, to get his point of view. Being what it is, such interpretation has necessarily to reckon with the laws of mental life. It is of two kinds, *general* and *individual*; general, insofar as it utilizes for its purpose the laws of mental and emotional life valid for all persons; individual, insofar as it seeks to trace the influence of an author's specific psychical traits upon the work he produces.

D. Psychological Interpretation

To speak in general, psychological interpretation is concerned chiefly with the laws of the association of ideas and those of emotional life. From the first it results that a given idea by reason of its natural relation to another idea summons up an image of the latter. This relation may be of various kinds, similarity, contrast, cause and effect, connection in time or place. Examples are: father and mother, peace and war, life and death, humiliation and exaltation, revolution and ruin. According to the laws of emotional life, the construction in the mind of a series of ideas is accompanied by emotional states or activities which influence in a definite manner the outward expression of ideas. From the emotional content which an author has put into his work, the reader may argue to the intellectual content which it was his purpose to express. By the same line of reasoning it is often possible to clear up seeming contradictions.

Psychological interpretation fixes its attention on the internal and external conditions which determine an author's psychical reactions. To grasp these conditions is often to reach the author's meaning with a success that would not be possible in any other way. Written history reflects as in a mirror the author's environment and times. However, one should not exaggerate, for purposes of interpretation, the importance of getting into personal contact with the physical backgrounds that reacted on an author psychologically, or conditioned historic situations and events. It is possible to write effectively on the history of lands one has never visited. Gibbon was never in Constantinople, nor Grote in Greece, nor Prescott in Mexico. At the same time, direct acquaintance with the physical setting of the events which he narrates can be a definite aid to the historian.—See John P. Mahaffy, *Problems in Greek History* (London, 1892), 24 f.

Among factors that react psychologically on an author's literary product, the following are particularly significant.

(a) *Origin, environment, station in life, personal experiences.* All these factors influence literary product by shaping or coloring thought, feeling, viewpoint, method and manner of expression. Environment, whether physical, social, political, religious, or economic, reacts on the literary content. Long association with physical surroundings of a particular type, such as mountains, woods, seashore, city streets, leaves its impression on an author's mentality. So also do the specific circumstances of his career. The autocratic, power-grasping Caesar; the modest provincial and stranger to politics, Livy; the aristocratic Tacitus, soured by despotism; the court bishop, Eusebius of Caesarea, instinctively critical but a dependent with his eyes fixed on imperial favor; the independent Dalmatian, St. Jerome, fiery and controversial—all thought and wrote differently in response to individual viewpoints and experiences. One does not fully appreciate the testimony of St. Paul unless the express commission he had received from Christ is taken into account, nor understand St. Peter's testimony unless one remembers that he was an eyewitness of the Transfiguration.

Albert J. Beveridge believed that "in a biography the subject should not be isolated from his environment and associates." His standard biographies of Marshall and Lincoln give probably a disproportionate amount of space to background and environment. He wrote in the preface to his *Marshall*:

> Vitally important in their effect upon the conduct and attitude of Marshall and of the leading characters of his time were the state of the country, the condition of the people, and the tendency of popular thought. Some reconstruction of the period has therefore been attempted. Without a background the picture and the figures in it lose much of their significance.—Tracy E. Strevey in W. T. Hutchinson, ed., *The Marcus W. Jernegan Essays in American History*, 381 f.

> It is now generally admitted that neither an individual nor a nation can be properly understood without a knowledge of their surroundings and means of support—in other words, of their geographical and economical conditions.—Alfred E. Zimmern, *The Greek Commonwealth: Politics and Economics in Fifth Century Athens* (Oxford, 1911), 51.

(b) *Cultural formation*. This may be taken to include native mental ability, knowledge as acquired by education, study and experience, philosophy of life, individuality of expression and presentation. Current intellectual fashions are reflected in a writer's own intellectual makeup. Hence, interpretation of his product requires that the general cultural conditions peculiar to his day be duly grasped.

(c) *Character, natural as well as acquired*. Interpretation must take account of this factor. An explanation of a text that does violence to its author's known character is ordinarily to be dismissed. The interpreter must therefore make it a point to know, as far as possible, the personality of the individual whose text he seeks to interpret, and be guided strictly by such knowledge in his effort to give a meaning to it or any part of it.

(d) *Writer's objective*. An interpreter of the Gospels will not lose sight of the fact Matthew composed a doctrinal treatise for the Jewish Christians of Palestine, while Mark wrote a simple narrative for converts from paganism residing in Rome. It is not an accident that in view of his didactic purpose Matthew frequently neglects chronological order. Livy wrote with a view to making his Roman readers proud of their historical past, a purpose which distinctly colors his work.

On the interpretation of literary texts, and by implication, also of historical, see C. M. Gayley and F. N. Scott, An *Introduction to the Methods and Materials of Literary Criticism*, 358 ff. Three factors in the production of a literary work are stressed: literary antecedents, national culture, author's individuality as affected by both.

> To know the characteristics of that time [the author's] is to understand one-half the work and mind of genius and the whole of the ordinary man's mind and work. This is only another way of transposing oneself to the author's point of vision—the first requisite of the best criticism.—Lorenzo Sears, *Principles and Methods of Literary Criticism*, 194.

E. Factual Interpretation

¶ 327 Factual interpretation deals with the facts of a document, not with the words. It aims to bring out the significance of the facts individually and in groups, their interrelations, especially in the category of cause and effect.

> The function of history is not merely to ascertain facts, but to interpret them aright. . . . It is certain that if a historian be not an interpreter, he is no more than a chronologist.—Sir John Fortescue, *The Writing of History* (London, 1926), 30 f.

In all historiography above the level of the mere recital of events, the rule holds, "no interpretation, no history." Beware of the merely antiquarian attitude; antiquarianism is not history [¶ 9].

As to the principle of dispensing with interpretation, of "letting the facts speak for themselves," see ¶ 330.

(a) The initial step in factual interpretation is to construct clear and distinct ideas or images of the persons, events, institutions, and other things about which the document informs us. Owing to the distance of time and space which separates us from the original source, the ideas and images we form in regard to such matters are often vague and hazy; we cannot clarify them simply with the aid of the document itself. In such cases we are under the necessity of building up anew in our minds the documentary content, and this indeed, from the author's viewpoint and within the circle of ideas that were familiar to him. This is possible only to the extent to which we can re-create mentally the entire religious, moral, and intellectual environment in which he moved. Failing this, we run the risk of "reading history backwards," that is, of making our own environment, with its particular viewpoints and other characteristics, the background of past conditions and events, with interpretation on them accordingly.

The manner in which Pharisees, Sadducees, Herodians, conduct themselves in the Gospels becomes intelligible through the history of the contemporary Jewish sects. The *Meditations* of Marcus Aurelius require for their correct interpretation broad knowledge of the cultural and political ideas current in the second century after Christ. Only exact knowledge of the opposition existing between the pagan Roman state and people, on the one hand, and the Christian religion as a guide of life, on the other, enables one to interpret the reasonings and allusions of the early Christian apologists. Anything like complete understanding of Shakespeare's plays is impossible without insight into English conditions contemporary with their production.

It is plain from these illustrations that factual interpretation often runs over into psychological. In the process of bringing out the true significance of the facts of a document, it thus becomes necessary to bring them into relation with the facts of the contemporary world. Facts recorded in a document may seem to be the effects of agencies or causes of which the document is silent; we should hardly get the meaning of the facts unless our knowledge of current conditions showed them to be reactions from contemporary facts not mentioned in the documents. The more we know of the environment and conditions coincident in time and place with the content of a historical source, the better we understand the content, the happier we are in recapturing it in the full range of its significance and color. Thus, an understanding of the Gospels as historical documents demands that we grasp their connection with the Old Testament, the synagogue, Jewish religious life, and in general, with the conditions, cultural and social, obtaining at the time in Palestine. The picture which the Gospels give us of the life and teaching of Christ has about it a distinct coloring caught from contemporary history and from certain limitations of time and place, while His person and teaching transcend all earthly bounds.

(b) Factual interpretation of a source of an unknown date, or of one in any way obscure in meaning, is often facilitated by a knowledge of the place in which it was found. This is especially the case with material remains. A pictured scene on a Greek vase may yield no meaning at all, even after long and serious efforts to interpret it. The clue to a solution of the problem may finally be at hand only when account is taken of the precise locality in the Greek world in which the vase was first unearthed. Thus, a clear connection can be established between the pictured scene and some local religious myth.

But interpretation based on place of discovery, though often yielding valuable results, is not always applicable. Numerous products of the arts, especially those of the ancient world, have been removed from their place of actual origin to other places, with no mark of any kind left on them to indicate the fact of removal. Thus, statues and other art objects were carried off from Greece in great numbers and scattered about in Rome and other localities in Italy. In the same way, numerous manuscripts originally in early medieval monasteries, such as Bobbio, Corbie, Tours, St. Gall, and Fulda, were removed thence to the libraries or archives of other institutions. Of course, if the precise places where such manuscripts were actually produced can be identified, factual interpretation based on their known *locus originis* can be safely attempted.

¶ 328 IMPORTANCE OF FACTUAL INTERPRETATION

The interpretation of facts is the end to which every other kind of interpretation in history is referred. The textual meaning of a document is subsidiary to the meaning of the facts which it contains. We interpret a historical document, whether strictly according to its words or in the light of its author's personality and environment, only in order to arrive at a knowledge of the data it contains, and especially of their significance in terms of present-day data.

Several more or less contemporary accounts of the coronation of Charlemagne, at Rome, in the year 800, are extant.—See Robert G. D. Laffan and Others, *Select Documents of European History* (3 vols., London, 1930), 1:6.

These accounts, however interpreted, have value chiefly as helps which enable us to answer the major question, What did this great ceremony mean? Further, what significance had it in the mind of Charlemagne, of the pope who crowned him, of the spectators who witnessed it, of the contemporary world which came to hear about it, of later generations which looked back to it? In fine, factual interpretation is the ultimate goal of all historical study and research. Obviously, in its attack on a document it summons to its aid verbal, psychological, and whatever other kinds of interpretation may be applicable.

¶ 329 FACTUAL INTERPRETATION ILLUSTRATED

Since hypothesis is of the nature of an assumed or conjectured interpretation, the examples of hypothesis given in ¶ 146, serve also to illustrate what is meant by factual interpretation. See also ¶ 433 ff.

Other illustrations.

(a) The rise of the modern capitalistic system has been variously explained as being caused by religious factors, Calvinism among them, but no single explanation holds the field decisively against the others.

George O'Brien, *An Essay on the Economic Effects of the Reformation* (London, 1923).
Richard H. Tawney, *Religion and the Rise of Capitalism* (New York, 1926).
James Brodrick, *The Economic Teachings of the Jesuits* (London, 1934).

Bernard W. Dempsey, "Religion and Capitalism," *HB*, 9 (1931): 25 ff.

(b) The only two contemporary sources for the life of St. Patrick are his *Confessions* and the *Epistle Against Coroticus*. There are interpretations of these documents in J. Eoin MacNeill, *St. Patrick, Apostle of Ireland* (New York, 1934); James F. Kenney, "St. Patrick and the Patrick Legend," *Thought*, 8 (1932): 5–34; 212–229.

The nature and significance of the Holy Roman Empire as an institution is analyzed in Francis X. Wernz, "Die Kaiseridee des Mittelalters," *Stimmen aus Maria-Laach*, 9 (1876): 198–212, 264–81.

Emil E. Michael, *Geschichte des deutschen Volkes seit dem dreizehnten Jahrhundert bis zum Ausgang des Mittelalters* (6 vols., Freiburg, 1897–1915), 1: 268 ff.

Émile Amann in Augustin Fliche and Victor Martin, eds., *Histoire de l'Église depuis les origines jusqu'à nos jours* (6 vols., Paris, 1935——), 6:160–65.

John B. Bury, *A History of the Later Roman Empire from Arcadius to Irene*, 2: 506–09.

(c) Three major interpretations of the Reign of Terror episode in the French Revolution: philosophical (Taine), political (Aulard), economic (Matthiez), are discussed in Greer, *The Incidence of the Terror during the French Revolution*.

All our institutions, instruments, laws, buildings, and writing derive from the Roman civilization of which we are still a department. —Hilaire Belloc, *A Short History of England* (New York, 1934), 21.

The English nation is of distinctly Teutonic or German origin. . . . From the Briton and the Roman of the fifth century we have received nothing. Our whole internal history testifies unmistakably to our inheritance of Teutonic institutions from the first immigrants.—William Stubbs, *Select Charters and Other Illustrations of English Constitutional History, from the Earliest Times to the Reign of Edward the First*, H. W. C. Davis, ed. (Oxford, 1929), 1.

Christopher Hollis, "Mr. Belloc's Interpretation of English History," *Dublin Review*, 197 (1935): 268–287.

What took place at Poitiers (1356) has been a stock matter of dispute between English and French historians.—A. H. Burne, "The Battle of Poitiers," *EHR*, 53 (1938): 28–52.

(d) The extant sources for a study of the route followed by Coronado in his expedition to Quivira, 1541, are brought together in George P. Winship, *The Coronado Expedition, 1540–1542* (U. S. Bureau of American Ethnology, Fourteenth Annual Report, 1892–1893, Washington, 1896), 329–637. On the bases of these sources as variously interpreted, Quivira, Coronado's objective, has been located in Kansas by Winship, Bandelier, Hodge, and others; in Nebraska by Michael A. Shine, "The Lost Province of Quivira," *CHR*, 2 (1916): 3–18; in Missouri by Louis Houch, *A History of Missouri* (3 vols., Chicago, 1908), 1: 119 ff; in Texas by David Donoghue, "The Route of the Coronado Expedition in Texas," Texas State Historical Association, Quarterly, 32 (1929): No. 3; and in "Coronado, Oñate and Quivira," MA, 17 (1936): 88-95; also in Texas by Carlos E. Castañeda, Our Catholic Heritage in Texas (5 vols., Austin, Tex., 1936-1942), 1: 82-108.

The location of San Miguel, Ayllon's settlement on the Atlantic Coast, 1526, has been placed by John G. Shea in Virginia, see Justin Winsor, ed., Narrative and Critical History in America, 2: 240; in South Carolina by Woodbury Lowery, Spanish Explorations Within the Present Limits of the United States, 1513-1561, 165 ff.; 447 ff.

Pineda's tarrying-place for forty days on the coast of the Gulf of Mexico, 1519, has been identified as Mobile Bay by Scaife, Bourne, Hamilton; as the mouth of the Rio Grande by Castañeda, Our Catholic Heritage in Texas, 1: 13-14.* The significance of the Spanish occupation of the Philippines is interpreted by Edward G. Bourne, in Emma H. Blair and James A. Robertson, eds. Philippine Islands, 1493-1898. (55 vols., Cleveland, 1903-1909), 1: 19-87.

(e) Different conclusions have been based on the same body of evidence regarding the place where De Soto crossed the Mississippi, 1541.—Dunbar Rowland, ed., A Symposium on the Place of Discovery of the Mississippi River by Hernando Soto (Jackson, Miss., 1927). See also the Final Report of the United States De Soto Expedition Commission, 234 ff.

Five contemporary sources exhaust the primary evidence available for the heroic exploit of Dollard and his youthful associates, who sacrificed their lives at the Long Sault, with the declared intention of thereby saving the Canadian colony from an Iroquois invasion (1660). The question whether the exploit was really effective in realizing this purpose is argued from opposite viewpoints by E. R. Adair and Gustave Lanctôt, in the Canadian Historical Review, 13 (1932): 121-46.

Why did France cede Louisiana to Spain in 1762? There are at least four answers to the question: France wished to get rid of it as a "white elephant"—a view now generally rejected. France wished to save it from England—a view also discredited. France wished to induce or bribe Spain by means of the cession to join her in accepting the terms offered by England at the close of the Seven Years War, 1763.—See Arthur S. Aiton, "The Diplomacy of the Louisiana Cession," AHR, 36 (1931): 701-720; E. Wilson Lyon, Louisiana in French Diplomacy, 1759-1804 (Norman, Okla., 1934). France wished by means of the cession to insure the permanence of her alliance with Spain through the "Family Compact."—See Richard R. Stenberg, "The Louisiana Cession and the Family Compact," Louisiana Historical Quarterly, 19 (1936): 204-209.

(f) In Dana C. Bailey, A New Approach to American History (Chi-

* As a matter of fact, we do not know, even approximately, the location of the river mentioned in the cédula of 1521.—J. Delanglez, El Rio del Espiritu Santo (New York, 1945), 13 f.—Ed.

cago, 1927), will be found an interpretative treatment of situations and events in American history.

In *The Quebec Act,* Charles H. Metzger analyzes the anti-Catholic feeling provoked in the American colonies by the passage of the Quebec Act (1774), which assured religious liberty to the Canadians.

Whether the Navigation Acts were a major factor alienating the American colonies from Great Britain is a question answered diversely by historians. —See Hugh E. Egerton, *Causes and Character of the American Revolution* (Oxford, 1923), 48–51; Lawrence A. Harper, "Mercantilism and the American Revolution," *Canadian Historical Review,* 23 (1942): 1–15.

Lawrence N. Kinard, "The Spanish Expedition Against Fort St. Joseph in 1781: A New Interpretation," *MVHR,* 19 (1932): 173–91. Four interpretations of an incident of the American Revolution in the West.

Warren H. Goodman, "The Origins of the War of 1812: A Survey of Changing Interpretations," *MVHR,* 28 (1941): 171–86.

Frederick J. Turner, "The Old West," *The Frontier in American History* (New York, 1920). Keen analysis and interpretation of the characteristics and spirit of the original "West," the region between the Atlantic seaboard and the Alleghenies, and the scene of the earliest stages of the Westward Movement.

"Lincoln's Election an Immediate Menace to Slavery in the States?" The pros and cons are discussed by Arthur C. Cole in *AHR,* 36 (1931), 740–67; by J. G. de Roulhac Hamilton, *ibid.,* 37 (1932), 700–712.

James G. Randall, *The Civil War and Reconstruction,* (Boston, 1937); idem, "The Civil War Restudied," *Journal of Southern History,* 6 (1940); 439–51; Carl R. Fish, *The American Civil War: An Interpretation,* ed. by William E. Smith (New York, 1937); Charles W. Ramsdell, "The Changing Interpretation of the Civil War," *Journal of Southern History,* 3 (1937): 3–27.

(g) Interpretations of historical characters are notoriously diverse. To Acton, voicing the traditional appreciation, Robespierre is "malignant and despotic." To Belloc he is an "honest fanatic, comparatively powerless, and consenting to the Terror only because he thought it popular." To Matthiez he is a "constructive, significant figure, not the evil genius of the French Revolution."

For an estimate of various appraisals made of the character of Queen Elizabeth of England, see Joseph B. Code, *Queen Elizabeth and the English Catholic Historians.*

Divergent appreciations of the character of Washington will be found in John C. Fitzpatrick, *George Washington Himself* (Indianapolis, 1933); in Bernard Knollenberg, *Washington and the Revolution: A Reappraisal* (New York, 1940).

On the interpretation of historical sources, see Maurice W. Keatinge, *Studies in the Teaching of History.* Though an elementary treatment, this is not without suggestions for the advanced student.

F. Letting the Facts Speak for Themselves

⟨ 330 A favorite contention among modern historians is that the facts, if correctly stated, will explain themselves. This abolishes (or is supposed to) the necessity of interpretation and comment on the part of the historian. In the French version, "The facts will speak for themselves," reads, "Je n'impose rien, je ne propose rien, j'expose." The principal is substantially sound, especially to the extent that it may be taken to be merely a way of stating the general ideal of objectivity in history. But as a practical direction to be followed in historical writing it has serious limitations.

(a) Clearly it is an abuse to be constantly pausing in the recital of facts to point out their implications, or to philosophize or speculate about them. Some historians have the annoying habit of repeatedly and unnecessarily interposing their personality between the facts and the reader, of saying what they think about the facts.

(b) On the other hand, how is it possible to write history without some measure of interpretation and comment? Causes must be indicated; to do so is to interpret. General truths must be interspersed among the individual facts if the facts are not to become a meaningless medley; to do this is to interpret. Often an individual fact reveals its significance only in the light of some psychological, economic, or social law; to connect the fact and the law is to interpret. Eliminate all statements of causation, all general truths, in a word, all interpretation, and how much history as record would be left? A mere annalistic narrative, nothing more. Over and over again the full implications of a group of facts fail to emerge clearly from the facts themselves as they are set down by the historian. This would be because of their restricted number, for space limitations do not allow the introduction of more. In this contingency nothing is left the historian but to supply for the omission out of his own presumed comprehensive grasp of the subject, by means of interpretation or comment; otherwise the reader would fail to grasp the full significance of the facts in question. Facts are not always self-explanatory, self-intelligible; they do not always "speak for themselves," or if they do, they do not always speak with the same voice, as can be seen for the divergent interpretations of the same fact or body of facts. Hence, unless one keeps in mind the limitations which regulate its practical applications, the principle of letting the facts speak for themselves is fallacious.

⟨ 331 Finding the course of history littered with the debris of exploded philosophies, the historians of the last century, unwilling to be forever duped, turned away (as they fondly hoped) from "interpretation" to the rigorous examination of the factual event just as it occurred. To establish the facts is always in order and is indeed the first duty of the historian; but to suppose that the facts, once established in all their fulness, will "speak for themselves" is an illusion. It was perhaps peculiarly the illusion of those historians of the last century who found some special magic in the word "scientific."—Carl L. Becker, "Every Man His Own Historian," AHR, 37 (1932): 232.

Facts when arranged justly interpret themselves. They tell the story. For this purpose a little fact is as important as what is called a big fact. The picture may be well-nigh finished, but it remains vague for want of one more fact.—Albert J. Beveridge, Abraham Lincoln, 1809–1858 (2 vols., Boston, 1928), 1: v.

The canon here enunciated by Beveridge did not go without challenge. It was pointed out that to arrange facts "justly," implies selection, interpretation, personal judgment as to what a "just" arrangement is. The facts left to themselves, have no arrangement at all, except a merely chronological arrangement. "The moment you say arrangement, you say interpretation." —Tracy E. Strevey in W. T. Hutchinson, ed., The Marcus W. Jernegan Essays in American Historiography, 384. See also, for a view similar to Beveridge's, Mark Sullivan, Our Times; The United States, 1900–1925 (6 vols., New York, 1926–1935), 6:70.

⁋ 332 Normal historical writing is, therefore, necessarily both factual and interpretative. Facts must be the substantial, the major element of the blend, but interpretation, though supplementary and accessory, is none the less indispensable. Therefore, the practical canon for guidance in history writing will be the following: give only the facts, avoid comment or interpretation, but only for as long as these can be omitted without prejudice to a really adequate and satisfactory presentation of the facts. This canon can often be obeyed for considerable portions of narrative. Just when the injection of comment may become expedient or necessary, is a problem which only the common sense of the writer can resolve.

Ray Stannard Baker's eight-volume work, *Woodrow Wilson: Life and Letters*, changes in the last two volumes from a largely interpretative treatment to a mere recital of facts. For comments on the effect produced by the change, see AHR, 46 (1941): 441–44.

Chapter Fifteen

EXTERNAL SYNTHESIS

A. The Problem of Selection . . . . Page 338
B. Organizing Data 341

⚆ 333 The major problem in the literary presentation of historical data is how to synthesize them, how to combine them to the best advantage in a unified and consistent whole. The data extracted from the sources, have been found to be certainly true, probably true, or false. Such as are selected for presentation, after such qualification as may be necessary, must find a place in the finished work according to the principle of unity, which is the first law of all literary composition.

The synthesis will be both external and internal. *External synthesis* is the grouping of data in order according to time, place, topic, or a combination of these categories; *internal synthesis* is the grouping of data according to inner relationships, chiefly those of cause, with a view to achieve, as far as practicable, a living picture of the past in which the true significance of it emerges from the retrospect.

A. The Problem of Selection

⚆ 334 The first problem before the historian when he sets about synthesizing the results of his research in written form, is that of selection. Obviously he cannot work all his notes, all his gathered material directly into the synthesis, except probably in those rare cases where thoroughgoing and exhaustive research has yielded only very meager results. The opinion has been expressed that on the average only about a tenth part of the notes and material assembled in a piece of historical research finds its way directly into the written product. This may have been nothing more than a surmise; but it lends point to the glaring contrast that generally obtains between the bulk of the material gathered and the bulk of the book.

⚆335 SELECTION OF MATERIAL NECESSARY

(a) *Limitations of space.* This factor generally determines the scale on which a work must be planned and written. Greatly detailed treatment of a topic may be impossible in the number of pages at an author's disposal. The experience that befell Macaulay in his *History of England* is often cited. He proposed to bring his narrative down to a period "within the memory of men still living," but miscalculated by a wide margin the space that would be required to complete the work according to this plan and in the minute detail with which he began it.

(b) *Artistic demands of the subject.* A narrative may well be the more effective, the fewer the details, provided these are aptly chosen. As a rule, skill in selecting out of a mass of available data the relatively few details packed with meaning, suggestion, picturesque or dramatic quality, is more important than multiplicity.

In selection the artist's instinct for adapting means to the end comes into play. The *ne quid nimis* of the ancients is the guiding principle. There is a standing temptation to crowd into a narrative irrelevant data of negative value, discovered in the sources. Regardless of their irrelevance to the final synthesis, they are still jealously retained by the writer who is loath to sacrifice direct use of material which it may have cost him much time and labor to acquire. Macaulay's notorious jibe at a book under review may be recalled: "Never was the truth of the axiom better illustrated, that the half is sometimes better than the whole." Incidentally, it may be remarked that Macaulay himself did not live up to his teaching. J. Cotter Morison deplored his "diffusiveness and excessive multiplicity of detail."

An exception to the principle here laid down is found in a type of history which aims at putting on record a mass of indifferently assorted data of varying value, which otherwise would not be easily accessible. A pertinent illustration is the Bancroft series of Pacific Coast histories. They are not likely to find many general readers, but they are indispensable for all workers in the fields they cover.

William A. Morris, "The Origin and Authorship of the Bancroft Pacific States Publications: A History of a History," *Oregon Historical Society Quarterly*, 4 (1903): 287 ff.

Michael Kraus, *A History of American History* (New York, 1937), 573–76.

J. Franklin Jameson, *History of Historical Writing in America* (Boston, 1891), 152–55.

❡ 336 THE VALUE OF MATERIAL NOT DIRECTLY UTILIZED

From the circumstance that a certain quota of his accumulated material will generally fail to find place in the synthesis, it does not follow that the researcher has nothing in this regard to show for his pains. Just as a certain amount of non-nutritious food, roughage, must be taken with food that is really nutritious, to promote assimilation, so a certain amount of non-usuable information will be gathered by the investigator in the process of acquiring usable information. Still more pertinent is the consideration that the bulk of the reading, study, research, which fails to come to the surface in the finished product, has gone to the creation of background, perspective, atmosphere, insight, that is, to broad, intelligent, and effective grasp of the subject treated. History may be written against a thin background of erudition and research, just as it may be written against a deep background of learning. Loyalty to his task, pride in his work, will save the conscientious worker from vain regrets that the toil of research does not always show itself openly on the printed page.—See Cyril C. Martindale, *Richard Philip Garrold: A Memoir* (London, 1921), 98.

❡ 337 PRINCIPLES OF SELECTION

An intelligent choice of facts must be made according to principles or standards of value. What appears significant and worthy of mention to one historian may not appear so to another. The significance of material for the historian's purpose depends on various factors, of which four are to be noted.

(a) *Purpose.* This may be: information, as in textbooks, monographs, scholarly works addressed to scholars, "historians' histories"; or entertainment, or a blend of information and entertainment, as in "popular" history, meant for the general reader; or inculcation of a theory, viewpoint, doctrine.

A designedly informative history will not hesitate to present topics, data, statistics, discussions of evidence on controverted points that would confuse or weary the general reader. On the other hand, a designedly popular history may, with an eye to vividness and human interest, embody data of picturesque or dramatic quality that might be out of place in scientific history. No principle of selection operates more decisively in the writing of history than the purpose the historian has in view. This is especially the case when he writes under the influence of a definite viewpoint or hypothesis. If, for instance, in discussing American Civil War beginnings, the historian approaches the subject with the conviction that the election of Abraham Lincoln made the war inevitable, he will very probably be guided by such conviction in his choice of data. Thucydides meant his history of the Peloponnesian War to be a species of repertoire of political lessons for future generations, while Livy wished to inspire the Romans of his day with pride in their past.

(b) *Available material.* Often a historian has had to restrict himself to certain facts, or to facts of a certain type, merely because his available sources offered him no other. This was particularly the case with historians of the pre-modern age. Their source material was liable to be jejune and limited in range. The use of diplomatic archives, inaugurated in the nineteenth century, opened up to contemporary investigators great masses of facts not previously available. In the United States the utilization of newspapers for sources, as instanced in McMaster, Rhodes, and Oberholzer, taps rich veins of data, political, social, and economic, from which the historian is free to make the selection that suits him best.

(c) *Preference for certain classes of facts.* Until relatively recent days, history was written largely from the military or from the political angle. Even today in histories of the general type politics in the broad sense probably outdistances any other single topic in allotment of space. But this is less the case in the United States than in England, where Freeman's creed that "history is past politics," still has a respectable following. How much politics, how much economics, how much sociology, are to go into a general history is a problem the author must settle for himself. In general, it is a problem ot proportion, to be solved by his sense of how far this or that class of facts fits in with the scope or purpose of his book. Where history of a specific type (political, social, economic or religious,) is intended, the problem of selection, as regards the particular class of facts to be stressed, solves itself.

(d) *Class of readers in view.* It makes a great difference whether a history is to be read by adults or young folk; it may also matter much whether it is addressed to people of this or of that country, this or that political or religious following. In all cases the intellectual caliber and development, sympathies, and prejudices of one's readers are to be reckoned with in the choice of facts. A child's history book neglects politics and economics, and is partial to stories of daring and adventure. A highschool text of ancient history, widely used, met with criticism on the ground that it gave excessive space to Roman constitutional development; the facts set forth in this connection were beyond the grasp of the average high school student. Even a narrative designed for the average adult reader must judiciously provide variety of facts, it it is to hold attention.

B. Organizing Data

¶ 338 GROUPING BY TIME

The most obvious arrangement of a body of historical facts is the chronological, for the facts of history follow one another in the order of time. Every kind of historical composition, no matter how planned, tends in some way to shape itself along chronological lines. Annals, chronicles, diaries, and similar types of record, set the facts down rigorously in the order in which they occurred, while any narrative of the topical sort must almost of necessity adopt a chronological scheme within the limits of the several topics. The more philosophical approach to history, such as stresses relations of cause and effect and resulting development, is also conditioned by factors of time-succession.

Albert H. Lybyer was able to demonstrate that the closing of the Oriental trade-routes at the close of the fifteenth century had nothing to do with starting contemporary interest in western maritime exploration, because the closing of the routes in question followed instead of preceded (according to the traditional view) the period of the exploration.—AHA, Report (1919), 371–88; EHR, 30 (1915): 577–88.

Democratic and representative forms of government cannot be the product of the Protestant Revolt, since, as Carlton H. Hayes points out, they were already in operation in Europe before the revolt took place.—CHR, 17 (1932): 416 f.

The claim made for Turner's frontier hypothesis, that it explains in substantial ways the origin of certain American democratic ideas and institutions, has been challenged on the ground that these ideas and institutions preceded rather than followed the Westward Movement.—Benjamin F. Wright, Jr., "American Democracy and the Frontier," Yale Review, 20 (1930): 349–65.

> Chronology reveals that in many of the policies that are considered reform the eastern states anticipated the western; the dates tell the story.
> —Marcus L. Hansen in D. R. Fox, ed., Sources of Culture in the Middle West, 105.

❮ 339 DATING EVENTS

Dates of known events are sometimes wanting in the documents. To supply them, methods are employed the general tenor of which is inferential reasoning from known dates and other evidence found in the sources. The specific method will vary for almost every individual case; it is scarcely practicable to formulate general rules of any value. Most critical histories furnish instances of missing dates supplied, in many cases, together with a statement of the reasoning or evidence used in arriving at the result.

Feder (Lehrbuch, 333) cites an illustration from Tacitus (Histories, I, 12, 18, 55; IV, 59), which concerns the revolt of the two Mayence legions against the Emperor Galba, January 1, A.D. 69. Roman couriers were immediately dispatched from Mayence to Rheims, headquarters of the governor of Belgic Gaul, and thence, carrying the latter's report, to Rome, which they reached before January 10. They covered the distance from Rheims to

Rome, 1,440 Roman miles (about 1,210 English miles) in fewer than nine days, having made, therefore, more than 160 miles a day. On what day had they reached Rheims? From the circumstance that Roman official couriers maintained a uniform speed on their journeys, and from the known distance between Rheims and Mayence (150 Roman miles), inference may be made that the couriers reached Rheims on January 2.

Date of the birth of Christ, in Fillion, *The Life of Christ*, 1:302. See also Peter Archer, *The Christian Calendar and the Gregorian Reform* (New York, 1941), 3.

When was Caesar born?—T. R. Holmes, *Caesar's Conquest of Gaul*, 556 f.; idem, "The Date of the Varian Disaster," *The Architect of the Roman Empire, 27 B.C.–A.D. 14* (2 vols., Oxford, 1931), 2:174–76.

Aubrey Gwynn, "The Date of St. Columban's Birth," *Studies*, 7 (1918): 274–484; 8 (1919): 59–68.

On the date of Columbus' birth, see J. B. Thatcher, *Christopher Columbus*, 1: 264–85.*

Date of signing of the Declaration of Independence, John H. Hazelton, *The Declaration of Independence, Its History* (New York, 1906); P. L. Ford, ed., *Autobiography of Thomas Jefferson*, 33; Edmund C. Burnett, *The Continental Congress* (New York, 1941).

❡ 340 GROUPING BY PLACE

Arrangement of historical data in groups according to geographical categories is common. Thus, a history of nineteenth-century Europe may distribute its contents into chapters or sections, each of these being assigned to a particular country. Moreover, the entire range of nineteenth-century history in a particular country, for example, in England, is progressively covered from beginning to end, and the same process repeated for each of the other members of the European family of nations. This pattern for the merely external synthesis of data, offers certain advantages. It enables one to see, by turning from section to section of the complete treatment, what was going on in various areas at the same time; further, it makes it possible to follow the course of events in a given area continuously and over a long stretch of time. But a rigidly geographical treatment of historical data may have serious drawbacks. Larger aspects of unity may have to be sacrificed in the process. Thus, to treat the modern democratic movement as it developed in one nation after another, may issue in failure to grasp the movement as a whole.

❡ 341 GROUPING BY TOPIC

In a topical arrangement the historical content is distributed under certain heads, categories, or leading considerations. Time and place as

---

* None of the dates mentioned in Thacher is correct. The Assereto document establishes that Columbus was born in 1451.—Ed.

principles in the ordering of material are made secondary. Various comprehensive or significant aspects of the subject as a whole are singled out for successive treatment, each aspect being disposed of *in toto* before the next is taken up. The main advantage resulting from topical grouping is that it affords a relatively complete and rounded view of one integrating phase after another of the general subject. Thus, a history of thirteenth-century France may assemble its facts under the five separate heads of political, economic, social, cultural, and religious life; or, in an alternative plan, under such topics as monarchy, nobility, clergy, peasants, universities, guilds. Thus, all data pertaining to the universities are brought together instead of being scattered among various chapters and sections of the book. On the other hand, topical grouping sometimes brings with it overlapping, repetition, and a distracting movement back and forth within the same chronological framework.

⟨ 342 Practically, especially where the subject ranges over a wide extent of time and place, all three principles of arrangement, namely, time, place, and topic, will come into play. In the conventional textbook of modern history the rise of the national European states is probably best treated as a distinct topic divided into sections according to countries, the facts for each section being marshalled chronologically.

In general, how best to order gathered material into a paper, monograph, or book is one of the most teasing problems that confront the writer of history. Any arrangement or grouping of parts adequate to his purpose will have to meet certain demands of clearness, unity, coherence, emphasis, logic, and comprehensiveness. Sometimes the nature and extent of the material at hand is the main factor determining the shape which the material shall have to take in the written work. Sometimes the writer's thesis, interpretation, or purpose, will suggest the proper distribution of the data. In any case, the importance of a well-planned and effective grouping of the contents of a history cannot be over-estimated.

⟨ 343 PLAN, OUTLINE

The necessity of some sort of plan or outline as a preparatory step in historical writing has been indicated in ⟨ 121 f. Two things are implied: the tentative character of the initial plan; and the subsequent modification of it to a greater or less extent. Modification will almost necessarily ensue as defects in the original plan reveal themselves during the process of composition, or as new material is discovered, or as the material under study is better understood. No distribution of one's material should be allowed to stand as definitive until it has been carefully checked for possible shortcomings and suitable remedies have been applied [¶ 338 f.].

The student can profit by careful perusal of the analytical table of contents often prefixed to histories of the scholarly kind. Thus, comparison of the various treatments of a given block of American or English history in standard works will reveal the great variety of arrangement of which virtually the same body of historical data is susceptible. Events of the Elizabethan period are ordered by Lingard and Green in a manner distinctive to each. McMaster, Rhodes, and Oberholzer show individuality in their respective marshalling of the facts of Reconstruction. Here, as in other phases of the history-writer's art, the author's ingenuity means much.

Chapter Sixteen

INTERNAL SYNTHESIS

A. The Synthesizing Faculty at Work . . . . . Page 346
B. Causation in History 350
C. Materialistic Determinism in History 353
D. Conditions and Means as Factors in History 357
E. Chance in History 359
F. Putting Oneself in The Past 362
G. The Philosophy of History 367

¶ 344 Merely to arrange a mass of facts in the order of time, of place, or of topic does not solve the entire problem of synthesis. However much the historian has to attend to such details in presenting the results of his research, these are only surface-arrangements. A more intimate and vital combination of data must be effected to make the synthesis complete. This inner combination consists essentially in binding together a series of facts on a basis of objective relationships, principally those of cause and effect. No single fact in history is completely isolated from other facts. Any single event owes its existence to other events which preceded it, and in turn, is followed by other events which owe their existence to it. Moreover, conditions, as distinct from causes, are at hand which make an event a possibility, and hence call for consideration. Thus, the thoroughgoing study of even a single historical fact carries one far afield, making it necessary to "look before and after" and to pursue research in many and divers directions.

For a suggested solution of a problem in historical synthesis, see Dixon R. Fox, "A Synthetic Principle in American Social History," AHR, 35 (1930): 256–266.

A. The Synthesizing Faculty at Work

¶ 345 CONNECTING FACTS

In the process of inner synthesis of his data, the historian either joins up recorded facts with other facts not directly recorded, such as come under the categories of cause, effect, condition, means; or he brings to light some hidden connection between the various facts of a given group. To make the matter simple, we consider here only causal relations, and we take this term in its broad sense, making it cover both efficient and final causes. The principle valid for the fixing of causal relations is also valid in substance for the fixing of other relations.

(a) We first take the case where to a given ascertained fact, another fact, the nature of which is not yet understood, is to be related as cause or effect. For example, we come upon the ruins of an old fort that was evidently destroyed by fire, and we set ourselves to discover the cause of the fire, whether lightning, accidental combustion, or bombardment. Investigation of the ruins may reveal definitely the cause of destruction; fragments of shell, let us suppose, are turned up, indicating bombardment. A concrete case of two facts related by cause and effect is thus established. On the other hand, searching investigation of the ruins may still leave their explanation very much in doubt. Often one has to be content to doubt; but it may happen that the study of the problem in the light of analogous cases may put one in the way, if not of a clear solution, at least of an explanation that has solid probability to recommend it.

(b) The search for immediate final causes, namely, for the motives that have inspired agents in historical events to act as they did, bristles with difficulty. When motives are avowed, and when there is no reason to suspect their sincerity, search for them will be unnecessary. More often one is reduced to the necessity of interpreting motives. This is a hazardous business, but frequently the historian cannot shirk it if the record of events is to be made complete. Motives can be elicited, with varying grades of assurance, from evidence of divers kinds: from the laws regulating normal human conduct; from the subject's character as revealed in various ways; from his behavior in analogous past situations. Every conclusion based on moral laws and on analogy will be the likelier, the more the subject conforms to the average human type; for the most part men choose the necessary or the useful or what is agreeable and easy. But if a person whose motivation we seek to explain rises above the average level in sentiments and ideals, his motives will reveal themselves as a rule only to those who can enter sympathetically into his outlook on life and its actual conduct.

(c) Another type of problem occurs when two or more facts are recorded and when it is sought to trace the causal relations that may exist between them. The problem grows in complexity the more numerous the effects to be correlated. In all such investigation of the causes of historical phenomena, various logical processes can be employed: hypothesis, analogy, analysis of effects, and the like. Numerous possibilities may have to be considered before finding the true causal nexus, if indeed it can be reached at all. In any case, the pursuit is not easy, as appears from the endless discussions that continue to this day over the cause or causes of such great historical phenomena as the fall of the Roman Empire, the Protestant Revolt, the French Revolution, the first World War.

After all, causes, while realities, are metaphysical realities, and as such are not apprehended with the distinctness with which we apprehend the realities under sight and hearing. Knowledge of them is the fruit of logical processes, and the evidence yielded is not always of a nature to issue in certainty. Yet any serious conception of history postulates an inquiry into causes. Merely to set down events one after another, with no attempt to show them as held together by the binding power of causation, is not even to cross the threshold of history. A human instinct urges us to know not only what things happen but why they happen. Hence, it becomes a practical necessity for the historian to know how to investigate causes in a manner consistent with logic and the objective evidence of the facts. "History should be a study of causes and effects, of distant as well as proximate causes, of the large, slow, and permanent evolution of things."—William E. H. Lecky, *Historical and Political Essays* (London and New York, 1910), 4.

Various possible explanations of a historical effect will generally have to be taken into account. Here, precisely, is where investigators often go astray in their conclusions, by discounting or even entirely overlooking possible explanations or causes, whether through prejudice or inadequate research.

It is interesting to note that with advancing research new and unsuspected causes of an important movement in history come into view, while previously accepted causes of the same movement are discounted. Max Weber, Richard Tawney, and others, see in certain theological systems, especially Calvinism, an influence on the rise of modern capitalism.— Richard H. Tawney, *Religion and the Rise of Capitalism*; George O'Brien, *An Essay on the Economic Effects of the Reformation*, chap. 2.

It is now recognized that economic factors had much more to do with the origins of the Protestant Revolt than was formerly supposed.— Carlton H. Hayes, "Significance of the Reformation in the Light of Contemporary Scholarship," CHR, 17 (1932): 415–16.

Van Tyne points out the bearing of religious prejudice on the beginnings of the American Revolution, a previously neglected factor in the study of the problem.—Claude H. Van Tyne, "Influence of the Clergy and of Religious and Sectarian Forces on the American Revolution," AHR, 19 (1924): 44–64.

In "The Oregon Pioneers and the Boundary," AHR, 19 (1924): 682 ff., Frederick Merk eliminates the presence of American settlers as a factor in the acquisition of the Oregon country by the United States, by stressing the circumstance that the territory which they occupied (Willamette Valley) was never in dispute between Great Britain and the United States.

(d) The case may occur where a historical effect stands in sharp contrast to the cause that brought it about. As a matter of fact, the contrast is only apparent, not real. Thus, ruthless repression of popular liberties has generally produced effects contrary to those intended; it has led to counter-violence and revolution. But the repression was none the less the true cause, at least partial, of the revolution.

(e) So-called negative facts may help the historian to an interpretation of causes. A country at a critical turn of its affairs may need a great statesman or ruler to meet the situation. With disastrous consequences, none appears. That Alexander the Great had no son capable of succeeding him, was a circumstance which visibly affected subsequent events. Lincoln's disappearance on the eve of Reconstruction had much to do with the radical turn which that movement took.

(f) As a rule, no great historical crisis or event is explicable by a single cause. A combination of causes has generally to be invoked to explain the phenomenon. Discussion of the causes of the first World War has been endless. What historians appear to agree upon, is that at least no single cause is adequate to explain the catastrophe. Facile explanations of it as the work of some single agency or influence, find no favor with the critical-minded. On the other hand, it may be argued that the whole course of European history for decades was determined by the personality of a single man, Napoleon.

> The historian has abandoned the single hypothesis for the multiple hypothesis. He creates a whole family of possible explanations of a given problem, and thus avoids the warping influence of partiality for a single theory.—Frederick J. Turner, *The Frontier in American History*, 331.
>
> In a discussion of the causes of the first World War at the Urbana meeting of the American Historical Association, in 1934, it was agreed that no single cause could be invoked to explain the epochal conflict; resort must be made to a multiplicity of causes. So it is with the frontier hypothesis. It explains much in American history; it does not explain everything, and this in the very nature of things, which postulates a plurality of causes for so intricate, so many-sided a phenomenon as the rise and growth of the American nation.—Gilbert J. Garraghan, "Noneconomic Factors in the Frontier Movement," MA, 23 (1941): 263.

B. Causation in History

❡ 346 THE CONCEPT OF CAUSE

A particular science—physics or history—connects things with their *proximate* causes; general science, or philosophy, connects things with their *ultimate* causes. This is a useful distinction, as pointing the way out of difficulties arising when discussion turns on the relations between history and philosophy. The concept of cause is not easy to analyze. In general, a cause is "anything that influences another thing either to exist at all or to exist in a particular way." (J. F. X. Pyne, *The Mind*, 20); or it is "that which makes a thing to be what it is" (Joyce, *Logic*, 220). The particular type of cause which confronts us in historical phenomena is mostly the *efficient* cause, the agent by whose activity the effect is produced. A *condition* is something helpful to the action of a cause: it does not itself "make a thing to be what it is."

For expositions of the doctrine of causality, see John Rickaby, *General Metaphysics* (London, 1905), 298 ff.; John F. McCormick, *Metaphysics* (Chicago, 1928), chap. 9; Patrick Coffey, *Ontology or the Theory of Being: An Introduction to General Metaphysics* (London, 1929), chaps. 13–15.

That the events of history are joined together by relations of cause and effect is a principle which the normal reason accepts without demur. Theoretically, one can attempt to question or deny the principle; practically, one has to proceed on the assumption that it is true. The tendency to seek out the why of things is irresistible. Historians, ancient and modern, as a matter of course, have accepted the notion of causality at its face value. "What does it profit the reader," exclaims Polybius (Bk. 11, chap. 19), "to wade through wars and battles and sieges of towns, and enslavements of peoples, if he is not to penetrate to the knowledge of the causes which have made one party succeed and the other fail in their respective situations?"—Toynbee, *Greek Historical Thought*, 170.

In our own day historians write books on "The Economic Causes of the Reformation," and "The Causes of the American Revolution."

❡ 347 CAUSALITY OR SEQUENCE?

Attempts to replace the concept of cause and effect by that of mere sequence are necessarily futile. Event two, it is contended, merely follows event one; that is all we can say. But this only removes the difficulty a step backward. If the traditional notion of causality brings or seems to bring metaphysical difficulties in its train, so does the notion of mere sequence.

It cannot but be admitted that the establishment of a sequence of events cannot satisfy the human mind, for the simple reason that the next question intrudes itself upon our notice, "Why this particular sequence and no other?" and the moment such a question is asked, immediately all the difficulties involved in the discussion of the causes of things become accentuated.—Alphonse M. Schwitalla, Jesuit Educational Association, Central States, *Proceedings* (1930), 92.

⁅ 348 It is to be noted that when the idea of a merely sequential order of events is assumed, there is no ground left for the rational forecasting of events on the principle that "similar causes produce similar effects." It is the doctrine of causation that gives history its value as a discipline and a guide. It is easy to lose one's way in a fog of speculation; but in history, as in everyday life, one gets nowhere without abiding by the principle of causal activity.

In any case [the law of causality] is a hypothesis which we are obliged to assume if the world is not to become a chaos and science to commit suicide. For as the function of science is to explain phenomena and explanation means the assignment of causes, it is clear that if a phenomenon containing lawless elements may occur, scientific research is impossible.—H. W. V. Temperley, ed., *Selected Essays of John B. Bury*, 60.

I suspect that all students are at the task of reducing history to order, dispelling the ignorance that makes events appear to be chaotic and without reason or to have been put together with what seems a false logic. We cannot imagine causeless happenings and we look everywhere for the orderly continuity of phenomena.—Regina F. Aragon, "History and the Fall of Rome," *Pacific Historical Review*, (1932): 153.

See also *The Month*, 150 (1932): 216–24, on the speculative difficulties raised against the principle of causality.

The Greek historians had the healthy mind's acquiescence in the principle of causality. Thucydides, and in a special way, Polybius, stressed causes; the first, those of the Peloponnesian War; the second, those which led to Roman domination of the Mediterranean region. Polybius philosophizes on causation as the "essence of history."

For an instance of the nebulosities of thought into which writers drift when they break with the common-sense notion of causality, see *Encyclopaedia of the Social Sciences*, 7:361.

⁅ 349 The following examples of analytic treatment of cause and effect in history are from Feder, *Lehrbuch*, 2 ed., 280.

The *proximate cause* of the victory of Augustus in the battle of Actium (31 B.C.) and the resulting establishment of the Roman Empire was the military skill of Agrippa, coupled with exhaustion of the enemy. *Remote causes* were the political dissensions and eventual prostration of the opposing parties, as also the ambition, shrewdness, and efficiency of Augustus, who was clever enough to turn circumstances to his own account. But there were still deeper causes for the rise of Roman Caesarism. The whole political and social life of the Romans had long been gravitating towards monarchy, an issue resulting especially from the increasing expansion of the commonwealth by force, from the gradual dissolution of internal order, and from the grasping power of the Senate. Moreover, the institution of monarchy was in close accord with the Roman character, which inclined to a government by force and pursued this inclination with a sense of the practical, with iron-like consistency, with firm confidence in ultimate success. But in God's designs, on its historical side antiquity was to terminate in the institution of the Empire and its worldwide domination. Rome was to take over all the acquisitions and developments of the past and pass them on to the modern age. The Roman commonwealth was to be a basis for the development of the Church and the Christian commonwealth.

Gibbon's five causes of the rise and spread of Christianity are discussed in John H. Newman, *Essay in Aid of a Grammar of Assent* (London, 1881), 457 ff.

¶ 350 The *proximate external cause* of the French Revolution was the meeting at Versailles, 1789, of the States-General, which had not been called into session since 1614. On August 4, the assembly, as the representative of the "sovereign people," decreed the renunciation of all privileges, thereby actually setting the Revolution in motion. The *proximate internal cause* of the upheaval was widespread resentment against existing institutions, spiritual and temporal, with their many abuses. *Remote causes* must be sought deeper down. They consisted in the political, intellectual, and moral factors which had brought about the prevailing conditions. Such were the growth of absolutism in government, luxuriousness, and other excesses at court and in the households of the nobility; general financial distress, the considerable immunities enjoyed by the clerical order, the subversive effects on religion and morality of the so-called Enlightenment (*Aufklärung,* philosophism); the vague, unimpeded drift of the common people toward freedom. God's design in permitting the Revolution was the purging of human society and the reanimation of the Church, as became manifest in the decades subsequent to the great upheaval.

¶ 351 SECONDARY CAUSES

The Christian philosophy of history, according to standard expositions of it from the time of St. Augustine, finds the key to history in the joint action of Providence and free human agency, issuing in the realization of certain divinely appointed ends [¶ 378]. This "providential view of history," while stressing the influence of a primary, supernatural cause, by no means excludes the influence of secondary or natural causes. Perhaps most of the disfavor with which secular-minded historians generally regard the "providential view of history," is a product of gross misunderstanding of it. The proper attitude of the Christian investigator in face of history and its innumerable problems, is expressed in the words of the Belgian scholar, Canon Cauchie: "Tout fidèle à sa foi admet le gouvernment du monde par la Providence, ce qui ne l'empêche pas d'étudier et de rechercher scientifiquement l'action des causes secondes."

C. Materialistic Determinism in History

❡ 352 MAN AND NATURE
The secondary causes which operate in history can be assigned to the two main categories of man and nature. Which of the two categories has exerted the greater influence? Determinist historians, such as Buckle, Taine, and Marx, answer that nature has. Denying the freedom of the human will, Henry Thomas Buckle took climate, food, and physical environment to be the decisive factors in history. Buckle attempted to explain what he considered to be the superstitions of Spain, Portugal, and Italy, by the earthquakes and volcanic eruptions of those countries. Briefly, in Buckle's view, fixed, immutable laws, and not free will govern the action of men, and therefore determine history.

Hippolyte Taine declares that Race, Surroundings (Milieu), Epoch (the Moment) are the three agencies which explain historical development in all its phases.—*History of English Literature*, trans. by H. Van Loon (4 vols., Philadelphia, 1908), 1:17.

Karl Marx (*Das Kapital*, and other writings) referred all historical results to social-economic causes, chiefly to the effort of the masses to obtain a livelihood, an effort developing into a class war between rich and poor, the haves and the have-nots. This is the economic or materialistic interpretation of history.

On Buckle, see Lord Acton, *Historical Essays and Studies*, chap. 10 f.; Charles K. Adams, *A Manual of Historical Literature* (New York, 1888), 4–6; 57; *Encyclopaedia Britannica* (11th ed.), 4:32.

On the Marxian philosophy of history, see Victor Cathrein, *Socialism: Its Theoretical Basis and Practical Application* (New York, 1904), 120–24.

Arthur J. Penty, *A Guildsman's Interpretation of History* (London, 1923), preface.

Martin C. D'Arcy, "The Exegetical Method of History in Modern Times," Edward Eyre, ed., *European Civilization*, 6: 1050 ff.; idem, *Christian Morals* (London, 1938).

Charles J. McFadden, *The Philosophy of Communism* (New York, 1939).

❡ 353 Marx's interpretation of history, called specifically "historical materialism," is indefensible on philosophical grounds, because it excludes free will and non-material realities generally from any share in history-making. Mandell M. Bober's analysis issues in the verdict: "Marx's theory is impotent to account for historical processes and the reason is that it fails to ascribe sufficient weight to the non-economic processes in history.—*Karl Marx's Interpretation of History* (Cambridge, Mass., 1927), 290.

Twenty-five years before the appearance of Bober's book, Edwin R. A. Seligman, Columbia University economist, had also shown the theory to be inadequate by reason of its elimination of non-economic factors. "As a philosophical system of universal validity, the theory of 'historical materialism,' can no longer be successfully defended."—*Economic Interpretation of History* (New York, 1902), 159.

Yet a qualified economic interpretation of history is inevitable. No one denies that physical and economic causes and conditions play a significant, sometimes a tremendous part in history. The mistake is to make them play the whole part.

¶ 354 PHYSICAL ENVIRONMENT

As a historical cause or condition, environment includes three groups of factors, all in the category of physical geography: topography; climate; potential wealth in soil, minerals, farms, flora. [¶ 79].

(a) The influence of geographical conditions on history has long been recognized. The failure of ancient Greece to achieve political unity was due largely to the physical configuration of the country, for the mountain ranges and valleys which intersect it, made communication between its parts difficult. The mid-Mediterranean position of Italy was favorable to empire. England's insular situation contributed to her centuries of peaceful, uninterrupted development; also, it turned her to seaborne commerce on a large scale, when it became necessary to import foodstuffs to support the population. Belgium's low-lying terrain made her inevitably a highway of armies and "the cockpit of Europe."

(b) Most of the large cities of the United States are located on the sea or other bodies of water. Chicago's economic greatness was originally determined by its location at the "Portage," a narrow ribbon of land connecting the two great water systems of the Mississippi and the St. Lawrence. The direction taken by the successive waves of emigration in the Westward Movement of the frontier era was fixed in the main by the relatively easy routes of travel offered by certain valleys and watercourses.

(c) Most of the great civilizations of history have arisen in the temperate zone. Excessive heat or cold reacts unfavorably on human exertion. Students and writers find that certain atmospheric conditions are more favorable than others to intellectual effort. The clear skies of Italy have been thought to account in part for the artistic predilections of its people. Yet the influence of weather and climate in history may be exaggerated and often is. Attempts to explain the intellectual vigor of the ancient Greeks by the plentiful sunshine, clear skies, and other climatic assets of their country, or to account for the fall of the Roman Empire by radical changes of climate, are of doubtful validity.

(d) Certain human occupations—agriculture, mining, hunting, furtrading—owe their development in the main to the opportunities at hand for pursuing them with success. The vast fertile prairies of the United States and Russia make wheat-raising a basic occupation in those countries. The wealth of fur-bearing animals in the forests of New France drew a considerable part of the population to traffic in furs and peltries. It was the abundance of free land of great agricultural possibilities to be found in the West that led the early American pioneers to move in that direction, just as it was a similar attraction that drew the early Germans to push their settlements east and beyond the Elbe. In both cases abundance of free land was the factor setting in motion "the advancing frontier." Briefly, environmental factors such as those mentioned can have their influence in shaping the course of history. Nevertheless, such influence is often subject to control or check by that incalculable element in life, the free will of man.

¶ 355 The dream of Buckle and other nineteenth-century determinists that history can be fitted into the mould of the exact sciences has not been realized.

> The first hopes of a science of society have been abandoned. The great mechanistic concept of man, measurable, responsive, predictable, now impresses us as a deceptive analogy borrowed in vain from the physical sciences.—Carl Sauer, "Historical Geography," in J. F. Willard and C. B. Goodykoontz, eds., The Trans-Mississippi West, 267.

Economically-minded though he be, Charles A. Beard expresses a similar judgment. He recalls the attempts made in the past to erect history into an exact science, only to comment on their plain futility. —"Written History as an Act of Faith," AHR, 31 (1934): 222-24.

¶ 356 No great history has ever been written on a platform of downright economic determinism. Reputable historians, no matter of what period, are at one in ascribing a large share of influence in history to human and other non-economic factors. Often, in fact, it is precisely here that they are deficient, for their disregard of physical and economic influences results in superficial, even in faulty interpretation.

Indirectly, the economic interpretation has done historiography a service by calling attention to certain forces at work in social development, which the older historians all too readily overlooked. Thus, it is clear that one must of necessity accept a modified version of the economic interpretation of history: that is, a version which gives due recognition to the action of material causes, but at the same time finds room for the play of Providence and free human agency, with the far-reaching historical results consequent thereon.

As to Carlyle's "great man theory" of history, it overstresses the human factor and ignores politics and economics. But it has this to its credit, that it reckons with the force which has operated more visibly and palpably than any other natural force in causing the stream of history to run in the definite and recognizable channels that we know.

¶ 357 Recent attempts to write history on a more or less economic basis include Lewis B. Namier, *The Structure of Politics at the Accession of George III* (London, 1929), which undertakes to throw new light on the political life of the period by investigating the financial standing of members of parliament (1761), as revealed in fiscal papers.

A similar line of investigation had already been followed by Charles A. Beard in his *Economic Interpretation of the Constitution* (New York, 1913), which aims to show from the financial status of the members of the Constitutional Convention, as made known by treasury records, that the Constitution was framed mainly in the interests of the monied and propertied classes. The same author adopts an analogous viewpoint in his *Economic Interpretation of Jeffersonian Democracy* (New York, 1915). His emphasis on economic factors and neglect of others has not escaped criticism.

(a) Turner's hypothesis of the "advancing frontier" has been called "economic" or "geographic-economic," though its author and most of his school have avoided describing it as such.—Gilbert J. Garraghan, "The Materialistic Interpretation of History," *Thought*, 14 (1929): 95–112; "Non-Economic Factors in the Frontier Movement," *MA*, 23 (1941): 263–71.

While stressing a geographic-economic factor (free land in the West), the Turner hypothesis does not really exclude non-economic factors, such as individual initiative and enterprise, and therefore may not be correctly described as materialistic; but it sometimes has the appearance of being materialistic through failure of its proponents to give due place to the operation of non-economic factors. According to Arthur M. Schlesinger, "advocates of the theory of economic determinism do not usually deny the existence of geographic, moral, religious and other forces in history nor the contribution made by great men"; but they maintain that "the ideas and ethical codes of any age are influenced, and in the long run controlled, by this economic background," and, further, that great men can "influence history only when society is ripe for them."—*New Viewpoints in American History*, 69 f.

(b) This last contention has its measure of truth; but the fact remains that great men, by sheer force of personality, a non-material entity, can influence the society of their day as much as, perhaps even more than they are influenced by it, and can and do on occasion act in flat contradiction to what their social environment would suggest. As to ethical and religious ideas, these often operate in history without relation to or dependence on economic conditions. The teaching of Christ in its character of divine revelation cannot in any manner be considered as having been "controlled" by economic conditions. The teaching of Francis of Assisi sprang from purely spiritual sources; economics had nothing to do with determining it in origin or content, and by no manner of means succeeded in "controlling" it.

D. Conditions and Means as Factors in History

¶ 358 CONDITIONS

Conditions (or occasions) as such have no causal efficacy; but they are necessary to prepare the ground, so to speak, for causes to act.

> The incidents of John's career are the occasions, not the causes, of the great national movement which laid the foundation of English liberties."—William S. McKechnie, *Magna Carta; A Commentary on the Great Charter of King John* (Glasgow, 1905), 3.

A circumstance making the American Revolution likely, if not inevitable, was the great distance separating the colonies from the mother country; but this circumstance was a condition only, not a cause of the Revolution. The shot fired at Sarajevo, June, 1914, marked the beginning of the first World War; but it was an occasion only, hardly a cause, certainly not a major one, of the great conflict.

For a discussion of the difference between an occasion and a true cause, see Polybius as cited in Toynbee, *Greek Historical Thought*, 170–72. See also on "condition and occasion," Bakewell R. Morrison and Stephen J. Rueve, *Think and Live* (Milwaukee, 1937), 53–63.

(a) The fact is that every historical event is dependent on a series of conditions in nature—physical or moral—which in a manner impress their character upon it. Any single event has conditions peculiar to itself, such as grow out of its own special concomitants of time, place, and other circumstances. But, apart from this aspect of the case, every fact in history presents itself against the background of a general condition, which, under limitations of time and place, comprises, on the one hand, physical surroundings, and on the other, the mental and moral life of the day. This general condition we call *environment*, which has therefore its physical as well as intellectual and moral aspects [¶ 354].

Every age has its specific cultural characteristics and every individual belonging to the age is exposed to their influence. The entire complex of his thoughts, feelings, volitions is affected by current opinion and tendencies, just as vision is affected by the various degrees and qualities of light in which it operates. The cultural conditions to which a man is subject, embrace everything that affects him in any manner whatever, from the cradle to the grave: domestic circumstances, family connections, home and school education, agencies of religious, moral, mental training; station and activities in a well-defined social circle; acquaintanceship and intercourse at home and abroad. The compelling fact has found expression in various formulas: "Everyone is a child of his age"; "Everyone feels the influence of his environment, his *milieu*" (Taine). What holds for the individual holds correspondingly for the masses, for the people as a unit; they also are constantly reacting to the influence of time and environment (*Zeitgeist*). The result of it all is that the facts of history are understood in the full range of their significance only when we have grasped the conditions in which they found their setting, and when we have fixed the relations between the conditions and the facts.

¶ 359 Time-conditions have affected and continue to affect human activity in various significant ways. Thus, the phases of the moon have played an important role in the liturgical life of peoples. The seasons help to determine the layout of dwelling houses, modes of clothing, choice of food, methods of travel, starting of wars. Nighttime favors thievery and crime. Economic facts are dependent in numerous ways on physical conditions, such as fertility of soil, size of crops, weather, and the like; so also they can be dependent on such conditions as peace, unrest, opportunities for labor and trade, spread of popular education. The precise intellectual level reached in a particular age is a factor which reacts necessarily on the historian's art. In time of uncritical mentality and crude investigation, as in many periods of antiquity and in the early Middle Ages, historiography deteriorates. Even in times of riper cultural development as a result of one-sided intellectual endeavor and lack of critical apparatus, it is possible for historical research to stand on a low level, as was the case, for example, in the later Middle Ages. During this period, it is true, theology, philosophy, jurisprudence, and the physical sciences were cultivated with ardor; but, at the same time, nearly all prerequisites for the growth of historical science were wanting, such as historical-mindedness, critical sense, facilities for pursuing investigation on the spot, archives, adequate libraries. Modern historiography has also had its reactions to intellectual environment. Historians of the age of humanism shared in the current exaggerated cult of antiquity. Those of the French Revolution went with the day in enthusiasm for personal liberty; those of the romantic school reflected the growing trend towards the artistic.——Feder, *Lehrbuch*, 304, 313.

¶ 360 MEANS

The concept of *means* or *instrument* is distinct from the concepts of cause and condition; yet, a means may be a true cause under another name. Hence, means and *instrumental cause* are, in general, convertible terms. The means or instrumental cause of a murder is the weapon in the murderer's hand. To grasp, then, a historical fact in all its implications, we must know the means by which it came about. Such means may be partly physical, partly moral. To estimate their effectiveness, investigation must be made of the relations they bear to the result they were meant to produce, as well as to the result they actually produced. Such investigation will show, in the case of failure, that there was no proportion between the means and the result intended, and in the case of success, that such proportion obtained. Victory in battle normally occurs when the victorious army is adequately equipped and is led by competent commanders. The rough violence of an excited mob is repressed only by ruthless counter-violence or by the influence of a personality who commands a high degree of moral authority. In the Middle Ages epidemics of disease were particularly disastrous, because adequate means of fighting them were unknown. Walter P. Webb [₵ 146-e] has offered the hypothesis that the new "technique of settlement" practised in the frontier period of the American West, was dependent for its success on such means or instrumental causes as barbed-wire, the six-shooter, windmills, and the like.

E. Chance in History

₵ 361 THE MEANING OF CHANCE

Chance is sometimes spoken of loosely as though it were a species of cause, a reason why something happens. Chance cannot be the cause of anything.

> We may say that true phenomena are conjoined by chance . . . meaning that they are in no way related by causation. . . . Facts conjoined by chance are separately the effects of causes, and therefore of laws; but of different causes and of facts not connected by any law.—John Stuart Mill cited in Joyce, *Logic*, 370.

When I unexpectedly meet an old friend in the street, I call the experience a "chance meeting." His presence at that precise time and place is an effect closing a series of causes, just as my presence at the same time and place is an effect closing an independent series of causes. The coming together of the two effects thus produced is called coincidence, conjuncture, chance. Chance or coincidence is therefore a real fact in human experience; but there is no causal virtue in it whatsoever. The two effects, each terminating its own separate series of antecedent causes, are in no way connected with one another by any relation of causality. When, therefore, one chooses to say that a certain event has happened by chance, the meaning to be conveyed should be that it involved a coincidence or conjuncture of effects in the sense just explained, though it was not itself without an adequate cause. Nothing happens without a cause. In a theistic world-view, everything, apart from moral evil, is to be referred ultimately to a First Cause. To speak strictly, there is nothing accidental in history. Everything in last analysis is either caused or at least permitted by God.—Joyce, *Logic*, 369–71; Coffey, *Science of Logic*, 2:268–72.

But the coincidence itself, the conjuncture of the terms of two or more independent series of causes, may be planned and actually brought about by an intelligent agent. Two servants, neither aware of the other's commission, may be dispatched by their common master to the same destination. Their meeting is mutually a surprise. As a matter of fact, it was an effect deliberately designed and brought about by the master. Similarly, coincidences, whether in private experience or on the larger stage of history, may be prearranged by Providence.

The English logician Baines remarked that only the superstitious would see any connection between the death of Oliver Cromwell and the furious storm raging at the moment over London. "Each event," he wrote, "rose out of its own independent series of causes . . . they concurred in time and that is all that should be said concerning them." The objection is inadmissible, since it implicitly denies the existence of a First Cause, which controls for its own purposes the operations of all secondary and finite causes.—Joyce, *Logic*, 37.

₡ 362 CONTINGENCY

The Cambridge historian, John B. Bury, attempted to erect chance or "contingency," as he preferred to call it, into a sort of fundamental law of history.—H. W. V. Temperley, ed., "Cleopatra's Nose," in *Selected Essays of John B. Bury*.

Every reader of history comes to realize how the most significant events sometimes seem to hinge on very trivial circumstances. The principle finds classic utterance in Pascal's saying that the shape of Cleopatra's nose determined all subsequent history, the reference being to Mark Antony's surrender, with such far-reaching results, to the charms of the Egyptian queen. In like fashion it has pleased Hilaire Belloc to trace the English Reformation back to Ann Boleyn's bewitching eyes and their baleful influence on an amorous king.

(a) Bury's definition of contingency, "the valuable collision of two or more independent chains of causes," is acceptable, unless one objects to the term "valuable" as having an implication not realized in every type of coincidence. It is such collisions or conjunctures, so Bury urges, which explain the major phenomena of history. Thus, if there is any cause accounting for the fall of the Roman Empire, it is the fact that "the German barbarians peacefully penetrated it," and finally occupied so many posts in the army that they rendered discipline impossible, with a consequent decline of the military spirit needed for imperial defense. But this situation alone need not necessarily have brought about collapse. It was a "complex of coincidences that proved decisive." Such coincidences or contingencies were: the Visigothic invasion, "a historical surprise"; Valens, "an incompetent Prince," was ruling at the time; Theodosius died prematurely—had he lived longer he might have averted the blunder of settling the Visigoths as a unit within the empire. Such circumstances had in them an element of chance. In view of the ordinary causes then shaping Roman affairs, they might easily not have happened, in which case subsequent history would have run off into vastly different channels.

❡ 363 Human history is full of accidents baffling to theory as well as to calculation. By the merest accident Napoleon becomes a French citizen. It seems that he had at one time thought of enlisting in the British navy. Had he been shot on the bridge of Lodi, or assassinated by Georges Cadoudal, both of which events were perfectly possible, the whole current of history would have changed. . . . Napoleon, it is true, would not have been what he was or have done what he did without predisposing forces. But the predisposing forces would not have produced the events without Napoleon, whose appearance on the scene, as it could not possibly have been foretold, was, if anything is, a chance. Such instances might be multiplied without number, and they are apparently fatal to the conception and verification of any scientific law.— Goldwin Smith, "The Treatment of History," AHA, Report (1904), 69.

❡ 364 Chance or contingency, rightly understood, sometimes plays a decisive part in historical development. The danger is in exaggerating its importance. Bury's viewpoint is suggestive, and within limits is correct, but two important considerations must control it. First, to repeat what is basic in this whole matter, contingency of itself is not a cause. Genuine causes at work, whether political, social, religious, or economic, must be allowed their respective influence, as far as determinable, in producing effects. One holding the theory of "climatic pulsations" to explain the breakdown of the Roman Empire, would scarcely allow that the contingencies listed by Bury had anything appreciable to do with the result. Secondly, theism posits a Divine Providence over the world, which regulates coincidences or contingencies and uses them to compass its own designs. Bury's rationalist outlook is without this necessary check on his tendency to overstate the influence of contingency as a factor in human affairs. His doctrine of historical contingencies is analyzed in *History*, 19 (1934): 106 ff.

> There is no human power that does not minister in spite of itself to other designs than its own. God only knows how to make everything subject to His will; and therefore everything is surprising if one considers only particular causes. . . . Let us talk no more of chance or of fortune or let us talk of them only as of a name with which we cover our ignorance. What is chance in regard to our uncertain counsels is a concerted design in a higher counsel, that is, in that eternal counsel which includes all causes and effects in one and the same order of things. Thus, everything concurs to the same end; and it is for want of understanding the whole that we find chance or irregularity in particular instances."—Jacques-Bénigne Bossuet, *Discourse on Universal History* (London, 1810), 560 f.

F. Putting Oneself in The Past

⟪ 365 There can be no vital, intimate synthesizing of historical data without projection of oneself into the past. This implies trying to share the impressions which events of other days made upon the people contemporary with them; and judging people of the past by the standards of their own day.

To react to past events in the same way that contemporaries reacted to them demands insight into their thoughts, emotions, viewpoints, likes, dislikes, prejudices; it also postulates intimate understanding of the events themselves in their full range of content and color. Both kinds of knowledge are difficult to obtain; but only to the degree that the historian approximates to them does he recapture the past and build up an animated picture of it in his own mind.

> (a) Nothing is more difficult than to realize existence in a bygone era. The perspective which years, as they roll by, give to past ages emphasizes certain salient points and leaves the background vague and it is only by saturating the mind in contemporary literature, diaries, and letters, that an idea can be formed of the ordinary life during a past period. But even then it is difficult to convey to a reader an impression of a time in which one has not lived; it is more—it is almost impossible.
> —Henry M. Stephens, *A History of the French Revolution* (2 vols., London and New York, 1902), 2:361.

> (b) Faithfulness to the truth of history involves far more than research, however patient and scrupulous, into special facts. The narrator must seek to imbue himself with the life and spirit of the time. He must study events in their bearing near and remote; in the character, habits and manners of those who took part in them. He must be, as it were,

a sharer or spectator of the action he describes.—John Fiske in the introductory essay to the Champlain edition of Parkman's works.

(c) The student must try to put life and blood into historical record by what he has learned of political human nature in watching the movements of his own time. He must think of the Past with the same keenness of interest as if it were the Present and of the Present with the same coolness of reflection as if it were the Past.—James, Viscount Bryce, *Modern Democracies*, 1:20. See also Arthur S. Turberville, "History, Objective and Subjective," *History*, 17 (1933): 298 f.

❡ 366 VIEWING THE PAST FROM WITHIN

To be in a position to portray a people, an age, an institution, intelligibly to others, it is generally necessary to view them from within; this does not differ materially from the process of projecting oneself into the past. The stained glass window suggests an analogy. Viewed from without, it is a meaningless pattern of dull glass and leaden joints; viewed from within, it is a colorful splendor lighting up a definitely traced picture. Thus, Belloc repeatedly comes around to the thought that really to understand Europe of the past, one must look at it from the inside, that is, from the vantage point of the Catholic Church, the institution which more than any other entered into its life and made it what it was.

(a) The same thought has been expressed by Feder, who writes that Christian phenomena in history can be seen in their true inwardness only by one who is himself a Christian. Only a person who has lived with Christ in sympathetic union of mind and heart, who has made himself one with Him through acceptance of His doctrine, will justly appraise His personality, or even from a merely historical point of view, the place He fills in the story of mankind. A person standing outside the Catholic Church is not in a position to appreciate adequately the worldwide influence of the papacy and its development through the ages; the objective basis for such appreciation is wanting. What has really been behind the relations between Church and State in all ages, especially in the Middle Ages, will almost certainly escape him; in general, the intimate meaning of events connected, whether proximately or remotely, with the papacy, will scarcely come within his ken. Accordingly, to cite these instances only, he will fail to grasp the true significance of the crowning of Charlemagne by Leo III, in 800, or to see the justice of the long and eventful struggle of Gregory VII with Henry IV of Germany.—Feder, *Lehrbuch*, 346 f.

In the same tenor, see also Christopher H. Dawson, *The Making of Europe: an Introduction to the History of European Civilization* (London, 1932), xvii–f.; William T. Walsh, *Isabella of Spain: The Crusades* (New York, 1930), vii–f.

(b) A clear instance of failure to see one's subject from the inside is Francis Parkman's treatment of the French Canadians. Parkman is conventionally referred to as the American historian who has best succeeded in turning out work that is at once good literature and good history. He was indeed a literary craftsman of the first rank; he wrote graphically and with dramatic effect. Further, he was a painstaking investigator, leaving on the products of his pen an impress of scholarship, which, however, was not without its limitations. More thoroughgoing research and study in his special field have in a measure outmoded his histories as authoritative.

What detracts more particularly from the adequacy of Parkman's historical work is his incapacity to understand or duly appreciate the element of the supernatural in men's lives. His mentality and outlook were distinctly naturalistic. The realities of religious faith, which escape eye or ear but which can be the most dynamic of all influences to stir men to action, had no place in his philosophy of life. Hence, his maladroit treatment of the famous Canadian missionaries. He could admire their courage and heroism, as he could admire the courage and heroism of any Spartan or Roman hero. But the lively religious faith that inspired them, the eager love of God that motivated their careers, were to him as sealed books. He did not rise to the fact that motivation of this order could account for the conduct of reasonable men. Miracles, mystical experience, exalted religious feeling, were to him "superstition" or "fanaticism."——Raymond Corrigan, "The Missions of New France; A Study in Motivation," MA, 18 (1936): 234–45.

James Truslow Adams says that Parkman "falls short of complete comprehension of the part that the Church and the Jesuits had in the contest."
—*Dictionary of American Biography*.

(c) The general principle that the historian should be able to view his subject from the viewpoint of the people, race, or institution he is concerned with, is not invalidated by the fact that one on the outside may occasionally succeed in looking at a subject more or less from within. It is significant that the two notable interpretations of American political institutions, De Tocqueville's *Democracy in America*, and Bryce's *American Commonwealth*, came from foreigners. Yet, while it is conceivable that one may write the history or describe the institutions of a country not one's own with genuine insight, the case of a non-Catholic historian handling Catholic topics presents special difficulties. Intimate understanding and technical knowledge of things Catholic will almost inevitably be wanting.—See *Speculum*, 7 (1932): 302–16; *The Month*, 126 (1915): 417, on knowledge of Catholic theology and canon law as a necessary equipment for handling certain issues in history.

❡ 367 JUDGING THE PAST BY ITS OWN STANDARDS

Equity demands that we measure the characters and institutions of history by the moral standards of their own age, not of our own. It is manifestly unfair to expect of a tenth-century Frank a loftiness of principle unknown to the age in which he lived. This does not mean that moral standards are relative, and that the virtue of one age becomes the vice of another. There are absolute values in morality, but they are apprehended less clearly in one age than in another, with the result that what was generally held to be morally licit in one age may be held illicit in another. Consequently, in placing praise or blame on historical characters, if the circumstances justify such procedure, one must take for standards of measurement the ideas of right and wrong that prevailed in their environment, ideas in which they presumably acquiesced in good faith. Moreover, circumstances sometimes determine attitudes and viewpoints which in other circumstances would be reprehensible. In the Middle Ages, when Catholicism was everywhere taken for granted, Catholics were much more free in criticizing church dignitaries than would be thought permissible in a day when the very authority of the Church is called into question. Frederick Ozanam wrote that the language of Dante and Jacopone da Todi in regard to Boniface VIII, would today be the language of impiety.

Lord Acton in his Cambridge inaugural lecture protested against the principle of judging the past by its own standards, as carrying with it the implication that there are no absolute values in morality.

> I exhort you never to debase the moral currency or to lower the standard of rectitude but to try others by the final maxims that govern your own lives and to suffer no man and no cause to escape the undying penalty which history has the power to inflict on wrong.—*Lecture on the Study of History*, 63.

Acton's position was contested by Henry C. Lea, in an address before the American Historical Association, in which on the opposite principle he exculpated Philip II of Spain from certain charges against him.—AHA Report (1903), 1:60.

Again, appealing to the same principle, that the figures of history are to be judged by the moral criteria of their own day, the Protestant Bishop of London, Dr. Mandell Creighton, made a plea as against Acton for one of the popes of the Renaissance.

W. E. H. Lecky repeats the same idea: "The men of each age must be judged by the ideal of their own age and not by the ideal of ours." Lecky remarks also that the opposite procedure is especially the error of novices in history.—"The Political Value of History," *Historical and Political Essays*, 39. See also Herbert Thurston, "Dr. Coulton's Medieval Village," *Studies*, 15 (1926): 571.

It is interesting to note that in the end Acton retracted his stand on the matter in question. "During what was almost our last conversation," writes his son, "he solemnly adjured me not to rash judge others, as he had done, but to take care to make allowance for human weakness."—G. P. Gooch, *History and Historians*, 393.

F. Putting Oneself in the Past

¶ 368 In the historian's outlook, past and present are duly correlated. Knowledge of the past helps him to knowledge of the present, and vice versa. The more he is alive to his own environment, the better he knows the men, manners, and institutions of other days. But he does not, as has been explained, attempt to measure a past age by the standards of his own day. No attitude in history has been more pernicious than that which assumes the present to show the high-water mark of human accomplishments, which commends or condemns the past according as it measures up to or falls short of present-day standards and ideals. The eighteenth century, having more than its share of blind spots, labeled the Middle Ages, "Gothic," or "barbarous." Macaulay, gaping in naive wonder at the accomplishments of his materialistic age, weighed the men and institutions of earlier days in its scales. In either case, the penalty of self-sufficiency was historical shortsightedness, inability to see the realities of the past in their true character and proportions.—See G. P. Gooch, *History and Historians*, 300.

¶ 369 MORAL JUDGMENTS IN HISTORY
The question is often raised whether it is any business of the historian to praise or blame, to express what are called moral judgments or values. The question has less practical bearing than may at first appear. Repeatedly the facts themselves, baldly stated, are eloquent of praise or blame. Comment by the author, especially if expressed with feeling, may easily detract from the effect, not heighten it. At the same time, if the historian finds himself moved on occasion to commend what is commendable or to blame what is blameworthy, there is nothing in logic, ethics, or the technical requirements of his art to forbid him.

(a) Materialistic-minded historians have regarded the matter differently.

> What matters it if Peter or Paul is a rascal? That is the business of his contemporaries; they suffered from his vices and ought to think only of despising and condemning him. Now we are beyond his reach and hatred has disappeared with danger. At this distance, and in the historic perspective, I see in him but a mental machine, provided with certain springs, animated by a primary impulse, affected by various circumstances.—Taine, *History of English Literature*, 4: 235.

Other authorities have deprecated moral judgments in history on the ground that they clash with the avowed purpose of the historian's art, which in their opinion is solely to record past events, not to pass judgment on their ethical values.

> To manifest bias against a liar like Titus Oates, whose perjuries sent innocent men to their death, or against such a disgusting publicist as Hébert, whose journal, *Le Père Duchesne*, reeked with foul and ribald

vituperation; or against any murderer, thief, or perpetrator of moral offences, is not culpable. It is commendable. No one is called upon to apologize for wrong or to mitigate his indignation when he meets with it.—E. Scott, History and Historical Problems, 192.

Since the historian's position resembles that of the judge, it is a mistake to suppose that the historian must not take sides, for if it is his deliberate and carefully considered judgment that one side was right, it is his duty to say so.—Sir Henry Lambert, The Nature of History, 70.

See also Sidney G. Fisher, "The Function of the Historian as a Judge of Historical Persons," AHA, Report (1898), 15 ff.; Arthur S. Turberville, "History, Objective and Subjective," History, 17 (1933); 289–302.

G. The Philosophy of History

⟨ 370   History and the philosophy of history deal with the same class of phenomena, but they do so in different ways. Both investigate causes, but not causes of the same order. History cannot content itself with a mere recording of the objective facts. It seeks also, in response to an irresistible urge of the human mind, to explain the facts, to interpret them. As we have seen, this is largely the same as to assign causes for them. The causes which history aims to bring to light may be immediate or mediate, proximate or remote; it stops short only of those causes which are ordinarily called last or ultimate. But as soon as we begin to explain, to assign causes, we begin to philosophize. Hence, a historical account which stresses causes is thereby philosophical in treatment. Macaulay and McMaster, confining themselves almost entirely to the factual, may be taken as types of the non-philosophical historian. Belloc, with his flair for interpretation, for the elucidation of facts in the light of general principles and movements, seems a fair instance of the philosophical historian.

⟨ 371   TRANSCENDENCY OF THE PHILOSOPHY
         OF HISTORY OVER HISTORY

Philosophical history is on a lower plane than the philosophy of history. The latter is an attempt to trace world-history to its farthest ascertainable causes, "to see it whole." To all intents and purposes it is the same thing as trying to solve "the enigma of life," or "the riddle of the universe." Allan Nevins says that "a philosophy of history springs from a writer's whole view of human destiny and thus embodies his philosophy of life."—The Gateway to History, 241.

It is plain that here we pass over into philosophy as such, and even into theology. A correct philosophy of history, inasmuch as it professes to explain things in the light of really ultimate causes, cannot ignore the most far-reaching cause of all, divine Providence, both in the natural and supernatural order. The *philosophy of history*, therefore, is essentially a theological concept, and cannot be formulated aright if divorced from a theistic and even Christian interpretation of life. Hence, valid formulations of the philosophy of history, like those of St. Augustine and of Bossuet, find their necessary basis in revelation. Hence also, the hostile attitude of many modern historians of rationalistic outlook, to the idea and the very name of the philosophy of history. To them it is, as usually conceived in the past, an impertinence, a superstition, an arbitrary lugging in of a *deus ex machina* to explain what in final analysis is, from their point of view, probably incapable of explanation at all.

⁋ 372 That there is no final interpretation of world-history without recourse to philosophy and religion, is a freely admitted truth.

> There are certain considerations with which science cannot deal and which therefore belong to religion and philosophy.—C. N. Cochrane, *Thucydides and the Science of History*, 176.
>
> [The historian] does not aspire to answer the riddle of the universe. —A. M. Schlesinger in W. Gee, ed., *Research in the Social Sciences*, 226.
>
> But history is not equipped for handling so vast, so intangible a problem. The significance of human history is a question which philosophy alone is qualified to answer.—Werner Sombart, "Economic Theory and Economic History," *Economic History Review*, 2 (1929): 2.
>
> The social sciences do not invade the field of religion; they have nothing to do with the ultimate; their problems are those of the City of Man, not the City of God.—James H. Shotwell, *AHR*, 18 (1913): 693.

It is pertinent to comment that history, even while dealing only with causes less than ultimate, cannot divorce itself entirely from religion and the problems raised by it. A right attitude toward religion qualifies true appreciation of even the proximate causes of historical events.

⁋ 373 NEED OF A PHILOSOPHY OF HISTORY
The history being written nowadays has been deprecated at times on the ground that it is weak on the philosophical side.—Harry Elmer Barnes, *The New History and the Social Studies* (New York, 1925), chap. 1.

The brunt of such criticism is that history, in its preoccupation with the factual, the episodical, the picturesque, has failed to search out and establish the fundamental laws or causes which explain the historical tory shows at a disadvantage as compared to the physical sciences, with process as a whole. In this respect, so it is contended, present-day his-

their well established and universally recognized laws and principles. The criticism is significant as implying the truth that the higher types of history must be philosophical in scope; it is misdirected if it assumes the possibility that there are certain undiscovered laws, of biological or like character, which regulate historical processes in some mechanical fashion, and which must be brought to light before history as reality will yield up its ultimate meaning as a whole. Only on the groundless assumption that history is an entirely mechanistic affair, may one predicate the existence of any such laws.

¶ 374   Eighteenth-century historians, most of them of the rationalist school (Voltaire, Hume, Gibbon), wrote history on a broad basis of philosophical interpretation. Voltaire, who coined the expression, "the philosophy of history," declared: "il faut écrire l'histoire en philosophe." Nineteenth-century historians, factually-minded, and deprecating, so they thought, any alliance between history and philosophy, confined or meant to confine themselves largely to an impersonal and merely factual statement of things "as they actually occurred." This is the type of history which Henry Adams thought he himself had written.

> He [Adams] had even published a dozen volumes of American history for no other purpose than to satisfy himself whether by the severest process of stating, with the least possible comment, such facts as seemed sure, in such order as seemed rigorously consequent, he could fix for a familiar movement a necessary sequence of human movement.—*The Education of Henry Adams*, 382.

Now the pendulum swings back, and twentieth-century historians tend to hold the view that history, if it is to discharge its function with adequacy, must get away from the merely factual, and give history a philosophical framework.

(a) At the New Orleans meeting (1903) of the American Historical Association, it was suggested by one of the speakers that sociology, then looked upon as an interloper in the circle of the sciences, was perhaps nothing more than that "ancient enemy of the historians," the philosophy of history, masquerading under another name. In truth, while usually treating the term with disdain and sometimes ridicule, as a thing inadmissible in scientific history, historians have never actually parted company with the thing itself. Unconsciously, and despite themselves they are always falling back on some ultimate interpretation of history.

Langlois and Seignobos, themselves of rationalist outlook, observe shrewdly that while historians profess to reject anything like a philosophy of history, they are really bringing the thing back in a "lay disguise," under cover of their theories about race, ideas, historical mission, and what not, as the determining factors in history.—*Introduction to the Study of History*, 287.

Historians are merely substituting one philosophy of history for another. The inference is obvious that what Langlois and Seignobos object to, is not the avowal of a philosophy of history as such, but the avowal of a theistic or Christian philosophy of history. Present-day historians of whatever school are beginning to stand very much on common ground in sensing the indispensable need of an interpretation of history in ultimate terms, if history is to have any meaning at all.

(b) In a presidential address before the American Historical Association (1933) Charles A. Beard said that history cannot be written without the aid of "a framework of reference," of some sweeping conception of the meaning of history as a whole, and although such conception cannot be proved, it must be accepted as a "deliberate conjecture," as an "act of faith." Keeping all religious postulates out of the picture, Beard lists three as the only explanations that can be advanced to interpret the historical movement in general or world history as a whole. His own theory or hypothesis, which he calls a "deliberate conjecture," an "act of faith," is in reality a philosophy of history, though he avoids using this term. His philosophy of history therefore, is that the world, society, the historical movement in general, is headed towards "a collectivist democracy," which is apparently but another name for socialism.—Charles A. Beard, "Written History as an Act of Faith," AHR, 39 (1934): 228.

> The question is not whether you have a philosophy of history or not, but whether the one you have is good for anything.—Frederick J. Turner, as cited by Carl L. Becker, in AHR, 45 (1940): 393.
>
> I cannot imagine the slightest theoretical importance in a collection of facts unless they mean something in terms of reason, unless we can hope to determine their vital connection in the whole system of reality. —John B. Bury, cited in History, 19 (1934): 103.
>
> Even the straitest school of scientific historians find it impossible to restrain their steps from divagations into the pasture of philosophy.— Norman Sykes in History, 19 (1934): 102.
>
> For the historian, the philosophy of history is by no means a superfluous luxury. . . . It is a fatal delusion for a specialist to be independent in his specialty of general views.—Ernest Bernheim, *Einleitung in die Geschichtswissenschaft* (2d ed., Berlin, 1920), 18.

❡ 375 HISTORISMUS

The label *historismus* has been affixed by way of reproach to the type of history associated with Leopold von Ranke and his school, which allegedly restricts the historian to a mere recording of facts without attempt to search out and interpret the deep-lying forces that operate below their surface. Historismus, so explained, is positivism in history; it ignores the existence of metaphysical, non-sensible factors, that is, such as are not open to physical investigation. It is rationalism in history: it accounts nothing as fact except what can be established as such by pure reason, thus excluding the data supplied to the historian by divine revelation. Finally, historismus precludes anything like a philosophy of history, the attempt to explain historical phenomena in terms of ultimate causation; as a result, it fails to provide an adequate framework for history in general or a proper method of writing it. One will easily admit that not a little history has been vitiated by the false standards thus described collectively as historismus.—Ross J. S. Hoffman, "Catholicism and Historismus, CHR, 24 (1939): 401 ff.

However, we should note, first, that it is mainly, if not exclusively, in the broader themes of history that the inadequacies of historismus become apparent. One can write a satisfactory history of Waterloo, Iowa, or of the free silver campaign of 1896, without employing therein any comprehensive philosophy of history. Secondly, historismus, to the extent that it is but another name for an exaggerated, impracticable objectivity of historical writing, is doubtless a fair target for criticism; but its excesses seem chargeable to the followers of Ranke rather than to Ranke himself. While the German historian was anything but objective in his treatment of Catholic religious issues, his conception of history did not exclude spiritual realities or broad synthetic views.

For a defence of the Rankean method as exemplified in American historiography, see Theodore C. Smith, "The Writing of American History, 1884-1934," AHR, 40 (1935): 438-49.

❡ 376 THE PHILOSOPHY OF HISTORY DEFINED

Philosophy in its generally accepted meaning is "the knowledge of things in their ultimate causes." The philosophy of history, as being a restriction of the general concept to a special field of reality, is "the knowledge (or meaning) of history in its ultimate causes" [❡ 370 f.].

In a narrow sense the philosophy of history refers to the attempts which have been made by sociologists and historians to interpret the meaning or significance of the historical process as a whole.—M. Mandelbaum, The Problem of Historical Knowledge, 305.

The essential feature of the philosophy of history is the attempt to envisage the history of mankind as a single whole, and to exhibit, so far as discernible, some plan or purpose, some "end" of intrinsic value, seen to be increasingly realized when the sequence of events is contemplated as a whole. Or to be more correct (since in a time sequence there is no absolute whole, and we ourselves stand in mediis rebus), a philosophy of history is the attempt to divine such a purpose and consummation, when we consider the apparent tendency or direction of the process, so far as it is open to our observation . . . but the fundamental thesis of a philosophy of history is the recognition, despite contingencies, of a providential purpose—a purpose of nature for the race, as Kant called it—which is worked out unconsciously by men and nations, each pursuing their private and discordant ends.—A. S. Pringle-Pattison, "The

Philosophy of History," in *Proceedings* of the British Academy, 9 (1924), 3 f.

¶ 377 An ultimate cause may be *efficient* (the agency by which an effect is produced), or *final* (the end or purpose in view of which an effect is produced). Again, an efficient cause may be *material* or *nonmaterial* (spiritual). Historians of materialistic outlook find or profess to find the last explanation of world-history in one or more causes of the material order, such as soil, climate, economics, human agency conceived as a merely material phenomenon [¶ 352]. Christian philosophy recognizes the tremendous influence of material causes in history, but does not recognize them as ultimate; other causes reach beyond them, affording the only ascertainable basis on which world-history in its totality becomes intelligible. The ultimate efficient causes in history are non-material, spiritual. Briefly, the joint action of human free will and Divine Providence (efficient causes), issuing in the realization of certain divine ends or objectives (final causes), explains history. This is the Christian philosophy of history as stated, with accidental differences of presentation, by St. Augustine, Dante, Bossuet, Schlegel, Vico.

¶ 378 FINAL CAUSES

The materialistic (economic) philosophy of history excludes the notion of final causes, which implies a supreme intelligence freely directing its activity to a certain end or purpose. A materialistic philosophy may, it is true, conceive of human affairs as moving automatically by some mystic, inexplicable impulse of their own in a definite direction and towards a definite goal, as for instance, the conception that the present social order is headed towards a "collectivist democracy"; but this is not to recognize an ultimate final cause in any consistent meaning of the term.

A final cause postulates a personal intelligence directing its activity to a known end. The philosophy of history denominated Christian is the only one strictly teleological (implying an ultimate purpose or end); it alone recognizes real final causes in the historical process as a whole. Such causes, from the Christian point of view are: the divine glory, the ultimate triumph of the Church, the eventual reward of the good and punishment of the wicked in another world. Human history is shaped by Divine Providence with a view to accomplishing these ends. This teleological view of history is especially stressed by St. Augustine.

Thus, it is clear that the Christian philosophy of history offers an explanation of the future as well as of the past. The history that is to be, will not differ essentially in determining causes, in final issue, from the history that was.

❡ 379 THE PHILOSOPHY OF HISTORY FORMULATED
The Christian conception of universal history was expressed by St. Paul in the words: "For of Him and by Him and in Him are all things" (Romans, 9:36).

The first elaborate attempt to state a philosophy of history was made by St. Augustine in his *City of God* (*De Civitate Dei*), one of the world's outstanding books. The capture and sack of Rome under Alaric (A.D. 409) gave occasion to the pagans to blame Christianity for the calamities that were overwhelming the empire. Augustine, taking up the defense of the Church, pointed out that the fall of the "earthly city" (*civitas terrestris*) mattered little; what did matter was the continued existence and ultimate triumph of the "City of God" (*civitas Dei*), the collective body of the good, especially as incorporated in the Church. Revelation and human records being alike drawn upon for illustration, history is interpreted in terms of a perennial conflict between the forces of good and the forces of evil, between the God-fearing and the wicked. The conflict began with the fall of the angels, and it will end only with the complete vindication and triumph of the good at the last judgment.

The Augustinian view of world-history is at once theological and teleological; it is based on revelation and it supposes a divine plan which finds its infallible execution in history. The *City of God* had a profound influence on the Middle Ages, supplying one of the great ideas which dominated those times, that of "Christendom" or a worldwide "Christian commonwealth"; in its essential groundwork, it is still a statement of the Christian philosophy of history.

> The first fact about a man for a thousand years after the *City of God* was written was not his race but his religion. That, I say, was held to be the prime fact of life and upon it the public order was professedly based.—William S. Lilly, *Christian and Modern Civilization*, 89.

On the *City of God*.
Pierre Labriolle, *History and Literature of Christianity from Tertullian to Boethius* (London, 1925), 408 ff.
Adhémar d'Alès, "En lisant la cité de Dieu," *Études*, 141 (1914): 318–32.
G. Sortais, *Traité de philosophie*, 1: 749.
Arnold J. Toynbee, *A Study of History* (6 vols., London, 1935–1939), 6: 365–69.
Ernest Bernheim, *Einleitung in die Geschichtswissenschaft*, 19–21.

❡ 380 St. Augustine's conception of history places the emphasis on supernatural rather than natural causes. But it has been pointed out that it does so to such an extent as to obscure unnecessarily the part played in history by natural or secondary causes. The operation of natural causes must be reckoned with in the Christian interpretation of history. Thus, the collapse of the Roman Empire had a significance in the divine scheme of things which the historian is at liberty to discover, if he can; but as a concrete phenomenon it was the issue of a whole vast network of natural or secondary causes producing their proportionate effects. Overtaxation, climatic changes, infiltration of foreign elements into the army and civil population, political and moral corruption—these and other factors in the category of secondary causes, proximate or remote, may have been responsible collectively for the collapse. It is the business of the historian, no matter what be his interpretation of history as a whole, to investigate whether and to what extent such factors were responsible. Yet the misconception is by no means uncommon that the historian who writes from the Christian point of view may dispense himself from laborious inquiry into the natural causes of historical phenomena by taking refuge in the facile blanket explanation of a divine decree.

> Grant that theology claims . . . that Rome fell and England arose, that America was discovered or remained so long undiscovered because 'God wills it.' That does not enlarge our knowledge of the process.—James T. Shotwell, *The History of History* (New York, 1939), 25

Admittedly, such a view does not enlarge our knowledge of the process, nor is it intended to do so. Knowledge of the process in question must be sought in study of the natural causes that were at work, a prescription which binds the Christian historian as well as any other.

> Since God operates in all secondary causes it is clear that divine providence uses them as intermediaries in its activities.—Robert L. Patterson, *The Conception of God in the Philosophy of Aquinas* (London, 1933), 476.

On the apparent lacuna in the Augustinian interpretation of history, see Moorhouse I. X. Millar, "Aquinas and the Missing Link in History," Peter Guilday, ed., *The Catholic Philosophy of History* (New York, 1936), 85–109.

¶ 381 Bossuet's *Discourse on Universal History*, written for the Dauphin and first published in 1681, elaborates at greater length than St. Augustine the idea of a superintending Providence in human affairs. It finds repeated manifestations of Providence in the great crises and movements of history.

> The idea of Providence is at the same time the law of history. If the crash of empires "falling one upon the other" does not in truth express some purpose of God regarding humanity, then history or what is called by that name, is indeed no longer anything but a chaotic chronology, the meaning of which we should strive in vain to disentangle. In that case Fortune or Chance would be the mistress of human affairs. . . . And why, after all, were there Greeks and Romans? Of what use was Salamis? Actium? Poitiers? Lepanto? Why was there a Caesar and a

Charlemagne? Let us frankly own, then, that unless something divine circulates in history, there is no history. . . . The hypothesis of Providence is the condition of the possibility of history, as the hypothesis of the stability of laws of nature is the condition of the possibility of science.—Ferdinand Brunetière in CE, 2:700.—See also Patrick J. Barry, "Bossuet's 'Discourse on Universal History,'" in Peter Guilday, ed., The Catholic Philosophy of History, 149–86.

¶ 382 MODERATE APPLICATION OF THE PROVIDENTIAL VIEW
While the Christian philosophy of life necessitates acceptance of "the providential view of history," it does not follow that one can always recognize a divine purpose in concrete human affairs. One may believe in "the hand through darkness moulding men," without being privileged thereby to see its workings clearly, if at all. The general principles on which Bossuet builds up his classic *Discourse on Universal History* can and should be accepted; but one may not always see eye to eye with him in his application of them to concrete cases. Salvian in his *De gubernatione Dei* interpreted events in the light of the doctrine of Providence; but he also laid down the principle, "I am a man, I do not know the secrets of God." The historian may on occasion qualify an event in history as "providential," in the theological sense; but he should not do so lightly. Moreover, such qualifications or interpretations are by their very nature subjective and personal to their authors; they do not require assent from the Christian believer.

Reason and faith teach us that all the activities of men on earth, even the least apparent, proceed under the Providence of an omniscient and omnipotent God and have in consequence, all of them, a significance in the world-process which is often of quite another kind than that we assume them to have in history. As the part which human activities play in God's great world-plan is concealed from us in many ways, they cannot ordinarily be considered from this point of view.—Feder, Lehrbuch, 5.

No one can deny that there is a divine design in history and that, despite human resistance, God makes a pattern. But what that pattern is and how, from our side, we are to interpret it, seems to many very obscure.—Martin C. D'Arcy in The Month, 174 (1939): 212.

¶ 383 Friedrich von Schlegel (1772–1829) follows conventional lines in the Christian interpretation of history. His point of departure is the fundamental revealed dogma of the fall of man. "The restoration in man of the lost image of God, so far as this relates to science," is "the first problem of history." "The greatest historical mystery, deepest and most complicated enigma of the world is the permission of evil on the part of God." The mystery finds its only solution in the free will of man and his being destined for a state of struggle. To divine Providence and human liberty, Schlegel accordingly added a third fundamental element in history, the principle of evil. His views on the philosophy of history are summarized in the introduction and in the tenth chapter of his *Philosophy of History*, trans. by J. B. Robertson (London, 1852).

¶ 384 The Italian, Giambattista Vico (1668–1744), conceived of history as a complex of three stages or cycles through which every people passes in the course of its historical development. These cycles are designated the divine, the heroic, the human. Vico's theory allows fully for the influence of Providence, whose decrees are executed by human societies. Objection has been made to this theory in that it stops with the law of the three cycles and does not answer the further question, "Does humanity as a whole, despite the periodic recurrence of the three cycles characteristic of every nation, really progress? If so, what is the law of its progress?"—G. Sortais, *Traité de philosophie*, 1: 749, note 1.

But Vico, it would appear, "had faith in the constant betterment of the race." See Paul C. Perotta, "Giambatista Vico, Philosopher-Historian," in Peter Guilday, ed., *The Catholic Philosophy of History*, 279; *The Autobiography of Giambattista Vico*, edited and translated by Max H. Fisch and Thomas G. Bergin, (Ithaca, N. Y., 1944).

¶ 385 George W. F. Hegel's *Lectures on the Philosophy of History*, trans. by J. Sieber (London, 1857), is an attempt to explain the historical process as a whole on the lines of the author's highly difficult philosophical system. To see things, not as isolated units but in the whole range of their knowable relationships, is a cardinal principle of Hegelian thought. The treatise accepts as its basic postulate the dictum of the Greek Anaxagoras, that "Reason governs the world." It concludes with the comprehensive formula that the "History of the World is the development of the Idea of Freedom." For the meaning of the latter concept we have Hegel's own perplexing definition: "The Nature of His [God's] will—that is, His Nature itself, is what is here called the Idea of Freedom." But in Hegelian doctrine "God is not a person, but a community of persons."—See John M. E. McTaggart, *Studies in Hegelian Cosmology* (Cambridge, Eng., 1918), 245.

In any case, God and the Idea of Freedom are here set before us as identical concepts.

The progressive evolution of the Idea of Freedom has proceeded, we are told, through four capital stages, Oriental history, Greek history, Roman history, Christian history as represented particularly by the achievements of the Germanic race. Here, then, is world-history knit together, and, so we are assured, rationally explained by the successive manifestations of a single all-embracing idea. The explanation so offered, with much apparatus of reasoning and historical illustration, is inadmissible. The Hegelian philosophy of history, like the Hegelian viewpoint in general, runs into pantheism; its theism is camouflage, being incompatible with the notion of a personal God; the Christianity it professes to adopt is of a distinctly rationalized type; it abuses logic by fitting facts into theory instead of fitting theory into facts; it anticipates the racial theories and totalitarian state pretensions of German National Socialism; it travesties Catholicism in which it recognizes the sworn enemy of its idol, the omnipotent state—the final development of the Hegelian "Idea." Finally, by its flood of vagaries, philosophical and historical, it is completely out of line with the genuine Christian philosophy of history. Hegel's interpretation of world-history is accordingly to be dismissed as unacceptable, on the same grounds as Hegelianism itself. —See Vernon J. Bourke, "The Philosophical Antecedents of German National Socialism," *Thought*, 14 (1937): 225–42.

❡ 386 PROVIDENCE IN HISTORY

This is the central idea in the Christian interpretation of history [❡ 379 ff.]. It is a commonplace of sound philosophy that God has a care of men, individually and collectively. The notion of a Divine Providence is a necessary corollary of belief in a personal God. If God exists, the conclusion is inevitable that He must exercise control and guidance over men and their affairs. St. Augustine gave expression to the thought in a famous sentence when he declared it to be absurd that while order and design reign in the material world, the social world, the rise and fall of kingdoms, should be left to blind chance. Since the time of the great Bishop of Hippo, the same thought has been a favorite with Christian thinkers. Frederick Ozanam calls Divine Providence and human liberty "the two great powers whose combined operation explains history."— *Dante and Catholic Philosophy in the Thirteenth Century* (New York, 1902), 63.

Boethius, followed by St. Thomas, defined Providence as "the all-regulating stable plan of God, the supreme Ruler of the universe."

The "providential view of history," being distinctly Christian in its implications, is repudiated by exponents of rationalist schools of thought. They qualify it by such terms as theological, teleological, mystical, arbitrary, unscientific, superstitious. Gibbon criticizes Salvian for seeing supernatural intervention in the catastrophic events which he relates. A more modern writer states the matter thus:

> Repudiating as false the notion that history teaches nothing, they [the historians] will nevertheless refrain from any attempt to find in it a

manifestation of the workings of Providence or a realization of the Idea or any other religious or metaphysical principle.——C. N. Cochrane, *Thucydides and the Science of History*, 168.

⁋ 387 From a Christian point of view the attempt to see Providence working in history is, with the caution emphasized [⁋ 382], perfectly reasonable. There are no intrinsic grounds on which it can be qualified as arbitrary or unscientific. One who seeks to understand events in the full range of their objective reality must take account not only of earthly and human causes, but also of the First Cause of everything that is or happens, namely, God. Without divine decree or permission, nothing happens or can happen, because the entire historical process is subject from beginning to end, to immediate divine government. Reason, even without the aid of revelation, makes it clear that God must refer all things to His glory, that this is the ultimate end at once of single historical phenomena and of history as a whole. Accordingly, it becomes possible to detect the ways and guiding hand of Providence, at least in remote events. Recorders of contemporary or nearly contemporary events will not ordinarily live to see the closing links in a given chain of events, and hence will not be in a position to grasp with clearness the drift and purposefulness of the development as a whole. On the other hand, one who records events of the remote past may conceivably find it possible both to follow the gradual development of some complex occurrence in its relation to the divine plan, and to appreciate the bearing of separate incidents on the larger historical process.

⁋ 388 Alexander's little army of thirty thousand, crossing the Hellespont, carried Greek culture with it to the banks of the Indus and the frontiers of Ethiopia, and thus helped to open up practicable avenues into those lands for the spread of the Gospel.

Scipio Africanus' destruction of the Carthaginian fleet assured Rome the mastery of the seas, and with it, world-dominion. This meant much for the expansion of Christianity at a later day.

In pursuance of a divine plan, the historical life of antiquity was to terminate in Rome with the setting up of the empire and the world-dominion it attained. Rome was to take over the acquisitions of all previous developments and hand them down to the new era to come; thus the Roman empire became a basis for the upbuilding of the Church and the Christian commonwealth.

A particularly striking instance of divine intervention in history is found in the Church. The influence of its guidance is manifest in numerous phenomena incapable of explanation by merely human causes. Such, for instance, was the spread of the Gospel with a rapidity that forestalled change or falsification in its content; its acceptance by nations of various types and by all classes and conditions of men; the constancy and perseverance of Christian martyrs; the numerous examples which the Gospel has furnished, of heroic holiness of life in the midst of a corrupt world; finally, the continued existence of the Church itself and of its teaching in the face of opposition from without and the frailities of its own members within.—Feder, *Lehrbuch*, 314.

❡ 389 Successive attempts to find a key to history independently of the notion of a controlling Divine Providence have been abortive. Evolution for its own sake, Darwinian selection, the Marxian class struggle; social disinterestedness, with the humanity of today sacrificing itself to furnish a nobler humanity to the morrow—these and similar attempted explanations of the human past break down under the stress of logic and fact. On the other hand the "providential view of history" (equivalently the Christian philosophy of history) is firmly grounded in right reason and the nature of things. It implies that God "has settled from eternity the final goal towards which the whole of His creation and each particular creature is to be directed, that He has ordained the means by which the end shall be reached, and that He rules in the course of the ages all events so perfectly that nothing shall occur to bar His final and absolute intention."—Bernard Boedder, *Natural Theology* (London, 1906), 382.

In summary, the Christian philosophy of history, the only one that is valid, is essentially theological in character.

> The Christian conception of history is inseparable from the Catholic faith. It is not a philosophic thing which has been elaborated by the intellectual effort of Christian scholars. It is an integral part of the Christian revelation.—Christopher H. Dawson, *Religion and the Modern State* (London, 1935), 73.

> To divorce, as the modernists do, the history of the world from the story of salvation, and God's government and sanctions of religion from the operation of matter is a fundamental apostacy from Christianity.— George Santayana, *Winds of Doctrine: Studies in Contemporary Opinion* (London, 1913), 34.

❡ 390 Three elaborate attempts in modern times, all more or less from the rationalist standpoint, to formulate a philosophy of history, may be noted.

(a) Otto Spengler in *The Decline of the West* (2 vols., New York, 1926–1928), reflects the disillusionment of the period subsequent to the first World War. History runs in cycles; civilizations are born, grow, decay, and die, after the analogy of the animal organism. As a general interpretation of history, it is fanciful, arbitrary, unsupported by valid evidence. Charles A.

Beard calls it "a fantastic morphological assumption."—*AHR*, 39 (1934): 223.

A brief summary of Spengler's theory is in Christopher H. Dawson, *Progress and Religion* (London, 1929), chap. 2.

(b) Arnold J. Toynbee, *A Study of History*. This is erudite comparative study of past civilizations, with an attempt to discover the laws that determined their growth.—See the review in *CHR*, 21 (1935): 314–22.

(c) Pitirim A. Sorokin, *Social and Cultural Dynamics* (3 vols., New York, 1937).—Reviewed in *America*, 57 (1937): 597.

On the Christian philosophy of history.
Franz Sawicki, *Geschichtesphilosophie* (Munich, 1923).
Charles S. Devas, *A Key to the World's Progress*.
Gilbert K. Chesterton, *The Everlasting Man* (London, 1926).
M. Legendre, *Liberté et Providence dans l'histoire* (Paris, 1927).
Christopher H. Dawson, "Communism and the Christian Interpretation of History," *Religion and the Modern State*, 73-101.
Moorhouse I. X. Millar, *Unpopular Essays in the Philosophy of History*.
Peter Guilday, ed., *The Catholic Philosophy of History*.
Jean du Plessis, *The Human Caravan*.
Shirley J. Case, *The Christian Philosophy of History* (Chicago, 1943).
Nicolas Berdyaev, *The Meaning of History*, trans. by G. Reavey (New York, 1936).

Chapter Seventeen

THE INDICATION OF SOURCES

A. The Necessity of Giving References . . . . Page 381
B. Footnotes: Rationale 382
C. Footnotes: Technique 385
D. Bibliography 390
E. The Documentary Appendix. Source Books. Consecutive Documents 393

A. The Necessity of Giving References

⟪ 391   Scholarly history rests on a solid substructure of research and criticism; but it may be asked how far the substructure ought to show in the finished work. The question is not of recent date. Henri Griffet, the eighteenth-century methodologist (*Traité*, 368 ff.), discussed it with cleverness and charm. The French church historian Fleury had objected to the appearance in a history text of any indications of sources or of critical discussions of evidence; he appealed in defense of his position to the analogy of the architect or builder, who after the house is finished, removes the scaffolding and machinery of construction. Griffet was quick to deny the parity. You may admire and make use of a building even though scaffolding and machinery have been put out of sight. But you cannot read with anything like satisfaction a history which reaches conclusions on doubtful and controversial matters, unless you know the process by which the conclusions were reached. Now, to make these processes clear to the reader means citing the sources which furnish the pertinent evidence; it means also revealing the lines of reasoning to which the evidence was subjected.

No doubt Griffet had the better of the argument. It is the architect's known professional competency which in last analysis is the real factor inspiring confidence in the solidity of the building. So also, the engineer constructs a bridge which people use without misgivings as to its stability. As with the architect, so with the engineer. It is the latter's general reputation for competency that inspires confidence in his work, not any evidence of a technical kind which he might produce. The historian is in similar case. He may prop up his statements with references to authorities and duly list his sources, but there always remains a residuum of research, supporting evidence, and personal judgment which he cannot in any practical way lay before the reader. In the end, what guarantees, at least for the ordinary reader, the trustworthiness of a narrative is the author's standing as a historian, in whatever way this standing be attested.

It is, therefore, an illusion to suppose that the footnotes and bibliographies of scientific history supply everything that is needed to check an author's accuracy. No doubt they are aids in this direction, and when elaborate, create a presumption in the author's favor, especially when he has not as yet achieved a reputation by previous work. But when all is said, one somehow or other always comes back to the author's established reputation for scholarship and general reliability as the main ground of confidence in his work.*

Three of the more familiar conventions of scientific historiography are: the bibliography or indication of sources; citation of authorities for individual statements, generally in the form of footnotes; appendixes of documents in illustration or proof of the text—what the French call *pièces justificatives*.

B. Footnotes: Rationale

❡ 392 Whether or not footnotes are necessary or even helpful to scholarly history writing, has been a moot question. The methodologists insist on their use; on the other hand, reputable historians have dispensed with them, and sometimes free lances in the field have made them a target of satirical criticism. The methodologists may be said to have the best of the argument. Young historians especially, with their eyes fixed on the approval of the profession rather than on that of the reading public, will do well to support all important statements, especially disputable statements, by citing their authorities in footnotes.

While footnotes may not easily be dispensed with in history writing that merits the scholarly name, they are not to be multiplied without need. A certain economy in their use must be practised. A statement of

---

* These statements are debatable. The "standing," the "established reputation" of not a few authors has proved to be spurious and undeserved. Their "general reliability has often no other basis than the assertions of those who belong to their group, their coterie, or their school of thought. There is much less objective appraisal of a book than one would expect from historians who claim for themselves the exclusive privilege of science and impartiality. Even a superficial reading of historical literature makes it apparent that many critics implicitly act on the principle: "Nul n'aura de l'esprit que nous et nos amis."—Ed.

common knowledge need not and should not be footnoted by way of support. If one writes: "Man's acquaintance with the geography of the New World has continued to expand ever since its discovery in 1492," no reference need or ought to be given for the date.

ℂ 393 THE USEFULNESS OF THE FOOTNOTE

(a) The critical reader requires a more explicit guarantee of the truth of a statement in the text than is afforded by the blanket authority or reputation of the author. The footnote affords this guarantee by indicating the sources or authority on which the truth of the particular statement is based.

(b) A statement sometimes embodies a conclusion arrived at by the sifting of a complex body of evidence. In such cases it is desirable that the line of reasoning pursued by the author be set before the reader, at least summarily, a thing which cannot always be done conveniently in the body of the text. The footnote is therefore the reader's resource for checking the author's accuracy; it is designed to make his statements verifiable, which is one of the hall-marks of scientific work [ℂ 53].

(c) It is desirable on occasion to enlarge on the point with fuller detail than can be done in the text without prejudice to its continuity and flow. The fuller discussion is then relegated to a footnote, which can also be made to include references to further reading or research on the topic involved. The footnote thus becomes a convenient receptacle for data and discussions of various kinds, supplementing the text, enriching it, and most important consideration of all, giving it weight, by linking it directly with its sources.

ℂ 394 THE NECESSITY OF FOOTNOTES IN SPECIFIC CASES

Particularized references by footnote are often mandatory, especially in the case of quotation, direct or indirect [ℂ 430].

(a) Words or passages quoted *directly* from writing not the author's own, should be credited to the proper source by a footnote, or otherwise, and set off by quotation marks, which indicate to the reader that the words or passages so set off are not the author's own, but those of another. If quotation marks (or other typographical device to show quotation) are not used, the author places himself in the position of claiming as his own, writing which is actually not his own—literary false pretence, or plagiarism.

(b) To summarize or paraphrase or interpret another's words in one's own, and then enclose the result in quotation marks is unpardonable, as the reader is thus left under the impression that he is getting the actual words of the writer quoted, whereas he is only getting a recasting. This is a malpractice charged against the English historian, Froude, who, however, was probably not aware of its impropriety.

(c) Matter quoted *indirectly* from a source, by way of paraphrase, summary, or interpretation, should be credited to the source in a footnote, or some other way, at least where statements of importance are concerned. Sometimes a general reference may suffice, as when the writer states explicitly that his account, say, of a battle or institution, or political crisis, is based on such and such a source or sources.

(d) By the ethics involved, in cases of extracted matter not subject to copyright law, and by such law itself where direct quotation or substantial paraphrase is made, permission of the proprietary is necessary, unless what is used from another falls under the accepted definition of "fair use." It is, for example, "fair use" on the part of this book to make—as it here does—the following extracts from Margaret Nicholson, *A Manual of Copyright Practice for Writers, Publishers, and Agents* (New York, Oxford University Press, 1945).

> 'Fair use' of copyright material has been defined by the courts as that extra-legal use that is usual, reasonable, and customary . . . quotation, either direct or by paraphrasing, is considered legitimate and the permission of the copyright owner is not required (p. 86).
>
> . . . The use of existing scholarly, legal, medical, and scientific works in the writing of new ones: Here again the serious scholar must take cognizance of the work done by his predecessors and colleagues. Earlier works can be commented on and discussed, and quoted at sufficient length to make the comments intelligible (p. 87).

A Manual of Copyright Practice is recommended as the most useful *vade mecum* for writers for publication; its approach is from the viewpoint of those without legal training. See also Stephen P. Ladas, *The International Protection of Literary and Artistic Property* (Harvard Studies in International Law, 2 vols., New York, 1938), an exhaustive treatise from the legalistic angle.

❡ 395 OBJECTIONS TO FOOTNOTES

(a) George Bancroft is said to have abandoned the use of footnotes on the ground that other writers copied his references without giving him credit for them. A similar grievance was voiced by John Gilmary Shea. But even if some historians have been unethical enough to pilfer a fellow craftsman's references and pass them off as their own, this is not a sufficient reason to sacrifice the undoubted advantages intrinsic to the device.

(b) A weightier objection to the footnote is that it is impossible in a great many cases to get into it references to all the sources and make it contain all the evidence that supports the statement in the text. Sometimes a footnote may be completely satisfying, as when, for example, it cites the single authority which alone is needed to substantiate a statement. But often it can present only a fraction of the evidence on which the author actually relies. The point is argued brilliantly by Belloc in the preface to his *Robespierre*, where he shows by a concrete instance how impracticable it is to pack into footnotes, without multiplying them endlessly, all the reasons that go to justify the text. "I could quote fifty places in that one page which would each demand a footnote to show from whence were drawn the threads of which the whole is woven." Belloc's position is well taken and brings home to us the limitations of the footnote; but it by no means disproves its general usefulness.

On Belloc's attitude towards the conventions of scientific history, see Joseph B. Code, *Queen Elizabeth and the English Catholic Historians,* 190–93.

(c) Publishers sometimes are said to be hostile to footnotes on the alleged grounds that they mar the appearance of the printed page, and are a nuisance to the general reader. As a compromise they relegate them to the end of the chapter or even of the volume, in either of which locations they are generally useless.

The volumes of the *Cambridge Modern History* carry no footnotes. Instead, these books are provided with detailed, but uncommented bibliographies, "to authenticate the text." As there are no specific or numbered references from text to bibliography, many statements of the text are not, as a matter of fact, "authenticated" in any practical way.

C. Footnotes: Technique

❡ 396 A full treatment of the techniques of handling footnotes, whether for the preparation of typescript copy or as eventually appearing on the printed page, is found in the *Appendix.** In amplification of some of the items of the *Appendix*, other items are supplied in ❡ 397–403.

❡ 397 THE PLACE OF THE FOOTNOTE IN TYPESCRIPT COPY
Where footnotes may be best placed in typescript copy, is a matter partly of personal preference, partly of convenience to those who must handle their collation to the foots of pages when finally in type.

---

* The forms of citation used in this book follow mainly the rules given in this appendix (Livia Appel, *Bibliographical Citation in the Social Sciences*). It was, however, considered more practically useful to readers of a work of this kind, to place bibliographical references either within the author's text or grouped at points where it applies to the matter treated, rather than to drop such material to its usual place at the foot of the page.—Ed.

PLACE IN MANUSCRIPT	COMMENT
(a) In manuscript immediately following the line of text containing the index number of the note, and set off from the text by lines of periods or ruled lines.	This avoids necessity of calculating space required when footnotes are disposed as in (b). Checking index numbers by author and makeup man is easiest and safest.
(b) At the foot of the manuscript page.	
(c) Consecutively, and properly labeled, at the end of each chapter or at the end of the whole manuscript.	This is useful if footnotes are not to appear on the same page with index numbers. But if they are so to appear, both checking and makeup may be hazardous.

⁋ 398 For the placing of footnotes in typescript and for other requirements of the mechanics of printing, it is well to consult the publisher before manuscript is typewritten. Publishers know their own "shop practices," found by experience to save time and the expense of "author's alterations."

⁋ 399 LATIN FORMS FOR SHORTENED CITATION

Though many of the Latin forms once common as a still shorter form of the shortened citation (see *Appendix*), are being discarded in more modern practice, students will encounter them frequently in general reading. A table of such devices follows:

AS USED	FULL FORM	MEANING
cf. (*not italicized*)	confer	compare, consult (see)
v., vide	vide	see
q. v.	quod vide	which see
s. v.	sub verbo, sub voce	under the (this, as given) word (heading)
ante	ante	before (as before)
post	post	after (as subsequently)
sup.; supra	supra	above
inf.; infra	infra	below
passim	passim	here and there (variously)
op. cit.	opere citato	in the work cited
loc. cit.	loco citato	in the place cited
ibid. [never ib.]	ibidem	in the same place
id.; idem	idem	the same (person, author)
et seq.	et sequentibus (paginis)	and on the (pages) following

⁋ 400 CITATION OF THE BIBLE AND OF STANDARD TEXTS

(a) Passages from the Bible (or from apocrypha arranged in the manner of the Bible), are cited by the name of the book, chapter, and verse. In the examples following, note: that the name of the book is generally abbreviated; that "St." is not used with the names of the Evangelists;

that an en-dash (not a hyphen) is used for continuation numbers; that an em-dash is used between continuation passages.

PREFERRED PRACTICE	ALSO FOUND
Gen. 5:22	Gen., chap. V, v.22 [V, 22; 5, 22]
John 6:34	[Similarly, as above]
Matt. 19:16–30	Matt. 19: 16–30 [16 ff.]
I Cor. 9:1—10:13	I Cor. 9:1 to 10:13
I Tim. 4:3, 4	I Tim. 4:3 f.

Lev. 7:6, 15, 21
   [Chapter 7: verses 6, 15, 21]
Lev. 7:6; 15
   [Chapter 7, verse 6, and all chapter 15]

(b) Many classical texts, works of theologians and philosophers, and of the masters in literature have been edited by experts in editions which have been accepted as standard for the parts into which the editors originally divided and published them. In such cases citation should follow the recognized standard editions. The examples following will illustrate the methods used.

Immanuel Bekker edited all the works of Aristotle (1831–1836). All subsequent editions and translations cite Bekker's pages and lines.

Aristotle, *Ethics*, 1094a–1181b.
Aristotle's "Doctrine of the Mean," *Nichomachean Ethics*, 1106a, 29–1106b, 10.

Henri Estienne (1531–1598), known as *Stephanus* [St.], edited Plato, in two volumes (1578). All subsequent editions and translations are divided according to Stephanus' pages and lines.

Plato, *Apology*, St. I, 17a–42a.
Plato, *Republic*, St. II, 327a–621d.
Plato's idea of "Philosopher Kings," *Republic*, St. II, 473c, 11–473e, 5.

The *Summa Theologica* of St. Thomas Aquinas is divided into four parts: *Pars Prima* [1a]; *Prima secundae* [1a. 2ae.]; *Secunda secundae* [2a. 2ae.]; and *Tertia* [3a.]. Further divisions are *Quaestiones*, which in turn consist of a number of *Articuli*. Each *Articulus* is divided into several points formulating objections to statements at the head of the *Articulus*; thus:

1. Videtur quod . . . non . . .
2. Videtur quod . . . non . . .
3. etc., etc.

The *Sed contra*, following, is generally a statement in agreement with a thesis taken from the Fathers or from Aristotle.

Respondeo dicendum . . . presents St. Thomas' own view in one paragraph. His answers to the objections previously proposed (*Videtur quod* . . .) are introduced in order by *Ad primum ergo dicendum* . . .; *ad secundum* . . .; etc.

A citation from St. Thomas, illustrating this method, would be, for example, on "the goodness of human acts":

St. Thomas [St. Th.], *Summa Theologica* [*Summa*], 1a. 2ae. Q. xviii, art. iv, ad tertium.

The citation of the classic poets is by author, work, book, line; giving, if necessary, reference to a particular edition used.

The citation of drama (Shakespeare), is by author, name of play, act, scene, and line, as in the edition used.

⁋ 401 THE NECESSITY AND USES OF STYLE

The matter of style as understood of a writer's personal and individual manner of literary expression, is treated in ⁋ 413–14. In this place, however, *style* is understood of the forms and arrangements, by rule and exception to rule, into which written language is cast and presented on the printed page: typographical style or practice.

The content of this chapter and of the *Appendix*, is only a small segment of the broad field of styling, in which—grammatically correct English presupposed—are included all rules and conventions that have accumulated, and of recent years have been codified and arranged, for the guidance of authors, publishers, and compositors. The corpus of such prescriptions for neat and orderly presentation, besides the matter in the *Appendix*, comprises such topics as capitalization, the use of italics, quotations, spelling and abbreviations, punctuation, compounding, division of words, transliteration of foreign-language names; how to treat legends and captions; how to indicate spacing; how to arrange tabular matter, formulas; how to prepare an index; and much more in the way of useful and necessary procedure.

Style or styling, and adequate knowledge of it, is a necessity for every writer, whether of history or in any other subject. It is beyond the compass of this book to present the full range of styling. The need for such material can be satisfied by the use of one of several manuals of style which various interested agencies have provided. In this there is liberty of an author's choice, for publishers will always respect well-reasoned preference and the needs arising from the nature of a particular work. What a simple logic demands and what every publisher asks, is that a fair consistency be followed.

The University of Chicago Press, *A Manual of Style*, remarks in point:

> Typography, like any art, is bound by conventions and rules. Perhaps in the deference which must be paid to consistency and uniformity of style it is as confined to precept as many an exact science. Since this is a manual of practice, the apparent dogmatism in many of the prescriptions will be understandable. The publisher must decide, or at least act as if a decision had been made, in cases where scholars are still de-

bating. Few of the rules contained in this book are absolutely inviolable. They were not devised to torment or to plague the author but to aid him in obtaining for his work the virtue of consistency (Preface).

❡ 402   STYLE MANUALS

A distinguished service to the needs of scholarly writing has been performed by the publication in this country and in England, of good manuals of style. The list following contains the books considered best by authors and publishers.

(a) American

The University of Chicago, *A Manual of Style: Containing Typographical Rules Governing the Publications of the University of Chicago, together with Specimens of Type Used at the University of Chicago Press* (10th ed., Chicago, 1937; 9th impression, 1945). This manual enjoys a deserved popularity in the United States. It is an example of the extension, through forty years, of local needs to the broad field of American publishing. The intelligence, clarity, restraint, and good taste in all its "rules" have been its chief recommendation.

United States Government Printing Office, *Manual of Style* (revised ed., Washington, D.C., 1945).

Style Manual of the Department of State (Washington, D.C., 1936).

Alice M. Ball, *Compounding in the English Language* (New York, 1939). This is the first complete study and thoroughly consistent treatment of this vexed phase of styling.

United States Government Printing Office, *Manual of Foreign Languages* (Washington, D.C., 1936).

Joseph Lasky, *Proofreading and Copy-preparation* (New York, 1941). An exhaustive, painstaking, and generally sound work, with a long and interesting bibliography.

C. O. Sylvester Mawson and John Robson, *The Complete Desk Book* (New York, 1939). In the first edition there are errors in the Greek accents. Otherwise this is a useful book.

Livia Appel, *Bibliographical Citation in the Social Sciences* (Madison, Wis., 1940). See Appendix.

John Benbow, *Manuscript and Proof* (New York, 1938).

William G. Campbell, *A Form Book for Thesis-writing* (Boston, 1938).

Many American publishers provide a manual of style especially adapted to their own preferences for "shop practice."

(b) British

Horace Hart, *Rules for Compositors and Readers at the University Press*, Oxford (London, 1925).

G. V. Carey, *Mind the Stop* (Cambridge, Eng., 1939). Written in friendly language, spiced with humor, this small book is a *tour de force* on punctuation.

❡ 403   USEFUL REFERENCE BOOKS FOR RESEARCHERS

Louis Shores, *Basic Reference Books* (2d ed., Chicago, 1939).

Isadore G. Mudge, *New Guide to Reference Books* (Chicago, 1936).

Directory of Special Libraries in the New York Metropolitan District (New York, 1937).

Special Libraries Directory of United States and Canada (New York, 1935).
American Library Directory (New York, 1939).
Webster's Dictionary of Biography (Springfield, Mass., 1944).
Henry P. Beers, Bibliographies in American History: Guide to Materials for Research (New York, 1938).

D. Bibliography

¶ 404 Devices for letting the reader of a history know what sources of information have been drawn upon in its making are not altogether of modern invention. As far back as the eighth century, Venerable Bede set down in the beginning of his *Ecclesiastical History of the English Nation* a brief statement of his sources of information, which included books and living persons. More than that, he entered on the margin of his manuscript references in the modern manner to authorities for many of the statements in the text, references which ignorant or careless copyists later failed to reproduce. But Bede's preoccupation with sources and references was rare in his day, as it was in the days that went before, and for a considerable time after. Griffet's *Histoire du règne de Louis XIII* (Paris, 1760), carries marginal references to authorities. Formal and systematic indication of sources as a recognized feature of scholarly history is scarcely older than the last century.

Bibliographical indication of sources generally takes one of two forms: formal bibliography (author, title, topical or other classification of source material, with or without critical comment); bibliographical essay, survey, excursus.*

¶ 405 COMPILATION OF A BIBLIOGRAPHY
Formal bibliography generally presents in alphabetical order and under distinct heads or categories, the various groups of material, printed or unprinted, which the author has used as the basis of his work [¶ 406]. Some cautions are to be heeded in compiling a bibliography meant to pertain to a specific work.

(a) *Only material actually put to account, or at least examined, should be listed.* Sources which have been examined, but which have furnished the author nothing for his purpose, may be mentioned as such. But to list material to which the author had no access, or which, if accessible, he failed for any reason to consult, is to make pretensions

---

* For another division of bibliography (not essentially different from the author's,) and for examples, see Livia Appel, *Bibliographical Citation in the Social Sciences* (Madison, Wis., 1940), printed as an appendix in this book.—Ed.

to a greater range of research than was actually performed. The implication latent in a bibliography is that it represents the actual basis of research on which a work is built; to make it represent more than this is disingenuous, and may lead readers and reviewers to attach more significance to a book than it actually deserves.

An exception may be noted. Sometimes lacunae in the material actually used are filled up in the bibliography to make it more complete, and so to enhance its value for other researchers. How far such procedure is permissible will depend on circumstances, which must be weighed for each particular case. At all events, the canon of literary propriety here stated must be duly observed. The reader must not be left under the impression that more or better material was used than was actually the fact, an impression that can hardly fail to be created by the admission of unused material into the bibliography without qualification or warning.

(b) *All material utilized, particularly if it is important, should be listed.* To draw on a source and then fail to give credit to it in the bibliography, or elsewhere, is an obvious impropriety. Moreover, it is a growing commendable practice among historians to give formal credit not only to written sources utilized, but also to individuals who have lent them direct personal aid in the preparation of their books. This laudable token of professional courtesy (though outside the scope of a formal bibliography), may be seen exemplified in forewords to dissertations, monographs, and larger works.

(c) *Material used indirectly should not be listed as though directly.* Thus, documents in the Archives Nationales, Paris, utilized only through photostat copies in the Library of Congress, should not be accredited directly to the Archives Nationales without mention in the bibliography of the photostat copies, in which form alone the documents were used. Otherwise, one would infer that the author worked in the Archives Nationales on the originals of the documents in question. This would be to credit him with more thoroughgoing research than he really carried on; for while a photostated or filmed copy may admittedly in many cases be as good as the original in the way of evidence, it will not usually be so in a question of authenticity, in which the quality of the paper, ink, and the like, may be important factors bearing on the problem. Similarly, archival material appropriated from a printed book should not be accredited directly to the archives, without mention of the book.

In the Edward E. Ayer Collection of the Newberry Library, Chicago, is a series of typewritten copies of documents from the Archives of the Indies, Seville. Citation of one of such documents may be made in either of two ways:

[Title]. Archivo General de Indias, Papeles de Cuba, [Call Number]. Typed copy in the Ayer Collection, Newberry Library, Chicago.

[Title]. Typewritten copy in the Ayer Collection, Newberry Library, Chicago. Original in Archivo General de Indias, Papeles de Cuba, [Call Number].

Reference to a document quoted at second hand may be made thus:

Isaac J. Cox, *West Florida Controversy, 1788–1813* (Baltimore, 1918), 288, citing Folch to Someruelos, January 26, 1809, Legajo 1566, Papeles de Cuba Archivo de Indias, General.

Or such reference may be made:

Folch to Someruelos [etc., as above]. Cited in Isaac J. Cox, *West Florida Controversy, 1798–1813; A Study in American Diplomacy* (Baltimore, 1918), 288.

If the document is known only through a particular book, it is improper to cite it without reference to that book.

¶ 406 ARRANGEMENT OF BIBLIOGRAPHY CONTENT

The content of a bibliography is arranged by groups, according to the nature and extent of the material used. The following scheme, which may be varied as needed, is typical.

BIBLIOGRAPHY

A. Unpublished sources:
   Archives, libraries, private collections. [These are listed severally by name, and with general description of the documentary material used, or with titles of individual documents put to account].
B. Published sources:
   1. Bibliographical aids
   2. Primary sources
   3. Secondary sources
      (a) General works
      (b) Special works, monographs.
      (c) Newspapers, periodicals

¶ 407 BIBLIOGRAPHICAL SURVEY

The formal bibliography is conventional in students' theses and in similar monographs of an academic nature. In other types of history its use is less general; its place is often taken by a connected survey of the source material requisitioned, in the form of a rather extended note or excursus. Often the purpose of such a survey is not so much to indicate the material used by the author, as to stimulate and direct further research and reading on the subject treated.

Examples of bibliographical note or survey.
Edward Channing, *History of the United States* (ends of chapters).
The American Nation Series, ed. by A. B. Hart.
The Chronicles of America, ed. by A. Johnson.
Original Narratives of Early American History, ed. by J. Franklin Jameson.
History of American Life, ed. by Arthur M. Schlesinger and Dixon R. Fox.
Horace K. Mann, *Lives of the Popes.*
Peter Guilday, *Life and Times of John Carroll, Archbishop of Baltimore.*

The chapters on sources in Justin Winsor's co-operative *Narrative and Critical History of America,* are generally recognized to be the most important feature of that elaborate work.

Charles H. Haskins, *Norman Institutions* (Cambridge, Mass., 1918), Appendix A, "The Documentary Sources of Early Norman History."

Thomas F. Tout, *Chapters on the Administrative History of Middle England; The Wardrobe, The Chamber and the Small Seals* (6 vols., London, 1920-1933), 1:36 ff.

E. The Documentary Appendix.
Source Books. Consecutive Documents.

¶ 408 THE DOCUMENTARY APPENDIX

It has long been the practice of history writers to supply in appendixes the complete text of documents previously unpublished, which have been utilized in the body of a history through reference, quotation, summary, or in other ways. Parkman made use of the documentary appendix; Pastor also, in his *History of the Popes.* The device is not common in the more recent-day historiography, though it can be usefully employed if space allows, and as may easily be the case, if the importance of the documents for illustrating or authenticating the text warrants their publication. Appendixes thus carry not only strictly documentary material, but may contain illustrative material of any kind; also notes or discussions of greater length than would be appropriate in the body of the work.

Further, the documents may be published separately from the text. A pertinent example of this arrangement is Thomas Hughes, *A History of the Society of Jesus in North America, Colonial and Federal* (New York, 1907-1917), a work in four volumes, two of text and two of documents. The documentary volumes, as regards the editorial principles and methods exemplified, follow the carefully worked-out plan for the critical editing of historical texts adopted in a Frankfurt (Germany) congress of historians (1895). The plan is ingenious. Summaries, introductory comments, footnotes explaining or enlarging on the text, connecting links of narrative, grouping of material under topical heads— these and other features result in a deftly constructed pattern of texts which can be read consecutively with the same sense of unity and progression with which one might read a continuous narrative.

❧ 409 SOURCE BOOKS AND CONSECUTIVE DOCUMENTS

While source books of the type now in vogue, namely, collections of selected texts, mainly primary, illustrating the history of particular periods, countries, or topics, are designed chiefly as aids to students or teachers, they may also have their use for the writer of history. The books listed here are not considered of equal editorial merit.

(a) *Source books in the English language*

Beresford J. Kidd, *Documents Illustrative of the History of the Church* (2 vols., London, 1920–1923).

Robert G. D. Laffan and Others, *Select Historical Documents of European History* (3 vols., London, 1930).

Ernest F. Henderson, *Select Historical Documents of the Middle Ages*, (London, 1921).

Frederick A. Ogg, *A Source Book of Mediaeval History* (New York, 1908).

Oliver J. Thatcher and Edgard McNeal, *A Source Book on Mediaeval History* (New York, 1905).

James H. Robinson, *Readings in European History* (2 vols., New York, 1904).

William Stubbs, *Select Charters and Other Illustrations of English Constitutional History from the Earliest Times to the Reign of Edward the First* (Oxford, 1929).

Roy C. Cave and Herbert H. Coulson, *A Source Book for Medieval Economic History* (Milwaukee, 1936).

Alfred E. Bland and Others, *English Economic History, Select Documents* (London, 1937).

R. Trevor Davies, *Documents Illustrating the History of Civilization in Medieval England, 1066–1500* (London, 1926).

Louis Kaplan, *Research Materials in the Social Sciences: An Annotated Guide for Graduate Students* (Madison, Wis., 1940). "A guide to bibliographies, newspapers and periodicals, government documents, manuscripts and other source materials, dissertations, book reviews, statistics, and general reference works; with instructions for obtaining materials through inter-library loans."

Raymond W. Chambers, *England before the Norman Conquest* (London, 1926).

Robert B. Morgan, *Readings in English Social History from Contemporary Literature* (5 vols., Cambridge, Eng., 1921–1922).

Frederick J. Furnivall, *The Fifty Earliest English Wills in the Court of Probate, London A.D. 1387–1439, with a Priest's of 1454* (London, 1882).

Leopold G. W. Legg, *Select Documents Illustrative of the History of the French Revolution: The Constituent Assembly* (2 vols., Oxford, 1905).

Different in scope from the ordinary source book are:

Frederic Duncalf and August C. Krey, *Parallel Source Problems in Mediaeval History* (New York, 1912).

Fred M. Fling and Helene D. Fling, *Source Problems in the French Revolution* (New York, 1913). See also Maurice W. Keatinge, *Studies in the Teaching of History* (London, 1913). Helpful on the interpretation of sources, and not without suggestions for the advanced student.

Albert B. Hart, *American History Told by Contemporaries* (5 vols., New York and London, 1897–1929).

William MacDonald, *Select Charters and Other Documents Illustrative of American History, 1606–1775* (New York, 1899).

Samuel E. Morison, *Sources and Documents Illustrating the American Revolution, 1764–1788* (Oxford, 1923).

Felix Flügel and Harold U. Faulkner, *Readings in the Economic and Social History of the United States* (New York, 1929).

Henry S. Commager, *Documents of American History* (2d ed., New York, 1940).

J. A. Nairn's *Classical Hand Book*, ed. B. H. Blackwell, Ltd. (2d ed., revised, enlarged, Oxford, 1939). Reference book for classics.

(b) Source books in languages other than English

Henry Denzinger, *Enchiridion Symbolorum, Definitionum et Declarationum de rebus fidei et morum* (10th rev. ed., by C. Bannwart, Freiburg, 1908, and many subsequent editions).

Conrad Kirch, *Enchiridion Fontium Historiae Ecclesiasticae Antiquae* (4th ed., Freiburg, 1923).

Charles Silva-Tarouca, *Fontes Historiae Ecclesiasticae Medii Aevi, I. saec. V–IX* (Rome, 1930).

Zaccaria Giacometi, *Quellen zur Geschichte der Trennung von Staat und Kirche* (Tübingen, 1926).

C. Mirbt, *Quellen zur Geschichte des Papsttums und des Römischern Katholizismus* (4th rev. ed., Tübingen, 1924).

Ernest Bernheim, *Quellen zur Geschichte der Entstehung des Kirchenstaates* (Leipzig, 1907).

Martin Grabmann and Francis Pelster, *Opuscula et textus historiam ecclesiae ejusque vitam atque doctrinam illustrantia* (Münster, 1929).

Charles V. Langlois, *La Sociètè française au XIII° siècle d'après dix Romans d'Aventure* (Paris, 1911).

Charles V. Langlois, *La vie en France au Moyen Age de la fin du XII° siècle d'après les moralistes du temps* (Paris, 1926).

Lending itself more readily to continuous reading than the conventional source book, is a type of compilation which seeks to enliven a historical topic by setting it out in the words of contemporary writers, especially eyewitnesses. Such compilations are called "consecutive documents."

August C. Krey, editor and translator, *The First Crusade; the Accounts of Eyewitnesses and Participants* (Princeton, 1921).

John Morris, *The Troubles of Our Catholic Forefathers Related by Themselves* (London, 1872).

G. Lenôtre, *The Last Days of Marie Antoinette* (Philadelphia, 1907).

Earl L. Higgins, *The French Revolution Told by Contemporaries* (New York, 1938).

Allan Nevins, *American Social History as Recorded by British Travelers* (New York, 1923).

Frank A. Mumby, *George III and the American Revolution: The Beginnings* (London, 1923).

Ina F. Woestemeyer and J. Montgomery Gambril, *The Westward Movement: a Book of Readings on our Changing Frontiers* (New York, 1939).

Chapter Eighteen

MAKING THE PRESENTATION EFFECTIVE

A. Reconstructing the Past . . . . Page 396
B. The Literary Element in History 397
C. Vivid Writing 401
D. Synthetic Views 404
E. Quotation: Direct and Indirect 407

¶ 410   That effective presentation is the acid test of the historian's competence in his art, is forcefully shown by Hilaire Belloc: "To make a history at once accurate, readable, useful, and new, is probably the hardest of all literary efforts; a man writing such history is driving more horses abreast in his team than a man writing any other kind of literary matter. He must keep his imagination active; his style must be not only lucid but also must arrest the reader; he must exercise perpetually a power of selection which plays over innumerable details; he must in the midst of such occupations preserve unity of design, as much as must the novelist or the playwright; and yet with all this, there is not a verb, an adjective, or a substantive, which, if it does not repose upon established evidence, will not mar the particular type of work on which he is engaged."—*First and Last* (6th ed., London, 1936), 129 f.

A. Reconstructing the Past

¶ 411   RECONSTRUCTION OF THE PAST:
        THE HISTORIAN'S IDEAL

All ideals may be approximated, but never fully realized. No phase of the historian's business puts him more on his mettle than the challenge to reconstruct the past. To picture in words one's actual environment or the play of events on the contemporary stage, is difficult, but the difficulty increases a hundredfold when environment and events lie hundreds, perhaps thousands of years behind. Yet, the historian must visualize the past, recapture its atmosphere and moods, and fix the picture successfully on the written page. The imagination is the faculty that helps most to carry out this manifold task successfully.

¶ 412 The poet's imagination is inventive, creative; the historian's is reproductive, such as enables him to reproduce, rebuild, reconstruct. The words, "the scientific use of the imagination," overflow with suggestion. They come to us from the English scientist, William Tyndall. The part which the reproductive imagination plays in physical research: to visualize phenomena inaccessible to the senses, as an aid to interpretation, is easily understood. There is a parallel "historical use of the imagination." At first thought, imagination would appear to be the last faculty the historian can legitimately call to his aid. Its product is ordinarily taken to be the unreal, the fictitious, the bizarre, whereas history pursues objective truth. The difficulty disappears when one reflects that the historical imagination is reproductive, not inventive in scope. Far from dealing with unrealities, it seeks only to make past realities live again. An indispensable means of achieving this result is to steep oneself in such primary sources as abound in intimate realistic details about the past.

I am a historian [wrote Niebuhr], for I can make a complete picture from separate fragments, and I know when the parts are missing and how to fill them up. No one believes how much of what seems to be lost can be restored. . . . On another occasion the historian is compared to a man in a cell whose eyes gradually become so accustomed to the darkness that he can perceive objects which one newly entering not only does not see but declares to be invisible.—G. P. Gooch, *History and Historians*, 19.

B. The Literary Element in History

¶ 413 Whether history is literature or science is an idle question. There is no reason why history, in conformity with the now prevailing attitude of trained historians towards it, should not be denominated a science [¶ 43]. If so, it has only a subordinate and accidental connection with literature. But this does not mean that the scientific and the literary cannot or should not unite in historical composition.

¶ 414 The ideal to be achieved, as something apart from the bare essentials in the writing of history, is a blend of science and literature. The Graeco-Roman era gave us literary history, at least the mature development of it, and while not discarding literary history, the nineteenth century gave us scientific history. The twentieth century looks to scientific-literary history as the true culmination of the historian's art. At all events, scientific method and literary form in history are not mutually exclusive; at times they are found together.

The advocates of history as literature sometimes argue as though making history a science necessarily means making it dull. This is misconception. To hold that history is a science, by no means implies that it may or ought to neglect questions of literary form. The dictum, "it is scientific to be dull," to quote Fortescue, is a libel on science, however much the manner of many scientific historians may give ground for the reproach.

❡ 415   At the same time, the tendency of scholarly history to become uninteresting is real, and calls for conscious resistance on the part of the writer. Charles G. Crump (*History and Historical Research*, 18), speaks of "the great enemy that lies in wait for all historians today, the enemy, who calls himself 'scientific method' and whose real name is 'meritorious dullness.'"

> They [the scientific historians] represent what is in itself the excellent reaction against superficiality and lack of research, but they have grown into the opposite and equally obnoxious belief that research is all in all, that accumulation of facts is everything. . . . The great historian must of course have the scientific spirit which gives the power of research, which enables one to marshal and weigh the facts; but unless his finished work is literature of a very high type, small will be his claim to greatness.—Theodore Roosevelt to Sir George Otto Trevelyan, January 23, 1904, in Joseph B. Bishop, *Theodore Roosevelt and His Times Shown in His Own Letters* (2 vols., New York, 1920), 1:140 f.
>
> Well, let us know what we mean by literary history. History in which the narrative of events is made subordinate to literary effect is an impudent swindle. But the history which has no quality of literature at all, neither power of expression nor imaginative insight, is nothing but materials—the bricks and stones out of which someone one day might build a house.—Frederick Harrison, *The Meaning of History* (New York, 1895), 131.
>
> Histories are written in order that the bulk of men may read and realize; and it is as bad to bungle the telling of a story as to lie, as fatal to lack a vocabulary as to lack knowledge. In no case can you do more than convey an impression, so various and complex is the matter. In the whole process there is a nice adjustment of means to ends which only the artist can manage. There is an art of lying—there is equally an art, an infinitely more difficult art—of telling the truth.—Woodrow Wilson, *Mere Literature* (Boston, 1913), 185 f.

❡ 416   The conventional types of historical composition are mostly three: textbooks; monographs and other learned works addressed to scholars; popular histories. In all three there is an irreducible minimum of literary requirement which consists in clear, correct, smoothly flowing language. These qualities can be present in a composition which shows no particular literary merit. But such qualities are the minimum one must require in any kind of history, for its presentation. Clearness or lucidity, the first of the stylistic virtues, may not be dispensed with, certainly not that substantial degree of it which saves writing from being unintelligible or obscure. Nor may one dispense with a certain smoothness and ease of movement, which makes the narrative readable. As to the more obvious elements of good composition, such as grammatical accuracy, correct structure of sentence and paragraph, propriety of diction—these are taken for granted. Slovenly, slipshod, incorrect writing is intolerable in any history book.

Minimum standards of expression are to be attained in any kind of history, whether textbook, student's thesis, critical monograph, or book for the general reader; in the last-named, a higher level of literary quality is expected than in history of other types.

¶ 417 The actual commitment of historical data to paper is a process of rhetoric, not of research. As such, it is governed by the rules of rhetoric, which one may take to be the art of effective expression through the medium of words. Particularly meaningful in this definition is the term *effective*. Expression is effective when it produces the result intended, whether this be to inform, convince, persuade, or entertain. Rhetoric is therefore a practical instrument or device for the successful transmission of human thought and feeling by means of language. It is a complex of principles, rules, practical directions, which enable the user to express himself in words to the best possible advantage. These principles and rules are partly natural, as being dictated by psychological and other laws of nature, partly artificial, as being based on recognized literary usage. In any case, the literary worker (and the historian is such when he begins to write), must conform to certain accepted canons of literary expression. Thus, account must be taken of the stylistic principles of unity, emphasis, coherence, and proportion. Moreover, the recognized prose types, namely, description, narration, exposition and argumentation (in the discussion of evidence), are all represented, as a rule, in any historical composition of length. Hence, knowledge of the rhetorical principles governing these types will be of practical use to the historian.

¶ 418 In every type of history writing, the general lesson to be learned is that the author must concern himself alike with substance and form. The young worker especially must take with seriousness the mechanics of composition and the rhetorical qualities which all good composition ought to show. Not much experience in composition will be needed to bring home to him his natural limitations in this regard, as distinct from shortcomings that are subject to remedy. "Look," exclaimed Quintilian, "there is a man trying to write better than he can!" With practice every writer gradually adjusts himself to a more or less uniform level in composition that is natural and practicable to him—one he can maintain steadily without affectation or strain.

> After all, the style, the art that carries all by storm and wins along the whole line is a God-given gift. Those who have it, cannot fail to make it felt, while those who have it not would do well to make no effort to affect it."—James H. Wylie, *The Council of Constance to the Death of John Hus* (London, 1900), 70.

⁋ 419 It is clear that historians who have achieved a popular success owe the result largely to their attractive prose. We see this to be true in the case of Macaulay, Green, Prescott, Parkman, Fiske, Belloc. The fact, then, stands, that if history is to appeal to the reading public, it can never be of the merely scientific kind. It must show at least some degree of literary merit by cultivating whatever graces of style the writer can command.

On the other hand, to cite a dissenting opinion, Justin Winsor thought that "the truest form of historical expression was the bare statement of fact in bald language."—Edward Channing, "Justin Winsor," *AHR*, 3 (1898), 201.

Another authority would have the historian "neglect the general reader." This may be a proper attitude in one who writes specialized history addressed to specialists; it is folly if the writer expects to be read beyond so narrow a circle. Macaulay wrote with the avowed purpose of producing a history which should "for a few days supersede the last fashionable novel on the tables of young ladies." The inscription on his monument in the chapel of Trinity College, Cambridge, reads: *Ita scripsit ut vera fictis libentius legerentur*. "He could not rest," wrote his biographer, "until every paragraph concluded with a telling sentence and every sentence flowed like water."—George O. Trevelyan, *The Life and Letters of Lord Macaulay* (2 vols., London, 1876), 2:250.

Macaulay is by no means a model historian according to modern standards or sound standards of any kind in historiography; but his preoccupation with style justified itself in its results and remains a warning to all followers of Clio's craft, that not by facts alone can history live. At the same time, it is pertinent to recall, Macaulay abused his great powers of expression. "Truth is bartered for a telling phrase, a sounding epithet."—G. P. Gooch, *History and Historians*, 300.

⁋ 420 A practical commentary on the topic of literary history is furnished by the action of the American Historical Association, in appointing a council of historians to investigate the admittedly unsatisfactory status of history-writing in the United States, and recommend means for its betterment.

The Council took notice of the general protest of a large portion of the public against the heaviness of style characteristic of much of the history now being written. They thought it necessary to do something to awaken young students and historians to a realization of the part good expression must play in enabling history to maintain a place in the world of letters. To them it did not seem advisable to accept the existing situation as the best to be expected nor to relinquish without a struggle the hope that historical information may be presented in such a manner as to make the reading of it pleasing if not delightful.—J. Jusserand and Others, *The Writing of History*, v.

C. Vivid Writing

¶ 421 Vivid writing may seem a rather impracticable issue to raise in the training of a historian. It suggests the prose of the great masters of historical style. This is certainly not an ideal to be pursued seriously by the average writer who grapples with the problem of putting the results of his research into readable form. Yet, vivid writing in the lesser degrees is really not as hopeless an objective as may at first sight appear; it depends, at least to some extent, on a technique which can be learned, and with varying degree of success, reduced to practice. The root-meaning of *vivid* is "living"; the term, as employed here, denotes the element which makes history as record live, by stirring the imagination and feelings, and in general, by filling one with a sense of the reality of what is told. Under the touch of a vivid writer past happenings take on the color and warmth perceived by contemporary witnesses. Vivid writing, therefore, is writing that is alive. It depends, among other things, on concrete, picturesque detail, and colorful diction.

¶ 422 CONCRETE DETAIL
By the working of a psychological law we are more impressed by the concrete than by the abstract. The concrete gives us an image or a series of images; it is food for the imagination, the faculty we chiefly rely upon in building up a mental picture of the past. The abstract engages the intellect, the superior faculty; but abstractions apart from images can be singularly unimpressive. Generalized descriptions are often feeble; particularize them by the introduction of concrete detail, and they become effective. Chesterton might have said that "charters were plentiful in the Middle Ages"; but he said that "the whole stuff of the Middle Ages was stiff with the parchments of charters."—Gilbert K. Chesterton, *A Short History of England* (New York, 1917), 27.

(a) But vivid expression is not necessarily figurative expression.

Macaulay's "famous third chapter" is a crowded canvas of factual details literally stated. What makes the picture effective is the rapid succession of well-chosen concrete particulars, in this case illustrating various sides of the English social scene at the accession of James II. The well-known trial scene in the same historian's *Warren Hastings*, is another example of effective use of the concrete. Belloc, himself a master of concrete writing, despite his flair for speculation and generalization, has written:

> I have often quoted and I here repeat that great phrase of Michelet's that "history should be a resurrection of the flesh." It is this which properly excuses, or rather makes praiseworthy the insistence upon physical details, upon color, weather, landscape, gesture, the aspect of a building, the hours of the day and of the night. Indeed, even as a mere record, a record will not be certain unless it lives.—Hilaire Belloc, *Danton* (New York and London, 1928), xvii.

(b) It is, then, a matter of importance to the writer of history that he learn to feel the value of concrete detail, and accustom himself to its use. Under its impact the reader is made to realize the broad, the typical, the general fact, which the historian seeks to make clear, as the most important business before him. But to succeed in this aim, the selection and arrangement of the details must be made with skill. Any mere heaping up of factual items will not suffice; like every other process in literary presentation the picturing of the general by means of the particular has its technique. To ignore this technique is to run the risk of producing the sort of thing which the critics qualify not by way of compliment, as encyclopedic. Any serious writer of history will be concerned to escape the reproach implicit in the hackneyed term.

❡ 423 Picturesque detail

The picturesque in literary expression is often identical with the concrete. Yet there are times when it is something more. The picturesque, whether the artist work in colors or in words, in the main is the element in things that makes them the right subjects for pictorial treatment. The artist's instinct tells him what details will make for an effective picture and what will not. The picturesqueness latent in certain facts, situations, and personalities of history is there independently of any notice of it by the historian.

> History cannot be made picturesque by the skill of the writer. It must be picturesque in itself if it is to be so at all. All the writer can claim is the artistic insight which discerns the elements of a forcible composition in unexpected places and reveals unknown beauties by compelling attention to what might otherwise be overlooked.—Mandell Creighton, *Historical Lectures and Addresses* (London, 1903), 264.

❡ 425   Chapter 18   403

Periods of great social stress and crisis, such as the Protestant Revolt and the French Revolution, tend to become picturesque. Striking characters, drawing together in their own personalities the tendencies characteristic of their day, stand out from the crowd and attract the attention of contemporaries, who may observe them at close range and set down the results of their observations in memoirs. Sometimes such characters become their own portrayers in personal reminiscence. All this means an abundance of intimate and often of dramatic detail available to the historian. It is largely the data supplied by memoirs that help to render history picturesque. Mandell Creighton was of the opinion that Italian history of the fifteenth century is highly picturesque, and that the same can be said of French but not of English history. He instances as the two most picturesque events in English history, the death of St. Thomas of Canterbury and that of Wolsey, and explains that the profound impression these events made on the people of the day and the ample detail concerning them, made them survive in contemporary sources.

❡ 424   But while revolutionary crises may be the most absorbing, they are not what is most instructive in history. Rather, that element in history is to note the hidden play of cause and effect, the slow growth of institutions, the step-by-step evolution of present-day civilization out of the welter of conditions in the past. To serious-minded readers such aspects of history may become more appealing, even more fascinating than the stirring dramatic situations that give one a momentary thrill. Historical beginnings are generally seen through an atmosphere of glamor and romance. "First things" have an interest all their own, and the more obscure and hazy they are, the more likely they are to intrigue.

Yet, often there is at work here nothing more than a psychological trick. A familiar line furnishes the key to the phenomenon: " 'Tis distance lends enchantment to the view." Participants in historical beginnings very probably found them quite as prosaic and uninspiring as people of today find their own actual environment, however true it be that past events very often take on with time a significance hidden from those who lived through them. Clarence Walworth Alvord pointed out that the most vital chapters in American history deal with the slow, undramatic shaping of a new American people out of various racial strains during the period of immigration, not with beginnings, however stirring these appear to us now.

❡ 425   Colorful diction

It is problematical how far conscious effort will enable a writer to acquire a vocabulary charged with color and warmth. A Cambridge don remarked to a student, apropos of brilliancy of style, "But that, you know, is a gift of God." Yet, the apprentice in history can profit by noting in his reading the life and movement which masters of historical prose put into their words. One may at least be placed in the way of acquiring a sense, always valuable, of the importance of color in the historian's style; one may be led to realize, and as a consequence, consciously to resist any tendency there may be to the anemic and spiritless use of words in one's personal style.

⟨ 426 Vividness through concrete detail and other rhetorical aids, is not a quality found in modern historians only. To Macaulay, the passage in Thucydides (Bk. VII) on the retreat from Syracuse, seemed the most graphic in written history. Tacitus is repeatedly vivid, as in his account of the accession of the emperor Otho to the throne (*Histories*, I, 59 ff.).

The medieval chroniclers were capable of lively writing: Matthew Paris on the attack made on the papal legate at Oxford and on the excommunication of Frederick II, at Lyons; Joinville's account of the death of St. Louis are graphic narratives. Froissart pictures the action at Crécy in glowing colors.

There are many examples of vivid, picturesque writing in the works of modern historians. Thus, Froude on the death of Caesar, in *Julius Caesar*; the "noche Triste" in Prescott's *History of the Conquest of Mexico*; Carlyle, "The Storming of the Bastille," in his *French Revolution*; "The Image Breakers of Antwerp," in Motley's *Rise of the Dutch Republic*; Gardiner, the defeat and death of Montrose, in *Commonwealth and Protectorate*; Parkman, "The Heights of Abraham," in *Wolf and Montcalm*.

D. Synthetic Views

⟨ 427 Concreteness is not the whole of historical composition. History must be concrete if it is to be vivid; it must offer broad, synthetic views if it is to be illuminating. In a telling passage Newman compares the student to a traveller who ascends a nearby height that he may look down on a city and get an idea of its topography as a whole. Similarly, the student must be above his subject, must be on a mental height that enables him to take it in as a whole, see the relation of part to part, and follow the unifying threads that bind them together. If he fails in this manner to rise above his subject, then he fails to see meaning or significance in it as a whole, and as a consequence will fail to convey its meaning or significance to others. Masses of details may have to be set out before the reader; but through the details the main drift and bearing of the subject must steadily show. Here we have an application of the principle of subordination of detail [⟨ 429].

Repeatedly, the historian must resort to synthesis, to sweeping comprehensive views. In the nature of things, he deals with many details. To repeat, it is imperative that he rise superior to them and not lie prostrate beneath their weight. He must feel their relation to a larger whole, see how they fit with the creation of a design or pattern of major scale.

The result of this comprehensive grasp is seen in the illuminating, and at the same time firmly-supported generalizations which he is able to set before his readers.

The nature and principles of generalization as a logical process applied to history have been dealt with in ¶ 132. Here we consider generalization rather as an element entering into and perfecting the presentation of the facts.

¶ 428 Historians vary in their capacity for synthesis. Some are competent in this regard, others less so, or not at all. Sometimes a single sentence will sum up an entire period, reveal its essential character, manifest the common drift and bearing of thousands of individual incidents and events.

(a) De Tocqueville conceived modern French history as a steady, forward movement towards centralized government, the Revolution itself aiding, not interfering with the process. To Madelin, the Revolution is a movement which continues to our own day, Napoleon having saved rather than destroyed its principles.

(b) To Bede Jarrett "not freedom but justice, not liberty but law, was the social ideal of the Middle Ages,"—*Social Theories of the Middle Ages* (London, 1920), 96.

> It is indeed the freedom of the spiritual life which the medieval Church was endeavoring to defend; it was the apprehension that there was some ultimate quality in human nature which stands and must stand outside of the direct or coercive control of society which lies behind all the confused clamor of the conflict of Church and State.—Alexander J. Carlyle, in Francis S. Marvin, ed., *Progress and History* (Oxford, 1916), 79.

A. J. Carlyle's essay develops the generalization that the Middle Ages, contrary to the traditional view, were not static but progressive in character. The work of the same author and his collaborator, in *History of Medieval Political Theory in the West*, is replete with judicious and striking generalizations. Thus, "to the Middle Ages the conception of an absolute or arbitrary monarchy was practically unknown" (5:474). "The Middle Ages remained faithful to the Gelasian principle that each power, the temporal and spiritual, derives its authority from God and that neither power has authority over the other in matters which belong to its own sphere" (5:440). Again, three legal conceptions are stressed as medieval, not Roman in origin: supremacy of law, sovereignty of the people, contractual nature of government (3:11–13). A. J. Carlyle summarizes the main generalizations of his elaborate work in *AHR*, 19 (1913): 3–12.

Ferdinand Brunetière emphasizes as a general fact the absence of individual, local, or regional characteristics in medieval literature and art. There is "nothing more French about a Gothic Cathedral in Paris than in Cologne, or more German about one in Cologne than in Canterbury."—*Manual of the History of French Literature* (New York, 1898), 4.

Belloc develops the thesis that the House of Commons has been essentially the organ of an aristocratic state. "That is the whole understanding of modern English History. As an ultimate result of the Reformation the Kings were broken and replaced by a governing Class of which the House of Commons was the organ."—Hilaire Belloc, *The House of Commons and Monarchy* (London, 1920), 38.

> The medieval king was "absolute" and irresponsible, but he was "limited." There were things beyond his legitimate power and if he overstepped that power his acts were *ultra vires*.—Charles H. McIlwain, *The Growth of Political Thought in the West from the Greeks to the End of the Middle Ages* (New York, 1932), 367.

(c) In American history suggestive and striking generalizations have been advanced by Frederick J. Turner in *The American Frontier in American History*, and in *The Significance of the Sections in American History*. For other generalizations, see Arthur M. Schlesinger, *New Viewpoints in American History*; Walter P. Webb, *The Great Plains*.

¶ 429 Subordination of detail

Subordination of detail means making a major historical idea or fact stand out in relief, while the particulars of the narrative fill in the background, and contribute to the general effect by way of illustration, supplementation, or proof. It is obviously a matter of right perspective and proportion, and therefore of effective presentation. Where details multiply and the broad lines of the picture fail to appear distinctly, we have the untoward result that "the woods cannot be seen for the trees."

> That particular feature which gives special character to the period under consideration must be selected and the relations of the others to it discerned, in order that in the pre-eminence of the one and the contributing subordination of the other, artistic unity of construction may be attained. Thus only can the mass of readers receive that correct impression of the general character and trend of a period which far surpasses in an instructive quality any volume of details, however accurate, the significance of which is not apprehended.—Alfred T. Mahan, "Subordination in Historical Treatment," AHA, *Report* (1902), 62.

Ranke's use of the typical, as described by E. G. Bourne, is substantially the same process as subordination of detail. "As a writer Ranke possessed a rare power of discerning in his material the typical. He draws in broad outline and then fills in with detail. The truth of the picture vitally depends upon the discrimination and honesty with which the choice of details is made."—*Essays in Historical Criticism*, 257.

The principle of subordination of detail coincides largely with the principle of synthetic views, as explained in ⁋ 427.

E. Quotation: Direct and Indirect

⁋ 430 Whether or not to quote directly from one's sources is a stock question in history-writing. Sir John Fortescue is decidedly against the practice, a stand in which he seems to have most of the English historians from Lingard's time, agreeing with him.—*The Writing of History*, 63.

Pastor quotes sparingly from his wealth of documents, the essence of which he extracts and lays before the reader. Objections urged against the formal quotation are that it checks the flow of the narrative, detracts from uniformity of style by introducing passages of varying literary merit, and in other ways militates against artistic form. It is argued from this point of view that sources are the raw material of history. It is the historian's business to work them over by paraphrase, summary, and other indirect means, not to transfer them bodily to the written page.

But much can be said for the direct quotation. "Wherever space permits, source material should be incorporated in the text. A paraphrase of a source never has the color of the source itself and there is furthermore the possibility of error in condensing it.—F. M. Fling, *The Writing of History*, 167.

There is no doubt that direct citation from the sources will often lend narrative a vividness and actuality that cannot be secured in any other way. Even a lengthy letter often makes delightful reading and may be many times more effective in portraying a person or situation than any paraphrase or summary of it could possibly be. "Wherever possible," said John Anthony Froude, an artist, if not a reliable historian, "let us not be told about this man or that. Let us hear the man himself speak, let us see him act and let us be left to form our own opinion about him."

A similar view was expressed by Cardinal Newman who held that biography is best written by means of liberal extracts from the subject's own letters. From the standpoint of good practice in historiography, there can be no doubt that direct quotation may be freely admitted into historical narrative, including that of the strictly scientific kind. At the same time, such a procedure may be overdone. Fortescue protests against the type of history which he calls "printed notebooks." One can string together extracts from the sources until the result is merely a loosely jointed mosaic, not the organic and unified whole which true history ought to be.

Chapter Nineteen

HISTORY—WRITTEN AND REWRITTEN

A. Studying Historians' Methods . . . . Page 408
B. Why History is Rewritten 412
C. Historical Revisions 420
D. Examples 421
E. Historical Problems 423

A. Studying Historians' Methods

❡ 431 Painters, sculptors, musicians study the technique of the masters in their respective arts. And yet, the technique of the masters is not something imitable in all its details; every artist's individual genius eventually works out a method that is peculiar to himself and would suit no one else. But a novice in any craft learns much by close examination of the finished product of its skilled practitioners. There are artifices in the craft that can be learned, even though one may not hope to turn out other masterpieces. Robert Louis Stevenson insisted that good writing was largely a matter of imitation. The technique of any art or craft has its general principles to which adepts in it consciously or unconsciously conform. Historiography, understood as "the art of writing history" (J. B. Black), not in the wider usage, as the literature of history, or the collective body of historical writings, falls under the same rule. A careful study of the working methods of almost any scholarly historian, as revealed in his written product, leads to practical results, is an object lesson of value. Thus three lines of examination of any book of history can be pursued.

(a) *Study of plan, distribution of material.* This is often made relatively easy if the work has an analytical table of contents. To go carefully through such a table is to ascertain the plan or structure of the work as a whole; the relations of part to part and the emphasis in space laid on each part; the efficacy of the plan as regards the general scope of the work.

(b) *Study of preface or introduction.* In these sections historians

¶ 431   Chapter 19

often disclose their methods. In the first book of his history, Thucydides distinguishes, after the manner of a modern historian, between firsthand and secondhand sources of information, and the use he has made of both. Livy introduces his history with an explicit statement of his purpose in writing it, but says nothing about his methods of research or composition. Tacitus is equally reticent on these points. On the other hand, Gregory of Tours, in his *History of the Franks*, discusses in a critical vein the different types of source material he used. So also Bede, in the preface to his *Ecclesiastical History of the English Nation*, is surprisingly modern in detailing the various groups of sources he put to account. The *Alexiad* of the Princess Anna Comnena [¶ 46-a] begins with announcing a strictly non-partisan attitude:

> I should counsel both parties, those attacked by us and our partisans alike, to take comfort from the fact that I have sought the evidence of the actual deeds themselves and the testimony of those who have seen the actions and the men and their actions [sic]—the fathers of some of the men now living and the grandfathers of others were actual eyewitnesses.

Lingard's preface to the second edition of his *History of England* informs the reader that he worked wherever possible with "original documents and the more ancient writers." He thus antedated in his scientific attitude towards history the Ranke school, whose first published work belongs to the eighteen-thirties. The preface to Prescott's *Conquest of Mexico* reveals the preoccupation of a successful historian with the factors that make for artistic and dramatic effect.

Questions of method are also touched on in the prefaces or introductions to Gardiner, *History of the Great Civil War, 1642–1649*; McMaster, *History of the People of the United States*; Osgood, *The American Colonies in the Seventeenth Century*; Bryce, *Modern Democracies*; Gasquet, *Henry VIII and the English Monasteries*; Pastor, *History of the Popes*.

(c) *Study of a historian's work as a whole.* This is not always particularly laborious or time-consuming, even when there is question of ascertaining a historian's method in general, and not that employed in a particular book. James Ford Rhodes read only one of Parkman's volumes, *Montcalm and Wolfe*, which had been recommended to him as the most typical of the New Englander's art; but he read it carefully and more than once, thus getting from the experience an insight into Parkman's manner of handling his material.

Another plan is to take up for study the treatment of the same topic at the hands of various authors, for instance, the American Revolution as presented by Bancroft, Channing, Van Tyne, Trevelyan. A comparative study of even so limited a range will bring to light interesting and instructive differences in manner of approach and general handling of a topic. But thoroughgoing study of a historian's method postulates a much broader acquaintance with his work as a safe basis for conclusions.

❡ 432 THE COMPARATIVE METHOD

A specific method of dealing with historical material is the comparative. This generally takes the form of a study of an institution or of a movement, as it existed in various times and places. Points of agreement or difference, according to the categories of time and place, are noted, and out of the comparison the true character of the institution or movement in question is seen to emerge.

Bryce in his *Modern Democracies* (vol. 1, chap. 2), adopts this method. See Harold D. Lasswell, "The Comparative Method of James Bryce," Stuart A. Rice, ed., *Methods in Social Science: A Case-book* (Chicago, 1931).

Similar comparative studies have been made of feudalism, the guild system, the medieval university, constitutional monarchy, and other topics.

Clarence C. Brinton in *The Anatomy of Revolution*, made a comparative study of four revolutions, English (Cromwellian), American, French, Russian.

> Historians of religion employ what is known as the comparative method of correlating and interpreting the facts with which their science deals, a method both fruitful and scientifically sound.—George C. Ring, *Gods of the Gentiles*, 94.

For the comparative method as applied to the history of religion, see Wilhelm Schmidt, *The Origin and Growth of Religion: Facts and Theories* (London, 1931), chap. 11; Pinard de la Boullaye, *L'étude comparée des religions* (2 vols., Paris, 1929), vol. 2, chap. 2.

❡ 433 A comprehensive study of the methods of the better known historians is recommended. Scattered treatment of the topic in studies of varying length and thoroughness, is available in books and articles.

❡ 434 Edward Fueter, *Geschichte der neueren Historiographie* (3d ed., Berlin, 1936). French translation by E. Jeanmaire, *Histoire de l'historiographie moderne* (Berlin, 1911; 3d ed., Berlin, 1936).

George P. Gooch, *History and Historians in the Nineteenth Century* (London and New York, 1913).

Paul M. Baumgarten, *Lea's Historical Writings; A Critical Inquiry into their Method and Merit* (New York, 1919).

Francis A. Gasquet, *Leaves from My Diary* (London, 1911).

Wilbur Cortez Abbott, "Some New History and Historians," *Adventures in Reputation*, 211-52.

Peter Guilday, ed., *Church Historians* (New York, 1926).

Thomas F. Peardon, *The Transition in English Historical Writing* (New York, 1933).

J. P. Code, *Queen Elizabeth and the English Catholic Historians*, on Lingard's method, 150–54; on Belloc's method, 190–93.

Sir Charles Firth, *A Commentary on Macaulay's History of England* (London, 1938).

Hilaire Belloc, prefaces to *Danton, Robespierre, Marie Antoinette.*

Bernadotte E. Schmidt, ed., *Some Historians of Modern Europe* (Chicago, 1941).

J. Franklin Jameson, *History of Historical Writing in America.*

Edward Channing, "Justin Winsor," *AHR*, 3 (1898): 197–202.

E. G. Bourne, *Essays in Historical Criticism*, includes studies of Parkman, Ranke, and others.

William A. Dunning, "A Generation of American Historiography," *AHA, Report* (1917), 347 ff.

J. S. Bassett, *The Middle Group of American Historians* (New York, 1917). Prescott, Sparks, Motley, Bancroft.

Merle E. Curti, "The Sections and the Frontier in American History: The Methodological Concepts of Fredrick Jackson Turner," Stuart A. Rice, ed., *Methods in Social Science: A Case-book*, 353–67.

William T. Hutchinson, ed., *The Marcus W. Jernegan Essays in American Historiography.* Critical appreciation of twenty-one American historians.

Studies in the *Mississippi Valley Historical Review*, of Schouler, 16 (1929): 212–27; of Bancroft, 19 (1932): 77–86; of Osgood, 19 (1932): 394–403.

Michael Kraus, *A History of American History.*

W. Stull Holt, ed., *Historical Scholarship in the United States as Revealed in the Correspondence of Herbert B. Adams* (Baltimore, 1938).

The published correspondence of historians sometimes throws light on their methods.

> It was not so much Carlyle the man as Carlyle the workman that was shown through his letters and that lead to a re-estimate of his work as a historian.—L. M. Salmon, *Historical Material*, 97.

⁋ 435 Biographies of historians can also be informative as to their methods of work.

> I will place the documents under his [the reader's] eyes; I will have him follow the way of my researches, my hesitations, my doubts. I will conduct him by the same route I followed myself. Moreover, I will point out to him the opinions opposite to my own and let him know for what reasons I fail to agree with them. I will, in fine, set my work before him as it was carried on almost from day to day and will furnish him at the same time the means of discussing my points of view. Whether this will be of use to anyone, I do not know. I have now been teaching twenty-five years and every year it has been my happiness to have four or five pupils. Above all things, I have taught them to investigate. What I impressed on them with most earnestness was not to think everything easy and never to pass problems by without recognizing them. The only truth I sought to bring home to them was that history

is the most difficult of the sciences.——N. D. Fustel de Coulanges, *Recherches sur quelques problèmes d'histoire*, iv.

The ideal historian would first collect and sift all the evidence until he has reached an assured basis of facts; holding all these facts in his mind at once, he would be able to relate them to each other in such a way as to see the relationship between them and so to arrive at their inner meaning; finally, he would set down this interpretation in such a way as to convey it most clearly to his readers, selecting for his purpose such facts as were most significant and most representative of the whole. ——R. E. Balfour, "History," Harold Wright, ed., *Cambridge Historical Studies* (Cambridge, Eng., 1933).

But the history will mature all the better for the delay. I [W. M. Thackeray] want to absorb the authorities gradually, so that when I come to write, I shall be filled with the subject and can sit down to a continuous narrative without jumping up every moment to consult somebody.——Lewis Melville (pseud., Lewis S. Benjamin), *William Makepeace Thackeray* (Garden City, N. Y., 1928), 410.

B. Why History is Rewritten

¶ 436 A characteristic of history as record is that it is not static, but is being constantly made over again. George M. Trevelyan describes it as "an eager aspiration destined to perpetual change, due to everlasting imperfection, but living, complex, broad as humanity itself." The opinion has been expressed that the average span of life of a history book in modern times is a hundred years. On the other hand, any narrative that preserves significant data not on record elsewhere, deserves to live, at least as a source for historians. Hence, every scrap of historical writing from ancient times has been jealously treasured, though a great part of this material is without interest or meaning for the general reader. Genuine literature is saved from oblivion largely because of its artistic form. The histories usually qualified as classic owe their distinction mainly to the fact that they are more than ordinarily well written [¶ 419].

When Thucydides planned his history to be an "everlasting possession," he did indeed base this expectation mainly on the ground that it was to be an accurate and informing piece of work, and as such would appeal to the select circle of readers who in all ages look for instruction rather than entertainment in history. Still, the fact remains that it is literary quality as much as anything else which gives his work the standing it has always had.

While some few histories, then, achieve an enviable immortality, the general fabric of history as record is being constantly altered, reshaped, done over again. What are the reasons for this? Why is history rewritten at all? Four factors, among others, account for the phenomenon: the errors and inadequacies of existing history; the discovery of new material; significant re-interpretations of old material; shifting attitudes and viewpoints in regard to the past.

¶ 437 THE PERVERSIONS OF HISTORY

A great deal of written history is inaccurate, or misleading, or positively false. On this matter there is only one opinion among scholars. It was under dominance of such a point of view that the *Cambridge Modern History* was projected, as appears from the general preface: "The long conspiracy against the revelation of truth has gradually given way, and competing historians all over the world have been zealous to take advantage of the change. . . . The honest student finds himself continually deserted, retarded, misled, by the classics of historical literature."

Belloc writes to similar effect: "Almost all the historical work worth doing at the present moment in the English language is the work of shovelling off heaps of rubbish inherited from the immediate past."

De Maistre's epigram is well known: "History for the last three hundred years has been a conspiracy against the truth."

The largest single factor explaining this phenomenon has been the Protestant revolt of the sixteenth century with the prejudices and the antipathies it aroused and its general influence on historiography. An illustration in point is the Statute of Appeals, 24, Henry VIII, c. 21, which was re-enacted by Elizabeth.

> The preamble to this is remarkable because it manufactured history on an unprecedented scale, but chiefly because it has operated from that day to this as a powerful incentive to its manufacture by others upon similar lines. In order to create the illusion that the new Anglican Church was indeed the same institution as the medieval Church, it was necessary to prove the historical continuity of these two very different institutions and obviously this could only be done by historical argument.—Sir William S. Holdsworth, *History of English Law* (3rd rev. ed., 9 vols., London, 1922-1923), 1: 591.

¶ 438 The result of such tampering with facts has been widespread misrepresentation in English history and in other fields of history as well. Froude's "incredible carelessness in detail" and "lack of impartiality" are notorious.—See G. P. Gooch, *History and Historians*, 337.

Macaulay and Green share the conventional bias, while George Macaulay Trevelyan's *History of England* has been characterized as "a gentlemen's version of the Protestant tradition." Even Samuel Rawson Gardiner (Rhodes "model historian," and often rated the leading English exponent of the modern scientific school in history), did not rise above inherited prejudices.

—*Times Literary Supplement* (London), Sept. 25; Dec. 18, 1919; "The Plague of Historical Falsehood"; *The Month*, 135 (1920): 70–72.

Frederick W. Maitland, *Roman Canon Law in the Church of England* (London, 1898), and James Gairdner, *Lollardry in England* (4 vols., London, 1908–1913) were probably the first of English scholars apart from Lingard to write English history on its Catholic side with understanding.

¶ 439 An exposé of the facile manner in which misstatements of fact are passed on from one historian to another may be read in Newman's *Present Position of Catholics in England*, lecture iii. (Newman, however, borrowed the illustration from Thomas Arnold, *Introductory Lectures on Modern History* (London, 1842, reprinted, New York, 1880), 105–108.

The church historian Mosheim had made an assertion derogatory to Catholic standards of morality in the Middle Ages, citing as evidence a statement from a medieval source. The statement, repeated after him by various historians, went unchallenged until an Anglican scholar, Dr. Waddington, thought of looking up the original authority cited. It was then discovered that the passage appealed to by Mosheim not only did not support his assertion, but supplied evidence to the contrary.

A similar instance of a libelous statement not to be found in the references cited for it, is in John Pollock, *The Popish Plot* (London, 1903), 201. See Malcolm V. Hay, *The Jesuits and the Popish Plot* (London, 1934), 2–4.

¶ 440 Henry J. Ford, "A Change of Climate," *CHR*, 12 (1925): 18–28.

Jeremiah D. M. Ford, "The Ciceronian Dictum on History," *CHR*, 21 (1936): 385–99.

A. L. Maycock, "To the Rescue of History," *The Month*, 145 (1925): 304–310.

Joseph Keating, "Truth in History," *The Month*, 155 (1930): 151–59.

Historical Textbooks and Readers (Westminster Catholic Federation, London, 1927, supplementary volume, 1928).

Brief critical notices of errata in Gibbon, Hume, Froude, Motley, Ranke, Acton, Prescott, Bancroft, Lea, Guizot, Taine, Parkman, Wells, and others in *HB*, 11 (1932): 17, 56–57, 75–76.

Malcolm V. Hay, *A Chain of Error in Scottish History; The Enigma of James II* (London, 1938).

William R. Thayer, "Fallacies in History," *AHR*, 25 (1920): 179–90.

¶ 441 Discovery of new material

A second reason why history is rewritten is that as time proceeds, more light is thrown on past events. Researchers at work in the British Museum and in the Public Record Office, London; the Archives Nationales, and Bibliothèque Nationale, Paris; the archives of Simancas and Seville, those of the Vatican, of the federal and state governments in the United States, and in other depositories in Europe and the Americas, have turned up a vast amount of important firsthand material unknown to historians a few generations ago. It is inevitable that such information should fill in gaps, clear up obscurities, and rectify errors in the record of the past.

Ranke's unearthing of diplomatic papers in the Venetian archives was a turning point in historiography, leading him as it did to bring to the attention of scholars the importance of basing history on new archival material. It became the ambition of every historian to be able to announce on the title page of his book that it is "based on hitherto unpublished documents." *

Edward G. Bourne said of John Cabot that no man owed more to historical research. It set the explorer right with posterity. Clarence W. Alvord, utilizing in *The Illinois Country, 1673-1818*, new material from the French archives, presents a more adequate picture of the political situation in New France than can be found in Parkman's more famous volumes in the same field. Even the contemporary historical novel shows the influence of the new light thrown on the past by scholarly research. Louis XI is more accurately portrayed in D. B. Wyndham Lewis' *King Spider* (1929) than in Walter Scott's *Quentin Durward* (1823).

⚆ 442 The lure of new material lying undiscovered in public archives or private collections ever attracts the genuine researcher. He covets the experience of turning up, it may be often after a long period of barren investigation, some precious document that solves a problem, or adds in some significant way to knowledge of the past. Sometimes by a happy inspiration fresh material is sought out in quarters where apparently no one thought of looking for it before. The American professor Charles W. Wallace, examining literally hundreds of thousands of papers in the Public Record Office, London, had the satisfaction, in 1910, of turning up six previously unknown Shakespeare documents, one of which bore the signature of the dramatist, the sixth known to exist.—C. W. Wallace, "Shakespeare as a Man Among Men," *Harper's Monthly Magazine*, 120 (1910): 489-510; Samuel A. Tannenbaum, *Problems in Shakespeare's Penmanship*, chap. 2.

John H. Rose, using fresh material from British archives, was enabled to throw new light on the much disputed question whether Napoleon's surrender to the English after Waterloo was voluntary or forced.—"The Detention of Napoleon at St. Helena," *Historical Essays by Members of the Owens College, Manchester* (London, 1902), 495-522.

William Barton and Louis Warren made their laborious way through thousands of old papers in Kentucky county archives in pursuit of fresh Lincoln material and were rewarded for their pains.

Stanley Pargellis, putting to account documents he discovered in Wind-

---

* For not a few historical writers this laudable "ambition" is a fetish; and it is not rare that the "hitherto unpublished documents" are of little or no importance at all with regard to our knowledge or our understanding of the events.—Ed.

sor Castle, was able to place Braddock's defeat in a new light.—*AHR*, 41 (1936): 253–69.

Randolph G. Adams, using the rich collection of the Clinton and Germain papers in the William L. Clements Library, Ann Arbor, Michigan, gave a new setting to the Yorktown campaign.—*AHR*, 37 (1931): 25 ff.

Carl Van Doren, also utilizing the Clinton papers in the same library, set out fresh data on what appeared to be a threadbare subject: *Secret History of the American Revolution* (New York, 1941).

Archer B. Hulbert, finding Major Pike's papers and maps in the Land Office, Washington, cleared up with their aid obscure points in the career of the explorer.—Stephen H. Hart and Archer B. Hulbert, eds., *Zebulon Pike's Arkansaw Journal* (Colorado Springs and Denver, Colo., 1932).

These instances are typical of hundreds of others in which historians have been privileged to capitalize on new material, in many cases brought to light by their own ingenuity and persistent research.

₡ 443   Though previously unknown material for the historian is constantly being recovered by archival and archaeological research, more or less obscurity will almost certainly continue to envelop many of the figures and events of history. It is not likely that any new data will be discovered about Julius Caesar or the Anglo-Saxon invasion of England, in 449. "Only two new Columbus documents have come to light in the twentieth century and there appears little hope of important additions in the future."—Charles E. Nowell, "The Columbus Question," *AHR*, 44 (1939): 802.

Virtually all sections of the historical field have benefited from recent discovery of new material, while the prospects of profitable investigation in hitherto unexplored directions seem unlimited.

₡ 444   Kenneth S. Latourette, "Chinese History as a Field of Research," *Historical Outlook*, 13 (1922): 13 f.

Walter T. Swinge, "Chinese Historical Sources," *AHR*, 25 (1921): 717–30.

₡ 445   Charles W. David, "American Historiography of the Middle Ages," *Speculum*, 10 (1933): 125–37.

Martin R. P. McGuire, "Medieval Studies in America," *CHR*, 22 (1936): 12–26.

Thomas Oestreich, "The Personality and Character of Gregory VII in Recent Historical Research," *CHR*, 7 (1921): 35–43; idem, "The Hildebrandine Reform and its Latest Historian," *CHR*, 17 (1931), 257–67.

Jeremiah D. M. Ford, "The Saint's Life in the Vernacular Literature of the Middle Ages," *CHR*, 17 (1931), 268–77.

James F. Kenney, "Early Irish Church History as a Field for Research by American Students," *CHR*, 17 (1931): 1–9.

It is not, however, one or two general works which are required—it is a whole series of monographs on important figures and specific aspects of the political and social life of the time and on the Oriental sources themselves. Not a single political figure prior to Saladin and the Third Crusade . . . has been studied in detail. . . . The criticism of Oriental sources, Arabic, Syriac, and Armenian, has not begun.——"Notes on the Arabic Material for the History of the Early Crusades," *Bulletin* of the School of Oriental Studies (London), part 7 (1935), 739.

¶ 446 John B. Stetson, "Florida as a Field for Historical Research," AHA Report (1922), 1:191 ff.

James A. Robertson, "The Spanish Manuscripts of the Florida State Historical Society," American Antiquarian Society, *Proceedings*, 39 (1929): 16–37; idem, "Notes on Early Church Government in Spanish Florida," CHR, 17 (1931): 151–74. Peter M. Dunne, "The Literature of the Jesuits of New Spain," CHR, 20 (1934): 248–59.

Herbert E. Bolton, "The Jesuits in America: an Opportunity for Historians," MA, 17 (1936): 223–33.

¶ 447 Edward P. Cheyney, "Report of the Conference on Research in English History," AHA, Report, (1908), 1: 89–108. In the same volume are reports on research in American colonial and revolutionary history.

Wallace Notestein, "The Stuart Period: Unsolved Problems," AHA, Report, (1908), 1: 391–99.

The adequate history of the Protestant Reformation in England has yet to be written. "To insure finality of judgment, however, or security against political views, considerable manuscript studies are still requisite."——John H. Pollen, cited in J. B. Code, *Queen Elizabeth and the English Catholic Historians*, 170.

George M. Dutcher, "Tendencies and Opportunities in Napoleonic Studies," AHA, Report (1914), 1: 181–220).

¶ 448 Alban W. Hoopes, "The Need for a History of the American Indian," *Social Studies*, 29 (1938): 26.

Solon J. Buck, "Some Materials for the Social History of the Mississippi Valley in the Nineteenth Century," Mississippi Valley Historical Association, *Proceedings*. 4 (1910–1911): 138–51.

Frank H. Garver, "Montana as a Field of Historical Research," Mississippi Valley Historical Association, *Proceedings*, 7, (1913–1914): 99–113.

William E. Dodd, "Profitable Fields of Investigation in American History, 1815–1860," AHR, 18 (1913): 522–36.

R. W. Kelsey, "Possibilities of Intensive Research in Agricultural History," AHA, Report (1919), 377–83.

James Truslow Adams, "The Unexplored Region in New England History," AHR, 28 (1923), 673 ff.

Samuel F. Bemis, "Fields for Research in the Diplomatic History of the United States to 900," AHR, 36 (1930): 68–75.

James G. Randall, "Has the Lincoln Theme been Exhausted?" AHR, 41 (1936): 270–94.

John C. Fitzpatrick, "The Significance to the Historian of the New Bicentennial Edition of the Writings of George Washington," AHA, Report, (1932), 99 ff.

Frederick J. Turner, "The West as a Field of Historical Study," *Early Papers of Frederick Jackson Turner* (Madison, Wis., 1938).

Asa E. Martin, "Research in State History: Its Problems and Opportunities," *Ohio Archaeological and Historical Quarterly*, 40 (1931): 565 ff.

¶ 449   J. Franklin Jameson urges that research "be directed towards things that are suffering to be done and away from fields already cultivated to the point of diminishing returns." Particular topics and fields recommended by him for exploration include "racial movements and their effects, the history of morals, industry, transportation, law and administration, the evolution of state policy in economic matters and the history of propaganda, journalism, education, and religious institutions."—*Historical Scholarship in America: Needs and Opportunities*, Report of the American Historical Association's Committee on the Planning of Historical Research, (New York, 1934), introduction.

¶ 450   The work possible for Catholic historians in the field of Western history is extensive. The harvest is rich enough for many laborers. The ultimate truth concerning the period of French discovery and settlement is still to be written, in spite of the fact that the greatest genius in American historiography devoted his life to the subject. Even Francis Parkman could not say the final word. Since his day many sources of information have been made available, giving all scholars equal opportunity to make their own interpretation."—Clarence W. Alvord, "Sources of Catholic History in Illinois," *Illinois Catholic Historical Review*, 1 (1918): 76.

Ecclesiastical administrators undertook comprehensive plans, the Catholic Church producing a group of colonizing bishops, Fenwick of Boston, Ireland of St. Paul, and Byrne of Little Rock, the activities of each of whom will repay study.—Marcus L. Hansen, "American Immigration a Field for Research," *AHR*, 32 (1927): 507.

R. J. White, "Some Opportunities of the Catholic Historian in the Reform and Progress of the Law, "*CHR*, 21 (1935): 49–64.

¶ 451   Exploitation of new material from home and foreign archives is a marked feature of recent writing in the American and the Hispanic-American history fields, as in others. The following are typical titles.

Charles A. Beard, *Economic Interpretation of the Constitution*.
Verner W. Crane, *The Southern Frontier*.
Clarence W. Alvord, *Mississippi Valley in British Politics*.
Arthur P. Whitaker, *The Spanish-American Frontier; The Mississippi Question*.
Samuel F. Bemis, *The Jay Treaty; The Pinckney Treaty; Diplomacy of the American Revolution*.
Arthur B. Thomas, *Forgotten Frontiers: After Coronado*.
Claude Van Tyne, *The American Revolution*.
Lesley B. Simpson, *The Encomienda in New Spain*.
Herbert E. Bolton, *The Rim of Christendom*.
Herbert I. Priestly, *Galvez*.
Arthur S. Alton, *Mendoza*.
William Robertson, *Miranda*.

¶ 452 REINTERPRETATION OF OLD MATERIAL
It is not altogether necessary that the historian set out new facts or use entirely new material. Interpretation is a vital part of history, and if he can present some significant reorganization, some illuminating interpretation of facts already known, his work will be worth while.

> It is no longer sufficient, therefore, for the modern historian of Kaskaskia and Cahokia to turn to the pages of Parkman and Shea and tell again in his own words the story of those romantic villages. This sort of history writing—the repetition of a story already told in what we call secondary works in contradistinction to original sources—is all too common. A new interpretation of old sources or an interpretation including new material, alone can justify the historian in breaking into print.—Clarence W. Alvord, *Illinois Catholic Historical Review*, 1 1918): 77.

¶ 453 Apart from modern archaeological and papyral discoveries, the available source material for Greek and Roman history has remained virtually the same for centuries. Scholarly works in these fields appearing in recent years, such as Holm's and Rostovtsev's, owe much of their value to rearrangement and reinterpretation of the traditional material. Newly discovered documents have doubtless played an important part in the recent rewriting of the history of the American Revolution; but it is a question whether the movement owes to this factor more than to reappraisement and reinterpretation of material long accessible to historians. So also, the American Civil War is being subjected to new interpretations. "The retelling of the Civil War is a matter of changed and changing viewpoints."—James G. Randall, "The Blundering Generation," *MVHR*, 27 (1940): 27.

In American universities it is not unusual for graduate students of history to be allowed to choose for their dissertations topics already treated. Freshness and originality of treatment are expected to compensate for lack of new facts or new material.

¶ 454 SHIFTING ATTITUDES TOWARDS THE PAST
Interest in the past is not set in a fixed direction, but turns now to this, now that class of historical facts. What seems important or significant to one age may not seem so to another. Up to the second half of the eighteenth century, social and economic conditions received but scant attention from the historians. Political and military exploits filled out the bulk of their product; even as late as the mid-nineteenth century a leading English historian declared that "history is past politics," and he has not lacked followers to this day. But with the growth of the democratic movement in Europe, there was a feeling that politics do not tell the whole story. Interest in the past was gradually focused less upon what government did and more upon what the common peo-

ple did, and were. This meant that history, if it was to keep in step with the altered viewpoint, would have to run in fresh channels. The new historiography was productive of works of the type of Green's *Short History of the English People*, and McMaster's *History of the People of the United States*.

Altered attitudes toward the past continue to assert themselves. It has been maintained, for example, that the human story is best presented from the viewpoint of growth in ideas and intellectual growth in general. Again, the first World War brought into relief the part played in modern warfare by the non-combatant elements of the population, the fighters "behind the lines." It may not be too much to say that adequate histories of the great conflict, when they come to be written, will stress as much as anything else what may be called the factor of lay participation. Similarly, now that the share of non-combatants in great military efforts has taken on a significance previously unrecognized, a history of the American Civil War could well be written from their standpoint and with emphasis on their contribution to the result. Finally, as has already been emphasized [❡ 3 f.], there is a certain relativity in history, not in its realities, which are absolute and immutable, but in men's attitude towards them, in what they think about them. The fact, then, that the world, as it moves along, does look at the past from shifting angles of interest and appreciation, makes it necessary to recast history as record, to rewrite it.

C. Historical Revisions

❡ 455 The British journal *History* once expressed editorially the opinion that the most important task before the historian today is the revision of hitherto accepted viewpoints and interpretations, now seen with the progress of research to be untenable. An identical opinion is elaborated in ❡ 442 f. Thus, certain traditional viewpoints in Hispanic-American history have been discredited by recent research, as exemplified in the work of Bourne, Moses, Bolton, and others.—See Lowell J. Ragatz, *Colonial Studies in the United States during the Twentieth Century* (Washington, 1934), 4 f.

On the general topic of Spanish constructive work in the western hemisphere, see E. G. Bourne, *Spain in America, 1450–1580*; H. E. Bolton, *Anza's California Expeditions*.

On the Philippine chapter of Spanish achievement, see the introduction by Edward G. Bourne to E. H. Blair and J. A. Robertson, eds., *The Philippine Islands, 1493–1898* (55 vols., Cleveland, 1903–1909), 1: 19–87.

❡ 456 The Puritan factor in New England history has received new

¶ 458   Chapter 19   421

treatment at the hands of James Truslow Adams, with resultant reversal of certain previously accepted views. The entire Reconstruction period has been subjected to pitiless re-examination. From this has emerged the rehabilitation of the more moderate politicians and statesmen, especially Andrew Johnson, and the discomfiture of their adversaries. The story of the American Revolution has undergone at least partial revision in a number of scholarly histories, beginning with Sidney G. Fisher's *True History of the American Revolution*, and including such later studies as those of Claude H. Van Tyne, and French. Books of the type indicated illustrate the inevitable tendency of a critical age to rewrite history in the interests of accuracy and truth. Justice is done to misunderstood or misrepresented personalities or groups, false impressions of whatsoever kind are removed, and the inadequacies of existing historical record gradually repaired.——See Charles H. McIlwain, "The Historian's Part in a Changing World," AHR, 42 (1937): 207–224.

D. Examples

¶ 457   Examples of historical judgments or viewpoints that have undergone revision with the progress of research.

Before the age of Columbus the earth was believed to be flat.——*History*, 22 (1937): 54–58.

The Middle Ages were a "night of a thousand years," "a wedge of barbarism" thrust in between the world's two great civilizations, ancient and modern.——C. G. Crump and E. F. Jacob, eds., *The Legacy of the Middle Ages*; Charles H. McIlwain, "Medieval Institutions in the Modern World," *Speculum*, 16 (1941): 275–81.

The traditional estimate of the Greek patriarch Photius is in accordance with the facts.——Émile Amann in A. Fliche and V. Martin, eds., *Histoire de l'Église depuis les origines jusqu' à nos jours*, 6: 483–501.

Peter the Hermit was the chief promoter of the first Crusade.——Dana C. Munro, "The Speech of Pope Urban II at Clermont," AHR, 11 (1906): 231–42; Ernest Barker, *The Crusades* (London, 1923).

There was no science in the Middle Ages.——Charles H. Haskins, *Studies in the History of Medieval Science*; Fielding R. Garrison, "Recent Realignment in the History of Medieval Medicine and Science," AHA, Report (1920), 715.

The Renaissance was ushered in with the fall of Constantinople and was a distinctly non-medieval movement.——Charles H. Haskins, *The Renaissance of the Twelfth Century*; Gerald G. Walsh, *Medieval Humanism* (New York, 1942); Arthur S. Turberville, "Changing Views of the Renaissance," *History*, 16 (1932); 288–95; Walter W. J. Wilkinson, "The Meaning of the Renaissance," *Thought*, 16 (1941): 444–56.

¶ 458   Pre-Reformation England refused to recognize the canon law of the Church.——F. W. Maitland, *Roman Canon Law in the Church of England*; Cuthbert Lattey, ed., *The Papacy* (Cambridge, Eng., 1934).

Trial by jury was established by Magna Carta.——William S. McKechnie, *Magna Carta: A Commentary on the Great Charter of King John with an Historical Introduction* (2d rev. ed., Glasgow, 1914).

Magna Carta was a national work inaugurating English constitutional liberties. Charles E. Petit-Dutaillis, *Studies and Notes Supplementary to Stubbs' Constitutional History down to the Great Charter* (Manchester, 1923), chap. 12; William A. Morris, *The Constitutional History of England to 1216* (New York, 1930), chap. 16.

All Europe was terror-stricken at the approach of the year A.D. 1000, which was expected to bring with it the end of the world.——George L. Burr, "The Year 1000 and the Antecedents of the Crusades," *AHR*, 6 (1901): 429–39.

❡ 459   English History is mainly Anglo-Saxon in its origins. "The Norman Conquest, despite the vehement protests of Anglo-historians, did in a real sense mark the beginning of English history, and it is no mere quibble that reckons the kings of England *post conquestum.*"——Albert F. Pollard, *The Evolution of Parliament* (London, 1926).

The traditional estimate of James II is in accord with the facts.——Malcolm V. Hay, *The Enigma of James II*; Hilaire Belloc, *James II* (Philadelphia, 1928); *The Month*, 135 (1920): 268 ff.

Judge Jeffreys was the villainous character he is depicted in tradition. ——Seymour Schofield, *Jeffreys of "The Bloody Assizes,"* (London, 1937).

❡ 460   Spanish and Portuguese maritime adventure and commerce at the close of the fifteenth century turned towards the West because the overland route to the Orient was closed by the Turks.——Albert H. Lybyer, "The Influence of the Rise of the Ottoman Turks upon the Routes of Oriental trade," *AHA, Report* (1919), 371–88; *EHR*, 30 (1915): 577–88.

The so-called *leyenda negra* regarding Spain's treatment of the natives in her New World colonies is based on fact.——Leslie B. Simpson, *The Encomienda in New Spain: Forced Labor in the American Colonies, 1492–1550* (Berkeley, Calif., 1929).

Menendez hung over his victims at Fort Caroline a placard reading "I do this not to Frenchmen, but to Lutherans."——Woodbury Lowery, *The Spanish Settlements within the Present Limits of the United States: Florida, 1562–1574* (New York, 1905), 178.

❡ 461   The French preceded the English in the Exploration of the Ohio Valley.——Clarence W. Alvord and Lee Bidgood, *The First Explorations of the Trans-Allegheny Country by the Virginians, 1560–1674* (Cleveland, 1912).

France supported the American colonies in the hope of recovering Canada and Louisiana.——Edward S. Corwin, *French Policy and the American Alliance of 1778* (Princeton, 1916); Claude H. Van Tyne, *The American Revolution, 1776–1783* (New York, 1905), 203–26; S. F. Bemis, *The Diplomacy of the American Revolution*, 60, 196 f.

The French regarded Louisiana as a "white elephant," which they were eager to turn over to Spain, and did so by the Treaty of Fontainebleau.—Arthur S. Aiton, "The Diplomacy of the Louisiana Cession," AHR, 36 (1931), 701–20.

❡ 462 The American Revolution was "a spontaneous uprising of the whole colonial population without faction or disagreement among them."—Sidney G. Fisher, *The True History of the American Revolution* (New York, 1902). John Adams declared that about one-third of the people were opposed to the Revolution in all its stages.—Arthur M. Schlesinger, *New Viewpoints in American History* (New York, 1922).

The Texan revolution of 1836 was engineered by American slaveholders.—Eugene C. Barker, *Mexico and Texas, 1821–1835* (Dallas, Tex., 1928).

The Dred Scott decision was the outcome of a "conspiracy" hatched by Buchanan, Taney, Douglas, and other Democrats high in office.—George F. Milton, *The Eye of Conflict: Stephen A. Douglas and the Needless War* (Boston, 1934); Carl B. Swisher, *Roger B. Taney* (New York, 1936).

The Compromise Bill of 1850 originated with Henry Clay.—Frank H. Godder, "The Authorship of the Compromise of 1850," MVHR, 22 (1936): 525–36.

Douglas' motive in introducing the Kansas-Nebraska Bill of 1854 was to win southern support in his ambition to become president.—Frank H. Godder, "The Railroad Background of the Kansas-Nebraska Act." MVHR, 12 (1925): 3–22.

The Reconstruction policy of the sixties was wise and "patriotic."—George F. Milton, *The Age of Hate: Andrew Johnson and the Radicals* (New York, 1930); James G. Randall, *The Civil War and Reconstruction* (Boston, 1937).

The German vote elected Lincoln in 1860.—Joseph Schafer, "Who Elected Lincoln?" AHR, 47 (1941): 51–63.

> The author's [Schafer] chief reason for calling sharp attention to the futility of the speculative method hitherto commonly used by historians in dealing with subjects of this kind, is to protest against an outworn methodology. "The 'guessing game' is no longer permissible to those who claim the right to be called historians, in the American field at least."

History (London, 1912) has carried from its first appearance a department which discusses traditional statements and viewpoints in history now calling for revision.

E. Historical Problems

❡ 463 "Study problems in preference to periods," advised Lord Acton, in his *Lecture on the Study of History*. Students preparing to write a doctor's or master's thesis are generally directed to throw their subject into the form of a problem.

"A historical problem" may be defined broadly as a situation or event capable of more than one explanation, and inviting examination and discussion as to its true explanation.

The subjects treated in students' theses are sometimes of such a nature that it is not easy to see how they offer anything in the nature of a genuine problem; but history does offer numerous examples of situations and events which exhibit all the characteristics we usually associate with the notion of a problem. They cannot be explained or readily accounted for; it is only after more or less investigation and weighing of evidence that they are explained, if indeed explanation be possible at all. It is presumably historical problems of this kind that are recommended for study, "in preference to periods." It is typical of the examples which follow that all take an interrogative form, involving, therefore, in each case, a question proposed for answer.

Examples of historical problems also occur in connection with the topics of hypothesis [⟨ 141 ff.], authenticity [⟨ 156 ff.], and factual interpretation [⟨ 327 ff.].

⟨ 464 "Did Richard II murder the Duke of Gloucester?"—This is the title of a paper by James Tait, in Thomas F. Tout and James Tait, eds., *Historical Essays First Published in 1902 in Commemoration of the Jubilee of Owens College, Manchester* (Manchester, 1907).

"Did Savonarola disobey the Pope?"—Stanislaus M. Hogan, *Blackfriars Magazine*, 11 (1930): 171–79; 224–41; 297–309. Herbert Lucas, *Fra Girolamo Savonarola: A Biographical Study Based on Contemporary Documents* (London, 1908). L. von Pastor, *History of the Popes at the Close of the Middle Ages*, 6: 3–54. James E. O'Neil, *Was Savonarola Really Excommunicated?* (Boston, 1900).

⟨ 465 Where was the Vinland of the Norsemen?—William S. Merrill, "The Vinland Problem Through Four Centuries," CHR, 21 (1935): 21–48.

What was the nationality of 'Columbus?—Charles E. Nowell, "The Columbus Question," AHR, 44 (1939): 807–10. J. B. Thacher, *Christopher Columbus*, 1: 230–63.

Did Columbus derive his geographical knowledge from the *Imago Mundi* of Pierre d'Ailly?—Edmond Buron, ed., *Ymago mundi de Pierre d'Ailly* (3 vols., Paris, 1930), 1: 23 ff. George P. Nunn, "The Imago Mundi and Columbus," AHR, 40 (1935): 646–61.

Did the Portuguese discover North America before Columbus?—Samuel E. Morison, *Portuguese Voyages to America in the Fifteenth Century*, (Cambridge, Mass., 1941).

⟨ 466 Was Elizabeth primarily responsible for the religious settlement made during her reign, or was she only a tool in the hands of her ministers, especially the Cecils?—Arnold O. Meyer, *England and the Catholic Church under Queen Elizabeth*, trans. by John R. McKee (London, 1916). John

H. Pollen, *The English Catholics in the Reign of Elizabeth* (London, 1920). Joseph B. Code, *Queen Elizabeth and the English Catholic Historians* (Louvain, 1935).

What was the Gunpowder Plot?—John Gerard, *What Was the Gunpowder Plot?* (London, 1897). Samuel R. Gardiner, *What Gunpowder Plot Was* (London, 1897), is a reply to Father Gerard's work. John Gerard, *The Gunpowder Plot . . . in reply to Professor Gardiner* (London, 1897); *Thomas Winter's Confession and the Gunpowder Plot* (London, 1898). Herbert Thurston "The Gunpowder Plot and the Witness Yates," *The Month*, 150 (1927): 385-98; "Another Powder Plot Forgery," *ibid.*, 500-510; *The Gunpowder Plot* (London, 1930). For a bibliography of periodical literature, see *Encyclopaedia Britannica*, 11:5.

❡ 467 Who was the Man in the Iron Mask?—Henri Griffet, *Traité des différentes sortes de preuves*, chap. 13. F. Funk-Brentano, *Legends of the Bastille*, chap. 4. Arthur S. Barnes, *The Man of the Mask* (London, 1912).

Did Robespierre shoot himself or was he shot by Meda?—F. M. Fling, *The Writing of History*, 175-81. Hilaire Belloc, *Robespierre: A Study* (New York, 1928): 409-12.

What became of the Dauphin, son of Louis XVI?—G. Lenôtre, *The Dauphin: the Riddle of the Temple* (London, 1927). Eric R. Bucken, *Monsieur Charles: the Tragedy of the True Dauphin* (London, 1927). John B. Morton, *The Dauphin* (London, 1937).

❡ 468 What was the route followed by Cabeza de Vaca?—Cleve Hallenbeck, *Alvar Nuñez Cabeza de Vaca: The Journey and Route of the First European to Cross the Continent of North America* (Glendale, Calif., 1940).

What was the route of the De Soto expedition of 1539-1542?—*Final Report of the United States De Soto Expedition Commission* (76th Congress, 1st Sess., House Doc. 71, Washington, 1939). Barbara Boston, "The Route of De Soto: Delisle's Interpretation," *MA*, 21 (1939): 277-97.

Where was Quivira, the region penetrated by Coronado's expedition of 1541?—See ❡ 329-d.

Did the La Vérendrye expedition of 1740 reach the Rocky Mountains? —Lawrence P. Burpee, ed., *Journals and Letters of Pierre Gaultier de Varenne de la Vérendrye and His Sons* (Toronto, 1927). Orin G. Libby, "Some Verendrye Enigmas," *MVHR*, 3 (1916): 143-60.

❡ 469 What influence, if any, did George Rogers Clark's military successes in the West have on the terms of the Treaty of Paris, 1783?— Clarence W. Alvord, "Virginia and the West: an Interpretation," *MVHR*, 3 (1916): 19 ff. Temple Bodley, *George Rogers Clark; his Life and Public Services* (Boston, 1926). James A. James, *The Life of George Rogers Clark* (Chicago, 1928); *idem*, "An Appraisal of the Contribution of George Rogers Clark to the History of the Northwest," *MVHR*, 17 (1930): 98-115. S. F. Bemis, *The Diplomacy of the American Revolution* (New York, 1935).

What was the Burr conspiracy?—Walter F. McCaleb, *The Aaron Burr Conspiracy* (New York, 1937).

Was the American Revolution inevitable?—Hugh E. Egerton, *The Causes and Character of the American Revolution*, 182–201.

Was the American Revolution justifiable from a legal or constitutional point of view?—Charles H. McIlwain, *The American Revolution: A Constitutional Interpretation* (New York, 1923), chap. 1. A. M. Schlesinger, *New Viewpoints in American History* (New York, 1922), 179.

Is the alleged Mecklenburg declaration of May 20, 1775, genuine?— Edward Channing, *A History of the United States* (6 vols., New York, 1905–1925), vol. 3. Charles G. Washburn, "Who was the Author of the Declaration of Independence?" American Antiquarian Society, Proceedings, 38 (1928): 51–62.

Was the American Civil War inevitable?—G. F. Milton, *The Eve of the Conflict: Stephen A. Douglas and the Needless War*. Arthur C. Cole, *The Irrepressible Conflict (1850–1865)*, (New York, 1935). Avery Craven, "Coming of the War Between the States," *Journal of Southern History*, 2 (1936): 303–22. J. G. Randall, *The Civil War and Reconstruction* (Boston, 1937). Charles W. Ramsdell, "Lincoln and Fort Sumter," *Journal of Southern History*, 3 (1937): 259–88. Avery Craven, *The Repressible Conflict* (University, La., 1939).

Additional examples will be found in John H. Wigmore, "A List of Thirty Historical Problems for the Application of the Principles of Judicial Proof," *The Nature of Judicial Proof*, 1003–1008; Fred M. Fling and Helene D. Fling, *Source Problems on the French Revolution* (New York, 1913); Andrew C. McLaughlin and Others, *Source Problems in the History of the United States* (New York, 1918).

BIBLIOGRAPHY OF HISTORICAL METHOD

THE FOLLOWING BIBLIOGRAPHY contains only those books which deal ex professo and systematically with historical method, and is restricted to books written in English, French, and German. There are manuals in other languages such as B. Albers, *Manuale di propaedutica*, or Z. García Villada, *Metodología y crítica históricas*, but there was no point in listing books not always easily accessible. For the same reason, there was no point in listing the numerous introductions to ecclesiastical history, most of which are written in Latin. Nor have we entered inaugural addresses, articles, or minor writings of many historians which touch upon some special point of methodology, since most of these are referred to in the text.

In the following brief survey, we have noted the main contributions of the earliest writers to the body of rules which today is called "historical method."

The *Methodus ad facilem historiarum cognitionem* (Paris, 1566), by Jean Bodin, is commonly considered as the foundation of historical methodology. The reason for this is difficult to understand. Not a few sixteenth-century writers made a sharper distinction between the value of original sources and derived sources than Bodin did in the sixth chapter of his book. Moreover, at least two of them anticipated Bodin with regard to this important distinction: Francesco Patrizzi, in the fifth, sixth, and seventh chapters of his *Dialogi X de historia* (Venice, 1560), and Melchior Cano in the eleventh book of his *De locis theologicis*, published posthumously at Salamanca, in 1563.

The contribution of Gerard J. Voss (Vossius) to methodology consists in his having been the first to claim that history is an independent subject of study, in his *Ars historica sive de historicis natura, historiaque scribenda praecepti commentatio* (Leyden, 1623). Another edition of this work appeared in 1653, and the treatise was reprinted in the fourth volume of his *Opera* (Amsterdam, 1701). The *Ars historica* is analyzed by Giovanni Gentile in the *Revue de synthèse historique*, 5 (1902): 132–38. Vossius' claim is clearly stated in the title of the third chapter: "Historicen non esse partem vel Grammaticae, vel Rhetoricae, vel Poëticae, vel Logicae. . . ."

Jean Mabillon's justly celebrated *De re diplomatica libri VI* (Paris, 1681), sometimes given as the first treatise on methodology, is in reality the first treatise on diplomatic; in fact, this auxiliary science owes its foundation to him. A supplement appeared in 1704, and the six books together with the supplement were reissued in 1709.

In 1696, Jean Le Clerc published at Amsterdam his *Ars critica* (2 vols.); a second edition enlarged and revised was published four years later. The full title of his book indicates its scope: *Ars critica, in qua ad studia linguarum Latinae, Graecae, & Hebraicae via munitur; Veterumque emendandorum, Spuriorum Scriptorum à Genuinis dignoscendorum, & judicandi de eorum Libris ratio traditur*. In the second volume he treats of errors of copyists and gives useful rules for restoring corrupted texts. He was the first to write on textual criticism.

In his *Réflexions sur les règles et sur l'Usage de la critique* (Paris, 1713), Father Honoré de Sainte-Marie (Honoratus a Sancta Maria) sets forth a number of useful rules for determining the trustworthiness of witnesses. His own applications of these rules, however, were not so critical. In the same year, Nicolas Lenglet du Fresnoy published his nine-volume *Methode pour etudier l'histoire*. A second edition appeared in 1729 and was reprinted in 1734.

The first of these nine volumes treats of "les sciences qui servents de fondement à l'étude de l'histoire," i.e., "la Geographie; la connoissance des Moeurs et des Coutumes, & la Chronologie." The second, third and fourth volumes, and most of the fifth, deal rather with historiography than with methodology. The titles of two chapters in the fifth volume indicate Lenglet du Fresnoy's contribution to the development of historical method: "Regles pour le discernement des ouvrages supposés" (Chapter lx), and "De l'usage qu'on peut faire des faits et des Ouvrages supposés et douteux, & des Historiens passionnes" (Chapter lxi).

None of these early writers considered the possibility of error in perception on the part of a witness. All took for granted that the testimony of a perfectly conscientious witness must be presumed to be true. The first writer to discuss the problem of error in perception is Johann M. Chladni or Chladenius in his *Allgemeine Geschichtswissenschaft*, published at Leipzig in 1752. Chladenius also warns against errors creeping in as testimony is repeated by various individuals. He calls attention to the importance of knowing whether the testimony which we have is that of an eyewitness. He rightly contends that errors may occur in the handing down of a story, for each one who repeats the testimony of the original witness may have a different point of view, and may add or detract from the original testimony.

The *Traité des différentes sortes de preuves qui servent à etablir la vérité de l'histoire*, by Henri Griffet, published at Liége in 1769 (2d edition, 1775) is generally recognized as containing the most precise formulation of the rules for getting at the truth which had as yet appeared [⁋ 56-e].

Between Griffet and Daunou, few books contribute anything of importance to the development of historical method. The following treatises may be mentioned. In *De la manière d'écrire l'histoire* (Paris, 1778; 2d ed., 1782; English translation, London, 1783), Gabriel Bonnot de Mably adopts the point of view of a writer of history rather than the point of view of a student. At the beginning of the nineteenth century, several short treatises on historical criticism were published in Germany, among these are Friedrich Rühs, *Entwurf einer Propädeutik des historischen Studiums* (Berlin, 1811); Whilhelm Wachsmuth, *Entwurf einer Theorie der Geschichte* (Halle, 1820); and Friedrich Rehm, who in his *Lehrbuch der historischen Propädeutik und Grundriss der algemeinen Geschichte* (Marburg, 1830), embodied the most useful observations and salient points of his predecessors.

Although Daunou is the first writer listed, Bernheim is the first who codified the observations and the rules of historical criticism formulated by previous methodologists and historians.

Bibliography

1842

DAUNOU, PIERRE C. F. *Cours d'études historiques.* 20 vols., Paris, 1842-1849. Volume 1 is a general treatise on methodology. In volume 2, Daunou deals with geography, in volumes 3 to 6, with chronology, as auxiliary sciences. Rules of exposition are given in volume 7.

1858

DROYSEN, JOHANN G. *Grundriss der Historik.* Printed as manuscript, in 1858. Third edition, Leipzig, 1882. See below, 1888 and 1893.

1882

TARDIF, ADOLPHE F. L. *Notions élémentaires de critique historique.* Paris, 1882.

1883

DE SMEDT, CHARLES. *Principes de la critique historique.* Liége and Paris, 1883.

1888

DORMAY, P. A. *Précis de la science de l'histoire.* Paris, 1888. Translation of Droysen's *Grundriss.* See above, 1858.

1889

BERNHEIM, ERNST. *Lehrbuch der historischen Methode.* Leipzig, 1889; second edition, 1894. The title of the third and fourth editions (Leipzig, 1903) reads: *Lehrbuch der historischen Methode und der Geschichtsphilosophie.* A sixth edition—the edition cited in this book—was published in Leipzig, 1908. A seventh edition appeared in 1914.

1893

ANDREWS, E. BENJAMIN. *Outline of the Principles of History.* Boston, 1893. Translation of Droysen's *Grundriss.* See above, 1858.

1894

MORTET, CHARLES, and V. *La science de l'histoire.* Paris, 1894.

1898

LANGLOIS, CHARLES-VICTOR, and SEIGNOBOS, CHARLES. *Introduction aux études historiques.* Paris, 1898. Reprinted, 1899, 1905.
———. *Introduction to the Study of History.* Translated into English by G. G. Berry. London and New York, 1898. Reprinted, 1912, 1925.

1899

FLING, FRED M. *Outline of Historical Method.* Lincoln, Neb., 1899.

1905

BERNHEIM, ERNST. *Einleitung in die Geschichtswissenschaft.* In Sammlung Göschen. Berlin and Leipzig, 1905. Abridgment of *Lehrbuch.* Reprinted 1909, 1912. Second edition, 1920; reprinted, 1926.

1908

FONCK, LEOPOLD. *Wissenschaftliches Arbeiten. Beiträge zur Methodik des academischen Studiums.* Innsbruck, 1908.

1909

GEORGE, HEREFORD B. *Historical Evidence.* Oxford, 1909.

1911

BOURG, J., and DÉCISIER, A. *Le travail scientifique. École—Pratique.* Paris, 1911. French adaptation of Fonck's *Wissenschaftliches Arbeiten.* See above, 1908.
VINCENT, JOHN M. *Historical Research: An Outline of Theory and Practice.* New York, 1911. Reprinted, New York: Peter Smith, 1929. This volume and Vincent's *Aids to Historical Research* (New York, 1934) form a complete treatise on historical method.
ERSLEV, KRISTIAN. *Historik Teknik.* Copenhagen, 1911.

1913

MEISTER, ALOYS. *Grundzüge der historischen Methode.* Leipzig, 1913. This short treatise on method is the eleventh part of volume 1, Meister, A., *Grundriss der Geschichtswissenschaft zur Einführung in das Studium der deutschen Geschichte des Mittelalters und der Neuzeit.* 2 vols., Leipzig, 1906–1927.

1919

FEDER, ALFRED. *Lehrbuch der historischen Methodik.* Regensburg, 1919. Second edition, 1921. The title of the third edition, revised and enlarged (Regensburg, 1924) reads: *Lehrbuch der geschichtlichen Methode.* Citations in this book are from the third edition.

CRUMP, CHARLES G. *The Logic of History.* London, 1919.—Marshall, Richard L. *The Historical Criticism of Documents.* London, 1920.—Johnson, Charles. *The Mechanical Processes of the Historian.* London, 1924. These three short treatises contain the essentials of historical method. They are Nos. 6, 28, and 50 of Charles Johnson, J. P. Whitney, and Harold W. V. Temperley, eds., *Helps for Students of History* (51 vols., London, 1918–1924).

1921

FLING, FRED M. *The Writing of History: An Introduction to Historical Method.* New Haven, 1920.

BAUER, WILHELM. *Einführung in das Studium der Geschichte.* Tübingen, 1921. Second edition, 1928.

1926

JOHNSON, ALLEN. *The Historian and Historical Evidence.* New York, 1926; reprinted, 1928.

1928

BRANDT, EBBA. *Historische Teknik.* Munich and Berlin, 1928. Translation of Erslev's *Historik Teknik.* See above, 1911.

CRUMP, CHARLES. *History and Historical Research.* London, 1928.

1930

SPAHR, WALTER E., and SWENSON, RINEHART J. *Methods and Status of Scientific Research.* New York and London, 1930.

ALMACK, JOHN C. *Research and Thesis Writing.* Boston, 1930.

1931

HOCKETT, HOMER C. *Introduction to Research in American History.* New York, 1931.

1938

NEVINS, ALLAN. *The Gateway to History.* Boston, 1938.

1939

OMAN, SIR CHARLES. *On the Writing of History.* New York, 1939.

INDEX OF AUTHORS*

Abbott, W. C., on miracles, 295; on historians, 434

Abel, A. H., editor of Chardon journal, 248

Acton, Lord
on Buckle, 352; on contemporary history, 20; on continuity of history, 24; errata in, 440; on forged letters of Marie Antoinette, 173-d; on impartial historian, 44, 46-a, e
on memoirs: of De Bouillé, 242-a; on French Revolution, 242-b; of Talleyrand, 242-a
on method, 49; on moral judgment, 367; on problems vs. periods, 463; on Robespierre, 329-g
on testimony: partisan, 282-g; self-incriminating, 311
on value of history, 17

Adair, E. R., on Dollard exploit, 329-e

Adams, C. K., on Buckle, 352

Adams, H., as factual historian, 374; and historical law, 138-d; on history as science, 39; and physical theory of history, 146-a; on value of history, 15-a

Adams, H. B., and American method, 434

Adams, J., on American Revolution, 462

Adams, J. Q., diary of, 247–48

Adams, J. T., on "new" biography, 240-a; on New England Puritanism, 456; on Parkman, 366-b; on unexplored New England fields, 448

Adams, R. G., on necessity of publication, 51-c; on Yorktown campaign, 442

Aiton, A. S., on Louisiana cession, 329-e, 461

Albert of Aix, historian of First Crusade, 91-a

Albright, W. F., and analogy, 130

Allard, P., on legal basis of early Christian persecutions, 146-b

Allen, C. E., on editorials, 252-b

Almack, J. C., on certainty, 69; on probability, 64; on psychoanalytic history, 240-c; on scientific method, 33; on Turner hypothesis, 146-d

Altamira, on "idolatry of document," 57-h

Alvord, C. W., on American social history, 424; on Clark expedition, 469; and discoveries on New France, 441; on Illinois Catholic sources, 450; on Mississippi Valley, 451; on reinterpretation, 452

Alvord, C. W., and Bidgood, L., on Ohio Valley exploration, 461

Amann, E., on Holy Roman Empire, 329-b; on Photius, 457

Anaxagoras, Hegelian derivation from, 385

Andrews, C. M., on archive administration, 115

Anna Comnena, impartial use of sources in, 431-b

Angle, P. M., on Lincoln document forgery, 173-f

Anselm, St., on belief, 62-a

Apollinaris, Sidonius, letters of, 251-c; on Thundering Legion, 303-a

Appel, L., on bibliographical citation, 396 (p. 385, n), 401-a, 404 (p. 390, n)'

Aquinas, see Thomas, St.

Aragon, R. F., on causality, 348

Archer, P., on birth date of Christ, 339; on calendar reform, 80-b; on fixing day of week in dating, 80-e

Arendzen, J., on source value of Gospels, 313-b

Aristotle, authentication of attributions to, 176-b; commentaries on, 214-g; edition of, 400-b; on history as science, 40-b; paraphrased by Themistius, 214-e; use of sources in, 54

Arnobius, and authorship of Octavius, 175

* (Numbers refer to paragraphs).

Index of Authors

Arnold, T., on antiquarianism, 9; on continuity of history, 24; on perversion of history, 439

Ashe, T., authenticity of Travels of, 189

Asquith, C., see Spender, J. A., and

Asquith, H. H., as autobiographer, 243

Asser, biographer of Alfred, 95-f; and earliest medieval history, 55-b

Attwater, D., see Thurston, H., and

Augustine, St., autobiographical candor of, 243; and Christian philosophy of history, 371, 377–79, 386; Latin of, 76, 165-b; legendary saying of, 261-a; on memory, 101; on natural causes, 380; on necessity of belief, 61; and omission of historical events, 152; self-authentication of, 162-c; "six ages" of 26-a

Aulard, as source on Reign of Terror, 329-c

Babbitt, I., on Croce's concept of history, 32

Bacchylides, single manuscript of, 216-b

Bacon, J. R., on legend, 272

Bailey, D. C., and interpretation of American history, 329-f

Bailly, spurious memorist, 173-d

Baines, on chance and causality, 361

Bainvel, J. V., on scriptural mistranslations, 323

Baker of Swinkind, on use of cannon at Crécy, 153

Baker, R. S., method of, 332; on sympathy, 46-c

Balfour, R. E., on method, 435

Ball, A. M., on style, American, 402-a

Bancroft, G., and authorship of Johnson's first message to Congress, 189; errata in, 440; on footnotes, 395-a; method of, 431-c, 434; and note-taking system, 102; subjectivity in, 46-e; verifiability in, 53

Bancroft, H. H., and use of interview, 111

Bandelier, on Coronado expedition, 329-d

Barbellion, spurious diaries of, 248-b

Bardenhewer, O., on apocryphal gospels, 173-a; on patristic authorships, 187

Barfield, O., on evidence of linguistics, 75

Baring, E., on bias, 46-e

Barker, E., on crusades, 91-a, 206, 457

Barker, E. C., on bias, 46-e

Barnes, A. S., on Bastille legends, 467

Barnes, H. E., on "new" history, 15-a, 373

Baronius, and Centuriators, 56-a; and Honorius controversy, 176-c

Barry, P. J., on Bossuet, 381

Barton, W. E., and Lincoln discovery, 442; on text of Gettysburg address, 210-b

Basler, R. T., on Lincoln legend, 270

Bassett, J. S., on Bancroft, 102, 434; on Motley, 434; on Prescott, 434; on Sparks, 434

Bates, E., diary of, 222, 248

Bates, E. S., on translation, 323

Battifol, and historical attitude in hagiography, 161-c

Bauer, W., on rumor, 255

Baumgarten, P. M., on method of Lea, 434

Baur, on martyrdom of St. Peter, 259-e

Beale, H. K., editor of Bates diary, 222, 248; on Welles diary, 313-d

Beard, C. A.
on Croce, 32; and economic theory of history, 357, 374-b, 451
on history: as exact science, 355, 374-b; as past actuality, 32
on Spengler, 390-a

Beck, A., on Pollard, Belloc, Abbé Constant, 287-c

Becker, C. L., on Declaration of Independence, 311; on fact vs. interpretation, 331; on Madame Roland, 313-d; on philosophy of history, 374-b

Bede, and earliest medieval history, 55-b; on periodization, 26-a; as secondary source, 91-c; trustworthiness of, 45-c; and use of sources, 55-a, 176-c, 404, 431-b

Beers, H. P., on Bibliography, American, 73, 403

Bekker, I., editor of Aristotle, 400-b

Bell, H. I., and Skeat, T. C., on papyri, 84-b

Bellarmine, St. Robert, on coronation of Charlemagne, 146-c

Beller, E. A., on propaganda, 253

Belloc, H., on Catholic Church in European history, 366; on English Reformation, 362-a; on footnotes, 395-b; on historian as judge, 44-b; on historical writing, 70; on British House of Commons, 428-b; on James II, 459; on legend, 271; on memoirs of Charlotte Robespierre, 188; method of, 370, 395-b, 410, 422-a, 434; on Michelet, 422-a; on need of rewriting history, 437; prefaces of, 434; on Robespierre, 329-f, 467; on Rome and modern civilization, 329-c; and style, 419

Bemis, S. F., on American Revolution, 451, 461; on Clark expedition, 469; on diplomatic correspondence, 251-a, 448; on Jay and Pinckney treaties, 451

Bemis, S. F., and Griffin, G. C., on bibliography, American, 73

Benbow, J., on style, American, 402-a

Berdyaev, N., on Christian view of history, 390-c

Bergin, T. C., see Fisch, M. H., and

Bergkamp, J. V., on Mabillon, 56-d

Bernard, St., biographer of St. Malachy, 95-f

Bernays, J., and restoration of lost passage of Tacitus, 204

Bernheim, E. E., editor of source book on Church, 409-b; on Giesbrecht restoration, 205; on miracles, 293-b, 296; on philosophy of history, 374-b; on St. Augustine, 379; on St. Bernard, 161-c, 292-b, 296; on single witness, 287; on steps of criticism, 157–58

on sources: credibility of, 237-a; dating of, 182-a; localization of, 185-d; in remains, 93-b

Bertin, G., on Lourdes, 231-a

Bertram, C. J., forger of Cirencester history, 173-b

Bestman, T., on bibliography, 73

Betten, F. S., on Kensington Stone, 173-f

Beveridge, A. J., on biography, 326-a; on fact vs. interpretation, 331

Bidgood, L., see Alvord, C. W., and

Bigelow, K. W., see Cole, A. H., and

Billington, R. A., on American antiCatholic legend, 259-e

Bingham, D. A., on Bastille Legend, 265

Binkley, R. C., on use of photography, 99-d

Birch, W. de G., on seals, 83

Bishop, J. B., on T. Roosevelt, 415

Bismarck, memoirs of, 242-b

Black, J. B., on historiography, 431

Blackburn, D., and Caddell, W., on handwriting, 165-d

Blair, E. H., and Robertson, J. A., on Philippines, 329-d, 455

Bland, A. E., and others, editors of English economics source books, 409-a, 455

Blount, E., memoirs of, 242-b

Boak, A. E. R., on Roman kingship, 259-e

Bober, M. M., on Marxism, 353

Bodin, J., on historical method, 56-e

Bodley, T., on Clark expedition, 469

Boedder, B., on providential causality, 389

Boethius, on providential causality, 386

Boissier, G., on Tacitus, 206

Bolingbroke, Lord, on purpose of history, 15

Bollandus, J., promoter of hagiography, 56-b

Bolton, H. E., on American Jesuit field, 446; on Christian field, 451; on continuity of history, 24; editor of Anza journal, 225, 248; and new views in Hispanic-American field, 455

Bond, J. J., on chronology, 80-e

Bordet, L., see Ponelli, L., and

Bossuet, J. B., on chance and contingency, 364; and Christian philosophy of history, 371, 377, 381

Boston, B., on De Soto, 468

Boswell-Stone, W. G., on Shakespeare's Holinshed, 206

Bouillé, de, memoirs of, 242-a

Bourke, V. J., on German National Socialism, 385

Bourne, E. G., on authorship of *Federalist*, 189; on Cabot problem, 311, 441; on Columbus biography, 190-c; and new views in Hispanic-American field, 455; on Parkman, 434; on Philippines, 329-d; on Pineda, 329-d; on Ranke, 46-f, 429, 434; on Seneca text, 321; on Whitman legend, 153, 260. See also Olson, J. E., and

Bourne, H. E., on evidence, 286-b

Bouscaren, T. L., on "historical causes," 284-c

Bowman, H. M., on discrepant sources, 308-h; on scientific method, 40-b

Bradley, H., on English place-names, 307-a, b

Breckenridge, J. M., on Cinq Hommes River, 307

Brewer, on inaccuracies of Froude, 51-d

Bridgett, T. E., on rumor, 265

Brigance, W. N., on Reconstruction sources, 313-d

Brigham, W. P., on geographic influences, 79-c

Brinton, C. C., comparative method in, 432; on historical laws, 15-c, 134; and use of statistics, 140-d

Brodrick, J., and hagiography, 161-c; on rise of modern capitalism, 329-a; and source indication in biography, 240-d

Brooks, P. C., on archive administration, 115

Browing, O. H., diary of, 248

Brown, J. L., on Bodin's method, 56-e

Brown, W. E., on Sulpicius Severus, 187, 313-c

Brunetière, F., and providential view of history, 381; on universality of medieval art and literature, 428-b

Bruno, F. de G. de, on Lourdes, 297

Bryant, A., and source indication in biography, 240-d

Bryce, J., on American democracy, 366-c; comparative method in, 431-b, 432; on range of history, 6; on self-projection into past, 365-c; on value of history, 17

Buchanan, G., and authorship of *Detectio*, 188

Buck, S. J., on Mississippi Valley materials, 448

Bucken, E. R., on Dauphin problem, 467

Buckle, H. T., determinist historian, 79-b, 138-d, 352, 355

Burke, E., on value of history, 17

Burne, A. H., on significance of Poitiers, 329-c

Burnet, J., on Plato, 313-a; on stylometry, 165-c

Burnett, E. C., on date of Declaration of Independence, 339

Buron, E., on Columbus, 465; editor of D'Ailly, 225

Burpee, L. P., on La Vérendrye, 468

Burr, G. L., on antecedents of Crusades, 458

Bury, J. B., on contingency, 362, 364; on defense of bias, 46-e; on face of Roman Empire, 146-b; on history as science, 39; on Holy Roman Empire, 329-b; on modern history, 20; on philosophy of history, 374-b; on Procopius, 91-c; on progress, 28; on range of history, 6

Butler, A., and hagiography, 161-c, 272

Caddell, W., see Blackburn, D., and

Caesar, J., bias in, 280-c, 326-a; dating of *Commentaries* of, 182, 182-b; on German customs, 280-b, 310; manuscripts of, 216-c; reliability of, 313-a

Calvin, J., on St. Peter, 259-e

Campbell, L., on linguistic evidence, 165-c

Campbell, W. C., on style, American, 402-a

Cappelli, A., on chronology, 80-e

Carcopino, J., on population of Rome, 77

Carey, G. V., on style, British, 402-b

Carlyle, A. J., on progressive trend of Middle Ages, 428-b. See also Carlyle, R. W., and

Carlyle, R. W., and Carlyle, A. J., on treatment of political theory, 38

Carlyle, T., on certainty, 69; and "great man" theory, 146-a, 356; inaccuracies in, 51-d; letters of, 434; and Squire

Papers, 173-c; thoroughness of, 52; and vivid style, 426
Carr, R. H., on Plutarch, 206
Carver, J., fictitious travel accounts of, 248-b
Case, S. J., on Christian view of history, 390-c
Case, S. J., and others, on bibliography of Church history, 73
Cassian, on necessary lies, 236-b
Castañeda, C. E., on Coronado expedition, 329-d; on Piñeda, 329-d
Castelein, A., on classification of facts, 7-d; on linguistic evidence, 165-c
Caterall, R. C. H., on Marat, 313-d
Cathrein, V., on Marxism, 352
Cauchie, on providential view of history, 351
Caulincourt, de, memoirs of, 241-a, 242-b
Cave, R. C., and Coulson, H. H., editors of source book on medieval economics, 409-a
Chambers, R. W., on anecdote, 255; on Bede, 55-a; on biography, 240-d; editor of source book on pre-Norman England, 409-a; on *History of Richard III*, 188
Channing, E., and bibliographical survey, 407; on Mecklenburg Declaration, 469; method of, 431-c; on Winsor, 47, 51-a, 419, 434
Channing, E., Hart, A. B., Turner, F. J., on bibliography, American, 73
Chardon, F. A., journal of, 247–48
Chateaubriand, and Romantic movement, 57-c
Chatelain, see Denifle and
Cheldowski, on Cenci legend, 261-a
Chesterton, G. K., on Christian view of history, 390-c; and concrete detail, 422; on legend, 271
Chevalier, U., on bibliography, medieval, 73
Cheyney, E. P., on laws of history, 134, 138-d; on research in English history, 447
Chladenius, J. M., on evidence, 56-e
Christopher, H. G. T., on transcription, 221

Cicero, authorship problem in, 172-a, 176-b; and dating of Caesar's Commentaries, 182; on Herodotus, 54-a; letters of, 177-b, 216-c, 251-c; method of, 54; on objectivity, 44, 46-a; text transmission of, 216-c, e; variable word forms in, 220
Clark, A. C., on copyists' errors, 218; on text transmission, 216-e
Clark, G. R., popular edition of, 222
Clark, W., see Lewis, M., and
Clarke, R. F., on metaphysical certainty, 63-c; on method, 33
Clement of Alexandria, on necessary lies, 236-b
Cochrane, C. N., on rationalist historians, 386; on Thucydides, 54-b, 372
Code, J. B., on Belloc, 395-b, 434; on English Catholic historians, 329-g, 447, 466; on Lingard's method, 57-g, 434
Coffey, P., on belief, 58, 61; on causality, 436; on probability, 64; on use of statistics, 140-d
Coke, and faulty analogy, 130
Cole, A. C., on American Civil War, 469; on Lincoln election and slavery, 329-f
Cole, A. H., and Bigelow, K. W., on note-taking, 109
Colum, P., on myths, 262-c
Columbus, F., biographical reliability of, 190-c
Commager, H. S., editor of American source book, 409-a
Comines, P. de, on continuity of history, 24; and earliest medieval history, 55-b
Comnena, Anna, on objectivity, 46-a
Comte, and positivism, 30
Concannon, and hagiography, 161-c
Condorcet, on social evolution, 28
Connor, T., diary of, 248
Conway, R. S., on Vergil's birthplace, 210-d
Coolidge, C., autobiography of, 243
Cornelius Nepos, errors in, 176-c
Corrigan, R., on missions of New France, 366-b
Corwin, E. S., on French policy in American Revolution, 461

Index of Authors

Coste, P., and source indication in biography, 240-d

Cotter, A. C., on analogy, 126

Cotton, J. S., and others, on Hindu inscriptions, 87

Coulson, H. H., See Cave, R. C., and

Coulter, E. M., and Gerstenfeld, M., on bibliography, 73

Coulton, G. G., inaccuracies in, 51-d

Craigie, W. A., and Hulbert, J. R., on Americanisms, 165-b

Crane, V. W., on Southern frontier, 451

Craven, A., on American Civil War, 469

Creighton, M., on moral judgment, 367; on picturesque epochs, 423

Croce, B., on certainty, 67; formula of, 22; on history as philosophy, 32; idealism of, 32, 67-b

Cromer, Lord, See Baring, E.

Crump, C. G., on Acton, 46-e; on alertness, 48; on note-taking, 109; on scientific method, 415; on use of official records, 277-c

Crump, C. G., and Jacob, E. F., on handwriting, 165-d; on Middle Ages, 457

Curti, M. E., on Turner method, 434

Daguerre, L. J. M., on photographic process, 57-j

Dahlmann, F. C., and Waitz, G., on bibliography, German, 73

D'Ailly, P., on Columbus, 223-a, 225, 465

Dalberg, J. E. E., see Acton, Lord

Dale, E., on newspaper sources, 252-e

D'Ales, A., on Christian epigraphy, 86; on St. Augustine, 379

Dalton, O. M., editor of Gregory of Tours, 225

Dante, on Christian philosophy of history, 377; and criticism of Church, 367

D'Arcy, M. C., on belief, 62-a; on Marxism, 352; on providential view of history, 382

David, C. W., on American historiography of Middle Ages, 445

Davies, G., on bibliography, English, 73

Davies, R. T., editor of source book on Medieval England, 409a

Davis, H .W. C., on English institutions, 329-c

Dawson, C. H., on Christian concept of history, 366-a, 389, 390-c; on cultural anthropology, 74, 146-a; on progress, 28, 28-d; on Spengler, 390-a

Delanglez, J., on LaSalle, 173-f, 311; on Piñeda, 329-d (p. 334, n.)

Delehaye, H., on Acts of the Martyrs, 283; on Bollandists, 56-b, c; on hagiographical method, 167-a; on history in Middle Ages, 55-a; on legends of saints, 263, (p. 269, n.), 270

Delisle, L., and internal tests, 96-a, 169-a, 182-b; on medieval text criticism, 55-a

Demosthenes, transmission of, 216-e

Dempsey, B. W., on rise of modern capitalism, 329-a

Denifle and Chatelain, and Paris University records, 96-d

Denis the Areopagite, attributions to, 153, 260

Denzinger, H., editor of collection of doctrinal decrees, 409-b

Devas, C. A., on Christian view of history, 390-c; on civilization, 27-a, b, d; on progress, 28; on retrogression, 28-c

Dickens, C., as source, 94-a, 276

Dickson, H. N., on cartography, 79-a

Dies, A., on linguistic evidence, 165-c

Diffie, B. W., on Markham mistranslation, 323

Dill, S., on Apollinaris Sidonius, 251-c; on Salvian, 277-b

Dingwall, E. J., on use of libraries, 96-a, 112-d

Dinsmore, C. A., on Boccaccio's Dante, 313-c

Diodorus of Agyrium, on value of history, 16

Diogenes Laertes, on authorship of Anabasis, 162-e

Dion Cassius, on Herculaneum and Pompeii, 154

Dionysius Exigiuus, on periodization, 26-a

Dionysius of Halicarnassus, on purpose of history, 15

Index of Authors

Dionysius the Areopagite, authorship of, 173-a
Dobson, A., editor of Evelyn's diary, 248
Dodd, W. E., on American history fields, 448
Döllinger, J. J. I., on errors in papal history, 176-c; on inscriptions, 176-d
Donaghue, D., on Coronado expedition, 329-d
Donat, J., criticism, 44, 45-a, 46-b
Doniol, H., bias in, 251-a
Donnand, E., editor of slave trade documents, 225
Dow, E. W., on note-taking, 109
Dowd, W. A., on criticism of New Testament, 209; on Gospels, 146-a, 162-e, 166-a
Draper, L. C., and use of interview, 111
Dreux-Breze, Mirabeau's reply to, 154
Du Cange, glossary of, 214-f
Duff, J. W., on Livy, 206; on Roman legend, 272
Duffy, C. G., on value of history, 17
Dugdale, dating of Monasticon of, 182-b
Dumond, D. L., on editorials, 252-b
Duncalf, F., and Krey, A. C., on Medieval source problems, 409-a
Dunn, J., on Brendan, 272
Dunne, P. M., on New Spain Jesuit literature, 446
Dunning, W. A., on American historiography, 434; on Johnson's first message to Congress, 189
Du Plessis, J., on Christian view of history, 390-c
Dutcher, G. M., on bibliography of diplomatic, 81; on English sources, 57-i; on Napoleonic studies, 447
Dutcher, G. M., and others, on bibliography, 73

Edgar, C. C., see Hunt, A. S., and
Edwards, E. E., on bibliography of frontier hypothesis, 146-d
Edwards, W., on medieval visitation reports, 44-b
Egbert, J. C., on Latin epigraphy, 86
Egerton, H. E., on American Revolution, 329-f, 469

Ehrle, F., and Liebaert, P., on handwriting, 84-a
Eichhorn, and legal history, 57-d
Einhard, on Charlemagne, 95-f, 150-b, 192-a, 313-c; and earliest medieval history, 55-b; *suppressio veri* in, 44-a
Eisenschiml, O., and circumstantial evidence, 301; on Lincoln proclamation forgery, 173-f
Emden, A. B., see Powicke, F. M., and
Eppstein, J., on international law, 38
Estella, D. de, and authorship of *Hundred Meditations*, 188
Estienne, H., editor of Plato, 400-b
Eusebius, editions of, 166-b; on Justin the Martyr, 162-c; leading historian of Christian antiquity, 55, 95-d; personal psychology of, 326-a; on Thundering Legion, 303-a; translations of, 214-d
Evans, T. W., memoirs of, 242-b
Evelyn, J., diary of, 248
Everett, C. W., on letters of Junius, 188

Fallon, V., on use of statistics, 140-d
Faries, H., diary of, 248
Farrand, M., on Federal Convention records, 225, 280-c
Faulkner, H. U., see Flügel, F., and
Feder, A., on art products as sources, 282-b; on Bernheim methodology, 237-a; on causality, 349; on Church history, 388; on copyists' errors, 218; on dating in Tacitus, 339; on derived sources, 193-g; and edition of St. Jerome, 216-e; on hagiographical apocrypha, 167-a; on Hilary of Poitiers, 176-c; on providential view of history, 382; on recension, 212-e; on relational significance, 8; on reliable tradition, 258; on restoration of lost sources, 204; on St. Augustine, 61, 152; on St. Bernard, 292-b; on sources, 90, 91-c; on text variants, 218; on time-conditions, 359; on understanding Christian history, 366-a; on women witnesses, 278-c
Feith, J. A., see Muller, S., Feith, J. A., and Fruin, R.
Fénelon, on neutrality, 46-a

Feuter, E., on Modern historiography, 434

Fillion, L. C., on birth date of Christ, 339; on Fouard's use of conjecture, 147-c; on Gospels, 166-a, 172, 182-b, 187, 190-b; and source indication in biography, 240-d

Filon, A., memoirs of, 242-b

Fink, C. G., and Polushkin, E. P., on Drake brass plate, 173-f

Finlay, G., on Belisarius, 261-c

Firth, C., on Macaulay, 44-a, 434

Fisch, M. H., and Bergin, T. C., on Vico, 384

Fish, C. R., on American Civil War, 329-f; on autobiographical material, 243

Fisher, G. S., on Bancroft, 53

Fisher, S. G., on American Revolution, 261-e, 456, 462; on moral judgment, 369-a

Fiske, J., on continuity of history, 24; on self-projection into past, 365-b; and style, 419

Fitzpatrick, J. C., on archive administration, 115; editor of Washington diary, 248; on Van Buren autobiography, 243; on Washington, 173-f, 329-g, 448

Fleming, W. L., editor of Reconstruction documents, 225

Fletcher, H., on date of Milton's Ad Patrem, 182-b

Fleure, H. J., on geographic influences, 79-c

Fleury, on citing sources, 391

Fliche, A., and Martin, V., on Church history, 457; on Holy Roman Empire, 329-b

Fling, F. M., on argument from silence, 154; on Bailly memoirs, 173-d; on conflicting sources, 311; on direct quotation, 430; on miracles, 296; on Robespierre, 467; on single witness, 287-b

Fling, F. M., and Fling, H. D., on French Revolution sources, 409-a, 469

Fling, H. D., see Fling, F. M., and

Flügel, F., and Faulkner, H. U., editors of American economic and social readings, 409-a

Fonck, L., on Catholic seminar, 37; on industry in research, 47; on primary vs. secondary sources, 123-a

Fontenelle, skepticism of, 68

Forau, W. A., on Marshall, 50

Ford, H. J., on rewriting of history, 440

Ford, J. D. M., on Ciceronian dictum, 440; on medieval vernacular hagiography, 445

Ford, P. L., on Declaration of Independence, 339; on Federalist, 189; on Jefferson Autobiography, 243

Ford, W. C., on Mecklenburg Declaration, 173-f

Fordham, H. G., on cartography, 79-a

Fortescue, G., on direct quotation, 430; on factual interpretation, 327; on scientific dulness, 414

Fouard, C., on conjectural detail, 147-c; on Josephus, 152

Fowler, R. C., on medieval episcopal records, 96-b

Fox, D. R., on Middle West culture, 338; and synthesis in American history, 138-g, 344; on Turner hypothesis, 146-d. See also Schlesinger, A. M., and

Frank, G., on chansons de geste, 268

Frank, T., on early Roman historiography, 306; on survey of sources, 240-d

Frederick II, on falconry, 182-b

Freeman, D. S., and source indication in biography, 240-d

Freeman, E. A., on certainty, 63-c, 69; on continuity of history, 23; on diplomatic correspondence, 251; on free will, 41-b; on history as "past politics," 29, 337-c

French, on American Revolution, 456

Froissart, and earliest medieval history, 55-b; on use of cannon at Crécy, 153; and vivid style, 426

Froude, J. A., inaccuracy of, 51–52, 440; perversions in, 438; and quotation, 394-b, 430; subjectivity in, 46-e; and vivid style, 426

Fruin, R., see Mullen, S., Feith, J. A., and

Fueter, E., on Bollandist Prolegomena, 56-b; on Loyola autobiography, 243

Fulk of Chartres, on First Crusade, 91-a

Index of Authors 441

Funck-Brentano, F., on Bastille legends, 265, 467; on Griffet's treatise, 56-e
Furnivall, F. J., editor of earliest English wills, 409-a
Fustel de Coulanges, N. D., on Caesar, 310; on "law of context," 319; on method, 52-a, 435; on post-classical Latin, 318; on Tacitus, 310, 321; and text interpretation, 312, 321; on value of history, 15-a

Gairdner, J., and English Catholic view, 438; editor of Paston letters, 251-c
Galbraith, V. H., on use of official records, 96-a
Gams, P. B., on Inquisition, 51-d
Gambrill, G. M., see Woestemeyer, I. F., and
Gardiner, S. R., bias in, 438; on Gunpowder Plot, 466; method of, 431-b; as secondary source, 91-c; subjectivity in, 46-e; verifiability in, 53; and vivid style, 426
Garraghan, G. J., on Croce, 22, 67-b; on frontier hypothesis, 146-d, 345-f, 357-a; on local tradition, 259-e; on parochial records, 96-b
Garrison, F. R., on medieval medicine and science, 457
Garver, F. H., on Montana field, 448
Gasquet, F. A., on method, 431-b, 434; on source interpretation, 316; on Wyclif's Bible, 154, 188
Gates, E. M., editor of northwest fur trader diaries, 248
Gathorne-Hardy, G. M., on Norse sagas, 259-e
Gayley, C. M., on classical myths, 262-c
Gayley, C. M., and Scott, F. N., on poetry, 38; on text interpretation, 326-d
Gee, W., and philosophy of history, 372
Gellinck, G. de, on Catholic seminar, 37
Gentile, G., on certainty, 67; on relativity in history, 4
George, H. B., on argument from silence, 153; on belief, 62-a; on conflicting testimony, 311; on improbability, 295; on place-names, 307-b
Gerard, J., on Gunpowder Plot, 466

Gerstenfeld, M., see Coulter, E. M., and
Giacometi, Z., editor of Church source book, 409-b
Gibbon, E., errata in, 440; rationalist historian, 374; on rise of Christianity, 349; on Salvian, 386
Giddings, F. H., on belief, 62-a
Giesebrecht, W. von, and restoration of mediaeval chronicle, 205
Giles, G. A., on English chronicles, 95-d
Gill, H. V., on A. Pope, 108-d
Gilson, J. P., on archives, 113
Godder, F. H., on Compromise Bill, 462; on Kansas-Nebraska Act, 462
Goethe, stylistic problem in, 172-a
Goldsmith, on natural history, 2
Gomme, G. L., and analogy, 128
Gooch, G. P., on Chateaubriand, 57-c; on diplomatic correspondence, 251; on Froude, 51-52, 438; on Fustel de Coulanges, 312; on judgement of past, 367-68; on Macaulay, 419; on Niebuhr, 412; on nineteenth-century historians, 46-e, 434; on objectivity, 46
Goode, J. P., on cartography, 79-a
Goodier, A., on relation of facts and theory, 46-b
Goodman, W. H., on War of 1812, 329-f
Goodykoontz, C. B., see Willard, J. F., and
Gosse, E., on biographical history, 95-f
Gougaud, L., on hagiography, 271; memoirs of, 242-b
Grabmann, M., and Pelster, F., editors of Church source books, 409-b
Grandmaison, L. de, on Acts of Apostles, 172; on Gospels, 166-a, 182-b, 187, 190-b; on Josephus, 168-c; and source indication in biography, 240-d
Grant, F. J., on heraldry, 83
Grant, J., on dating of documents, 180-g
Grant, U. S., memoirs of, 243
Gratz, S., on handwriting, 165-d
Gray, E. F., on saga transmission, 259-e
Greeley, H., letters of, 250, 252-d
Green, J. R., bias in, 438; and faulty analogy, 130; modern viewpoint in, 29, 454; and organization of data, 343; and style, 419

Greer, D., on Reign of Terror, 329-c; and use of statistics, 140-d
Gregg, and authorship of Commerce of the Prairies, 189
Gregoire, H., on Herodotus text, 321
Gregory of Tours, and earliest medieval history, 55-b; and Germanic ballad sources, 98-c; source treatment in, 55-a, 431-b; trustworthiness of 45-c, 314
Gregory the Great, St., on Theodoric the Great, 269
Greville, P. W., diary of, 248
Grierson, on date of Milton's Ad Patrem, 182-b
Griffet, H., on memoirs, 242-b; on method, 56-e, 91-c; and source citation, 91-c, 391, 404
Griffin, G. C., see Bemis, S. F., and
Grimm, J., and German history, 176-c
Grisar, H., on argument from silence, 153; on Bastille legends, 467; on Luther, 231, 260
Griscum, A., editor of Geoffrey of Monmouth, 225
Grose, C. L., on bibliography, English, 73
Grosjean, P., on psuedo-Malachy, 173-b
Gross, G., on bibliography, English, 73
Gross, H., on circumstantial evidence, 300-a
Grosseteste, R., spurious letter of, 173-b
Grote, subjectivity in, 46-e
Grotefend, H., on chronology, 80-e
Gudeman, A., on authorship of De oratoribus, 162-c
Gui, B., medieval expert on documents, 55-a
Guilday, P., and bibliography, 73, 407; on Catholic philosophy of history, 380–81, 384, 390-c; on Church historians, 56-a, b, 73, 434; on periodization, 26-b; and source indication in biography, 240-d
Guizot, F. P. G., errata in, 440; on history of civilization, 27-a
Gwynn, A., on St. Columban, 339

Haggard, J. V., on text transcription, 221; on translation, 323

Hall, F. W., on conjectural emendation, 219; on copyists' errors, 218; on interpolation, 160; on recension, 212-e, 216-e; on textual criticism, 224
Hallenbeck, C., on Cabeza de Vaca, 468
Halphen, L., on Einhard, 313-c
Hamilton, G. de R., on Pineda, 329-d; on Lincoln election and slavery, 329-f
Hanoteau, J., editor of De Caulaincourt, 241-a
Hansbery, J. E., on Children's Crusade, 91-a
Hansen, M. L., on American immigration field, 450; on interpretative use of dates, 338
Harnack, A., on New Testament, 172; on St. Peter, 259-e
Harper, L. A., on American Revolution, 329-f
Harpocration, lexicon of, 214-b
Harrison, H., on literary historian, 415
Harsin, P., on witnesses, 91-c
Hart, A. B., on American sources, 409-a; and bibliographical survey, 407. See also Channing, E., Hart, A. B., Turner, F. J.
Hart, H., on style, British, 402-b
Hart, S. H., and Hulbert, A. B., on Pike explorations, 442
Harwood, D., on newspaper sources, 252-e
Haselden, R. B., on text transcription, 221
Haskins, C. H., and bibliographical survey, 407; on falconry treatise of Frederick II, 182-b; on medieval science, 457; on medieval student letters, 251-c; on method, 19; on Renaissance, 457
Hastings, H., and Church records, 96-c
Hatch, E., and faulty analogy, 130
Havet, J., and bibliotics, 165-d
Hay, M. V., on mistranslation of missa, 323; on Pollock perversion, 439; on Scottish history, 440, 459
Hayden, M., and Moonan, G. A., on Irish legend, 272
Hayes, C. H., on Protestant revolt, 345-c; on rise of democracy, 338
Hayes, R. B., autobiography of, 243

Hazelton, J. H., on Declaration of Independence, 339
Hébert, journal of, 369-a
Hegel, G. W. F., on certainty, 67; and concept of state, 29; and pantheistic theory, 385
Henderson, B. W., on place-names, 307-b
Henderson, E. F., editor of source book on Middle Ages, 409-a
Henderson, T. F., on Casket Letters, 173-c
Hennepin, travel accounts of, 276
Henry, H. T., on authorship of Adeste Fideles and Stabat Mater, 187
Henry, P., treason speech of, 246
Herder, J. G. von, genetic historian, 18, 57-a
Héritier, J., on Casket Letters, 173-c
Herodotus, errors in, 176-c; "father of history," 54-a; as literary historian, 31; manuscript transmission of, 162-d, 267; methodology of, 40-b; as narrative historian, 14, 54; as secondary source, 91-c; textual interpretation of, 321; trustworthiness of, 45-c
Herondas, single manuscript of, 216-b
Herrick, F. H., on Ashe, 189
Hesdin, R., forged authorship of, 173-d
Hesseltine, W. B., on American Reconstruction, 146-d
Hickey, E. J., on Church mission records, 96-b
Hicks, E. L., on Greek epigraphy, 86
Higgins, E. L., editor of French Revolution source readings, 409
Hilary of Poitiers, St., restoration of Tractatus of, 204; single manuscript of, 216-b
Hill, G. F., on Greek coins, 88
Hinkhouse, F. J., on newspaper sources, 252-e
Hinsdale, B. A., on value of history, 17
Hoar, G. F., autobiography of, 242–43; on recollection, 241–42
Hockett, H. C., on conjecture, 148-b; on Federal Convention records, 280-c; on miracles, 296; on note-taking, 109
Hodder, F. H., on Turner hypothesis, 146-d

Hodge, F. W., on Coronado expedition, 329-d
Hodge, F. W., and Lewis, T. H., on Castañeda narrative, 283; on De Soto sources, 313-d
Hodgkin, T., on Attila legend, 261-e; on Salvian, 277-b
Hoffman, R. J. S., on historismus, 375; on progress, 28
Hogan, S. M., on Savonarola, 464
Holand, H. R., on Kensington Stone, 173-f
Holdsworth, W. S., on perversion of history, 437
Hollis, C., on Belloc, 329-c
Holm, on Graeco-Roman history, 453
Holmes, T. R., on Caesar, 313-a, 339; on Commentaries, 182-b, 216-c
Holmstrom, J. E., on translation of sogenannt, 323
Holt, W. S., on Adams, H. B., 434
Holzapfel, H., on candor, 50; on Franciscan records, 96-b
Honoré de Sainte-Marie, on criticism, 56-e
Hoopes, A. W., on American Indian study, 448
Horace, reattributions to, 176-b
Houch, L., on Coronado expedition, 329-d
How, W. W., and Wells, J., on Herodotus, 313-a
Howe, J. W., as informal American Civil War source, 94-a
Hugh the Chanter of York, on Canterbury-York controversy, 310
Hughes, T. A., on American Jesuit sources, 96-b, 225; and documentary appendix, 408
Hughes, T. W., on newspapers and law of evidence, 252-a
Huillard-Bréholles, J. L. A., on Frederick II, 96-a
Hulbert, A. B., on physical environment, 79-c; and Western mission records, 96-c. See also Hart, S. H., and
Hulbert, J. R., see Craigie, W. J., and
Hull, E. R., on civilization, 27-e
Hull, R., on Gelasius, 320
Hume, errata in, 440; on Mary Tudor,

91-c; on miracles, 294–95; rationalist historian, 374
Hunt, A. S., and Edgar, C. C., on papyri, 84-b
Huntington, E., on Roman Empire, 146-b
Hutchins, M., on libraries, 96-a
Hutchins, M., Johnson, A. S., and Williams, M. S., on libraries, 96-a, 112-d
Hutchinson, W. T., on fact vs. interpretation, 331; on Jernegan essays, 434; on newspaper sources, 252-e
Huxley, on miracles, 295
Hyma, A. A., on authorship of *Imitation of Christ*, 188
Hypereides, single manuscript of, 216-b

Ihne, E., on etiological saga, 98-d
Ingulf, and Croyland history, 173-b
Isidore of Seville, on periodization, 26-a

Jacob, E. F., see Crump, C. G., and
Jacobus de Varagine, see Varagine
Jacopone da Todi, and criticism of Church, 367
James, J. A., on Clark memoir, 313-d, 469
James, M. R., on archive administration, 115; on text transmission, 216-e
James, W., on historical law, 138-d
Jameson, J. F., on American historians, 335-b, 434; and bibliographical survey, 407; on early American Sources, 313-d; and hypothesis, 143; and lost Pinckney plan, 205; on needed research, 449
Janelle, P., and source indication in biography, 240-d
Janssen, J., on Pirkheimer diary, 247
Jarrett, B., on social ideal of Middle Ages, 428-b
Jefferson, T., autobiography of, 243
Jenkins, C., on Church records, 96-c
Jenkinson, H., on archive administration, 115; on palaeography, 84-a
Jenks, E., on Anglo-Saxon texts, 321
Jerome, St., bibliographer of Church writers, 216-e; on contextual interpretation, 319; on critical sense, 45-a; editor-translator of Eusebius, 55, 95-d, 214-d; errors in, 176-c; on periodization, 26-a; personal psychology of, 326-a; and Vulgate, 209
Jerome, T. S., on Tacitus, 313-a
Jerphanion, G. de, on Antioch chalice, 173-a
Jerrold, D., on progress, 28
Jocher, K., see Odum, H. W., and
Johnson, A., on beginnings of historical science, 56-e; and bibliographical survey, 407; on certainty, 68; and conjectural detail, 148-b; and experiments in testimony, 229-d; on Griffet's treatise, 56-e; on hypothesis, 142-b; on idealism, 67-a; on preconceptions, 46-e; on single witness, 287-b
Johnson, A. S., see Hutchins, M., Johnson, A. S., and Williams, M. S.
Johnson, C., on archive administration, 115; on handwriting, 165-d
Johnson, D., on Pliny manuscript, 216-a
Johnson, S., on knowledge, 72
Joinville, biographer of St. Louis, 95-f; and vivid style, 426
Jones, W. L., on Arthurian legend, 272
Jones, O. W., on circumstantial evidence, 300-b
Jordanes, and Germanic ballad sources, 98-c
Jorgensen, J., on Lourdes, 231-a; on St. Francis of Assisi, 313-c; and source indication in biography, 240-d
Josephus, on burning of Temple, 204; interpolation in, 168-c; method of, 54-e; on objectivity, 46-a; and silence on infant massacre, 152
Jousse, M., on illiterate tradition, 259-e
Joyce, G. H., on analogy, 126, 131; on causality, 346, 361; on chance, 361; on hypothesis, 141, 145-c; on probability, 64
Joyce, P. W., on Irish place-names, 307-b
Julian, J., on authorship of *Stabat Mater*, 187
Jusserand, J., on conjecture, 148-b; on value of history, 17
Jusserand, J., and others, on impartiality, 46-a, e; on style, American, 420
Justin the Martyr, archetype text of, 216-b

Index of Authors

Kane, M., on safety valve doctrine, 146-d; on Turner hypothesis, 146-d
Kane, W. T., on libraries, 112-d
Kant, I., on certainty, 67; on providential purpose, 376
Kaplan, L., editor of graduate research guide, 409-a
Kastner, L. E., and Marks, J., on language criteria, French, 165-b
Kavanagh, J., on argument from silence, 154
Keatinge, M. W., on dating of Monasticon, 182-b; on source interpretation, 329-g; on teaching-problems, 409-a
Kellar, C., on periodization, 26-a
Kellogg, L. P., on Carver travel accounts, 248-b; on Kinzie history of Northwest, 313-d; and translation of St. Cosme letter, 210-c
Kelsey, R. W., on agricultural history field, 448
Kenney, J. F., on early Irish Church history as research field, 445; on Irish bibliography, 73; on St. Patrick, 329-b
Kenny, L. J., on local tradition, 259-e
Kent, S., on note-taking, 109
Kepler, and astronomical hypothesis, 142-a
Kidd, B. J., on early Christian documents, 282-c; editor of church source book, 409-a
Kinard, L. N., on West in American Revolution, 329-f
Kingford, H. S., on seals, 83
Kirben, R. P., on editorials, 252-b
Kirch, C., editor of ancient Church sources, 409-b
Klarwill, V. van, editor of Fugger letters, 251-c
Klibansky, R., and Paton, H. J., on relativity in history, 4
Knollenberg, B., on Washington, 329-g
Knox, R., on exaggerations of internal criticism, 171
Koch, H., and Stiglmayer, J., on authorship of Areopagitica, 173-a
Kraus, M., on American historians, 335-b, 434
Krey, A. C., editor of First Crusade sources, 410; See also Duncalf, F., and

Kuhnmuench, O. J., on hymns of St. Gregory the Great, 154
Kurth, K., on Gregory of Tours, 314

La Boullaye, P. de, and comparative religious history, 432
Labriolle, P., on St. Augustine, 379
Ladas, S. P., on copyright practice, 394-d
Laffan, R. G. D., and others, on Charlemagne sources, 328; editors of European source book, 409-a
La Gorce, de, on impartiality, 46-e
Lahonton, travel account of, 276
Laistner, M. L., on hagiography, 271
Lambert, H., on history as science, 39; on moral judgment, 369-a; on objectivity, 46-a
Lanciani, R., on St. Peter, 259-e
Lanctot, G., on Dollard exploit, 329-e
Lang, A., on Casket Letters, 173-c; on Froude, 51-d; on Homeric legend, 272; on Theocritus, 94-a
Langlois, C. V., on French medieval society, 409-b; rationalist historian, 374-a; skepticism of, 67-b
Langlois, C. V., and Seignobos, C., on miracles, 296; on philosophy of history, 374-a; on single witness, 287-b; skepticism in, 68
Lanzoni, F., on legend, 263–64, 266, 268–69
La Rochefoucauld, de, memoirs of, 242-b
Larson, L. M., on Kensington Stone, 173-f; on Norse sagas, 259-e
Las Casas, on Columbus journal, 190-c
Las Cases, on Napoleon, 242-b, 308-f
Lasky, J., on style, American, 402-a
Lasswell, H. D., on Bryce, 432
Latourette, K. S., on Chinese field, 444; Church records, 96-c
Lattey, C., on Church in pre-Reformation England, 458
Laurand, L., on abuses of higher criticism, 172-a; on archaeology, 85; on classical prose, 220; on conjectural emendation, 219–20; on textual criticism, 224
La Vaissière, C. de, on illusion and hallucination, 231-a
Lavay, J. B., on handwriting, 165-d, 173-f

Lavine, H., and Wachsler, J., on propaganda, 253
Lea, H. C., inaccuracies in, 51-d, 440; method of, 434; on moral judgment, 367
Le Bec, E., on medical proof of miracles, 297
Lecky, W. E. H., on causality, 345-c; on moral judgment, 367
Le Clerc, J., on critical method, 56-e
Le Clercq, H., on Antioch chalice, 173-a; on Mabillon, 56-d
Lee, J. T., on authorship of *Commerce of the Prairies,* 189
Lee, S., on biography, 240-d; on Shakespeare, 173-c, 188
Legendre, M., on Christian view of history, 390-c
Legg, L. G. W., editor of French Revolution sources, 409-a
Leibnitz, and methodology, 56-e
Lenglet du Fresnoy, N., on method, 56-e
Lenotre, C., on Dauphin problem, 467; editor of French Revolution documents, 409-b
Leo XIII, on truth in history, 44
Lester, see Morgan and
Lewis, C., on credibility of early Roman history, 91-c
Lewis, D. B. W., on Louis XI, 441
Lewis, L., on Lincoln legend, 270
Lewis, M., and Clark, W., journal of, 248
Lewis, T. H., on counterfeit tradition, 161-a. See also Hodge, F. W., and
Libaire, G., editor of De Caulaincourt, 241-a
Libby, O. G., on La Vérendrye, 468
Liebaert, P., see Ehrle, F., and
Liebermann, F., on Nennius, 206
Lilly, W. S., on medieval Christendom, 379; on periodization, 26-b
Lindworsky, J., on illusions of memory, 235
Lingard, on direct quotation, 430; exponent of English Catholic view, 438; on Joan of Arc, 231-a; method of, 57-g, 176-c, 343, 434; objectivity in, 46-e; **political historian,** 29; on primary vs.

secondary sources, 123-a; scientific attitude in, 431-b
Linglebach, W. E., on diplomatic correspondence, 251
Livy, Method of, 54-d, 190-a, 431-b; personal psychology of, 326-a; purpose of, 326-d, 337-a; reliability of 54-d, 176-c, 313-a
  as source: primary, 12-b, 91-c; secondary, 91-c
  sources of: 12-b, 98-c, 206, 272; subjectivity in, 46-e
Llewellyn, M., on microphotography, 99-d
Llorente, on Inquisition, 51-d
Loomis, L. R., see Shotwell, J. T., and
Lord, L. E., on Tacitus, 313-a
Lorimer, E. O., translator of Carcopino, 77
Lounsbury, T. R., on printed transmission of Shakespeare, 213-e
Lowe, E. A., on handwriting, 84-a
Lowery, W., on De Soto sources, 313-d; on Fray Marcos, 313-d; on location of San Miguel, 329-d; on Spanish rule in Florida, 460
Loyola, St. Ignatius, autobiography of, 243
Lucas, H., on Savonarola, 464
Lucian of Samosata, on value of history, 16
Ludde, A. J., on St. Bernard, 292-b
Lunt, W. E., and papal records, 96-b
Lutoslawski, W., on linguistic evidence, 165-c; on Plato, 287-c
Lybyer, A. H., on Western Hemisphere exploration, 338, 460
Lyett C., on argument from silence, 154
Lyon, E. W., on Louisiana cession, 329-e
Lyons, E., on news censorship, 252-d

Mabillon, founder of diplomatic, 81; vs. Papebroch, 56-c; and source criticism, 312
McCaleb, W. F., on Burr conspiracy, 469
Macan, R. W., on Herodotus, 313-a; on myths and legends, 267
McCann, on St. Benedict, 161-c
Macaulay, detail in, 335-a, 422-a; and

Index of Authors

judgment of past, 368; non-philosophical historian, 370; partisanship in, 282-g, 438; and popular appeal, 419; and style, 419; subjectivity in, 46-e; *suppressio veri* in, 44-a; on Thucydides, 426

Mace, W. H., on institutional history, 27-b; on periodization, 25

McClure, E., on British place-names, 307-b

McCormick, J. F., on causality, 346

McCracken, H. M., on conjectural emendation, 219

McDonald, G., on Greek coins, 88

McDonald, J. C., on chronology, 80-e

McDonald, W., editor of American source book, 409-a

McDonnell, J., diary of, 248

McDougall, W. M., on racial theories, 146-a

McDowell, R. H., on numismatics, 88

McFadden, C. J., on communism, 352

McGuire, M. R. P., on medieval studies in America, 445

McIlwain, C. H., on American Revolution, 469; on changing viewpoints, 456; on medieval institutions, 428-b, 457

McKechnie, W. S., on Magna Carta, 272, 358, 458

McKerrow, R. B., on bibliography, 73; on handwriting, 165-d; on printed transmission, 213-e, 218

McLaughlin, A. C., and others, on American source problems, 469

McLaughlin, J. A., on analogy, 126, 131; on induction, 132-a

McLeod, A. N., diary of, 248

McMaster, J. B., method of, 343, 431-b; modern viewpoint in, 454; and newspaper sources, 252-e, 337-b; non-philosophical historian, 370; as source, 12-b

McMurray, C. A., and McMurray, F. M., on generalization in history, 40-b

McMurray, F. M., see McMurray, C. A., and

McNeal, E., see Thatcher, O. A., and

MacNeill, E., on oral tradition, 259-e; on St. Patrick, 329-b

McNutt, F. A., and diaries, 241-a

Macpherson, J., and Ossian forgery, 173-c

McTaggart, J. M. E., on Hegelianism, 385

McWilliams, J. A., on miracles, 297

Madelin, on French Revolution, 428-a

Maden, F., on copyists' errors, 218; on manuscripts, 216-e, 224; on textual criticism, 224

Madison, J., as reporter, 280-c

Madvig, and emendations of Cicero and Seneca, 219

Mahan, A. T., on detail, 429

Maher, M., on illusion and hallucination, 231-a

Mahon, R. A., on Buchanan, 188; on Casket Letters, 173-c

Maine, H., and analogy, 128

Maistre, de, on "conspiracy against truth," 437

Maitland, F. W., on Church in pre-Reformation England, 458; exponent of English Catholic view, 438

Major, J. C., on memoirs, 242

Malaise, J., on authorship of *Imitation of Christ*, 188

Malone, D., on biography, 240-d

Mandelbaum, M., on philosophy of history, 376; on relativity in history, 4

Mandeville, J., travel accounts of, 276

Manley, J. M., and Rickert, E., on note-taking, 109

Mann, H. K., and bibliographical survey, 407

Mannhardt, F. X., on Pirkheimer diary, 247; on text criticism in Middle Ages, 55-a

Marchand, R., on *Lourdes* and medicine, 297

Marco Polo, travel accounts of, 276

Marcus Aurelius, forged letter of, 303-a; interpretation of, 327-a

Marks, J., see Kastner, L. E., and

Marsh, F. B., on Tacitus, 206, 313-a

Marshall, J., historianship of, 50

Marshall, R. L., on forgeries, 173-b; on Ingulf authorship, 173-b; on Squire Papers, 173-c

Marshall, W. I., on Whitman legend, 153

Marsilius of Padua, on St. Peter, 259-e

Index of Authors

Martin, A. E., on state history field, 448
Martin, V., see Fliche, A., and
Martindale, C. C., on indirect use of sources, 336; on Lourdes, 231-a
Marucchi, O., on Christian archaeology, 85; on Christian epigraphy, 86
Marvin, F. S., editor of *Progress and History*, 428-b
Marx, K., determinist historian, 30, 138-d, 352
Matthew Paris, see Paris, M.
Matthiez, on Reign of Terror, 329-c; on Robespierre, 329-g
Mattingly, H., on Roman coins, 88
Mawer, A., on English place-names, 307-b
Mawson, C. O. S., and Robson, J., on style, American, 402-a
Maycock, A. L., on rewriting of history, 440
Meany, E. S., on *Ulster County (N. Y.) Gazette*, 216-a
Meister, A., on methodology, 1, 36
Melville, L., on Thackeray, 435
Mencken, H. L., on Americanisms, 165-b
Mercier, D., on idealism, 67
Meres, F., and Shakespeare plays, 182
Merk, F., on Oregon acquisition, 345-c
Merrill, D. K., on autobiography, 243; on biography, 240-d
Merrill, E. T., on Pliny letters, 216-a
Merrill, W. S., on Norse tradition, 259-e, 465
Merz, J. T., on impartiality, 46-e
Metzger, C. H., on newspaper sources, 252-e; on propaganda in American Revolution, 253; on Quebec Act, 329-f
Meyer, A. O., on Church under Elizabeth, 466
Meyers, F. W. H., on Joan of Arc, 231-a
Michael, E. E., on Holy Roman Empire, 329-b
Michelet, on reconstruction of past, 422-a
Migne, and evidence of miracles, 292-b
Mill, J. S., and analogy, 131; on chance, 361; on induction, 138-b; on miracles, 295; on value of history, 17
Millar, M. I. X., on Aquinas view of natural causes, 380; on Christian view of history, 390-c; on civilization, 27-e
Miller, J. C., on propaganda, 253
Miller, W. J., on fixing day of week in dating, 80-e
Milne, J. S., on numismatics, 88
Milton, G. F., on American Civil War, 469; on American Reconstruction, 462; on Dred Scott decision, 462
Minucius Felix, and authorship of *Octavius*, 175
Mirabeau, and reply to Dreux-Brézé, 154; secret correspondence of, 242-b
Mirbt, C., editor of papal sources, 409-b
Mitchell, B., on note-taking, 101
Mitchell, C. A., on handwriting, 165-d
Molinier, A., on bibliography, French, 73
Mommsen, T., and conjectural detail, 147-c; on bias, 46-e; and inscriptions, 95; on *jus coercitionis*, 146-b; on linguistic evidence, 75; on periodization, 25-b; refuted by archaeology, 306-a; on Roman history, 176-c, 204; subjectivity in, 46-e
Monaghan, F., and authorship of Junius letters, 188
Monroe, J., diary of, 248
Montague, W. P., on belief, 62-a
Montesquieu, C. de, and methodology, 56-e
Montholon, memoirs of, 242-b
Montmorency, J. E. G. de, on authorship of *Imitation of Christ*, 188
Moonan, G. A., see Hayden, M., and
Moore, C. E., on women witnesses, 278-c
More, T., and authorship of *History of Richard III*, 188
Morgan and Lester, on photography, 99-d
Morgan, R. B., editor of source book on English social history, 409-a
Morison, J. C., on Macaulay's detail, 335-b
Morison, S. E., on Columbus, 465; editor of American Revolution source book, 409-a
Morley, Lord, on relation of modern and medieval history, 21

Morrell, P., editor of Greville diary, 248

Morris, J., editor of Catholic source documents, 409-b; on False Decretals; on rumor, 265; on St. Thomas Becket, 313-c; on St. Thomas of Canterbury, 260

Morris, W. A., on Bancroft series, 335-b

Morrison, B. R., and Rueve, S. J., on condition and occasion, 358

Morton, J. B., on Dauphin problem, 467

Moses, and Hispanic-American field, 455

Mosheim, on Catholic medieval morality, 439

Motley, errata in, 440; method of, 434; subjectivity in, 46-e; and vivid style, 426

Mudge, I. G., on reference books, 403

Mueller, F. H., see Sieber, S. A., and

Müller, M., myth theory of, 262-c; and philological history, 146-a

Muller, S., Feith, J. A., and Fruin, R., on archive administration, 115

Muller-Thym, B. J., on history as science, 39

Mumby, F. A., editor of American Revolution source readings, 409-b

Munro, D. C., editor of crusader letters, 251-c; on Peter the Hermit, 457

Munro, J. A. R., on Thucydides, 284-a

Muntsch, A., on cultural anthropology, 74; on Müller hypothesis, 146-a; on origin of myths, 262-c

Murray, G., on Homeric legend, 272

Nairn, J. A., editor of classical handbook, 409-a

Namier, L. B., and economic theory of history, 357

Nansen, F., on Norse Sagas, 259-e

Neilson, W. A., and Thorndike, A. H., on Bacon-Shakespeare controversy, 188; on conjectural emendation, 219

Nelson, W., on newspaper source, 252-e

Nennius, and authorship of Historia Brittonum, 206

Nevins, A., on biography, 240-d; editor of J. Q. Adams diary, 24-j; editor of readings in American Social History, 409-b; on editorials, 252-b; on philosophy of history, 371

Newman, J. H., and autobiographic candor, 242; on biography, 430; on English Anti-Catholic legend, 259-e; on Gibbon on rise of Christianity, 349; on perversion of history, 439; on Scott historical novels, 277-a; on synthesis, 427

Nicholson, M., on copyright practice, 394-d

Niebuhr, B. G., and early Roman history, 57-f, 176-c; genetic historian, 18; on heuristic, 90-a; on Livy, 98-c; on reconstruction of past, 412; on source critique, 57-h

Notestein, W., on biography, 240-d; on diaries and journals, 248-a; on Stuart period, 447

Nowell, C. E., on Columbus, 443, 465

Nunn, H. P. V., on Christian epigraphy, 86

Nute, G. L., on archive administration, 115, 224; on text transcription, 221

Nys, E., edtior of Franciscus de Vittoria, 225

Oberholzer, and newspaper sources, 337-b; and organization of data, 343; subjectivity in, 46-e

O'Brien, G., on rise of modern capitalism, 329-a, 345-c

O'Brien, L., on famous sayings, 261-a; on witnesses, 91-c, 287-a

Odum, H. W., and Jocher, K., on method, 34

Oestreich, T., on Gregory VII, 445

Ogg, F., A., editor of medieval source book, 409-a

Oldenburg, on Great Plague, 154

Olson, J. E., and Bourne, E. G., on Norse tradition, 259-e, 304

Oman, C. W. C., on bias, 46-e; on industry in research, 47; on methodology, 36; on necessity of publication, 51-c; on neutrality, 46-a; on rumor in first World War, 266

O'Neil, J. E., on Savonarola, 464

O'Neill, E. H., on biography, 240-d

O'Neill, G., editor of Golden Legend, 272

Ordericus Vitalis, and earliest medieval history, 55-b
Origen, on necessary lies, 236-b
O'Rourke, W. T., on libraries, 112-d
Osborn, A. S., on bibliotics, 165-d
Osgood, method of, 52, 431-b, 434; subjectivity in, 46-e
Otto of Freising, source critique of, 55-a
Oxenham, J., on Lourdes, 297
Ozanam, F., on criticism of Church, 367; on "golden ages," 28-e; on Providence and free will, 386

Paetow, L. J., on bibliography, medieval, 73; on diplomatic correspondence, 251
Page, W. H., correspondence of, 251
Pais, E., on archaeological evidence, 85; on Roman legend, 272
Paley, on circumstantial evidence, 300-a; on human testimony, 237-a
Palmer, R. R., and use of statistics, 140-d
Panvinio, O., source of pseudo-Malachy, 173-b
Papebroch, D., vs. Mabillon, 56-c
Pargellis, S., on Braddock's defeat, 313-d, 442
Paris, Matthew, bias in, 91-a; and earliest medieval history, 55-b; and Grosseteste letter, 173-b; subjectivity in, 46-e; and vivid style, 426
Parker, E. C., on Texan revolution, 462
Parkman, F., on American West, 450; and documentary appendix, 408; errata in, 440; on French Canadians, 366-b; 441; method of, 365–66, 431-c, 434; subjectivity in, 46-e; and vivid style, 419, 426
Parrot, T. M., on emendation of Shakespeare, 219
Parry, E. P., on Casket Letters, 173-c
Parsons, R., on Giordano Bruno, 154
Partington, W., on Wise forgeries, 173-f
Pascal, on Antony and Cleopatra, 362-a
Paston, letters of, 251-c
Pastor, L. von, on Cenci legend, 261-a; on direct quotation, 430; and documentary appendix, 408; method of, 431-b; on Savonarola, 464; as secondary source, 91-c

Paton, H. J., see Klibansky, R., and
Patrick, St., writings of, 329-b
Patterson, R. L., on St. Thomas on natural causes, 380
Paul, St., personal psychology of, 326-a
Paul the Deacon, and Germanic ballad sources, 98-c; and Tractatus of St. Hilary, 204
Paxson, F. L., on Turner hypothesis, 146-d
Peardon, T. F., on English methods, 434
Pearson, L., on Herodotus, 54-a
Pelster, F., see Grabmann, M., and
Penty, A. J., on economic view, 352
Pepys, diary of, 247–48
Perotta, P. C., on Vico theory, 384
Pershing, J. W., memoirs of, 243
Peter, St., personal psychology of, 326-a
Peterson, H. C., on propaganda, 253
Petit-Dutaillis, C. E., on Magna Carta, 458
Petrarch, critical essay of, 55-a
Petrie, W. M. F., and archaeological method, 85, 182-c
Phelps, W. L., and use of diaries, 241-a
Philip, A., on chronology, 80-e
Phillimore, W. P., on genealogy, 89
Phillips, R. P., on miracles, 297
Philo, on necessary lies, 236-b
Photius, lexicon of, 214-b
Pirenne, H., medieval cities, 146-c
Pirkheimer, C., diary of, 247
Pius X, on criticism, 45-a; on teaching of scientific method, 37
Plato, chronology in, 165-c; commentaries on, 214-g; edition of, 400-b; manuscripts of, 216-d; on necessary lies, 236-b
Plessis, J. de, on progress, 28
Pliny the Elder, authenticity of works of, 162-c; natural history of, 2; and omissions on Herculaneum and Pompeii, 154
Pliny the Younger, on authorship of De oratoribus, 162-c; letters of, 177-b, 216-a, 251-c
Plutarch, on authorship of Anabasis, 162-e; sources of, 206; trustworthiness of, 45-c

Index of Authors

Poland, W. F., on belief, 58; on epistemology, 66
Pollard, A. F., on Barbellion diaries, 248-b; on evolution of Parliament, 459; on origins of English history, 459
Pollen, J. H., on Casket Letters, 173-c; on Church under Elizabeth, 447, 466
Pollock, J., on Popish Plot, 439
Pollux, lexicon of, 214-b
Polonus, M., interpolated chronicle of, 176-c
Polushkin, E. P., see Fink, C. G., and
Polybius, on causality, 346, 348, 358; didactic historian, 15, 54-c; on function of historian, 54-c; on value of history, 16
Pond, P., diary of, 248
Ponelli, L., and Bordet, L., on source indication in biography, 240-d
Ponsonby, A., on English diaries, 248-a
Poole, R. L., on chronology, 80-e; on diplomatic, 56-d; on English royal charters, 182-b; on evolution of chronicles, 95-d; on numismatics, 88; on papal chancery practice, 96-b; on seals, 83
Pope, H., on *Comma Johanninum*, 160-c; on Gospels, 166-a, 313-b; on higher criticism, 157; on Old Testament and archaeology, 306-a
Postgate, J. P., on translation, 323
Potthast, A., on bibliography, medieval, 73
Powicke, F. M., on place-names, 307-b
Powicke, F. M., and Emden, A. B., revisers of Rashdall, 72
Prescott, W. H., artistic aim in, 431-b; errata in, 440; method of, 434; as secondary source, 91-c; and vivid style, 419, 426
Priscillian, single manuscript of, 216-b
Priestly, H. I, on Galvez, 451
Pringle-Pattison, A. S., on philosophy of history, 376
Probus, on Vergil, 210-d
Procopius, on Belisarius, 91-c
Prosper, false attribution to, 176-c
Prou, M., on palaeography, 84-a
Pyne, J. F. X., on concept of cause, 346;

on definition of science, 40-b; on epistemology, 66

Quaife, M. M., on Kensington Stone, 173-f; on Kinzie history of Northwest, 313-d; and popular editing, 222; on sources for American West, 313-d
Quintilian, on history as rhetoric, 54, 418; on necessary lies, 236-b

Raby, F. J. B., on authorship of *Stabat Mater*, 187
Ragatz, L. J., on Hispanic-American field, 455
Raglan, Lord, on Norse tradition, 259-e
Raisz, E., on cartography, 79-a
Ramband, A., on Inquisition, 51-d
Ramsay, W. R., on Gospel of St. Luke, 284-a
Ramsdell, C. W., on American Civil War, 329-f, 469
Rand, E. K., on handwriting, 165-d; on Vergil, 210-d
Randall, J. G., on American Civil War and Reconstruction, 329-f, 462, 469; editor of Browing diary, 248; on Lincoln field, 448; on reinterpretation, 453
Ranke, L., von, on Albert of Aix, 91-a; antedated by Lingard, 431-b; on Catholicism, 375; errata in, 440; "father of modern scientific history," 46-f, 57-h, 441; formula of, 3-a, 46, 46-e, 55-a, 374; and historismus, 375; method of, 46-f, 176-c, 434; on range of history, 6; and selection of detail, 429; and seminar, 57-h; on sources, 12-c; subjectivity in, 46-f
Rashdall, on medieval universities, 72
Ratzeberger, on Luther, 153
Ratzel, F., and anthropo-geography, 79-c
Ray, M. A., on American anti-Catholic legend, 259-e
Raymund of Agiles, on First Crusade, 91-a
Reeder, W. G., on interview and questionnaire, 111
Reeves, E. A., on cartography, 79-a
Reid, C., on bibliography, English, 73
Reid, J. S., on Tacitus, 313-a

Retz, memoirs of, 242-b
Rhenanus, B., publisher of Paterculus, 216-a
Rhodes, J. F., on Greeley letter, 252-d; and newspaper sources, 252-d, e, 337-b; and note-taking system, 102; and organization of data, 343; and Parkman, 431-c; subjectivity in, 46-e
Rice, O. S., on newspaper sources, 252-e
Rice, S. A., on method, 432, 434
Rice-Oxley, L., on value of memoirs, 242
Richard of Cirencester, spurious attribution to, 173-b
Rickaby, J., on argument from silence, 154; on causality, 346; on miracles, 296; on single witness, 287-a
Rickert, E., see Manley, J. M.
Ring, G. C., on religious history, 262-c, 432
Rivers, W. H., on ethnology, 74
Robertson, J. A., on Florida Spanish documents, 446. See also Blair, E. H., and
Robertson, W., on Miranda
Robespierre, C., memoirs of, 188
Robinson, J. H., editor of European source book, 409-a; on progress, 28; on value of history, 15-a
Robson, J., see Mawson, C. O. S., and
Roemer, T., on American Church society records, 96-b
Rogers, J. E. T., and statistical history, 139
Rogers, T., and argument from silence, 154
Roland, Mme., correspondence of, 249
Rollings, P. A., editor of Oregon Trail records, 225
Roosevelt, T., autobiography of, 243; on Clark memoir, 313-d; on scientific historian, 415; on Theocritus, 94-a
Rose, J. H., on Napoleon, 442
Ross, E., on culture, 74
Rossi, J. B. de, and archaeological research, 85, 95; collector of inscriptions, 95; on early Christian community, 142-c; method of, 45-c, 63-a
Rostovtsev, M. I., on Graeco-Roman history, 146-b, 453; on method, 34

Rother, J., on moral certainty, 63-a
Round, J. H., on English feudal sources, 313-c
Roussel, J., on Joan of Arc, 231-a
Rowell, H. T., editor of Carcopino, 77
Rowland, D., on De Soto, 329-e
Rowley, T., and Chatterton forgery, 173-c
Roy, J. E., on Lahontan, 313-d
Ruch, E. J., on False Decretals, 173-b
Rueve, S. J., see Morrison, B. R., and
Ryan, A. J., as Civil War source, 94-a
Ryan, E. A., on Counter-Reformation, 56-a
Rye, W., on genealogy, 89

Sacchini, F., on *suppressio veri*, 44-b
Sahagun, B. de, as primary source, 91-c
St. Cosme, B. F., and Guardian Angel Mission, 210-c, 307
St.-Pierre, de, on social evolution, 28
Sainte-Beuve, on letter-writing, 249
Saintsbury, G., on Shakespeare biographies, 148-b; on treatment of literature, 38
Sallust, manuscripts of, 216-d; and Thucydides, 54-d
Salmon, L. M., on Carlyle, 51-d, 434; on editorials, 252-b; on legend, 272; on Lincoln forgery, 173-f; on linguistic evidence, 75; on newspaper sources, 252-e; on numismatics, 88; on Roman sources, 272
Salvian, method of, 55-b; and providential view, 382, 386; source value of, 277-b
Sandys, J. E., on Latin epigraphy, 86; on Madvig reading of Cicero, 219; on palaeography, 84-a; on textual criticism, 224
Santayana, G., on modernist view, 389
Sarton, G., on bibliography, medieval, 73
Sauer, C., on determinist history, 355; on Fray Marcos, 313-d; on historical geography, 79
Savigny, and legal history, 57-d
Sawicki, F., on Christian view, 390-c
Sayce, A. H., on argument from silence, 154
Scaife, on Pineda, 329-d

Schafer, J., on Lincoln, 462

Schindler, M. C., on fictitious biography, 173-f

Schlegel, F. von, on Christian philosophy of history, 377; on evil, 383

Schlesinger, A. M., on American history, 428-c, 462; on American Revolution, 469; on economic determinism, 357-a; on philosophy of history, 372; on physical environment, 79-c; on range of history, 6; on use of statistics, 140-d

Schlesinger, A. M., and Fox, D. R., and bibliographical survey, 407

Schliemann, H., and archaeological research, 85, 176-a, 267

Schmidt, B., on modern European historians, 434

Schmidt, W., on culture, 74; on ethnology, 38; on religious history, 432

Schluter, W. C., on interview and questionnaire, 111

Schmeckebier, L. F., on official records, 96-a

Schofield, S., on Jeffreys, 459

Schouler, method of, 434

Schrader, C. E., on Canterbury-York controversy, 310

Schumacher, on Synoptic Problem, 190-b

Schwitalla, A. M., on causality, 347

Scott, C. W., on heraldry, 83

Scott, E., on Croce, 32; on faulty analogy, 130; on Mommsen, 46-e; on moral judgment, 369-a

Scott, F. N., see Gayly, C. M., and

Scott, J. A., on Gospel of St. Luke, 166-a, 313-b; on Homeric Poems, 171, 267

Scott, W., and historical novel, 277-a; journal of, 248; on Louis XI, 441

Sears, L., on environmental interpretation, 326-d; on literature as source, 94-b

Seebohm, F., on Tacitus text, 321

Seignobos, C., rationalist historian, 374-a; skepticism of, 67-b. See also Langlois and

Seligman, E. R. A., on materialism, 353

Seltman, C., on Greek coins, 88

Semple, E. C., on physical environment, 79-c

Seneca, textual interpretation of, 219, 321

Seton-Watson, R. W., on contemporary history, 20

Sévigné, Mme. de, letters of, 94-a, 251-c

Seward, S. S., Jr., on note-taking, 109

Shea, J. G., on footnotes, 395-a; on location of San Miguel, 329-d; on St. Cosme letter, 210-c

Shewring, H., on authorship of *Passio* of Sts. Felicity and Perpetua, 187

Shine, M. A., on Coronado expedition, 329-d

Shores, L., on basic reference books, 403

Shorey, P., on Homeric poems, 171

Shotwell, J. T., on Herodotus, 54-a; on school of St. Maur, 56-d; on social sciences and religion, 372; on theological view, 380

Shotwell, J. T., and Loomis, L. R., on tradition, 267

Showerman, G., on Roman archaeology, 85

Shurtleff, H. R., on log-cabin tradition, 259-e

Sieber, S. A., and Mueller, F. H., on culture, 74

Simon, J. M., on Gospel of St. Luke, 313-b

Simpson, L. B., on encomienda in New Spain, 451, 460

Skeat, T. C., on Chatterton forgery, 173-c. See also Bell, H. I., and

Smedt, C. de, on conflicting testimony, 308-h; on inscription reading, 176-d; on legend, 269; on Pragmatic Sanction of Bourges, 146-c, 153; on research, 45-c; on single witness, 287, 287-a; on tradition, 258, 264–65

Smith, A. L., on Grosseteste letter, 179-b

Smith, G., on history as science, 39, 41-e, 363

Smith, S., on miracles, 297

Smith, T. C., on American historiography, 375

Smith, W. E., on American Civil War, 329-f

Socrates (Scholasticus), source derivation of, 202

Sombart, W., on hypothesis, 141, 143; on philosophy of history, 372

Sorokin, P. A., on social-cultural dynamics, 390-c

Sortais, G., on St. Augustine, 379; on single witness, 287; on Vico theory, 384

Southwell, R., and authorship of *Hundred Meditations*, 188; biographical sources on, 240-d

Sozomen, source derivation of, 202

Spahn, W. E., and Swenson, R. J., on miracles, 296

Sparks, method of, 434

Spender, J. A., and Asquith, C., on Lord Asquith biography, 243

Spengler, O., on civilization, 28-d; and cyclical history, 390-a

Squire, W., forger of Cromwell letters, 173-c

Stenberg, R. R., on Louisiana cession, 329-e

Stephens, H. M., on self-projection into past, 365-a

Stephanus, St., see Estienne, H.

Stephenson, C., on community origins, 146-c

Stetson, J. B., on Florida research, 446

Stevenson, R. L., on writing technique, 431

Stewart, G. R., on place-names, 307-b

Stiglmayer, J., see Koch, H., and

Stock, L. F., editor of Parliament debates on American colonies, 225

Strabo, confirmed by archaeology, 306-a

Strachey, L., and psychological biography, 240-b

Strevey, T. E., on Beveridge, 326-a; on fact vs. interpretation, 331

Stubbs, W., on bias, 46-e; editor of English constitutional source book, 409-a; on English institutions, 329-c

Studer, P., on critical editing, 224

Sturlason, S., and Norse sagas, 259-e

Sturm, J., on note-taking, 101

Suetonius, biographer of Augustus, 192-a; and omission on Herculaneum and Pompeii, 154

Suidas, lexicon of, 214-b

Sullivan, M., on fact vs. interpretation, 331

Sully, memoirs of, 242-b

Sulpicius Severus, and authorship of life of St. Martin of Tours, 187; and Tacitus, 204

Summers, W. C., on conjectural emendation, 219; on Tacitus, 206

Sweet, W. H., on American Church records, 96-c

Swenson, R. J., see Spahn, W. E. and

Swinge, W. T., on Chinese sources, 444

Swisher, C. B., on Dred Scott decision, 462

Sybel, on Albert of Aix, 91-a

Sykes, N., on philosophy of history, 374-b

Tacitus, and authorship of *De oratoribus*, 162-c; on German customs, 280-b, 310, 321; on Herculaneum and Pompeii, 154; literary historian, 31, 54-d; manuscripts of, 216-b, c; method of, 431-b; misconceptions of Christianity in, 54-d; on Nero in burning of Rome, 261-a; personal psychology of, 54-d, 278-d, 326-a; pragmatic trend in, 54-d; reliability of, 313-a; restoration of lost passage of, 204; as source, 91-c, 339; sources of, 190-a, 206; and style, 165-c, 172-a, 426; on sympathy, 46-c; on Tiberius, 7-c

Taine, H., determinist historian, 352, 358-a; errata in, 440; on moral judgment, 369-a; on Reign of Terror, 329-c

Tait, J., on Richard II, 464. See also Tout, T. F., and

Tannenbaum, S. A., on bibliotics, 165-d; on Shakespeare penmanship, 442; on textual falsification, 169

Tarouca, C. S., editor of medieval Church source book, 409-b

Tate, V. D., on Daguerre, 57-j; on microphotography, 99-d

Tawney, R., on rise of modern capitalism, 329-a, 345-c

Taylor, I., on silence, 151-b

Teggart, F. J., on science as method, 40-b

Temperley, H. W. V., on Bury theory of contingency, 362; on causality, 348;

on history as science, 39; on Ranke, 46-e
Tennyson, stylistic problem in, 172-a
Tertullian, editions of, 166-b; editor of *Passio* of Sts. Perpetua and Felicity, 187; on Thundering Legion, 303-a
Thackeray, W. M., method of, 435
Thatcher, O. A., and McNeal, E., editors of medieval source book, 409-a
Thatcher, J. B., on Columbus, 190-c, 339
Thayer, W. R., on fallacies, 440; on historical law, 138-d
Themistius, and paraphrasing of Aristotle, 214-e
Theobald, and Shakespeare emendation, 219
Theocritus, as informal source, 94-a
Theodoret of Cyrrhus, source derivation of, 202
Theophylactus, Simocatta, on value of history, 16
Thomas, A. B., on forgotten frontiers, 451
Thomas Aquinas, St., edition of, 400-b; on providential causality, 386
Thomas a Kempis, and authorship of *Imitation of Christ*, 155, 188
Thompson, A. H., on parochial records, 96-b
Thompson, E. M., on palaeography, 84-a; on papyri, 84-b; on Shakespeare handwriting, 165-d
Thompson, J. W., on Mabillon, 56-d; on medieval town, 146-c; and use of statistics, 140-d
Thorndike, A. H., see Neilson, W. A., and
Thorndike, L., on history of civilization, 27-a
Thucydides, and causality, 348; confirmed by archaeology, 306-a; on continuity of history, 24; on Cretan empire, 267; and critical attitude, 190-a; direct testimony in, 284-a; first didactic historian, 54-b; first scientific historian, 54-b; and graphic style, 426; heuristic of, 54-b; manuscript transmission of, 162-d; method of, 40-b, 54-b; on Peloponnesian War, 54-b, 91-c; permanent quality in, 436; purpose of, 337-a; source values in, 12-b, 91-c; speeches in, 54-b; on value of history, 15–16
Thurston, H., on Antioch chalice, 173-a; and circumstantial evidence, 301; on Coulton, 51-d; on False Decretals, 173-b; on Gunpowder Plot, 466; on hypothesis qua fact, 145-e; on illusion and hallucinations, 231-a; on institutional origins in Western Europe, 146-c; on Lea, 51-d; on moral judgment, 367; on pseudo-Malachy, 173-b; on St. Joseph of Arimathea, 272
Thurston, H., and Attwater, D., editors of *Golden Legend*, 272
Thurston, H., and others, and hagiography, 161-c
Thwaites, R. G., editor of *Jesuit Relations*, 225; on Lahontan, 313-d; and scholarly editing, 222
Tocqueville, de, on American democracy, 366-c; on modern French history, 428-a
Tolman, H. C., on translation, 323
Tout, T. F., and bibliographical survey, 407; on forgeries, 173-b; on Ingulf authorship, 173-b; on medieval chronicles, 95-d; on medieval text criticism, 55-a
Tout, T. F., and Tait, J., on Richard II, 464
Toynbee, A. J., on civilizations, 27-e; and comparative view, 390-b; on contemporary history, 20–21; on Greek historical thought, 15-b, 346, 358; on Herodotus, 54-a, b; on St. Augustine, 379; on translation of *Barbaros*, 323
Toynbee, Mrs. P., editor of Walpole letters, 251-c
Trevelyan, G. M., bias in, 438; on literature as source, 94-b; on living history, 436; on Macaulay, 419; method of, 431-c; on range of history, 6
Trochu, F., on Curé d'Ars, 284-b
Tschan, F., on Helmold, 206
Tucker, W. J., on Shakespeare as source, 277-a
Turberville, A. S., on Croce, 32; on objective and subjective history, 365-c, 369-a; on Renaissance, 457

Turenue, memoirs of, 242-b
Turner, F. J., on American sectional development, 146-d; on American West fields, 448; and economic view, 357-a; frontier hypothesis of, 138-g, 142-c, 146-d, 338, 428-c; and generalization, 138-g; method of, 434; on multiple hypothesis, 345-f; on "Old West," 329-f; on philosophy of history, 374-b. See also Channing, E., Hart, A. B., and
Turpin, unreliability of, 150-b, 153
Twemlow, J. A., on forgeries, 173-b
Tylor, E. B., on culture, 74
Tyndall, W., on imagination, 413

Vaganay, L., on text criticism of New Testament, 209
Valla, L., and early criticism, 56
Van Buren, M., autobiography of, 243
Van der Velde, L. G., on diaries, 245
Van Doren, C., on American Revolution, 442
Van Dyke, P., on Jesuit doctrine of truth in historiography, 44-b
Van Hoesen, H. B., and Walter, F. K., on bibliography, 73; on note-taking, 109
Van Loon, H., on Taine, 352
Van Tyne, C., on American Revolution, 345-c, 451, 456, 461; method of, 431-c
Varagine, Jacobus de, and Golden Legend, 272
Varro, archetype text of, 216-b
Velleius Paterculus, lost manuscript of, 216-a
Vergennes, diplomatic correspondence of, 251-a
Vermeersch, A., on inaccurate figures, 51-c
Vico, on Christian philosophy of history, 377; and cyclical history, 384
Villani, on use of cannon at Crécy, 153
Viller, M., on autobiographies of saints, 243
Vincent, J. M., on informal sources, 93-b
Vinogradoff, P. G., on institutional origins in Western Europe, 146-c

Voltaire, and *Kulturgeschichte*, 57-b; rationalist historian, 374
Von Holst, H. E., on newspaper sources, 252-e; subjectivity in, 46-e
Voss, G. J., on history as science, 56-e

Wachsler, J., see Lavine, H., and
Waddington, on Mosheim perversion, 439
Waitz, G., see Dahlmann, F. C., and
Wallace, C. W., and Shakespeare discoveries, 442
Walley, H. R., on literary dating, 178
Wallis, J. E. on English regnal years, 80-c; on medieval documents, 81
Walpole, H., letters of, 251-c
Walsh, G. G., on medieval humanism, 457
Walsh, W. T., on understanding Christian history, 366-a
Walter, F. K., see Van Hoesen, H. B., and
Warner, B. E., on Shakespeare as popular source, 277-a
Warren, L., see Barton, W., and
Washburn, C. G., on Mecklenburg Declaration, 469
Webb, W. P., on frontier technique, 360; and generalization, 138-g; and Great Plains theory, 146-d, 428-c
Weber, M., on rise of modern capitalism, 345-c
Wedekind, and source localization, 185-d
Weekley, E., on linguistic evidence, 75
Weicht, C. L., on newspaper sources, 252-e
Wellman, F. L., on discrepant Lincoln stories, 311; on Parnell forgery, 173-e
Wells, J., see How, W. W., and
Wernz, F. X., on Holy Roman Empire, 329-b
Westermann, W. L., on Ancyra monument, 254
Wex, K., on Bertram forgery, 173-b
Whateley, on Napoleon, 68
Wheatley, H. B., editor of Pepys diary, 248
Wheatley, L. A., and authorship of *Imitation of Christ*, 188

Index of Authors 457

Whitaker, A. P., on Spanish-American frontier, 451
White, R. J., on legal reform as Catholic field, 450
Whibley, L., on Greek epigraphy, 86; on textual criticism, 224
Wigmore, J. H., on discrepant sources, 309; on judicial proof, 300–1; on research problems, 469
Wilkinson, W. W. J., on Renaissance, 457
Willard, J. F., and Goodykoontz, C. B., on bias, 46-e; on mechanistic concept of man, 355
William of Malmsbury, on Canterbury-York controversy, 310
William of Tyre, historian of crusades, 206
Williams, B., on manuscript migrations, 216-e
Williams, J. J., on ethnologists, 74
Williams, L. F. R., on use of official records, 96-a
Williams, M. S., see Hutchins, M., Johnson, A. S., and
Wilmart, A., on Hilary of Poitiers, 176-c
Wilson, W., on art of truth, 415
Windle, B. C. A., on miraculous healings, 297
Winship, G. P., on Coronado sources, 329-d
Winsor, J., on American sources, 313-d; and bibliographical survey, 407; inaccuracy of, 51-a; industry of, 47; on location of San Miguel, 329-d; and style, 419
Winter, J. G., on papyri, 84-b
Wise, T. J., bibliographical imposter, 173-f
Wissler, C., on Sahagun, 91-c
Witiking, errors in, 176-c
Wittke, C., and American saga, 263-e
Woestemayer, I. F., and Gambrill, J. M., editors of source readings on American frontier, 146-d, 409
Wolf, F. A., on Homeric poems, 57-e, 171
Wolf, G., on French memoirs, 242-b
Wooley, C. L., and archaeological dating, 182-c
Wright, B. F., Jr., on rise of American democracy, 338
Wright, H., editor of Cambridge Historical Studies, 435
Wyclif, and Bible translation, 154
Wylie, J. H., on style, 418

Xenophon, and authorship of Anabasis, 162-e; false attribution to, 166-c; status of among ancients, 54-c; trustworthiness of, 45-c, 54-c

Young, A., travel accounts of, 276

Zema, D. B., on civilization, 27-e
Zimmern, A. E., on environmental interpretation, 326-a
Zweig, S., on Marie Antoinette memoir literature, 242-b

INDEX OF MATTER *

A priori reasoning, see argument a priori
Abbreviations, for books of Bible, 400-a; in citations, 399; as internal evidence, 165-d; interpretations of, 176-d
Abnormality, organic, in witness, 280-a
Accretion in legend, 261-d
Accuracy, basic requisite in historian, 51–52; in classics, 437; in figures, 51-d; proved by detail, 284; relative character of, 51-b; and revision of views, 456; in translation, 322; in witness, 59-c. See also Credibility
Acropolis, dating of, 180-d
Acta Sanctorum, critical method in, 56-b; Prolegomena of, 56-b
Acts, official, see Records, official
Acts of Barnabas, ascription of, 167-a
Acts of the Apostles, authorship of, 165-c; source value of, 313-b; "we"-sections of, 172
Acts of the Martyrs, "air of sincerity" in, 283; as legend, 98-f; as primary source, 91-c
Ad Patrem (Milton), 182-b
Adeste Fideles, authorship of, 187
Adversus gentes (Arnobius), 175
Advertisements, Socio-economic data in, 252-c
Age factor, in witness, 278-b
Agencies, see Causality
Alertness, 48
Agreement of sources, 192–93
Agricola (Tacitus). 54-d, 216-c
"Air of Sincerity," 283
Alexander the Great, Christian view of, 388; empire of, 345-e; Sagas of, 98-d
Allgemeine Geschichtswissen-schaft (Chladenius), 56-e
American Board of Foreign Missions, archives of, 96-c
American Civil War, see Civil War, American
American Historical Association, and listing of research projects, 118-a

American history and catholic research, 450; changing view points in, 456, 461–62; colonial era of, 26-b; "critical period" in, 26-b, 40-b; frontier in, 146-d, 354-d, (see also Frontier hypothesis); generalizations in, 138-g; geographical factor in, 354-b; library resources on, 112; natural resources as factor in 354-d; new material in, 210, 451; research opportunities in, 449; and "technique of settlement," 360
American Revolution causes of, 469; French policy in, 461; legality of, 469; new documents on, 442; reinterpretation of, 44, 453, 456, 462
American Society of Church History, 96-c
American State Papers, 96-a
Anabasis (Xenophon), 54-c, 162-e
Anachronisms, 166-c, 168-c
Analogy, defined, 126; examples of, 128; faulty, 129–30; use of, 127, 131, 345-c; validity of, 126
Ancient history, see Antiquity, Graeco-Roman history Periodization
Anecdote as counterfeit tradition, 161-d; as source, 98-a, 255
Anglo-Saxon Conquest, and English language, 75
Ann Rutledge legend, 260
Annales ecclesiastici (Baronius), 56-a
Annales Rosenveldenses, 185-d
Annals, as medieval type, 238; as narrative history, 14, 95-d; organization of, 338; Source value of, 238, 276
Annals, Livy, 54-d
Annals of Lorsch, 182-a
Annals, (Tacitus), 54-d, 204, 261-a
Anthropo-geography, 79-c. See also Geography
Anthropology, 40-a, 70, 74, 146-a
Antioch chalice, 173-a
Antiquarianism vs. history, 9, 327
Antiquity, access to facts of, 68; cult of,

* (Numbers refer to paragraphs).

Index of Matter 459

359; historiography of, 359; humanistic cult of, 359. *See also* Historiography, ancient
Antiquities, see Archaeology, Remains
Anza's California Expedition, 225
Apocrypha, citation of, 400-a; early christians, 172–73; earmarks of, 167–68; hagiographical, 167-a
Apologetic (Tertullian), 166-b
Apologetics, christian, and source treatment, 91
Apologia pro Vita Sua (Newman), 242
Apothegms, see sayings
Apparatus criticus, 223
Appendix, documentary, 391, 408; Frankfurt Type, 408
Archaeology, and anthropology, 74; as auxiliary science, 124; and chronology, 182-c; Christian, 124; defined, 85; high evidential value of, 85; *and* new discoveries, 443; in place-names, 307, 307-a, b; refuting formal testimony, 306-a; *and* tradition, 258, 267. *See also* Remains
"Contemporary" history, 20–22
Architectural remains, see Remains
Archives, administration of, 115; American, 441–42; British, 441–42; defined, 113–14; diplomatic, 337-b; discoveries of new material in, 441–42; French, 114, 441–42; Spanish, 441; use of, 115; Vatican, 114, 441. *See also* Documents, Records
Archives Nationales (Paris), 114, 441
Archivo Vaticano, 114
Areopagitica, authorship of, 173-a
Argument *a priori*, abuse of 155; basis of, 155; examples of, 155
Argument from silence aim of, 149–54; application of, 149-b; examples of, 150-a, b; invalid, 44-b, 154; uses of, 150–51; valid, 149-a, 153. *See also* Suppression of data, Veracity
Aristeas, letter of, 176-c
Arles Manuscript of St. Hilary, 216-b
Armorial bearings, 83, 99-a, b, 100-a
Arrangement of data, see method organization of data, plan, presentation
Ars critica (Le Clerc), 56-e
Ars historica (Voss), 56-e

Art products, comparative test in, 165-e; dating of, 181-c; localization of, 327-b; misidentification of, 176-e; as sources, 274, 282-b. *See also* Remains
Arthurian legend, 272
Assyria, annal sources for, 95-d
Athenian State, authorship of, 166-c
Attila legend, 261-a, d, e
Attitudes toward past, see Viewpoints
Augustinian view, 378
Augustus, Suetonius biography of, 192-a
Authentication, see References, Sigillography
Authenticity, vs. credibility, 312; criteria of: external, 162–64; internal, 165–73; defined, 157, 159-a; and environmental correlations, 166, 166-a, b; of Gospels, 162-e; incomplete, 168, of manuscripts, 162-c, d; as misused term, 159-a; tests of: by content, 168-c; exemplified, 169-a; lingual, 168-b; palaeographical, 168-a; stylistic, 165-a, 168-b; and use of facsimiles, 405-c. *See also* Authorship Diplomatic Documents
Authority, attitudes on, 62-a; *and* evidence, 62-a; *and* historical fact, 58; *and* science, 61
Authorship, attribution of, 165-a, e, 168-c; and borrowing, 192-b; and character factor, 326-c; criteria of: external, 162–64; internal, 165–73; determination of, 156-c, 186–89; and individuality of treatment, 343; mannerisms in, 192-b; objective in, 326-d; *and* personal background, 326, 326-a, b, 327-a; problems of, 187–89; pseudo, 176-b; psychological factor in, 326–27; and selection of data, 334–37; spurious, 166-b, c, 167-a, b; and type of viewpoint, 337-a, c; *and* use of sources, 214-a, 218, 314, 391; variations of method in 192-b; *and* verbal usage, 318. *See also* Bibliotics, Diplomatic, Palaeography, Style
Autobiographies, American, 243; credibility of, 243; liability of error in, 233; *and* memoirs, 243; as narrative sources, 95-g; of saints, 243
Auxiliary Sciences, 70–89

Ayer Collection Newberry Library, 112, 405-c
Axiom of history, 15-b

Babylon, archaeological finds on, 85
Background orientation, 120, 336
Bacon-Shakespeare controversy, 155, 188, 192-a
Ballads, 14, 98-c, 324
Bamberg manuscript of St. Jerome, 216-e
Bancroft series, 335-b
Barbarossa legend, 261-a, e
Bastille legends, 274, 467
"Battle history," 15. See also Military history
"Battle Hymn of the Republic," (Howe), 94-a
Beatification processes, 284-b, 292-b
Behistun Inscription, 95, 254
Belgian history, geographical factor in, 354-a
Belief, and authority, 62; and critical attitude, 62; defined, 58; dictum of Anselm on, 62-a; divine, 62-a; doctrinal, 62-a; as essential factor of life, 61; and evidence, 62; historical, 62-a; human, 62-a; motive of, 62
Belisarius legend, 261-c
Bella diplomatica, 56-c
Benedictines, and critical history, 56-c, e
Beowulf manuscript, 216-b
Bernadette Soubirous, St., 231-a
Bias, vs. objectivity, 46-g; 345-c; prevalence of, 46-e. See also Impartiality, Partisanship, Subjectivity
Bible, citation of, 400-a; internal criticism of, 170, 181-b; polychrome, 172; rainbow, 172; text integrity of, 212-e; Wyclif's, 188. See also Gospels, New Testament, Old Testament
Bibliography, American, 73; on archive administration, 115; arrangement of, 406; for authentication, 395-c; of Church history, 73; compilation of, 405, 405-a, c; defined, 72; earliest, 404; English, 73; essay type, 404; examples of, 404 (p. 390, n.), 405-c; excursus type, 404, 407; formal, 404-5, 407; French, 73; general, 73; German, 73; Irish, 73; medieval, 73; as proof of accuracy, 391; in research work, 118, 118-a, b; of St. Augustine, 162-c; Survey type, 404, 407; on teaching-value of history, 17
Biblioteca Nazionale (Rome), 114
Biblioteca Vaticana, 114. See also Vatican archives
Bibliothèque Nationale, 112, 114, 441
Bibliotics, 84-a, 165-d, 169
Biography, credibility of, 239–40; "debunking," 240-a; dictionary of, 403; of historians, 435; Medieval, 95-f; as narrative source, 95-f, g; "new," 240, 240-a, c; psychoanalytic, 240-c; psychological, 240-b; of saints, 95-f, 98-f, 236-c (See also Hagiography); sources indication in, 240-d; source problems in, 239; untruthfulness in, 236-d
Bollandists, and scientific history, 45-c, 56-b
Books, printed, 183
Borrowing, in use of sources, 192–202, 394–95. See also Plagiarism, Quotation
Brackets, use of, 223-a
Brendan, St., 272
British Museum, 112, 116, 441
Bruno, burning of, 154
Burr conspiracy, 155, 469

Cabeza de Vaca route, 468
Caesarism, Roman, 349
Calendars, as narrative sources, 95-c. See also chronology
Calligraphy, 185-b. See also Handwriting, Manuscripts, Script
Calvinism, 329-a, 345-c
Cambridge Ancient History, 85
Cambridge History of India, 88
Cambridge Modern History, 437
Canadian Historical Review, and history of research projects, 118-a
Canadian history, natural resources as factor in, 354-d; Parkman treatment of, 366-b, 441
Candor, 44-a, c, 50; See also Criticism
Canonization processes, 284-b, 292-b
Capitalism, Modern, origins of, 329-a, 345-c
Cartography, 79-a
Casket Letters, 155, 173-c

Index of Matter 461

Catenae, 214-b
Cathedrals, 93-b
Catholic history, American, 112, 450; and outside authorship, 366-c. See also Christian history, Church
Causality, agent vs. condition in, 346; analysis of: exemplified, 349-51; relational, 345, 345-a, f; attitudes on, 346-57; in Augustinian concept, 380; and chance, 361-64; Christian view of, 378; and conditions, 358-59; defined, 346; efficient, 377; ethical, 357-b; final, 377-90; and forecast, 347; human, 352, 356-57, 377; and instrumentality, 360; material, 377-78; and means, 360; in modern historiography, 373; multiple, 356; natural, 352; nonmaterial, 377-78; and philosophy of history, 370; physical, 352, 354; as principle of synthesis, 71, 330-b, 338, 344-48; problems of, exemplified, 345-c, d; religious, 357-b; secondary, 351-52; vs. sequence, 347-48; social-economic, 352; supernatural, 380 (See also First cause, revelation); ultimate, 346, 370, 377. See also Interpretation
Celtic words in English, 75
Cenci legend, 261-a
Certainty, from converging probabilities, 69
Certainty, defined, 63; in evidence: archaeological, 302-a, b; circumstantial, 300; concurrent, 299; cumulative, 301; grounds of, 69; metaphysical, 63-c; moral, 63-a, c, 69; nature of, 63, 63-a, c; 69; and number of witnesses, 305-b, c; and personal experience, 69; physical, 63-b; possibility of, 65, 237, 237-a, b; in tradition, 258
Chance vs. causality, 361-64
Change, as principle of history, 2
Chanson de geste, 266, 268
Character factor in interpretation, 326-c
Charlemagne, coronation of, 26-a, 146-c, 328; legend of, 261-a, c
Charles Martel legend, 261-c
Chatterton forgery, 173-c
Children as witnesses, 278-b
Christ, historical career of, 46-e

Christian Apologists, environmental interpretation of, 327-a
Christian commonwealth medieval idea of, 379
Christian Era, as time-division, 26-a
Christian history, 55-56, 146-b. See also Catholic history, Church, Religious history
Christian philosophy of history, 351, 374-a, 377-80, 386-90
Christianity, earliest records of, 84-85; rise of, 349; Tacitus on, 54-d; See also Church, Gospels, Historians
Chronicle (Eusebius), 55, 95-d, 214-d
Chronicle of the Slavs (Helmold), 206
Chronicles, credibility of, 238, 276; critical method in, 55, 55-a, b; as medieval type, 95-d, 238; as narrative sources, 14, 95-d; organization of, 338; and vivid style, 426
Chronological history, 338
Chronology, archaeological aid in, 182-c; arrangement of data by, 338; "eye of history," 79; Gregorian, 80; Julian, 80; New Style, 80; Old Style, 80; Scientific beginnings of, 56-d; system of, 80, 80-a, e. See also Dating
Church, Catholic, under Elizabeth, 466; and European past, 366; medieval criticism of, 367; in pre-Reformation England, 458; providential history of, 388; and scientific method, 37. See also Catholic history, Christian history, Religious history
Church records, see Records
Cid as cultural source, 268
Circumstantial evidence, see Evidence
Citation, from apocrypha, 400-a; of Aristotle, 400-b; in Bede, 404; biblical, 400-a; bibliographical, 404; of classics, 400-b; direct vs. indirect, 430; in footnotes, 392-93, 397-98; in Griffet, 404; necessity of, 391; by paraphrasing, 394-b; of Plato, 400-b; by quotation, 394-a; of St. Thomas Aquinas, 400-b; shortened, 399; of standard texts, 400-a, b; by summerization, 394-b; See also Bibliography, Reference
City of God (St. Augustine), 379
Civil War, American, Anonymous diary

of, 189; causes of, 469; noncombatant participation in, 3-c, 454; reinterpretation of, 453–54

Civilization, defined, 27, 27-d; variant concepts of, 27-a, e. See also Culture

Clark expedition, 469
and Christian view of history, 389; theory of, 352

Classics, citation of, 400-b; conjectural readings in, 220

Climate, and causality, 354, 354-c, 364, 377; and economic facts, 359

Cluny Museum, 116

Coats-of-arms, 83, 99-a, b, 100-a

Code Napoléon, authorship of, 216-b

Codex Laurentianus, 216-b

Codex Mediceus, 216-b

Codex Murbacensis, 216-a

Codex Parisiensis, 175, 216-b

Codex Sinaiticus, 162-d

Codex Vaticanus, 162-d

Codex Vercellensis, 162-d

Codex Wirceburgensis, 216-b

Codices, 85

Codices Mixtae, 215

Coincidence, 361

Coins Roman, 88, 185-a; science of, 88; source values in, 93-b, 100-a, 276. See also Remains

Collections, comprehensive, 57-i; private, 442

Collectivism, Beard theory of, 374-b, 378

College of the Propaganda, 253

Collegia tenuiorum, theory of, 142-c

Columbus documents, 190-c, 223-a, 225, 443, 465

Comma Johanninum, 160-c

Comment, see Interpretation, Judgment

Commentaries (Caesar), 182, 182-b, 216-c, 280-c

Commentary, defined, 214-g

Communication, error in, 234–35; immediate, 234; mediate, 235

Community of origin, in sources, 191, 191-a, d

Comparative method, 390-b, 422

Composition, method in, 108-e; scale in, 122; unity in, 333

Compromise Bill, changing views on, 462

Concentration, requisite in historian, 48

Concordances, 318

Concreteness of detail, 422, 422-a, b

Concurrence of Testimony, see Testimony

Conditions, climatic, 359; cultural, 358-a; defined, 346; environmental, 358-a; geographical, 359; intellectual, 358–59; moral, 358-a; of place, 358-a; of season, 359; social, 359; of time, 358–59. See also Causality

Confessions (St. Augustine), 242

Conflict of evidence, see Evidence, Testimony, Witness

Congregatio de Propaganda Fide, 253

Conjecture, defined, 147; of detail, 147-c; in emendation, 147-a, 219–20; exemplified, 219, 329-a, g; interpretative, 329; in restoration, 147-b; use of, 148-a, b. See also Hypothesis

Conjuncture, 361

"Conquered Banner" (Ryan), 94-a

Considérations . . . (Montesquieu), 56-e

Conspiracy of Cataline, (Sallust), 54-d

Constantine, legend of, 261-a; reign of, 26-a

Constantinople, fall of, 26-a

Consularia Italica, 204

Contemporary reports, 276. See also Newspaper Sources

Content, as basis of dating, 181–82; in related sources, 192–93

Contents, table of, analytical, 343, 431-a

Context, verbal defined, 319

Contingency, Bury theory of, 362, 362-a, 364; vs. cause, 364

Continuity in history, 23–24

Contradiction, principle of, 63-c; see testimony conflicting

Conventions of style, 401–2

Copernican theory, 144

Copies, see Criticism, textual; Documents; Sources

Copyright practice, 394-d

Coronado expedition, 185-a, 329-d, 468

Corpus inscriptionum latinarum, 254

Correction, textual, 218–20; of viewpoints, see Reinterpretation

Correspondence, see Letters

Corroboration, a priori, 289-a, e; and in-

Index of Matter

dependence of testimony, 303; intrinsic, 288-a, c; of single witness, 305-b

Counter-Reformation, 56-a

Counterfeiting, in hagiography, 161-c; motives for, 161, 161-c; in Sagas, 161-b. In tradition: De Soto, 161-a; exemplified, 161-d; local, 161-a; oral, 161-d. See also Falsification, Forgeries

Credibility, of annuals, 238; vs. authenticity, 312; of autobiographies, 243; of biographies, 239–40; of chronicles, 238; of conflicting sources, 309; and detail, 227–28; of diaries, 244; evaluation of, 156–57, 314; of evidence, see Evidence; fluctuating, 190, 190-a, c; of formal testimony, 227-a; general postulates of, 279, 279-a, b; of inscriptions, 254; and laws of possibility, 288-a, c; of letters, 249–51; of memoirs, 241–42; of newspapers, 252, 252-a, e; and probability test, 289-c, d; of sayings, 261-a; of source types, 237–54; of tradition, 255–60; of witnesses, see Witness

Credits, 192-b, 450-b. See also bibliography, Footnotes, Quotations, References

Credo ut intelligam, 62-a

Credulity as cause of error, 175

Cretan-Mycenean civilization, 180-d

Critical apparatus, 223–24

Critical history, accuracy in, 51, 51-a, c, 456; candor in, 50; hallmarks of, 49–53; and missing dates, 339; thoroughness in, 52, 52-a; verifiability in, 53. See also Criticism Method

Critical sense, 45

Criticism, apparatus of, 223–24; *in bella diplomatica*, 56-c; and credibility problems, 313–14; defined, 156; vs. evidence, 158; excessive, 45-b, 175; exemplified, 173-a, f; external, 157–58; higher, 57-e, 157; internal, 157, 170; and interpretation, 315; lack of, 45-a; lower, 157; in Middle Ages, 55-a, 238; Niebuhr influence on, 57-f; in Protestant Revolt, 56-a; in Renaissance, 56; and revision of views, 456; as step

method, 33; Technique of, 313-d; Textual, 157, 207–25

Croyland monastery, history of, 173-b

Crusades, changing views on, 457–58; historians of, 91-a; and Oriental Sources, 445

Cult of document, 57-h

Culture, and civilization, 27-a, 74; concept of, 27-c; as condition, 358-a; medieval, 133; retrogressions in, 28-c; theory of: Anthropologic, 74, 146-a; diffusion, 74; evolutionary of, 74

Customs, as corroborative evidence, 306-a; of oral-tradition origin, 256

Cyclical view of history, 390-a

Darwinism, and Christian view of history, 389; and social evolution, 28

Dating, absence of, 177–78, 339; by archaeological evidence, 180-c, 182-c; by comparison, 181-a; by content, 181–82; criteria of: external, 179–80; internal, 179, 181–83; by day of week, 80-e; and epigraphy, 86; in fragmentary sources, 180-f; importance of, 156, 178, 180-a; and interpretation, 338; by literary traits, 181-b; medieval practice in, 177-a; methods of, 339; by physical evidence, 180-g; in printed works, 177-a, 183; by regnal years, 80, 80–c; by related sources, 180-a, c; and reliability of testimony, 178; by saints and feast days, 80-c; by silence on significant events, 181-c; by technical evidence, 180-e; by termini, 182–83; by tree-rings, 182-c. See also Chronology Diplomatic

Dauphin problem, 467

Day of week, method of ascertaining, 80-e

De arte venandi cum avibus (Frederick II), 182-b

De Civitate Dei (St. Augustine), 379

De gubernatione Dei (Salvian), 55-b, 277-b, 382

De Indis et de Jure Belli Selectiones (Franciscus de Vittoria), 225

De lingua latina (Varro), 216-b

De Oratore (Cicero), 220

De re diplomatica (Mavillon), 56-c, e

De rudibus catechezandis (St. Augustine), 76
De situ Britanniae, authorship of, 173-b
De Soto expedition, 313-d, 468
De viris illustribus (St. Jerome), 216-e
Declaration of Independence, 29
Deduction, 71
Defensor pacis (Marsilius of Padua), 259-e
Democracy, collectivist, 374-b, 378; rise of: American, 338; European, 454
Dendrochronology, 182-c
Dependent source, *see* sources
Derived source, *see* sources
Detail, concrete, 422-a, b, 426–27; contradiction in, 308–9; dramatic, 423–24; and effective presentation, 421–22; footnote supplementation of, 393-c; picturesque, 423–24; and presumption of accuracy, 284; selection of, 422-b; subordination of, 427–429
Detectio, (Buchanan), 188
Determinism, materialistic, *see* Materialistic determinism
Dialect, 185-c, 214-f. *See also* Language Linguistics
Dialectics, in training of historian, 71
Diaries, accuracy test for, 248-b; American, 248; credibility of, 244; English, 248; examples of, 248; factual, 245; intimate, 245; introspective, 245; as narrative sources, 95-g; objective, 245; organization of, 338; value of: in contemporaneousness, 241-a, 244; for corroboration, 241-a, 246; in dating, 246; for detail, 247; indirect, 245
Diction, as internal test, 165, 165-b, c, 168-b, 193-b, 196-e; as means of dating, 181-b; and presentation, 421, 425; in source comparison, 192-a, 196-e. *See also* Style
Dictionaries, 318
Dictionary of American Biography, errata in, 51-b
Dictionary of National Biography, errata in, 51-b
Didactic history, 13, 15–18, 54-b, d, 337-a, 424
Diocletian, era of, 26-a
Diplomata, 96

Diplomatic, application of, 81, 124; Defined, 81; palaeography in, 81; as science, 56-c, 81; scope of, 81
Directories, library, 403
Disagreement of Sources, *see* Testimony, conflicting
Discourse on Universal History, (Bossuet), 381-82
Discoveries, ambition for, 441; in American field, 451; by archaeology, 443, 453; in archives: national and state, 441, private, 442, Vatican, 441; in Hispanic-American field, 451; in papyri, 453; possibilities for 443–50; of Ranke, 441
Discovery of the Oregon Trail, 225
Discrepancy of sources, *see* Testimony, conflicting
Dishonesty, 50. *See also* Counterfeiting, Plagiarism
Dissertations, bibliography in, 407; lists of, 118-a; reinterpretative, 118-b, 453; and source credits, 405-b; style requirements in, 416; and subject selection, 463
Distribution of material, 431-a
Divine place, *see* First Cause
Doctrinal history, 337-a
Documentary History of Reconstruction, 225
Documents, ancient, 436; "Authentic," 91-c; changing of, 168; classical, 81; collation of, 213-b, c; consecutive, 409-b; copies of, 212-b; corroborative, 306-b; critical editing of, 217–20, 222; dating of, 75, 80–81, 165-d, 177–83; defined, 12, 12-a, c; emendation of, 212-e, 218–20; forged, 55-a (*see also* Forgeries); "idolatry" of, 57-h; interpolation in, 160, 168, 173-f; medieval, 55-a, 81, 91-d, 165-a, d; modern, 81; non-official, 91-d, 96-d; official, 91-d, 96-d, (*See also* Formalities); "original," 12-b; primary, 91-c; printed editions of, 216-a; public, 324; reproduction of, 222, 391; transmission of, *see* Recension; unpublished, *see* Discoveries; written, 12-b. *See also* Citation, Diplomatic, Manuscripts, Records, Sources

Index of Matter 465

Documents Illustrative of the History of the Slave Trade in America, 225
Documents inédits, 57-i
Dogma and scientific method, 37
Dogmatism, as source of error, 175
Domesday Book, 12-b, 277-c
Dominion Archives (Ottawa), 114
Donation of Constantine, 56, 153, 269
Drake brass plate, 173-f
Drama, see Plays
Dred Scott decision, 462
"Drum-and-trumpet history," 15. See also Military History
Dynamic view of history, 390-c

Early Ionian Historians, (Pearson), 54-a
Ecclesiastical history, see Catholic history, Christian history, Church
Ecclesiastical History (Eusebius), 166-b
Ecclesiastical History of the English Nation (Bede), 55-a, 176-c, 404, 431-b
Economic history, 146-a, 337-c, 377, 454. See also Materialistic determinism
Economics, auxiliary to history, 70, 124
Economics, as social science, 40-a
Edda, as cultural source, 268
Editing, critical, 217–20; Frankfurt plan of, 408; textual, 222–25
Editions, of classics, 400-b, printed, and recension, 213-e; scholarly, 225; up-to-dateness in, 72
Editorials, newspaper, 252-b
Education factor, 278-e
Egyptian history, dating of, 182-c; in papyri, 84-b
Egyptian Museum (Turin), 116
Egyptology, 85, 182-c
Ellipses, textual, 223-b
Emendation, conjectural, 219–20; defined, 212-e; by selection, 218
Emotional factor, historiography, 326
Encyclopedia Britannica, 79-a
Encyclopedia of the Social Sciences, 138-d
Encyclopedic history, 422-b
English history, dating of reigns in, 80-c; dissolution of lesser monasteries in, 80-c; era of political reform in, 26-b; geographical factor in, 354-a, gregorian calendar in, 80-b; industrial revolution in, 26-b; medieval, 3-c (see also Medieval history, Middle Ages); origins of, 459; picturesqueness of, 423; Tudor era of, 26-b
English language of Chaucer, 317; evolution of, 75; period differences in, 317; of Shakespeare, 317
Environment, affecting historian, 326, 326-a, 327-a; as cause, 352–54; as condition, 358-a; as factor in testimony, 278-e; and free will, 354-d; physical, 79-c, 354, see also Geography
Epic, as popular tradition, 266, 324. See also Saga
Epidemics, Medieval, 360
Epigraphy, see Inscriptions
Epistemology, 19, 66, 71
Epitoma Chronicon (Prosper), 176-c
Epoch, affecting historian, 359; as historical determinant, 352; and morality, 367
Epopéc, 266
Errata, see Accuracy, Error
Error, in authentication, 174–76; in communication, 234–35; compositor's, 213-e, 218; copyists', 218, 259-e; in criticism, 176-b, c; in dating remains, 176-a; examples of, 176-c; through hallucination, 230; through illusion, 230; in imagination, 229-c; in judgment, 229-e; through language limitations of, 234-a; in reproduction of perceptions, 233; and revision of views, 456; in sense-perception, 229-a, d; in sources: formal, 227–35, informal, 226; through suggestion, 234-c; in synthesis of perceptions, 232. See also Inaccuracy, Misconception
Érudit, 210-a
Esprit des lois (Montesquieu), 56-e
Essai sur les moeurs (Voltaire), 57-b
Ethics and causality, 357-b; in training of historian, 71
Ethnology, 74
Euhemerism, 262-a
Eulogies, 324
Evidence, archaeological, 302-b; vs. authority, 62-a; circumstantial, 300–1; citation of, 391; contemporaneous, 162-e; contradiction in, 288-a; converg-

ing, 301; corroboration of, 288–89; cumulative, 301–2; discussion of, 391, 393-b, 395-b; evaluation of, 156, 275; extrinsic, 162-a, d, 164, 212-a; from facsimiles or reproductions, 405-c; indirect, 285–86; internal, 158, 165–73 (see also Authenticity, Integrity); linguistic, 165-b; mediate, 285–86; on miracles, 288-b; numismatic, 88; testimonial, 300, 300-b. See also Testimony, Witnesses

Evil, Schlegel's problem of, 383

Evolution theory, 144, 389

Evolutionary history, see Genetic history

Exaggeration, in legend, 261-a

Excerpts, see Quotation

Exposition, 34, 315

Experience, as individual history, 15-b

Extracts, see Quotation

Fable, defined, 263-a

Fabrication, in hagiography, 161, 161-c, d; in oral tradition, 161; in sagas, 161-b. See also Apocrypha, Counterfeiting, Falsification, Forgeries, Lies

Facts, general, 68; historically significant, 7-e, 454; vs. interpretation, 330–35. See also Interpretation

Factual history, 374

"Fair use" in quotation, 394-d

False confessions, 282-f

False Decretals, and argument from silence, 153; authorship of, 173-b; late appearance of, 260; localization of, 177; as social source, 269

Falsehood, see Fabrication, Falsification, Lies

Falsification, in antiquity, 236-c; in biography, 236-d; in indirect transmission, 286-b; in legend, 263 (see also Legend); in Middle Ages, 161, 236-c; by omission, 159-b, 169; in source material, 159–61. See also Error, Fabrication, Lies, Perversions

"Father of history," 54-a

Faust legend, 98-f

Feast days, ecclesiastical, in dating, 80-d

Federalist, authorship of, 189

Festivals of oral-tradition origin, 256

Feudalism, as research problem, 52-a.

See also, Medieval history, Middle Ages

Figured Sources, 99, 99-a, d, 274. See also Art products

Fingerprints, 99-c

First Cause, 361, 376–77, 387. See also Causality, Providential view

Flores temporum, 176-c

Florilegia, 214-b

Folklore, see Legend, Myth, Saga, Tradition

Footnotes, for discussion of evidence, 393-b; economy in, 392; inaccuracy in, 53-a; limitations of, 395-b; objections to, 395-a, c; pilfering from, 395-a; as proof of accuracy, 391; for quotation credits, 394-a, c; rationale of, 392; for source citation, 393-a; specific necessity of, 394; for supplementation of detail, 393-c; technique of, 396; in typescript, 396–98; usefulness of, 393-a, c, 395-b, c

Forecast, 41-e, 132-b

Forewords, 405-b

Forgeries, American, 173-f; and bibliotics, 169; early Christian, 173-a; English, 173-c; examples of, 161-a, d, 173-a, f; and internal tests, 167-b, 169-a; Irish, 173-e; French, 173-d; medieval, 55-a, 173-b; Motives in, 161, 161-a, c. See also Counterfeiting, Falsification, Fraud

Formalities, as internal test, 65, 165-a, 168-b, 212-a; interpretation of, 324

Francis of Assisi legend, 266

Free will, as cause, 377, 386; as factor, 41-d, 351, 383; vs. environment, 354-d; limitations of, 136–37

French history, concepts of, 428-a; periods in, 26–27; picturesqueness of 423

French language, 78

French Revolution, and analogies, 128; causality in, 345-c, 350; as era, 26-b; historians of, 359; Reign of Terror in, 329-c; social effects of, 27-b

French School of Rome, 96-b

Freudian analysis, in biography, 240-c

Frontier hypothesis, bibliography of, 146-d; as economic determinism,

357-a; and medieval German eastward expansion, 146-d; and principle of multiple causality, 345-f; Turner's, 138-g, 142-c, 146-d, 338, 428-c
"Froude's disease" ("Frouditis"), 51-d
Fugger letters, 251-c
Funeral orations, 324

Gelasian principle, 428-b
Genealogies, 14, 89, 95-b
Generalization, in American history, 138-g, 428-c, as basis of science, 40-b; exemplified, 7-b, 137, 428-a, b; in French modern history, 428-a; and historical law, 132–35, 373; as interpretation, 330-b; limits of certainty in, 140-d; in medieval history, 428-b; moral vs. rigid applicability of, 41-a; and objective truth, 138-e; probability in, 140-d; in social sciences, 134; sweeping, 138-g, 427; as synthesis, 427; types of, 132; value of, 133. See also Induction, Interpretation, Synthesis
Genetic history, 13, 18, 338, 424
Génie du Christianisme (Chateaubriand), 57-c
Genuineness of sources, see Authenticity
Geographical history, 79-b, c, 354, 354-a, d
Geography, defined, 79; "eye of history," 79; historical, 70, 79; human, 79-c; organization of data by, 340; physical, 79, 79-b, c, 354; political, 79
German history, and medieval eastward expansion, 146-d; soil wealth as factor in, 354-d
German language, 78, 323
German National Socialism, 385
Germania (Tacitus), 54-d, 216-c
Gesta Francorum, 91-a
Glossarium (Du Cange), 214-f
Glosses, 160-c, 214-f
"Golden ages," 28-e
Golden Legend (Varagine), 272
Gospel, of John, 187, 279-a; of Luke, 165-c; of Mark, 197-b, 326-d; of Matthew, 197-b, 326-d
Gospels, "air of sincerity" in, 283; apocryphal, 173; authenticity of, 146-a, 166-a; confirmed by remains, 306-a; credibility of, 280-a, 282-e, 313-b; and critical method, 37; dates of composition of, 182-b; environmental interpretation of, 327-a; oral source element in, 98; parables of, 263-b; Synoptic Problem in, 190-b; text integrity of, 212-e; variant manuscript readings in, 218. See also Bible, New Testament, Scriptures
Government publications (U. S.), 96-a
Graffiti, 85, 100-b
Grammar, and interpretation, 319, 325
Graphic transmission, 99-c
"Great man" theory, 146-a, 356
Greek history, annal sources for, 95-d; archaelogical, 85; climate factor in, 354-c; epigraphic, 86; geographical factor in, 354-a; literary quality in, 414; reinterpretation of, 453; writers of, 54, 54-a, c
Greek language, translation of, 323
Gregorian calendar, 80, 80-b
Gregory VII, correspondence of, 96-b
Gregory XIII, calendar reform of, 80-b
Gregory the Great, St., as hymn writer, 154
Group psychology, 124. See also Psychology
Gunpowder Plot, 466

Hagiography, Bollandist influence in, 56-b; confusion in, 261-c; fabrication in, 161, 161-c, d, 167-a; purpose in 271; as social history, 271; as special field, 95-f. See also Legend, Tradition
Hallucination, 230, 235, 280-a
Handwriting, history of, 84; as internal tests, 165, 165-d, 212-a. See also Bibliotics
Hegelianism, 29, 385
Hellenica (Xenophon), 54-c
Heraldry, 83, 99-a, b, 100-a
Herculaneum, 154
Hero-tale, 98-d, f. See also Legend, Myth, Saga, Tradition
Hesiod, commentaries on, 214-g
Heuristic, defined, 156; purpose of, 34, 49, 90-a; in Thucydides, 54-b. See also Research

Higher criticism, 57-e, 157. See also Criticism

Hilary of Poitiers, St., 176-c

Hindus, see India

Hispanic-American history, changing view points in, 455, 460; valuation of sources on, 313-d; linguistic requisite for, 76; new material in, 451

Historia de las Indias (Las Casas), 190-c

Historia de vita Caroli Magni et Roland (Turpin), 150-b

Historia Regum Britanniae, 225

Historia Sacra (Severus), 204

Historian, Christian, 380; competent, 19, 44–48, 141, 391; ideal of, 414; and individual method, 431; and new contribution, 452; and personal style, 418, 426; and reconstruction of past, 412, 421; and self-projection into past, 365–66. See also, Historians, Historiography, Method, Presentation

Historians, ancient, 54–55; biographies of, 435; correspondence of, 434; eighteenth-century, 259, 374; Jesuit, 56-b, e; medieval, 55-a, b, 359; modern, 359, 414, 426, 438; motivations of, 10; nineteenth-century, 359, 374; in Protestant Revolt, 56-a; Rennaissance, 56; Romantic, 359; study of method of, 431–35; twentieth-century, 374. See also Historian, Historiography, History

"Historical causes," 284-c

Historical mission and causality, 374-a

Historical Section of Sacred Congregation of Rites, 284-c

Histories, average life span of, 436; for children, 337-d; classic, 436; general, 416; historians' 335-b, 337-a; secondary, 452. See also Historians, Historiography, History

Histories (Tacitus), 54-d, 216-b

Historiography, American, 138-g, 313, 420; ancient, 359; defined, 431; European, 313; in Graeco-Roman era, 54, 54-a, e, 414; and intellectual fashions, 326–27, 359; land marks in, 57-f, g; medieval, 55-a, 359; modern, 359, 373, 454; scholarly, 335-b, 337-a, 343, 391, 414–15; scientific, 56-b, e, 57-f, h, 337-a, 391–92, 413–15; specialized, 419; types of, 13, 416. See also Historian, Historians, Histories, Method, Presentation

Historismus, 375

History, vs. antiquarianism, 9; as art, 31, 42; "as it actually occurred," 374, (see also Rankean formula); of civilization, 27-a, 57-b; concepts of, 1–2, 31–32, 42; continuity of, 23–24; defined, 7–8; as description, 40-b; as discipline, 10, 15-a, 17; as evolution, 57-a; as experience, 15-b; immediate purpose of, 31; and individuals, 7-e, f; as inquiry, 1, 19; as knowledge, 1, 3-a, 7-a, c, e, 32; laws of, 132, 373 (see also Generalization, Uniformities); vs. legend, 55-a (see also Legend); as literature, 42; as "living past," 9; as magistra vitae, 132-b; material of, 2, 7-b, e, 15-c, 40-b, 41-c; meaning of, 1–32, 374-a; misconceptions in, 29–32; objective, 11; outmoded viewpoints in, 462; as past actuality, 1–3, 15-b, 32, 134; as past politics, 29, 337-c, 454; periods of 23–27, 463; and philosophy, 1, 32; range of, 2, 5–6; as record: absolute vs. relative in, 2, 67-a, b; concept of, 1–4, 79; earliest form of, 98-c; remaking of, 436, 454; subjective element in, 11; types of, 13 and rhetoric, 54 (see also Literary history); as science, 18, 39–43, 57-f, 413–15; as social memory, 15-b; and sociology, 7-b, 30, 374-a; as technique, 1, 19, 40-b; unity of, 23–24. See also Historians, Historiography

History (Sallust), 54-d

History of England (Froude), 46-e

History of England (Lingard), 46-e, 57-g

History of Greece (Grote), 46-e

History of Richard III, 188

History of Rome (Mommsen), 46-e

History of the Commonwealth (Gardiner), 46-e

History of the Franks (Gregory of Tours), 55-a, 225

History of the Monastery of Croyland, 173-b

Index of Matter 469

History of the Peloponnesian War (Thucydides), 54-b
History of the People of the United States (McMaster), 454
History of the Society of Jesus in North America, Colonial and Federal, 225
Hittites, historicity of, 154
Holinshed: The Chronicle of the Historical Plays Compared (Boswell-Stone), 206
Holland, introduction of Gregorian calendar in, 80-b
Holograph, 211
Holy Grail legend, 98-d, f
Homeric poems, and archaeological research, 85, 267; commentaries on, 214-g; as cultural source, 268; and internal criticism, 57-e, 170-71, 181-b; text transmission of, 216-e. See also Iliad, Odyssey
Homoioteleuton, 218
Honorius Controversy, 176-c
Household articles, cultural evidence, 306-b
Human activity, products of, as sources, 90
Human remains, see Relics
Humanism, 56, 359
Hundred Meditations on the Love of God, 188
Huntington Library, 112
Hypercriticism, 45-b, 175. See also Criticism
Hypothesis, and a priori corroboration, 289-e; and analysis of data, 145-a; dangers of, 142-b; defined, 141, 329; descriptive, 143; discredited, 142-b, c; disproved, 142-c; exemplified, 146-a, e; explanatory, 142-a, c; vs. facts, 145-e; faulty, 144; integration of, 145-g; multiple, 345-f; probability in, 145-b; vs. theory, 144; use of, 141, 145-a, g, 345-b; working, 46-b, 143

Icelandic Saga, 259-e, 263-e. See also Norse Tradition, Saga
Idealism, 32, 67, 67-a, b
Ideen zur Philosophie der geschichte ... (Herder), 57-a
Ideological history, 374-a, 454

Identity of sources, 193-a
Iliad, 171, 261-b, 268. See also Homeric poems
Illiteracy, in witness, 278-e
Illusion, mass, 235; in witness, 230, 280-a
Imagination, 229-c, 412
Imago Mundi (D'Ailly), 223-a, 225, 465
Imitation of Christ, 155, 185-c, 188
Impartiality, 44, 44-a, c, 46. See also Objectivity
"Impression of truth," 283
Inaccuracy, 51-d, 437. See also Accuracy, Error, Misconception
Indian (East) history, 87–88
Indian Office (U. S.), 114
Indicitions, 80
Induction, in Criticism, 71; four methods of verification in, 138-b; and historical laws, 134; incomplete, 132, 132-a, b; limits of certainty in, 138-a; and principle of causality, 132-a, b, 138-g; probability in, 138, 138-f; use of, 138-a, g; validity of, 132-a, b. See also Generalization
Industry, requisite in historian, 47
Inference, in dating, 339; pitfalls of, 302-c. See also Conjecture
Informant, see Authorship, Source, Testimony, Witness
Innocent III, on detection of forged documents, 55-a
Innocent IV, correspondence of, 96-b
Inscriptions, as corroborative evidence, 306-b; errors in interpretation of, 176-d; Hindu, 87; Mommsen's work on, 254; as oldest records, 95-a, 100-a; reliability of, 254, 276; Roman, 93-b; Science of, 86; as sources, 90
Institutional history, and concept of civilization, 27-b; American, 366-c; English, 146-c, 329; French, 146-c; in inscriptions, 254; in oral tradition, 256; political, 70; Roman, 3-b. See also Social History
Instrument, see Means
Integrity of sources, see Sources, integrity of
Intellectual history, 374-a, 454
Interpolation, 160, 168, 173-f

Interpretation, abuse of, 330-a; of authors intent, 324; Christian, 371, 386–89; comparative, 390-b; conjectural, 329, (See also Hypothesis); cyclical, 390-a; dynamic, 390-c; economic, 330-b, 352–53; factual: defined, 327; exemplified, 328–29; method in, 327-a, b; priority of, 328, 331–32; false, 261-e; function of, 315, 328, 330-b; and grammar, 319, 325; inferential, 302-c; of literary form, 324; logical, 325; materialistic, 352–57; (see also Materialistic Determinism) methods of, 316; mystical, 386; of motives, 345-b; of names, 261-e; necessity of, 330–32; psychological, 316, 326, 327-a, 330-b; rationalistic, 371, 374, 374-a, 390; social, 29, 330-b; 337-c, 454; technical, 324; teleological, 378, 386; theistic, 371–72, 386–89; and translation, 322–23; verbal, 261-e, 315–23. See also Causality, Philosophy of history, Reinterpretation, Synthesis
Interview, use of, 111
Introductions, study of, 431-b
Investigation, See Criticism, Research
Inwardness, see Projection
Isidorian decretals, see False Decretals
Italian History, climatic factor in, 354-a, c; picturesqueness of, 423

James II, revision of views on, 459
Jeffreys, changing view on, 459
Jesuit Relations and Allied Documents, 225, 253
Jesuits, and scientific history, 56-c, e. See also Bollandists
Jesus Christ (Grandmaison), 240-d
Jewish Antiquities (Josephus), 54-e
Jewish history, 54-e
Jewish War (Josephus), 54-e
Joan, Popess, 153, 176-c, 260
Joan of Arc, St., 231-a
John XXII, correspondence of, 96-b
John, the Evangelist, legend of, 261-a
John Carter Brown Library, 112
John England (Guilday), 240-d
Johnson message (first) to Congress, 189
Joseph of Arimathea, St., 272

Journal intime, 245
Journals, as aid to reliability, 241-a; credibility of, 244; as narrative sources, 95-g
Judgment, by contemporary standards, 367–69; as factor in error, 229-e; moral, 369, 369-a; and objectivity, 46-d; and self-projection into past, 365-69; suspension of, 308-9. See also Criticism
Julian calendar, 80, 80-b
Jugurthine War, (Sallust), 54-d
Junius letters, 188
Jus coercitionis, 146-b
Justinian Code, 177-b

Kalevala, 268
Kansas-Nebraska Act, 462
Kensington Stone, 173-f
King Charles II (Bryant), 240-d
Knowledge, of ancient and medieval history, 68; derivation of, 72; meaning of, 58; of witness, 59-a. See also History as record
Kulturgeschichte, 27-a, 57-b

Lacunae, textual, 223-b
Language, in choice of variants, 218; as corroborative evidence, 306-a; dialect, 185-c, 214-f; foreign, 76; French, 78; German, 78, 323; Greek, 323; as internal test, 165-b, c, 168-b; and interpretation, 77, 317–23; Latin, see Latin; limitations of, 234-a; and localization, 185-c; period differences in, 317; in presentations, 417; relation of Semitic and Indo-European, 237-b; in source identification, 237-b; Spanish, 76; in translations, 214-d, 322. Usage in, 318. See also Linguistics
La Salle expedition, 173-f
Latin, of Bede, 318; of Caesar, 318; classical, 76, 317; medieval, 76, 317; Merovingian, 318; period differences in, 317; postclassical, 317; for shortened citation, 399; of Tacitus, 318
La Vérendrye expedition, 185, 468
Laws of classical prose, 220; historical: application of 132-b; classified, 135; defined, 134; exemplified, 132, 132-a;

limits of, 138-d; mechanistic view of, 138-d, 373, (see also Generalization); moral, 63-a, 288-c; natural, 294; physical, 63-b; of possibility, 288–89, 293–94

Lawyers' pleas, Source value of, 324

Layard excavations, 306-b

Lee R. E. (Freeman), 240-d

Legal history, methodology, 57-d

Legend, accretion in, 261-d; Christian, 269; concentration in, 261-b; confusion in, 261-c; defined, 263, 263-d; development of, 261, 261-a, e; dissemination of, 263-d; early Roman sources in, 272; exaggeration in, 261-a; false enterpretation in, 261-e; Legends, weather, 130; "kernel of truth" in, 264; liturgical, 98-f; in medieval historiography, 55-a; origin of, 266;

of saints: confusion in, 261-c; as counterfeit tradition, 161-d; as cultural source, 259-a; and faulty analogy, 130; values in, 270–72, (see also Hagiography); social history in, 268–69, 272–73; as source, 98-c, 176-c, 263–73; as technical term, 98-f; types of, 263, 263-a, e; written, 263-d. See also Myth, Saga, Tradition, Transmission

Leif Erikson saga, 259-e

Leo XIII, and opening of Vatican archives, 96-b

Letters, as aid to reliability, 241-a; as corroborative evidence, 306-b; credibility of, 249–51; diplomatic, 251, 251-b; of historians, 434; official, 251; private, 250; public, 250; source values in, 95, 95-g, 249, 278-f

"Letting facts speak for themselves," 330–35

Lewis and Clark journals, editing of, 222

Legenda negra of colonial Spain, 460

Lex continuitatis of Leibnitz, 56-e

Liberty, national, and historiography, 57-b

Libraries, catalogue systems of, 112-b; and inter-library loans, 112-c; outstanding for specific resources, 112; references, 403; use of, 112, 112-a, d

Library of Congress, 112, 112-d, 114

Lies, for art's sake 236-c; defined, 236; formal, 236; material, 236; in modern biography, 236-d; of necessity and utility, 236-b; of omission 44-a; pathological, 236, 281-b; recognition of, 236-a. See also Fabrication, Falsification, Perversions of history

Life and Labours of St. Vincent de Paul (Coste), 240-d

Life and Times of John Carroll (Guilday), 240-d

Life and Works of Blessed Robert Francis Cardinal Bellarmine (Broderick), 240-d

Life of Christ (Fillion), 240-d

Life of William Shakespeare (Lee), 240-d

Lincoln, addresses of, 94-a, 89, 210-b; documentary problems on, 173-f, 442; election of, 462; saga of, 263-e

Linguistics, and dating, 75; requisites in, 76, 78; use of, exemplified, 77. See also Language

Lists of official persons, 14; of research projects, 118-a

Literacy factor, in witness, 278-e

Literary history, 42, 176-b, 413–15, 420, 436

Literary style, see Style

Literature, corroborating remains, 306-b; as source, 94, 94-a, b, 324

Lives, see Autobiography, Biography, Hagiography

Localizations, by art technique, 185-b; by calligraphy, 185-b; caution in, 185-a; and critical process, 156-b; as interpretative factor, 184, 327-b; by language, 185-c; by style, 185-c; by typography, 185-b

Locus originis, see Localization

Log-cabin tradition, 259-e

Logic, of a priori reasoning, 155; of analogy, 126–32; of argument from silence, 149–54; of conjecture, 147–48; contextual, 325; of generalization, 132–38; and historical method, 37; of hypothesis, 141–46; inferential, 302-c; and method, 71, 125; of statistics, 139–40

London Institute of Historical Research, 118-a

Louisiana cession, 329-e, 461
Louvre, 116
Luther legend, 153, 260
Lycurgus legend, 261-a

Magdeburg Centuries, 56-a
Magistra vitae role of history, 132-b
Magna Carta, 272, 458
Malachy, St., spurious prophesies of, 173-b
Man in the Iron Mask, 467
Manuals of style, 402-a, b
Manuscripts, archetype in, 215; conflated, 215; copies of, 162-d; filiation of, 213-b, 216-e; genealogy of, 213-b, 216-e; genuineness of, 85, 162-d (see also Authenticity); localization of, 327-b; mixed, 215; pedigree of, 213-b, 216-d; prototype in, 215; sources of, 214-a; tradition of: direct, 213-a, d, indirect, 214, 214-a, g; transmission of, 214-15. See also Bibliotics, Documents. Palaeography, Texts
Maps, 79-a
Marcus Aurelius legend, 261-b
Marie Antoinette, forged letters of, 173-d
Martin of Tours, St., biography of, 187
Martyrology, 282-c. See also Acts of the Martyrs
Martyrs (Les) (Chateaubriand), 57-c
Marxism, 352–53, 389
Mary Stuart, and Casket Letters, 155, 173-c
Materialistic determinism, attitudes of, 30, 79-b, c, 146-a, 369-a, 377–78; exemplified, 352–57
Mayan history, 85
Means, and causality, 360; moral, 360; physical, 360
Mechanistic history, 355, 373
Mecklenburg Declaration, 173-f, 469
Medals, as sources, 100-a
Medical science, in historical research, 124
Medieval Academy of America, 118-a
Medieval history, and language, 76; resources on: Bibliothèque Nationale, 112; British Museum, 112; Vatican Library, 112. See also Middle Ages, Periodization

Meditations (Marcus Aurelius), 327-a
Memoirs, and autobiography, 243; credibility of, 241–42; of first World War, 242-b; of Franco-Prussian War, 242-b; of French Revolution, 188, 242-b; of French Second Empire, 242-b; liability of error in, 233, 241, 241-a; of Marie Antoinette, 242-b; Napoleonic, 242-b; as narrative sources, 95-g; personal equation in, 241-b; and picturesque detail, 423; use of journals, diaries, etc., in, 241
Memoranda, as aid to reliability, 241-a
Memorials, as sources, 99-a
Memory, defined, 280-b
Mendelian law, 138-d
Metaphysical possibility, 288–89
Metaphysics, and principle of causality, 71
Method, in American history, 462; of ancient historians, 54, 54-a, e; attitudes on, 36; in bella diplomatica, 56-c, d; bibliography on, 433–34; Bollandist contribution to, 56-b; capital function of, 36, 40-b, 49, 63; comparative, 390-b, 432; in controversies of Protestant Revolt, 56-a; critical, 34, 36, 49 (see also Criticism); defined, 33; development of, 54, 57-a, j; of differentials, 140-b; of early Christian historians, 55; ecclesiastical teaching of, 37; eighteenth-century, 56-e; and epistemology, 19; expositional, 34; and footnotes, 392–94; and hermeneutic, 37; heuristic, 34, 49, 54-b, 90-a, 156; qua history, 19; and history of dogma, 37; Lingard's, 57-g; as means to certainty, 237, 237-a; of medieval historians, 55-a, b; Niebuhr's, 57-f, h; nineteenth-century advances in, 57, 57-a, j; in philosophy, 37; Rankean, 57-h, 375, 431-b (See also Rankean formula); of Renaissance historians, 56; rules of, 33; scientific, 37, 56-e, 144 (see also Criticism); in social sciences, 38; in Scripture exegesis, 37; speculative, 37, 462; study of, 431–35; synthetic, 34; in theology, 37; three steps of, 34; uses of, 35–37. See also Historians, Historiography

Méthode pour étudier l'histoire (Lenglet du Fresnoy), 56-e
Methodology, see Method
Methodus ad facilem historiarum cognitionem (Bodin), 56-e
Metropolitan Museum of Art, 116
Microfilm, 99-d
Microprint, 99-d
Middle Ages, access to facts of, 68; "age of faith," 25-b; art of, 428-b; changing views on, 21, 368, 457; and Christian legends, 269; conflict of church and state in, 428-b; critical spirit in, 258-b; historiography in, 55-a, 359; legal concepts of, 428-b; limits of, 26-a; political thought of, 428-b; progressivism of, 428-b; science of, 457; social theories of, 428-b. See also Medieval history
Milieu, 352, 358-a. See also Environment
Military history, 15, 337-c, 454
Mineral wealth, as cause, 354
Mira, 290-b, 291, 296
Miracles, a priori corroboration of, 289-e; controversy on, 296; criteria of provenance of, 292-a; critics of, 293–97; defined, 290-a, b; evidential value of, 294; as historical facts, 296; knowability of, 292; as natural phenomena, 296; possibility of, 291, 294; testimony on, 292-b
Misconceptions, of history, 29–32; of objectivity, 46-a, g. See also Error, Reinterpretation
Misrepresentation, see Error, Falsification, Lies
Missouri Historical Society Library, 112
Mistakes, see Error, Misconceptions
Modern history, as new cycle, 25-b; rationalistic, 390. See also Criticism, Historiography, Method
Monasteries, and origination of manuscripts, 327-b
Monasticon (Dugdale), 182-b
Monographs, bibliography of, 407; needed, 445; and selection of data, 337-a; source credits in, 405-b; style requirements in, 416
Monumenta Germaniae historica, chronicle history in, 95-d; credibility of, 238; Crusade sources in, 91-a; dating in, 182-a, 185-d; motto of, 46-a; on St. Bernard, 292-b; significance of, 57-i; and transcription errors, 165-d
Monuments, 99-a. See also Art products, Remains
Monumentum Ancyranum, 95, 254
Moral backgrounds, in historiography, 327-a
Moral judgments, 369, 369-a
Moral laws, defined, 288-c; examples of, 63-a; exception in, 63-a
Moral possibility, 288-89, 298
Morey-Motley letter forgery, 173-f
Moving pictures, 99-d, 274
Museums, 116
Myth, classical, 261–63; defined, 98-e, 263-c; explanation of: euhemeristic, 262-a; historical, 262-c; philological, 146-a, 261–62; symbolical, 262-a; Graeco-Roman, 261–63; Greek, 146-a; hero, 98-d, f; local, 327-b; as narrative history, 14; nature, 98-e; origin of, 262-a, c; religious, 146-a, 262, 262-a, c; as sources, 98-e, f, 176-c. See also Legend, Saga, Tradition, Transmission

Names, of oral-tradition origin, 256. See also Place-names
Napoleon, and European history, 57-b, 345-f, 363; legend of, 261-b, e; new data on, 442
Narrative history, in annals, 14; in chronicles, 14; function of, 13, 192-a; in genealogies, 14; in Herodotus, 54-a; in lists of official persons, 14; organizations of, 192-a, 338; types of, 95, 95-a, g
"Narrative recital," 54-a
National Archives (U. S.), 114
National Museum (Naples), 116
Nationalism, and Kulturgeschichte, 57-b
Nationality factor, in witness, 278-a
"Natural history," 2
Natural resources, as cause, 354, 354-d
Nature myths, see Myth
Near East, archaeological research in, 85
Negative argument, 149. See also Argument from silence
Ne quid nimis, 335-b

Nero legend, 261-a, b
Neutrality, 46-a. See also Objectivity
New France, 354-d, 366-b
"New history," attitude of, 15-a. See also Criticism, Method, Modern history
New Style calendar, 80-b
New Testament, doubtful passages in, 209; and internal criticism, 172; manuscript transmission of, 162-d; textual restoration of, 209. See also Bible, Gospels, Scriptures
Newberry Library, 112, 405-c
Newspapers, as aid in dating, 252-d; American Civil War, 252-d; in American historiography, 337-b; censorship of, 252-d; credibility of, 252, 252-a, e; critical use of, 252, 252-e, 303; liability of error in, 252-a; as narrative sources, 95
Niebelungenlied, 261-b, 258
Norse tradition accuracy of, 259-e, 286-b; concurrence in, 304; in Icelandic saga, 259-e, 263-e; of Vinland, 259-e, 304, 465. See also Saga
North American explorations field, 313-d
Note-taking, bibliographical, 105-a, 108-c; blank book, 102–3; on cards, 102–4; chronological, 107; for comments, 105-a, 108-d; for extracts, 105-a, 108-a, b; for factual data, 108-e; per item, 105-c; looseleaf, 102, 104; for references, 108-c; self-indexed, 106; on slips, 102; source entry in, 108-a, b; for summaries, 105-a, 108-a, b; topical, 107
Notitiae, 204
Notre Dame University collection on U. S. Catholic Church history, 112
Novels, as sources, 277-a, 324, 441
Numismatics, 88

Objective history, 11, 46-g
Objectivity, and circumstantial completeness, 46-e; defined, 46, 46-e; ideal of, 46-g, 330; and judgments, 46-d; misconceptions of, 46-a, g; and philosophy of life, 46-b, g; Rankean, 375; and sympathy, 46-c, g; and working hypotheses, 46-b. See also Subjectivity
Occasion, and causality, 358

Occupation factor, in witness, 278-f, 280-a
Octavius (Minucius Felix), erroneous attribution of, 175
Odyssey, 171, 268. See also Homeric poems
Office Records, see Documents, Records
Official papers, see Documents, Records
Old Style calendar, 80-b
Old Testament, confirmed by archaeology, 306-a; manuscript transmission of, 162-d; theory of multiple authorship of, 172; translations of, 214-d. See also Bible, Scriptures
Omissio, in copying, 218
Oral transmission, see Sources; Tradition; Transmission, oral
Orations, 54-b, 176-b, 324. See also Rhetoric
Organization of data, chronological, 338; combined methods in, 342; criteria of, 342; genetic, 338; geographical, 340; topical, 341. See also Presentation
Oriental history, archaeological, 85; epigraphic, 86; unworked, 445
Ornamental transmission, 99-b
Ossian forgery, 173-c
Outline, see Plan

Palaeography, beginnings of, 56-c, d; bibliography on, 84-a; and bibliotics, 84-a; as branch of diplomatic, 81, 124, 168-a; defined, 84; and papyrology, 84-b; purpose of, 84
Paleontology, 74
Pantheon, dating of, 180-c
Papal history, Vatican Library resources on, 112
Papebroch-Mabillon controversy, 56-c, d
Paper, as transmission medium, 100-b
Papers, see Documents, Records
Papyrology, 84-b, 220
Papyrus, as transmission medium, 100-b
Parables, 263-b
Parallel texts, 319
Paraphrase, 214-e, 394-b, 430
Parchment, as transmission medium, 100-b
Parnell letter forgery, 173-e

Partisanship, 46-a, c, 308-e. See also Bias, Impartiality, Subjectivity
Passion of St. Alban, ascription of, 167-a
Passion of St. Andrew, ascription of, 167-a
Past, reconstruction of, 412, 421
Patrologia Latina (Migne), 292-b
Pedigree, science of, 89
Perception, see Sense-perception
Periodization, in American history, 26–27; as convention, 23, 26-a, b, 463; in English history, 26-b; in French history, 26–27; reasons for, 25–26
Personal equation, in testimony, 279–81, 326–27. See also Authorship, Witnesses
Personal recollections, see Autobiographies, Memoirs, Witnesses
Perspective, see Judgment, Philosophy of history, Projection, Synthesis
Perversions of history, 437–39
Phantasy, see Imagination
Philology, as critical tool, 57-e; in explaining myths, 146-a, 261–62. See also Linguistics
Philosophical history, 338, 371
Philosophy, qua history, 1, 32; and proof by probabilities, 63-a; in training of historian, 71
Philosophy of history, Augustinian, 379–80; Christian, 351, 374-a, 377–80, 386–90; cyclical, 384, 390-a; defined, 371, 376; dynamics, 390-c; economic, 378; eighteenth-century, 374; as "framework of reference," 374-b; materialistic, 378; naturalistic, 366-b; need of, 373–74; Pauline, 379; present-day, 373–74; providential, 381–83, 386–87; nationalistic, 364, 371–75, 390; socialistic, 374-b; sociological, 374-a; teleological, 378–79; theistic, 361, 364, 371–72, 374-a; theological, 371, 379, 389; transcendency of, 371–72; transitions in, 374-a; Voltairean concept of, 374
Photographic transmission, 57-j, 99-d, e
Photostat, 99-d
Physical backgrounds, see Environment
Physical possibility, 288–89
Pictorial sources, 99, 99-a, d, 274

Picturesqueness, 423–24
Piéces authentiques, 91-c
Piéces justicatives, 391
Pipe rolls, and compiled sources, 277-c
Place, see Geography, Localization
Place-names, 258, 302-a, b, 307
Placidus, St., apocryphal biography of, 167-a
Plagiarism, 50, 394–95
Plan, 343, 431-a. See also Method
Plays, citation from, 400-b; source values of, 277-a, 324. See also Shakespeare, plays of
Poetry, citation of, 400-b; as source, 324. See also Homeric poems, Saga
Political backgrounds, see Environment
Political history, 29, 337-c, 454
Political science, 70
Pompeii, 116, 154
Popes, dating of reigns of, 80-c
Popular history, 337-a, 416, 419
Porta Nigra of Treves, dating of, 180-d
Positivist history, 30, 375
Possibility, moral, 288–89, 298; physical, 288–89
Pottery, as cultural evidence, 306-b
Pragmatic Sanction of Bourges, 146-c, 153, 155
Prediction, 41-e, 132-b
Prefaces, 431-b
Pre-history, dating in, 80. See also Remains
Prejudice, see Bias, Partisanship
Pre-literate period, dating in, 80
Prepossessions, see Bias, Partisanship
Presentation, concreteness in, 422–23; dullness in, 414–15; literary, 413–14; plan in, 343; quotation in, 430; reconstruction of past in, 411–12; requirements of, 410; rhetoric in, 417–19, 425–26; scholarly, 414; subordination of detail in, 429; synthesis in, 427–28; types of, 416; vivid, 421–26. See also References, Style
Press reports, as evidence, 303. See also Newspapers
Prevarication, see Lies
Printing, as transmission medium, 100-b
Pro Marcello (Cicero), 176-b
Probability, antecedent, 155; in archae-

ological remains, 302-a, b; "beyond reasonable doubt," 68; circumstantial, 300; *in* conjectural detail, 148-a, b; *in* contradictory sources, 308-a, h; cumulative, 301; defined, 289-c; extrinsic, 289-c; historical vs. mathematical, 64; intrinsic, 289-c, d

Problems, defined, 463; examples of, 464–69 (*see also* Authenticity, Hypothesis, Interpretation); vs. periods, 463; as thesis subjects, 463

Proceedings and Debates of the British Parliaments Respecting North America, 225

Procedure, see Method, Technique

Pro Coelio (Cicero), 219

Professional courtesy, 405-b

Progress, defined, 28; postulate of, 28-b; vs. retrogression, 28-c

Projection, personal, 365–66. See also Reconstruction of past

Prolegomena (Wolf), 57-e

Propaganda, defined, 253; *in* literature, 324; source value of, 253, 282-g; variant connotations of, 253

Protestant Revolt, causality in, 345-c; criticism, 56-a; diary account of, 247; and perversion of history, 437–40; as terminating medieval era, 26-a

Provenance, see Authenticity, Authorship, Manuscripts

Proverbs, 98-a

Providence, see First Cause, Providential view

Providential view, bibliography of, 390; exemplified, 388; formulation of: by Boethius, 386; by Bossuet, 381–82; by St. Augustine, 378–80; by St. Thomas, 386; moderate application of, 382; and natural causes, 351; *and* problem of evil, 383; rationalist rejection of, 386, 389; subjectivity of, 382; validity of, 387. See also Philosophy of history

Pseudo authorships, 176-b

Psychological backgrounds, 326–27

Psychological interpretation, see Interpretation, psychological

Psychology, as auxiliary science, 124; *and* concurrent evidence, 304; group, 7-b, 70

Ptolemaic theory, 142–43

Public documents, see Documents, Records

Public opinion, and testimony, 278-e

Public Record Office (London), *archives of*, 114, 441

Public records, see Records, official

Publication, copyright practice in, 394-d; footnote problem in, 395-c, 397–98; urgency of, 51-c; value of, 57-i

Pyramids, 306-b

Pythagoras legend, 261-a

Quatuor tempora, 76

Questionnaire, use of, 110

Quivira problem, 468

Quotation, and copyright law, 394-d; of corrupt or lost source, 214-c; direct, 394-a, d, 430; *and* "fair use," 394-d; indirect, 394-c, d, 430; *and* necessary reference, 394; quotation marks in, 394-a, b

Race, as cause, 352, 374-a; as factor in witness, 278-a; in Hegelian theories, 385

Ramayana, 268

Rankean formula, 3-a, 46, 46-e, 55-a, 374

Rationalistic history, 364, 371–75, 390

Reasoning, 125. See also logic

Recension, *and* author's sources, 214-a; *and* commentaries, 214-g; defined, 212-e; *and* excerpts, 214-b; *and* glosses, 214-f; *and* paraphrases, 214-e; *and* printed editions, 213-e, 216-a; *and* quotations, 214-c; *and* relation of manuscripts, 215–16; *and* scholia, 214-g; *and* text tradition: direct, 213-a, d; indirect, 213–14; *and* translations, 214-d

"Recent" history, see Contemporary history

Reconstruction, American, 26-b, 146-d, 345-e, 456, 462; Reconstruction of past, 412, 421

Records, American trading company, early, 96-d; church: American colonial, 96-c; Anglican, 96-c; Catholic, 96-a, b; Oriental, 96-c; Protestant, 96-c; diplomatic, 337-b; episcopal, 96-b; govern-

Index of Matter 477

ment, 96-a, 277-c; guild, 96-d; medieval university, 96-d; mission-aid society, 96-b; monastic, 96-b; official, 91-d, 96, 96-a, d; papal, 96-b; parish, 96-b; private organization, 96-d, 277-c; types of, 90. See also Archives, Documents

Records of the Federal Convention, 225

References, in Bede, 404; bibliographical, 404–7; in Griffet, 404; inaccuracy in, 53-a; limitations of footnotes for, 395-b; necessity of, 391; for quotations, 394. See also Bibliography Footnotes

Réflexions surles règles et sur l'usage de la critique (Honoré de Sainte-Marie), 56-e

Regnal years, dating by, 80, 80-c

Reign terror, 329-c

Reinterpretation, in American history, 453–56, 462; and changing viewpoints, 454–56; in English history, 458–59; in French-American history, 461; in Graeco-Roman history, 453; in Hispanic-American history, 455, 460; instances of, 457–62; in medieval history, 457; of traditional material, 452–53. See also Problems, Research

Relativity in history, 3–4, 67-b, 454

Relics, 90, 93-b, 116. See also Remains

Religion, as cause, 357-b; as interpretative factor, 329-a, 372. See also Philosophy of history

Religious background, in historian, 326–27

Religious history, 337-c, 432. See also Christian history, Christianity

Remains, Assyrian, 306-b; Babylonian, 306-b; classified, 93-b; confirmed by formal testimony, 306-b; confirming formal testimony, 302, 302-a, b, 306-a; corroborating tradition, 258; as cultural evidence, 306-b; dating of, 176-a, 182-c; Egyptian, 306-b; factual interpretation of, 327-b; human, 90, 93-b; as informal sources, 226; in museums, 116; reliability of, 237-b. See also Archaeology

Renaissance history, changing views on, 457; critical spirit in, 56; Italian, 56; as organic cycle, 25-b; Vatican Library resources on, 112

Repetition, in history, 15-b

Reporting, contemporary, 282-d; in Gospels, 282-e. See also Testimony, Witnesses

Republic (Plato), 236-b

Reputation, and reliability, 391

Res gestae Saxonicae (Witiking), 176-c

Research, auxiliary sciences in, 124; availability of material in, 119; background orientation in, 120; bibliographical helps in, 118, 118-a, b, 403; choice of topic in, 117; initial step in, 117; mechanical aids in, 101–24; plan in, 121; recent contributions of, 451; reports on, 447, 449; scale in, 122; source work in, 123–24; unworked fields of, 443–50. See also Problems, Reinterpretation

Research and Reports, Manual on (Amos Tuck School), 111

Restoration of sources, 147-b, 203–5, 217

Revelation, 91, 379

Revision of history, see Reinterpretation, Research

Rewriting of history, 436–39, 441–51. See also Reinterpretation, Research

Rhetoric, 54, 417–19, 425–26. See also Literacy history, Presentation, Style

Rhythm in classical prose, 220

Richard the Lion-Hearted, legend of, 261-e

Rise of the Dutch Republic (Motley), 46-e

Rivière des Pères, origin of name of, 307

Robert Southwell (Janelle), 240-d

Robespierre problem, 467

Römische Geschichte, (Niebuhr), 57-f

Rolls Series, 57-i, 238

Roman Congregations, records of, 96-b

Roman Empire, and development of Christianity, 388; fall of: causality in, 345-c, 380; theories on, 55-b, 146-b, 362-a, 364; rise of, 349

Roman history, annal sources for, 95-d; and archaeology, 85; climatic factor in, 354-c; epigraphic, 86; geographical factor in, 354-a; legend sources of, 176-c, 264, 268, 272; literary quality

in, 414; political institutions in, 3-b; reinterpretation of, 453. See also Historians, Historiography
Romantic movement, 57-c, 359
Rosetta Stone, 95, 254
Rudes, 76
Rumor, 98-a, 176-c, 255, 265–66
Russian history, of Gregorian calendar in, 80-b; soil wealth as factor in, 354-d
Russian Revolution, 128

Sacramentum, in early usage, 76
Safety valve doctrine, 146-d
Saga, confirmed by remains, 306-a; counterfeit, 161, 161-b, d; and criticism, 176-c; cultural evidence in, 237-b; defined, 263-e; East Indian, 98-d; etiological, 98-d, 161-d; Icelandic, 259-e, 263-e (see also Norse tradition); literary version of, 259-e; as narrative history, 14; oral transmission of, 98, 98-d, 259-e; Scandinavian, 263-e (see also Norse tradition); as source, 98, 98-c, d, f; wandering, 98-d, 161-b, d. See also Legend, Myth, Tradition, Transmission
St. Denys, Abbey of, 56-c
St. Francis of Assisi (Jorgensen), 240-d
St. Germain-des-Prés, 56-d
St. Maur, Congregation of, 56-c, d
St. Philip Neri (Ponelli-Bordet), 240-d
Saints, See Hagiography, Legends of Saints
Saints' days, in dating, 80-d
Savonarola problem, 464
Sayings, 161-d, 261-a
Scandinavian saga, see Saga
Scholia, 214-g
Science, and authority, 61; defined, 40-b; of documents, see Diplomatic; of handwriting, see Bibliotics; in historical method, 39–43, 70 (see also Criticism, Method); social vs. exact, 39–40 (see also Social science)
Sciences, auxiliary to history, 70–89
Scientific history, Bollandist contribution to, 56-b, e; and cult of document, 57-h; earliest, 54-a, b; and indication of references, 391–92; and literary quality, 413–15; modern, 414, 438; Niebuhr influence in, 57-f; Ranke influence in, 57-h; selection of data in, 337-a; theory in, 141. See also Criticism, Method
Scientific method, see Criticism, Method
Script, evolution of, 84; of medieval documents, 165-d. See also Documents, Handwriting, Manuscripts
Scriptures, commentaries on, 214-g; and holographic survival, 211; mistranslations in, 323. See also Bible, Gospels, New Testament, Old Testament
Seals, as authentication, 212-a; Carolingian, 176-e; science of, 82; as signatures, 82; as sources: figured, 99-a; written, 100 a
Selection of data, and artistic demands, 335-b; and availability, 337-b; and mass compilations, 335-b; and personal outlook, 337-a; preferential, 337-c; principles of, 337, 337-a, d; by purpose, 337-a; by reader type, 337-d; and space limitation, 335-a; and synthesis, 334
Seminar, 37, 57-h
Seminaries, ecclesiastical, 37
Sense-perception, 229-a, b, d, 232. See also Witnesses
Septuagint, attribution of, 176-c
Sequence vs. causality, 347–48
Series episcoporum (Gams), 89
Sermons, as popular sources, 277-b
Seville archives (Spain), 441
Sex factor in witness, 278-c
Shakespeare, biography of, 148-b; document finds on, 442; editions of, 222; and forgeries, 173-c; holography of, 211, 213-e, 442; plays of: authorship problem in, 155, 188, 192-a; citation of, 400-b; dating of, 182, 182-b; interpretation of, 327–29; printed transmission of, 213-e; as source, 94-a, 277-a
Shanameh, 268
Short History of the English People (Green), 130, 454
Siècle de Louis XIV (Voltaire), 57-b
Sigillography, 82. See also Seals
Signatures, see Formalities, Seals, Sigillography
Silence, see Argument from silence

Index of Matter

Simancas archives (Spain), 441
Sine ira et studio, 46-c
Singularity, in material of history, 40-b
"Six ages" of St. Augustine, 26-a
Skepticism, 66–69
Social backgrounds, see Environment
Social history, 29, 330-b, 337-c, 454
"Social memory," 15-b
Social science, as category of related sciences, 40-a; historical method in, 38; qua history, 7-b, 30, 374-a, 355
Socialism, 374-b
Sociological history, see Social history
Sociology, see Social history, Social science
Socrates legend, 261-a, b
Soil wealth, *as* cause, 354, 377; as condition, 359
Solon legend, 261-a
Source books, bibliography of, 409; *in* English, 409-a; *in* foreign languages, 409-b
Sources (analysis)
 additions to, 160-a, b, 193-c, 196-c; agreement of, 192–93, 305; and analytical principles, 191, 191-a, d; comparison of, 192-b; contradictory, 308–11; copies of, 212-b, d; corroboration of, 288–89; derived: criteria in, 193-a, g; and principle of common origin, 191, 191-d; tests of relation in, 195–202; doubtful, 159; form variations in, 192-b; genuineness of, 157, 159, 159-a, b, 162-c, d; and glosses, 160-c; and heuristic, 54-b, 90-a, 156; identical, 193-a, integrity of: criteria of, 212-a, e; and critical process, 156–57, 207–25, 312; defined, 211; lost, 203; meaning of analysis of, 156-d, 190; origin of, 91, 91-a, d, 191–202; original vs. derived, 91-c, 194–202; related, 192–93; spurious, 159–61, 167, 167-a, b (*see also* Forgeries); typical problems in, 206; untruthful, 227-a, 236, 236-a, d. See *also* Authenticity, Authorship, Credibility, Criticism, Dating, Testimony, Witnesses
Sources (classification)
 apocryphal, 159, 167-a; classified: by aim, 93–94; by content, 92; by origin, 91, 91-a, d; contemporary, 91-a, 94, 94-a, 100-b, 276; diplomatic, 337-b; divine, 91, 379; domestic, 91-b; economic, 92; foreign, 91-b; formal, 90, 93, 93-a, 100-b; formal-informal, 93-b; human, 91, 93-b; immediate, 91-c; informal, 90, 93, 93-b, 100-b; informative, 93, 275–77, 324; mediate, 91-c; narrative, see Narrative history; official, 91-d, 96-d; political, 92; primary, 91-c, 100-b, 123, 192-c, 412; private, 91-d, 96-d; propaganda, 253, 282-g, 324; quasi-contemporary, 91-a; religious, 92, 277-b; remote, 91-a, 100-b; secondary, 91-c, 100-b, 123, 123-a; social, 92. See *also* Archives, Documents, Records
Sources (treatment)
 editing of, 217–20, 222–25, 408; emendation of, 218–20; publication of, 57-i; restoration of, 147-b, 203–5, 217; unworked, 441–51; use of: direct, 90-a; and imagination, 412; indirect, 336; requisites in, 124. See *also* Appendix, Citation, Interpretation, Localization, Method, Organization of data, Selection of data, Synthesis
Sources (types)
 defined in general, 90, 90-a; figured, 99, 99-a, d, 274; oral, 97–98 (*see also* Legend, Myth, Saga, Tradition, Transmission, oral); pictorial, 99, 99-a, d; translated, see Translations; written, 100, 100-a, b. See *also* Annals, Autobiographies, Biography, Chronicles, Diaries, Hagiography, Inscriptions, Letters, Memoirs, Newspapers, Novels, Plays, Travel books
Spanish history, see Hispanic-American history
Spanish language, 76
Speculum, 118-a
Speeches, 54-b, 176-b, 324. See *also* Rhetoric
Sphragistics, 82. See *also* Seals
Squire Papers, 173-c
Staaten geschichte, 6
Stabat Mater, authorship of, 187
Standards, moral, 367–69
State papers, see Documents, Records
Statism, 29, 385

Statistics, and certainty, 140-d; defined, 139; economics, 139; English, 139; Government, 139; method of differentials in, 140-b; Roman, 139; use of, 140-a; validity of, 140-c
Statute of Appeals (Henry VIII), 437–38
Stoics, lies, 236-b
Story, defined, 263-b
Sufficient reason, principle of, 301–2, 304
Style, as aid in localization, 185-c; in American presentation, 420; as authorship test, 165, 165-c, 168-b, 193-b, 196-e; in choice of variant readings, 218; manuals of, 401-2; as means of dating, 181-b; minimum requirements of, 416; necessity of, 401; and popular success, 419; typographical, 401–2; uses of, 401; vivid, 421–22, 426–27. See also Presentation
Stylometry, 165-c
Subjectivity, 11, 46-e, 330-a, 382. See also Authorship, Interpretation, Objectivity
Suggestion, and error, 234-c; mass, 235
Sumerian civilization, 182-c
Summa Theologica (St. Thomas), 400-b
Suppressio veri est assertio falsi, 44-a
Suppression of data, 44-a, b
Surroundings, see Environment
Survivals, 93-b. See also Remains
Sympathy, in historian, 46-c
Synoptic Problem, 190-b
Synthesis, and causal problems, 345-a, f; defined, 333; exemplified, 345-a; external, 333-43; individual capacity for, 428; initial plan in, 343; internal, 344–90; by motives, 344-b; organization of data in: chronological, 338; by combined methods, 342; geographical, 340; topical, 341; of perceptions, 232; and presentation, 427; relational categories in, 344–45; as requisite to generalization, 427; and selection, 334–37; and self-projection into past, 365–66; and subordination of detail, 429. See also Generalization

Tablets (clay, wax), 100-b
Tale, defined, 176-c, 263-b
Talkie, 99-d
Tamia Palladis (Meres), 182
Teaching-value of history, 10, 15-a, 17
Technical interpretation, 324
Technique, qua history, 1, 19; training in, 36. See also Criticism, Method
Teleological history, 378, 386
Temperament factor in witness, 278-d
Temples, 306-b
Termini in dating, 182, 182-a
Terminology, Technical, 41-b
Testimony, conflicting, 288-a, 308–11; concurrent: certainty vs. probability in, 299; circumstantial, 300–1; minor divergences in, 305-d; in remains, 302-a, b; criteria: of knowledge in, 280-a, c; of veracity in, 282–84; defined, 58; dependability of, 69; direct, 279–84; fact of, 60; formal: concurrence in, 303–5; confirmed by remains, 306-a; confirming remains, 306-b; error in, 227-a; independent, 303–4; indirect, 285–86; oral, 300-a; partisan, 282-g; at personal risk, 282-e. See also Evidence, Witness
Tests, lingual, 165-b, c; palaeographical, 168-a; in related sources, 192–202; stylistic, 181-b. See also Authenticity, Criticism, Integrity
Texan Revolution, 462
Textbooks, 337-a, d, 416
Texts citation of, 400-a, b; cuneiform, 306-b; editing of, 210, 210-a, d, 213-a, d, 216-e, 222–25; emendation of, 217–20; parallel, comparison of, 319; source-book collections of, 409; transcription of, 221; transmission of, see Recension; variant readings in, 218. See also Documents, Manuscripts, Sources
Textual criticism, see Criticism
Textual interpretation, see Interpretation, verbal
Theism, see Philosophy of history
Theodicy, 71
Theodoric legend, 261-b, 269
Theodosius legend, 269
Theology, 91, 124. See also Philosophy of history, Religious history
Theory, see Hypothesis

Thermodynamics, 146-a
Theses, see Dissertations
Thomas More (Chambers), 240-d
Thomas of Canterbury, St., legend of, 260
Thoroughness, 52, 52-a
Thundering legion, 303-a
Time-divisions, see Chronology, Periodization
Tombs, 306-b
Topical history, 338, 341
Topography, 354. See also Geography
Totalitarianism, see Hegelianism
Tractatus mysteriorum (St. Hilary), 204, 216-b
Tradition, anti-catholic, 259-e; content of, 257–258; corroborative value of, 259-a; counterfeit, 161-a, d, 259-d; credibility of, 255–60, 264, 286-b; criticism of, 176-c, 259-a, e; defined, 256; Icelandic, 259-e; illiterate, 259-e; "in possession," 258; late-appearing, 260; legal, 306-a; local, 161-a, d, 259-e; Norse, 259-e, 286-b; oral: concurrence in, 305-a; confirmed by remains, 267, 306-a; and rumor, 265–66; as source category, 90; stages of, 256; as "peoples memory," 259-e; pictured, 256; popular, 98-b, 255–60, 263-d; recurrent, 259-c; source value of: direct, 267; formal, 259-a; indirect, 268–73; informal, 259-a; textual, see manuscripts, recension; witnesses in, 257–58; written, 256, 259-b, e. See also Legend, Myth, Saga, Transmission
Training, see Method, technique
Traité des différentes sortes de preuves. (Griffet), 56-e
Transcription, textual, 221
Translations, ancient, 214-d; from German, 323; from Greek, 323; limitations of, 214-d, 322; of Scriptures, 323; and text integrity, 212-c; as verbal interpretation, 322–23
Transmission, direct, 213-a, d; figured, 274; graphic, 99-c; indirect, 213–14; monumental, 99-a; oral, 97–98, 255–56; ornamental, 99-b; phonographic, 99-e; photographic, 99-d; physical media of, 100-g; pictorial, 99, 99-a, d, 274; printed, 213-e; 216-a; by sound recording, 99-d, e; types of, 274; 97–98, written, 100-a, b, 274. See also Communication, Recension, Sources, Tradition
Travel books. Source value of, 91-b, 276, 280-b
Travels in America (Ashe), 189
Treaties, 324
Tree-rings, as means of dating, 182-c
Troy, historicity of, 85
Truth, human capacity for, 66; and methodology, 237, 237-a; zeal for, 44. See also Accuracy, Veracity
Two Cities (Otto of Freising), 55-a
Typescript, 396–98
Typography, 185-b

Ubication, 79
Ulster County (N. Y.) *Gazette*, 216-a
Uniformities, in historical events, 15-c, 134, 137–38, 144, (see also generalization; Laws); statistical, 140-c, d
Uniqueness of historical events, 15-c
Unitary hypothesis, 145-d
United States, see American history
Unity of history, 23–24. See also Synthesis
Universal history, see Philosophy of history
Up-to-dateness, and linguistics, 78
Urban II, reconstruction of lost sermon of, 205
Usage, see Customs, Language
Utensils as cultural evidence, 306-b

Vanity Fair (Thackeray), 94-a
Variants, Textual, 218. See also Manuscripts, Sources
Vatican Archives, 96-b, 114, 441
Vatican Library, 112, 114
Venice archives, 441
Veracity, in contemporary reporting, 282-d, e; criteria of, 282–83; and detail particularity, 284, 284-a, c; in impersonal matters, 282-g; and moral character, 281-a; negative proofs of, 281–82; in public testimony, 282-d; in propaganda, 282-g; revision for, 456;

vs. self-interest, 279-b, 282-f. See also Accuracy, Truth, Witnesses
Verbal interpretation, 261-e, 315–23
Vergil, biographical sources on, 240-d; birthplace problem in 210-d; text transmission of, 162-d, 216-e
Verifiability, 53
Versification, as internal test, 165
Victoria-Albert Museum, 116
Viewpoints, revision of, see Reinterpretation, Research
Vinland saga, 259-e, 304, 465. See also Norse tradition, Saga
Vita Caroli (Einhard), 192-a
Vita S. Pauli (St. Jerome), 176-c
Vita Virgilii (Probus), 210-d
Vitae Vergilianae, 240-d
Vividness, see Presentation, Style
Vocabulary, and interpretation, 318. See also Latin, Linguistics
Volition, see Free will
Vulgate, textual restoration of, 209

Wandering Jew, legend of, 98-f
Wars, see Military history, World War
Washington, diaries of, 245, 248; forged letters of, 155, 173-f; legend of, 98-f; and Sparks corrections, 222
Watermarks, as internal test, 165-d
West, American, and settlement technique, 360. See also Frontier hypothesis
Whitman legend, 153, 260
Wie es eigentlich gewisen ist, see Rankean formula
Will, see Free will
William L. Clements Library, 112, 441
Witnesses, abnormality in, 227-c; accuracy of, 59, 59-c, 279-a; authority of, 62, 279-a; contemporary, 162-e; contradictory, 289-b, 308-a, c; credibility of, 59, 59-a, c, 62, 227–35, 278, 278-a, f, 286-a, b; and date factors, 178; direct, 255, 279–84; evaluation of, 62; function of, 58, 280-a, c; in Gospel transmission, 162-e; independent, 303–5; knowledge of, 59, 59-a, 62, 279–80; lying, 281–82; of miraculous occurrences, 288-b, 294; objectivity in, 280-b; and religious motivation, 282-c; self-contradictory, 308-f; self-incriminating, 282-f; single, 286–87, 289-d, 303-a, 305–6; in tradition, 257–58; types of, 278, 278-a, f; veracity of, 59-b, 62, 278–82; virtual, 93-b. See also Evidence, Testimony
Women, as witnesses, 278-c
"Wonders," see Mira
Word-of-mouth transmission. See Sources oral; Tradition, oral; Transmission, oral
World-history, see Philosophy of history
World-kingdoms, ancient, 26-a
World-view, see Philosophy of history
World war, noncombatant participation in, 3-c; first, 345-c, f, 454; and progress, 28-d
Written Sources, see Documents, Manuscripts, Records, Sources, Tradition, Transmission
Writer, see Authorship, Historian
Writing, ancient, 84, 84-a, b; of history, see Historian; Historiography
Writing material, as internal test, 165-d, 212

X. Y. Z. letters, 251-a

Year, beginning of, 80-a
Ymago Mundi (D'Ailly), 223-a, 225, 465

Zeitgeist, 358-a

Bibliographical Citation in the Social Sciences

A HANDBOOK OF STYLE

by
LIVIA APPEL
Managing Editor
University of Wisconsin Press

MADISON
THE UNIVERSITY OF WISCONSIN PRESS

Copyright 1940 by the UNIVERSITY OF WISCONSIN

Fourth printing, 1957

Printed in the United States of America

CONTENTS

THE FOOTNOTES

- I. GENERAL PRINCIPLES 7
  - THE FUNCTION OF FOOTNOTES 7
  - ARRANGEMENT 7
  - THE NUMBERING OF THE NOTES 8
  - THE PLACING OF INDEXES IN THE TEXT 8
  - THE COMBINATION OF CITATIONS 9
  - COMPLETE BIBLIOGRAPHICAL INFORMATION 10
- II. THE CITATION OF BOOKS AND PAMPHLETS. 11
  - THE COMPLETE CITATION 11
    - THE AUTHOR'S NAME 11
    - THE FULL TITLE 12
    - CAPITALIZATION 14
    - THE FACTS OF PUBLICATION 15
    - VOLUME AND PAGE CITATIONS 17
  - THE SHORTENED CITATION 17
- III. REPORTS, PROCEEDINGS, AND YEARBOOKS. 19
  - THE COMPLETE CITATION 19
  - THE SHORTENED CITATION 20
- IV. GOVERNMENT DOCUMENTS 20
- V. NEWSPAPERS 21
- VI. PARTS OF PUBLICATIONS 21
- VII. MANUSCRIPT MATERIALS 22
  - DIARIES, JOURNALS, AND LETTER BOOKS 22
  - COLLECTIONS OF MANUSCRIPTS 23
  - INDIVIDUAL MANUSCRIPTS 23
  - UNPUBLISHED DISSERTATIONS 24

THE BIBLIOGRAPHY

- I. TYPES OF BIBLIOGRAPHY 25
- II. ORGANIZATION 25
- III. ANNOTATIONS 25
- IV. ALPHABETIZATION 26
  - INDEX 29

PREFACE

AT NO POINT, a recent survey reveals, are publishers of scholarly works agreed upon a uniform style of bibliographical citation. Indeed it is doubtful whether a body of rules could be formulated that would be equally acceptable to all scholars in the social sciences, or even unfailingly applicable to all the materials of research. This is not to say, however, that there is no basic doctrine, or that traditional practices can be discarded at will. For the chief desideratum of any system of citation is that the essential data be given in a form which allows of no misinterpretation and which helps one to locate the materials cited. It is in response to requests for a brief guide to some such system, and in the hope that it will prove helpful to the uninitiated, that this little manual has been compiled for publication. The rules it embodies are those governing bibliographical style in publications of the University of Wisconsin Press.

I am indebted to several members of this faculty for their interest and many helpful suggestions, especially to Dean George C. Sellery, Professor William B. Hesseltine, and Professor Frederic A. Ogg; to Miss Alice E. Smith, curator of manuscripts in the State Historical Society of Wisconsin, whose counsel I have sought on the problem of manuscript citations; and to Mr. Louis Kaplan, assistant librarian in the University, who has enlightened me on various library practices.

L. A.

The University of Wisconsin
  February, 1940

THE FOOTNOTES

I. GENERAL PRINCIPLES

THE FUNCTION OF FOOTNOTES

Footnotes are used to cite the sources upon which the text is based, to call to the reader's attention still other materials on a given topic, to amplify statements made in the text, and to give cross references. They protect the writer against the charge of plagiarism or improper use of his sources, and help other students to continue the investigation. In works based on original research, references to source should be given for all important statements of fact requiring substantiation and for all inferences and conclusions borrowed from other writers.

ARRANGEMENT

In works addressed to scholars, annotations are usually printed at the foot of the text pages. In books written primarily for the layman, who may not be interested in following the sources, formal citations are sometimes placed at the end of the volume, and only those annotations which elaborate upon the text itself are treated as footnotes. This plan obviously calls for two sets of index symbols.

When the manuscript is typed, care should be taken to avoid crowding the notes. In preparing a work for publication the notes as well as the text should be double-spaced to allow for editorial revision and typographical instructions. Some publishers prefer that the notes be grouped either at the end of each chapter or at the end of the entire manuscript, regardless of what the ultimate arrangement is to be. This facilitates the printer's task, inasmuch as the setting of each size of type is in any case a separate operation.

The first line of each note should be indented to align with paragraph indentions in the text. Long discursive footnotes, which should be included only with good reason, should be further paragraphed. The note number should be typed as a superscript (that is, slightly elevated) without period or parentheses. A series of formal citations should be separated by semicolons (see note 1 below and others throughout).

[1] Gustavus Ohlinger, *Their True Faith and Allegiance* (New York, 1916), 42; Johann H. von Bernstorff, *My Three Years in America* (London, 1920), 19; James C. Child, *The German-Americans in Politics, 1914–1917* (Madison, Wisconsin, 1939), 8.

[A manuscript edited for publication should include instructions to the printer to use an en dash, not a hyphen, wherever a dash is used in lieu of the word "to," as in: 1914–1917; pp. 10–20; vols. 3–6; etc.]

THE NUMBERING OF THE NOTES

In Short Publications.—In articles and short monographs not divided into chapters, notes are ordinarily numbered consecutively throughout. If, however, the notes are few and so widely scattered as to make a single numerical sequence undesirable, the notes on each page may be treated as a separate series, either numbers or symbols (*, †) being used as indexes. This practice, however, should be adopted only for sparsely annotated studies. While it has the advantage of permitting the insertion of new notes with a minimum of change in numbers or symbols, it increases the cost of typesetting, for the reason that most of the notes will need to be indexed anew after type is "made up" into pages. Obviously the printed pages will rarely correspond with those of the manuscript.

In Longer Publications.—Each chapter should begin with footnote 1, and unless the manuscript is only sparsely annotated the numbering should continue consecutively throughout the chapter rather than page by page, for the reason given above. If a chapter contains many more than one hundred notes, it is a good plan to begin numbering anew after note 99 to prevent the rather unsightly gap that occurs between words in the text when the three-digit figures are used as indexes. As in shorter publications, other symbols may be used if annotations are sparse.

Notes to a table should be placed directly below it and should be indexed with a separate series of symbols to prevent confusion with the series annotating the text.

THE PLACING OF INDEXES IN THE TEXT

The index referring to the footnote is, like the note number itself, a superior figure. It should be placed, preferably, at the end of a sentence rather than within it unless it is essential to annotate specific phrases, and should come after the punctuation mark closing the sentence. It should follow, not precede, a quoted passage. Before a manuscript is put into final form, a check should be made to insure the agreement of each note with the text index referring to it.

[Though in general practice the note number in the footnote itself is also a superior figure, there is a growing tendency to print the note number as a regular figure, aligning with the text. In this style the note number is easier to read, and cost of typesetting is reduced.]

THE COMBINATION OF CITATIONS

Other things being equal, a single note combining a group of references is often preferable to a number of shorter annotations, for numerous indexes in the text tend to distract the reader, to cause unnecessary duplication of references, to mar the appearance of the printed page, and to complicate the problem of page "make-up."

In grouping citations it is desirable to combine those that relate to a paragraph or group of paragraphs on the same general topic, the index being placed at the close of the last paragraph. This plan is especially feasible when the discussion is based on comparatively few sources and wherever the relation of text to sources is obvious. In the following excerpt, for example, from William W. Folwell's *History of Minnesota*, 4:353 (St. Paul, 1930), the relation of each footnote citation to the author's statements in the text is so clear as to make more specific annotation unnecessary:

> In 1857 the legislative body of South Australia, at the instance of Francis S. Dutton, passed a bill to insure the secrecy of the ballot. Similar laws were soon passed in other Australian provinces. The English Parliament, after long debates and bitter opposition, embodied the principle in its Ballot Act of 1872. American states also took time to consider the plan. Henry George, the author of *Progress and Poverty*, in an article in the *North American Review* in 1883, described in graphic paragraphs the iniquities of political machines and recommended the adoption of the Australian system. But there was no haste. The state of Kentucky was the first to adopt it, but not until February 24, 1888. Massachusetts was a close second on May 30 of the same year. The next year many legislatures had it under consideration. Minnesota was one of the few that then, in 1889, adopted it, but only for cities of ten thousand or more; two years later, however, the system was extended to all election districts of the state.[2]
>
> [2] John H. Wigmore, *The Australian Ballot System as Embodied in the Legislation of Various Countries* (Boston, 1889), 3–8, 15, 22–28, 37–151; Henry George, "Money in Elections," in the *North American Review*, 136:201–211 (March, 1883); Andrew C. McLaughlin and Albert B. Hart, eds., *Cyclopedia of American Government* (New York and London, 1914), 1:101; *General Laws of Minnesota*, 1889, pp. 12–40; 1891, pp. 37–45.

So far as practicable, the order of citations in the note should conform to that of the text which it documents, except that similar materials—newspapers, manuscripts, etc.—should be grouped. All the page references to a given volume should follow consecutively; such citations as Adams, *Tendency of History*, 113, 56, 24, 156, should be avoided.

If the normal order of page references is likely to cause confusion, it is best to forego grouping them and to document more specifically.

Supplementary information and observations by the author should follow the citations for the text. If the references are the same, they need not be repeated. If they are not the same, the additional references should be given in connection with the statements which they cover, as in the following examples:

> [3] On the trading colony see Wilhelm Roscher and Robert Jannasch, *Kolonien, Kolonialpolitik, und Auswanderung* (3d ed., Leipzig, 1885), 12. [*This citation supports a text statement on the trading colony of the Phoenicians.*] Carthaginian, Greek, and Roman trading posts continued the process, and a continental trade was developed. The routes of this trade have been ascertained. Karl Müllenhoff, *Deutsche Altertumskunde* (2 vols., Berlin, 1890–91), 1:212. [*Supports the two sentences preceding.*]
>
> [4] Indian Office, *Report*, 1901, pt. 1, pp. 68, 247. [*Reference for the text.*] The *Minneapolis Journal* for April 20, 1901, pt. 2, p. 1, contains an elaborate account of the operations of the preceding winter of cutting dead and down timber. Secretary Hitchcock put a stop to it on April 24, 1901. See the *Minneapolis Journal*, April 24, 1901, p. 1. [*Supports the preceding sentence.*] The secretary in his report for the year makes no reference to the transactions. Captain Mercer was relieved of his duties at the close of 1901. Indian Office, *Report*, 1902, pt. 1, p. 221. [*Supports the two sentences preceding.*]

As suggested above, long discursive footnotes should be broken into paragraphs. They should conform to the text in particulars of style, and they should be in equally good literary form. The omission of articles before nouns and similar contractions of phraseology have nothing to recommend them, for the space thus saved is negligible. Write "see the maps on page 6," not "see maps"; consult the index," not "consult index," etc.

COMPLETE BIBLIOGRAPHICAL INFORMATION

Full bibliographical data—that is, the name of the author, the title, and the facts of publication as defined below—should be given at least once for every work cited. If there is a formal bibliography, an abridged citation is sometimes used throughout the notes for all the titles listed therein. If no bibliography is included, the bibliographical data must be given at least upon the first occurrence of the title in the footnotes, and if the work is a long one, heavily annotated, it is advisable to repeat the full citation in connection with the first occurrence of the title in each chapter.

In published works containing many footnotes but no comprehensive bibliography, a short form of each title is sometimes included in the index, in distinctive type, under the name of the author, with references to the pages upon which bibliographical and other information is given. This is a helpful extension of the index that might well be more frequently employed.

MÜLLENHOFF, KARL, *Deutsche Altertumskunde,* 175n
WIGMORE, JOHN H., *Australian Ballot,* 3n, 6n

II. THE CITATION OF BOOKS AND PAMPHLETS

THE COMPLETE CITATION

The bibliographical data on a book or pamphlet include (1) the name of the author, editor, or compiler; (2) the full title italicized; (3) where applicable, the series title, series volume number, and identification of the edition; (4) the publisher or place of publication, or both, and the date of publication; and (5) volume and page references.

THE AUTHOR'S NAME

The author's name is cited in normal, not inverted, order in the footnotes. The full first name, if available, and middle initial should be given (except for writers invariably cited otherwise—as, for example, Edgar Lee Masters, John Middleton Murry, G. Lowes Dickinson). The citation of the first name helps to identify the author and facilitates the location of the work in a library catalog. Honorary and professional titles, such as Colonel, Dr., Professor, Reverend, and the like, as well as academic degrees and affiliations, may usually be omitted.

When the name of an editor or compiler appears on the title page in place of that of author, it should be followed by the abbreviation "ed." or "comp."

[5] Josephine K. Piercy, ed., *Modern Writers at Work* (New York, 1930), 93–110.

When both an editor's or translator's name and that of author appear on the title page, both should be given in the complete citation. The phraseology of the title page and the form to be used in subsequent citations will determine which of the following is the most appropriate form for the first citation:

[6] Gideon D. Scull, ed., *The Voyages of Pierre Esprit Radisson, Being an Account of His Travels and Experiences among the North American Indians from 1652 to 1684* (Publications of the Prince Society, vol. 16, Boston, 1885), 105.

Subsequent citations: Scull, *Voyages of Radisson,* 110.

[7] Louis Hennepin, *A Description of Louisiana,* translated and edited by John G. Shea (New York, 1880), 135.

Subsequent citations: Hennepin, *Louisiana* (Shea ed.), 112.

⁸ *The Story of Bayreuth as Told in the Bayreuth Letters of Richard Wagner*, translated and edited by Caroline V. Kerr (Boston, 1912).

Subsequent citations: Wagner, *Bayreuth Letters*, 160.

When the author, editor, or compiler of an anonymously published work has been identified, his name should be included, but should be enclosed in brackets (not parentheses) to indicate that it is supplied from some source other than the title page:

⁹ [John Mitchell], *The Contest in America between Great Britain and France* (London, 1757), 237.

¹⁰ [John Filson, ed.], *Life and Adventures of Colonel Daniel Boon, the First White Settler of the State of Kentucky* (Brooklyn, 1823).

Subsequent citations: Mitchell, *Contest in America*, 240; Filson, *Daniel Boon*, 19.

When an institution or organization named on the title page is the author, it should be so cited in the usual form:

¹¹ International Labour Office, *The International Labour Organization: The First Decade* (London, 1931), 570.

¹² Auslandstelle des Kriegspresseamts, Germany, *Handbuch der Auslandpresse* (Berlin, 1918), 150.

¹³ Hoover War Library, Stanford University, *Catalog of Paris Peace Conference Delegation Propaganda in the Hoover War Library* (Stanford University, 1926), 13.

¹⁴ Library of Congress, *List of Publications on Publicity for the States* (Select List no. 107, Washington, 1916).

¹⁵ Committee on Uniform Street and Sanitation Records, Chicago, *How to Prepare an Annual Public Works Report* (Chicago, 1933).

If the name of the agency is included in the title, it is unnecessary to cite it also as author:

¹⁶ *Report of the Central Committee for National Patriotic Organizations* (London, 1916), 27.

THE FULL TITLE

In the full citation of a work the title is given, in italics, as it appears on the title page (not the cover). Normally it includes all of the subtitle, separated from the main title by a colon or semicolon if not grammatically dependent on it. Since the subtitle often elucidates a main title that does not fully reveal the subject matter and scope of the work, its inclusion may be helpful to the reader. The subtitle of the work cited below, for instance, may tell the reader exactly what he would like to know about the contents:

¹⁷ Charles M. Gates, ed., *Five Fur Traders of the Northwest, Being the Narrative of Peter Pond and the Diaries of John Macdonell, Archibald N. McLeod, Hugh Faries, and Thomas Connor* (Minneapolis, 1933).

Generally speaking, even very long titles of several lines should be cited in full in the bibliography. If, on the other hand, there is no bibliography and all the bibliographical data must be given in the footnotes, so cumbersome a title as the following may be abridged, even in the first instance:

> 18 *Observations on the North-American Land Company, Lately Instituted in Philadelphia, Containing an Illustration of the Object of the Company's Plan, the Articles of Association, with a Succinct Account of the States Wherein Their Lands Lie; to Which Are Added Remarks on American Lands in General, More Particularly the Pine-Lands of the Southern and Western States, in Two Letters from Robert G. Harper, Esquire, Member of Congress for South Carolina, to a Gentleman in Philadelphia* (London, 1796).

Retaining the salient phrases, we may have some such citation as this:

> 19 *Observations on the North-American Land Company . . . Remarks on American Lands in General . . . in Two Letters from Robert G. Harper, Member of Congress . . .* (London, 1796).
>
> Subsequent citations: Harper, *North-American Land Company*, 29.

Occasionally supplementary information is available from the title page or other source which ought to be cited for the light it throws on the nature of the material. Such information may be added in a sentence of explanation:

> 20 J. Lynn Barnard and Others, *The Teaching of Community Civics* (United States Bureau of Education Bulletin no. 650, Washington, 1915). This is the report of a special committee of the Commission on the Reorganization of Secondary Education, National Education Association.

or, if the title is followed by other references, as a part of the citation itself:

> 21 J. Lynn Barnard and Others, *The Teaching of Community Civics* (United States Bureau of Education Bulletin no. 650, Washington, 1915; a report of a special committee of the Commission on the Reorganization of Secondary Education, National Education Association), 12; John Drinkwater, *Patriotism in Literature* (New York, 1924), 35.
>
> 22 First report, for 1916, of the St. Paul branch of the Fatherless Children of France, an eight-page pamphlet published under the title *The Fatherless Children of France* (St. Paul, 1917); *St. Paul Pioneer Press*, 1914: October 2, p. 3; 7, p. 2; 21, p. 4.
>
> 23 William C. Edgar, *The Millers' Belgian Relief Movement, 1914–15* (Minneapolis, 1915), 64–72, which constitutes the director's final report; *Weekly Northwestern Miller* (Minneapolis), November 11, 1914–January 20, 1915.
>
> 24 *Radio in the Classroom: Experimental Studies in the Production and Classroom Use of Lessons Broadcast by Radio* (Madison, 1942; report of the Wisconsin Research Project in School Broadcasting, conducted 1937–1939), 19; Zaufig, *Folk Songs and Ballads*, 16.

CAPITALIZATION

In all languages capitalize the first word of the title.

In English titles capitalize also all other words except prepositions, conjunctions, and the definite and indefinite articles.

In French titles capitalize the first two words if they consist of article and noun, and the first three words if they consist of article, adjective, and noun in this order; do not capitalize the adjective if it follows the noun. If the title begins with any word other than le, la, les, un, une, or an adjective, the word following is not capitalized. Capitalize all proper nouns but not the adjectives derived from them:

[25] Charles Benoist, Les Lois de la politique française (Paris, 1928), 160.

[26] Georges Lefèbvre, La Grande Peur de 1789 (Paris, 1932).

[27] Pierre le Rohu, "Le Premier Congrès international contre le duel," in the Correspondant, 231:1204–1214 (1908).

[28] Louis Bréhier, L'Art chrétien (Paris, 1918), 26.

[29] Georges Sorel, Réflexions sur la violence (Paris, 1912).

In Italian, Spanish, Swedish, and Norwegian titles capitalize proper nouns but not the adjectives derived therefrom:

[30] Ettore Pais, Storia della Sicilia (Milan, 1894), 168.

[31] Ernesto Vercesi, Il movimento cattolico in Italia, 1870–1922 (Florence, 1923).

[32] Leon Trotsky, La revolución española (Madrid, 1931).

[33] Oscar Montelius, Om lifet i Sverige under hednatiden (Stockholm, 1905).

[34] Johan R. Reiersen, Veiviser for norske emigranter til de forenede nordamerikanske stater og Texas (Christiania, 1844).

In German titles capitalize all nouns and the adjectives derived from personal names, but not the adjectives derived from other proper nouns:

[35] Joseph Lenz, "Grundbegriffe der Marxistisch-Leninistischen Strategie und Taktik," in his Proletarische Politik im Zeitalter des Imperialismus und der sozialistischen Revolution (Berlin, 1931).

In Dutch titles capitalize all nouns and the adjectives derived from proper nouns:

[36] Cornelis Veth, De Humor in de moderne Nederlandsche Literatur (Amsterdam, 1929).

In Latin titles capitalize all proper nouns and the adjectives derived from them:

[37] Philipp Jaffé, Regesta pontificum Romanorum (2 vols., Leipzig, 1885).

THE FACTS OF PUBLICATION

Place and Date of Publication.—The number of volumes comprising the work cited, the place of publication or the publisher, or both, and the date of publication normally follow the title within parentheses:

[38] John B. McMaster, *A History of the People of the United States from the Revolution to the Civil War* (8 vols., New York, 1883-1913), 1:326.

Inclusion of the place of publication has long been conventional practice; but it must be said that the citation of publisher instead of place, or in addition to place, has much to recommend it, especially in the case of works that are presumably still in print.

If only one or two volumes of a many-volume work published over a considerable period have been used in the research, it may be preferable to give specific publication dates for those volumes, particularly if the dates are significant in the light of the conclusions based on the material:

[39] John B. McMaster, *A History of the People of the United States from the Revolution to the Civil War*, 1:326 (New York, 1883).

Note that here the place and date of publication follow rather than precede the volume citation, to make it clear that only this volume, and not the entire work, appeared in 1883.

If the date of publication does not appear on the title page or in a copyright notice but is available from the Library of Congress card or other authentic source, it should be included in the citation, but within brackets:

[40] William E. Griffis, *Sir William Johnson and the Six Nations* (New York [1819]).

If the date is not available, the abbreviation "n. d." (no date) is used; the abbreviation "n. p." (no place) signifies that the place of publication is not known:

[41] John P. Hale, *Daniel Boone: Some Facts and Incidents Not Hitherto Published* (Wheeling, West Virginia, n. d.).

[42] Isaac Adams, *Persia, by a Persian: Personal Experiences, Manners, Customs, Habits, Religious and Social Life in Persia* (n. p., 1900), 302.

[43] C. R. Bardeen, *Public Needs to be Met by the Proposed State of Wisconsin General Hospital* (n. p., n. d.).

In citing foreign cities and towns as places of publication the accepted English form should be used: Brussels, *not* Bruxelles; Florence, *not* Firenze; Cologne, *not* Köln, etc. The number of volumes comprising the work and the number of the edition should also be cited in English.

The Series Title.—If the work cited is one of a series, the series title and the series volume number, if there is one, should precede the place and date of publication within the parentheses. Italicize the name of a series of which the work cited is a component part:

⁴⁴ Albert Koocurek and John H. Wigmore, *Primitive and Ancient Legal Customs* (The Evolution of Law, vol. 2, Boston, 1915), 165.

⁴⁵ Frederick J. Turner, *Rise of the New West, 1819-1829* (The American Nation, a History, edited by Albert B. Hart, vol. 14, New York, 1906), 260.

⁴⁶ Frederic Seebohm, *The Era of the Protestant Revolution* (Epochs of European History, edited by Edward E. Morris, London, 1877), 11.

also the titles of historical society *Collections* and of the serial *Studies, Monographs, Contributions,* etc., published by colleges, universities, and other institutions:

⁴⁷ Gordon C. Davidson, *The North West Company* (University of California Publications in History, vol. 7, Berkeley, 1918), 260.

⁴⁸ Caroline E. MacGill, *History of Transportation in the United States before 1860* (Carnegie Institution Contributions to American Economic History, Washington, 1917), 13.

⁴⁹ Peter Charanis, *Church and State in the Later Roman Empire: The Religious Policy of Anastasius the First, 491-518* (University of Wisconsin Studies in the Social Sciences, no. 26, Madison, 1939), 63.

⁵⁰ Merle E. Curti, *Bryan and World Peace* (Smith College Studies in History, vol. 16, nos. 3-4, Northampton, Massachusetts, 1931), 130.

⁵¹ J. Fletcher Williams, *History of the City of Saint Paul and of the County of Ramsey, Minnesota* (Minnesota Historical Collections, vol. 4, St. Paul, 1876), 256-257.

⁵² John R. Brodhead, "Memoir on the Early Colonization of New Netherland," in *New York Historical Collections*, 2d series, 2:355-366 (New York, 1849).

Publishers' series titles which merely designate format, such as Modern Library, Loeb Classical Library, Pelican Books, etc., are not italicized.

Identification of the Edition.—When more than one edition of a work has been published, the data identifying the edition should also be included in the first citation, and in subsequent citations if necessary to prevent confusion:

⁵³ Karl Jaspers, *Psychologie der Weltanschauungen* (3d ed., Berlin, 1925).

⁵⁴ G. Lowes Dickinson, *Revolution and Reaction in Modern France* ([3d ed.], New York, n. d.).

The brackets indicate that the information was obtained from some source other than the title page—in this instance from the prefaces.

⁵⁵ Francis Parkman, *Pioneers of France in the New World* (Frontenac ed., 2 vols., Boston, 1907), 2:161.

Mimeographed, multigraphed, photoprinted, and other materials reproduced by processes other than letterpress, if issued for general distribution, should be regarded as published titles and italicized in the same way, with a notation on the form of publication:

[56] Library of Congress, *List of References on Political and Social Psychology* (Select List of References no. 726, mimeographed, Washington, 1922), 3.

VOLUME AND PAGE CITATIONS

It will have been observed that throughout this manual Arabic numbers are used for both volume and page citations, separated by a colon. It should be said, however, that it is still common practice among scholars to use Roman numerals for the volume and Arabic for the page citations, the usual form being as follows:

[57] Allan Nevins, *Frémont, the West's Greatest Adventurer* (2 vols., New York and London, 1928), I, 473–491; II, 69.

But the use of the Arabic figures for volume as well as page citations has certain advantages that would seem to justify more general acceptance of this form: it is simpler and easier to read, and it coincides with the form commonly used by libraries in stamping serial numbers on periodical sets and rebound volumes.

Exact page references are preferable to the terms "f." (the page following), "ff." (the pages following), and "passim" (here and there), except where these latter forms greatly simplify a citation. The criterion should be the convenience of the reader, not that of the writer. Such a citation as that in note 58 below, containing a long series of consecutive page references, is not only cumbersome but actually less convenient to use than the form given in note 59.

[58] For frequent mention of the bear as an item of diet and article of barter, see Gates, *Five Fur Traders of the Northwest*, 148, 240, 259, 260, 261, 262, 263, 264, 265.

[59] For frequent mention of the bear as an item of diet and article of barter, see Gates, *Five Fur Traders of the Northwest*, 148, 240, 259–265 passim.

If the reference to a given source is derived from another work, the note should so state:

[60] Henry Cabot Lodge, *A Short History of the English Colonies in America* (New York, 1881), 152, cited in *The Early Writings of Frederick Jackson Turner* (Madison, 1938), 204.

THE SHORTENED CITATION

An abridged form of citation may be used throughout the footnotes for any title that appears in the bibliography, and in any event after its first appearance in the manuscript or a given chapter of it (see page 10). This shorter form need include only (1) the surname of the author, editor, or compiler; (2) a shortened form of the title, if it is a long one; and (3) volume and page references (also part or section if the volume is not paged consecutively throughout).

Ordinarily a title should be shortened by omitting unnecessary phrases, not by abbreviating individual words. So far as possible, the key words—that is, the distinctive portion of the title—should be retained. While there is an advantage in beginning the citation with the first word of the title, it will be recognized that such general terms as *History, Summary, Introduction, Description, Survey*, etc., when used alone, are not very illuminating to the reader unfamiliar with the literature of the subject under discussion.

For some works usage has established a particular form for the shortened citation. For example, the monumental collection of *Documents Relative to the Colonial History of the State of New York*, edited by Edmund B. O'Callaghan, is generally known as *New York Colonial Documents*. Another is *Die grosse Politik der europäischen Kabinette, 1871–1914: Sammlung der diplomatischen Akten des auswartigen Amtes*, which is sometimes abridged to *Die grosse Politik*, more frequently to *G. P.* When such an abbreviation is used, or any other short title that requires explanation, it is well to state in connection with the full citation how the work will be cited thereafter.

EXAMPLES

The citations below are shortened forms of some of those given in full above. For convenience of comparison they have been numbered to correspond with the earlier citations.

1 Child, *German-Americans in Politics*, 34.

2 Wigmore, *Australian Ballot*, 22–28.

3 Roscher and Jannasch, *Kolonien*, 12.

5 Piercy, *Modern Writers at Work*, vii–xi.

6 Scull, *Voyages of Radisson*, 28.

7 Hennepin, *Louisiana* (Shea ed.), 32. [The Shea edition must be specified, since another edition has been published.]

8 Wagner, *Story of Bayreuth*, 127.

9 Mitchell, *Contest in America*, 200.

10 Filson, *Daniel Boon*, 16.

11 International Labour Office, *International Labour Organization*, 570.

13 Hoover War Library, *Peace Conference Delegation Propaganda*, 13.

14 Library of Congress, *Publicity for the States*, 10.

17 Gates, *Five Fur Traders*, 150.

18 Harper, *North-American Land Company*, 6.
40 Griffis, *Sir William Johnson*, 20.
48 MacGill, *Transportation in the United States*, 13.
49 Charanis, *Church and State in the Later Roman Empire*, 8.
51 Williams, *Saint Paul*, 256.
54 Dickinson, *Modern France*, 27.

Instead of the shortened title some writers use the term *op. cit.*, for the Latin *opere citato* ("the work cited"). This practice, once common, is no longer in general use, for it has obvious disadvantages. It may not, of course, be employed if more than one work of a given author is cited. Moreover, it places upon the reader the burden of keeping in mind, or of relocating, the earlier citations if he is endeavoring to follow the sources. To the person who consults a book only for a particular topic treated therein, it offers no help until he has located the first citation. Reference librarians and others who have occasion to consult a large number of works more or less cursorily will be grateful to the writer who cites enough of a title to make it easily identifiable rather than the indefinite *op. cit.*, especially if there is no bibliography to which to turn.

When a footnote is immediately followed on the same page by another reference to the same work, the abbreviation *ibid.*, for the Latin *ibidem* ("in the same place") may be used. Note in the examples below that the term *ibid.* is used to cover as much of the previous citation as remains the same.

60 Channing, *United States*, 6:400.
61 *Ibid.*, 4:300.
62 *Ibid.* [that is, 4:300.]
63 *Ibid.*, 5:123; 6:148; 8:296, 298.

Most of the other Latin abbreviations, such as *et seq., cf., vide, v., id., idem., loc. cit., ante*, and *post*, are being discarded.

III. REPORTS, PROCEEDINGS, AND YEARBOOKS

THE COMPLETE CITATION

The complete citation of a volume in a series of official reports, proceedings, minutes, catalogs, or yearbooks should give the exact title of the series as it appears on the title page and the year or years which it covers. It is common practice not to italicize the latter. This procedure, while not altogether logical, has the advantage of permitting the omission of such cumbersome phrases as *for the Two Years Ending on June 30*, etc. The place of publication is not essential except in the case of the less well-known organizations and institutions, nor is the date of publication.

[64] *Report of the President of the University of Minnesota*, 1918, p. 10.
[65] *First Annual Report of the Bureau of Ethnology*, 1879–80, p. 324.
[66] *Catalogue of the University of Wisconsin*, 1888–89, pp. 95–97.
[67] *Proceedings of the Thirty-Sixth Annual Meeting of the State Historical Society of Wisconsin*, 1889, p. 90.

Note that in the preceding citations the abbreviations "p." and "pp." have been used to prevent the juxtaposition of two numerals representing different items of information.

THE SHORTENED CITATION

In subsequent citations the organization or institution may be treated as author and the title shortened as follows:

[68] University of Minnesota, *President's Report*, 1918, p. 10; 1919, p. 4; 1921, p. 2.
[69] Bureau of Ethnology, *Report*, 1879–80, p. 326.
[70] University of Wisconsin, *Catalogue*, 1888–89, p. 98.
[71] Wisconsin Historical Society, *Proceedings*, 1889, p. 91; 1890, p. 12.

IV. GOVERNMENT DOCUMENTS

A government document having a distinctive title and published under the name of the author (or editor or compiler) should be cited by author and title in the same form as non-governmental publications. In addition, the citation should include (1) the series title if it has one; (2) the number of the Congress and session if it is a congressional document; and (3) the serial number if it appears in the "serial" set of congressional documents, since in most libraries these are shelved numerically rather than by subject.

[72] William F. Switzler, *Report on the Internal Commerce of the United States* (50 Congress, 1 session, House Executive Document no. 6, pt. 2, serial 2552, Washington, 1888).

[73] *Inland Water Transportation in the United States* (Bureau of Foreign and Domestic Commerce, Miscellaneous Series, no. 119, Washington, 1923).

[74] *Treaties and Conventions Concluded between the United States and Other Powers since July 4, 1776* (48 Congress, 2 session, Senate Executive Document no. 47, vol. 1, pt. 2, serial 2262, Washington, 1889), 380.

[75] *Public Schools of the District of Columbia* (56 Congress, 1 session, Senate Report no. 711, serial 3889, Washington, 1900), 5.

Citations of other federal and state documents are illustrated in the notes below:

[76] *Annals of Congress*, 16 Congress, 2 session (1820–21), 715–716.
[77] *Congressional Globe*, 35 Congress, 1 session (1857–58), 1403.
[78] *Congressional Record*, 65 Congress, 1 session (1917), 103.
[79] *United States Statutes at Large*, 11:285.
[80] *Senate Journal*, 38 Congress, 1 session (1863–64, serial 1236), 30, 32.
[81] Thomas H. Benton, "Highway to the Pacific," in the *Congressional Globe*, 31 Congress, 2 session (1850–51), 56–58.
[82] *Wisconsin Session Laws*, 1937, pp. 68–69.

V. NEWSPAPERS

A citation of a newspaper should include (1) the title in italics and the place of publication, (2) the date of issue, (3) for the larger papers, the section and page, and (4) for obscure items, the column number. The official title of a newspaper is that given in the masthead, which sometimes differs from the bannerhead.

[83] *New York Times*, January 2, 1916, sec. 2, p. 6, col. 7.
[84] *New York Evening Post*, March 10, April 1, 1863.
[85] *New Ulm Post* (Minnesota), April 30, 1916.

When the place of publication is a part of the title (note 83 above), it is included in each citation unless the reference is clear without it. In a work in which the *New York Times*, for example, is the chief newspaper source and in which it is frequently cited, the reference may be simply to the *Times* after the first citation in each chapter.

When the place of publication is not a part of the title (note 84), it is included, without italics, in the first citation in each chapter and wherever it is necessary to identify the paper. If the references are few and widely scattered, the place of publication should appear in each citation.

When several issues of a single year are cited with page references, a convenient form of citation is the following:

[86] *Minneapolis Journal*, 1917: January 15, p. 22; March 4, p. 11; July 17, p. 20; 1918: March 31, p. 10; May 19, p. 2; 1920: August 1, p. 1.

VI. PARTS OF PUBLICATIONS

The title of an article, essay, or document in a larger work or in a periodical or newspaper is enclosed in quotation marks, and the book or periodical in which it appears is italicized. The first citation of a book referred to in such a connection should be complete:

[87] James Ewing, "Cancer as a Public Health Problem," in Leiv Kreyberg and Others, *A Symposium on Cancer* (Madison, 1938), 73–77.

and the title of the book should be repeated in subsequent citations:

> [88] Ewing, "Cancer as a Public Health Problem," in Kreyberg and Others, *Symposium on Cancer*, 80.

In citing well-known periodicals the place of publication is commonly omitted, but at least the year of issue should be included in addition to volume and page references. Both of the forms below are in common use:

> [89] John D. Hicks, "The Birth of the Populist Party," in *Minnesota History*, 9:219–247 (September, 1928).
>
> [90] Alvin H. Hansen, "The Effect of Price Fluctuations on Agriculture," in the *Journal of Political Economy*, 33 (1925):196–213.

The word "in" may be omitted before an italicized title, the relation between quoted and italicized titles being perfectly clear without it:

> [91] John D. Hicks, "The Birth of the Populist Party," *Minnesota History*, 9:219–247 (September, 1928).

but in such citations as those below it is obvious that the preposition is needed:

> [92] Harold D. Lasswell, "The Study and Practice of Propaganda," in Harold D. Lasswell, Ralph D. Casey, and Bruce L. Smith, *Propaganda and Promotional Activities: An Annotated Bibliography* (Minneapolis, 1935), 3–27.
>
> [93] Lasswell, "Study and Practice of Propaganda," in Lasswell, Casey, and Smith, *Propaganda*, 3–27.

VII. MANUSCRIPT MATERIALS

A reference to a manuscript should enable the reader to identify it readily and to locate it for his own use if he has occasion to do so. Therefore it is important to cite the author and date of the manuscript, the title and location of the collection in which it is included, the location of copies known to the writer, and whatever other information may be valuable to the reader, who will probably not have easy access to the material. If a handwritten or typewritten copy has been used, that fact, too, should be stated, since such a copy may be less authentic than the original.

DIARIES, JOURNALS, AND LETTER BOOKS

Titles of manuscripts are capitalized but neither italicized nor enclosed in quotation marks. References to diaries, journals, letter books, and other manuscripts presenting a chronology should be cited by date even if the manuscript is paged. In citing correspondence it is customary to omit the word "letter," as in notes 95, 96, and 98.

⁹⁴ The Jeremiah Stevens Diary and the Stevens Papers, upon which this article is based, are in the possession of the writer. Microfilm copies of the diary for the period from 1850 to 1858 are available at the State Historical Society of Wisconsin.

Subsequent citations: Stevens Diary, January 2, 1856.

⁹⁵ Jacob Brown to Governor Lewis Cass, September 27, 1819, in the Brown Letter Books, vol. 2, in the Library of Congress. These two volumes of letter books contain copies of letters sent and received.

Subsequent citations: Brown to Cass, September 27, 1819, in Brown Letter Books, vol. 2.

⁹⁶ Governor William Clark to the Secretary of War, May 28, 1816, in Letters Received, War Department, Adjutant General's Office, Old Records Division. These volumes contain accurate digests of the letters relating to military affairs received by the secretary of war from the adjutant general. The letters themselves are filed and can be found readily. The ledgers are so detailed and so accurate that they compensate to some extent for the loss of occasional letters.

Subsequent citations: Clark to the Secretary of War, May 28, 1816, in Letters Received, Adjutant General's Office, Old Records Division.

⁹⁷ Order of General Edmund P. Gaines, July 14, 1821, in Department Orders, War Department, Adjutant General's Office, Old Records Division. This volume contains the orders issued by the commander of the Ninth Department from 1819 to 1821 and the orders of the commander of the Northwestern Frontier, the Western Wing of the Western Department, and the Western Department from 1821 to 1825.

⁹⁸ Aratus Kent to the Reverend Absalom Peters, May 10, 1830, in the American Home Missionary Papers at the University of Chicago. A photostatic copy is in the possession of the State Historical Society of Wisconsin.

Subsequent citations: Kent to Peters, May 10, 1830, in American Home Missionary Papers.

COLLECTIONS OF MANUSCRIPTS

Collections of personal and other papers are usually designated by some such inclusive title as the Pierre Chouteau Papers, the Clinton Papers, the Richard Graham Collection, the Draper MSS, Governor's Archives. The particular form used by the depository possessing the manuscripts should be followed.

INDIVIDUAL MANUSCRIPTS

If a manuscript bears a distinctive title or has been entitled by the depository in which it is located, it should be cited by that title. In this group are included reminiscences, narratives, and historical sketches. Such titles are sometimes enclosed in quotation marks for greater clarity, but the practice is not general.

[99] Jared W. Daniels, Sisseton Agency, p. 5, in the Daniels Reminiscences, manuscript in the possession of the Minnesota Historical Society.

[100] For details of this transaction see a small manuscript volume entitled "Winnebago Debt 1841," in the Hercules L. Dousman Papers, in the possession of the Minnesota Historical Society.

Subsequent citations: Winnebago Debt 1841, in the Dousman Papers.

[101] Raphael P. Thian, Notes Illustrating the Military Geography of the United States, in the United States Adjutant General's Office, Old Records Division.

UNPUBLISHED DISSERTATIONS

The same form is used for master's theses, doctoral dissertations, and similar unpublished works:

[102] John R. Smith, The Panic of 1837 in Wisconsin, p. 89, unpublished master's thesis, dated 1928, in the library of the University of Wisconsin.

Subsequent citations: Smith, Panic of 1837, p. 89.

THE BIBLIOGRAPHY

I. TYPES OF BIBLIOGRAPHY

Bibliographies are of two general types: the author bibliography, comprising the works of a single author, and the subject bibliography, comprising works on a given subject. The latter may be (1) a comprehensive list of all the materials available on the subject; (2) a list of the materials drawn upon in the preparation of a work; or (3) a select list of titles that will prove most helpful to the general reader.

II. ORGANIZATION

Unless some good reason exists for a different treatment, the bibliography should be arranged as a single list alphabetized by author. The long bibliography which includes many different kinds of material usually requires some classification. How best to organize such a mass of diverse materials is often a problem for which no hard and fast rules can be laid down. Classification may be on the basis of kind of material —manuscripts, government publications, reports and proceedings, books and articles, and newspapers; or it may be chronological or topical. The problem should be considered in the light of the materials to be included and the number of titles falling within the several classes.

III. ANNOTATIONS

The usefulness of any bibliography is also enhanced if it includes succinct annotations on (1) the scope of each work or its bearing on the subject under discussion, when these are not clearly revealed by the title; (2) the purpose or bias of the author, if the account is not strictly impartial; and (3) the particular merit or limitations of the work if there is reason to comment upon either.

The following examples of bibliographical entries have been selected from John D. Hicks, *The Populist Revolt: A History of the Farmers' Alliance and the People's Party* (Minneapolis, 1931). They illustrate not only the form of entry but an expert use of brief annotations stating the salient features of each title in the light of the text discussion.

ALLEN, EMORY A. *Labor and Capital.* Cincinnati, 1891. Contains chapters on each of the important farm orders of the period.

BOGART, ERNEST L. *An Economic History of the United States.* New York, 1922. Useful for general background.

BREWTON, WILLIAM W. *The Life of Thomas E. Watson.* Atlanta, 1926. Poorly done, but draws upon manuscript materials not yet generally available.

BROOKS, ROBERT P. *The Agrarian Revolution in Georgia, 1865–1912.* Madison, 1914. Perhaps the best study of the economic background of Populism in the South.

BUCHANAN, JOHN R. "The Great Migration into Northern Nebraska." *Proceedings and Collections of the Nebraska State Historical Society,* 15:25–34. Lincoln, 1907. Buchanan was one of the advertisers for a local Nebraska railroad.

BURNAP, WILLARD A. *What Happened during One Man's Lifetime.* Fergus Falls, Minnesota, 1923. Contains some interesting chapters on the settlement of the West.

LA FOLLETTE, ROBERT M. *Autobiography.* Madison, 1913. The conditions that produced La Follette were in large part the conditions that produced Populism.

MAITLAND, WILLIAM. "The Ruin of the American Farmer." *Nineteenth Century,* 32:733–743 (November, 1892). A conservative English view.

POWDERLY, TERENCE V. *Thirty Years of Labor.* Columbus, 1889. Presents the side of labor.

WEAVER, JAMES B. *A Call to Action.* Des Moines, 1892. The standard farmers' arguments, by one of their best-known leaders.

IV. ALPHABETIZATION

Alphabetization should be by (1) author (as above) if there is an author (or editor or compiler);

(2) by title for general reference works, anonymously published works, and periodicals:

Appletons' Annual Cyclopaedia, 1880–1908. Contains information on the Populist movement in the various states.

Cartoons from Punch. 4 vols. London, 1906. Covers the period 1841–1901.

"Communists in Java." *Living Age,* 332:298–301. February 15, 1927.

New Republic, 1914–1917.

Outlook, 1914–1917.

(3) by title for newspapers when the city or state of publication constitutes the first word of the title; by city of publication for other papers, as in the citations of the New York *World* and St. Louis *Westliche Post* below. Note that the place of publication is not italicized when it is not a part of the title.

Cincinnatier Freie Presse, 1914–18.

Illinois Staats-Zeitung (Chicago), 1914–18.

Milwaukee Germania-Herold, 1914–18.

Milwaukee Sonntagspost, 1914–18.

Mississippi Blätter (St. Louis), 1914–18.

New York Times, 1914–18.

New York *World,* 1914–17.

Providence Journal, 1914–17.
St. Louis *Westliche Post*, 1914–18.

(4) by state or UNITED STATES for public documents relating to government departments:

COLORADO: *Governor's Message*, 1895.
MINNESOTA:
 House Journal, 1857–65.
 Senate Journal, 1857–65.
UNITED STATES:
 Congressional Globe, 1818–25.
 Journals of the Continental Congress, 1784–1789. 4 vols. Washington, 1823.
 Malloy, William M., comp. *Treaties, Conventions, International Acts, Protocols, and Agreements between the United States and Other Powers, 1776–1902*. 2 vols. Washington, 1910.

INDEX

Anonymously published works, 12, 26
Articles, citation of, 21
Author's name, citation of 11-12, 18

Bibliographical data in footnotes, 10; for books and pamphlets, 11-19; for reports, proceedings, and yearbooks, 19-20; for government documents, 20-21; for articles, essays, etc., 21; for manuscripts, 22-24
Bibliography, types of, 25; organization of, 25; annotation of, 25; alphabetical arrangement of, 26
Books, citation of, in footnotes, 11-19; in bibliography, 25-26; the full citation, 11-17; the shortened citation, 17-19
Brackets, use of, 12, 15, 16

Capitalization, in titles, 14
Catalogs, citation of, 19-20
Compiler, citation of, 11, 18
Complete citation, of books and pamphlets, 11-17; of reports, proceedings, and yearbooks, 19-20; of public documents, 20; of articles and essays, 21; of manuscripts, 23-24; of dissertations, 24
Congressional documents, 20

Date of publication, 11, 15; for periodicals, 22
Diaries, manuscript, 22
Dissertations, 24
Documents, see Government documents: Manuscript materials
Dutch titles, capitalization in, 14

Edition, citation of, 16
Editor, citation of, 11, 18
Essays, citation of, 21

Footnotes, function of, 7; arrangement, 7; typing of, 7; numbering, 8; indexes to, 8; combination of citations in, 9-10; information supplementing the text, 10; literary form of, 10; bibliographical data to be included in, 10

Foreign-language publications, 14, 15
French titles, capitalization in, 14

German titles, capitalization in, 14
Government documents, 20-21, 27

Honorary titles of authors, 11
House documents, 20

Ibid., use of, 19
Indexes to footnotes, 8
Institution, as author, 12, 20
Italian titles, capitalization in, 14
Italicization of titles, 11, 12, 16, 19, 21, 22

Journals, manuscript, 22

Latin titles, capitalization in, 14
Letter books, manuscript, 22

Manuscripts, 22-24
Mimeographed materials, 17
Multigraphed materials, 17

Newspapers, 21, 26
Norwegian titles, capitalization in, 14
Numbering of footnotes, 8

Op. cit., use of, 19
Organization, as author, 12, 20

Page references, citation of, 9, 17
Pamphlets, citation of, 11-19
Passim, use of, 17
Periodicals, articles and essays in, 21; place of publication generally omitted, 22; in bibliographies, 26
Photoprinted materials, 17
Place of publication, for books and pamphlets, 11, 15; for newspapers, 21; foreign, 15; omitted for periodicals, 22
Proceedings of organizations, citation of, 19-20
Professional titles of authors, 11
Public documents, 20-21, 27
Publication, facts of, 15-17, 19, 20, 21, 22

Publisher, name of, 11, 15
Quotation marks, use of, 21, 23
Reports of organizations, 19–20
Senate documents, 20
Serial numbers, of congressional documents, 20
Serial titles, 16, 19–20, 21
Shortened citation, of books and pamphlets, 17–19; of reports, proceedings, and yearbooks, 19; of articles and essays, 21
Spanish titles, capitalization in, 14

Subtitles, 12
Swedish titles, capitalization in, 14
Tabular material, notes to, 8
Titles, of books and pamphlets, 12–13, 17–19; of series, 16; of reports, proceedings, and yearbooks, 19–20; of government documents, 20; of newspapers, 21
Titles, honorary and professional, of authors, 11
Volume numbers, citation of, 15–16, 17
Yearbooks, 19–20